2016

U.S.
COIN
Digest

The Complete Guide to Current Market Values

David C. Harper, Editor
Harry Miller, Market Analyst

Copyright ©2015 F+W Media, Inc.

All rights reserved. No portion of this publication may be reproduced or
transmitted in any form or by any means, electronic or mechanical, including
photocopy, recording, or any information storage and retrieval system, without
permission in writing from the publisher, except by a reviewer who may quote
brief passages in a critical article or review to be printed in a magazine or
newspaper, or electronically transmitted on radio, television, or the Internet.

Published by

Krause Publications, a division of F+W, A Content + eCommerce Company
700 East State Street • Iola, WI 54990-0001
715-445-2214 • 888-457-2873
www.krausebooks.com

To order books or other products call toll-free 1-800-258-0929
or visit us online at www.shopnumismaster.com

ISSN 1544-8517
ISBN-13: 978-1-4402-4408-7
ISBN-10: 1-4402-4408-1

Cover Design by Jana Tappa
Designed by Sandi Carpenter
Edited by George Cuhaj

Printed in China

Contents

Preface

Since 1952, Krause Publications has built its business and reputation by serving the needs of coin collectors. Three questions dominate every collector's thinking.

The first is: "What is it?" We hope the photographs in this price guide will help you identify the coins you own.

The second question is: "What's it worth?" The prices contained in this volume are intended to serve as a retail guide. That means if you want to buy a specific coin in a specific grade, the price listed will be approximately what you would have to pay at the time this book was compiled. The prices listed are neither an offer to buy nor an offer to sell the coins listed. They are simply a guide assembled for your convenience by the authors. Remember that prices fluctuate. What dealers will pay to buy coins from you is a question beyond the scope of this book.

The third question is: "How do I buy a specific coin?" There are several thousand coin dealers across America who are ready, willing and able to serve your needs. To find them, you can consult the phone book in your local area, but beyond that, there is a whole hobby world out there and newspapers and magazines that feature advertisements by dealers who want to fill your needs. For more information on numismatic products and pricing go to www.numismaster.com.

Photo Credits

We wish to thank the following auction houses and individuals for the fabulous color images contained within these pages.

Mike Locke   **Jay M. Galst, M.D.**   **Chester L. Krause**

Heritage Numismatic Auctions, Inc.
www.HeritageCoins.com

Stack's
www.stacks.com

Ken Potter
www.koinpro.com

Professional Coin Grading Service
www.pcgs.com

Introduction

The authors have organized this book in a manner that we hope you will find both logical and useful.

Value listings

Values listed in the price guide are average retail prices. These are the approximate prices collectors can expect to pay when purchasing coins from dealers. They are not offers to buy or sell. The pricing section should be considered a guide only; actual selling prices will vary.

The values were compiled by Krause Publications' independent staff of market analysts. They derived the values listed by monitoring auction results, business on electronic dealer trading networks and at major shows, and in consultation with a panel of dealers. For rare coins, when only a few specimens of a particular date and mintmark are known, a confirmed transaction may occur only once every several years. In those instances, the most recent auction result is listed.

Grading

Values are listed for coins in various states of preservation, or grades. Standards used in determining grade for U.S. coins are those set by the American Numismatic Association (www.money.org). See Chapter 3 for more on grading.

Precious metal content

Throughout this book precious metal content is indicated in troy ounces. One troy ounce equals 480 grains, or 31.103 grams. This is followed by ASW or AGW, which stand for Actual Silver (Gold) Weight.

Dates and mintmarks

The dates listed are the individual dates that appear on each coin. The letter that follows the date is the mintmark and indicates where the coin was struck: "C" – Charlotte, N.C. (1838-1861); "CC" – Carson City, Nev. (1870-1893); "D" – Dahlonega, Ga. (1838-1861), and Denver (1906-present); "O" – New Orleans (1838-1909); "P" – Philadelphia (1793-present), coins without mintmarks also were struck at Philadelphia; "S" – San Francisco (1854-present); and "W" – West Point, N.Y. (1984-present).

A slash mark in a date indicates an overdate. This means a new date was engraved on a die over an old date. For example, if the date is listed as "1899/8," an 1898 die had a 9 engraved over the last 8 in the date. Portions of the old numeral are still visible on the coin.

A slash mark in a mintmark listing indicates an overmintmark (example: "1922-P/D"). The same process as above occurred, but this time a new mintmark was engraved over an old.

See Chapter 6, "U.S. Minting Varieties and Errors," for more information on overdates and overmintmarks.

1 Type Identification Guide

United States coins are often given nicknames based on their obverse design. This Type Identification Guide is a start for coin identification. It also shows the changes in the sizes of various denominations over time.

Half Cent

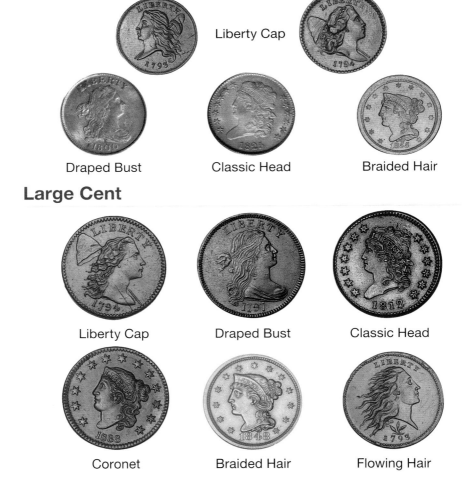

Liberty Cap

Draped Bust

Classic Head

Braided Hair

Large Cent

Liberty Cap

Draped Bust

Classic Head

Coronet

Braided Hair

Flowing Hair

Small Cent

Flying Eagle

Indian Head

Lincoln

Shield

Silver 3 Cents

Coronet

Half Dime

Flowing Hair

Draped Bust

Liberty Cap

Seated Liberty

Nickel

Shield

Liberty

Buffalo

Jefferson

Jefferson
large profile

Jefferson
large facing portrait

Dime

Draped Bust

Liberty Cap

Seated Liberty

Barber

Mercury

Roosevelt

Twenty Cents

Seated Liberty within circle of stars

Quarter

Draped Bust

Liberty Cap

Seated Liberty

Barber

Standing Liberty

Washington

50 State

Half Dollar

Flowing Hair

Draped Bust

Capped Bust

Seated Liberty

Barber

Walking Liberty

Franklin

Kennedy

Dollar

Flowing Hair

Draped Bust

Gobrecht

Seated Liberty

Trade

Morgan

Peace

Eisenhower

Dollar

Susan B. Anthony

Sacagawea

 Liberty Head - Type 1

 Indian Head - Type 2

 Indian Head - Type 3

$2.50 Gold Quarter Eagle

Liberty Cap   Turban Head   Coronet Head   Indian Head

$3.00 Gold

Indian Head with headress

$5.00 Gold Half Eagle

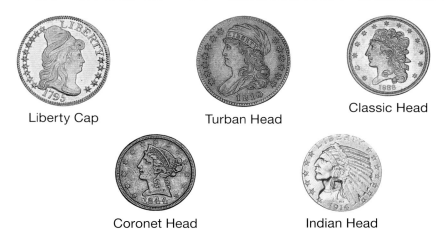

Liberty Cap

Turban Head

Classic Head

Coronet Head

Indian Head

$10.00 Gold Eagle

Liberty Cap

Coronet Head

Indian Head

$20.00 Gold Double Eagle

Coronet Head

Saint-Gaudens

2 Care and Storage of Your Coins

Use caution to retain coin's value

Once you find a coin you love, or begin to build a collection that you are dedicating time and money to, you really need to consider proper care and storage methods. Careless handling of your coins can quickly lead to loss of value.

Here is some quick and simple advice, which you should always follow when handling your coins:
- Always hold your coin by the edge.
- Never touch your coin on its large surfaces.

You leave fingerprints on surfaces that you touch and fingerprints on coins cause long-term damage which degrades the quality of your coin. If you are not comfortable handling your coins, it is best to wear special gloves available through coin supply dealers and to do your work over a jeweler's tray for your coins safety.

Another quick and simple bit of advice regarding cleaning your coins:
- Don't clean coins.

Some coins you acquire may seem dirty to you and an early impulse may be to clean them. Many inexperienced collectors degrade or even destroy their coins value through cleaning. Most cleaning methods are abrasive and remove not only the dirt, but also the metal surface of the coin. In most instances you will damage your coins value by attempting to clean them, so don't.

Most collectors enjoy examining the coins they have acquired and some collectors concentrate on finding varieties. Close examination requires magnification. The following instruments are commonly used to examine coins more closely:
- Magnifying glass
- Jeweler's loupe
- Microscope

Magnifiers come in different strengths and all shapes and sizes. Most coin collectors find a 5x magnifying glass quite versatile for checking out a coin's surface for wear. When looking for varieties, a 10x loupe works pretty well. For a closer look, many specialists use a 10x to 60x adjustable microscope. Each of these tools has its proper use and appropriate cost. Start simple with a nice 5x magnifier and see how it works for you.

Spend a little time at a coin show or in a coin shop and you will see that there are many different methods of storing your coins. The simplest are coin envelopes, which are produced in various colors of paper and are usually 2-inch by 2-inch in size. Information can be written on these holders, the coin inserted and the flap tucked in so that the coin does not easily fall out if the envelope is tipped or dropped. If you use coin envelopes, it is best to stick with plain white paper, as colored paper will tone your coin over time. When writing information on the envelope, do so before you insert the coin and use a ball-point pen or pencil, as a felt-tip marker may bleed through and harm your coin.

For standard sized U.S. coins, coin boards have been used for many years as a simple cataloging and storage method for beginning collectors. Coin boards provide several useful services. Coin boards:
- Organize your collection.
- Focus your attention on a single type of coin.
- Offer a cheap method of storage.

Sounds pretty good? Yes, for common circulating coins, the coin board is a great way to get started. However, there are drawbacks to this system that you may notice over time. You may find that it is difficult to insert your coins in the board and to get them to stay put. Because of this, you may find that you are handling your coins too much. If you don't place a soft cloth over the coin before you push it into the board, you will leave a fingerprint on the coin's surface. Over time you will notice that material from which the board was manufactured may have added a color tint to your coins. This is called toning. Some collectors like toning and some do not, so toning may hamper or help in your collection's appreciation over time.

If you like the display feature of boards, but do not care for some of these drawbacks, you can consider using any number of the vast array of containment storage methods available. There are hard plastic holders, tight plastic capsules, plastic envelopes called flips, and die-cut cardboard holders with Mylar lining. The last three of these can be inserted in pocket sheets for three ring binder display or simply placed into special coin boxes for storage.

The simplest and most widely used of these individual storage methods is the die cut cardboard holder with Mylar lining. These holders come in different size die cuts. To use this type of holder, follow these simple steps:
- Choose a die cut that is slightly larger than your coin.
- Place your coin on the Mylar over the die cut hole.
- Carefully fold the top over your coin.
- Grasp the holder and coin between your thumb and forefinger.
- Carefully staple the three open sides of the holder to secure your coin.
- Flatten the staples with a set of pliers.

Once this process is complete, you can write information on the outer edges of the cardboard to catalog, value and grade or otherwise identify the attributes of your coin.

Plastic flip envelopes are made from different materials. There are soft plastic types and hard plastic types. The soft plastic should only be used for short term storage. Soft plastic flips contain polyvinylchloride or PVC which, over time, can cause serious damage to your coins in the form of a green corrosive slime which eats away at the coin's surface. The hard plastic is normally made from Mylar, which does not contain PVC, but does get brittle and can crack as it ages. Both types of flips are constructed with two pockets, one for your coin and one for a small, square piece of paper or thin cardboard on which you can write your coin's catalog information.

The storage methods mentioned above are good for low to medium value coins. If your collecting advances into coins of higher value, you may want to consider a third party grading service. These services will grade and encapsulate your coin in an airtight hard plastic holder containing both your coin and coin information.

Use your common sense in choosing appropriate methods of care and storage for maintaining your coins. Here are a few more basic rules to remember:

- Keep you coins in a cool, dry place.
- Make sure your coins are secure from tampering or theft.
- Do not store your coins in a leather pouch or bag.
- Do not allow you coins to knock or slide against each other.
- Put your coins in some sort of holder that protects them.
- Be sure that your choice of holder does not cause damage to your coins.
- Examine your coins regularly and check for any changes.

Your collection can provide you with both an enjoyable hobby and a valuable investment, but it is your responsibility to organize, store, care for and maintain your coins properly.

3 How to Grade

Better condition equals better value

Grading is one of the most important factors in buying and selling coins as collectibles. Unfortunately, it's also one of the most controversial. Since the early days of coin collecting in the United States, buying through the mail has been a convenient way for collectors to acquire coins. As a result, there has always been a need in numismatics for a concise way to classify the amount of wear on a coin and its condition in general.

A look back

In September 1888, Dr. George Heath, a physician in Monroe, Mich., published a four-page pamphlet titled *The American Numismatist*. Publication of subsequent issues led to the founding of the American Numismatic Association, and *The Numismatist*, as it's known today, is the association's official journal. Heath's first issues were largely devoted to selling world coins from his collection. There were no formal grades listed with the coins and their prices, but the following statement by Heath indicates that condition was a consideration for early collectors:

"The coins are in above average condition," Heath wrote, "and so confident am I that they will give satisfaction, that I agree to refund the money in any unsatisfactory sales on the return of the coins."

As coin collecting became more popular and *The Numismatist* started accepting paid advertising from others, grading became more formal. The February 1892 issue listed seven "classes" for the condition of coins (from worst to best): mutilated, poor, fair, good, fine, uncirculated, and proof. Through the years, the hobby has struggled with developing a grading system that would be accepted by all and could apply to all coins. The hobby's growth was accompanied by a desire for more grades, or classifications, to more precisely define a coin's condition. The desire for more precision, however, was at odds with the basic concept of grading: to provide a concise method for classifying a coin's condition.

For example, even the conservatively few classifications of 1892 included fudge factors.

"To give flexibility to this classification," *The Numismatist* said, "such modification of find, good and fair, as 'extremely,' 'very,' 'almost,' etc., are used to express slight variations from the general condition."

The debate over grading continued for decades in *The Numismatist*. A number of articles and letters prodded the ANA to write grading guidelines and endorse them as the association's official standards. Some submitted specific suggestions for terminology and accompanying standards for each grade. But grading remained a process of "instinct" gained through years of collecting or dealing experience.

A formal grading guide in book form finally appeared in 1958, but it was the work of two individuals rather than the ANA. *A Guide to the Grading of United States Coins* by Martin R. Brown and John W. Dunn was a break-through in the great grading debate. Now collectors had a reference that gave them specific guidelines for specific coins and could be studied and restudied at home.

The first editions of Brown and Dunn carried text only, no illustrations. For the fourth edition, in 1964, publication was assumed by Whitman Publishing Co. of Racine, Wis., and line drawings were added to illustrate the text.

The fourth edition listed six principal categories for circulated coins (from worst to best): good, very good, fine, very fine, extremely fine, and about uncirculated. But again, the desire for more precise categories was evidenced. In the book's introduction, Brown and Dunn wrote, "Dealers will sometimes advertise coins that are graded G-VG, VG-F, F-VF, VF-XF. Or the description may be ABT. G. or VG plus, etc. This means that the coin in question more than meets minimum standards for the lower grade but is not quite good enough for the higher grade."

When the fifth edition appeared, in 1969, the "New B & D Grading System" was introduced. The six principal categories for circulated coins were still intact, but variances within those categories were now designated by up to four letters: "A," "B," "C" or "D." For example, an EF-A coin was "almost about uncirculated." An EF-B was "normal extra fine" within the B & D standards. EF-C had a "normal extra fine" obverse, but the reverse was "obviously not as nice as obverse due to poor strike or excessive wear." EF-D had a "normal extra fine" reverse but a problem obverse.

But that wasn't the end. Brown and Dunn further listed 29 problem points that could appear on a coin – from No. 1 for an "edge bump" to No. 29 for "attempted re-engraving outside of the Mint." The number could be followed by the letter "O" or "R" to designate whether the problem appeared on the obverse or reverse and a Roman numeral corresponding to a clock face to designate where the problem appears on the obverse or reverse. For example, a coin described as "VG-B-9-O-X" would grade "VG-B"; the "9" designated a "single rim nick"; the "O" indicated the nick was on the obverse; and the "X" indicated it appeared at the 10 o'clock position, or upper left, of the obverse.

The authors' goal was noble – to create the perfect grading system. They again, however, fell victim to the age-old grading-system problem: Precision comes at the expense of brevity. Dealer Kurt Krueger wrote in the January 1976 issues of *The Numismatist*, "Under the new B & D system, the numismatist must contend with a minimum of 43,152 different grading combinations! Accuracy is apparent, but simplicity has been lost." As a result, the "New B & D Grading System" never caught on in the marketplace.

The 1970s saw two important grading guides make their debut. The first was *Photograde* by James F. Ruddy. As the title implies, Ruddy uses photographs instead of line drawings to show how coins look in the various circulated grades. Simplicity is also a virtue of Ruddy's book. Only seven circulated grades are listed (about good, good, very good, fine, very fine, extremely fine, and about uncirculated), and the designations stop there.

In 1977 the longtime call for the ANA to issue grading standards was met with the release of *Official A.N.A. Grading Standards for United States Coins*. Like Brown and Dunn, the first edition of the ANA guide used line drawings to illustrate coins in various states of wear. But instead of using adjectival descriptions, the ANA guide adopted a numerical system for designating grades.

The numerical designations were based on a system used by Dr. William H. Sheldon in his book *Early American Cents*, first published in 1949. He used a scale of 1 to 70 to designate the grades of large cents.

"On this scale," Sheldon wrote, "1 means that the coin is identifiable and not mutilated – no more than that. A 70-coin is one in flawless Mint State, exactly as it left the dies, with perfect mint color and without a blemish or nick."

(Sheldon's scale also had its pragmatic side. At the time, a No. 2 large cent was worth about twice a No. 1 coin; a No. 4 was worth about twice a No. 2, and so on up the scale.)

With the first edition of its grading guide, the ANA adopted the 70-point scale for grading all U.S. coins. It designated 10 categories of circulated grades: AG-3, G-4, VG-8, F-12, VF-20, VF-30, EF-40, EF-45, AU-50, and AU-55. The third edition, released in 1987, replaced the line drawings with photographs, and another circulated grade was added: AU-58. A fourth edition was released in 1991.

Grading circulated U.S. coins

Dealers today generally use either the ANA guide or *Photograde* when grading circulated coins for their inventories. (Brown and Dunn is now out of print.) Many local coin shops sell both books. Advertisers in *Numismatic News*, *Coins* magazine, and *Coin Prices* must indicate which standards they are using in grading their coins. If the standards are not listed, they must conform to ANA standards.

Following are some general guidelines, accompanied by photos, for grading circulated U.S. coins. Grading even circulated pieces can be subjective, particularly when attempting to draw the fine line between, for example, AU-55 and AU-58. Two longtime collectors or dealers can disagree in such a case.

But by studying some combination of the following guidelines, the ANA guide, and *Photograde*, and by looking at a lot of coins at shops and shows, collectors can gain enough grading knowledge to buy circulated coins confidently from dealers and other collectors. The more you study, the more knowledge and confidence you will gain. When you decide which series of coins you want to collect, focus on the guidelines for that particular series. Read them, reread them, and then refer back to them again and again.

AU-50

AU-50 (about uncirculated): Just a slight trace of wear, result of brief exposure to circulation or light rubbing from mishandling, may be evident on elevated design areas. These imperfections may appear as scratches or dull spots, along with bag marks or edge nicks. At least half of the original mint luster generally is still evident.

Indian cent

Lincoln cent

Buffalo nickel

Jefferson nickel

AU-50

Mercury dime

Standing Liberty quarter

Washington quarter

Walking Liberty half dollar

Morgan dollar

Barber coins

XF-40

XF-40 (extremely fine): The coin must show only slight evidence of wear on the highest points of the design, particularly in the hair lines of the portrait on the obverse. The same may be said for the eagle's feathers and wreath leaves on the reverse of most U.S. coins. A trace of mint luster may still show in protected areas of the coin's surface.

Indian cent

Lincoln cent

Buffalo nickel

Jefferson nickel

XF-40

Mercury dime

Standing Liberty quarter

Washington quarter

Walking Liberty half dollar

Morgan dollar

Barber coins

VF-20

VF-20 (very fine): The coin will show light wear at the fine points in the design, though they may remain sharp overall. Although the details may be slightly smoothed, all lettering and major features must remain sharp.

Indian cent: All letters in "Liberty" are complete but worn. Headdress shows considerable flatness, with flat spots on the tips of the feathers.

Lincoln cent: Hair, cheek, jaw, and bow-tie details will be worn but clearly separated, and wheat stalks on the reverse will be full with no weak spots.

Buffalo nickel: High spots on hair braid and cheek will be flat but show some detail, and a full horn will remain on the buffalo.

Jefferson nickel: Well over half of the major hair detail will remain, and the pillars on Monticello will remain well defined, with the triangular roof partially visible.

Mercury dime: Hair braid will show some detail, and three-quarters of the detail will remain in the feathers. The two diagonal bands on the fasces will show completely but will be worn smooth at the middle, with the vertical lines sharp.

Standing Liberty quarter: Rounded contour of Liberty's right leg will be flattened, as will the high point of the shield.

Washington quarter: There will be considerable wear on the hair curls, with feathers on the right and left of the eagle's breast showing clearly.

Indian cent

Lincoln cent

Buffalo nickel

Jefferson nickel

VF-20

Walking Liberty half dollar: All lines of the skirt will show but will be worn on the high points. Over half the feathers on the eagle will show.

Morgan dollar: Two-thirds of the hair lines from the forehead to the ear must show. Ear should be well defined. Feathers on the eagle's breast may be worn smooth.

Barber coins: All seven letters of "Liberty" on the headband must stand out sharply. Head wreath will be well outlined from top to bottom.

Mercury dime

Standing Liberty quarter

Washington quarter

Walking Liberty half dollar

Morgan dollar

Barber coins

F-12

F-12 (fine): Coins show evidence of moderate to considerable but generally even wear on all high points, though all elements of the design and lettering remain bold. Where the word "Liberty" appears in a headband, it must be fully visible. On 20th century coins, the rim must be fully raised and sharp.

Indian cent

Lincoln cent

Buffalo nickel

Jefferson nickel

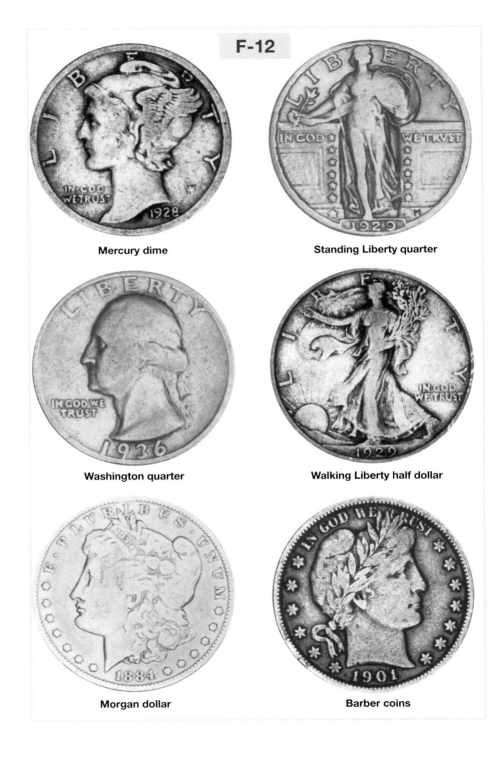

F-12

Mercury dime

Standing Liberty quarter

Washington quarter

Walking Liberty half dollar

Morgan dollar

Barber coins

VG-8

VG-8 (very good): The coin will show considerable wear, with most detail points worn nearly smooth. Where the word "Liberty" appears in a headband, at least three letters must show. On 20th century coins, the rim will start to merge with the lettering.

Indian cent

Lincoln cent

Buffalo nickel

Jefferson nickel

VG-8

Mercury dime

Standing Liberty quarter

Washington quarter

Walking Liberty half dollar

Morgan dollar

Barber coins

G-4

G-4 (good): Only the basic design remains distinguishable in outline form, will all points of detail worn smooth. The word "Liberty" has disappeared, and the rims are almost merging with the lettering.

About good or fair: The coin will be identifiable by date and mint but otherwise badly worn, with only parts of the lettering showing. Such coins are of value only as fillers in a collection until a better example of the date and mintmark can be obtained. The only exceptions would be rare coins.

Indian cent

Lincoln cent

Buffalo nickel

Jefferson nickel

G-4

Mercury dime

Standing Liberty quarter

Washington quarter

Walking Liberty half dollar

Morgan dollar

Barber coins

Grading uncirculated U.S. coins

The subjectivity of grading and the trend toward more classifications becomes more acute when venturing into uncirculated, or mint-state, coins. A minute difference between one or two grade points can mean a difference in value of hundreds or even thousands of dollars. In addition, the standards are more difficult to articulate in writing and illustrate through drawings or photographs. Thus, the possibilities for differences of opinion on one or two grade points increase in uncirculated coins.

Back in Dr. George Heath's day and continuing through the 1960s, a coin was either uncirculated or it wasn't. Little distinction was made between uncirculated coins of varying condition, largely because there was little if any difference in value. When *Numismatic News* introduced its value guide in 1962 (the forerunner of today's Coin Market section in the *News*), it listed only one grade of uncirculated for Morgan dollars.

But as collectible coins increased in value and buyers of uncirculated coins became more picky, distinctions within uncirculated grade started to surface. In 1975 *Numismatic News* still listed only one uncirculated grade in Coin Market, but added this note: "Uncirculated and proof specimens in especially choice condition will also command proportionately higher premiums than these listed."

The first edition of the ANA guide listed two grades of uncirculated, MS-60 and MS-65, in addition to the theoretical but non-existent MS-70 (a flawless coin). MS-60 was described as "typical uncirculated" and MS-65 as "choice uncirculated." *Numismatic News* adopted both designations for Coin Market. In 1981, when the second edition of the ANA grading guide was released, MS-67 and MS-63 were added. In 1985 *Numismatic News* started listing six grades of uncirculated for Morgan dollars: MS-60, MS-63, MS-65, MS-65+, and MS-63 prooflike.

Then in 1986, a new entity appeared that has changed the nature of grading and trading uncirculated coins ever since. A group of dealers led by David Hall of Newport Beach, Calif., formed the Professional Coin Grading Service. For a fee, collectors could submit a coin through an authorized PCGS dealer and receive back a professional opinion of its grade.

Collectors have a variety of grading services to choose from. This set of Arkansas half dollars that appeared in an Early American History Auctions sale used two of the services.

The concept was not new; the ANA had operated an authentication service since 1972 and a grading service since 1979. A collector or dealer could submit a coin directly to the service and receive a certificate giving the service's opinion on authenticity and grade. The grading service was the source of near constant debate among dealers and ANA officials. Dealers charged that ANA graders were too young and inexperienced, and that their grading was inconsistent.

Grading stability was a problem throughout the coin business in the early 1980s, not just with the ANA service. Standards among uncirculated grades would tighten during a bear market and loosen during a bull market. As a result, a coin graded MS-65 in a bull market may have commanded only MS-63 during a bear market.

PCGS created several innovations in the grading business in response to these problems:

1. Coins could be submitted through PCGS-authorized dealers only.

2. Each coin would be graded by at least three members of a panel of "top graders," all prominent dealers in the business. (Since then, however, PCGS does not allow its graders to also deal in coins.)

3. After grading, the coin would be encapsulated in an inert, hard-plastic holder with a serial number and the grade indicated on the holder.

4. PCGS-member dealers pledged to make a market in PCGS-graded coins and honor the grades assigned.

5. In one of the most far-reaching moves, PCGS said it would use all 11 increments of uncirculated on the 70-point numerical scale: MS-60, MS-61, MS-62, MS-63, MS-64, MS-65, MS-66, MS-67, MS-68, MS-69, and MS-70.

Numerous other commercial grading services followed in the steps of PCGS and third-party grading is an accepted part of the hobby.

How should a collector approach the buying and grading of uncirculated coins? Collecting uncirculated coins worth thousands of dollars implies a higher level of numismatic expertise by the buyer. Those buyers without that level of expertise should cut their teeth on more inexpensive coins, just as today's experienced collectors did. Inexperienced collectors can start toward that level by studying the guidelines for mint-state coins in the ANA grading guide and looking at lots of coins at shows and shops.

Study the condition and eye appeal of a coin and compare it to other coins of the same series. Then compare prices. Do the more expensive coins look better? If so, why? Start to make your own judgments concerning relationships between condition and value. Experience remains the best teacher in the field of grading.

Grading U.S. proof coins

Because proof coins are struck by a special process using polished blanks, they receive their own grading designation. A coin does not start out being a proof and then become mint state if it becomes worn. Once a proof coin, always a proof coin.

In the ANA system, proof grades use the same numbers as circulated and uncirculated grades, and the amount of wear on the coin corresponds to those grades. But the number is preceded by the word "proof." For example, Proof-65, Proof-55, Proof-45, and so on. In addition, the ANA says a proof coin with many marks, scratches or other defects should be called an "impaired proof."

4 10 Ways to Buy Coins

But not all are smart

Coin collecting is not a complicated concept. Collectors want to know what something is. They want to know what it is worth and they want to know how to buy one if it appeals to them.

What could be simpler?

Coin Digest is compiled to tell readers the answers to the first two questions. This book helps identify the many coin issues of the United States and it will tell you what each coin is worth on the retail market in many states of preservation by the terms of the official American Numismatic Association grading system that uses a 1-70 scale in ranking quality. Coins that show no wear are at the top end in the Mint State grades MS-60 to MS-70.

It is the final question of how to buy something that will set the average collector off on a lifetime of acquisitions. It also sets off discussions among collectors as to whether there might be other ways of making purchases, or better ways.

Let's look at 10 purchase methods and see what you think. Most are good. Some are not. Most collectors will use multiple methods to reach their goals.

1. Coin shops

The first method of buying coins is to walk into a traditional coin shop and talk to the person behind the counter about what it is you are interested in purchasing.

That person would then direct you to a specific tray in the display case, a three-ring binder of coins in 2x2 holders, or a display of slabs (coins graded by a third-party grading firm and then encapsulated in plastic) that the business might have on hand. You might even get a kick out of going through their junk box from time to time, if they have one.

Shops generally have a good working inventory of the popularly collected coin series, but they cannot own everything. If you don't see what you are looking for, you can ask about it. Sometimes they can get it for you. Sometimes they can't.

But let's say you find a few items you want to add to your collection. What then? How do you make a purchase?

Shops generally are the most retail oriented numismatic businesses. Prices are often marked and the purchase process is like checking out at the grocery store. However, depending on the size of the purchase, or whether you have become a regular customer, prices might be reduced a bit for you.

The advantages of buying at shops is that if you are near one, it is quick. You can see what you are buying and you get immediate satisfaction. You might also become a regular customer and that can provide you with valuable noncash benefits.

Knowledge is king in this hobby. The more you know, the better you get at buying right. If you become a regular shop customer, you open the door to many discussions with the owner/employees. These discussions can often be highly valuable educational tools. If a shop operator knows you are collecting a particular series, he very likely will not only sell you coins, but he will serve as a tutor so you can learn the ins and outs of specific sets. You want to know what "FBL" means? The shop owner can tell you all about full bell lines on the Liberty bell on the reverse of the Franklin half dollar.

You get the idea.

2. Coin shows

Another way of making purchases is to attend a coin show. Most localities have at least one coin show a year. These range in size from 20 dealers in a VFW Hall to hundreds of dealers in a downtown convention center.

No matter the show's size, the purpose is the same. The dealers who are paying for the privilege of sitting behind an 8-foot table would like to do business with you.

Coins are displayed in glass-topped display cases. You ask a dealer to show you things and he will do so. If you see something you like, know that prices are usually not marked.

You might say something like, "What can you do for me on this?"

The dealer will reply with a price. Because it is a show, some dickering is expected. But if you have never done business with the dealer before, keep your counterproposal reasonable. Valuable lasting relationships are made at coin shows because the larger ones offer the collector access to specialists in various coin series. If you like large cents, for example, you will be encountering a highly specialized community of collectors and dealers who will enrich your hobby experience.

You can find coins at flea markets and antique malls, but the people handling them often have no background in numismatics and may knowingly or unknowingly offer you coins. You have to learn your stuff to be able to spot the difference.

3. Online auctions

Online auctions sites, such as eBay, are another popular way to buy coins. You can look at as few, or as many of the listed coins as you want and you can participate in the bidding. You can set up alerts for coins posted in your area of interest.

Some people get hooked on the process and enjoy sniping at the last second of bidding before a sale closes.

The advantage of online auctions is you might get a better price on the coin you are looking for. The disadvantage is you can't see the coin, hold it closely and examine it. You must depend on the accuracy of the description and the quality of the posted images.

Not being able to see a coin first-hand brings up the necessity of return privileges. Don't do business with someone who won't let you send a coin back. Even the best descriptions and photos might miss something that you consider important.

eBay has PayPal, which as a convenient payment mechanism also provides an important consumer protection. If a transaction does not go appropriately PayPal can retrieve payments from sellers and get your money back for you.

Online auctions have the benefit of being available to you from the comfort of your own home.

There are pitfalls, but with *Coin Digest* in your hands, you will likely not fall for sales that pop up from time to time of the rare 1804 dollar of which there are just 15 known. Naturally, the whereabouts of the 15 are known, so the seller is not likely to have a real one.

4. Traditional auctions

Owners of the great rarities are likely to sell them by the traditional auction method. These bring the highest prices of any sales method on average for top quality coins.

Traditional auctions where buyers gather in a ballroom to bid on lots are still quite popular for this reason, though all but the smallest usually have an online component.

For bidders in the room, it is expected that you have examined the lots beforehand during the lot viewing hours and any bids you then win generally are not refundable. However, if you bid online and you did not see anything more than a lot description, you will have a return privilege.

Traditional auctions are conducted by the very largest numismatic firms to the very smallest estate sales.

5. Mail order

Advertisements in newspapers and magazines are another way to buy coins. Care must be taken. Compare grades in the description with those in this book. Compare prices.

If nonstandard grading terminology is employed in an advertisement, say brilliant uncirculated instead of MS-63, you might want to keep up your guard. If prices of all listed coins are well below price guide prices, you might be on your guard as well. After all, if the retail market enables the dealer to get guide book prices, why would he be offering his coins for much less?

In that case, something is likely wrong. The coin might not be what average collectors would presume it is supposed to be. It might be called a grade that is far higher than what it turns out to be.

To protect yourself, look for the return privilege in all ads. Buying a coin you cannot personally examine before the sale makes it extremely important that you can send it back if you are not satisfied when you get the chance to examine it closely.

There are specialty coin publications like the weekly *Numismatic News* hobby newspaper that make the process of buying by mail easier, but even here it is important to assure yourself of a return privilege before sending in your money.

All terms usually are spelled out. The ads will tell you what the postage and handling charges are, what a minimum order size needs to be if any, how coins are graded, the details of the return privilege, sales tax applicability and what forms of payment are accepted. It is expected that coins must stay in the holders in which they were sent to you in order to get a refund.

The ad will also tell you where to send mail orders, or what number to telephone to reach the firm.

6. Online retail advertisements

Online versions of ads have links to coin retailing Web sites that should also spell out sales terms just like an ad in a newspaper. Treat them as you would a newspaper or magazine ad. Look for the sales terms before you do anything else.

Purchases can be completed online, but depending on your payment method, it doesn't hurt to see if the firm is part of the regular numismatic industry, or is actually operated by someone hiding in Kazakhstan.

The Web site for *Numismatic News* is www.numismaticnews.com. It is a good portal to learn about coins in the online numismatic world.

7. TV coin shows

Another way of buying coins, especially if you like to stay up into the wee hours of the morning, is through television coin programs.

Watch yourself here. The sales pitches are so perfectly made that you can hardly contain your excitement and you will want to telephone the number immediately to get your very rare and unusual coin that will only be available for the next half hour at a very special price.

If you are going to buy through programs like this, keep *Coin Digest* handy and see how the TV price compares to the retail prices listed in the book.

If you discover that the TV prices are higher, you will at least be aware that there are cheaper coins available elsewhere, but you will just have to wait until you can go online, or to a coin show to get those better deals.

Sometimes higher prices are justified. It is up to you to make that determination. TV time is costly. The coins they are selling might be hard to find otherwise. Know your alternatives before you pick up the phone.

8. Phone solicitations

Sometimes the telephone can be your enemy. If you get a telephone call out of the blue and the caller wants to sell you coins, hang up. Don't talk. Hang up. Telephone solicitations that you haven't asked for are dangerous to the health of your checkbook balance. The caller could just as easily be trying to sell you oil leases in Patagonia. The sales pressure starts immediately and the end result of any purchase is not usually good.

9. Coin club meetings

An old-fashioned way to buy coins is at a meeting of a local coin club. There are fewer clubs nowadays, but they are still out there. One of the primary aspects of club meetings is providing a time for members to trade coins among themselves.

Each club is different. Find out what their rules and habits are.

The learning aspect to the social occasions provided by clubs is invaluable. You also might find that you will become a better collector by learning what the other members can teach you for free.

Coin collectors love to share what they know. If you enjoy coins as much as they do, the benefits to you can be large.

10. The U.S. Mint

The final method to purchase coins is to go right to the United States Mint. It produces coins every year for use in your change and it sells collector versions of these coins directly to collectors.

Visit the Web site at www.usmint.gov to see what is available, or telephone (800) USA-MINT.

Just remember that the Mint sells new coins for the most part. The older ones you have to find out there yourself.

Beware of firms that put the word "mint" in their title. There is only one official government mint in the United States. It operates minting facilities in Philadelphia, Pa., West Point, N.Y., Denver, Colo., and San Francisco, Calif. These minting plants do not sell coins directly to collectors, unless you happen to stop by the gift shops in Philadelphia and Denver.

Private firms with "mint" in their names might offer you something you want to buy, but don't mistake them for the U.S. government. There is only one United States Mint and that is its formal name.

Summary

There is no great mystery to coin buying for Americans who have been raised on shopping. The process is the same, but the hunt for specific coins might take just a bit longer than the hunt for a new car.

What makes coin collecting so interesting is the challenge that it presents. Some coins are easy to find. Some are not so easy. Some are downright hard and you may only get one or two chances in your lifetime to buy them.

If you get out there and try the various coin buying methods, you will not only find out which methods suit you best, you will also find out how to recognize the difference between contrived rarity and when those very rare coins have genuinely come your way.

Get out there and get started.

10 ways to buy coins

1. Coin shops	6. Online retail ads
2. Coin shows	7. TV coin shows
3. Online auctions	8. Phone solicitations (Avoid)
4. Traditional auctions	9. Coin club meetings
5. Mail order	10. United States Mint

5 Five Tips on Selling

And five ways to do it

Selling coins is more challenging than buying them. The first thing to remember is you cannot force anybody to buy your coins. There is no automatic process. You have to work at it.

The smarter you work at it, the better the result. There are do's and don'ts to follow.

There are five tips to keep in mind as you prepare to sell your coins and there are five popular methods of selling coins.

Tip 1: Know prices

When you want to sell coins, you usually cannot obtain retail coin prices listed in Coin Digest. Dealers have to make a profit on what they buy and you must expect them to offer less than the prices printed here in this book.

How much less?

The answer can be a shock. For accurately graded and described material, offers will come in depending on how long the dealer expects that he will have to hold the material in inventory before he can in turn sell it to someone else.

For coins that might hang around for awhile, you are likely to get no more than 60 percent of retail. Coins that contain precious metals trade at far less of a discount to retail. Because metals were hot as this is written, many U.S. coins that trade close to bullion prices were actually trading at premium prices. These include many of the common circulated U.S. gold coin dates

Knowing what is easily traded will help you accurately determine what has the higher values. Lincoln cents are expected to be hot in 2009, but to sell a Lincoln cent set that is anything less than Mint State, a dealer will look for the keys, the 1909-S, 1909-S VDB, 1910-S, 1914-D, 1922 and 1931-S. He might pass altogether if they are not there.

Series like Jefferson nickels are very hard to sell at premium prices. Most circulated dates are just returned to the bank. Even the Mint State grade coins are not in particularly high demand.

If your collection contains classically rare coins, the prices you will get for them will be closer to retail value. Age does not automatically translate to value, but it has given the hobby time to establish pricing relationships that hold up year after year. Learn what these are and profit from them.

Tip 2. Complete inventory

It is crucial to have an accurate inventory of what you are trying to sell, whether it is two coins you want to get rid of because you have others, or whether it is a lifetime collection.

A buyer needs solid information on which to base his calculations of what he will pay. An inventory is usually a starting point for discussion. It doesn't mean the dealer doesn't want to see what you have. He will ask if and when he is ready for the next step. A look at an inventory list will give him the opportunity to say that even if the coins are as you represent them, he just doesn't have a need for them. That saves you the trouble of hauling them around.

Specialists in Seated Liberty coinage, for example, are less likely to spend time analyzing the value of coins outside of their area, but a generalist, which coin shop proprietors usually are, might be interested in everything.

Tip 3. Complete sets are better

It is far easier to sell complete sets of various American coins for better prices than hodgepodge accumulations. Accumulations can have some good values hidden in them, but it is harder for a would-be buyer to make that judgment.

A complete set of large cents speaks volumes in a few words. The same is true of Morgan dollars or Standing Liberty quarters or almost any other set.

These are easier to evaluate and to sell to others. Thus, prices offered to sellers will tend to be higher.

Tip 4. Be up-front and honest

If you don't know something, the would-be buyer will figure this out in a hurry. If your lack of knowledge paints you as an unreasonable person, say trying to pass off AU-58 coins as MS-65, the buyer will not want to do business with you, or he will lowball you to protect himself.

Just being honest won't make a deal happen, but it is a critical foundation to eventually making a satisfactory deal happen.

Tip 5. Don't ship coins without permission

Shipping coins to someone without being asked is a frequent mistake and it is a stupid one. Make sure that the recipient knows something is coming to him, that he knows precisely what is coming and that he wants them to come.

Nothing is so irritating as getting coins in the mail that are unexpected and perhaps unneeded.

Think about this for your own protection. A dealer who doesn't need something is going to offer you less money if he makes an offer at all. A dealer for whom you've made things difficult is going to discount his prices to pay for the trouble that is caused.

A would-be buyer might not want your coins at all and you are on the hook for the return shipping costs.

Five ways to sell

You have educated yourself about prices, you have a full and accurate inventory and you are ready to courteously contact would-be buyers.

What's next?

Method 1. Sell to a shop

Walking into a coin shop can be the best way to sell your coins. This is especially true if this shop is where you purchased many of your prize pieces and the owner helped you along the way.

If the owner knows you, not only will that facilitate the negotiating process, but it is to be expected that he will also know your coins. After all, he handled many of them. Coin dealers as a group have remarkable memories. They can discourse, if you let them, on the salient details of the XF-45 1909-S VDB cent that you bought from them a decade ago.

A dealer who helped you build a set will know the quality of your coins and if there are any problems. He will know how to make you feel most comfortable with the whole selling process.

And from the perspective of the seller, knowing the buyer can make all the difference. Who would you rather deal with, someone you know or someone you don't know?

If you don't happen to know the person in the shop doing the buying, your complete inventory and straight-forward manner will keep the process on track on a businesslike basis.

If there is anything in a shop scenario that makes you uncomfortable, you are best able to make the changes necessary face to face with the other party. If it turns into a high-pressure session, something has gone wrong and it might be best to go somewhere else, or try some other sales method.

Method 2. Sell in traditional auction

Since the turn of the 21st century, public auctions have been doing better and better at getting the maximum value for coins.

If your collection is of a certain size and quality, it might be in your best interest to consider consigning the coins to an auction firm. Naturally, the larger your collection and the higher the expected values, the bigger the firm that you might choose to deal with.

Auction firms usually charge the seller fees. These vary and can even be waived entirely for desirable material. The auctioneer calculates the public relations value of having your coins in his sale. You can even negotiate the option to buy back a piece that appears to be going too cheaply.

Almost anything that is mutually agreeable is possible, but you have to negotiate the terms ahead of time.

What if your collection won't be making headlines in the next Heritage or Stack's auction? Don't give up. Most collections don't.

Smaller auction firms might want to handle your coins. Here again, your accurate inventory will help these firms in making a decision quickly in determining whether they will sell your coins. They can quickly determine whether you make their financial threshold.

And, as is the case with shops, if you were a regular buyer at the auctions conducted by these firms, they will remember you and be just as delighted to help you sell your coins as they were to help you buy them.

For successful collectors, personal relationships between them and their dealers are as close or closer than a collector and his doctor.

Method 3. Sell in online auction

The arrival of eBay in the 1990s opened a new door for collectors interested in selling their coins themselves. You can sell one coin at a time at any pace you choose. You can sell a whole collection this way or any part of one. The choice is yours.

You simply need to prepare yourself to write accurate descriptions and post high-quality photos. Once again, that inventory that you prepared will serve you well.

Selling online has the advantage that you can get the highest possible price for individual coins. There are many retail buyers online who will be willing to pay higher prices than a dealer who is watching his profit margin. This is to your benefit.

The downside is the time element and your comfort level with computers and dealing with many persons otherwise unknown to you. Your commitment to being up-front and honest in your approach will serve you well here.

Method 4. Sell at a show

Sometimes the dealer or dealers you know best do business at shows and it is at a show that you would like to sell your coins.

This works well for portable quantities of coins. However, the larger the quantities, the more you will have to consider the logistics.

If you want to sell your Proof-65 1895 Morgan dollar to your favorite Morgan dollar specialist at a coin show, go for it. This is quick and convenient and you probably will maximize the value you receive.

However, if you are going to show up unannounced with bag quantities of medium value circulated Mercury dimes, unless you know the dealer is prepared to handle them, you might be handicapping your effort to get the best value for your coins.

The show dealer you sell them to will be mentally figuring in his shipping and insurance costs to get them back to his base of operation. It might be better to sell this kind of thing in a shop or in a pre-arranged deal.

Nevertheless, shows in the United States do billions of dollars' worth of deals in the course of a year and logistical issues are built right into everybody's plans.

Method 5. Sell at a club

This is selling as a social activity. Many coin collectors who are longtime club members might remember their favorite collector.

"Old Joe" has attended all the meetings you have ever been at, and he just always happens to have a few nice pieces in his pocket that he is getting rid of for the benefit of younger collectors.

You might discover someday that it is you who are Old Joe. You can enjoy the society of fellow collectors. You can educate the newcomers, and you can get a fair but not an incredible price for the pieces you choose to sell this way.

This, of course, depends on the rules of each club, but if you already know Old Joe, you already know the rules.

Summary

It is your choice which way you choose to sell your coins. There is no right or wrong way. It is a matter of getting the best prices possible.

You can choose to sell in multiple ways over time. You can break collections up and sell your best Morgans to the specialist, your bulk circulated silver coin sets to a shop owner and put a few medals online to see what they will bring.

But remember one final bit of advice. As a collector, it is up to you to be ready to sell when the time comes. This means test your sales skills from time to time.

Even when you are most interested in buying, plan to sell a piece here and there just to see who treats you the best and who gives you the best prices.

Desirable outcomes aren't always a given, but if you practice, the odds tilt in your favor. People change over the years as old-timers leave the business and newcomers enter. A bitter divorce might change the nature of a dealer's business dealings. He might become less pleasant to deal with.

You might hate dealing with online buyers, but you won't find this out if you don't do a little advance preparation.

It is up to the collector to be ready to sell his collection when the time comes. A part of this process is to do some test runs with a few pieces over the years.

If you do that when the time comes, you will be ready to get the best prices for the collection that you have built. That is the name of the game. We collectors are merely custodians of our collections. Sooner or later, we have to give them up. A properly prepared collector will achieve the most satisfactory result.

Good luck. Now get out there and mix it up a little.

10 Tips and ways to sell coins

1. Know prices
2. Complete inventory
3. Complete sets are better
4. Be up-front and honest
5. Don't ship coins without permission
6. Sell to a shop
7. Sell at traditional auction
8. Sell at a online auction
9. Sell at a show
10. Sell at a club

6 U.S. Minting Varieties and Errors

Most are common, some are rare

Introduction

The P.D.S. cataloging system used here to list minting varieties was originally compiled by Alan Herbert in 1971. PDS stands for the three main divisions of the. minting process, "planchet," "die" and "striking." Two more divisions cover collectible modifications after the strike, as well as non-collectible alterations, counterfeits and damaged coins.

This listing includes 445 classes, each a distinct part of the minting process or from a specific non-mint change in the coin. Classes from like causes are grouped together. The PDS system applies to coins of the world, but is based on U.S. coinage with added classes for certain foreign minting practices.

Price ranges are based on a U.S. coin in MS-60 grade (uncirculated.) The ranges may be applied in general to foreign coins of similar size or value although collector values are not usually as high as for U.S. coins. Prices are only a guide as the ultimate price is determined by a willing buyer and seller.

To define minting varieties, "A coin which exhibits a variation of any kind from the normal, as a result of any portion of the minting process, whether at the planchet stage, as a result of a change or modification of the die, or during the striking process. It includes those classes considered to be intentional changes, as well as those caused by normal wear and tear on the dies or other minting equipment and classes deemed to be "errors."

The three causes are represented as follows:
1. (I) = Intentional Changes
2. (W) = Wear and Tear
3. (E) = Errors
Note: A class may show more than one cause and could be listed as (IWE).

Rarity level

The rarity ratings are based on the following scale:

1 - Very Common. Ranges from every coin struck down to 1,000,000.

2 - Common. From 1,000,000 down to 100,000.

3 - Scarce. From 100,000 down to 10,000.

4 - Very Scarce. From 10,000 down to 1,000.

5 - Rare. From 1,000 down to 100.

6 - Very Rare. From 100 down to 10.

7 - Extremely Rare. From 10 down to 1.

Unknown: If there is no confirmed report of a piece fitting a particular class, it is listed as Unknown. Reports of finds by readers would be appreciated in order to update future presentations.

An Unknown does not mean that your piece automatically is very valuable. Even a Rarity 7 piece, extremely rare, even unique, may have a very low collector value because of a lack of demand or interest in that particular class.

Classes, definitions and price ranges are based on material previously offered in Alan Herbert's book, The Official Price Guide to Minting Varieties and Errors and in Coin Prices Magazine.

Pricing information has also been provided by John A. Wexler and Ken Potter, with special pricing and technical advice from Del Romines.

Also recommended is the Cherrypicker's Guide to Rare Die Varieties by Bill Fivaz and J.T. Stanton. Check your favorite coin shop, numismatic library or book seller for availability of the latest edition.

Quick check index

If you have a coin and are not sure where to look for the possible variety:

If your coin shows doubling, first check V-B-I.

Then try II-A, II-B, II-C, II-I (4 & 5), III-J, III-L, or IV-C.

If part of the coin is missing, check III-B, III-C, or III-D.

If there is a raised line of coin metal, check II-D, II-G.

If there is a raised area of coin metal, check II-E, II-F, or III-F.

If the coin is out of round, and too thin, check III-G.

If coin appears to be the wrong metal, check III-A, III-E, III-F-3 and III-G.

If the die appears to have been damaged, check II-E, II-G. (Damage to the coin itself usually is not a minting variety.)

If the coin shows incomplete or missing design, check II-A, II-E, III-B-3, III-B-5 or III-D.

If only part of the planchet was struck, check III-M.

If something was struck into the coin, check III-J and III-K.

If something has happened to the edge of the coin, check II-D-6, II-E-10, III-I, III-M and III-O.

If your coin shows other than the normal design, check II-A or II-C.

If a layer of the coin metal is missing, or a clad layer is missing, check III-B and III-D.

If you have an unstruck blank, or planchet, check I-G.

If your coin may be a restrike, check IV-C.

If your coin has a counterstamp, countermark, additional engraving or apparent official modifications, check IV-B and V-A-8.

Do not depend on the naked eye to examine your coins. Use a magnifying lens whenever possible, as circulation damage, wear and alterations frequently can be mistaken for legitimate minting varieties.

The planchet varieties

DIVISION I

The first division of the PDS System includes those minting varieties t hat occur in the manufacture of the planchet upon which the coins will ultimately be struck and includes classes resulting from faulty metallurgy, mechanical damage, faulty processing, or equipment or human malfunction prior to the actual coin striking.

●PLANCHET ALLOY MIX (I-A)

This section includes those classes pertaining to mixing and processing the various metals which will be used to make a coin alloy.

I-A-1 Improper Alloy Mix (WE), Rarity Level: 3-4, Values: $5 to $10.

I-A-2 Slag Inclusion Planchet (WE), Rarity Level: 5-6, Values: $25 up.

●DAMAGED AND DEFECTIVE PLANCHETS (I-B)

To be a class in this section the blank, or planchet, must for some reason not meet the normal standards or must have been damaged in processing. The classes cover the areas of defects in the melting, rolling, punching and processing of the planchets up to the point where they are sent to the coin presses to be struck.

I-B-1 Defective Planchet (WE), Rarity Level: 6, Values: $25 up.

I-B-2 Mechanically Damaged Planchet (WE), Rarity Level: –, Values: No Value. (See values for the coin struck on a mechanically damaged planchet.)

I-B-3 Rolled Thin Planchet (WE), Rarity Level: 6 - (Less rare on half cents of 1795, 1797 and restrikes of 1831-52.) Values: $10 up.

I-B-4 Rolled Thick Planchet (WE), Rarity Level: 7 - (Less rare in Colonial copper coins. Notable examples occur on the restrike half cents of 1840-52.) Values: $125 up.

I-B-5 Tapered Planchet (WE), Rarity Level: 7, Values: $25 up.

I-B-6 Partially Unplated Planchet (WE), Rarity Level: 6, Values: $15 up.

I-B-7 Unplated Planchet (WE), Rarity Level: 6-7, Values: $50 up.

I-B-8 Bubbled Plating Planchet (WE), Rarity Level: 1, Values: No Value.

I-B-9 Included Gas Bubble Planchet (WE), Rarity Level: 6-7, Values: $50 up.

I-B-10 Partially Unclad Planchet (WE), Rarity Level: 6, Values: $20 up.

I-B-11 Unclad Planchet (WE), Rarity Level: 6-7, Values: $50 up.

I-B-12 Undersize Planchet (WE), Rarity Level: 7, Values: $250 up.

I-B-13 Oversize Planchet (WE), Rarity Level: 7, Values: $250 up.

I-B-14 Improperly Prepared Proof Planchet (WE), Rarity Level: 7, Values: $100 up.

I-B-15 Improperly Annealed Planchet (WE), Rarity Level: - , Values: No Value.

I-B-16 Faulty Upset Edge Planchet (WE), Rarity Level: 5-6, Values: $10 up.

I-B-17 Rolled-In Metal Planchet (WE), Rarity Level: 6-7, Values: $50 up.

I-B-18 Weld Area Planchet (WE), Rarity Level: Unknown, Values: No Value Established. (See values for the coins struck on weld area planchets.)

I-B-19 Strike Clip Planchet (WE), Rarity Level: 7, Values: $150 up.

I-B-20 Unpunched Center-Hole Planchet (WE), Rarity Level: 5-7, Values: $5 and up.

I-B-21 Incompletely Punched Center-Hole Planchet (WE), Rarity Level: 6-7, Values: $15 up.

I-B-22 Uncentered Center-Hole Planchet (WE), Rarity Level: 6-7, Values: $10 up.

I-B-23 Multiple Punched Center-Hole Planchet (WE), Rarity Level: 7, Values: $35 up.

I-B-24 Unintended Center-Hole Planchet (WE), Rarity Level: Unknown, Values: -.

I-B-25 Wrong Size or Shape Center-Hole Planchet (IWE), Rarity Level: 5-7, Values: $10 up.

●CLIPPED PLANCHETS (I-C)

Clipped blanks, or planchets, occur when the strip of coin metal fails to move forward between successive strokes of the gang punch to clear the previously punched holes, in the same manner as a cookie cutter overlapping a previously cut hole in the dough. The size of the clip is a function of the amount of overlap of the next punch.

The overlapping round punches produce a missing arc with curve matching the outside circumference of the blanking punch. Straight clips occur when the punch overlaps the beginning or end of a strip which has had the end sheared or sawed off. Ragged clips occur in the same manner when the ends of the strip have been left as they were rolled out.

The term "clip" as used here should not be confused with the practice of clipping or shaving small pieces of metal from a bullion coin after it is in circulation.

I-C-1 Disc Clip Planchet (WE), Rarity Level: 3-5, Values: $5 up.

I-C-2 Curved Clip Planchet - (To 5%) (WE), Rarity Level: 5-6, Values: $5 up.

I-C-3 Curved Clip Planchet - (6 to 10%) (WE), Rarity Level: 6, Values: $10 up.

I-C-4 Curved Clip Planchet - (11 to 25%) (WE), Rarity Level: 5-6, Values: $15 up.

I-C-5 Curved Clip Planchet - (26 to 60%) (WE), Rarity Level: 6-7, Values: $25 up.

I-C-6 Double Curved Clip Planchet (WE), Rarity Level: 6, Values: $10 up.

I-C-7 Triple Curved Clip Planchet (WE), Rarity Level: 5-6, Values: $25 up.

I-C-8 Multiple Curved Clip Planchet (WE), Rarity Level: 6-7, Values: $35 up.

I-C-9 Overlapping Curved Clipped Planchet (WE), Rarity Level: 6-7, Values: $50 up.

I-C-10 Incompletely Punched Curved Clip Planchet (WE), Rarity Level: 6, Values: $35 up.

I-C-11 Oval Curved Clip Planchet (WE), Rarity Level: 6-7, Values: $50 up.

I-C-12 Crescent Clip Planchet - (61% or more) (WE), Rarity Level: 7, Values: $200 up.

I-C-13 Straight Clip Planchet (WE), Rarity Level: 6, Values: $30 up.

I-C-14 Incompletely Sheared Straight Clip Planchet (WE), Rarity Level: 6, Values: $50 up.

I-C-15 Ragged Clip Planchet (WE), Rarity Level: 6-7, Values: $35 up.

I-C-16 Outside Corner Clip Planchet (E), Rarity Level: -, Values: No Value.

I-C-17 Inside Corner Clip Planchet (E), Rarity Level: -, Values: No Value.

I-C-18 Irregularly Clipped Planchet (E) Rarity Level: -, Values: Value not established.

I-C-19 Incompletely Punched Scalloped or Multi-Sided Planchet (E), Rarity Level: 7, Values: $25 up.

I-C-2

● **LAMINATED, SPLIT, OR BROKEN PLANCHET (I-D)**

For a variety of reasons the coin metal may split into thin layers (delaminate) and either split completely off the coin, or be retained. Common causes are included gas or alloy mix problems. Lamination cracks usually enter the surface of the planchet at a very shallow angle or are at right angles to the edge. The resulting layers differ from slag in that they appear as normal metal.

Lamination cracks and missing metal of any size below a split planchet are too common in the 35 percent silver 1942-1945 nickels to be collectible or have any significant value.

I-D-1 Small Lamination Crack Planchet (W), Rarity Level: 4-5, Values: $1 up.

I-D-2 Large Lamination Crack Planchet (W), Rarity Level: 3-4, Values: $5 up.

I-D-3 Split Planchet (W), Rarity Level: 5-6, Values: $15 up.

I-D-4 Hinged Split Planchet (W), Rarity Level: 6-7, Values: $75 up.

I-D-5 Clad Planchet With a Clad Layer Missing (W), Rarity Level: 5-6, Values: $35 up.

I-D-6 Clad Planchet With Both Clad Layers Missing (W), Rarity Level: 6-7, Values: $75 up.

I-D-7 Separated Clad Layer (W), Rarity Level: 5, Values: $25 up.

I-D-8 Broken Planchet (WE), Rarity Level: 3-4, Values: $5 up.

● **WRONG STOCK PLANCHET (I-E)**

The following classes cover those cases where the wrong coin metal stock was run through the blanking press, making blanks of the correct diameter, but of the wrong thickness, alloy or metal or a combination of the wrong thickness and the wrong metal.

I-E-1 Half Cent Stock Planchet (IE), Rarity Level: Unknown, Values: No Value Established.

I-E-2 Cent Stock Planchet (IE), Rarity Level: Unknown, Values: No Value Established.

I-E-3 Two Cent Stock Planchet (E), Rarity Level: Unknown, Values: No Value Established.

I-E-4 Three Cent Silver Stock Planchet (E), Rarity Level: Unknown, Values: No Value Established.

I-E-5 Three Cent Nickel Stock Planchet (E), Rarity Level: Unknown, Values: No Value Established.

I-E-6 Half Dime Stock Planchet (E), Rarity Level: Unknown, Values: No Value Established.

I-E-7 Dime Stock Planchet (E), Rarity Level: 7, Values: $200 up.

I-E-8 Twenty Cent Stock Planchet (E), Rarity Level: Unknown, Values: No Value Established.

I-E-9 Quarter Stock Planchet (E), Rarity Level: Unknown, Values: No Value Established.

I-E-10 Half Dollar Stock Planchet (E), Rarity Level: Unknown, Values: No Value Established.

I-E-11 Dollar Stock Planchet (E), Rarity Level: 7, Values: $300 up.

I-E-12 Token or Medal Stock Planchet (E), Rarity Level: Unknown, Values: No Value Established.

I-E-13 Wrong Thickness Spoiled Planchet (IWE), Rarity Level: Unknown, Values: No Value Established.

I-E-14 Correct Thickness Spoiled Planchet (IWE), Rarity Level: Unknown, Values: No Value Established.

I-E-15 Cut Down Struck Token Planchet (IWE), Rarity Level: Unknown, Values: No Value Established.

I-E-16 Experimental or Pattern Stock Planchet (IE), Rarity Level: Unknown, Values: No Value Established.

I-E-17 Proof Stock Planchet (IE), Rarity Level: Unknown, Values: No Value Established.

I-E-18 Adjusted Specification Stock Planchet (IE), Rarity Level: 7, Values: $25 up.

I-E-19 Trial Strike Stock Planchet (IE), Rarity Level: Unknown, Values: No Value Established.

I-E-20 U.S. Punched Foreign Stock Planchet (E), Rarity Level: 7, Values: $75 up.

I-E-21 Foreign Punched Foreign Stock Planchet (E), Rarity Level: 7, Values: $75 up.

I-E-22 Non-Standard Coin Alloy Planchet (IE), Rarity Level: 7, Values: Unknown.

●EXTRA METAL ON A BLANK, OR PLANCHET (I-F)

True extra metal is only added to the blank during the blanking operation. This occurs as metal is scraped off the sides of the blanks as they are driven down through the thimble, or lower die in the blanking press. The metal is eventually picked up by a blank passing through, welded to it by the heat of friction.

A second form of extra metal has been moved to this section, the sintered coating planchet, the metal deposited on the planchet in the form of dust during the annealing operation.

I-F-1 Extra Metal on a Type 1 Blank (W), Rarity Level: 7, Values: $50 up.

I-F-2 Extra Metal on a Type 2 Planchet (W), Rarity Level: 6-7, Values: $75 up.

I-F-3 Sintered Coating Planchet (W), Rarity Level: 7, Values: $75 up.

●NORMAL OR ABNORMAL PLANCHETS (I-G)

This section consists of the two principal forms – the blank as it comes from the blanking press – and in the form of a planchet after it has passed through the upsetting mill. It also includes a class for purchased planchets and one for planchets produced by the mint.

I-G-1 Type I Blank (IWE), Rarity Level: 3-5, Values: $2 up.

I-G-2 Type II Planchet (IWE), Rarity Level: 3-4, Values: 50 up.

I-G-3 Purchased Planchet (I), Rarity Level: 1, Values: No Value.

I-G-4 Mint Made Planchet (I), Rarity Level: 1, Values: No Value.

I-G-5 Adjustment-Marked Planchet (I), Rarity Level: Unknown, Values: No Value.

I-G-6 Hardness Test-Marked Planchet (I), Rarity Level: -, Values: No Value Established.

Note: There are no classes between I-G-6 and I-G-23

I-G-23 Proof Planchet (IE), Rarity Level: 6-7, Values: $1 up.

●COIN METAL STRIP (I-H)

When the coin metal strip passes through the blanking press it goes directly to a chopper. This cuts the remaining web into small pieces to be sent back to the melting furnace. Pieces of the web or the chopped up web may escape into the hands of collectors.

I-H-1 Punched Coin Metal Strip (IWE), Rarity Level: 4-6, Values: $5 up, depending on size, denomination and number of holes showing.

I-H-2 Chopped Coin Metal Strip (IE), Rarity Level: 3-5, Values: $5 up.

The die varieties

DIVISION II

Die varieties may be unique to a given die, but will repeat for the full life of the die unless a further change occurs. Anything that happens to the die will affect the appearance of the struck coin. This includes all the steps of the die making:

- Cutting a die blank from a tool steel bar.
- Making the design.
- Transferring it to a model.
- Transferring it to the master die or hub.
- The hubbing process of making the die.
- Punching in the mintmark.
- Heat treating of the die.

The completed dies are also subject to damage in numerous forms, plus wear and tear during the striking process and repair work done with abrasives. All of these factors can affect how the struck coin looks.

●ENGRAVING VARIETIES (II-A)

In all cases in this section where a master die, or master hub is affected by the class, the class will affect all the working hubs and all working dies descending from it.

Identification as being on a master die or hub depends on it being traced to two or more of the working hubs descended from the same master tools.

II-A-1 Overdate (IE), Rarity Level: 1-7, Values: $1 up.

II-A-2 Doubled Date (IE), Rarity Level: 1-7, Values: $1 up.

II-A-3 Small Date (IE), Rarity Level: 2-5, Values: $1 up.

II-A-4 Large Date (IE), Rarity Level: 2-5, Values: $1 up.

II-A-5 Small Over Large Date (IE), Rarity Level: 4-6, Values: $15 up.

II-A-6 Large Over Small Date (IE), Rarity Level: 3-5, Values: $10 up.

II-A-7 Blundered Date (E), Rarity Level: 6-7, Values: $50 up.

II-A-8 Corrected Blundered Date (IE), Rarity Level: 3-5, Values: $5 up.

II-A-9 Wrong Font Date Digit (IE), Rarity Level: 5-6, Values: Minimal.

II-A-10 Worn, Broken or Damaged Punch (IWE), Rarity Level: 5-6, Values: $5 up.

II-A-11 Expedient Punch (IWE), Rarity Level: 5-6, Values: $10 up.

II-A-12 Blundered Digit (E), Rarity Level: 4-5, Values: $50 up.

II-A-13 Corrected Blundered Digit (IE), Rarity Level: 3-6, Values: $10 up.

II-A-14 Doubled Digit (IWE), Rarity Level: 2-6, Values: $2 up.

II-A-15 Wrong Style or Font Letter or Digit (IE), Rarity Level: 3-5, Values: Minimal.

II-A-1

II-A-2

II-A-2

II-A-16 One Style or Font Over Another (IE), Rarity Level: 4-6, Values: $10 up.

II-A-17 Letter Over Digit (E), Rarity Level: 6-7, Values: $25 up.

II-A-18 Digit Over Letter (E), Rarity Level: 6-7, Values: $25 up.

II-A-19 Omitted Letter or Digit (IWE), Rarity Level: 4-6, Values: $5 up.

II-A-20 Blundered Letter (E), Rarity Level: 6-7, Values: $50 up.

II-A-21 Corrected Blundered Letter (IE), Rarity Level: 1-3, Values: $10 up.

II-A-22 Doubled Letter (IWE), Rarity Level: 2-6, Values: $2 up.

II-A-23 Blundered Design Element (IE), Rarity Level: 6-7, Values: $50 up.

II-A-24 Corrected Blundered Design Element (IE), Rarity Level: 3-5, Values: $10 up.

II-A-25 Large Over Small Design Element (IE), Rarity Level: 4-6, Values: $2 up.

II-A-26 Omitted Design Element (IWE), Rarity Level: 5-7, Values: $10 up.

II-A-27 Doubled Design Element (IWE), Rarity Level: 2-6, Values: $2 up.

II-A-28 One Design Element Over Another (IE), Rarity Level: 3-6, Values: $5 up.

II-A-29 Reducing Lathe Doubling (WE), Rarity Level: 6-7, Values: $50 up.

II-A-30 Extra Design Element (IE), Rarity Level: 3-5, Values: $10 up.

II-A-31 Modified Design (IWE), Rarity Level: 1-5, Values: No Value up.

II-A-32 Normal Design (I), Rarity Level: 1, Values: No Extra Value.

II-A-33 Design Mistake (IE), Rarity Level: 2-6, Values: $1 up.

II-A-34 Defective Die Design (IWE), Rarity Level: 1, Values: No Value.

II-A-35 Pattern (I), Rarity Level: 6-7, Values: $100 up.

II-A-36 Trial Design (I), Rarity Level: 5-7, Values: $100 up.

II-A-37 Omitted Designer's Initial (IWE), Rarity Level: 3-7, Values: $1 up.

II-A-38 Layout Mark (IE), Rarity Level: 5-7, Values: Minimal.

II-A-39 Abnormal Reeding (IWE), Rarity Level: 2-5, Values: $1 up.

II-A-40 Modified Die or Hub (IWE), Rarity Level: 1-5, Values: No Value up.

II-A-41 Numbered Die (I), Rarity Level: 3-5, Values: $5 up.

II-A-42 Plugged Die (IW), Rarity Level: 5-6, Values: Minimal.

II-A-43 Cancelled Die (IE), Rarity Level: 3-6, Values: No Value up.

II-A-44 Hardness Test Marked Die (IE), Rarity Level: 7, Values: $100 up.

II-A-45 Coin Simulation (IE), Rarity Level: 6-7, Values: $100 up, but may be illegal to own.

II-A-46 Punching Mistake (IE), Rarity Level: 2-6, Values: $1 up.

II-A-47 Small Over Large Design (IE), Rarity Level: 4-6, Values: $5 up.

II-A-48 Doubled Punch (IE), Rarity Level: 5-7, Values: $5 up.

II-A-49 Mint Display Sample (I) Rarity Level: 7, Values not established

II-A-50 Center Dot, Stud or Circle (IE) Rarity Level: 7, much more common on early cents, Values not established

●Hub doubling varieties (II-B)

This section includes eight classes of hub doubling. Each class is from a different cause, described by the title of the class. At the latest count over 2,500 doubled dies have been reported in the U.S. coinage, the most famous being examples of the 1955, 1969-S and 1972 cent dies.

II-B-I Rotated Hub Doubling (WE), Rarity Level: 3-6, Values: $1 up

II-B-II Distorted Hub Doubling (WE), Rarity Level: 3-6, Values: $1 up.

II-B-III Design Hub Doubling (IWE), Rarity Level: 3-6, Values: $1 up to five figure amounts.

II-B-IV Offset Hub Doubling (WE), Rarity Level: 4-6, Values: $15 up.

II-B-V Pivoted Hub Doubling (WE), Rarity Level: 3-6, Values: $10 up.

II-B-VI Distended Hub Doubling (WE), Rarity Level: 2-5, Values: $1 up.

II-B-VII Modified Hub Doubling (IWE), Rarity Level: 2-5, Values: $1 up.

II-B-VIII Tilted Hub Doubling (WE), Rarity Level: 4-6, Values: $5 up.

●Mintmark varieties (II-C)

Mintmarks are punched into U.S. coin dies by hand (Up to 1985 for proof coins, to 1990 for cents and nickels and 1991 for other denominations). Variations resulting from mistakes in the punching are listed in this section. Unless exceptionally mispunched, values are usually estimated at 150 percent of numismatic value. Slightly tilted or displaced mintmarks have no value.

II-C-1 Doubled Mintmark (IE), Rarity Level: 2-6, Values: 50 cents up.

II-C-2 Separated Doubled Mintmark (IE), Rarity Level: 5-6, Values: $15 up.

II-C-3 Over Mintmark (IE), Rarity Level: 3-6, Values: $2 up.

II-C-4 Tripled Mintmark (IE), Rarity Level: 3-5, Values: 50 up.

II-C-5 Quadrupled Mintmark (IE), Rarity Level: 4-6, Values: $1 up.

II-C-6 Small Mintmark (IE), Rarity Level: 2-5, Values: No Extra Value up.

II-C-7 Large Mintmark (IE), Rarity Level: 2-5, Values: No Extra Value up.

II-C-8 Large Over Small Mintmark (IE), Rarity Level: 2-5, Values: $2 up.

II-C-9 Small Over Large Mintmark (IE), Rarity Level: 3-6, Values: $5 up.

II-C-10 Broken Mintmark Punch (W), Rarity Level: 5-6, Values: $5 up.

II-C-11 Omitted Mintmark (IWE), Rarity Level: 4-7, Values: $125 up.

II-C-12 Tilted Mintmark (IE), Rarity Level: 5-7, Values: $5 up.

II-C-13 Blundered Mintmark (E), Rarity Level: 4-6, Values: $5 up.

II-C-14 Corrected Horizontal Mintmark (IE), Rarity Level: 4-6, Values: $5 up.

II-C-15 Corrected Upside Down Mintmark (IE), Rarity Level: 4-6, Values: $5 up.

II-C-16 Displaced Mintmark (IE), Rarity Level: 4-6, Values: $5 to $10.

II-C-17 Modified Mintmark (IWE), Rarity Level: 1-4, Values: No Extra Value up.

II-C-18 Normal Mintmark (I), Rarity Level: 1, Values: No Extra Value.

II-C-19 Doubled Mintmark Punch (I), Rarity Level: 6-7, Values: No Extra Value up.

II-C-20 Upside Down Mintmark (E) Rarity Level 6-7, Values: $5 up.

II-C-21 Horizontal Mintmark (E) Rarity Level 6-7, Values: $5 up.

II-C-22 Wrong Mintmark (E) Rarity Level 6-7, Values $15 up. (Example has a D mintmark in the date, but was used at Philadelphia.)

II-C-3

II-C-3

II-C-1

II-C-4

●**DIE, COLLAR AND HUB CRACKS (II-D)**

Cracks in the surface of the die allow coin metal to be forced into the crack during the strike, resulting in raised irregular lines of coin metal above the normal surface of the coin. These are one of the commonest forms of die damage and wear, making them easily collectible.

Collar cracks and hub cracks are added to this section because the causes and effects are similar or closely associated.

Die cracks, collar cracks and hub cracks are the result of wear and tear on the tools, with intentional use assumed for all classes.

II-D-1 Die Crack (W), Rarity Level: 1-3, Values: 10 to $1, $25 up on a proof coin with a rarity level of 6-7.

II-D-2 Multiple Die Cracks (W), Rarity Level: 1-3, Values: 25 cents to $2.

II-D-3 Head-To-Rim Die Crack (Lincoln Cent) (W), Rarity Level: 2-6, Values: 25 to $10 for multiple die cracks.

II-D-4 Split Die (W), Rarity Level: 5-6, Values: $10 up.

II-D-5 Rim-To-Rim Die Crack (W), Rarity Level: 2-5, Values: $1 up.

II-D-6 Collar Crack (W), Rarity Level: 4-6, Values: $10 up.

II-D-7 Hub Crack (W), Rarity Level: 3-5, Values: $1-$2.

●**DIE BREAKS (II-E)**

Breaks in the surface of the die allow coin metal to squeeze into the resulting holes, causing raised irregular areas above the normal surface of the coin. Die chips and small die breaks are nearly as common as the die cracks, but major die breaks, which extend in from the edge of the coin, are quite rare on the larger coins.

If the broken piece of the die is retained, the resulting design will be above or below the level of the rest of the surface.

II-E-1 Die Chip (W), Rarity Level: 1-2, Values: 10 to $1.

II-E-2 Small Die Break (W), Rarity Level: 1-3, Values: 10 to $2.

II-E-3 Large Die Break (W), Rarity Level: 3-5, Values: $1 to $50 and up.

II-E-4 Rim Die Break (W), Rarity Level: 2-3, Values: 25 cents to $5.

II-E-5 Major Die Break (WE), Rarity Level: 3-6, Values: $5 to $100 and up.

II-E-6 Retained Broken Die (W), Rarity Level: 3-5, Values: $1 to $10 and up.

II-E-7 Retained Broken Center of the Die (W), Rarity Level: 6-7, Values: $100 up.

II-E-8 Laminated Die (W), Rarity Level: 3-5, Values: 10 cents to $5.

II-E-9 Chipped Chrome Plating (W), Rarity Level: 4-5, Values: $10 to $25 on proofs.

II-E-10 Collar Break (W), Rarity Level: 4-6, Values: $5 to $25 and up.

II-E-11 Broken Letter or Digit on an Edge Die (W), Rarity Level: 4-6, Values: Minimal.

II-E-12 "Bar" Die Break (W), Rarity Level: 3-5, Values: 25 to $20.

II-E-13 Hub Break (W), Rarity Level: 4-6, Values: 50 to $10 and up.

●**"BIE" VARIETIES (II-F)**

A series of small die breaks or die chips in the letters of "LIBERTY" mostly on the wheat-reverse Lincoln cent are actively collected. The name results from the resemblance to an "I" between the "B" and "E" on many of the dies, but they are found between all of the letters in different cases. Well over 1,500 dies are known and cataloged. Numerous more recent examples are known.

II-F-1 ILI Die Variety (W), Rarity Level: 4-5, Values: 25 cents to $10.

II-F-2 LII Die Variety (W), Rarity Level: 3-5, Values: 50 cents to $15.

II-F-3 IIB Die Variety (W), Rarity Level: 3-5, Values: 50 cents to $15.

II-F-4 BIE Die Variety (W), Rarity Level: 3-5, Values: $1 to $20.

II-F-5 EIR Die Variety (W), Rarity Level: 3-5, Values: 50 to $15.

II-F-6 RIT Die Variety (W), Rarity Level: 4-5, Values: $2 to $25.

II-F-7 TIY Die Variety (W), Rarity Level: 4-5, Values: $5 to $30.

II-F-8 TYI Die Variety (W), Rarity Level: 4-5, Values: $2 to $25.

●**WORN AND DAMAGED DIES, COLLARS AND HUBS (II-G)**

Many dies are continued deliberately in service after they have been damaged, dented, clashed or show design transfer, since none of these classes actually affect anything but the appearance of the coin. The root cause is wear, but intent or mistakes may enter the picture.

II-G-1 Dented Die, Collar or Hub (IWE), Rarity Level: 3-5, Values: 25 to $5.

II-G-2 Damaged Die, Collar or Hub (IWE), Rarity Level: 3-5, Values: 25 to $5.

II-G-3 Worn Die, Collar or Hub (IWE), Rarity Level: 2-3, Values: No Extra Value to Minimal Value.

II-G-4 Pitted or Rusted Die, Collar or Hub (IWE), Rarity Level: 3-4, Values:No Extra Value, marker only.

II-G-5

II-G-5 Heavy Die Clash (IWE), Rarity Level: 4-5, Values: $1 to $10 and up.

II-G-6 Heavy Collar Clash (IWE), Rarity Level: 3-4, Values: $1 to $5 and up.

II-G-7 Heavy Design Transfer (IWE), Rarity Level: 3-4, Values: 10 cents to $1.

● **Die progressions (II-H)**

The progression section consists of three classes. These are useful as cataloging tools for many different die varieties, but especially the die cracks and die breaks which may enlarge, lengthen or increase in number.

II-H-1 Progression (W), Rarity Level: 3-5, Values: $1 up.

II-H-2 Die Substitution (IW), Rarity Level: 2-4, Values: No Extra Value to Minimal Value.

II-H-3 Die Repeat (I), Rarity Level: 2-4, Values: No Extra Value to Minimal Value.

● **Die scratches, polished and abraded dies (II-I)**

This section consists of those classes having to do with the use of an abrasive in some form to intentionally polish proof dies, or repair the circulating die surface. Several classes which previously were referred to as "polished" now are listed as "abraded."

II-I-1 Die Scratch (IW), Rarity Level: 1-2, Values: No Extra Value to 10 cents to 25 cents, as a marker.

II-I-2 Polished (proof) Die (IW), Rarity Level: 1, Values: No Extra Value.

II-I-3 Abraded (Circulation) Die (IW), Rarity Level: 1-2, Values: No Extra Value up to $10.

II-I-4 Inside Abraded Die Doubling (IW), Rarity Level: 1-3, Values: No Extra Value to $1.

II-I-5 Outside Abraded Die Doubling (IW), Rarity Level: 1-3, Values: No Extra Value to $1.

II-I-6 Lathe Marks (IW), Rarity Level: 5-7, Values: No Extra Value, marker only.

Striking varieties

DIVISION III

Once the dies are made and the planchets have been prepared, they are struck by a pair of dies and become a coin. In this division, we list the misstrikes resulting from human or mechanical malfunction in the striking process. These are one-of-a-kind varieties, but there may be many similar coins that fall in a given class.

Multiples and combinations of classes must be considered on a case by case basis. The first several sections match the planchet sections indicated in the title.

● **Struck on defective alloy mix planchets (III-A)**

This section includes those classes of coins struck on planchets that were made from a defective alloy.

III-A-1 Struck on an Improper Alloy Mix Planchet (IE), Rarity Level: 2-3, Values: 10 cents to $2.

III-A-2 Struck on a Planchet With Slag Inclusions(IE), Rarity Level: 5-6, Values: $10 up.

● **Struck on damaged, defective or abnormal planchet (III-B)**

Coins get struck on many strange objects. The more common of course are planchets which have been damaged in some way in the production process. In most of the classes in this section intent is at least presumed, if not specifically listed as a cause.

III-B-1 Struck on a Defective Planchet (IWE), Rarity Level: 4-6, Values: $5 to $10 and up.

III-B-2 Struck on a Mechanically Damaged Planchet (IWE), Rarity Level: 5-6, Values: $10 to $20 and up.

III-B-3 Struck on a Rolled Thin Planchet (IWE), Rarity Level: 5-6, Values: $2 to $5 and up.

III-B-4 Struck on a Rolled Thick Planchet (IWE), Rarity Level: 5-6, Values: $35 to $50 and up.

III-B-5 Struck on a Tapered Planchet (WE), Rarity Level: 4-6, Values: $2 to $5 and up.

III-B-6 Struck on a Partially Unplated Planchet (WE), Rarity Level: 5, Values: $10 up.

III-B-7 Struck on an Unplated Planchet (WE), Rarity Level: 6-7, Values: $100 up.

III-B-11

III-B-19

III-B-29

III-B-8 Struck on a Bubbled Plating Planchet (IWE), Rarity Level: 1, Values: No Value.

III-B-9 Struck on an Included Gas Bubble Planchet (WE), Rarity Level: 5-6, Values: $5 up.

III-B-10 Struck on a Partially Unclad Planchet (WE), Rarity Level: 5-6, Values: $5 up.

III-B-11 Struck on an Unclad Planchet (WE), Rarity Level: 4-5, Values: $5 and up.

III-B-12 Struck on an Undersize Planchet (WE), Rarity Level: 4-6, Values: Minimal.

III-B-13 Struck on an Oversize Planchet (WE), Rarity Level: 6-7, Values: Minimal.

III-B-14 Struck on an Improperly Prepared Proof Planchet (IWE), Rarity Level: 3-5, Values: $5 up.

III-B-15 Struck on an Improperly Annealed Planchet (IWE), Rarity Level: 4-5, Values: $5 up.

III-B-16 Struck on a Faulty Upset Edge Planchet (IWE), Rarity Level: 4-5, Values: $1 to $2.

III-B-17 Struck on a Rolled In Metal Planchet (WE), Rarity Level: 4-6, Values: $2 up.

III-B-18 Struck on a Weld Area Planchet (WE), Rarity Level: 6, Values: $25 to $50.

III-B-19 Struck on a Strike Clip Planchet (W), Rarity Level: 6-7, Values: $25 up.

III-B-20 Struck on an Unpunched Center Hole Planchet (WE), Rarity Level: 4-6, Values: $1 and up.

III-B-21 Struck on an Incompletely Punched Center Hole Planchet (WE), Rarity Level: 6-7, Values: $5 up.

III-B-22 Struck on an Uncentered Center Hole Planchet (WE), Rarity Level: 6-7, Values: $10 up.

III-B-23 Struck on a Multiple Punched Center Hole Planchet (WE), Rarity Level: 7, Values: $25 up.

III-B-24 Struck on an Unintended Center Hole Planchet (WE), Rarity Level: 6-7, Values: $25 and up.

III-B-25 Struck on a Wrong Size or Shape Center Hole Planchet (WE), Rarity Level: 5-7, Values: $5 up.

III-B-26 Struck on Scrap Coin Metal (E), Rarity Level: 4-6, Values: $10 up.

III-B-27 Struck on Junk Non Coin Metal (E), Rarity Level: 4-6, Values: $15 up.

III-B-28 Struck on a False Planchet (E), Rarity Level: 3-5, Values: $35 up.

III-B-29 Struck on Bonded Planchets (E), Rarity Level: 6-7, Values: $50 up.

●**STRUCK ON A CLIPPED PLANCHET (III-C)**

Coins struck on clipped blanks, or planchets, exhibit the same missing areas as they did before striking, modified by the metal flow from the strike which rounds the edges and tends to move metal into the missing areas. Values for blanks will run higher than planchets with similar clips.

III-C-3

III-C-1 Struck on a Disc Clip Planchet (WE), Rarity Level: 4-5, Values: $1 on regular coins, $20 and up for clad coins.

III-C-2 Struck on a Curved Clip Planchet - to 5% (WE), Rarity Level: 3-5, Values: 50 cents up.

III-C-3 Struck on a Curved Clip Planchet - (6 to 10%) (WE), Rarity Level: 4-5, Values: $1 up.

III-C-4 Struck on a Curved Clip Planchet - (11 to 25%) (WE), Rarity Level: 4-5, Values: $2 up.

III-C-5 Struck on a Curved Clip Planchet - (26 to 60%) (WE), Rarity Level: 4-6, Values: $10 up.

III-C-15

III-C-6 Struck on a Double Curved Clip Planchet (WE), Rarity Level: 3-4, Values: $2 up.

III-C-7 Struck on a Triple Curved Clip Planchet (WE), Rarity Level: 4-5, Values: $5 up.

III-C-8 Struck on a Multiple Curved Clip Planchet (WE), Rarity Level: 4-6, Values: $5 up.

III-C-9 Struck on an Overlapping Curved Clipped Planchet (WE), Rarity Level: 5-6, Values: $15 up.

III-C-10 Struck on an Incomplete Curved Clip Planchet (WE), Rarity Level: 4-5, Values: $10 up.

III-C-11 Struck on an Oval Clip Planchet (WE), Rarity Level: 5-6, Values: $20 up.

III-C-12 Struck on a Crescent Clip Planchet - (61% or more) (WE), Rarity Level: 6-7, Values: $100 up.

III-C-13 Struck on a Straight Clip Planchet (E), Rarity Level: 4-6, Values: $10 up.

III-C-14 Struck on an Incomplete Straight Clip Planchet (WE), Rarity Level: 5-6, Values: $20 up.

III-C-15 Struck on a Ragged Clip Planchet (E), Rarity Level: 4-6, Values: $15 up.

III-C-16 Struck on an Outside Corner Clip Planchet (E), Rarity Level: 7, Values: $100 up.

III-C-17 Struck on an Inside Corner Clip Planchet (E), Rarity Level: Unknown outside mint., Values: -.

III-C-18 Struck on an Irregularly Clipped Planchet (E), Rarity Level: 6-7, Values: $20 up.

III-C-19 Struck on an Incompletely Punched Scalloped or Multi-Sided Planchet (E), Rarity Level: 7, Values: $20 up.

●**STRUCK ON A LAMINATED, SPLIT OR BROKEN PLANCHET (III-D)**

This section has to do with the splitting, cracking or breaking of a coin parallel to the faces of the coin, or at least very nearly parallel, or breaks at right angles to the faces of the coin.

Lamination cracks and missing metal of any size below a split planchet are too common in the 35-percent silver 1942-1945 nickels to be collectible or have any significant value.

III-D-1 Struck on a Small Lamination Crack Planchet (W), Rarity Level: 3-4, Values: 10 up.

III-D-2 Struck on a Large Lamination Crack Planchet (W), Rarity Level: 3-6, Values: $1 up.

III-D-3 Struck on a Split Planchet (W), Rarity Level: 4-6, Values: $5 up.

III-D-4 Struck on a Hinged Split Planchet (W), Rarity Level: 5-6, Values: $35 up.

III-D-5 Struck on a Planchet With a Clad Layer Missing (W), Rarity Level: 4-5, Values: $15 up.

III-D-6 Struck on a Planchet With Both Clad Layers Missing (W), Rarity Level: 4-5, Values: $25 up.

III-D-7

III-E-2

III-D-7 Struck on a Separated Clad Layer or Lamination (W), Rarity Level: 6-7, Values: $75 up.

III-D-8 Struck on a Broken Planchet Before the Strike (W), Rarity Level: 3-5, Values: $10 up.

III-D-9 Broken Coin During or After the Strike (W), Rarity Level: 4-6, Values: $20 up.

III-D-10 Struck Coin Fragment Split or Broken During or After the Strike (W), Rarity Level: 3-5, Values: $5 up.

III-D-11 Reedless Coin Broken During or After the Strike (W), Rarity Level: Unknown, Values: -.

●STRUCK ON WRONG STOCK PLANCHETS (III-E)

These classes cover those cases where the wrong stock was run through the blanking press, making planchets of the correct diameter, but of the wrong thickness, alloy or metal or a combination of incorrect thickness and metal.

III-E-1 Struck on a Half Cent-Stock Planchet (IE), Rarity Level: Unknown, Values: No Value Established.

III-E-2 Struck on a Cent-Stock Planchet (IE), Rarity Level: Unknown, Values: No Value Established.

III-E-3 Struck on a Two-Cent-Stock Planchet (E), Rarity Level: Unknown, Values: -.

III-E-4 Struck on a Three-Cent-Silver Stock Planchet (E), Rarity Level: Unknown, Values: -.

III-E-5 Struck on a Three-Cent-Nickel Stock Planchet (E), Rarity Level: Unknown, Values: -.

III-E-6 Struck on a Half Dime-Stock Planchet (E), Rarity Level: Unknown, Values: -.

III-E-7 Struck on a Dime-Stock Planchet (E), Rarity Level: 5-6, Values: $20 up.

III-E-8 Struck on a Twenty-Cent-Stock Planchet (E), Rarity Level: Unknown, Values: -.

III-E-9 Struck on a Quarter-Stock Planchet (E), Rarity Level: 6, Values: $50 up.

III-E-10 Struck on a Half Dollar-Stock Planchet (E), Rarity Level: 6-7, Values: $100 up.

III-E-11 Struck on a Dollar-Stock Planchet (E), Rarity Level: 6-7, Values: $300 up.

III-E-12 Struck on a Token/Medal-Stock Planchet (E), Rarity Level: 7, Values: No Value Established.

III-E-13 Struck on a Wrong Thickness Spoiled Planchet (IWE), Rarity Level: 7, Values: $50 up.

III-E-14 Struck on a Correct Thickness Spoiled Planchet (IWE), Rarity Level: Unknown, Values: No Value Established.

III-E-15 Struck on a Cut Down Struck Token (IWE), Rarity Level: 6-7, Values: $50 up.

III-E-16 Struck on an Experimental or Pattern-Stock Planchet (IE), Rarity Level: 7, Values: $50 up.

III-E-17 Struck on a Proof-Stock Planchet (IE), Rarity Level: 7, Values: $100 up.

III-E-18 Struck on an Adjusted Specification-Stock Planchet (IE), Rarity Level: 3-7, Values: No Value to $5 and up.

III-E-19 Struck on a Trial Strike-Stock Planchet (IE), Rarity Level: Unknown, Values: No Value Established.

III-E-20 U.S. Coin Struck on a Foreign-Stock Planchet. (E), Rarity Level: 5, Values: $35 up.

III-E-7

III-G-18

III-E-21 Foreign Coin Struck on a Foreign-Stock Planchet (E), Rarity Level: 5-6, Values: $25 up.

III-E-22 Struck on a Non-Standard Coin Alloy (IE), Rarity Level: 4-7, Values: $20 up.

●EXTRA METAL (III-F)

The term "extra metal" for the purpose of this section includes both extra metal added to the blank during the blanking operation and metal powder added to the planchet during the annealing operation.

III-F-1 Struck on a Type 1 Blank With Extra Metal (W), Rarity Level: Unknown, Values: -.

III-F-2 Struck on a Type 2 Planchet With Extra Metal (W), Rarity Level: 4-5, Values: $10 up.

III-F-3 Struck on a Sintered Coating Planchet (W), Rarity Level: 6-7, Values: $35 up.

●STRUCK ON NORMAL OR ABNORMAL BLANKS, OR PLANCHETS (III-G)

This section includes coins struck on either a blank, as it comes from the blanking press, or as a planchet that has passed through the upsetting mill. Added to this section are those planchets which are normal until they are struck by the wrong dies. These differ from the wrong stock planchets because the wrong stock planchets are already a variety before they are struck.

III-G-1 Struck on a Type 1 Blank (IWE), Rarity Level: 4-6, Values: $10 up.

III-G-2 Struck on a Type 2 Planchet (I), Rarity Level: 1, Values: No Extra Value.

III-G-3 Struck on a Purchased Planchet (I), Rarity Level: 1, Values: No Extra Value.

III-G-4 Struck on a Mint-Made Planchet (I), Rarity Level: 1, Values: No Extra Value.

III-G-5 Struck on an Adjustment-Marked Planchet (I), Rarity Level: 4-7, Values: Minimal, and may reduce value of coin in some cases.

III-G-6 Struck on a Hardness Test-Marked Planchet (I), Rarity Level: 6-7, Values: $10 up.

III-G-7 Wrong Planchet or Metal on a Half Cent Planchet (IE), Rarity Level: 5-7, Values: $100 up.

III-G-8 Wrong Planchet or Metal on a Cent Planchet (IE), Rarity Level: 3-6, Values: $25 up.

III-G-9 Wrong Planchet or Metal on a Nickel Planchet (E), Rarity Level: 4-6, Values: $35 up

III-G-10 Wrong Planchet or Metal on a Dime Planchet (E), Rarity Level: 4-6, Values: $50 up.

III-G-11 Wrong Planchet or Metal on a Quarter Planchet (E), Rarity Level: 4-6. Values: $100 up.

III-G-12 Wrong Planchet or Metal on a Half Dollar Planchet (E), Rarity Level: 6-7, Values: $500 up.

III-G-13 Wrong Planchet or Metal on a Dollar Planchet (E), Rarity Level: 7, Values: $500 up.

III-G-14 Wrong Planchet or Metal on a Gold Planchet (E), Rarity Level: 7, Values: $1000 up.

III-G-15 Struck on a Wrong Series Planchet (IE), Rarity Level: 6-7, Values: $1500 up.

III-G-16 U.S. Coin Struck on a Foreign Planchet (E), Rarity Level: 5-7, Values: $35 up.

III-G-17 Foreign Coin Struck on a U.S. Planchet (E), Rarity Level: 6-7, Values: $50 up.

III-G-18 Foreign Coin Struck on a Wrong Foreign Planchet (E), Rarity Level: 6-7, Values: $50 up.

III-G-19 Struck on a Medal Planchet (E), Rarity Level: 6-7, Values: $100 up.

III-G-20 Medal Struck on a Coin Planchet (IE), Rarity Level: 3-5, Values: $10 up.

III-G-21 Struck on an Official Sample Planchet (IE), Rarity Level: Unknown, Values: No Value Established.

III-G-22 Struck Intentionally on a Wrong Planchet (I), Rarity Level: 6-7, Values: Mainly struck as Presentation Pieces, full numismatic value.

III-G-23 Non-Proof Struck on a Proof Planchet (IE), Rarity Level: 6-7, Values: $500 up.

●STRUCK ON COIN METAL STRIP (III-H)

Pieces of the coin metal strip do manage at times to escape into the coin press.

III-H-1 (See I-H-1 Punched Coin Metal Strip), Rarity Level: Impossible, Values: -.

III-H-2 Struck on Chopped Coin Metal Strip (E), Rarity Level: 6-7, Values: $25 up.

●DIE ADJUSTMENT STRIKES (III-I)

As the dies are set up and adjusted in the coin press, variations in the strike occur until the dies are properly set. Test strikes are normally scrapped, but on occasion reach circulation.

III-I-1 Die Adjustment Strike (IE), Rarity Level: 5-6, Values: $35 up.

III-I-2 Edge Strike (E), Rarity Level: 5-6, Values: $10 to $20 and up.

III-I-3 Weak Strike (W), Rarity Level: 1, Values: No Extra Value.

III-I-4 Strong Strike (IWE), Rarity Level: 1, Values: No value except for the premium that might be paid for a well struck coin.

III-I-5 Jam Strike (IE), Rarity Level: 7, Values: $50 up.

III-I-6 Trial Piece Strike (I), Rarity Level: 6-7, Values: $100 up.

III-I-7 Edge-Die Adjustment Strike (I), Rarity Level: 5-7, Values: $5 up.

III-I-8 Uniface Strike (I), Rarity Level 7, Values: $50 up.

III-I-3

●INDENTED, BROCKAGE AND COUNTER-BROCKAGE STRIKES (III-J)

Indented and uniface strikes involve an extra unstruck planchet between one of the dies and the planchet being struck. Brockage strikes involve a struck coin between one of the dies and the planchet and a counter-brockage requires a brockage coin between one of the dies and the planchet.

A cap, or capped die strike results when a coin sticks to the die and is squeezed around it in the shape of a bottle cap.

III-J-1 Indented Strike (W), Rarity Level: 3-6, Values: $5 up.

III-J-2 Uniface Strike (W), Rarity Level: 3-5, Values: $15 up.

III-J-3 Indented Strike By a Smaller Planchet (WE), Rarity Level: 5-7, Values: $100 up.

III-J-4 Indented Second Strike (W), Rarity Level: 3-5, Values: $10 up, about the same as a regular double strike of comparable size.

III-J-5 Partial Brockage Strike (W), Rarity Level: 3-6, Values: $15 up.

III-J-6 Full Brockage Strike (W), Rarity Level: 3-6, Values: $5 up.

III-J-7 Brockage Strike of a Smaller Coin (WE), Rarity Level: 6-7, Values: $200 up.

III-J-8 Brockage Strike of a Struck Coin Fragment (WE), Rarity Level: 4-6, Values: $5 up.

III-J-9 Brockage Second Strike (WE), Rarity Level: 3-5, Values: $5 up.

III-J-10 Partial Counter-Brockage Strike (WE), Rarity Level: 3-5, Values: $10 up.

III-J-11 Full Counter-Brockage Strike (WE), Rarity Level: 5-7, Values: $100 up.

III-J-12 Counter-Brockage Second Strike (WE), Rarity Level: 4-6, Values: $10 up.

III-J-13 Full Brockage-Counter-Brockage Strike (WE), Rarity Level: 6-7, Values: $150 up.

III-J-14 Multiple Brockage or Counter-Brockage Strike (WE), Rarity Level: 5-7, Values: $100 up.

III-J-15 Capped Die Strike (WE), Rarity Level: 6-7, Values: $500 up.

III-J-16 Reversed Capped Die Strike (WE), Rarity Level: 7, Values: $1,000 up.

III-J-1

III-J-3

III-J-4

III-J-6

III-K-1

III-K-7

●STRUCK THROUGH ABNORMAL OBJECTS (III-K)

This section covers most of the objects or materials which might come between the planchet and the die and be struck into the surface of the coin. Unless noted, the materials - even the soft ones - are driven into the surface of the coin.

> III-K-1 Struck Through Cloth (IWE), Rarity Level: 3-6, Values: $35 up.
>
> III-K-2 Struck Through Wire (IWE), Rarity Level: 3-6, Values: $5 up.
>
> III-K-3 Struck Through Thread (IWE), Rarity Level: 3-6, Values: $5 up.
>
> III-K-4 Struck Through Dirt-and-Grease-Filled Die (IWE), Rarity Level: 1-4, Values: 10 cents to 25 cents up, but no value on a worn or circulated coin.
>
> III-K-5 Struck Through a Dropped Filling (IWE), Rarity Level: 5-6, Values: $10 up.
>
> III-K-6 Struck Through Wrong Metal Fragments (IWE), Rarity Level: 4-6, Values: $1 up.
>
> III-K-7 Struck Through an Unstruck Planchet Fragment (IWE), Rarity Level: 3-5, Values: $1 up.

III-K-7

III-K-8

III-K-8

III-K-8 Struck Through a Rim Burr (IWE), Rarity Level: 3-5, Values: $1 to $2 and up.

III-K-9 Struck Through plit-Off Reeding (IWE), Rarity Level: 5-6, Values: $25 up.

III-K-10 Struck Through a Feed Finger (IWE), Rarity Level: 5-7, Values: $25 to $50 and up.

III-K-11 Struck Through Miscellaneous Objects (IWE), Rarity Level: 4-6, Values: $1 up.

III-K-12 Struck Through Progression (IWE), Rarity Level: 4-6, Values: $1 up.

Note: Some 1987 through 1994 quarters are found without mintmarks, classed as III-K-4, a Filled Die. Values depend on market conditions. Filled dies have value ONLY on current, uncirculated grade coins.

●Double strikes (III-L)

Only coins which receive two or more strikes by the die pair fall in this section and are identified by the fact that both sides of the coin are affected. Unless some object interferes, an equal area of both sides of the coin will be equally doubled.

The exception is the second strike with a loose die, which will double only one side of a coin, but is a rare form usually occurring only on proofs. A similar effect is flat field doubling from die chatter.

III-L-1 Close Centered Double Strike (WE), Rarity Level: 4-6, Values: $15 up.

III-L-2 Rotated Second Strike Over a Centered First Strike (WE), Rarity Level: 4-6, Values: $15 up.

III-L-3 Off-Center Second Strike Over a Centered First Strike (WE), Rarity Level: 4-6, Values: $15 up.

III-L-4 Off-Center Second Strike Over an Off-Center First Strike (WE), Rarity Level: 4-6, Values: $10 up.

III-L-5 Off-Center Second Strike Over a Broadstrike (WE), Rarity Level: 5-6, Values: $20 up.

III-L-6 Centered Second Strike Over an Off-Center First Strike (WE), Rarity Level: 5-6, Values: $50 up.

III-L-7 Obverse Struck Over Reverse (WE), Rarity Level: 5-6, Values: $25 up.

III-L-8 Nonoverlapping Double Strike (WE), Rarity Level: 5-6 Values: $20 up.

III-L-9 Struck Over a Different Denomination or Series (WE), Rarity Level: 6, Values: $300 and up.

III-L-10 Chain Strike (WE), Rarity Level: 6, Values: $300 up for the pair of coins that were struck together.

III-L-11 Second-Strike Doubling From a Loose Die (W), Rarity Level: 6-7, Values: $200 up.

III-L-12 Second-Strike Doubling From a Loose Screw Press Die (W), Rarity Level: 5-6, Values: $100 up.

III-L-13 Second Strike on an Edge Strike (WE), Rarity Level: 5-6, Values: $20 up.

III-L-14 Folded Planchet Strike (WE), Rarity Level: 5-7, Values: $100 up.

III-L-15 Triple Strike (WE), Rarity Level: 6-7, Values: $100 up.

III-L-16 Multiple Strike (WE), Rarity Level: 6-7, Values: $200 up.

III-L-17 U.S. Coin Struck Over a Struck Foreign Coin (WE), Rarity Level: 6-7, Values: $300 up.

III-L-18 Foreign Coin Struck Over a Struck U.S. Coin (WE), Rarity Level: 6-7, Values: $400 up.

III-L-19 Foreign Coin Struck Over a Struck Foreign Coin (WE), Rarity Level: 7, Values: $500 up.

III-L-20 Double Strike on Scrap or Junk (E), Rarity Level: 6, Values: $50 up.

III-L-21 Struck on a Struck Token or Medal (E), Rarity Level: 5-6, Values: $100 up.

III-L-22 Double-Struck Edge Motto or Design (E), Rarity Level: 6-7, Values: $200 up.

III-L-23 One Edge Motto or Design Struck Over Another (E), Rarity Level: 7, Values: $300 up.

III-L-24 Flat Field Doubling (W), Rarity Level: 2-3, Values: $1 to $5.

III-L-25 Territorial Struck over Struck U.S. Coin: (I) Rarity Level: 6-7, Values: $200 up.

III-L-26 Pattern Struck over Struck U.S. Coin: (I) Rarity Level: 6-7, Values: $200 up.

III-L-27 Pattern Struck over Struck Pattern:(I) Rarity Level 6-7, Values: $200 up.

III-L-28 Pattern Struck Over Foreign Coin:(I) Rarity Level 6-7, Values - $200 up.

●COLLAR STRIKING VARIETIES (III-M)

The collar is often referred to as the "Third Die," and is involved in a number of forms of misstrikes. The collar normally rises around the planchet, preventing it from squeezing sideways between the dies and at the same time forming the reeding on reeded coins.

If the collar is out of position or tilted, a partial collar strike results; if completely missing, it causes a broadstrike; if the planchet is not entirely between the dies, an off-center strike.

III-M-1 Flanged Partial Collar Strike (WE), Rarity Level: 5-6, Values: $20 up.

III-M-2 Reversed Flanged Partial Collar Strike (WE), Rarity Level: 6-7, Values: $35 up.

III-M-3 Tilted Partial Collar Strike (WE), Rarity Level: 5-6, Values: $20 up.

III-M-4 Centered Broadstrike (WE), Rarity Level: 5-6, Values: $5 up.

III-L-3

III-L-3

III-L-4

III-M-5

III-M-8

III-M-5 Uncentered Broadstrike (WE), Rarity Level: 5, Values: $3 up.

III-M-6 Reversed Broadstrike (WE), Rarity Level: 6, Values: $10 up.

III-M-7 Struck Off-Center 10-30% (W), Rarity Level: 3-6, Values: $3 up.

III-M-8 Struck Off-Center 31-70% (W), Rarity Level: 4-6, Values: $5 up.

III-M-9 Struck Off-Center 71% or More (W), Rarity Level: 3-5, Values: $2 up.

III-M-10 Rotated Multi-sided Planchet Strike (W), Rarity Level: 5-6, Values: $10 up.

III-M-11 Wire Edge Strike (IWE), Rarity Level: 1-2, Values: No Extra Value.

III-M-12 Struck With the Collar Too High (WE), Rarity Level: 6-7, Values: $20 up.

III-M-13 Off-Center Slide Strike (W), Rarity Level:3-6 $4 up.

●MISALIGNED AND ROTATED (DIE) STRIKE VARIETIES (III-N)

One (rarely both) of the dies may be Offset Misaligned, off to one side, or may be tilted (Vertically Misaligned). One die may either have been installed so that it is turned in relation to the other die, or may turn in the holder, or the shank may break allowing the die face to rotate in relation to the opposing die.

Vertical misaligned dies are rarely found, and like rotated dies, find only limited collector interest. Ninety and 180 degree rotations are the most popular. Rotations of 14 degrees or less have no value. The 1989-D Congress dollar is found with a nearly 180 degree rotated reverse, currently retailing for around $2,000. Only about 30 have been reported to date.

III-N-1 Offset Die Misalignment Strike (WE), Rarity Level: 3-5, Values: $2 up.

III-N-2 Vertical Die Misalignment Strike (WE), Rarity Level: 4-6, Values: $1 up.

III-N-3 Rotated Die Strike - 15 to 45 Degrees (IWE), Rarity Level: 4-6, Values: $2 up.

III-N-4 Rotated Die Strike - 46 to 135 Degrees (IWE), Rarity Level: 5-6, Values: $10 up.

III-N-5 Rotated Die Strike - 136 to 180 Degrees (IWE), Rarity Level: 5-6, Values: $25 up.

●LETTERED AND DESIGN EDGE STRIKE VARIETIES (III-O)

Early U.S. coins and a number of foreign coins have either lettered edges, or designs on the edge of the coin. Malfunctions of the application of the motto or design to the edge fall in this section.

III-O-1 Overlapping Edge Motto or Design (WE), Rarity Level: 3-4, Values: $5 to $10 and up.

III-O-2 Wrong Edge Motto or Design (WE), Rarity Level: 5-6-7, Values: $50 up.

III-O-3 Missing Edge Motto, Design or Security Edge (IWE), Rarity Level: 5-6-7, Values: $50 up.

III-O-4 Jammed Edge Die Strike (W), Rarity Level: 6, Values: $10 up.

III-O-5 Misplaced Segment of an Edge Die (E), Rarity Level: 4-7, Values: $25 up.

III-O-6 Reeded Edge Struck Over a Lettered Edge (IE), Rarity Level: 3-6, Values: No Extra Value up.

●DEFECTIVE STRIKES AND MISMATCHED DIES (III-P)

The final section of the Striking Division covers coins which are not properly struck for reasons other than those in previous classes, such as coins struck with mismatched (muled) dies. The mismatched die varieties must be taken on a case by case basis, while the otherclasses presently have little collector demand or premium.

III-P-1 Defective Strike (WE), Rarity Level: 1, Values: No Extra Value.

III-P-2 Mismatched Die Strike (E), Rarity Level: 4-7, Values: $25 up.

III-P-3 Single-Strike Proof (WE), Rarity Level: 4-5, Values: Minimal.

III-P-4 Single Die-Proof Strike (IE), Rarity Level: 5-6, Values: $100 up.

III-P-5 Reversed Die Strike (I), Rarity Level: 4-5, Values: No Extra Value to Minimal.

Official Mint modifications

DIVISION IV

Several mint produced varieties occur after the coin has been struck, resulting in the addition of the fourth division to my PDS System. Since most of these coins are either unique or are special varieties, each one must be taken on a case by case basis. All classes listed here are by definition intentional.

I have not listed values as the coins falling in these classes which are sold through regular numismatic channels, are cataloged with the regular issues or are covered in specialized catalogs in their particular area.

●MATTE PROOFS (IV-A)

Matte proofs as a section include several of the forms of proof coins which have the striking characteristics of a mirror proof but have been treated AFTER striking to give them a grainy, non-reflective surface.

IV-A-1 Matte Proof (I), Rarity Level: 3-5, Values: Normal Numismatic Value.

IV-A-2 Matte Proof on One Side (I), Rarity Level: 7, Values: Normal Numismatic Value.

IV-A-3 Sandblast Proof (I), Rarity Level: 4-6, Values: Normal Numismatic Value.

●ADDITIONAL ENGRAVING (IV-B)

This section includes any added markings which are placed on the struck coin and struck coins which later were cut into pieces for various purposes. The warning is repeated: Anything done to a coin after the strike is extremely difficult to authenticate and is much easier to fake than a die struck coin.

IV-B-1 Counterstamp and Countermark (I), Rarity Level: 3-6, Values: Normal Numismatic Value.

IV-B-2 Perforated and Cut Coins (I), Rarity Level: 4-6, Values: Normal Numismatic Value.

●RESTRIKES (IV-C)

Restrikes cover a complicated mixture of official use of dies from a variety of sources. Whether or not some were officially sanctioned is always a problem for the collector.

IV-C-1 Restrike on the Same Denomination Planchet (I), Rarity Level: 4-6, Values: Normal Numismatic Value.

IV-C-2 Restrike on a Different Denomination or Series Planchet (I), Rarity Level: 4-6, Values: Normal Numismatic Value.

IV-C-3 Restrike on a Foreign Coin (I), Rarity Level: 6-7, Values: Normal Numismatic Value.

IV-C-4 Restrike on a Token or Medal (I), Rarity Level: 5-6, Values: Normal Numismatic Value.

IV-C-5 Restruck With the Original Dies (I), Rarity Level: 4-6, Values: Normal Numismatic Value.

IV-C-6 Restruck With Mismatched Dies (I), Rarity Level: 4-6, Values: Normal Numismatic Value.

IV-C-7 Copy Strike With New Dies (I), Rarity Level: 3-5, Values: Normal Numismatic Value.

IV-C-8 Fantasy Strike (I), Rarity Level: 4-6, Values: Normal Numismatic Value.

After strike modifications

DIVISION V

This division includes both modifications that have value to collectors – and those that don't. I needed a couple of divisions to cover other things that happen to coins to aid in cataloging them. This avoids the false conclusion that an unlisted coin is quite rare, when the exact opposite is more likely to be the case.

●COLLECTIBLE MODIFICATIONS AFTER STRIKE (V-A)

This section includes those classes having to do with deliberate modifications of the coin done with a specific purpose or intent which makes them of some value to collectors. Quite often these pieces were made specifically to sell to collectors, or at least to the public under the guise of being collectible.

V-A-1 Screw Thaler, Rarity Level: 5-6, Values: Normal Numismatic Value.

V-A-2 Love Token, Rarity Level: 3-6, Values: $10 up.

V-A-3 Satirical or Primitive Engraving, Rarity Level: 6-7, Values: $5 up.

V-A-4 Elongated Coin, Rarity Level: 2-7, Values: 50 cents to $1 and up.

V-A-5 Coin Jewelry, Rarity Level: 2-5, Values: $1 up.

V-A-6 Novelty Coin, Rarity Level: 1-3, Values: No Value up to $5 to $10.

V-A-7 Toning, Rarity Level: 3-6, Values: No value up, depending on coloration. Easily faked.

V-A-8 Mint Modification, Rarity Level: 4-7, Values: $5 up. Easily faked.

V-A-9 Mint Packaging Mistake, Rarity Level: 5-7, Values: Nominal $1. Very easily faked.

●ALTERATIONS AND DAMAGE AFTER THE STRIKE(V-B)

This section includes those changes in a coin which have no collector value. In most cases their effect on the coin is to reduce or entirely eliminate any collector value - and in the case of counterfeits they are actually illegal to even own.

V-B-1 Machine Doubling Damage: NOTE: Machine doubling damage is defined as: "Damage to a coin after the strike, due to die bounce or chatter or die displacement, showing on the struck coin as scrapes on the sides of the design elements, with portions of the coin metal in the relief elements either displaced sideways or downward, depending on the direction of movement of the loose die." Machine doubling damage, or MDD, is by far the most common form of doubling found on almost any coin in the world. Rarity Level: 0, Values: Reduces the coin's value.

V-B-2 Accidental or Deliberate Damage, Rarity Level: 0, Values: Reduces the coin's value.

V-B-3 Test Cut or Mark, Rarity Level: 0, Values: Reduces value of coin to face or bullion value.

V-B-4 Alteration, Rarity Level: 0, Values: Reduces value to face or bullion value.

V-B-5 Whizzing, Rarity Level: 0, Values: Reduces value sharply and may reduce it to face or bullion value.

V-B-6 Counterfeit, Copy, Facsimile, Forgery or Fake, Rarity Level: 0, Values: No Value and may be illegal to own.

V-B-7 Planchet Deterioration. Very common on copper-plated zinc cents. Rarity level: 0, Values: No Value.

7 American Coin History

U.S. Mint founded in 1792

At peak production, the U.S. Mint strikes nearly 30 billion coins a year. Who would have thought it possible at its founding? In July 1792, a site for the new U.S. Mint not yet having been secured, 1,500 silver half dismes were struck on a small screw press in the cellar of a Philadelphia building owned by sawmaker John Harper. Though some have since categorized these early emissions of the fledgling U.S. Mint as patterns, it is clear that first President George Washington – who is said to have deposited the silver from which the coins were struck – considered this small batch of half dismes to be the first official U.S. coins.

The law establishing the Mint dates to April 2, 1792. From that early legislative birth has flowed the coins that have underpinned the workings of U.S. commerce for over two centuries. It must be remembered that the Mint was born

First United States Mint, 1854 Philadelphia Pa.

in chaos. It was a time shortly after the Revolutionary War and as hard as it was to win independence from Great Britain, setting up American government finances on a sound basis was to prove almost as daunting.

At first a cumbersome system was proposed by Robert Morris, a Revolutionary War financier and first superintendent of finance. Refinements tendered by Thomas Jefferson and Alexander Hamilton then firmly placed the nation on an easily understood decimal system of coinage. They were working with a hodgepodge system that grew up in the Colonial period.

Despite a dire need for coinage in the Colonies, Great Britain considered it a royal right and granted franchises sparingly. Much of the Colonial economy, therefore, revolved around barter, with food staples, crops, and goods serving as currency. Indian wampum or bead money also was used, first in the fur trade and later as a form of money for Colonial use.

Copper pieces were produced around 1616 for Sommer Islands (now Bermuda), but coinage within the American Colonies apparently didn't begin until 1652, when John Hull struck silver threepence, sixpence and shillings under authority of the General Court of Massachusetts. This coinage continued, with design changes (willow, oak, and pine trees), through 1682. Most of the coins were dated 1652, apparently to avoid legal problems with England.

In 1658 Cecil Calvert, second Lord Baltimore, commissioned coins to be struck in England for use in Maryland. Other authorized and unauthorized coinages – including those of Mark Newby, John Holt, William Wood, and Dr. Samuel Higley – all became part of the landscape of circulating coins. In the 1780s there were influxes of counterfeit British halfpence and various state coinages.

The Articles of Confederation had granted individual states the right to produce copper coins. Many states found this to be appealing, and merchants in the mid-1780s traded copper coins of Vermont, Connecticut, Massachusetts, New Jersey, and New York. Not all were legal issues; various entrepreneurs used this as an invitation to strike imitation state coppers and British halfpence. Mutilated and worn foreign coins also circulated in abundance. Included among these were coins of Portugal, Great Britain, and France, with the large majority of the silver arriving from Spain.

The accounting system used by the states was derived from the British system of pounds, shillings, and pence. Each state was allowed to set its own rates at which foreign gold and silver coins would trade in relation to the British pound.

In 1782 Robert Morris, newly named superintendent of finance, was appointed to head a committee to determine the values and weights of the gold and silver coins in circulation. Asked simply to draw up a table of values, Morris took the opportunity to propose the establishment of a federal mint. In his Jan. 15, 1782, report (largely prepared by his assistant, Gouverneur Morris), Morris noted that the exchange rates between the states were complicated.

He observed that a farmer in New Hampshire would be hard-pressed if asked to determine the value of a bushel of wheat in South Carolina. Morris recorded that an amount of wheat worth four shillings in his home state of New Hampshire would be worth 21 shillings and eightpence under the accounting system used in South Carolina.

Morris claimed these difficulties plagued not only farmers, but that "they are perplexing to most Men and troublesome to all." Morris further pressed for the adoption of an American coin to solve the problems of the need for small change and debased foreign coinages in circulation.

In essence, what he was advocating was a monometallic system based on silver.

He said that gold and silver had fluctuated throughout history. Because these fluctuations resulted in the more valuable metal leaving the country, any nation that adopted a bimetallic coinage was doomed to have its gold or silver coins disappear from circulation.

Gouverneur Morris calculated the rate at which the Spanish dollar traded to the British pound in the various states. Leaving out South Carolina, because it threw off his calculations, Gouverneur Morris arrived at a common denominator of 1,440. Robert Morris, therefore, recommended a unit of value of 1/1,440, equivalent to a quarter grain of silver. He suggested the striking of a silver 100-unit coin, or cent; a silver 500-unit coin, or quint; a silver 1,000-unit coin, or mark; and two copper coins, one of eight units and the other of five units.

On Feb. 21, 1782, the Grand Committee of Congress approved the proposal and directed Morris to press forward and report with a plan to establish a mint. Morris had already done so. Apparently feeling confident that Congress would like his coinage ideas, Morris (as shown by his diary) began efforts at the physical establishment prior to his January 1782 report. He had already engaged Benjamin Dudley to acquire necessary equipment for the mint and hoped to have sample coins available to submit with his original report to Congress.

It wasn't until April 23, 1783, that Morris was able to send his Nova Constellatio patterns to Congress and suggest that he was ready to report on establishing a mint. Apparently nothing came of Morris' efforts. Several committees looked into the matter, but nothing was accomplished. Dudley was eventually discharged as Morris' hopes dimmed.

Thomas Jefferson was the next to offer a major plan. Jefferson liked the idea of a decimal system of coinage, but disliked Morris' basic unit of value. As chairman of the Currency Committee, Jefferson reviewed Morris' plan and formulated his own ideas.

To test public reaction, Jefferson gave his "Notes on Coinage" to The Providence Gazette, and Country Journal, which published his plan in its July 24, 1784, issue. Jefferson disagreed with Morris' suggestion for a 1/1,440 unit of value and instead proposed a decimal coinage based on the dollar, with the lowest unit of account being the mil, or 1/1,000.

"The most easy ratio of multiplication and division is that by ten," Jefferson wrote. "Every one knows the facility of Decimal Arithmetic."

Jefferson argued that although Morris' unit would have eliminated the unwanted fraction that occurred when merchants converted British farthings to dollars, this was of little significance. After all, the original idea of establishing a mint was to get rid of foreign currencies.

Morris' unit, Jefferson said, was too cumbersome for use in normal business transactions. According to Jefferson, under Morris' plan a horse valued at 80 Spanish dollars would require a notation of six figures and would be shown as 115,200 units.

Jefferson' coinage plan suggested the striking of a dollar, or unit; half dollar, or five-tenths; a double tenth, or fifth of a dollar, equivalent to a pistareen; a tenth, equivalent to a Spanish bit; and a one-fifth copper coin, relating to the British farthing. He also wanted a gold coin of $10, corresponding to the British double guinea; and a copper one-hundredth coin, relating to the British halfpence.

In reference to his coinage denominations, Jefferson said, it was important that the coins "coincide in value with some of the known coins so nearly, that the people may by quick reference in the mind, estimate their value." The Spanish dollar was the most commonly used coin in trade, so it was natural basis for the new U.S. silver dollar. In the Spanish system, the coin was called an eight reales, or piece of eight.

More than a year, however, passed without any further action on his plan or that proposed by Morris. In a letter to William Grayson, a member of the Continental Congress, Washington expressed concern for the establishment of a national coinage system, terming it "indispensably necessary." Washington also complained of the coinage in circulation: "A man must travel with a pair of scales in his pocket, or run the risk of receiving gold at one-fourth less than it counts."

On May 13, 1785, the 13-member Grand Committee, to whom Jefferson's plan had been submitted, filed its report, generally favoring Jefferson's coinage system. The committee did, however, make slight alterations, including the elimination of the gold $10 coin, the addition of a gold $5 coin, and the dropping of Jefferson's double tenth, which it replaced with a quarter dollar. The committee also added a coin equal to 1/200 of a dollar (half cent). On July 6, 1785, Congress unanimously approved the Grand Committee's plan. It failed, however, to set a standard weight for the silver dollar or to order plans drawn up for a mint.

Several proposals were offered for a contract coinage. On April 21, 1787, the board accepted a proposal by James Jarvis to strike 300 tons of copper coin at the federal standard. Jarvis, however, delivered slightly less than 9,000 pounds of his contract. The contract was voided the following year for his failure to meet scheduled delivery times, but helped to delay further action on a mint. Concerted action on a coinage system and a mint would wait until the formation of the new government.

Alexander Hamilton, named in September 1789 to head the new Treasury, offered three different methods by which the new nation could achieve economic stability, including the funding of the national debt, establishment of the Bank of North America and the founding of the U.S. Mint. On Jan. 21, 1791, Hamilton submitted to Congress a "Report on the Establishment of a Mint."

Hamilton agreed with Jefferson that the dollar seemed to be best suited to serve as the basic unit, but believed it necessary to establish a proper weight and fineness for the new coin. To do so, Hamilton had several Spanish coins assayed to determine the fine weight of the Spanish dollar. He also watched the rate at which Spanish dollars traded for fine gold (24 3/4 grains per dollar) on the world market.

From his assays and observations he determined that the Spanish dollar contained 371 grains of silver. He then multiplied 24 3/4 by 15 (the gold value of silver times his suggested bimetallic ratio) and arrived at 371 1/4 as the proper fine silver weight for the new silver dollar.

The Spanish dollar actually contained 376 grains of pure silver when new, 4 3/4 grains more than Hamilton's proposed silver dollar.

Hamilton also wanted a bimetallic ratio of 15-to-1. Hamilton said his ratio was closer to Great Britain's, which would be important for trade, and Holland's, which would be important for repaying loans from that country.

His report suggested the striking of a gold $10; gold dollar; silver dollar; silver tenth, or disme; and copper one-hundredth and half-hundredth. Hamilton felt the last of these, the half cent, was necessary because it would enable merchants to lower their prices, which would help the poor.

Congress passed the act establishing the U.S. Mint April 2, 1792. It reinstated several coin denominations left out by Hamilton and dropped his gold dollar. In gold, the act authorized at $10 coin, or "eagle"; a $5 coin, or "half eagle"; and a $2.50 coin, or "quarter eagle." In silver were to be a dollar, half dollar, quarter dollar, disme, and half disme, and in copper a cent and half cent.

Though it established a sound system of U.S. coinage, the act failed to address the problem of foreign coins in circulation. It was amended in February 1793 to cancel their legal-tender status within three years of the mint's opening.

Coinage totals at the first mint in Philadelphia were understandably low. Skilled coiners, assayers and others who could handle the mint's daily operations were in short supply in the United States. Also in want were adequate equipment and supplies of metal for coinage. Much of the former had to be built or imported. Much of the latter was also imported or salvaged from various domestic sources, including previously struck tokens and coins, and scrap metal.

Coinage began in earnest in 1793 with the striking of half cents and cents at the new mint located at Seventh Street between Market and Arch streets in Philadelphia. Silver coinage followed in 1794, with half dimes, half dollars, and dollars. Gold coinage did not begin until 1795 with the minting of the first $5 and $10 coins. Silver dimes and quarters and gold $2.50 coins did not appear until 1796.

Under the bimetallic system of coinage by which gold and silver served as equal representations of the unit of value, much of the success and failure of the nation's coinage to enter and remain in circulation revolved around the supply and valuation of precious metals. From the Mint's beginning, slight miscalculations in the proper weight for the silver dollar and a proper bimetallic ratio led gold and silver to disappear from circulation. The U.S. silver dollar traded at par with Spanish and Mexican dollars, but because the U.S. coin was lighter, it was doomed to be exported.

A depositor at the first mint could make a profit at the mint's expense by sending the coins to the West Indies. There they could be traded at par for the heavier Spanish or Mexican eight reales, which were then shipped back to the United States for recoinage. As a result, few early silver dollars entered domestic circulation; most failed to escape the melting pots.

Gold fared no better. Calculations of the bimetallic ratio by which silver traded for gold on the world market were also askew at first and were always subject to fluctuations. Gold coins either disappeared quickly after minting or never entered circulation, languishing in bank vaults. These problems led President Jefferson to halt coinage of the gold $10 and the silver dollar in 1804.

The gold $10 reappeared in 1838 at a new, lower weight standard. The silver dollar, not coined for circulation since 1803, returned in 1836 with a limited mintage. Full-scale coinage waited until 1840.

Nor was the coinage of copper an easy matter for the first mint. Severe shortages of the metal led the mint to explore various avenues of obtaining sufficient supplies for striking cents and half cents.

Witness, for example, the half-cent issues of 1795 and 1797 struck over privately issued tokens of the New York firm of Talbot, Allum & Lee because of a shortage of copper for the federal issue. Rising copper prices and continued shortages forced the mint to lower the cent's weight from 208 grains to 168 grains in 1795.

In 1798, because of the coinage shortage, the legal-tender status of foreign coins was restored. Several more extensions were given during the 1800s, ending with the withdrawal of legal-tender status for Spanish coins in 1857.

A new law made the mint lower the standard weight of all gold coins in 1834. This reflected market conditions and in effect recognized a higher gold price when bought with silver coins. For example, $5 in silver coins bought a new, lighter $5 gold piece, meaning the buyer got less gold. This led to the melting of great numbers of the older, heavier gold coins as speculators grabbed a 4.7 percent profit.

By the 1850s discovery of gold in California made silver more expensive in terms of gold. All silver quickly disappeared from circulation. Congress reacted in 1853 by lowering the weight of the silver half dime, dime, quarter, and half dollar, hoping to keep silver in circulation. A new gold coin of $20 value, the "double eagle," was introduced to absorb a great amount of the gold from Western mines.

Not long after, silver was discovered in Nevada. By the mid-1870s the various mines that made up what was known as the Comstock Lode (named after its colorful early proprietor, Henry P. Comstock) had hit the mother lode. Large supplies of silver from the Comstock, combined with European demonetization, caused a severe drop in its value. Silver coins were made heavier as a result in 1873.

Also, it was believed that the introduction of a heavier, 420-grain silver dollar in 1873, known as the Trade dollar, would create a market for much of the Comstock silver, bolster its price, and at the same time wrest control from Great Britain of lucrative trade with the Orient. It didn't. Large numbers of Trade dollars eventually flooded back into the United States. They were demonetized in 1887.

Morgan dollars were introduced in 1878 as a panacea to the severe economic problems following the Civil War. Those who proudly carried the banner of free silver contended that by taking the rich output of the Comstock mines and turning it into silver dollars, a cheaper, more plentiful form of money would become available. This was supposed to give the economy a boost.

The Free Silver Movement reached its peak in 1896 when William Jennings Bryan attempted to gain the White House on a plank largely based on restoration of the free and unlimited coinage of the standard 412.5-grain silver dollar. He failed. Silver failed. In 1900 the United States officially adopted a gold standard.

Silver continued to be a primary coinage metal until 1964, when rising prices led the Mint to remove it from the dime and quarter. Mintage of the silver dollar had ended in 1935. The half dollar continued to be coined through 1970 with a 40 percent silver composition. It, too, was then made of copper-nickel clad metal.

Gold coinage ended in 1933 and exists today only in commemorative issues and American Eagle bullion coins with fictive face values. A clad composition of copper and nickel is now the primary coinage metal. Even the cent is no longer all copper; a copper-coated zinc composition has been used since 1982.

Precious-metal supplies were also linked to the opening of additional mints, which served the parent facility in Philadelphia. The impact of gold discoveries in the 1820s in the southern Appalachian Mountains was directly tied to the construction of branch mints in Dahlonega, Ga., and Charlotte, N.C., in 1838. These new mints struck only gold coins. New Orleans also became the site of a branch mint in the same year as Dahlonega and Charlotte. It took in some of the outflow of gold from Southern mines, but also struck silver coins.

Discovery of gold in California in the late 1840s created a gold rush, and from it sprang a great western migration. Private issues of gold coinage, often of debased quality, were prevalent, and the cost of shipping the metal eastward for coinage at Philadelphia was high. A call for an official branch mint was soon heard and heeded in 1852 with the authorization of the San Francisco Mint, which began taking deposits in 1854.

The discovery of silver in the Comstock Lode led to yet another mint. Located only a short distance via Virginia & Truckee Railroad from the fabulous Comstock Lode, the Carson City mint began receiving bullion in early 1870.

Denver, also located in a mineral-rich region, became the site of an assay office in 1863 when the government purchased the Clark, Gruber & Co. private mint. It became a U.S. branch mint in 1906. Now four mints exist. They are in Denver, Philadelphia, San Francisco and West Point, N.Y. The latter strikes current precious metal coinage for collectors and investors.

8 How Are Coins Made?

Mints are really factories

Copper, nickel, silver, and gold are pretty much the basic coin metals for the United States. When mixed with tin, copper becomes bronze, and this alloy was used in cents. Current cents have a pure zinc core. There have been patterns made of aluminum, but these never were issued for use in circulation. Platinum joined gold and silver as a precious metal used in U.S. coinage starting in 1997.

There are three basic parts of the minting process: (1) the making of the planchet, which is divided into the selection and processing of the metal and the preparation of the planchets, (2) the making of the dies, and (3) the use of the dies to strike the planchets. To help you remember these three parts, think of "P," "D," and "S" for planchet, die, and striking.

Making the 'blanks'

The piece of metal that becomes a coin is known as a "blank." This is a usually round, flat piece that has been punched or cut from a sheet or strip of coin metal.

Before a blank can become a coin it has to be processed, cleaned, softened, and given what is known as an "upset edge" – a raised ridge or rim around both sides. The blank then becomes a "planchet" and is ready to be struck into a coin by the dies. First they go through what looks like a monstrous cement mixer. A huge cylinder revolves slowly as the planchets are fed in at one end and spiral their way through. This is an annealing oven, which heats the planchets to soften them. When they come out the end, they fall into a bath where they are cleaned with a diluted acid or soap solution. As the final step, they go through the upsetting mill, the machine that puts the raised rim on the blank and turns it into a planchet, ready to be struck. In a different department the process of making the dies used to strike the coins has already begun.

Preparing the dies

For those who haven't studied metallurgy, the concept of hard metal flowing about is pretty hard to swallow, but this is actually what happens. It is basically the same process as the one used in an auto plant to turn a flat sheet of steel into a fender with multiple curves and sharp bends. The cold metal is moved about by the pressure applied.

To make the metal move into the desired design, there has to be a die. Actually, there have to be two dies, because one of the laws of physics is that for every action there has to be an equal and opposite reaction. You cannot hold a piece of metal in midair and strike one side of it. Instead you make two dies, fix one, and drive the other one against it – with a piece of metal in between to accept the design from each die.

A die is a piece of hard metal, like steel, with a design on its face that helps to form a mirror image on the struck coin. Early dies were made by hand. Engravers used hand tools, laboriously cutting each letter, each digit, and each owl or eagle or whatever design was being used into the face of the die. Notice that this is "into" the surface of the die. Each part of the die design is a hole or cavity of varying shape and depth.

This is because we want a mirror image on the coin, but we want it raised, or in "relief." To make a relief image on a coin, the image on the die has to be recessed into the face of the die, or "incuse." Of course, if we want an incuse image on the coin, such as the gold $2.50 and $5 coins of 1908-1929, the design on the die face would have to be in relief.

To fully understand this, take a coin from your pocket and a piece of aluminum foil. Press the foil down over the coin design and rub it with an eraser. When you take the foil off and look at the side that was in contact with the coin, you have a perfect copy of a die. Everywhere there is a relief design on the coin there is an incuse design on your foil "die."

From sketchbook to coin

The design process begins with an artist's sketch. This is translated into a three-dimensional relief design that is hand-carved from plaster or, in recent years, from a form of plastic.

The plaster or plastic design is then transformed into a "galvano," which is an exact copy of the design that has been plated with a thin layer of copper. This is used as a template or pattern in a reducing lathe, which cuts the design into a die blank.

This die becomes the master die, from which all of the following steps descend. The process can be reversed so that the designs will be cut in relief, forming a tool called a "hub," which is simply a piece of steel with the design in relief, exactly the same as the relief design on the intended coin.

To make working dies, pieces of special steel are prepared, with one end shaped with a slight cone. The die blank is softened by heating it. Then the hub is forced into the face of the die, forming the incuse, mirror-image design in the face of the die.

The process usually has to be repeated because the die metal will harden from the

A galvano of the 1976 half dollar goes on the reducing lathe.

pressure. The die is removed, softened, and returned to the hubbing press for a second impression from the hub. As you can imagine, it takes several hundred tons per square inch to force the hub into the die. Logically, this process is called "hubbing" a die.

The advantage of hubbing a die is that thousands of working dies can be made from a single hub, each one for all practical purposes as identical as the proverbial peas in a pod. This enables, for example, U.S. mints to strike billions of one-cent coins each year, each with the identical design.

Die making has come a long way from the early days. Philadelphia used to make all dies and then shipped them to the branch mints. Now Denver has its own die shop and creates dies of its own.

Striking the coin

Yesterday's die might strike only a few hundred coins. Today it is not unusual for a die to strike well over a million coins.

The coin press used to strike modern coins is a complicated piece of equipment that consists basically of a feed system to place the planchets in position for the stroke of the hammer die to form a coin. This process takes only a fraction of a second, so the press has to operate precisely to spew out the hundreds of coins that are struck every minute.

The end of the early hammered coinage came with the introduction of the collar, which often is called the "third" die. The collar is nothing more than a steel plate with a hole in it. This hole is the exact diameter of the intended coin and often is lined with carbide to prolong its life. It surrounds the lower, or fixed, die. Its sole purpose is to contain the coin metal to keep it from spreading too far sideways under the force of the strike.

If the intended coin has serrations, or "reeds," on the edge, then the collar has the matching design. The strike forces the coin metal against the serrations in the collar, forming the reeded edge at the same time that the two dies form the front and back, or obverse and reverse, of the coin.

Lettered-edge coins are produced usually by running the planchets through an edge-lettering die, or by using a segmented collar that is forced against the edge of the planchet during the strike by hydraulic pressure.

Several hundred tons were required to drive a hub into a die. Not as much but still significant amounts of force are needed to strike coins. A cent requires about 30 tons per square inch. A silver dollar took 150 tons. Other denominations fall between.

Modern coin presses apply pressure in a variety of ways. A ram, carrying the moving or "hammer" die, is forced against the planchet. Most commonly this is with the mechanical advantage of a "knuckle" or connected pieces to which pressure is applied from

A binful of blanks are ready for the coin press.

the side. When the joint straightens – like straightening your finger – the ram at the end of the piece is driven into the planchet. Once the strike is complete, at the final impact of the die pair, the coin has been produced. It is officially a coin now, and it's complete and ready to be spent.

Making proof coins

Proof coins started out as special presentation pieces. They were and still are struck on specially prepared planchets with specially prepared dies. Today the definition of a proof coin also requires that it be struck two or more times.

Currently all proof versions of circulating U.S. coins are struck at the San Francisco Mint, but some of the proof commemorative coins have been struck at the other mints. West Point currently strikes proof American Eagles of silver, gold, and platinum, and they carry a "W" mintmark.

After the proof blanks are punched from the strip, they go through the annealing oven, but on a conveyor belt rather than being tumbled in the revolving drum. After cleaning and upsetting they go into a huge vibrating machine where they are mixed with steel pellets that look like tiny footballs. The movement of the steel pellets against the planchets burnishes, or smooths, the surface so any scratches and gouges the planchets pick up during processing are smoothed over.

Proof dies get an extra polishing before the hubbing process. They are made at Philadelphia and shipped to the branch mints. When the proof dies arrive at San Francisco, they are worked on by a team of specialists who use diamond dust and other polishing agents to turn the fields of the proof dies into mirrorlike surfaces. The incuse design is sandblasted to make the surface rough, producing what is known as a "frosted" design. Because collectors like the frosted proofs, the design is periodically swabbed with acid to keep the surface rough and increase the number of frosted proofs from each die. This process has been around about a quarter century, so frosted examples of earlier proofs are considerably scarcer.

The presses that strike proof coins usually are hand-operated rather than automatic. Some of the newer presses use equipment such as vacuum suction devices to pick up the planchets, place them in the coining chamber, and then remove the struck coins. This avoids handling the pieces any more than necessary.

On a hand-operated press, the operator takes a freshly washed and dried planchet and, using tongs, places it in the collar. The ram with the die descends two or more times before the finished coin is removed from the collar and carefully stored in a box for transport to storage or the packaging line. After each strike the operator wipes the dies to make sure that lint or other particles don't stick to the dies and damage the coins as they are struck.

Proof dies are used for only a short time. Maximum die life is usually less than 10,000 coins, varying with the size of the coin and the alloy being struck.

CIRCULATION COINAGE

HALF CENT

Liberty Cap Half Cent
Head facing left.
KM# 10 • 6.74 g., Copper, 22 mm. • **Designer:**
Henry Voigt

Date	Mintage	G4	VG8	F12	VF20	XF40	MS60
1793	35,334	3,900	6,100	10,750	15,500	27,000	72,000

Head facing right.
KM# 14 • Copper, 6.74 g. (1794-95) and 5.44 g.
(1795-97), 23.5 mm. • **Designer:** Robert Scot
(1794) and John Smith Gardner (1795) **Note:** The
"lettered edge" varieties have TWO HUNDRED FOR
A DOLLAR inscribed around the edge. The "pole"
varieties have a pole upon which the cap is hanging,
resting on Liberty's shoulder. The "punctuated date"
varieties have a comma after the 1 in the date. The
1797 "1 above 1" variety has a second 1 above the
1 in the date.

Date	Mintage	G4	VG8	F12	VF20	XF40	MS60
1794 Normal Relief Head, lg letters	81,600	485	700	1,135	2,500	5,000	20,000
1794 High Relief Head, Lt wreath	Inc. above	485	700	1,135	2,500	5,000	20,000
1795 lettered edge, pole	25,600	535	750	1,450	2,900	5,400	17,500
1795 plain edge, no pole	109,000	485	775	1,400	2,750	5,250	16,000
1795 lettered edge, punctuated date	Inc. above	560	700	2,500	3,750	8,000	50,000
1795 plain edge, punctuated date	Inc. above	485	1,000	1,450	2,800	5,250	57,500
1796 pole	5,090	20,000	50,000	53,500	75,000	75,000	—
1796 no pole	1,390	32,000	42,500	47,500	75,000	—	—
1797 plain edge	119,215	485	750	1,250	2,000	6,500	57,500
1797 lettered edge	Inc. above	1,850	5,700	12,600	27,500	40,000	—
1797 1 above 1	Inc. above	505	750	1,000	2,500	5,000	50,000
1797 gripped edge	Inc. above	140	250	1,135	2,500	—	—

Draped Bust Half Cent
Draped bust right, date at angle below. Value within thin wreath.
KM# 33 • 5.44 g., Copper, 23.5 mm. • **Obv.
Legend:** LIBERTY **Rev. Legend:** UNITED STATES
OF AMERICA **Designer:** Robert Scot **Note:** The
wreath on the reverse was redesigned slightly in
1802, resulting in "reverse of 1800" and "reverse
of 1802" varieties. The "stems" varieties have stems
extending from the wreath above and on both
sides of the fraction on the reverse. On the 1804
"crosslet 4" variety, a serif appears at the far right
of the crossbar on the 4 in the date. The "spiked
chin" variety appears to have a spike extending from
Liberty's chin, the result of a damaged die. Varieties
of the 1805 strikes are distinguished by the size of
the 5 in the date. Varieties of the 1806 strikes are
distinguished by the size of the 6 in the date.

Stemless   Stems

Date	Mintage	G4	VG8	F12	VF20	XF40	MS60
1800	211,530	75.00	90.00	160	205	600	5,500
1802/0 rev. 1800	14,366	23,500	55,000	—	—	—	—
1802/0 rev. 1802	Inc. above	875	2,000	6,500	9,000	—	—
1803	97,900	75.00	95.00	140	325	950	7,000
1804 plain 4, stemless wreath	1,055,312	60.00	80.00	125	215	385	1,400
1804 plain 4, stems	Inc. above	60.00	110	175	325	1,850	15,000
1804 crosslet 4, stemless	Inc. above	65.00	90.00	135	240	410	1,350
1804 crosslet 4, stems	Inc. above	62.00	90.00	160	260	450	1,500
1804 spiked chin	Inc. above	75.00	105	190	260	435	1,500
1805 small 5, stemless	814,464	65.00	90.00	140	240	410	3,500
1805 small 5, stems	Inc. above	1,850	2,350	5,400	8,000	35,000	—
1805 large 5, stems	Inc. above	85.00	125	135	305	650	3,000

Date	Mintage	G4	VG8	F12	VF20	XF40	MS60
1806 small 6, stems	356,000	500	475	750	1,350	5,750	—
1806 small 6, stemless	Inc. above	65.00	85.00	135	260	435	1,350
1806 large 6, stems	Inc. above	65.00	85.00	135	260	460	1,500
1807	476,000	75.00	95.00	190	275	485	1,400
1808/7	400,000	300	400	600	1,500	4,250	57,500
1808	Inc. above	95.00	130	175	295	600	5,000

Classic Head Half Cent
Classic head left, flanked by stars, date below.   Value within wreath.

KM# 41 • 5.44 g., Copper, 23.5 mm. • **Rev. Legend:** UNITED STATES OF AMERICA **Designer:** John Reich **Note:** Restrikes listed were produced privately in the mid-1800s. The 1831 restrikes have two varieties with different sized berries in the wreath on the reverse. The 1828 strikes have either 12 or 13 stars on the obverse.

Date	Mintage	G4	VG8	F12	VF20	XF40	MS60Brn
1809/6	1,154,572	60.00	95.00	100	125	300	1,000
1809	Inc. above	59.00	80.00	90.00	107	185	800
1809 circle in 0	—	76.00	95.00	150	375	750	5,100
1810	215,000	66.00	105	150	325	600	3,550
1811 Close Date	63,140	300	950	1,650	2,400	5,500	—
1811 Wide Date Inc. Above	—	290	725	1,550	2,550	4,750	—
1811 restrike, reverse of 1802, uncirculated	—	—	—	—	—	—	57,500
1825	63,000	56.00	75.00	85.00	110	155	950
1826	234,000	53.00	72.00	82.00	99.00	125	750
1828 13 stars	606,000	51.00	70.00	75.00	82.00	105	235
1828 12 stars	Inc. above	61.00	80.00	125	160	275	850
1829	487,000	53.00	73.00	82.00	102	125	500
1831 original	2,200	—	—	—	—	65,000	—
1831 1st restrike, lg. berries, reverse of 1836	—	—	—	—	—	—	6,500
1831 2nd restrike, sm. berries, reverse of 1840, proof	—	—	—	—	—	—	55,000
1832	154,000	51.00	70.00	75.00	82.00	105	235
1833	120,000	51.00	70.00	75.00	82.00	105	235
1834	141,000	51.00	70.00	75.00	82.00	105	235
1835	398,000	51.00	70.00	75.00	82.00	105	235
1836 original, proof	—	—	—	—	—	—	6,000
1836 restrike, reverse of 1840, proof	—	—	—	—	—	—	50,000

Braided Hair Half Cent
Head left, braided hair, within circle of stars, date below.   Value within wreath.

KM# 70 • 5.44 g., Copper, 23 mm. • **Rev. Legend:** UNITED STATES OF AMERICA **Designer:** Christian Gobrecht **Note:** 1840-1849 and 1852 strikes, both originals and restrikes, are known in proof only; mintages are unknown. The small-date varieties of 1849, both originals and restrikes, are known in proof only. The restrikes were produced clandestinely by Philadelphia Mint personnel in the mid-1800s.

Date	Mintage	G4	VG8	F12	VF20	XF40	MS60	PF60Brn
1840 original	—	—	—	—	—	3,000	—	3,250
1840 1st restrike	—	—	—	—	—	3,000	—	3,250
1840 2nd restrike	—	—	—	—	—	3,000	—	5,500
1841 original	—	—	—	—	—	3,000	—	3,250
1841 1st restrike	—	—	—	—	—	3,000	—	3,250
1841 2nd restrike	—	—	—	—	—	3,000	—	6,000
1842 original	—	—	—	—	—	3,000	—	3,250
1842 1st restrike	—	—	—	—	—	3,000	—	3,250
1842 2nd restrike	—	—	—	—	—	3,000	—	6,000
1843 original	—	—	—	—	—	3,000	—	3,250
1843 1st restrike	—	—	—	—	—	3,000	—	3,250
1843 2nd restrike	—	—	—	—	—	3,000	—	6,500
1844 original	—	—	—	—	—	3,000	—	3,250
1844 1st restrike	—	—	—	—	—	3,000	—	3,250
1844 2nd restrike	—	—	—	—	—	3,000	—	6,000
1845 original	—	—	—	—	—	3,000	—	6,000
1845 1st restrike	—	—	—	—	—	3,000	—	3,250
1845 2nd restrike	—	—	—	—	—	3,000	—	6,000

Date	Mintage	G4	VG8	F12	VF20	XF40	MS60	PF60Brn
1846 original	—	—	—	—	—	3,000	—	3,250
1846 1st restrike	—	—	—	—	—	3,000	—	3,250
1846 2nd restrike	—	—	—	—	—	3,000	—	6,000
1847 original	—	—	—	—	—	3,000	—	3,250
1847 1st restrike	—	—	—	—	—	5,500	—	3,250
1847 2nd restrike	—	—	—	—	—	3,000	—	6,000
1848 original	—	—	—	—	—	3,000	—	6,000
1848 1st restrike	—	—	—	—	—	3,000	—	3,250
1848 2nd restrike	—	—	—	—	—	3,000	—	6,000
1849 original, small date	—	—	—	—	—	3,000	—	3,250
1849 1st restrike small date	—	—	—	—	—	3,000	—	3,250
1849 large date	39,864	58.00	76.00	82.00	92.00	150	300	—
1850	39,812	58.00	76.00	82.00	92.00	110	340	—
1851	147,672	54.00	71.00	77.00	84.00	96.00	220	—
1852 original	—	15,000	55,000	30,000	35,000	40,000	—	90,000
1852 1st restrike	—	1,000	1,500	1,850	2,600	3,000	—	5,000
1852 2nd restrike	—	1,000	1,500	1,850	2,600	3,000	—	7,000
1853	129,694	54.00	71.00	77.00	84.00	96.00	220	—
1854	55,358	54.00	71.00	77.00	84.00	96.00	220	—
1855	56,500	54.00	71.00	77.00	84.00	96.00	220	3,250
1856	40,430	54.00	71.00	77.00	84.00	96.00	220	3,250
1857	35,180	59.00	78.00	87.00	110	175	295	3,250

CENT

Flowing Hair Cent
Chain.

KM# 11 • 13.48 g., Copper, 26-27 mm. • **Designer:** Henry Voigt

Date	Mintage	G4	VG8	F12	VF20	XF40	MS60
1793 AMERI	36,103	9,950	14,850	25,500	45,500	96,000	245,000
1793 AMERICA	Inc. above	6,950	10,600	17,750	36,500	71,500	140,000
1793 periods after "LIBERTY"	Inc. above	7,850	12,350	19,850	38,500	73,500	147,000

Wreath.

KM# 12 • 13.48 g., Copper, 26-28 mm. • **Designer:** Henry Voigt

Date	Mintage	G4	VG8	F12	VF20	XF40	MS60
1793 vine and bars edge	63,353	3,150	4,450	7,750	12,000	22,500	48,500
1793 lettered edge	Inc. above	3,450	5,150	8,850	14,000	25,500	56,000
1793 strawberry leaf; 4 known	—	350,000	550,000	875,000	—	—	—

Liberty Cap Cent

KM# 13 • Copper, 13.48 g., 29 mm. • **Designer:** Joseph Wright **Note:** The heavier pieces were struck on a thicker planchet. The Liberty design on the obverse was revised slightly in 1794, but the 1793 design was used on some 1794 strikes. A 1795 "lettered edge" variety has ONE HUNDRED FOR A DOLLAR and a leaf inscribed on the edge.

Date	Mintage	G4	VG8	F12	VF20	XF40	MS60
1793 cap	11,056	5,500	12,500	23,500	45,000	98,500	—
1794 NO FRACTION BAR	Inc. above	500	800	1,350	3,000	8,000	40,000
1794 head '93	918,521	1,550	2,600	4,250	9,850	21,500	85,000
1794 head '94	Inc. above	445	710	1,200	2,425	4,500	16,500
1794 head '95	Inc. above	530	775	1,265	2,775	5,000	20,000
1794 starred rev.	Inc. above	13,500	23,500	44,500	115,000	275,000	—
1795 Lettered Edge	Inc. above	515	650	1,375	3,200	4,500	16,500
1795 plain edge	501,500	375	610	1,050	1,775	3,800	12,500

CENT

CENT

Date	Mintage	G4	VG8	F12	VF20	XF40	MS60
1795 reeded edge	Inc. above	350,000	700,000	—	—	—	—
1795 Jefferson head plain edge	Inc. above	24,500	49,500	95,000	150,000	—	—
1795 Jefferson head lettered edge	Inc. above	75,000	95,000	155,000	250,000	—	—

KM# 13a • 10.89 g., Copper, 29 mm. • **Designer:** John Smith Gardner

Date	Mintage	G4	VG8	F12	VF20	XF40	MS60
1795 lettered edge, "One Cent" high in wreath	37,000	445	735	1,100	2,175	4,800	15,000
1796	109,825	425	610	1,650	3,850	9,500	36,500

Draped Bust Cent
Draped bust right, date at angle below. Value within wreath.

KM# 22 • 10.98 g., Copper, 29 mm. • **Obv. Legend:** LIBERTY **Rev. Legend:** UNITED STATES OF AMERICA **Designer:** Robert Scot **Note:** The 1801 "3 errors" variety has the fraction on the reverse reading "1/000," has only one stem extending from the wreath above and on both sides of the fraction on the reverse, and UNITED in UNITED STATES OF AMERICA appears as "Iinited."

Stemless Stems

Date	Mintage	G4	VG8	F12	VF20	XF40	MS60
1796 reverse of 1794	363,375	300	450	1,050	2,800	6,850	—
1796 reverse of 1795	Inc. above	260	375	850	3,250	9,500	36,500
1796 reverse of 1797	Inc. above	240	350	1,050	2,150	4,250	11,000
1796 Liberty error	Inc. above	450	850	1,800	5,500	13,500	75,000
1797 reverse of 1795 plain edge	897,510	165	300	600	3,450	5,500	38,500
1797 reverse of 1795 gripped edge	Inc. above	185	425	850	1,450	4,750	—
1797 stems	Inc. above	165	325	450	1,275	2,650	9,000
1797 stemless	Inc. above	300	495	750	1,850	4,750	38,500
1797 reverse of 1795	—	—	—	—	—	—	9,500
1798 (1797) reverse of 1795	—	—	—	—	—	—	7,000
1798 reverse of 1796	Inc. above	150	250	600	1,750	3,600	9,500
1798 1st hair style	Inc. above	90.00	130	325	800	4,450	9,850
1798 2nd hair style	Inc. above	85.00	125	310	750	2,850	8,000
1798/7	1,841,745	200	325	650	2,100	5,100	22,000
1799	42,540	2,750	4,650	11,500	24,500	85,000	650,000
1799/98	Inc. above	2,600	4,300	11,000	34,000	110,000	—
1800	2,822,175	100	165	375	1,850	3,000	12,500
1800/798 (1800)	Inc. above	85.00	225	550	1,550	4,000	—
1800/79	Inc. above	80.00	200	375	1,500	3,300	16,500
1801	1,362,837	75.00	100	250	700	2,025	7,750
1801 3 errors	Inc. above	225	500	1,150	2,400	6,850	35,000
1801 1/000	Inc. above	80.00	175	475	1,350	2,650	9,850
1801 100/000	Inc. above	150	325	850	1,650	4,200	12,500
1802	3,435,100	65.00	100	250	535	1,500	4,500
1802 stemless	Inc. above	68.00	95.00	200	515	1,800	5,000
1802 1/000	Inc. above	80.00	135	325	750	1,750	7,500
1803 small date, small fraction	2,471,353	65.00	100	225	425	1,200	3,850
1803 small date, large fraction	Inc. above	65.00	100	225	435	1,250	4,050
1803 large date, small fraction	4,600	11,500	14,500	42,000	75,000	—	—
1803 large date, large fraction	Inc. above	80.00	135	450	1,550	3,150	—
1803 1/100 over 1/1000	—	95.00	165	360	900	2,600	10,000
1803 Stemless wreath	—	80.00	150	350	650	2,100	6,950
1804	96,500	1,650	2,650	4,000	8,950	16,500	80,000
1804 Restrike of 1860	—	—	—	650	750	875	1,750
1805	941,116	60.00	90.00	245	425	1,600	4,650
1806	348,000	70.00	110	305	600	2,075	7,500
1807 small fraction	727,221	65.00	100	265	625	2,200	4,600
1807 large fraction	Inc. above	65.00	100	225	510	1,400	3,850
1807/6 large 7/6	Inc. above	65.00	175	225	625	1,700	—

Date	Mintage	G4	VG8	F12	VF20	XF40	MS60
1807/6 small 7/6	Inc. above	1,900	4,250	9,500	24,500	49,500	—
1807 Comet Variety	Inc. above	95.00	175	345	1,100	3,200	16,500

Classic Head Cent
Classic head left, flanked by stars, date below. Value within wreath.
KM# 39 • 10.89 g., Copper, 29 mm. • **Rev. Legend:** UNITED STATES OF AMERICA **Designer:** John Reich

Date	Mintage	G4	VG8	F12	VF20	XF40	MS60
1808	1,109,000	121	160	535	700	1,850	9,500
1809	222,867	135	285	450	1,050	3,350	13,500
1810/09	1,458,500	90.00	160	515	910	1,850	10,500
1810	Inc. above	75.00	110	415	910	1,550	9,500
1811/10	218,025	175	300	700	1,950	4,650	60,000
1811	Inc. above	110	225	575	1,300	3,350	11,000
1812 small date	1,075,500	90.00	155	440	885	2,125	8,000
1812 large date	—	90.00	155	440	895	2,175	8,500
1813	418,000	60.00	175	400	800	1,950	9,000
1814 Plain 4	357,830	90.00	160	400	910	1,925	6,800
1814 Crosslet 4	Inc. above	90.00	155	390	885	1,825	6,650

Coronet Cent
Coronet head left, within circle of stars, date below. Value within wreath.
KM# 45 • 10.89 g., Copper, 28-29 mm. • **Rev. Legend:** UNITED STATES OF AMERICA **Designer:** Robert Scot

Date	Mintage	G4	VG8	F12	VF20	XF40	MS60
1816	2,820,982	31.00	42.00	60.00	117	245	1,350
1817 13 obverse stars	3,948,400	29.00	33.00	44.00	74.00	155	650
1817 15 obverse stars	Inc. above	35.00	56.00	90.00	225	675	2,650
1818	3,167,000	29.00	35.00	42.00	74.00	150	450
1819 Large date, 9/8	2,671,000	—	—	—	—	—	—
1819	—	31.00	38.00	46.00	116	315	1,000
1819/8	—	—	—	—	—	—	—
1819 Large date	Inc. above	29.00	33.00	42.00	78.00	183	600
1819 Small date	Inc. above	30.00	35.00	45.00	82.00	203	675
1820 Large date, 20/19	4,407,550	31.00	38.00	50.00	88.00	250	950
1820 Large date	—	33.00	39.00	60.00	117	335	1,600
1820 Small date	—	29.00	36.00	46.00	78.00	188	450
1821	389,000	45.00	72.00	200	525	1,375	7,500
1822	2,072,339	31.00	45.00	45.00	150	365	1,500
1823 Included in 1824 mintage	—	90.00	200	450	1,350	3,950	30,000
1823/22 Included in 1824 mintage	—	80.00	165	425	975	3,250	—
1823 Restrike	—	600	650	700	800	900	1,850
1824	1,262,000	31.00	35.00	46.00	210	450	1,950
1824/22	Inc. above	40.00	49.00	110	440	1,000	5,500
1825	1,461,100	30.00	35.00	45.00	125	400	2,150
1826	1,517,425	30.00	35.00	45.00	87.00	265	950
1826/25	Inc. above	40.00	55.00	95.00	275	1,200	4,250
1827	2,357,732	29.00	33.00	42.00	92.00	260	800
1828 Large date	2,260,624	29.00	33.00	44.00	87.00	225	900
1828 Small date	—	32.00	37.00	49.00	110	265	1,650
1829 Large letters	1,414,500	29.00	33.00	40.00	93.00	208	1,100
1829 Medium letters	Inc. above	32.00	45.00	90.00	275	675	5,250
1830 Large letters	1,711,500	25.00	29.00	36.00	70.00	188	650
1830 Medium letters	Inc. above	45.00	90.00	265	650	1,650	7,500
1831 Large letters	3,359,260	25.00	31.00	36.00	70.00	193	500
1831 Medium letters	—	29.00	34.00	41.00	76.00	225	950
1832 Large letters	2,362,000	25.00	31.00	36.00	70.00	158	525
1832 Medium letters	—	27.00	32.00	39.00	74.00	178	850
1833	2,739,000	25.00	31.00	36.00	70.00	158	475
1834 Large 8, stars and letters	1,855,100	75.00	120	145	250	625	2,350
1834 Large 8 & stars, medium letters	Inc. above	190	275	600	1,100	3,250	6,200

CENT

Date	Mintage	G4	VG8	F12	VF20	XF40	MS60
1834 Large 8, small stars, medium letters	Inc. above	25.00	29.00	36.00	70.00	158	650
1834 Small 8 & stars	Inc. above	25.00	29.00	36.00	70.00	145	750
1835 Large 8 & stars	3,878,400	25.00	31.00	39.00	74.00	168	1,000
1835 Head '36	—	25.00	31.00	39.00	74.00	158	550
1835 Small 8 & stars	—	25.00	29.00	36.00	70.00	158	650
1836	2,111,000	25.00	29.00	36.00	70.00	125	290
1837 Plain hair cords, medium letters	5,558,300	25.00	29.00	36.00	70.00	125	290
1837 Plain hair cords, small letters	Inc. above	25.00	31.00	39.00	74.00	133	485
1837 Head '38	Inc. above	25.00	31.00	39.00	74.00	125	250
1838	6,370,200	25.00	29.00	36.00	70.00	125	250
1839 Head '38, beaded hair cords	3,128.661	29.00	33.00	40.00	74.00	130	450
1839/36 Plain hair cords	Inc. above	300	600	1,250	2,450	6,800	75,000
1839 Silly head	Inc. above	35.00	40.00	50.00	90.00	165	900
1839 Booby head	Inc. above	34.00	38.00	47.00	85.00	153	875

Braided Hair Cent
Head left, braided hair, within circle of stars, date below. Value within wreath.

KM# 67 • 10.89 g., Copper, 27.5 mm. • **Rev. Legend:** UNITED STATES OF AMERICA **Designer:** Christian Gobrecht **Note:** 1840 and 1842 strikes are known with both small and large dates, with little difference in value. A slightly larger Liberty head and larger reverse lettering were used beginning in 1843.

Date	Mintage	G4	VG8	F12	VF20	XF40	MS60
1839 Petite Head	3,128,661	29.00	33.00	47.00	62.50	100	825
1840 Large date	2,462,700	25.00	28.00	36.00	51.50	80.00	440
1840 Small date	Inc. above	30.00	35.00	42.00	53.50	90.00	550
1840 Small date over large 18	Inc. above	40.00	50.00	75.00	125	210	1,150
1841	1,597,367	25.00	28.00	36.00	51.50	79.00	450
1842 Small date	2,383,390	25.00	28.00	36.00	51.50	69.00	400
1842 Large date	Inc. above	28.00	32.00	42.00	57.50	100	365
1843 Petite Head, small date	2,425,342	25.00	28.00	35.00	51.50	69.00	360
1843 Petite Head, (rev '44)	Inc. above	27.00	30.00	37.00	51.50	79.00	550
1843 Mature Head	—	28.00	32.00	50.00	140	260	600
1844	2,398,752	25.00	28.00	36.00	51.50	69.00	375
1844/81	Inc. above	40.00	60.00	80.00	100	225	1,900
1845	3,894,804	25.00	28.00	33.00	51.50	69.00	300
1846 Small date	4,120,800	23.00	27.00	31.00	51.50	69.00	225
1846 MD	Inc. above	25.00	28.00	35.00	53.50	72.00	375
1846 TD	Inc. above	36.00	45.00	80.00	125	260	1,650
1847	6,183,669	23.00	27.00	31.00	47.50	65.00	250
1847/7	Inc. above	37.00	50.00	90.00	150	385	1,350
1848	6,415,799	25.00	28.00	33.00	47.50	61.00	215
1849	4,178,500	25.00	28.00	33.00	47.50	61.00	225
1850	4,426,844	25.00	28.00	33.00	39.50	61.00	225
1851	9,889,707	23.00	26.00	31.00	37.50	59.00	195
1851/81	Inc. above	36.00	45.00	60.00	90.00	175	700
1852	5,063,094	23.00	26.00	31.00	37.50	59.00	195
1853	6,641,131	23.00	26.00	31.00	37.50	59.00	195
1854	4,236,156	23.00	26.00	31.00	37.50	59.00	195
1855 Slanted 5's	1,574,829	43.00	56.00	65.00	74.50	95.00	245
1855 Upright 5's	Inc. above	23.00	26.00	33.00	37.50	59.00	195
1855 Slanted 5's Knob on Ear	Inc. above	27.00	34.00	46.00	70.00	99.00	450
1856 Slanted 5	2,690,463	23.00	26.00	31.00	37.50	59.00	195
1856 Upright 5	Inc. above	30.00	40.00	52.00	63.50	80.00	250
1857 Large date	333,456	90.00	125	175	235	310	600
1857 Small date	Inc. above	75.00	100	160	195	265	550

Flying Eagle Cent
Flying eagle above date. Value within wreath.

KM# 85 • 4.67 g., Copper-Nickel, 19 mm. • **Obv. Legend:** UNITED STATES OF AMERICA **Designer:** James B. Longacre **Note:** On the large-letter variety of 1858, the "A" and "M" in AMERICA are connected at their bases; on the small-letter variety, the two letters are separated.

Large letters — AM touch at bottom

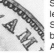
Small letters — Space between AM

Date	Mintage	G4	VG8	F12	VF20	XF40	AU50	MS60	MS65	Prf65
1856	Est. 2500	6,250	7,250	9,000	10,750	12,850	13,500	16,500	65,000	28,500
1857	17,450,000	27.50	39.00	40.00	47.00	140	210	425	3,500	29,000
1858/7	Inc. below	65.00	92.50	175	380	760	1,500	3,300	60,000	—
1858 large letters	24,600,000	28.00	41.00	43.50	56.00	160	230	445	3,850	24,500
1858 small letters	Inc. above	27.50	39.00	42.00	47.00	140	210	425	3,650	30,000

Indian Head Cent
Indian head with headdress left above date. Value within wreath.

KM# 87 • 4.67 g., Copper-Nickel, 19 mm. • **Obv. Legend:** UNITED STATES OF AMERICA **Designer:** James B. Longacre

Date	Mintage	G4	VG8	F12	VF20	XF40	AU50	MS60	MS65	Prf65
1859	36,400,000	13.00	16.00	22.50	48.00	100	175	230	3,650	5,200

Indian head with headdress left above date. Value within wreath, shield above.

KM# 90 • 4.67 g., Copper-Nickel, 19 mm. • **Obv. Legend:** UNITED STATES OF AMERICA **Designer:** James B. Longacre

Date	Mintage	G4	VG8	F12	VF20	XF40	AU50	MS60	MS65	Prf65
1860 Rounded Bust	20,566,000	11.00	15.00	22.00	46.00	68.00	110	190	965	3,600
1860	1,000	—	—	—	—	—	—	—	—	—
1860 Pointed Bust	Inc. above	20.00	30.00	42.00	60.00	100	160	300	6,000	—
1861	10,100,000	23.00	30.00	42.00	58.00	95.00	160	180	975	7,250
1862	28,075,000	11.50	11.50	12.50	15.00	28.00	60.00	80.00	1,050	2,350
1863	49,840,000	9.00	9.25	11.00	12.50	25.00	58.00	75.00	1,050	3,100
1864	13,740,000	20.00	28.50	35.00	72.00	125	175	220	1,400	3,200

KM# 90a • 3.11 g., Bronze, 19 mm. • **Obv. Legend:** UNITED STATES OF AMERICA **Designer:** James B. Longacre **Note:** The 1864 "L" variety has the designer's initial in Liberty's hair to the right of her neck.

1864 "L"

Date	Mintage	G4	VG8	F12	VF20	XF40	AU50	MS60	MS65	Prf65
1864	39,233,714	13.00	20.00	25.00	44.00	65.50	85.00	110	335	10,500
1864 L pointed bust	Inc. above	50.00	75.00	145	190	270	320	410	1,700	200,000
1865 plain 5	35,429,286	13.00	14.00	22.50	27.00	42.00	58.00	90.00	485	6,750
1865 fancy 5	Inc. above	12.75	13.50	21.00	24.00	37.50	54.00	85.00	465	—
1866	9,826,500	53.00	62.00	92.00	115	195	235	280	1,350	4,500
1867	9,821,000	52.00	68.50	115	120	187	230	285	1,350	6,100
1867/1867	Inc. above	68.00	160	230	400	550	775	565	1,950	—
1868	10,266,500	39.00	48.00	75.00	115	172	235	265	985	5,750
1869/9	6,420,000	175	295	530	670	1,000	1,150	1,250	2,350	—
1869	Inc. above	85.00	115	220	305	1,076	575	625	1,750	3,100
1870 Bold N	5,275,000	59.00	120	225	305	460	470	600	1,400	2,650
1870 Shallow N	Inc. above	80.00	140	245	560	575	590	—	—	—
1871 Bold N	3,929,500	89.00	125	275	310	435	480	610	2,400	2,500
1871 Shallow N	Inc. above	135	150	320	600	700	750	—	—	—
1872 Bold N	4,042,000	110	185	365	410	555	600	840	3,850	4,250
1872 Shallow N	Inc. above	120	210	380	665	725	755	—	—	—
1873 closed 3	11,676,500	27.00	36.50	75.00	110	220	275	400	2,850	2,950
1873 open 3	Inc. above	21.50	32.50	63.00	79.00	170	210	250	1,300	—
1873 Double Liberty die 1	Inc. above	350	750	1,250	1,850	3,250	4,650	7,500	—	—
1873 Double Liberty die 2	Inc. above	—	100	275	450	540	975	4,500	—	—
1874	14,187,500	15.50	21.00	45.00	61.00	110	145	225	700	2,850
1875	13,528,000	16.50	29.50	54.00	63.00	110	157	215	800	8,500
1876	7,944,000	30.00	38.50	74.00	125	205	280	325	975	2,600
1877	852,500	595	725	1,025	1,500	2,550	2,850	3,450	13,000	12,500
1878	5,799,850	27.50	33.00	69.00	140	240	285	350	875	1,375
1879	16,231,200	6.75	9.00	15.75	32.00	69.00	73.00	100	365	1,250
1880	38,964,955	4.00	4.75	5.75	10.50	27.50	46.00	66.00	360	1,250

Date	Mintage	G4	VG8	F12	VF20	XF40	AU50	MS60	MS65	Prf65
1881	39,211,575	4.30	4.35	5.75	7.50	21.50	28.50	43.00	325	1,250
1882	38,581,100	3.75	4.00	5.00	9.25	21.50	28.50	40.00	325	1,450
1883	45,589,109	3.25	3.50	4.00	6.75	17.00	28.50	42.00	325	1,600
1884	23,261,742	4.00	4.25	6.50	11.00	28.00	39.00	60.00	460	1,250
1885	11,765,384	8.75	9.00	11.00	26.50	60.00	78.00	105	625	1,500
1886 Type 1 obverse	17,654,290	4.25	6.25	19.00	55.00	145	155	190	1,250	2,650
1886 Type 2 obverse	Inc. above	7.00	10.00	28.00	235	180	235	325	2,500	7,500
1887	45,226,483	2.00	2.10	3.00	5.00	18.00	26.50	50.00	400	6,200
1888	37,494,414	2.90	3.05	3.80	7.25	19.25	25.00	48.00	900	5,400
1888/7	Inc. above	1,850	2,850	4,500	8,500	10,000	13,000	—	—	—
1889	48,869,361	1.70	2.00	2.50	4.25	9.25	21.00	40.00	400	1,900
1890	57,182,854	1.85	2.55	2.90	4.60	12.00	20.50	37.50	400	1,800
1891	47,072,350	1.65	2.95	4.10	5.15	17.75	23.00	37.00	400	2,150
1892	37,649,832	1.70	2.55	2.90	4.60	9.25	20.50	35.00	400	1,325
1893	46,642,195	5.50	6.00	13.00	17.50	48.00	61.00	30.00	340	1,250
1894/94	16,752,132	2.25	2.30	3.00	3.75	11.00	20.50	85.00	6,000	1,350
1894	Inc. above	35.00	45.00	100	275	325	485	800	375	—
1895	38,343,636	2.25	2.30	2.75	3.85	12.00	24.00	32.00	200	1,275
1896	39,057,293	1.65	2.00	2.35	3.75	9.25	21.00	34.00	225	1,900
1897	50,466,330	1.65	2.10	2.40	3.75	9.25	21.00	34.00	195	1,600
1898	49,823,079	1.65	2.00	2.30	3.75	9.50	21.00	34.00	195	1,275
1899	53,600,031	1.65	2.00	2.30	3.60	12.00	21.50	34.00	165	1,275
1900	66,833,764	1.65	2.00	2.30	3.60	10.50	21.00	34.00	175	1,275
1901	79,611,143	1.65	2.00	2.30	3.60	9.25	20.00	33.00	165	1,275
1902	87,376,722	1.70	2.00	2.30	3.60	9.25	20.00	32.00	165	1,325
1903	85,094,493	1.50	2.00	2.30	3.60	9.25	20.00	32.00	165	1,275
1904	61,328,015	1.40	2.00	2.30	3.60	8.00	19.00	32.00	165	1,275
1905	80,719,163	1.40	2.00	2.30	3.60	8.00	20.00	32.00	165	1,350
1906	96,022,255	1.40	2.00	2.30	3.60	8.00	19.00	32.00	165	1,275
1907	108,138,618	1.40	2.05	2.30	3.60	8.00	19.00	32.00	165	1,950
1908	32,327,987	80.00	85.00	100	125	160	215	32.00	165	1,275
1908S	1,115,000	10.50	12.50	13.00	15.00	19.50	29.00	275	700	—
1909	14,370,645	12.50	13.50	14.00	14.50	18.00	27.00	35.00	150	1,275
1909S	309,000	485	500	535	600	750	800	1,125	2,250	—

Lincoln Cent
Wheat Ears.

KM# 132 • 3.11 g., Bronze, 19 mm. • **Designer:**
Victor D. Brenner **Note:** The 1909 "VDB" varieties
have the designer's initials inscribed at the 6 o'clock
position on the reverse. The initials were removed
until 1918, when they were restored on the obverse
• MS60 and MS63 prices are for brown coins and
MS65 prices are for coins that are at least 90%
original red.

1922 Plain

Date	Mintage	G4	VG8	F12	VF20	XF40	AU50	MS60	MS65	Prf65
1909 VDB	27,995,000	11.50	12.00	12.50	13.50	14.00	16.50	24.00	95.00	2,750
1909 VDB Doubled Die Obverse	Inc. above	—	—	55.00	75.00	100	120	200	1,500	—
1909S VDB	484,000	660	675	695	800	1,025	1,325	1,575	2,950	—
1909	72,702,618	3.65	3.50	4.35	4.75	5.50	12.50	14.50	85.00	625
1909S	1,825,000	89.00	105	110	150	225	245	340	750	—
1909S/S S over horizontal S	Inc. above	115	135	148	200	275	290	365	850	—
1910	146,801,218	0.50	0.60	0.75	1.00	4.25	10.00	17.50	120	610
1910S	6,045,000	16.50	21.00	21.00	28.00	47.50	72.00	98.00	425	—
1911	101,177,787	0.45	0.60	1.60	2.35	6.75	11.00	18.50	175	525
1911D	12,672,000	4.75	5.75	9.00	22.50	50.00	75.00	90.00	750	—
1911S	4,026,000	49.00	53.00	55.00	59.00	75.00	105	175	1,100	—
1912	68,153,060	1.60	1.75	2.35	5.50	13.50	26.00	33.00	235	625
1912D	10,411,000	6.50	9.25	10.00	26.00	70.00	110	165	800	—
1912S	4,431,000	24.00	26.00	29.00	42.00	78.00	118	175	1,250	—
1913	76,532,352	0.80	1.00	1.45	3.25	18.50	28.50	34.50	240	625
1913D	15,804,000	2.75	3.25	3.60	11.00	49.00	62.00	105	875	—
1913S	6,101,000	13.50	16.50	21.00	31.00	57.00	110	195	2,100	—
1914	75,238,432	0.60	0.95	2.10	6.00	18.50	40.00	52.00	240	625
1914D	1,193,000	190	200	245	365	760	1,475	2,000	9,500	—
1914S	4,137,000	25.00	27.50	30.00	40.00	85.00	175	310	3,250	—
1915	29,092,120	2.25	2.90	4.00	18.00	60.00	70.00	82.00	375	625
1915D	22,050,000	2.25	2.85	4.50	6.85	24.00	44.00	72.00	350	—
1915S	4,833,000	21.00	24.50	28.50	32.00	70.00	96.00	190	2,600	—
1916	131,833,677	0.45	0.55	0.85	2.40	8.00	14.50	19.00	135	650
1916D	35,956,000	1.35	2.00	3.10	6.50	17.50	38.00	88.00	850	—
1916S	22,510,000	1.65	3.25	4.40	9.50	27.50	48.00	105	1,100	—

Date	Mintage	G4	VG8	F12	VF20	XF40	AU50	MS60	MS65	Prf65
1917	196,429,785	0.30	0.40	0.55	1.85	4.75	14.50	18.50	150	—
1917 Doubled Die Obverse	Inc. above	175	225	2.75	350	1,350	2,000	3,200	15,000	—
1917D	55,120,000	1.00	1.50	2.85	5.00	36.50	44.00	72.00	850	—
1917S	32,620,000	0.55	0.90	1.40	2.60	11.50	26.00	74.00	1,350	—
1918	288,104,634	0.30	0.40	0.50	1.00	4.40	10.00	13.50	185	—
1918D	47,830,000	0.95	1.45	2.45	5.50	15.50	36.00	76.00	1,200	—
1918S	34,680,000	0.40	0.90	1.45	3.65	11.00	33.00	70.00	1,750	—
1919	392,021,000	0.30	0.40	0.50	0.80	1.60	5.75	8.00	85.00	—
1919D	57,154,000	0.80	1.20	1.60	4.85	12.75	35.00	60.00	775	—
1919S	139,760,000	0.40	0.60	1.50	2.45	5.75	17.50	48.00	1,175	—
1920	310,165,000	0.25	0.35	0.75	1.25	2.80	7.50	15.50	225	—
1920D	49,280,000	1.00	1.65	2.90	6.85	18.50	37.00	70.00	650	—
1920S	46,220,000	0.60	0.80	1.50	2.75	13.00	34.50	105	2,150	—
1921	39,157,000	0.55	0.80	1.15	3.00	10.75	22.50	42.00	175	—
1921S	15,274,000	1.50	2.00	3.50	6.25	36.50	68.00	110	1,100	—
1922D	7,160,000	23.50	24.50	25.50	27.00	37.50	75.00	105	475	—
1922D Weak Rev	Inc. above	22.00	23.00	24.00	25.50	34.00	65.00	95.00	400	—
1922D Weak D	Inc. above	30.00	44.00	48.00	60.00	135	190	285	7,500	—
1922 No D Die 2 Strong Rev	Inc. above	550	580	730	925	2,050	4,250	10,500	85,000	—
1922 No D Die 3 Weak Rev	Inc. above	300	375	575	750	1,650	3,350	8,500	45,000	—
1923	74,723,000	0.40	0.60	0.85	1.50	5.75	10.50	13.50	160	—
1923S	8,700,000	5.85	7.00	8.50	12.50	42.00	105	190	2,850	—
1924	75,178,000	0.25	0.35	0.45	1.00	5.25	11.00	17.50	120	—
1924D	2,520,000	37.50	45.00	50.00	62.00	118	170	255	1,800	—
1924S	11,696,000	1.25	1.50	2.75	5.35	34.50	68.00	110	2,350	—
1925	139,949,000	0.25	0.35	0.45	0.70	3.00	6.50	9.50	65.00	—
1925D	22,580,000	1.00	1.65	3.10	6.25	15.50	30.00	62.00	625	—
1925S	26,380,000	0.80	1.20	1.85	2.75	11.75	31.50	85.00	3,650	—
1926	157,088,000	0.25	0.35	0.45	0.60	1.65	5.25	7.50	70.00	—
1926D	28,020,000	1.50	1.70	3.40	5.25	15.50	34.00	82.00	800	—
1926S	4,550,000	9.00	10.00	11.75	16.50	35.00	72.00	140	5,500	—
1927	144,440,000	0.20	0.25	0.35	0.60	1.60	5.25	7.50	60.00	—
1927D	27,170,000	1.15	1.70	2.25	3.35	7.50	25.00	60.00	525	—
1927S	14,276,000	1.40	1.85	2.65	5.25	14.50	42.00	65.00	2,550	—
1928	134,116,000	0.20	0.25	0.35	0.60	1.45	4.00	7.50	82.00	—
1928D	31,170,000	0.90	1.40	2.15	3.65	6.75	19.00	37.50	300	—
1928S Small S	17,266,000	1.00	1.65	2.60	4.00	9.50	31.00	71.50	800	—
1928S Large S	Inc. above	1.65	2.85	4.25	7.50	16.50	55.00	135	1,250	—
1929	185,262,000	0.20	0.25	0.35	0.55	2.75	5.25	7.00	55.00	—
1929D	41,730,000	0.50	1.00	1.40	2.75	5.85	13.50	25.00	145	—
1929S	50,148,000	0.60	1.10	1.85	2.80	6.75	14.75	20.00	100	—
1930	157,415,000	0.20	0.25	0.35	0.60	1.25	2.75	4.00	45.00	—
1930D	40,100,000	0.25	0.35	0.60	0.90	2.00	5.50	11.00	55.00	—
1930S	24,286,000	0.25	0.35	0.55	0.80	1.50	6.50	9.50	48.00	—
1931	19,396,000	0.65	0.75	1.10	2.00	4.00	9.50	19.00	85.00	—
1931D	4,480,000	5.00	5.85	6.50	8.00	13.00	33.50	48.50	375	—
1931S	866,000	60.00	66.00	71.00	77.00	135	140	160	350	—
1932	9,062,000	1.60	1.95	2.85	3.50	6.75	13.00	17.50	65.00	—
1932D	10,500,000	1.50	1.90	2.50	2.85	4.15	11.00	18.50	65.00	—
1933	14,360,000	1.50	1.80	2.65	2.85	6.50	11.50	16.50	65.00	—
1933D	6,200,000	3.50	4.25	5.65	7.50	13.50	19.00	24.00	60.00	—
1934	219,080,000	0.15	0.25	0.30	0.45	1.25	4.00	9.00	25.00	—
1934D	28,446,000	0.35	0.50	0.80	1.25	5.50	9.00	20.00	30.00	—
1935	245,338,000	0.15	0.20	0.25	0.40	0.90	1.50	5.00	20.00	—
1935D	47,000,000	0.20	0.30	0.40	0.55	0.95	2.50	5.50	20.00	—
1935S	38,702,000	0.25	0.35	0.60	1.75	3.00	5.00	11.00	44.00	—
1936 (Proof in Satin Finish)	309,637,569	0.15	0.20	0.30	0.40	0.85	1.40	1.90	10.00	600
1936 Brilliant Proof	Inc. above	—	—	—	—	—	—	—	—	800
1936 DDO	Inc. above	—	—	25.00	50.00	80.00	125	175	1,000	—
1936D	40,620,000	0.20	0.30	0.40	0.55	0.90	1.50	4.00	15.00	—
1936S	29,130,000	0.20	0.30	0.45	0.60	1.50	2.25	5.00	18.00	—
1937	309,179,320	0.15	0.20	0.30	0.40	0.50	0.75	1.75	13.50	110
1937D	50,430,000	0.20	0.30	0.40	0.60	0.80	1.20	2.65	15.00	—
1937S	34,500,000	0.20	0.30	0.40	0.55	0.90	1.25	2.75	16.50	—
1938	156,696,734	0.15	0.20	0.30	0.40	0.50	1.20	2.25	18.00	90.00
1938D	20,010,000	0.20	0.30	0.45	0.60	1.00	1.50	3.50	20.00	—
1938S	15,180,000	0.30	0.40	0.50	0.70	1.00	1.75	3.00	15.00	—
1939	316,479,520	0.15	0.20	0.30	0.40	0.45	0.75	1.00	16.00	60.00
1939D	15,160,000	0.35	0.45	0.50	0.60	0.95	1.75	3.00	18.00	—
1939S	52,070,000	0.30	0.40	0.50	0.60	0.80	1.20	2.50	16.00	—
1940	586,825,872	0.10	0.20	0.30	0.35	0.45	0.75	1.00	12.00	65.00
1940D	81,390,000	0.20	0.30	0.40	0.55	0.75	1.10	2.00	11.00	—
1940S	112,940,000	0.20	0.30	0.40	0.55	0.70	1.25	2.50	12.50	—
1941	887,039,100	0.10	0.20	0.30	0.35	0.45	0.60	1.25	10.00	60.00
1941 Doubled Die Obv	Inc. above	35.00	50.00	70.00	80.00	95.00	135	200	1,000	—
1941D	128,700,000	0.20	0.30	0.40	0.55	0.90	1.35	2.20	12.50	—
1941S	92,360,000	0.20	0.30	0.40	0.55	0.95	1.75	2.50	15.00	—

CENT

Date	Mintage	G4	VG8	F12	VF20	XF40	AU50	MS60	MS65	Prf65
1942	657,828,600	0.10	0.20	0.30	0.35	0.40	0.55	0.85	11.00	65.00
1942D	206,698,000	0.20	0.25	0.30	0.35	0.45	0.60	1.00	12.00	—
1942S	85,590,000	0.25	0.35	0.45	0.85	1.25	2.50	5.00	18.00	—
1943 Copper planchet error	—	—	—	35,000	42,000	45,000	80,000	155,000	—	—
1943S Copper planchet error	—	—	—	125,000	150,000	185,000	275,000	—	—	—

KM# 132a • 2.70 g., Zinc Coated Steel, 19 mm. •
Designer: Victor D. Brenner

Date	Mintage	G4	VG8	F12	VF20	XF40	AU50	MS60	MS65	Prf65
1943	684,628,670	0.20	0.30	0.35	0.45	0.60	0.85	1.25	18.00	—
1943D	217,660,000	0.35	0.40	0.45	0.50	0.70	1.00	1.50	—	—
1943D/D RPM	Inc. above	30.00	38.00	50.00	65.00	90.00	125	200	—	—
1943S	191,550,000	0.40	0.45	0.50	0.65	0.90	1.40	4.00	28.00	—

KM# A132 • 3.11 g., Brass, 19 mm. • **Designer:**
Victor D. Brenner **Note:** KM#132 design and
composition resumed • MS60 prices are for brown
coins and MS65 prices are for coins that are at least
90% original red.

1955 Double die

Date	Mintage	XF40	MS65	Prf65
1944	1,435,400,000	0.30	8.00	—
1944D	430,578,000	0.40	14.00	—
1944D/S Type 1	Inc. above	220	3,750	—
1944D/S Type 2	Inc. above	175	1,600	—
1944S	282,760,000	0.35	8.00	—
1945	1,040,515,000	0.40	13.50	—
1945D	226,268,000	0.40	8.00	—
1945S	181,770,000	0.40	7.50	—
1946	991,655,000	0.25	13.50	—
1946D	315,690,000	0.30	10.00	—
1946S	198,100,000	0.30	13.50	—
1946S/D	—	70.00	650	—
1947	190,555,000	0.45	18.50	—
1947D	194,750,000	0.35	7.50	—
1947S	99,000,000	0.35	8.00	—
1948	317,570,000	0.35	18.50	—
1948D	172,637,000	0.40	12.00	—
1948S	81,735,000	0.40	12.00	—
1949	217,775,000	0.40	18.00	—
1949D	153,132,000	0.40	15.00	—
1949S	64,290,000	0.50	10.00	—
1950	272,686,386	0.35	16.50	65.00
1950D	334,950,000	0.35	12.50	—
1950S	118,505,000	0.30	9.00	—
1951	295,633,500	0.40	16.50	62.00
1951D	625,355,000	0.30	8.50	—
1951S	136,010,000	0.40	9.00	—
1952	186,856,980	0.40	16.00	36.00
1952D	746,130,000	0.30	8.50	—
1952S	137,800,004	0.60	12.00	—
1953	256,883,800	0.25	18.00	37.00
1953D	700,515,000	0.25	8.50	—
1953S	181,835,000	0.40	8.00	—
1954	71,873,350	0.25	20.00	19.00
1954D	251,552,500	0.25	8.50	—
1954S	96,190,000	0.25	10.00	—
1955	330,958,000	0.25	9.00	14.00
1955 Doubled Die	Inc. above	1,900	37,500	—

Note: The 1955 "doubled die" has distinct doubling of the date
and lettering on the obverse.

Date	Mintage	XF40	MS65	Prf65
1955D	563,257,500	0.20	8.00	—
1955S	44,610,000	0.35	7.50	—

Date	Mintage	XF40	MS65	Prf65
1956	421,414,384	0.20	12.00	5.00
1956D	1,098,201,100	0.20	7.00	—
1957	283,787,952	0.20	7.50	4.00
1957D	1,051,342,000	0.20	6.00	—
1958	253,400,652	0.20	9.00	6.50
1958D	800,953,300	0.20	7.00	—

Lincoln Memorial.

KM# 201 • 3.11 g., Brass, 19 mm. • **Rev. Designer:**
Frank Gasparro **Note:** MS60 prices are for brown
coins and MS65 prices are for coins that are at least
90% original red. The dates were modified in 1960,
1970 and 1982, resulting in large-date and small-
date varieties for those years. The 1972 "doubled
die" shows doubling of IN GOD WE TRUST. The
1979-S and 1981-S Type II proofs have a clearer
mint mark than the Type I proofs of those years.
Some 1982 cents have the predominantly copper
composition; others have the predominantly zinc
composition. They can be distinguished by weight.

Small date | Large date

Small date | Large date

Date	Mintage	XF40	MS65	Prf65
1959	610,864,291	—	15.00	10.00
1959D	1,279,760,000	—	7.50	—
1960 small date, low 9	588,096,602	1.85	12.00	16.00
1960 large date, high 9	Inc. above	—	8.00	7.50
1960 small over large date	Inc. above	—	—	600
1960D small date, low 9	1,580,884,000	—	10.00	—
1960D large date, high 9	Inc. above	—	8.00	—

Date	Mintage	XF40	MS65	Prf65
1960D/D small over large date	Inc. above	—	300	—
1961	756,373,244	—	8.50	9.00
1961D	1,753,266,700	—	18.00	—
1962	609,263,019	—	8.00	8.00
1962D	1,793,148,400	—	14.00	—
1963	757,185,645	—	10.00	6.00
1963D	1,774,020,400	—	12.00	—
1964	2,652,525,762	—	8.50	6.00
1964D	3,799,071,500	—	10.00	—
1965	1,497,224,900	—	10.00	—
1965 SMS	Inc. above	—	7.50	—
1966	2,188,147,783	—	10.00	—
1966 SMS	Inc. above	—	8.00	—
1967	3,048,667,100	—	12.00	—
1967 SMS	Inc. above	—	8.00	—
1968	1,707,880,970	—	12.00	—
1968D	2,886,269,600	—	12.50	—
1968S	261,311,510	—	10.00	4.50
1969	1,136,910,000	—	7.00	—
1969D	4,002,832,200	—	10.00	—
1969S	547,309,631	—	15.00	5.50
1969S Doubled Die Obverse	Inc. above	10,000	125,000	100,000
1970	1,898,315,000	—	8.00	—
1970D	2,891,438,900	—	6.00	—
1970S small date, level 7	Inc. above	30.00	65.00	60.00
1970S large date, low 7	Inc. above	—	15.00	5.00
1970S Doubled Die Obverse	Inc. above	—	20,000	15,000
1971	1,919,490,000	—	20.00	—
1971D	2,911,045,600	—	6.50	—
1971S	528,354,192	—	7.50	5.50
1971S Doubled Die Obverse	Inc. above	—	—	400
1972	2,933,255,000	—	6.00	—
1972 Doubled Die Obverse	Inc. above	290	785	—
1972D	2,665,071,400	—	12.00	—
1972S	380,200,104	—	26.50	5.50
1973	3,728,245,000	—	8.00	—
1973D	3,549,576,588	—	11.00	—
1973S	319,937,634	—	10.00	5.50
1974	4,232,140,523	—	12.00	—
1974D	4,235,098,000	—	9.00	—
1974S	412,039,228	—	12.00	5.00
1975	5,451,476,142	—	8.00	—
1975D	4,505,245,300	—	13.50	—
1975S	2,845,450	—	—	5.00
1976	4,674,292,426	—	14.00	—
1976D	4,221,592,455	—	16.00	—
1976S	4,149,730	—	—	6.00
1977	4,469,930,000	—	16.00	—
1977D	4,149,062,300	—	16.00	—
1977S	3,251,152	—	—	5.00
1978	5,558,605,000	—	16.00	—
1978D	4,280,233,400	—	14.00	—
1978S	3,127,781	—	—	5.00
1979	6,018,515,000	—	12.00	—
1979D	4,139,357,254	—	8.00	—
1979S type I, proof	3,677,175	—	—	5.00
1979S type II, proof	—	—	—	10.00
1980	7,414,705,000	—	6.50	—
1980D	5,140,098,660	—	12.00	—
1980S	3,554,806	—	—	5.00
1981	7,491,750,000	—	8.50	—
1981D	5,373,235,677	—	9.00	—
1981S type I, proof	4,063,083	—	—	5.00
1981S type II, proof	—	—	—	42.00
1982 large date	10,712,525,000	—	7.00	—
1982 small date	Inc. above	—	9.00	—
1982D large date	6,012,979,368	—	7.50	—
1982S	3,857,479	—	—	5.00

KM# 201a • 2.50 g., Copper Plated Zinc, 19 mm.
• **Note:** MS60 prices are for brown coins and MS65 prices are for coins that are at least 90% original red.

Date	Mintage	XF40	MS65	Prf65
1982 large date	—	—	6.00	—
1982 small date	—	—	9.00	—
1982D large date	—	—	8.00	—
1982D small date	—	—	6.00	—

KM# 201b • Copper Plated Zinc, 19 mm. • **Note:** MS60 prices are for brown coins and MS65 prices are for coins that are at least 90% original red.

Date	Mintage	XF40	MS65	Prf65
1983	7,752,355,000	—	7.00	—
1983 Doubled Die	Inc. above	135	450	—
1983D	6,467,199,428	—	5.50	—
1983S	3,279,126	—	—	3.50
1984	8,151,079,000	—	7.50	—
1984 Doubled Die	Inc. above	100	325	—
1984D	5,569,238,906	—	6.50	—
1984S	3,065,110	—	—	3.50
1985	5,648,489,887	—	4.50	—
1985D	5,287,399,926	—	4.50	—
1985S	3,362,821	—	—	3.50
1986	4,491,395,493	—	5.00	—
1986D	4,442,866,698	—	8.00	—
1986S	3,010,497	—	—	3.50
1987	4,682,466,931	—	7.50	—
1987D	4,879,389,514	—	5.50	—
1987S	4,227,728	—	—	3.50
1988	6,092,810,000	—	10.00	—
1988D	5,253,740,443	—	6.00	—
1988S	3,262,948	—	—	3.50
1989	7,261,535,000	—	6.50	—
1989D	5,345,467,111	—	6.50	—
1989S	3,220,194	—	—	5.00
1990	6,851,765,000	—	5.00	—
1990D	4,922,894,533	—	5.50	—
1990S	3,299,559	—	—	3.50
1990 no S, Proof only	Inc. above	—	—	4,650
1991	5,165,940,000	—	6.50	—
1991D	4,158,442,076	—	5.50	—
1991S	2,867,787	—	—	3.50
1992	4,648,905,000	—	5.50	—
1992D	4,448,673,300	—	5.50	—
1992D Close AM, Proof Reverse Die	Inc. above	—	—	—
1992S	4,176,560	—	—	3.50
1993	5,684,705,000	—	5.00	—
1993D	6,426,650,571	—	4.50	—
1993S	3,394,792	—	—	3.50
1994	6,500,850,000	—	6.00	—
1994D	7,131,765,000	—	4.50	—
1994S	3,269,923	—	—	3.50
1995	6,411,440,000	—	5.00	—
1995 Doubled Die Obverse	Inc. above	20.00	60.00	—
1995D	7,128,560,000	—	4.50	—
1995S	2,707,481	—	—	3.50
1996	6,612,465,000	—	4.50	—
1996D	6,510,795,000	—	4.50	—
1996S	2,915,212	—	—	3.50
1997	4,622,800,000	—	3.00	—
1997D	4,576,555,000	—	3.50	—
1997S	2,796,678	—	—	4.00
1998	5,032,155,000	—	3.00	—
1998 Wide AM, reverse from proof die	Inc. above	—	110	—
1998D	5,255,353,500	—	3.00	—
1998S	2,957,286	—	—	4.00

CENT

Date	Mintage	XF40	MS65	Prf65
1999	5,237,600,000	—	3.00	—
1999 Wide AM, reverse from proof die	Inc. above	—	450	—
1999D	6,360,065,000	—	3.00	—
1999S	3,362,462	—	—	3.50
2000 Wide AM, reverse from proof die	Inc. above	—	45.00	—
2000	5,503,200,000	—	3.00	—
2000D	8,774,220,000	—	3.00	—
2000S	4,063,361	—	—	3.50
2001	4,959,600,000	—	3.00	—
2001D	5,374,990,000	—	3.00	—
2001S	3,099,096	—	—	3.50
2002	3,260,800,000	—	3.00	—
2002D	4,028,055,000	—	3.00	—
2002S	3,157,739	—	—	3.50
2003	3,300,000,000	—	3.50	—
2003D	3,548,000,000	—	3.50	—
2003S	3,116,590	—	—	3.50
2004	3,379,600,000	—	3.50	—
2004D	3,456,400,000	—	3.50	—
2004S	2,992,069	—	—	3.50
2005	3,935,600,000	—	2.50	—
2005 Satin Finish	1,160,000	—	4.00	—
2005D	3,764,450,000	—	2.50	—
2005D Satin Finish	1,160,000	—	4.00	—
2005S	3,273,000	—	—	3.50
2006	4,290,000,000	—	2.00	—
2006 Satin Finish	847,361	—	4.00	—
2006D	3,944,000,000	—	2.50	—
2006D Satin Finish	847,361	—	4.00	—
2006S	2,923,105	—	—	3.50
2007	3,762,400,000	—	2.00	—
2007 Satin Finish	895,628	—	4.00	—
2007D	3,638,800,000	—	2.00	—
2007D Satin Finish	895,628	—	4.00	—
2007S	2,577,166	—	—	3.50
2008	2,558,800,000	—	2.25	—
2008 Satin Finish	745,464	—	4.00	—
2008D	2,849,600,000	—	2.25	—
2008D Satin Finish	745,464	—	4.00	—
2008S	2,169,561	—	—	4.50

Lincoln Bicentennial
Bust right.   Log cabin.

KM# 441 • 2.50 g., Copper Plated Zinc, 19 mm. • **Subject:** Early Childhood in Kenturcky **Rev. Designer:** Richard Masters and James Licaretz

Date	Mintage	XF40	MS65	Prf65
2009P	284,400,000	—	1.50	—
2009D	350,400,000	—	1.50	—

KM# 441a • 3.31 g., Brass, 19 mm. • **Subject:** Early childhood in Kentucky **Rev. Designer:** Richard Masters and James Licaretz

Date	Mintage	XF40	MS65	Prf65
2009P Satin finish	784,614	—	4.00	—
2009D Satin finish	784,614	—	4.00	—
2009S	2,995,615	—	—	4.00

Lincoln seated on log.

KM# 442 • 2.50 g., Copper Plated Zinc, 19 mm. • **Subject:** Formative years in Indiana **Rev. Designer:** Charles Vickers

Date	Mintage	XF40	MS65	Prf65
2009P	376,000,000	—	1.50	—
2009D	363,600,000	—	1.50	—

KM# 442a • 3.11 g., Brass, 19 mm. • **Subject:** Formative years in Indiana **Rev. Designer:** Charles Vickers

Date	Mintage	XF40	MS65	Prf65
2009P Satin finish	784,614	—	4.00	—
2009D Satin finish	784,614	—	4.00	—
2009S	2,995,615	—	—	4.00

Lincoln standing before Illinois Statehouse.

KM# 443 • 2.50 g., Copper Plated Zinc, 19 mm. • **Subject:** Professional life in Illinois **Rev. Designer:** Joel Iskowitz and Don Everhart

Date	Mintage	XF40	MS65	Prf65
2009P	316,000,000	—	1.50	—
2009D	336,000,000	—	1.50	—

KM# 443a • 3.11 g., Brass, 19 mm. • **Subject:** Professional life in Illinois **Rev. Designer:** Joel Iskowitz and Don Everhart

Date	Mintage	XF40	MS65	Prf65
2009P Satin finish	784,614	—	4.00	—
2009D Satin finish	784,614	—	4.00	—
2009S	2,995,615	—	—	4.00

Capitol Building.

KM# 444 • 2.50 g., Copper Plated Zinc **Subject:** Presidency in Washington, DC **Rev. Designer:** Susan Gamble and Joseph Menna **Shape:** 19

Date	Mintage	XF40	MS65	Prf65
2009P	129,600,000	—	1.50	—
2009D	198,000,000	—	1.50	—

KM# 444a • 3.11 g., Brass, 19 mm. • **Subject:** Presidency in Washington, DC **Rev. Designer:** Susan Ganmble and Joseph Menna

Date	Mintage	XF40	MS65	Prf65
2009P Satin finish	784,614	—	4.00	—
2009D Satin finish	784,614	—	4.00	—
2009S	2,995,615	—	—	4.00

Lincoln - Shield Reverse
Lincoln bust right.   Shield.

KM# 468 • 2.50 g., Copper Plated Zinc, 19 mm. •
Obv. Designer: Victor D. Brenner **Rev. Designer:**
Lyndall Bass and Joseph Menna

Date	Mintage	XF40	MS65	Prf65
2010P	1,963,630,000	—	1.50	—
2010P Satin finish	583,912	—	—	—
2010D	2,047,200,000	—	1.50	—

Date	Mintage	XF40	MS65	Prf65
2010D Satin finish	583,912	—	—	—
2010S	1,689,364	—	—	4.00
2011P	2,006,800,000	—	1.50	—
2011D	2147483647	—	1.50	—
2011S	1,673,010	—	—	4.00
2012P	3,132,000,000	—	1.50	—
2012D	2,883,200,000	—	1.50	—
2012S	1,237,415	—	—	4.00
2013P	3,750,400,000	—	1.50	—
2013D	3,319,600,000	—	1.50	—
2013S	1,237,926	—	—	4.00
2014P		—	1.50	—
2014D		—	1.50	—
2014S		—	—	4.00
2015P		—	1.50	—
2015D		—	1.50	—
2015S		—	—	4.00

2 CENTS

Shield in front of crossed arrows, banner above, date below.   Value within wheat wreath.

KM# 94 • 6.22 g., Copper-Tin-Zinc, 23 mm. • **Rev. Legend:** UNITED STATES OF AMERICA **Designer:** James
B. Longacre **Note:** The motto IN GOD WE TRUST was modified in 1864, resulting in small-motto and large-
motto varieties for that year.

Small motto   Large motto

Date	Mintage	G4	VG8	F12	VF20	XF40	AU50	MS60	MS65	Prf65
1864 small motto	19,847,500	140	210	285	425	650	725	1,125	3,000	45,000
1864 large motto	Inc. above	16.50	18.50	20.00	27.50	42.50	72.00	88.00	375	1,100
1865 fancy 5	13,640,000	16.50	18.50	20.00	27.50	42.50	72.00	88.00	375	—
1865 plain 5	Inc. above	16.50	18.50	21.00	29.00	45.00	75.00	92.00	400	650
1866	3,177,000	17.00	20.00	21.50	29.00	46.00	77.00	98.00	395	650
1867	2,938,750	18.00	21.00	36.00	46.00	60.00	96.00	125	395	650
1867 double die obverse	Inc. above	—	80.00	165	250	350	500	650	4,750	—
1868	2,803,750	18.00	22.00	37.50	47.50	65.00	105	135	465	650
1869	1,546,000	20.00	23.00	40.00	50.00	79.00	125	165	550	650
1869 repunched 18	Inc. above	35.00	45.00	75.00	150	325	550	—	—	—
1869/8 die crack	Inc. above	150	185	375	435	650	900	—	—	—
1870	861,250	31.00	42.00	60.00	82.00	135	190	280	550	650
1871	721,250	43.50	49.00	70.00	110	150	215	285	650	650
1872	65,000	400	550	700	900	1,200	1,800	3,150	5,500	850
1873 closed 3 proof only	Est. 600	1,250	1,400	1,535	1,650	1,750	2,000	—	—	3,850
1873 open 3 proof only	Est. 500	1,275	1,400	1,575	1,700	1,875	2,150	—	—	4,200

SILVER 3 CENTS

Silver 3 Cents - Type 1
Shield within star, no outlines in star.   Roman numeral in designed C, within circle of stars.

KM# 75 • 0.80 g., 0.750 Silver, 14 mm. • **Obv.
Legend:** UNITED STATES OF AMERICA **Designer:**
James B. Longacre

Date	Mintage	G4	VG8	F12	VF20	XF40	AU50	MS60	MS65	Prf65
1851	5,447,400	32.00	48.50	51.00	58.50	68.00	145	180	825	—
1851O	720,000	38.50	58.50	61.00	95.00	160	275	500	3,100	—
1852	18,663,500	32.00	48.50	51.00	58.50	68.00	145	180	825	—
1853	11,400,000	32.00	48.50	51.00	58.50	68.00	145	180	825	—

Silver 3 Cents - Type 2
Shield within star, three outlines in star. Roman numeral in designed C, within circle of stars.

KM# 80 • 0.75 g., 0.900 Silver, 14 mm. • **Obv.**
Legend: UNITED STATES OF AMERICA **Designer:**
James B. Longacre

Date	Mintage	G4	VG8	F12	VF20	XF40	AU50	MS60	MS65	Prf65
1854	671,000	32.00	48.50	51.00	59.50	112	205	340	2,700	33,500
1855	139,000	44.00	57.50	75.00	125	200	325	520	7,400	15,000
1856	1,458,000	34.00	50.50	54.00	67.00	119	205	260	3,250	15,500
1857	1,042,000	34.00	50.50	54.00	67.00	112	223	285	2,375	13,500
1858	1,604,000	33.00	49.50	52.00	62.00	122	205	230	2,350	6,400

Silver 3 Cents - Type 3
Shield within star, two outlines in star. Roman numeral in designed C, within circle of stars.

KM# 88 • 0.75 g., 0.900 Silver, 14 mm. • **Obv.**
Legend: UNITED STATES OF AMERICA **Designer:**
James B. Longacre

Date	Mintage	G4	VG8	F12	VF20	XF40	AU50	MS60	MS65	Prf65
1859	365,000	40.00	53.50	56.00	64.00	87.00	160	195	975	2,150
1860	287,000	40.00	53.50	56.00	64.00	83.00	160	195	1,050	4,000
1861	498,000	40.00	53.50	56.00	64.00	83.00	160	195	1,050	1,800
1862	343,550	46.00	55.50	58.00	66.00	88.00	180	235	935	1,400
1862/1	Inc. above	43.00	57.50	62.00	71.00	94.00	177	210	865	—
1863	21,460	375	420	450	485	520	725	825	2,250	1,350
1863/62 proof only; Rare	Inc. above	—	—	—	—	—	—	—	—	5,400
1864	12,470	375	420	450	485	520	725	850	1,675	1,350
1865	8,500	475	525	550	620	665	700	875	1,650	1,350
1866	22,725	375	420	450	485	520	675	775	1,950	1,325
1867	4,625	475	525	575	625	675	725	850	2,750	1,300
1868	4,100	475	535	585	640	690	750	875	5,750	1,400
1869	5,100	475	535	585	640	690	750	875	2,450	1,400
1869/68 proof only; Rare	Inc. above	—	—	—	—	—	—	—	—	—
1870	4,000	450	460	525	600	665	750	950	5,650	1,350
1871	4,360	440	450	535	625	670	710	835	1,800	1,450
1872	1,950	465	485	550	645	690	750	875	5,500	1,350
1873 proof only	600	—	—	—	—	950	1,050	—	—	2,950

NICKEL 3 CENTS

Coronet head left, date below. Roman numeral value within wreath.

KM# 95 • 1.94 g., Copper-Nickel, 17.9 mm. • **Obv.**
Legend: UNITED STATES OF AMERICA **Designer:**
James B. Longacre

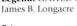

Date	Mintage	G4	VG8	F12	VF20	XF40	AU50	MS60	MS65	Prf65
1865	11,382,000	15.50	16.50	17.50	22.50	37.50	60.00	100	550	6,500
1866	4,801,000	15.50	16.50	17.50	22.50	37.50	60.00	100	550	1,725
1867	3,915,000	15.50	16.50	17.50	22.50	37.50	60.00	100	670	1,575
1868	3,252,000	15.50	16.50	17.50	22.50	37.50	60.00	100	550	1,450
1869	1,604,000	16.50	17.50	19.50	25.50	40.50	61.00	120	730	1,050
1870	1,335,000	17.50	18.50	20.50	26.50	41.50	62.00	135	725	2,250
1871	604,000	17.50	19.00	22.50	27.50	42.50	64.00	155	740	1,200
1872	862,000	19.00	22.50	24.50	29.00	43.50	68.00	175	995	910
1873 Closed 3	1,173,000	16.50	18.50	22.50	25.50	40.50	62.00	145	1,050	1,125
1873 Open 3	Inc. above	16.50	18.50	22.50	26.00	41.50	68.00	180	4,500	—
1874	790,000	17.50	20.50	22.50	27.50	42.50	66.00	160	950	950
1875	228,000	19.00	22.50	27.50	30.50	45.50	82.00	190	750	1,500
1876	162,000	20.50	23.50	26.50	34.50	49.50	97.00	225	1,290	1,025
1877 proof	Est. 900	1,100	1,150	1,175	1,250	1,275	1,350	—	—	3,750
1878 proof	2,350	615	645	720	770	795	830	—	—	1,200
1879	41,200	70.00	80.00	96.00	110	122	180	320	750	690
1880	24,955	100	115	130	165	185	235	375	730	700
1881	1,080,575	15.50	16.50	19.00	23.50	39.50	60.00	100	585	680
1882	25,300	130	150	180	225	300	325	425	1,025	700
1883	10,609	200	225	265	305	375	425	480	4,850	690
1884	5,642	400	445	550	600	645	730	800	6,250	700
1885	4,790	470	520	645	700	745	775	900	12,000	720
1886 proof	4,290	320	330	345	385	385	420	—	—	715

Date	Mintage	G4	VG8	F12	VF20	XF40	AU50	MS60	MS65	Prf65
1887/6 proof	7,961	350	390	415	450	460	515	—	—	940
1887	Inc. above	305	355	395	440	455	500	540	1,200	1,125
1888	41,083	54.00	63.00	70.00	80.00	100	170	315	650	690
1889	21,561	90.00	115	145	180	230	260	320	775	690

HALF DIME

Flowing Hair Half Dime

KM# 15 • 1.35 g., 0.892 Silver 0.0387 oz. ASW, 16.5 mm. • **Designer:** Robert Scot

Date	Mintage	G4	VG8	F12	VF20	XF40	MS60
1794	86,416	1,325	1,625	2,150	3,125	7,325	19,000
1795	Inc. above	1,050	1,350	1,875	2,900	5,800	13,000

Draped Bust Half Dime
Draped bust right.   Small eagle.

KM# 23 • 1.35 g., 0.892 Silver 0.0387 oz. ASW, 16.5 mm. • **Designer:** Robert Scot

Date	Mintage	G4	VG8	F12	VF20	XF40	MS60
1796	10,230	1,435	1,550	3,150	4,850	8,650	17,550
1796 LIKERTY	Inc. above	1,485	1,600	3,200	4,900	8,700	17,600
Note: In 1796 the word LIBERTY was spelled LIKERTY on a die.							
1796/5	Inc. above	1,555	1,700	3,300	5,000	8,800	17,700
1797 13 stars	44,527	2,100	2,650	4,250	5,950	9,750	30,750
1797 15 stars	Inc. above	1,385	1,500	3,100	4,800	8,600	17,500
1797 16 stars	Inc. above	1,535	1,750	3,350	5,050	8,850	17,750

Draped bust right, flanked by stars, date at angle below.   Heraldic eagle.

KM# 34 • 1.35 g., 0.892 Silver 0.0387 oz. ASW, 16.5 mm. • **Obv. Legend:** LIBERTY **Rev. Legend:** UNITED STATES OF AMERICA **Designer:** Robert Scot

Date	Mintage	G4	VG8	F12	VF20	XF40	MS60
1800	24,000	1,000	1,250	1,875	2,550	6,500	13,500
1800 LIBEKTY	Inc. above	1,000	1,250	1,875	2,550	7,000	15,050
1801	33,910	1,225	1,500	2,125	2,800	6,750	17,750
1802	3,060	44,500	65,000	95,000	135,000	300,000	—
1803 Large 8	37,850	1,100	1,375	2,000	2,675	6,625	13,625
1803 Small 8	Inc. above	1,325	1,625	2,250	2,925	6,875	15,850
1805	15,600	1,225	1,525	2,350	3,025	9,900	31,000

Liberty Cap Half Dime
Classic head left, flanked by stars, date below.   Eagle with arrows in talons, banner above.

KM# 47 • 1.35 g., 0.892 Silver 0.0387 oz. ASW, 15.5 mm. • **Rev. Legend:** UNITED STATES OF AMERICA **Designer:** William Kneass

Date	Mintage	G4	VG8	F12	VF20	XF40	AU50	MS60	MS65
1829	1,230,000	60.00	75.00	85.00	148	190	275	365	2,750
1830	1,240,000	52.50	67.50	75.00	118	160	225	350	2,600
1831	1,242,700	52.50	67.50	75.00	118	160	225	350	2,600
1832	965,000	52.50	67.50	75.00	118	160	225	350	2,600
1833	1,370,000	52.50	67.50	75.00	118	160	225	350	2,600
1834	1,480,000	52.50	67.50	75.00	118	160	225	350	2,600
1835 large date and 5C.	2,760,000	52.50	75.00	87.00	133	175	245	350	2,600
1835 large date, small 5C.	Inc. above	52.50	67.50	75.00	118	160	225	410	3,800
1835 small date, large 5C.	Inc. above	52.50	67.50	75.00	118	160	225	375	3,500
1835 small date and 5C.	Inc. above	52.50	67.50	75.00	118	160	225	350	2,600
1836 large 5C.	1,900,000	52.50	67.50	75.00	118	160	225	350	2,600
1836 small 5C.	Inc. above	54.50	70.50	79.00	128	172	237	362	3,100
1837 large 5C.	2,276,000	52.50	67.50	83.00	136	175	245	395	3,800
1837 small 5C.	Inc. above	59.50	77.50	90.00	148	240	465	950	11,000

Seated Liberty Half Dime

Seated Liberty, no stars around border, date below. Value within wreath.

KM# 60 • 1.34 g., 0.900 Silver 0.0388 oz. ASW, 15.5 mm. • **Rev. Legend:** UNITED STATES OF AMERICA **Designer:** Christian Gobrecht **Note:** A design modification in 1837 resulted in small-date and large-date varieties for that year.

Date	Mintage	G4	VG8	F12	VF20	XF40	AU50	MS60	MS65
1837 small date	Inc. above	35.00	46.50	75.00	135	220	495	750	4,450
1837 large date	Inc. above	39.00	49.50	82.00	150	235	445	620	3,650
1838O	70,000	110	130	250	475	975	1,450	2,500	29,500

Seated Liberty, stars around top 1/2 of border, date below. Value within wreath.

KM# 62.1 • 1.34 g., 0.900 Silver 0.0388 oz. ASW, 15.5 mm. • **Rev. Legend:** UNITED STATES OF AMERICA **Designer:** Christian Gobrecht **Note:** The two varieties of 1838 are distinguished by the size of the stars on the obverse. The 1839-O with reverse of 1838-O was struck from rusted reverse dies. The result is a bumpy surface on this variety's reverse.

Date	Mintage	G4	VG8	F12	VF20	XF40	AU50	MS60	MS65
1838 large stars	2,255,000	22.50	25.50	29.00	36.00	88.00	198	265	2,475
1838 small stars	Inc. above	26.50	31.50	46.00	115	189	299	595	3,950
1839	1,069,150	23.50	26.50	30.00	37.00	93.00	203	265	2,000
1839O	1,034,039	27.50	30.50	34.00	41.00	88.00	198	715	6,850
1839O reverse 1838O	Inc. above	500	700	1,200	1,750	3,000	—	—	—
1840	1,344,085	24.50	27.50	31.00	38.00	80.00	190	255	2,275
1840O	935,000	29.50	32.50	38.00	48.00	138	368	1,235	—

KM# 62.2 • 1.34 g., 0.900 Silver 0.0388 oz. ASW, 15.5 mm. • **Rev. Legend:** UNITED STATES OF AMERICA **Designer:** Christian Gobrecht **Note:** In 1840 drapery was added to Liberty's left elbow. Varieties for the 1848 Philadelphia strikes are distinguished by the size of the numerals in the date.

Date	Mintage	G4	VG8	F12	VF20	XF40	AU50	MS60	MS65
1840	Inc. above	21.50	18.00	75.00	135	210	350	490	3,850
1840O	Inc. above	52.50	60.00	115	225	650	1,350	6,500	—
1841	1,150,000	18.50	21.50	23.50	31.00	60.50	127	180	1,325
1841O	815,000	21.50	24.50	30.00	50.00	125	300	650	6,750
1842	815,000	18.50	21.50	23.50	28.00	57.50	127	175	1,750
1842O	350,000	39.50	45.00	75.00	225	550	1,050	2,250	16,500
1843	1,165,000	18.50	21.50	23.50	28.00	57.50	122	175	1,365
1844	430,000	20.50	24.50	26.50	34.00	60.50	127	180	1,150
1844O	220,000	80.00	110	210	600	1,300	2,650	5,400	27,500
1845	1,564,000	18.50	21.50	23.50	35.00	60.50	122	175	1,150
1845/1845	Inc. above	20.50	24.50	26.50	38.00	85.00	132	190	1,200
1846	27,000	410	550	850	1,250	2,475	3,600	11,500	—
1847	1,274,000	18.50	21.50	23.50	28.00	57.50	127	175	1,150
1848 medium date	668,000	20.50	24.50	26.50	34.00	67.50	137	215	3,150
1848 large date	Inc. above	24.00	28.00	48.00	65.00	145	275	635	4,250
1848O	600,000	21.50	25.50	33.00	62.00	135	265	450	2,350
1849/8	1,309,000	28.50	35.00	47.50	67.50	140	250	785	2,950
1849/6	Inc. above	24.00	26.00	30.00	56.50	110	200	425	2,800
1849	Inc. above	20.50	18.50	27.50	52.50	67.50	137	190	1,825
1849O	140,000	29.00	40.00	95.00	225	540	1,100	2,350	—
1850	955,000	20.50	24.50	26.50	34.00	62.50	127	190	1,300
1850O	690,000	21.50	24.50	35.00	65.00	125	280	685	4,450
1851	781,000	17.50	21.50	23.50	28.00	59.90	122	175	1,350
1851O	860,000	20.50	24.50	26.50	41.50	110	220	500	4,350
1852	1,000,500	17.50	21.50	23.50	28.00	59.50	122	175	1,150
1852O	260,000	26.50	44.50	79.00	135	275	475	885	11,500
1853	135,000	40.00	60.00	90.00	175	300	525	850	2,850
1853O	160,000	285	325	450	850	1,800	3,500	6,450	27,500

HALF DIME

KM# 76 • 1.24 g., 0.900 Silver 0.0359 oz. ASW **Rev. Legend:** UNITED STATES OF AMERICA **Designer:** Christian Gobrecht

Date	Mintage	G4	VG8	F12	VF20	XF40	AU50	MS60	MS65	Prf65
1853	13,210,020	17.75	21.50	22.50	28.00	58.00	135	195	1,410	—
1853O	2,200,000	20.75	29.50	30.50	36.00	66.00	143	310	3,260	—
1854	5,740,000	17.75	21.50	24.50	30.00	60.00	137	205	1,410	15,000
1854O	1,560,000	18.75	22.50	32.50	38.00	88.00	165	235	3,560	—
1855	1,750,000	18.75	22.50	24.50	30.00	60.00	137	200	1,810	15,000
1855O	600,000	22.75	27.50	38.50	54.00	140	220	540	4,260	—

KM# A62.2 • 1.24 g., 0.900 Silver 0.0359 oz. ASW **Rev. Legend:** UNITED STATES OF AMERICA **Designer:** Christian Gobrecht **Note:** On the 1858/ inverted date variety, the date was engraved into the die upside down and then re-engraved right side up. Another 1858 variety has the date doubled.

Date	Mintage	G4	VG8	F12	VF20	XF40	AU50	MS60	MS65	Prf65
1856	4,880,000	17.50	21.00	23.00	27.00	52.50	115	175	1,200	15,000
1856O	1,100,000	18.50	22.00	26.00	28.00	97.50	260	470	2,150	—
1857	7,280,000	17.50	21.00	23.00	27.00	52.50	115	175	1,050	5,600
1857O	1,380,000	18.50	22.00	24.00	28.00	62.50	185	320	1,750	—
1858	3,500,000	17.50	21.00	23.00	27.00	52.50	115	175	1,150	5,500
1858 inverted date	Inc. above	30.00	43.50	62.50	100	225	300	675	3,950	—
1858 double date	Inc. above	45.00	60.00	90.00	175	285	425	800		—
1858O	1,660,000	18.50	22.00	24.00	28.00	71.50	137	245	1,650	—
1859	340,000	19.50	23.00	25.00	29.00	54.50	117	225	1,350	4,000
1859O	560,000	20.50	24.00	26.00	42.00	128	200	285	1,850	—

Seated Liberty, date below.
Value within wreath.

KM# 91 • 1.24 g., 0.900 Silver 0.0359 oz. ASW **Obv. Legend:** UNITED STATES OF AMERICA **Designer:** Christian Gobrecht

Date	Mintage	G4	VG8	F12	VF20	XF40	AU50	MS60	MS65	Prf65
1860	799,000	17.00	20.00	23.00	26.00	47.00	77.00	155	825	1,550
1860O	1,060,000	18.00	20.00	23.00	29.00	49.00	79.00	180	1,175	—
1861	3,361,000	17.00	20.00	22.00	25.00	45.00	75.00	155	825	1,600
1861/0	Inc. above	26.00	32.50	59.00	125	260	435	560	3,650	—
1862	1,492,550	21.00	25.00	34.00	44.00	64.00	94.00	164	825	1,550
1863	18,460	200	250	300	400	485	550	800	1,375	1,550
1863S	100,000	35.00	45.00	70.00	95.00	165	300	750	3,450	—
1864	48,470	375	475	575	750	950	1,100	1,375	2,350	1,600
1864S	90,000	60.00	75.00	115	175	250	450	785	3,750	—
1865	13,500	375	475	575	750	950	1,100	1,350	1,950	1,550
1865S	120,000	30.00	40.00	60.00	85.00	145	375	975	5,450	—
1866	10,725	350	475	550	700	875	1,000	1,225	2,375	1,550
1866S	120,000	30.00	40.00	60.00	85.00	145	285	485	5,000	—
1867	8,625	550	650	775	900	1,100	1,200	1,375	2,350	1,550
1867S	120,000	30.00	40.00	60.00	85.00	150	325	850	3,850	—
1868	89,200	60.00	90.00	190	225	300	425	625	2,400	1,550
1868S	280,000	21.00	25.00	35.00	42.00	59.00	125	335	3,250	—
1869	208,600	21.00	25.00	35.00	42.00	59.00	135	210	1,175	1,560
1869S	230,000	19.00	24.00	30.00	35.00	55.00	125	320	4,150	—
1870	536,600	19.00	24.00	30.00	35.00	55.00	125	195	775	1,550
1870S unique	—	—	—	—	—	—	—	—	—	—
Note: 1870S, Superior Galleries, July 1986, brilliant uncirculated, $253,000.										
1871	1,873,960	17.00	20.00	22.00	25.00	45.00	75.00	145	775	1,550
1871S	161,000	26.00	30.00	45.00	60.00	90.00	175	320	2,225	—
1872	2,947,950	17.00	20.00	22.00	25.00	45.00	75.00	145	775	1,550
1872S mint mark in wreath	837,000	17.00	20.00	22.00	25.00	45.00	75.00	145	775	—
1872S mint mark below wreath	Inc. above	18.00	21.00	24.00	27.00	47.00	80.00	145	775	—
1873	712,600	17.00	20.00	22.00	25.00	45.00	75.00	145	1,175	1,550
1873S	324,000	21.00	25.00	30.00	42.00	62.00	90.00	160	775	—

HALF DIME

5 CENTS

Shield Nickel
Draped garland above shield, date below. Value within center of rays between stars.

KM# 96 • 5.00 g., Copper-Nickel, 20.5 mm. • **Obv. Legend:** IN GOD WE TRUST **Rev. Legend:** UNITED STATES OF AMERICA **Designer:** James B. Longacre

Date	Mintage	G4	VG8	F12	VF20	XF40	AU50	MS60	MS65	Prf65
1866	14,742,500	29.00	38.00	55.00	80.00	150	250	280	2,050	3,450
1867	2,019,000	37.00	45.50	63.50	90.00	180	280	330	3,850	75,000

Draped garland above shield, date below. Value within circle of stars.

KM# 97 • 5.00 g., Copper-Nickel **Obv. Legend:** IN GOD WE TRUST **Rev. Legend:** UNITED STATES OF AMERICA

Date	Mintage	G4	VG8	F12	VF20	XF40	AU50	MS60	MS65	Prf65
1867	28,890,500	18.50	28.00	30.00	37.50	64.00	115	150	825	2,500
1868 Rev'67	28,817,000	18.50	28.00	30.00	37.50	64.00	115	150	675	1,325
1868 Rev'68	Inc. above	22.00	34.00	36.00	45.00	77.00	144	188	—	—
Note: Star points to center of A in STATES.										
1869	16,395,000	18.50	28.00	30.00	37.50	64.00	115	150	700	900
1870	4,806,000	27.00	35.00	54.00	69.00	100	150	210	1,600	1,060
1871	561,000	72.00	95.00	140	210	310	365	415	2,100	910
1872	6,036,000	39.00	48.00	85.00	96.00	135	180	235	1,350	715
1873 Open 3	4,550,000	29.00	39.00	54.00	68.00	80.00	135	230	1,950	—
1873 Closed 3	Inc. above	36.00	48.00	70.00	100	150	220	350	3,250	715
1874	3,538,000	31.00	45.00	74.00	94.00	120	165	245	1,400	800
1875	2,097,000	46.00	62.00	90.00	125	170	230	290	1,500	1,500
1876	2,530,000	40.00	54.00	84.00	125	165	200	255	1,350	825
1877 proof	Est. 900	—	—	—	2,100	2,150	2,300	—	—	4,850
1878 proof	2,350	—	—	—	1,100	1,250	1,450	—	—	2,100
1879	29,100	390	485	625	660	720	800	970	1,900	750
1879/8	Inc. above	—	—	—	—	—	—	—	—	825
1880	19,995	500	575	700	850	1,275	1,700	3,250	47,500	730
1881	72,375	260	340	430	500	600	675	735	1,800	700
1882	11,476,600	18.50	28.00	28.00	30.00	37.50	64.00	115	150	635	645
Note: Many exist with excess metal at numeral 2 & 3 these should not be confused with the following overdate.										
1883	1,456,919	18.50	28.00	32.00	39.50	67.00	135	160	750	645
Note: Many exist with excess metal at numeral 2 & 3 these should not be confused with the following overdate.										
1883/2	Inc. above	220	300	535	850	1,250	1,750	2,000	3,750	—

Liberty Nickel
Liberty head left, within circle of stars, date below. Roman numeral value within wreath, without CENTS below.

KM# 111 • 5.00 g., Copper-Nickel, 21.2 mm. • **Rev. Legend:** UNITED STATES OF AMERICA **Designer:** Charles E. Barber

Date	Mintage	G4	VG8	F12	VF20	XF40	AU50	MS60	MS65	Prf65
1883	5,479,519	7.00	7.75	8.50	8.75	9.25	12.00	25.50	215	1,075

Liberty head left, within circle of stars, date below. Roman numeral value within wreath, CENTS below.

KM# 112 • 5.00 g., Copper-Nickel, 21.2 mm. • **Rev. Legend:** UNITED STATES OF AMERICA

Date	Mintage	G4	VG8	F12	VF20	XF40	AU50	MS60	MS65	Prf65
1883	16,032,983	19.00	29.50	39.50	55.00	85.00	120	160	625	610
1884	11,273,942	22.50	33.50	39.50	59.00	92.00	135	190	1,675	610
1885	1,476,490	585	635	875	1,050	1,350	1,650	1,950	8,650	3,150
1886	3,330,290	285	335	400	500	685	850	1,950	7,250	1,950
1887	15,263,652	16.00	25.00	31.00	44.00	78.00	115	150	1,025	585
1888	10,720,483	28.00	44.00	68.00	130	185	250	295	1,500	585

Date	Mintage	G4	VG8	F12	VF20	XF40	AU50	MS60	MS65	Prf65
1889	15,881,361	14.50	19.50	30.00	52.50	77.00	125	155	850	585
1890	16,259,272	10.50	20.50	26.00	39.50	68.50	115	165	1,365	585
1891	16,834,350	5.75	11.00	22.00	37.50	60.00	120	160	1,050	585
1892	11,699,642	6.50	11.00	22.50	39.00	65.00	120	165	1,300	585
1893	13,370,195	5.50	11.00	24.00	37.50	60.00	120	155	1,050	585
1894	5,413,132	16.50	31.00	98.00	165	230	295	350	1,500	585
1895	9,979,884	5.75	7.50	24.00	45.00	66.00	120	145	2,200	585
1896	8,842,920	9.00	21.00	41.50	68.50	98.00	150	205	1,950	585
1897	20,428,735	3.25	4.50	12.50	27.50	46.00	69.50	95.00	925	585
1898	12,532,087	2.15	4.25	11.00	23.50	40.00	68.50	130	1,025	585
1899	26,029,031	1.80	3.00	8.50	19.50	34.00	62.50	89.00	560	585
1900	27,255,995	1.60	2.50	8.50	19.00	34.00	69.50	84.00	650	585
1901	26,480,213	1.60	2.50	7.00	14.50	34.00	65.00	100	550	585
1902	31,480,579	1.60	2.50	4.00	15.00	32.00	65.00	102	550	585
1903	28,006,725	1.80	2.50	4.75	14.50	32.00	60.00	77.00	500	585
1904	21,404,984	1.60	2.40	4.75	11.50	30.00	65.00	96.00	500	585
1905	29,827,276	1.60	2.40	4.00	12.00	30.00	65.00	96.00	550	585
1906	38,613,725	1.80	2.40	4.00	11.50	30.00	65.00	96.00	650	585
1907	39,214,800	1.50	2.20	4.00	12.00	30.00	65.00	96.00	1,000	585
1908	22,686,177	1.80	2.20	4.00	12.00	30.00	68.00	104	1,100	585
1909	11,590,526	2.50	2.80	4.35	13.00	33.00	80.00	112	1,075	585
1910	30,169,353	1.50	1.85	4.00	10.00	30.00	52.00	62.00	550	585
1911	39,559,372	1.50	1.85	4.00	10.00	30.00	52.00	62.00	500	585
1912	26,236,714	1.50	1.85	4.00	10.00	30.00	52.00	62.00	570	585
1912D	8,474,000	2.75	3.60	11.50	38.00	70.00	170	280	2,200	—
1912S	238,000	165	190	220	480	810	1,300	1,475	5,900	—
1913 5 known	—	—	—	—	—	—	—	—	—	—

Note: 1913, Heritage Sale, January 2010, Proof-64 (Olsen), $3,737,500. Private treaty, 2007, (Eliasburg) Proof-66 $5 million.

Buffalo Nickel

American Bison standing on a mound.

KM# 133 • 5.00 g., Copper-Nickel, 21.2 mm. •
Designer: James Earle Fraser

Date	Mintage	G4	VG8	F12	VF20	XF40	AU50	MS60	MS65	Prf65
1913	30,993,520	12.00	15.50	17.00	18.50	20.00	24.50	32.50	150	3,150
1913D	5,337,000	16.00	19.50	21.00	28.00	35.00	55.00	60.00	300	—
1913S	2,105,000	43.00	46.00	50.00	60.00	70.00	95.00	125	660	—

American Bison standing on a line.

KM# 134 • 5.00 g., Copper-Nickel, 21.2 mm. • **Designer:** James Earle Fraser **Note:** In 1913 the reverse design was modified so the ground under the buffalo was represented as a line rather than a mound. On the 1 937D 3-legged variety, the buffalo's right front leg is missing, the result of a damaged die.

1918/17D	1937D 3-legged

Date	Mintage	G4	VG8	F12	VF20	XF40	AU50	MS60	MS65	Prf65
1913	29,858,700	12.00	13.00	13.00	14.00	19.00	25.00	32.50	325	2,500
1913D	4,156,000	125	155	156	160	210	235	285	1,150	—
1913S	1,209,000	340	375	385	415	550	650	875	3,850	—
1914	20,665,738	20.00	22.00	23.00	25.00	27.50	35.00	47.00	420	2,250
1914/3	Inc. above	150	300	425	525	700	1,050	2,850	30,000	—
1914D	3,912,000	90.00	110	145	180	295	375	456	1,450	—
1914/3D	Inc. above	115	225	335	450	625	900	3,500	—	—
1914S	3,470,000	26.00	35.00	42.00	56.00	90.00	145	165	2,000	—
1914/3S	Inc. above	250	500	750	1,000	1,450	2,260	4,300	—	—
1915	20,987,270	7.00	8.00	8.50	11.00	20.00	37.50	50.00	325	2,100
1915D	7,569,500	21.50	31.00	38.50	60.00	115	150	225	1,600	—
1915S	1,505,000	49.00	68.00	105	155	315	490	625	3,000	—
1916	63,498,066	7.50	6.50	7.00	8.00	13.50	22.00	42.00	300	3,250
1916 2 Feathers	Inc. above	35.00	—	45.00	—	—	—	—	150	—
1916/16	Inc. above	3,950	5,200	8,750	11,000	16,500	34,500	49,500	375,000	—
1916D	13,333,000	16.50	26.50	27.50	35.00	82.50	110	165	1,850	—
1916S	11,860,000	11.00	14.00	22.50	33.00	75.00	125	195	1,900	—
1917	51,424,029	7.50	8.00	8.75	9.00	14.00	32.50	56.00	510	—
1917 2 Feathers	Inc. above	40.00	—	50.00	—	—	—	—	165	—
1917D	9,910,800	26.00	31.00	52.50	75.00	135	255	345	2,650	—

5 CENTS

Date	Mintage	G4	VG8	F12	VF20	XF40	AU50	MS60	MS65	Prf65
1917S	4,193,000	23.00	42.00	80.00	105	180	285	395	4,000	—
1917S 2 Feathers	Inc. above	50.00	70.00	95.00	—	—	—	—	315	—
1918	32,086,314	7.00	7.25	8.00	15.00	31.00	48.50	105	1,400	—
1918/17D	8,362,314	1,000	1,550	2,750	4,950	8,750	11,000	36,500	350,000	—
1918D	Inc. above	22.50	39.00	63.00	120	220	330	420	3,750	—
1918 2 Feathers	Inc. above	50.00	—	95.00	—	—	—	—	315	—
1918S	4,882,000	14.00	27.50	52.50	95.00	175	300	485	20,000	—
1919	60,868,000	2.60	3.50	3.90	7.00	13.50	32.00	57.00	465	—
1919D	8,006,000	15.50	31.00	72.00	125	235	335	560	6,500	—
1919S	7,521,000	8.00	21.00	48.00	100	225	360	535	16,500	—
1920	63,093,000	1.50	2.75	3.25	8.00	14.50	30.00	57.00	675	—
1920D	9,418,000	8.50	19.00	35.00	110	260	340	550	5,250	—
1920S	9,689,000	4.50	12.75	30.00	95.00	204	285	525	21,000	—
1921	10,663,000	4.00	7.75	8.50	25.00	49.00	70.00	115	775	—
1921S	1,557,000	64.00	98.00	165	350	785	1,150	1,575	7,350	—
1923	35,715,000	1.70	3.25	4.25	7.00	13.50	36.00	58.00	575	—
1923S	6,142,000	8.00	10.00	24.00	100	265	315	625	9,500	—
1924	21,620,000	1.50	2.40	4.50	9.00	18.50	40.00	70.00	825	—
1924D	5,258,000	8.00	10.50	27.50	80.00	210	315	375	4,000	—
1924S	1,437,000	16.50	32.00	85.00	325	1,050	1,700	2,300	11,500	—
1925	35,565,100	3.00	4.00	4.25	8.50	16.50	32.00	42.00	350	—
1925D	4,450,000	10.00	22.00	35.00	70.00	160	265	425	4,650	—
1925S	6,256,000	4.00	8.50	16.50	72.00	170	250	435	25,500	—
1926	44,693,000	1.50	2.00	2.80	5.40	11.50	22.00	30.00	210	—
1926D	5,638,000	10.00	17.50	28.50	95.00	170	285	335	4,650	—
1926S	970,000	20.00	42.00	95.00	235	725	2,450	4,750	115,000	—
1927	37,981,000	1.40	1.75	2.50	4.50	12.50	22.00	35.00	275	—
1927D	5,730,000	2.50	6.00	7.00	30.00	75.00	115	155	7,250	—
1927S	3,430,000	1.50	2.50	4.00	32.00	80.00	160	490	17,000	—
1928	23,411,000	1.40	1.75	2.50	4.50	12.50	25.00	32.50	285	—
1928D	6,436,000	1.90	2.50	3.50	14.50	40.00	46.50	53.00	645	—
1928S	6,936,000	1.75	2.35	2.50	10.50	27.50	100	225	3,650	—
1929	36,446,000	1.40	1.75	2.25	4.50	13.00	21.00	35.00	315	—
1929D	8,370,000	1.50	1.85	2.25	6.75	32.50	42.50	60.00	1,150	—
1929S	7,754,000	1.50	1.85	2.00	2.50	12.50	25.00	49.50	435	—
1930	22,849,000	1.40	1.75	2.25	4.50	11.00	21.00	32.50	235	—
1930S	5,435,000	1.50	2.00	2.75	4.50	14.50	37.50	65.00	400	—
1931S	1,200,000	15.00	16.00	17.00	19.00	32.00	46.00	59.00	300	—
1934	20,213,003	1.00	1.30	2.25	4.50	11.00	19.00	47.50	320	—
1934D	7,480,000	2.00	3.00	4.25	9.60	22.00	50.00	76.00	550	—
1935	58,264,000	0.90	1.20	1.50	1.90	3.50	7.00	25.50	125	—
1935 Double Die Rev.	Inc. above	50.00	75.00	125	250	675	1,800	4,000	75,000	—
1935D	12,092,000	1.60	2.50	3.00	9.00	22.00	48.00	72.00	415	—
1935S	10,300,000	1.35	1.75	2.00	2.50	3.75	17.50	48.50	225	—
1936	119,001,420	0.90	1.20	1.50	1.90	3.00	6.50	25.00	90.00	1,650
1936 Brilliant	Inc. above	—	—	—	—	—	—	—	—	2,450
1936D	24,814,000	1.35	1.75	2.00	2.50	5.00	11.50	33.50	115	—
1936D 3-1/2 leg	Inc. above	750	1,250	2,000	3,500	6,000	10,500	17,500	—	—
1936D/S	Inc. above	—	—	10.00	16.00	25.00	—	—	—	—
1936S	14,930,000	1.35	1.75	2.00	2.50	4.00	11.50	33.50	110	—
1937	79,485,769	0.90	1.20	1.50	1.90	3.00	6.50	25.00	52.50	2,100
1937D	17,826,000	1.35	1.75	2.00	2.50	4.00	9.00	29.00	60.00	—
1937D 3-legged	Inc. above	535	585	615	725	965	1,225	2,375	37,000	—
1937S	5,635,000	1.35	1.75	2.00	2.50	4.00	9.50	27.50	58.00	—
1938D	7,020,000	3.50	3.75	3.90	4.00	4.50	12.00	25.00	52.50	—
1938D/D	Inc. above	3.75	4.50	6.00	8.00	10.00	18.50	35.00	100	—
1938D/S	Inc. above	4.50	6.75	9.00	12.50	18.00	30.00	50.00	150	—

Jefferson Nickel
Monticello, mintmark to right side.

KM# 192 • 5.00 g., Copper-Nickel, 21.2 mm. •
Designer: Felix Schlag **Note:** Some 1939 strikes
have doubling of the word MONTICELLO on the
reverse.

Date	Mintage	VG8	F12	VF20	XF40	MS60	MS65	65FS	Prf65
1938	19,515,365	0.50	0.75	1.00	2.25	7.50	18.00	125	—
1938D	5,376,000	1.00	1.25	1.50	2.00	4.00	15.00	95.00	—
1938S	4,105,000	1.75	2.00	2.50	3.00	5.25	12.00	165	—
1939 T I, wavy steps, Rev. of 1939	120,627,535	—	—	—	—	3.00	30.00	300	70.00
1939 T II, even steps, Rev. of 1940	Inc. above	—	0.20	0.25	0.30	4.00	45.00	50.00	130
1939 doubled MONTICELLO T II	Inc. above	40.00	60.00	90.00	165	300	1,250	2,000	—
1939D T IT I, wavy steps, Rev. of 1939	3,514,000	—	—	10.00	17.50	75.00	160	275	—
1939D T III II, even steps, Rev. of 1940	Inc. above	4.00	5.00	8.00	14.00	55.00	105	400	—
1939S T IT I, wavy steps, Rev. of 1939	6,630,000	0.45	0.60	1.50	4.00	17.00	45.00	250	—

5 CENTS

Date	Mintage	VG8	F12	VF20	XF40	MS60	MS65	65FS	Prf65
1939S T IIT II, even steps, Rev. of 1940	Inc. above	—	—	—	5.00	24.00	250	275	—
1940	176,499,158	—	—	—	0.25	1.00	12.00	60.00	125
1940D	43,540,000	—	0.20	0.30	0.40	1.50	2.75	25.00	—
1940S	39,690,000	0.25	0.40	0.50	1.25	4.50	20.00	55.00	—
1941	203,283,720	—	—	—	0.20	0.75	20.00	55.00	—
1941D	53,432,000	—	0.20	0.30	0.50	2.25	7.50	25.00	—
1941S	43,445,000	0.25	0.40	0.50	1.35	5.00	14.00	60.00	—
1942	49,818,600	—	—	—	0.40	5.00	22.00	75.00	—
1942D	13,938,000	1.00	1.75	3.00	5.00	38.00	65.00	85.00	—
1942D D over horizontal D	Inc. above	35.00	60.00	100	165	750	10,000	25,000	—

Note: Fully Struck Full Step nickels command higher prices. Bright, Fully Struck coins command even higher prices. 1938 thru 1989 - 5 Full Steps. 1990 to date - 6 Full Steps. Without bag marks or nicks on steps.

Monticello, mint mark above.

KM# 192a • 0.350 Copper-Silver-Manganese, 21.2 mm. • **Designer:** Felix Schlag **Note:** War-time composition nickels have the mint mark above MONTICELLO on the reverse.

1943/2P

Date	Mintage	VG8	F12	VF20	XF40	MS60	MS65	65FS	Prf65
1942P	57,900,600	1.87	1.93	2.13	2.00	9.00	20.00	75.00	150
1942S	32,900,000	1.87	1.93	2.13	2.45	8.00	19.00	170	—
1943P	271,165,000	1.87	1.93	2.13	2.00	5.00	20.00	40.00	—
1943PDDO	Inc. above	—	—	32.00	54.00	125	575	1,100	—
1943/2P	Inc. above	35.00	50.00	75.00	110	300	775	1,000	—
1943D	15,294,000	2.12	2.18	2.38	2.05	4.00	18.00	40.00	—
1943S	104,060,000	1.87	1.93	2.13	2.15	6.75	18.50	48.00	—
1944P	119,150,000	1.87	1.93	2.13	2.15	10.00	28.00	75.00	—
1944D	32,309,000	1.92	1.98	2.18	2.25	10.00	22.50	65.00	—
1944S	21,640,000	1.92	1.98	2.18	2.15	8.50	20.00	185	—
1945P	119,408,100	1.87	1.93	2.13	2.15	6.00	28.00	120	—
1945D	37,158,000	1.97	2.03	2.28	2.30	5.50	20.00	40.00	—
1945S	58,939,000	1.87	1.93	2.13	2.15	5.00	18.00	250	—

Note: Fully Struck Full Step nickels command higher prices. Bright, Fully Struck coins command even higher prices. 1938 thru 1989 - 5 Full Steps. 1990 to date - 6 Full Steps. Without bag marks or nicks on steps.

Pre-war design resumed.

KM# A192 • 5.00 g., Copper-Nickel, 21.2 mm. • **Edge:** Plain **Designer:** Felix Schlag

Date	Mintage	XF40	MS65	Prf65
1946	161,116,000	0.25	35.00	—
1946D	45,292,200	0.35	22.00	—
1946D/D	Inc. above	—	1,750	—
1946S	13,560,000	0.40	15.00	—
1947	95,000,000	0.25	18.00	—
1947D	37,822,000	0.30	18.00	—
1947S	24,720,000	0.25	20.00	—
1948	89,348,000	0.25	25.00	—
1948D	44,734,000	0.35	19.00	—
1948S	11,300,000	0.50	15.00	—
1949	60,652,000	0.30	40.00	—
1949D	36,498,000	0.40	18.00	—
1949D/S	Inc. above	65.00	550	—
1949S	9,716,000	0.90	25.00	—
1950	9,847,386	0.75	25.00	75.00
1950D	2,630,030	10.00	25.00	—
1951	28,609,500	0.50	35.00	70.00
1951D	20,460,000	0.50	22.00	—
1951S	7,776,000	1.10	28.00	—
1952	64,069,980	0.25	35.00	42.00

Date	Mintage	XF40	MS65	Prf65
1952D	30,638,000	0.45	30.00	—
1952S	20,572,000	0.25	30.00	—
1953	46,772,800	0.25	26.00	45.00
1953D	59,878,600	0.25	25.00	—
1953S	19,210,900	0.25	35.00	—
1954	47,917,350	—	37.50	20.00
1954D	117,136,560	—	40.00	—
1954S	29,384,000	0.20	35.00	—
1954S/D	Inc. above	20.00	350	—
1955	8,266,200	0.45	25.00	13.50
1955D	74,464,100	—	25.00	—
1955D/S	Inc. above	25.00	300	—
1956	35,885,384	—	16.00	3.00
1956D	67,222,940	—	26.00	—
1957	39,655,952	—	35.00	2.50
1957D	136,828,900	—	22.00	—
1958	17,963,652	0.20	36.00	8.00
1958D	168,249,120	—	13.00	—

Note: Fully Struck Full Step nickels command higher prices. Bright, Fully Struck coins command even higher prices. 1938 thru 1989 - 5 Full Steps. 1990 to date - 6 Full Steps. Without bag marks or nicks on steps.

Date	Mintage	XF40	MS65	Prf65
1959	28,397,291	—	22.00	1.40
1959D	160,738,240	—	22.00	—
1960	57,107,602	—	30.00	1.25
1960D	192,582,180	—	25.00	—
1961	76,668,244	—	40.00	1.00
1961D	229,342,760	—	35.00	—
1962	100,602,019	—	24.00	1.00
1962D	280,195,720	—	110	—
1963	178,851,645	—	4.00	1.00
1963D	276,829,460	—	100	—
1964	1,028,622,762	—	5.00	1.00
1964D	1,787,297,160	—	12.00	—

5 CENTS

5 CENTS

Date	Mintage	XF40	MS65	Prf65
1965	136,131,380	—	12.00	—
1965SMS	2,360,000	—	12.00	—
1966	156,208,283	—	10.00	—
1966SMS	2,261,583	—	15.00	—
1967	107,325,800	—	8.00	—
1967SMS	1,863,344	—	12.00	—
1968 none minted	—	—	—	—
1968D	91,227,880	—	6.00	—
1968S	103,437,510	—	5.00	0.75
1969 none minted	—	—	—	—
1969D	202,807,500	—	5.00	—
1969S	123,099,631	—	7.50	0.75
1970 none minted	—	—	—	—
1970D	515,485,380	—	12.00	—
1970S	241,464,814	—	30.00	0.75
1971	106,884,000	—	9.00	—
1971D	316,144,800	—	4.50	—
1971S	3,220,733	—	—	1.00
1972	202,036,000	—	4.00	—
1972D	351,694,600	—	3.00	—
1972S	3,260,996	—	—	1.00
1973	384,396,000	—	5.00	—
1973D	261,405,000	—	4.00	—
1973S	2,760,339	—	—	0.75
1974	601,752,000	—	12.00	—
1974D	277,373,000	—	5.00	—
1974S	2,612,568	—	—	0.75
1975	181,772,000	—	6.00	—
1975D	401,875,300	—	6.00	—
1975S	2,845,450	—	—	0.75
1976	367,124,000	—	8.00	—
1976D	563,964,147	—	6.00	—
1976S	4,149,730	—	—	0.75
1977	585,376,000	—	8.50	—
1977D	297,313,460	—	6.50	—
1977S	3,251,152	—	—	0.75
1978	391,308,000	—	7.00	—
1978D	313,092,780	—	5.00	—
1978S	3,127,781	—	—	0.75
1979	463,188,000	—	8.50	—
1979D	325,867,672	—	5.50	—
1979S type I, proof	3,677,175	—	—	0.75
1979S type II, proof	—	—	—	2.00
1980P	593,004,000	—	6.50	—
1980D	502,323,448	—	5.50	—
1980S	3,554,806	—	—	0.75
1981P	657,504,000	—	5.00	—
1981D	364,801,843	—	6.00	—
1981S type I, proof	4,063,083	—	—	2.00
1981S type II, proof	—	—	—	2.50
1982P	292,355,000	—	15.00	—
1982D	373,726,544	—	14.00	—
1982S	3,857,479	—	—	1.50
1983P	561,615,000	—	9.00	—
1983D	536,726,276	—	6.00	—
1983S	3,279,126	—	—	1.50
1984P	746,769,000	—	5.00	—
1984D	517,675,146	—	4.75	—
1984S	3,065,110	—	—	1.50
1985P	647,114,962	—	4.75	—
1985D	459,747,446	—	4.75	—
1985S	3,362,821	—	—	1.50
1986P	536,883,483	—	5.00	—
1986D	361,819,140	—	4.75	—
1986S	3,010,497	—	—	3.00
1987P	371,499,481	—	5.00	—
1987D	410,590,604	—	4.50	—
1987S	4,227,728	—	—	1.25
1988P	771,360,000	—	4.50	—
1988D	663,771,652	—	5.00	—
1988S	3,262,948	—	—	1.75
1989P	898,812,000	—	4.50	—
1989D	570,842,474	—	6.00	—
1989S	3,220,194	—	—	1.50
1990P	661,636,000	—	4.50	—
1990D	663,938,503	—	5.50	—
1990S	3,299,559	—	—	1.50
1991P	614,104,000	—	4.50	—
1991D	436,496,678	—	4.50	—
1991S	2,867,787	—	—	1.50
1992P	399,552,000	—	5.00	—
1992D	450,565,113	—	4.00	—
1992S	4,176,560	—	—	1.00
1993P	412,076,000	—	4.00	—
1993D	406,084,135	—	4.00	—
1993S	3,394,792	—	—	1.00
1994P	722,160,000	—	4.00	—
1994P Special Uncirculated matte finish	167,703	—	—	—
1994D	715,762,110	—	4.00	—
1994S	3,269,923	—	—	1.00
1995P	774,156,000	—	4.00	—
1995D	888,112,000	—	4.50	—
1995S	2,707,481	—	—	1.50
1996P	829,332,000	—	4.00	—
1996D	817,736,000	—	4.00	—
1996S	2,915,212	—	—	1.50
1997P	470,972,000	—	4.75	—
1997P Special Uncirculated matte finish	25,000	—	—	—
1997D	466,640,000	—	4.50	—
1997S	1,975,000	—	—	1.50
1998P	688,272,000	—	3.75	—
1998D	635,360,000	—	3.75	—
1998S	2,957,286	—	—	1.25
1999P	1,212,000,000	—	3.75	—
1999D	1,066,720,000	—	3.75	—
1999S	3,362,462	—	—	1.25
2000P	846,240,000	—	3.75	—
2000D	1,509,520,000	—	3.75	—
2000S	4,063,361	—	—	1.00
2001P	675,704,000	—	3.75	—
2001D	627,680,000	—	3.75	—
2001S	3,099,096	—	—	1.00
2002P	539,280,000	—	3.75	—
2002D	691,200,000	—	3.75	—
2002S	3,157,739	—	—	1.00
2003P	441,840,000	—	3.75	—
2003D	383,040,000	—	3.75	—
2003S	3,116,590	—	—	1.00

Jefferson - Westward Expansion - Lewis & Clark Bicentennial

Jefferson era peace medal design: two clasped hands, pipe and hatchet.

KM# 360 • 5.00 g., Copper-Nickel, 21.2 mm.
• **Obv. Designer:** Felix Schlag **Rev. Designer:** Norman E. Nemeth

Date	Mintage	MS65	Prf65
2004P	361,440,000	1.50	—
2004D	372,000,000	1.50	—
2004S	2,992,069	—	5.00

Lewis and Clark's Keelboat.

KM# 361 • 5.00 g., Copper-Nickel, 21.2 mm. • **Obv. Designer:** Felix Schlag **Rev. Designer:** Al Maletsky

Date	Mintage	MS65	Prf65
2004P	366,720,000	1.50	—
2004D	344,880,000	1.50	—
2004S	2,965,422	—	5.00

Thomas Jefferson large profile right. American Bison right.

KM# 368 • 5.00 g., Copper-Nickel, 21.2 mm. • **Obv. Designer:** Joe Fitzgerald and Don Everhart II **Rev. Designer:** Jamie Franki and Norman E. Nemeth

Date	Mintage	MS65	Prf65
2005P	448,320,000	1.50	—
2005P Satin Finish	1,160,000	4.00	—
2005D	487,680,000	1.50	—
2005D Satin Finish	1,160,000	4.00	—
2005S	3,344,679	—	6.50

Thomas Jefferson large profile right. Pacific coastline.

KM# 369 • 5.00 g., Copper-Nickel, 21.2 mm. • **Subject:** Ocean in View!, oh the joy! **Obv. Designer:** Joe Fitzgerald and Don Everhart **Rev. Designer:** Joe Fitzgerald and Donna Weaver

Date	Mintage	MS65	Prf65
2005P	394,080,000	1.25	—
2005P Satin Finish	1,160,000	4.00	—
2005D	411,120,000	1.25	—
2005D Satin Finish	1,160,000	4.00	—
2005S	3,344,679	—	5.50

Jefferson large facing portrait - Enhanced Monticello Reverse

Jefferson head facing. Monticello, enhanced design.

KM# 381 • 5.00 g., Copper-Nickel, 21.2 mm. • **Subject:** Jefferson facing head **Obv. Designer:** Jamie N. Franki and Donna Weaver **Rev. Designer:** Felix Schlag and John Mercanti

Date	Mintage	MS65	Prf65
2006P	693,120,000	2.50	—
2006P Satin finish	847,361	4.00	—
2006D	809,280,000	2.50	—
2006D Satin finish	847,361	4.00	—
2006S	3,054,436	—	5.00
2007P	571,680,000	2.50	—
2007P Satin finish	895,628	4.00	—
2007D	626,160,000	2.50	—
2007D Satin finish	895,628	4.00	—
2007S	2,577,166	—	4.00
2008P	279,840,000	2.50	—
2008P Satin finish	745,464	4.00	—
2008D	345,600,000	2.50	—
2008D Satin finish	745,464	4.00	—
2008S	2,169,561	—	4.00
2009P	39,840,000	3.50	—
2009P Satin finish	784,614	4.00	—
2009D	46,800,000	1.75	—
2009D Satin finish	784,614	4.00	—
2009S	2,179,867	—	3.00
2010P	260,640,000	1.50	—
2010P Satin finish	—	4.00	—
2010D	229,920,000	1.50	—
2010D Satin finish	—	4.00	—
2010S	1,689,216	—	3.00
2011P	450,000,000	1.50	—
2011D	540,240,000	1.50	—
2011S	1,673,010	—	4.00
2012P	464,640,000	1.50	—
2012D	558,960,000	1.50	—
2012S	1,237,415	—	4.00
2013P	607,440,000	1.50	—
2013D	615,600,000	1.50	—
2013S	1,237,926	—	3.00
2014P	—	1.50	—
2014D	—	1.50	—
2014S	—	—	3.00
2015P	—	2.50	—
2015D	—	2.50	—
2015S	—	—	3.00

DIME

Draped Bust Dime

Draped bust right. Small eagle.

KM# 24 • 2.70 g., 0.892 Silver 0.0774 oz. ASW, 19 mm. • **Designer:** Robert Scot

Date	Mintage	G4	VG8	F12	VF20	XF40	MS60
1796	22,135	2,850	3,600	5,500	7,000	12,350	24,500
1797 13 stars	25,261	3,100	3,950	6,050	8,000	13,150	70,000
1797 16 stars	Inc. above	3,000	3,850	5,800	7,150	13,650	36,500

DIME

Draped bust right. Heraldic eagle.

KM# 31 • 2.70 g., 0.892 Silver 0.0774 oz. ASW,
19 mm. • **Obv. Legend:** LIBERTY **Rev. Legend:**
UNITED STATES OF AMERICA **Designer:** Robert
Scot **Note:** The 1805 strikes have either 4 or 5
berries on the olive branch held by the eagle.

Date	Mintage	G4	VG8	F12	VF20	XF40	MS60
1798 large 8	27,550	725	1,250	1,550	2,100	3,625	8,850
1798 small 8	Inc. above	975	1,450	2,350	3,250	6,000	53,500
1798/97 13 stars	Inc. above	2,150	3,850	5,650	8,850	13,850	59,000
1798/97 16 stars	Inc. above	775	1,125	1,800	2,650	4,600	10,500

Note: The 1798 overdates have either 13 or 16 stars under the clouds on the reverse; Varieties of the regular 1798 strikes are distinguished by the size of the 8 in the date

Date	Mintage	G4	VG8	F12	VF20	XF40	MS60
1800	21,760	700	1,075	1,400	2,700	4,350	37,500
1801	34,640	750	1,150	1,650	3,100	6,250	49,500
1802	10,975	1,750	2,650	3,500	4,750	10,000	37,500
1803	33,040	675	1,150	1,900	2,750	5,900	49,500
1804 13 stars	8,265	2,650	4,450	10,500	19,000	41,500	—
1804 14 stars	Inc. above	4,850	6,500	12,500	24,500	46,500	—
1805 5 berries	Inc. above	625	1,000	1,400	2,100	3,700	9,100
1805 4 berries	120,780	615	920	1,225	1,650	2,950	7,350
1807	165,000	575	900	1,200	1,650	2,950	6,850

Liberty Cap Dime
Draped bust left, flanked by stars, date below. Eagle with arrows in talons, banner above, value below.

KM# 42 • 2.70 g., 0.892 Silver 0.0774 oz. ASW, 18.8
mm. • **Rev. Legend:** UNITED STATES OF AMERICA
Designer: John Reich **Note:** The 1820 varieties are
distinguished by the size of the 0 in the date. The
1823 overdates have either large E's or small E's in
UNITED STATES OF AMERICA on the reverse.

Date	Mintage	G4	VG8	F12	VF20	XF40	AU50	MS60	MS65
1809	51,065	140	220	450	700	1,500	2,850	4,500	24,500
1811/9	65,180	110	175	275	650	1,350	2,000	4,000	33,500
1814 small date	421,500	60.00	80.00	145	300	650	1,250	2,000	19,500
1814 large date	Inc. above	43.00	56.00	75.00	168	450	720	1,425	17,000
1814 large date with period	Inc. above	46.00	60.00	85.00	195	500	775	2,000	—
1814 STATESOF	Inc. above	70.00	88.00	160	335	750	1,400	2,350	24,500
1820 large O	942,587	42.00	54.00	71.00	155	445	715	1,410	14,750
1820 small O	Inc. above	43.00	56.00	75.00	170	465	800	1,675	17,250
1820 STATESOF	Inc. above	43.00	56.00	75.00	168	450	720	1,425	16,500
1821 large date	1,186,512	42.00	54.00	71.00	155	445	715	1,410	14,750
1821 small date	Inc. above	43.00	56.00	75.00	170	465	800	1,675	19,000
1822	100,000	1,000	1,850	3,250	4,500	6,250	7,850	13,500	70,000
1823/22 large E's	440,000	42.00	54.00	71.00	163	465	735	1,460	16,850
1823/22 small E's	Inc. above	42.00	54.00	71.00	163	465	735	1,460	15,600
1824/22	—	50.00	80.00	145	300	650	1,250	2,000	19,500
1825	510,000	39.00	50.00	65.00	145	425	675	1,350	14,850
1827	1,215,000	39.00	50.00	65.00	145	425	675	1,350	14,500
1827/7	Inc. above	250	—	—	750	1,100	1,500	—	—
1828 large date	125,000	70.00	110	175	375	750	1,250	3,100	17,250

KM# 48 • Silver, 18.5 mm. • **Rev. Legend:** UNITED
STATES OF AMERICA **Designer:** John Reich **Note:**
The three varieties of 1829 strikes and two varieties
of 1830 strikes are distinguished by the size of
"10C." on the reverse. On the 1833 "high 3" variety,
the last 3 in the date is higher thatn the first 3. The
two varieties of the 1834 strikes are distinguished by
the size of the 4 in the date.

Date	Mintage	G4	VG8	F12	VF20	XF40	AU50	MS60	MS65
1828 small date	Inc. above	41.50	52.00	80.00	155	425	625	1,250	12,500
1829 very large 10C.	770,000	60.00	75.00	120	235	550	800	1,500	—
1829 large 10C.	Inc. above	54.00	65.00	110	200	400	600	1,150	9,250
1829 medium 10C.	Inc. above	37.50	46.00	54.00	85.00	255	400	900	8,500
1829 small 10C.	Inc. above	37.50	46.00	56.00	90.00	270	460	920	8,700
1829 curl base 2	Inc. above	7,750	10,500	16,500	27,500	38,500	44,000	—	—
1830 large 10C.	510,000	37.50	46.00	56.00	85.00	255	440	900	8,500
1830 small 10C.	Inc. above	37.50	46.00	54.00	90.00	270	465	950	10,500
1830/29	Inc. above	53.50	79.00	120	220	430	815	1,625	—

DIME

Date	Mintage	G4	VG8	F12	VF20	XF40	AU50	MS60	MS65
1831	771,350	37.50	46.00	54.00	85.00	255	440	900	8,500
1832	522,500	37.50	46.00	54.00	85.00	255	440	900	8,500
1833	485,000	37.50	46.00	54.00	85.00	260	455	915	8,500
1833 last 3 high	Inc. above	37.50	46.00	54.00	85.00	260	455	945	11,000
1834 small 4	635,000	37.50	46.00	54.00	85.00	255	440	900	8,650
1834 large 4	Inc. above	37.50	46.00	54.00	85.00	255	440	900	8,500
1835	1,410,000	37.50	46.00	54.00	85.00	255	440	900	8,500
1836	1,190,000	37.50	46.00	54.00	85.00	255	440	900	8,500
1837	1,042,000	37.50	46.00	56.00	90.00	270	460	920	8,650

Seated Liberty Dime
Seated Liberty, date below. Value within wreath.

KM# 61 • 2.67 g., 0.900 Silver 0.0773 oz. ASW, 17.9 mm. • **Rev. Legend:** UNITED STATES OF AMERICA **Designer:** Christian Gobrecht

Date	Mintage	G4	VG8	F12	VF20	XF40	AU50	MS60	MS65
1837 flat top	Inc. above	44.00	58.00	110	285	515	700	1,050	6,500
1837 curly top	Inc. above	40.00	52.00	95.00	250	465	750	1,000	6,500
1838O	406,034	47.50	70.00	125	375	725	1,250	3,500	21,000

Seated Liberty, stars around top 1/2 of border, date below. Value within wreath.

KM# 63.1 • 2.67 g., 0.900 Silver 0.0773 oz. ASW, 17.9 mm. • **Obv. Designer:** Christian Gobrecht **Rev. Legend:** UNITED STATES OF AMERICA **Note:** The 1839-O with reverse of 1838-O variety was struck from rusted dies, it has a bumpy reverse surface.

No drapery at elbow

Date	Mintage	G4	VG8	F12	VF20	XF40	AU50	MS60	MS65
1838 small stars	1,992,500	27.00	38.00	55.00	85.00	175	400	625	—
1838 large stars	Inc. above	22.00	25.50	34.50	45.00	135	260	375	8,500
1838 partial drapery	Inc. above	35.00	50.00	85.00	150	225	350	550	—
1839	1,053,115	19.00	23.50	28.50	40.00	125	245	315	3,000
1839O	1,323,000	23.50	30.00	47.00	140	150	280	650	6,000
1839O reverse 1838O	Inc. above	165	225	375	550	1,150	—	—	—
1840	1,358,580	19.00	24.50	28.50	40.00	125	245	315	4,000
1840O	1,175,000	23.00	28.50	36.50	60.00	165	325	2,750	6,500

KM# 63.2 • 2.67 g., 0.900 Silver 0.0773 oz. ASW, 17.9 mm. • **Rev. Legend:** UNITED STATES OF AMERICA **Designer:** Christian Gobrecht **Note:** Drapery added to Liberty's left elbow

Drapery at elbow

Date	Mintage	G4	VG8	F12	VF20	XF40	AU50	MS60	MS65
1840	Inc. above	32.00	50.00	90.00	175	300	400	2,400	—
1841	1,622,500	17.50	20.00	22.50	29.00	50.00	150	310	2,700
1841O	2,007,500	23.50	28.50	33.00	41.50	90.00	250	1,500	5,000
1841O large O	Inc. above	600	900	1,200	2,500	—	—	—	—
1842	1,887,500	16.50	18.00	22.00	28.50	47.00	150	280	2,700
1842O	2,020,000	25.00	30.00	37.50	75.00	225	1,350	2,900	—
1843	1,370,000	16.50	18.00	22.00	28.50	47.00	150	280	3,000
1843/1843	Inc. above	16.00	18.50	22.50	30.00	75.00	200	295	—
1843O	150,000	50.00	75.00	135	300	1,100	3,450	—	—
1844	72,500	200	300	375	600	1,350	1,850	3,000	—
1845	1,755,000	17.50	18.00	22.00	28.50	47.00	150	280	2,600
1845/1845	Inc. above	17.00	20.00	35.00	55.00	100	175	—	—
1845O	230,000	32.00	48.00	90.00	225	650	1,350	—	—
1846	31,300	150	250	365	575	1,600	6,500	30,000	—
1847	245,000	19.50	30.00	40.00	70.00	125	350	950	9,000
1848	451,500	19.50	25.00	28.50	52.50	95.00	175	750	7,000
1849	839,000	19.50	21.50	25.00	37.50	55.00	150	500	4,000
1849O	300,000	26.00	33.00	50.00	125	275	750	2,200	—

Date	Mintage	G4	VG8	F12	VF20	XF40	AU50	MS60	MS65
1850	1,931,500	19.50	21.50	24.50	34.50	50.00	150	280	5,900
1850O	510,000	25.00	32.00	40.00	75.00	135	300	1,250	—
1851	1,026,500	19.50	21.50	24.50	32.50	50.00	150	335	5,000
1851O	400,000	25.00	34.00	42.50	85.00	175	475	1,850	—
1852	1,535,500	16.50	18.00	20.00	26.50	45.00	150	280	2,550
1852O	430,000	28.50	34.00	53.50	145	250	400	1,800	—
1853	95,000	95.00	145	220	300	425	575	750	—

Seated Liberty, stars around top 1/2 of border, arrows at date. Value within wreath.

KM# 77 • 2.49 g., 0.900 Silver 0.072 oz. ASW **Rev. Legend:** UNITED STATES OF AMERICA **Designer:** Christian Gobrecht

Date	Mintage	G4	VG8	F12	VF20	XF40	AU50	MS60	MS65	Prf65
1853	12,078,010	16.00	18.00	19.00	25.00	44.00	145	260	2,500	31,500
1853O	1,100,000	18.00	20.00	24.00	45.00	125	285	900	—	—
1854	4,470,000	16.00	18.00	19.00	22.00	44.00	145	260	2,500	31,500
1854O	1,770,000	17.00	20.00	22.00	26.00	60.00	160	600	—	—
1855	2,075,000	16.00	18.00	19.00	22.00	48.00	150	350	3,800	31,500

Seated Liberty, stars around top 1/2 of border, date below. Value within wreath.

KM# A63.2 • 2.49 g., 0.900 Silver 0.072 oz. ASW **Rev. Legend:** UNITED STATES OF AMERICA **Designer:** Christian Gobrecht

Date	Mintage	G4	VG8	F12	VF20	XF40	AU50	MS60	MS65	Prf65
1856 small date	5,780,000	15.50	17.00	18.50	21.00	42.00	138	250	7,050	38,000
1856 large date	Inc. above	20.00	23.50	27.00	34.00	65.00	175	475	—	—
1856O	1,180,000	19.00	22.00	23.50	32.00	70.00	225	625	5,250	—
1856S	70,000	135	185	360	575	1,150	1,750	—	—	—
1857	5,580,000	15.50	17.00	18.50	21.00	42.00	138	250	2,600	3,400
1857O	1,540,000	16.50	18.00	19.50	26.00	55.00	175	375	2,600	—
1858	1,540,000	15.50	17.00	18.50	21.00	42.00	138	260	2,600	3,400
1858O	290,000	16.50	25.00	36.00	85.00	120	280	800	5,000	—
1858S	60,000	135	200	265	475	1,000	1,650	—	—	—
1859	430,000	16.00	20.00	23.50	38.00	55.00	138	350	—	3,400
1859O	480,000	16.00	20.00	25.00	40.00	80.00	240	550	—	—
1859S	60,000	100	175	350	600	1,350	2,750	—	—	—
1860S	140,000	37.50	55.00	70.00	145	325	625	—	—	—

UNITED STATES OF AMERICA replaced stars. Value within wreath.

KM# 92 • 2.49 g., 0.900 Silver 0.072 oz. ASW **Obv. Legend:** UNITED STATES OF AMERICA **Obv. Designer:** Christian Gobrecht **Note:** The 1873 "closed-3" and "open-3" varieties are distinguished by the amount of space between the upper left and lower left serifs of the 3 in the date.

Date	Mintage	G4	VG8	F12	VF20	XF40	AU50	MS60	MS65	Prf65
1860	607,000	17.50	19.00	29.00	32.00	44.00	115	275	1,350	1,400
1860O	40,000	400	600	900	1,950	3,650	6,500	8,500	—	—
1861	1,884,000	16.50	18.00	20.00	23.00	32.00	85.00	150	1,250	1,400
1861S	172,500	55.00	90.00	150	200	400	650	1,400	—	—
1862	847,550	17.50	19.00	21.00	24.00	45.00	75.00	165	1,250	1,400
1862S	180,750	45.00	60.00	95.00	175	300	675	1,000	—	—
1863	14,460	425	500	650	900	1,050	1,100	1,300	—	1,400
1863S	157,500	45.00	55.00	75.00	145	250	500	1,200	—	—
1864	11,470	425	500	650	800	1,000	1,150	1,200	—	1,400
1864S	230,000	35.00	45.00	75.00	120	225	375	1,200	—	—
1865	10,500	475	575	700	875	1,250	1,200	1,350	—	1,400
1865S	175,000	45.00	55.00	85.00	200	350	775	—	—	—
1866	8,725	500	600	775	950	1,300	1,200	1,800	—	1,750
1866S	135,000	50.00	65.00	100	150	275	400	1,900	—	—
1867	6,625	600	700	950	1,100	1,450	1,600	1,800	—	1,750
1867S	140,000	45.00	80.00	135	200	365	675	1,200	—	—
1868	464,000	25.00	30.00	36.00	50.00	90.00	175	300	—	1,400
1868S	260,000	32.00	38.00	50.00	115	175	275	600	—	—
1869	256,600	30.00	35.00	45.00	110	145	250	600	—	1,400
1869S	450,000	25.00	30.00	40.00	55.00	90.00	160	400	—	—
1870	471,000	17.50	22.00	30.00	40.00	50.00	85.00	150	—	1,400
1870S	50,000	300	375	500	650	850	1,050	2,000	—	—

DIME

Date	Mintage	G4	VG8	F12	VF20	XF40	AU50	MS60	MS65	Prf65
1871	907,710	16.50	18.00	20.00	30.00	45.00	160	300	—	1,400
1871CC	20,100	2,000	3,500	4,500	9,500	12,500	25,000	—	—	—
1871S	320,000	35.00	55.00	85.00	135	195	325	900	—	—
1872	2,396,450	15.00	16.50	18.50	21.50	30.00	85.00	175	—	1,400
1872CC	35,480	650	1,250	1,850	3,000	7,500	—	—	—	—
1872S	190,000	40.00	65.00	85.00	165	250	400	1,100	—	—
1873 closed 3	1,568,600	16.50	18.00	20.00	24.00	32.50	75.00	200	—	1,400
1873 open 3	Inc. above	28.00	35.00	60.00	90.00	140	220	650	—	—
1873CC	12,400	—	—	—	—	—	—	—	—	—

Note: 1873-CC, Heritage Sale, April 1999, MS-64, $632,500.

Seated Liberty, arrows at date.
Value within wreath.

KM# 105 • 2.50 g., 0.900 Silver 0.0723 oz. ASW
Obv. Legend: UNITED STATES OF AMERICA
Designer: Christian Gobrecht

Date	Mintage	G4	VG8	F12	VF20	XF40	AU50	MS60	MS65	Prf65
1873	2,378,500	17.00	20.00	27.50	60.00	118	280	500	4,500	4,500
1873CC	18,791	1,350	2,850	4,250	9,500	16,500	—	—	—	—
1873S	455,000	22.00	30.00	40.00	80.00	200	425	1,500	—	—
1874	2,940,700	16.00	19.00	26.00	60.00	118	280	500	4,500	4,500
1874CC	10,817	5,000	7,000	10,500	18,500	34,000	—	—	—	—
1874S	240,000	50.00	60.00	85.00	150	265	450	1,500	—	—

Seated Liberty, date below.
Value within wreath.

KM# A92 • 2.50 g., 0.900 Silver 0.0723 oz. ASW
Obv. Legend: UNITED STATES OF AMERICA
Designer: Christian Gobrecht **Note:** On the 1876-CC doubled-obverse variety, doubling appears in the words OF AMERICA in the legend.

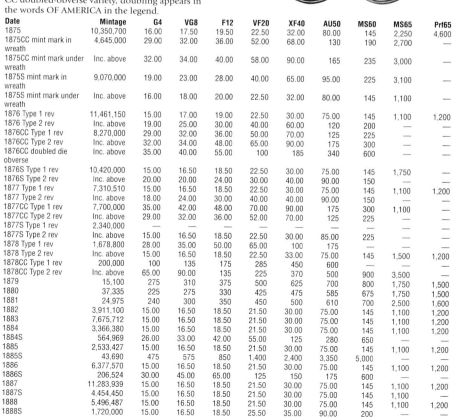

Date	Mintage	G4	VG8	F12	VF20	XF40	AU50	MS60	MS65	Prf65
1875	10,350,700	16.00	17.50	19.50	22.50	32.00	80.00	145	2,250	4,600
1875CC mint mark in wreath	4,645,000	29.00	32.00	36.00	52.00	68.00	130	190	2,700	—
1875CC mint mark under wreath	Inc. above	32.00	34.00	40.00	58.00	90.00	165	235	3,000	—
1875S mint mark in wreath	9,070,000	19.00	23.00	28.00	40.00	65.00	95.00	225	3,100	—
1875S mint mark under wreath	Inc. above	16.00	18.00	20.00	22.50	32.00	80.00	145	1,100	—
1876 Type 1 rev	11,461,150	15.00	17.00	19.00	22.50	30.00	75.00	145	1,100	1,200
1876 Type 2 rev	Inc. above	19.00	25.00	30.00	40.00	60.00	120	200	—	—
1876CC Type 1 rev	8,270,000	29.00	32.00	36.00	50.00	70.00	125	225	—	—
1876CC Type 2 rev	Inc. above	32.00	34.00	48.00	65.00	90.00	175	300	—	—
1876CC doubled die obverse	Inc. above	35.00	40.00	55.00	100	185	340	600	—	—
1876S Type 1 rev	10,420,000	15.00	16.50	18.50	22.50	30.00	75.00	145	1,750	—
1876S Type 2 rev	Inc. above	20.00	20.00	24.00	30.00	40.00	90.00	150	—	—
1877 Type 1 rev	7,310,510	15.00	16.50	18.50	22.50	30.00	75.00	145	1,100	1,200
1877 Type 2 rev	Inc. above	18.00	24.00	30.00	40.00	40.00	90.00	150	—	—
1877CC Type 1 rev	7,700,000	35.00	42.00	48.00	70.00	90.00	175	300	1,100	—
1877CC Type 2 rev	Inc. above	29.00	32.00	36.00	52.00	70.00	125	225	—	—
1877S Type 1 rev	2,340,000	—	—	—	—	—	—	—	—	—
1877S Type 2 rev	Inc. above	15.00	16.50	18.50	22.50	30.00	85.00	225	—	—
1878 Type 1 rev	1,678,800	28.00	35.00	50.00	65.00	100	175	—	—	—
1878 Type 2 rev	Inc. above	15.00	16.50	18.50	22.50	33.00	75.00	145	1,500	1,200
1878CC Type 1 rev	200,000	100	135	175	285	450	600	—	—	—
1878CC Type 2 rev	Inc. above	65.00	90.00	135	225	370	500	900	3,500	—
1879	15,100	275	310	375	500	625	700	800	1,750	1,500
1880	37,335	225	275	330	425	475	585	675	1,750	1,500
1881	24,975	240	300	350	450	500	610	700	2,500	1,600
1882	3,911,100	15.00	16.50	18.50	21.50	30.00	75.00	145	1,100	1,200
1883	7,675,712	15.00	16.50	18.50	21.50	30.00	75.00	145	1,100	1,200
1884	3,366,380	15.00	16.50	18.50	21.50	30.00	75.00	145	1,100	1,200
1884S	564,969	26.00	33.00	42.00	55.00	125	280	650	—	—
1885	2,533,427	15.00	16.50	18.50	21.50	30.00	75.00	145	1,100	1,200
1885S	43,690	475	575	850	1,400	2,400	3,350	5,000	—	—
1886	6,377,570	15.00	16.50	18.50	21.50	30.00	75.00	145	1,100	1,200
1886S	206,524	30.00	45.00	65.00	125	150	175	600	—	—
1887	11,283,939	15.00	16.50	18.50	21.50	30.00	75.00	145	1,100	1,200
1887S	4,454,450	15.00	16.50	18.50	21.50	30.00	75.00	145	1,100	—
1888	5,496,487	15.00	16.50	18.50	21.50	30.00	75.00	145	1,100	1,200
1888S	1,720,000	15.00	16.50	18.50	25.50	35.00	90.00	200	—	—

DIME

Date	Mintage	G4	VG8	F12	VF20	XF40	AU50	MS60	MS65	Prf65
1889	7,380,711	15.00	16.50	18.50	21.50	30.00	75.00	145	1,100	1,200
1889S	972,678	15.00	18.50	25.00	45.00	70.00	150	475	4,500	—
1890	9,911,541	15.00	16.50	18.50	21.50	30.00	75.00	145	1,100	1,200
1890S	1,423,076	15.00	16.50	24.00	44.00	85.00	145	400	4,900	—
1891	15,310,600	15.00	16.50	18.50	21.50	30.00	75.00	145	1,100	1,200
1891O	4,540,000	16.00	17.50	20.50	25.50	35.00	90.00	175	1,750	—
1891O /horizontal O	Inc. above	65.00	95.00	125	175	225	400	—	—	—
1891S	3,196,116	15.00	17.00	19.00	21.50	30.00	75.00	175	1,650	—
1891S/S	Inc. above	25.00	30.00	40.00	85.00	135	250	—	—	—

Barber Dime
Laureate head right, date at angle below. Value within wreath.
KM# 113 • 2.50 g., 0.900 Silver 0.0723 oz. ASW, 17.9 mm. • **Obv. Legend:** UNITED STATES OF AMERICA **Designer:** Charles E. Barber

Date	Mintage	G4	VG8	F12	VF20	XF40	AU50	MS60	MS65	Prf65
1892	12,121,245	8.75	9.50	16.00	22.00	27.50	66.00	115	620	1,485
1892O	3,841,700	11.00	15.00	36.00	58.00	78.00	96.00	150	1,275	—
1892S	990,710	66.00	115	215	245	285	340	425	4,250	—
1893/2	3,340,792	135	155	175	225	300	325	675	6,000	—
1893	Inc. above	8.25	12.50	20.00	30.00	46.00	80.00	165	1,000	1,485
1893O	1,760,000	31.00	45.00	135	168	195	250	315	2,950	—
1893S	2,491,401	14.00	25.00	39.00	50.00	92.50	155	300	3,750	—
1894	1,330,972	25.00	45.00	122	165	190	235	310	1,150	1,485
1894O	720,000	70.00	105	215	280	425	650	1,550	15,500	—
1894S	24	—	—	—	—	—	—	—	2,850,000	—
Note: 1894S, Eliasberg Sale, May 1996, Prf-64, $451,000.										
1895	690,880	85.00	180	355	480	565	650	750	2,650	1,485
1895O	440,000	385	575	900	1,350	2,550	3,650	6,000	24,500	—
1895S	1,120,000	43.50	60.00	135	210	240	320	500	7,500	—
1896	2,000,762	11.50	23.00	58.00	82.00	100	120	155	1,450	1,485
1896O	610,000	80.00	155	305	375	465	700	975	9,500	—
1896S	575,056	85.00	160	310	345	385	525	775	4,650	—
1897	10,869,264	4.00	5.00	8.00	15.00	32.00	76.00	265	620	1,485
1897O	666,000	69.50	115	290	385	480	600	975	4,450	—
1897S	1,342,844	21.00	45.00	98.00	130	185	265	435	3,950	—
1898	16,320,735	4.00	5.00	7.50	15.00	28.00	71.00	135	620	1,485
1898O	2,130,000	13.50	27.50	95.00	150	210	285	450	3,850	—
1898S	1,702,507	8.50	15.00	36.00	52.00	78.00	160	370	3,750	—
1899	19,580,846	4.00	5.00	7.50	12.00	26.00	71.00	120	620	1,485
1899O	2,650,000	10.00	19.50	72.00	115	150	230	415	4,450	—
1899S	1,867,493	9.00	16.00	36.00	39.00	48.50	105	300	3,550	—
1900	17,600,912	4.00	5.00	7.00	11.00	26.00	66.00	115	650	1,485
1900O	2,010,000	19.50	38.50	122	168	225	355	595	5,350	—
1900S	5,168,270	5.00	6.25	12.50	19.50	32.00	75.00	155	1,850	—
1901	18,860,478	4.00	5.00	6.50	10.00	27.50	66.00	115	665	1,485
1901O	5,620,000	4.00	5.50	16.00	27.50	68.00	175	450	4,350	—
1901S	593,022	80.00	150	360	475	520	675	985	5,350	—
1902	21,380,777	4.00	5.00	7.00	8.00	25.00	66.00	115	665	1,485
1902O	4,500,000	4.00	5.50	15.00	32.50	62.50	145	350	4,500	—
1902S	2,070,000	8.00	21.00	58.00	95.00	135	195	375	3,950	—
1903	19,500,755	4.00	5.00	7.00	8.00	27.00	66.00	115	1,100	1,485
1903O	8,180,000	4.00	5.50	14.50	23.50	54.00	110	250	4,850	—
1903S	613,300	84.00	130	365	500	750	840	1,100	3,150	—
1904	14,601,027	5.00	5.50	7.75	10.25	28.00	66.00	115	1,650	1,485
1904S	800,000	45.00	75.00	175	245	335	465	725	4,500	—
1905	14,552,350	3.79	5.25	7.00	10.25	28.00	66.00	115	645	1,485
1905O	3,400,000	4.25	10.00	36.50	57.50	100	155	285	1,650	—
1905O micro O	Inc. above	35.00	50.00	75.00	140	235	375	1,750	12,500	—
1905S	6,855,199	4.00	5.00	9.00	18.50	43.50	96.00	210	975	—
1906	19,958,406	2.79	3.10	4.75	7.75	25.00	61.00	110	645	1,485
1906D	4,060,000	3.29	5.00	7.00	15.00	35.00	78.00	175	1,650	—
1906O	2,610,000	5.50	13.00	50.00	78.00	105	135	195	1,150	—
1906S	3,136,640	3.79	5.80	13.00	24.00	49.00	110	240	1,350	—
1907	22,220,575	2.79	3.10	4.75	7.75	25.00	61.00	110	610	1,485
1907D	4,080,000	3.29	4.60	10.50	10.00	43.50	115	275	2,350	—
1907O	5,058,000	3.79	7.50	35.00	50.00	63.50	110	210	1,350	—
1907S	3,178,470	3.79	5.50	17.00	27.50	68.50	150	410	2,450	—
1908	10,600,545	2.79	3.10	4.75	7.75	25.00	61.00	110	610	1,485
1908D	7,490,000	2.79	3.10	6.00	10.25	32.00	66.00	125	990	—
1908O	1,789,000	5.25	11.00	46.00	68.00	93.00	150	290	1,350	—
1908S	3,220,000	4.04	5.80	12.00	22.00	49.00	175	310	2,350	—
1909	10,240,650	2.79	3.10	4.75	7.75	25.00	61.00	110	610	1,485
1909D	954,000	7.25	18.50	60.00	100	135	225	485	2,850	—

Date	Mintage	G4	VG8	F12	VF20	XF40	AU50	MS60	MS65	Prf65
1909O	2,287,000	4.00	7.25	13.00	23.00	50.00	92.50	185	1,650	—
1909S	1,000,000	8.75	19.50	92.00	135	182	315	525	2,850	—
1910	11,520,551	2.79	3.10	4.75	10.25	25.00	61.00	110	610	1,485
1910D	3,490,000	3.04	4.00	9.50	19.00	49.00	100	210	1,650	—
1910S	1,240,000	5.25	9.00	52.50	74.00	112	195	425	2,450	—
1911	18,870,543	2.79	3.10	4.75	7.50	25.00	61.00	110	610	1,485
1911D	11,209,000	2.79	3.10	4.75	7.50	27.00	61.00	110	610	—
1911S	3,520,000	3.54	4.30	9.50	18.50	39.50	105	195	1,050	—
1912	19,350,700	2.79	3.10	4.75	7.50	25.00	61.00	110	610	1,485
1912D	11,760,000	2.79	3.10	4.75	7.50	25.00	61.00	110	710	—
1912S	3,420,000	3.04	4.10	5.60	12.50	34.00	92.50	155	775	—
1913	19,760,622	2.79	3.10	4.75	7.50	25.00	61.00	110	610	1,485
1913S	510,000	35.00	50.00	120	190	240	325	480	1,375	—
1914	17,360,655	2.79	3.10	4.75	7.50	25.00	61.00	110	610	1,485
1914D	11,908,000	2.79	3.10	4.75	7.50	25.00	61.00	110	610	—
1914S	2,100,000	3.04	4.10	8.50	17.50	39.50	78.00	150	1,250	—
1915	5,620,450	2.79	3.10	5.00	7.50	25.00	61.00	110	610	1,485
1915S	960,000	7.50	11.50	36.00	49.50	68.50	135	250	1,550	—
1916	18,490,000	2.79	3.10	4.75	7.50	25.00	61.00	110	610	—
1916S	5,820,000	3.04	3.60	5.00	7.75	27.00	66.00	115	620	—

Mercury Dime

KM# 140 • 2.50 g., 0.900 Silver 0.0723 oz. ASW, 17.8 mm. • **Designer:** Adolph A. Weinman **Note:** All specimens listed as -65FSB are for fully struck MS-65 coins with fully split and rounded horizontal bands on the fasces.

Mint mark

Full split bands

Date	Mintage	G4	VG8	F12	VF20	XF40	AU50	MS60	MS63	MS65	65FSB
1916	22,180,080	3.75	4.75	6.00	7.00	10.50	22.50	29.00	46.50	110	165
1916D	264,000	800	1,540	2,500	4,100	6,900	9,450	14,350	16,600	25,500	48,500
1916S	10,450,000	3.80	5.00	9.25	15.00	25.00	28.00	44.00	57.50	200	800
1917	55,230,000	3.40	3.60	5.15	5.50	8.00	12.50	27.00	63.50	155	375
1917D	9,402,000	4.00	5.50	12.50	26.00	52.50	90.00	120	292	1,050	5,650
1917S	27,330,000	3.40	3.60	2.35	7.50	15.00	28.00	59.00	161	400	1,265
1918	26,680,000	3.40	4.00	5.75	12.00	34.00	42.00	69.00	110	345	1,325
1918D	22,674,800	3.50	3.90	6.50	13.00	32.00	46.00	100	205	575	27,500
1918S	19,300,000	3.40	3.60	4.00	11.00	24.00	38.50	92.00	215	630	7,450
1919	35,740,000	3.40	3.60	4.00	5.50	12.00	23.00	36.00	215	350	685
1919D	9,939,000	3.65	6.00	13.50	31.00	46.00	70.00	175	390	1,315	38,500
1919S	8,850,000	3.50	4.25	11.00	20.00	42.00	70.00	175	410	1,200	14,350
1920	59,030,000	3.40	3.60	4.00	4.50	8.50	14.00	27.50	66.00	240	540
1920D	19,171,000	3.50	3.90	5.00	9.00	24.00	43.00	105	315	565	4,750
1920S	13,820,000	3.50	3.60	7.50	10.00	21.00	39.00	105	290	1,250	8,250
1921	1,230,000	55.00	6,000	800	1,240	1,340	2,050	1,150	2,325	3,000	4,350
1921D	1,080,000	69.00	450	55.00	57.00	63.00	80.00	1,275	2,700	3,075	5,200
1923	50,130,000	3.25	4.00	3.75	4.50	7.00	15.00	26.50	43.50	120	340
1923S	6,440,000	3.25	3.90	8.50	20.00	75.00	100	150	355	1,265	7,450
1924	24,010,000	3.25	3.60	3.75	4.50	13.50	26.50	40.00	84.00	165	500
1924D	6,810,000	3.25	4.30	9.00	23.50	69.00	100	167	437	975	1,365
1924S	7,120,000	3.25	3.60	5.00	12.00	58.00	95.00	212	486	1,050	16,750
1925	25,610,000	3.25	3.60	3.75	5.50	11.00	16.00	27.00	71.00	205	990
1925D	5,117,000	4.00	5.00	12.75	46.50	130	185	335	690	1,745	3,500
1925S	5,850,000	3.35	3.75	7.75	18.50	85.00	100	177	443	1,200	4,650
1926	32,160,000	3.25	3.60	3.75	4.25	5.75	12.00	24.50	51.50	235	525
1926D	6,828,000	3.35	4.00	5.00	12.50	32.00	43.00	120	247	515	2,500
1926S	1,520,000	11.50	13.75	29.00	65.00	250	385	850	1,400	2,825	6,750
1927	28,080,000	3.25	3.60	3.75	4.25	6.00	11.00	25.50	97.50	150	350
1927D	4,812,000	3.65	5.00	7.75	27.00	88.00	95.00	172	350	1,200	8,500

DIME

Date	Mintage	G4	VG8	F12	VF20	XF40	AU50	MS60	MS63	MS65	65FSB
1927S	4,770,000	3.35	3.75	5.50	13.00	30.00	46.00	330	520	1,350	7,600
1928	19,480,000	3.25	3.60	3.75	4.25	16.00	16.00	27.75	57.50	131	345
1928D	4,161,000	3.55	4.30	11.50	27.50	62.50	85.00	167	385	825	2,750
1928S Large S	7,400,000	4.00	5.50	7.50	12.00	40.00	85.00	225	475	750	6,500
1928S Small S	Inc. above	3.35	3.75	3.75	6.50	19.00	36.00	138	340	405	2,000
1929	25,970,000	3.25	3.60	3.75	4.25	4.50	10.00	21.50	32.00	67.00	175
1929D	5,034,000	3.35	3.75	3.75	8.00	15.00	21.00	32.00	35.00	76.00	225
1929S	4,730,000	3.35	3.75	3.75	5.00	7.50	20.00	32.00	39.00	115	560
1929S Doubled Die Obv	Inc. above	5.00	9.00	16.00	25.00	40.00	60.00	95.00	150	335	1,150
1930	6,770,000	3.25	3.60	3.75	4.25	7.00	13.00	25.50	46.00	110	575
1930S	1,843,000	3.35	3.75	4.25	6.50	19.00	45.00	80.00	150	210	685
1931	3,150,000	3.35	3.75	3.75	8.00	12.50	22.50	33.00	73.00	130	800
1931D	1,260,000	7.75	10.00	15.00	21.00	48.00	53.00	97.00	125	275	375
1931 Doubled Die Obv & Rev	Inc. above	—	20.00	27.50	50.00	70.00	90.00	135	225	485	650
1931S	1,800,000	3.80	5.00	5.50	11.00	23.50	42.50	105	145	275	2,500
1931S Doubled Die Obv	Inc. above	7.50	10.00	13.00	25.00	35.00	60.00	140	220	425	3,850
1934	24,080,000	1.50	1.55	1.60	2.31	6.50	10.00	27.75	33.00	42.00	130
1934D	6,772,000	2.05	2.25	3.30	7.50	14.00	27.50	54.00	59.50	75.00	320
1935	58,830,000	1.50	1.55	1.60	2.01	4.25	7.50	10.00	14.50	28.50	68.00
1935D	10,477,000	1.65	2.05	2.40	6.50	13.00	25.00	35.75	44.00	88.00	500
1935S	15,840,000	1.65	1.95	2.10	2.71	5.50	14.00	23.50	27.00	36.00	360
1936	87,504,130	1.50	1.55	1.60	2.01	2.22	6.50	9.00	14.50	25.50	84.00
1936 Doubled Die Obv	Inc. above	—	—	8.00	15.00	25.00	35.00	50.00	105	165	—
1936D	16,132,000	1.65	1.95	2.00	4.25	8.50	17.00	27.00	36.00	51.00	290
1936S	9,210,000	1.65	1.95	2.00	2.41	6.00	12.50	26.00	32.00	32.00	88.00
1937	56,865,756	1.50	1.55	1.60	2.01	3.75	6.00	8.50	12.00	24.50	52.00
1937 Doubled Die Obv	Inc. above	—	—	—	6.00	9.00	12.00	20.00	40.00	95.00	175
1937D	14,146,000	1.65	1.95	2.00	2.51	6.00	12.50	22.50	30.00	42.00	105
1937S	9,740,000	1.65	1.95	2.00	2.41	5.50	10.00	21.50	25.75	36.00	190
1937S Doubled Die Obv	Inc. above	—	—	—	5.00	8.00	12.00	28.00	45.00	125	275
1938	22,198,728	1.50	1.55	1.60	2.01	3.75	7.50	13.00	14.50	25.50	80.00
1938D	5,537,000	1.65	1.95	2.00	5.00	6.00	12.00	18.50	22.50	33.00	62.00
1938S	8,090,000	1.65	1.95	2.00	2.41	5.00	12.00	20.50	30.00	40.00	160
1939	67,749,321	1.50	1.55	1.60	1.81	2.22	5.00	8.50	9.75	25.50	170
1939 Doubled Die Obv	Inc. above	—	—	—	4.00	6.00	8.00	14.00	22.00	35.00	450
1939D	24,394,000	1.65	1.75	1.85	2.11	3.50	5.50	8.00	9.50	25.50	49.00
1939S	10,540,000	2.00	2.05	2.20	2.51	6.75	14.00	25.00	32.00	39.00	765
1940	65,361,827	1.50	1.55	1.60	1.81	2.22	3.00	6.00	10.75	28.50	48.00
1940D	21,198,000	1.65	1.75	1.85	2.11	3.62	6.00	8.00	11.75	31.00	48.00
1940S	21,560,000	1.65	1.75	1.80	2.11	3.62	6.50	8.50	11.75	31.00	95.00
1941	175,106,557	1.50	1.55	1.60	1.81	2.22	3.00	6.00	9.75	28.50	46.00
1941 Doubled Die Obv	Inc. above	—	—	—	10.00	16.00	30.00	55.00	95.00	165	295
1941D	45,634,000	1.65	1.75	1.80	2.11	2.62	0.50	10.00	13.00	24.00	46.00
1941D Doubled Die Obv	Inc. above	—	—	—	9.00	14.00	20.00	30.00	62.00	125	250
1941S Small S	43,090,000	1.65	1.75	1.80	2.11	2.62	4.50	7.50	11.00	28.50	46.00
1941S Large S	Inc. above	4.00	5.00	8.00	15.00	25.00	60.00	110	150	250	425
1941S Doubled Die Rev	Inc. above	4.00	4.50	5.00	5.50	6.00	7.50	18.00	28.00	60.00	85.00
1942	205,432,329	1.50	1.55	1.60	1.81	2.22	3.00	6.00	10.75	24.00	46.00
1942/41	Inc. above	490	505	530	565	710	920	2,760	4,650	14,500	35,000
1942D	60,740,000	1.65	1.75	1.80	2.11	2.62	0.50	7.75	12.00	26.50	46.00
1942/41D	Inc. above	440	450	460	495	610	1,045	2,750	5,050	10,000	26,500
1942S	49,300,000	1.65	1.75	1.80	2.11	2.62	0.50	9.75	13.75	24.00	145
1943	191,710,000	1.50	1.55	1.60	1.81	2.22	3.00	6.00	10.75	27.00	50.00
1943D	71,949,000	1.65	1.75	1.80	2.11	2.62	3.30	7.50	11.75	27.50	47.00
1943S	60,400,000	1.65	1.75	1.80	2.11	2.62	0.50	9.00	12.75	26.50	66.00
1944	231,410,000	1.50	1.55	1.60	1.81	2.22	3.00	6.00	9.75	24.00	75.00
1944D	62,224,000	1.65	1.75	1.80	2.11	2.62	3.30	7.75	15.00	24.00	46.00
1944S	49,490,000	1.65	1.75	1.80	2.11	2.62	0.50	9.25	15.00	27.50	50.00
1945	159,130,000	1.50	1.55	1.60	1.81	2.22	3.00	6.00	9.75	24.00	97.50
1945D	40,245,000	1.65	1.75	1.80	2.11	2.62	0.50	7.50	9.75	24.00	46.50
1945S	41,920,000	1.65	1.75	1.80	2.11	2.62	0.50	11.00	11.75	24.00	105
1945S micro S	Inc. above	3.25	4.00	6.00	9.00	13.00	20.00	27.00	38.00	89.00	685

Roosevelt Dime

KM# 195 • 2.50 g., 0.900 Silver 0.0723 oz. ASW, 17.9 mm. • **Designer:** John R. Sinnock

Mint mark 1946-64

Date	Mintage	G4	VG8	F12	VF20	XF40	AU50	MS60	MS65	Prf65
1946	225,250,000	—	—	—	—	1.47	1.73	2.25	9.00	—
1946D	61,043,500	—	—	—	—	1.47	1.93	2.25	10.00	—
1946S	27,900,000	—	—	—	—	1.47	1.98	2.25	10.00	—
1947	121,520,000	—	—	—	—	1.47	1.63	2.75	12.00	—
1947D	46,835,000	—	—	—	—	1.47	1.63	4.00	16.00	—

DIME

Date	Mintage	G4	VG8	F12	VF20	XF40	AU50	MS60	MS65	Prf65
1947S	34,840,000	—	—	—	—	1.47	1.63	3.50	12.00	—
1948	74,950,000	—	—	—	—	1.47	1.63	3.25	10.00	—
1948D	52,841,000	—	—	—	—	1.47	1.63	5.00	14.00	—
1948S	35,520,000	—	—	—	—	1.47	1.63	4.50	15.00	—
1949	30,940,000	—	—	1.32	1.37	4.00	8.50	12.00	25.00	—
1949D	26,034,000	—	—	1.32	1.37	2.27	5.50	7.00	20.00	—
1949S	13,510,000	—	—	1.32	3.50	8.00	15.00	35.00	60.00	—
1950	50,181,500	—	—	—	1.37	1.47	3.50	6.00	12.00	55.00
1950D	46,803,000	—	—	—	—	—	1.63	3.25	10.00	—
1950S	20,440,000	—	—	1.32	1.37	3.75	9.00	23.00	35.00	—
1951	102,937,602	—	—	—	—	—	1.83	2.60	13.00	60.00
1951D	56,529,000	—	—	—	—	—	1.73	2.80	12.00	—
1951S	31,630,000	—	—	—	1.37	1.47	4.00	10.00	18.00	—
1952	99,122,073	—	—	—	—	—	1.63	2.25	22.00	35.00
1952D	122,100,000	—	—	—	—	—	1.63	2.25	10.00	—
1952S	44,419,500	—	—	—	1.37	1.87	2.13	5.50	16.00	—
1953	53,618,920	—	—	—	—	—	1.63	2.25	12.00	38.00
1953D	136,433,000	—	—	—	—	—	1.63	2.60	11.00	—
1953S	39,180,000	—	—	—	—	—	2.03	3.00	12.50	—
1954	114,243,503	—	—	—	—	—	1.63	2.25	10.00	18.00
1954D	106,397,000	—	—	—	—	—	1.63	2.25	15.00	—
1954S	22,860,000	—	—	—	—	—	1.63	2.35	10.00	—
1955	12,828,381	—	—	—	1.40	1.47	1.63	2.50	8.50	17.00
1955D	13,959,000	—	—	—	1.40	1.47	1.63	2.50	8.50	—
1955S	18,510,000	—	—	—	1.40	1.47	1.63	2.50	8.00	—
1956	109,309,384	—	—	—	—	—	1.63	2.25	9.50	8.00
1956D	108,015,100	—	—	—	—	—	1.63	2.35	9.00	—
1957	161,407,952	—	—	—	—	—	1.63	2.25	8.50	5.00
1957D	113,354,330	—	—	—	—	—	1.63	2.25	7.50	—
1958	32,785,652	—	—	—	—	—	1.63	2.25	11.00	6.00
1958D	136,564,600	—	—	—	—	—	1.63	2.25	10.00	—
1959	86,929,291	—	—	—	—	—	1.63	2.25	8.00	4.50
1959D	164,919,790	—	—	—	—	—	1.63	2.25	8.50	—
1960	72,081,602	—	—	—	—	—	1.63	2.25	8.50	4.50
1960D	200,160,400	—	—	—	—	—	1.63	2.25	7.50	—
1961	96,758,244	—	—	—	—	—	1.63	2.25	8.00	4.00
1961D	209,146,550	—	—	—	—	—	1.63	2.25	6.50	—
1962	75,668,019	—	—	—	—	—	1.63	2.25	6.50	4.00
1962D	334,948,380	—	—	—	—	—	1.63	2.25	7.00	—
1963	126,725,645	—	—	—	—	—	1.63	2.25	7.50	3.75
1963D	421,476,530	—	—	—	—	—	1.63	2.25	7.00	—
1964	933,310,762	—	—	—	—	—	1.63	2.25	7.50	3.75
1964D	1,357,517,180	—	—	—	—	—	1.63	2.25	7.00	—

KM# 195a • 2.27 g., Copper-Nickel Clad Copper, 17.91 mm. • **Designer:** John R. Sinnock **Note:** The 1979-S and 1981-S Type II proofs have clearer mint marks than the Type I proofs of those years. On the 1982 no-mint-mark variety, the mint mark was inadvertently left off.

Mint mark 1968- present   1982 No mint mark

Date	Mintage	MS65	Prf65
1965	1,652,140,570	6.00	—
1965SMS	—	2.00	—
1966	1,382,734,540	6.50	—
1966SMS	—	2.25	—
1967	2,244,007,320	7.00	—
1967SMS	—	3.50	—
1968	424,470,000	6.50	—
1968D	480,748,280	6.50	—
1968S	3,041,506	—	4.00
1968 no S error	—	—	7,500
1969	145,790,000	7.00	—
1969D	563,323,870	6.00	—
1969S	2,934,631	—	4.00
1970	345,570,000	5.50	—
1970D	754,942,100	5.00	—
1970S	2,632,810	—	4.00
1970S No S	—	—	1,300

Date	Mintage	MS65	Prf65
1971	162,690,000	10.00	—
1971D	377,914,240	8.00	—
1971S	3,220,733	—	4.00
1972	431,540,000	7.50	—
1972D	330,290,000	8.50	—
1972S	3,260,996	—	4.00
1973	315,670,000	6.00	—
1973D	455,032,426	5.50	—
1973S	2,760,339	—	4.00
1974	470,248,000	5.50	—
1974D	571,083,000	4.50	—
1974S	2,612,568	—	4.00
1975	585,673,900	4.50	—
1975D	313,705,300	4.50	—
1975S	2,845,450	—	4.00
1976	568,760,000	4.50	—
1976D	695,222,774	4.50	—
1976S	4,149,730	—	4.00
1977	796,930,000	4.50	—
1977D	376,607,228	8.00	—
1977S	3,251,152	—	4.00
1978	663,980,000	5.00	—
1978D	282,847,540	4.50	—
1978S	3,127,781	—	4.00
1979	315,440,000	5.50	—
1979D	390,921,184	5.00	—
1979S type I	3,677,175	—	5.00
1979S type II	—	—	2.00
1980P	735,170,000	6.00	—
1980D	719,354,321	5.00	—
1980S	3,554,806	—	4.00

DIME

Date	Mintage	MS65	Prf65
1981P	676,650,000	4.00	—
1981D	712,284,143	4.00	—
1981S type I	—	—	4.00
1981S type II	—	—	6.50
1982	519,475,000	8.50	—
1982 no mint mark	Inc. above	300	—
1982D	542,713,584	3.20	—
1982S	3,857,479	—	4.00
1983P	647,025,000	6.00	—
1983D	730,129,224	4.00	—
1983S	3,279,126	—	4.00
1984P	856,669,000	4.00	—
1984D	704,803,976	3.50	—
1984S	3,065,110	—	4.00
1985P	705,200,962	5.00	—
1985D	587,979,970	3.50	—
1985S	3,362,821	—	4.00
1986P	682,649,693	3.50	—
1986D	473,326,970	3.50	—
1986S	3,010,497	—	4.00
1987P	762,709,481	4.50	—
1987D	653,203,402	4.50	—
1987S	4,227,728	—	4.00
1988P	1,030,550,000	5.50	—
1988D	962,385,488	5.50	—
1988S	3,262,948	—	3.00
1989P	1,298,400,000	4.00	—
1989D	896,535,597	5.00	—
1989S	3,220,194	—	4.00
1990P	1,034,340,000	4.50	—
1990D	839,995,824	5.50	—
1990S	3,299,559	—	4.00
1991P	927,220,000	5.00	—
1991D	601,241,114	5.00	—
1991S	2,867,787	—	3.00
1992P	593,500,000	4.50	—
1992D	616,273,932	4.50	—
1992S	2,858,981	—	4.00
1993P	766,180,000	3.50	—
1993D	750,110,166	4.50	—
1993S	2,633,439	—	7.00
1994P	1,189,000,000	4.00	—
1994D	1,303,268,110	5.50	—
1994S	2,484,594	—	5.00
1995P	1,125,500,000	4.00	—
1995D	1,274,890,000	4.50	—
1995S	2,010,384	—	20.00
1996P	1,421,163,000	3.00	—
1996D	1,400,300,000	5.00	—
1996W	1,457,949	24.00	—
1996S	2,085,191	—	3.50
1997P	991,640,000	4.00	—
1997D	979,810,000	3.00	—
1997S	1,975,000	—	14.00
1998P	1,163,000,000	2.75	—
1998D	1,172,250,000	2.75	—
1998S	2,078,494	—	4.00
1999P	2,164,000,000	2.75	—
1999D	1,397,750,000	2.75	—
1999S	2,557,897	—	4.00
2000P	1,842,500,000	2.75	—
2000D	1,818,700,000	2.75	—
2000S	3,097,440	—	1.00
2001P	1,369,590,000	2.75	—
2001D	1,412,800,000	2.75	—
2001S	2,249,496	—	3.75
2002P	1,187,500,000	2.75	—
2002D	1,379,500,000	3.00	—
2002S	2,268,913	—	2.50
2003P	1,085,500,000	3.00	—
2003D	986,500,000	3.00	—
2003S	2,076,165	—	2.60
2004P	1,328,000,000	3.00	—
2004D	1,159,500,000	3.00	—
2004S	1,804,396	—	4.75
2005P	1,412,000,000	2.75	—
2005P Satin Finish	—	4.00	—

Date	Mintage	MS65	Prf65
2005D	1,423,500,000	2.75	—
2005D Satin Finish	—	4.00	—
2005S	2,275,000	—	2.60
2006P	1,381,000,000	2.50	—
2006P Satin Finish	—	4.00	—
2006D	1,447,000,000	2.50	—
2006D Satin Finish	—	4.00	—
2006S	2,000,428	—	2.50
2007P	1,047,500,000	2.00	—
2007P Satin Finish	—	3.00	—
2007D	1,042,000,000	2.00	—
2007D Satin Finish	—	3.00	—
2007S	1,702,116	—	2.50
2008P	391,000,000	1.25	—
2008 Satin Finish	—	2.50	—
2008D	624,500,000	1.25	—
2008D Satin Finish	—	2.50	—
2008S	1,405,674	—	2.50
2009P	96,500,000	1.25	—
2009P Satin Finish	—	1.00	—
2009D	49,500,000	1.25	—
2009D Satin Finish	—	1.00	—
2009S	1,482,502	—	2.50
2010P	557,000,000	4.00	—
2010P Satin Finish	—	2.00	—
2010D	562,000,000	4.00	—
2010D Satin Finish	—	2.00	—
2010S	1,103,815	—	2.50
2011P	748,000,000	4.00	—
2011D	754,000,000	4.00	—
2011S	1,098,835	—	2.50
2012P	808,000,000	4.00	—
2012D	868,000,000	4.00	—
2012S	841,972	—	2.50
2013P	1,086,500,000	4.00	—
2013D	1,025,500,000	4.00	—
2013S	821,031	—	2.50
2014P	—	2.00	—
2014D	—	2.00	—
2014S	—	—	2.50
2015P	—	2.00	—
2015D	—	2.00	—
2015S	—	—	2.50

KM# 195b • 2.50 g., 0.900 Silver 0.0723 oz. ASW, 17.9 mm. • **Designer:** John R. Sinnock

Date	Mintage	Prf65
1992S	1,317,579	5.00
1993S	761,353	7.00
1994S	785,329	7.00
1995S	838,953	8.00
1996S	830,021	7.00
1997S	821,678	14.00
1998S	878,792	7.00
1999S	804,565	7.00
1999S	1,317,579	7.00
1999S	761,353	7.00
1999S	785,329	7.00
1999S	838,953	7.00
2000S	965,921	5.50
2001S	849,600	5.00
2002S	888,826	5.00
2003S	1,090,425	4.75
2004S	1,175,934	5.00
2005S	1,069,679	5.00
2006S	1,054,008	4.50
2007S	875,050	6.00
2008S	763,887	6.50
2009S	697,365	6.75
2010S	585,401	6.75
2011S	574,175	6.75
2012S	395,443	6.75
2013S	821,031	6.75
2014S	—	6.75
2015S	—	6.75

DIME

20 CENTS

Seated Liberty within circle of stars, date below. Eagle with arrows in talons, value below.

KM# 109 • 5.00 g., 0.900 Silver 0.1447 oz. ASW, 22 mm. • **Rev. Legend:** UNITED STATES OF AMERICA **Designer:** William Barber

Date	Mintage	G4	VG8	F12	VF20	XF40	AU50	MS60	MS65	Prf65
1875	39,700	165	210	270	325	415	550	835	5,500	9,500
1875S Clear S	Inc. above	110	120	135	200	235	350	600	5,500	—
1875S	1,155,000	100	110	120	175	210	320	500	4,900	—
Note: 1875-S exists as a branch mint proof										
1875S over horizontal S	Inc. above	100	110	120	175	210	320	500	4,900	—
Note: Also known as filled S										
1875S as	Inc. above	—	120	130	150	225	260	375	1,300	—
1875CC	133,290	335	385	475	600	775	1,150	1,650	10,000	—
1876	15,900	185	225	285	350	410	535	800	5,600	9,400
1876CC	10,000	—	—	—	—	—	60,000	—	—	175,000
Note: Only one circulated example known. Eliasberg Sale, April 1997, MS-65, $148,500. Heritage 1999 ANA, MS-63, $86,500.										
1877 proof only	510	—	—	2,700	2,900	3,300	3,500	—	—	10,000
1878 proof only	600	—	—	2,000	2,300	2,400	2,800	—	—	9,500

QUARTER

Draped Bust Quarter
Draped bust right. Small eagle.

KM# 25 • 6.74 g., 0.892 Silver 0.1933 oz. ASW, 27.5 mm. • **Designer:** Robert Scot

Date	Mintage	G4	VG8	F12	VF20	XF40	AU50	MS60	MS65
1796	6,146	12,000	17,500	25,500	36,500	55,000	59,000	83,000	410,000

Draped bust right, flanked by stars, date at angle below. Heraldic eagle.

KM# 36 • 6.74 g., 0.892 Silver 0.1933 oz. ASW, 27.5 mm. • **Obv. Legend:** LIBERTY **Rev. Legend:** UNITED STATES OF AMERICA **Designer:** Robert Scot

Date	Mintage	G4	VG8	F12	VF20	XF40	AU50	MS60	MS65
1804	6,738	5,500	6,750	9,250	14,500	32,500	56,500	92,500	425,000
1805	121,394	555	690	1,085	1,965	3,900	6,000	11,500	95,000
1806/5	206,124	585	725	1,160	2,365	4,200	6,300	12,500	100,000
1806	Inc. above	525	650	985	1,865	4,100	5,850	11,000	116,000
1807	220,643	525	650	985	1,865	4,100	5,850	11,500	117,500

Liberty Cap Quarter
Draped bust left, flanked by stars, date below. Eagle with arrows in talons, banner above, value below.

KM# 44 • 6.74 g., 0.892 Silver 0.1933 oz. ASW, 27 mm. • **Rev. Legend:** UNITED STATES OF AMERICA **Designer:** John Reich **Note:** Varieties of the 1819 strikes are distinguished by the size of the 9 in the date. Varieties of the 1820 strikes are distinguished by the size of the 0 in the date. One 1822 variety and one 1828 variety have "25" engraved over "50" in the denomination. The 1827 restrikes were produced privately using dies sold as scrap by the U.S. Mint.

Date	Mintage	G4	VG8	F12	VF20	XF40	AU50	MS60	MS65
1815	89,235	120	160	250	550	1,725	2,250	4,600	39,000
1818/15	361,174	120	180	310	750	1,650	2,600	5,000	31,000
1818	Inc. above	110	135	215	515	1,675	2,400	4,550	30,000
1819 small 9	144,000	95.00	135	215	595	1,875	2,525	4,550	35,000
1819 large 9	Inc. above	95.00	145	225	655	1,975	2,600	5,550	42,500
1820 small 0	127,444	95.00	135	215	515	1,675	2,400	4,550	35,000
1820 large 0	Inc. above	95.00	140	220	800	1,950	3,150	5,500	42,500
1821	216,851	115	160	240	540	1,675	2,350	4,350	30,000
1822	64,080	150	240	350	850	1,800	3,000	4,250	38,500
1822 25/50C.	Inc. above	2,750	6,500	7,850	11,000	18,500	25,000	36,500	125,000
1823/22	17,800	35,000	35,000	48,500	70,000	85,000	110,000	150,000	—
1824/2	—	950	1,350	2,250	4,000	5,850	9,000	22,500	—
1825/22	168,000	170	275	400	2,250	5,500	8,800	18,500	40,000
1825/23	Inc. above	160	235	375	700	1,875	2,600	4,650	35,000
1825/24	Inc. above	140	225	350	650	1,650	2,500	4,550	32,500
1827 original curl base 2	4,000	—	—	—	70,000	75,000	80,000	—	—
1827 restrike, square base 2	Inc. above	—	—	—	—	—	—	—	—
1828	102,000	95.00	135	215	515	1,575	2,300	4,350	30,000
1828 25/50C.	Inc. above	500	850	1,550	1,900	3,000	4,250	9,500	—

Draped bust left, flanked by stars, date below. Eagle with arrows in talons, value below.

KM# 55 • 0.892 Silver, 24.3 mm. • **Rev. Legend:** UNITED STATES OF AMERICA **Designer:** William Kneass **Note:** Varieties of the 1831 strikes are distinguished by the size of the lettering on the reverse.

Date	Mintage	G4	VG8	F12	VF20	XF40	AU50	MS60	MS65
1831 small letter rev.	398,000	68.00	120	145	185	425	850	1,875	29,000
1831 large letter rev.	Inc. above	90.00	135	165	220	470	895	1,920	29,000
1832	320,000	68.00	110	135	170	400	825	1,850	31,000
1833	156,000	80.00	120	145	185	435	860	1,885	26,500
1834	286,000	68.00	110	135	170	400	825	1,850	29,000
1834 No period after 25C	Inc. above	75.00	120	149	190	430	870	1,925	27,500
1834 0 over 0	Inc. above	—	—	—	—	—	—	—	—
1835	1,952,000	68.00	110	135	170	400	875	1,900	26,500
1836	472,000	68.00	110	135	170	400	825	1,850	29,000
1837	252,400	68.00	110	135	170	400	825	1,850	26,500
1838	832,000	68.00	110	135	170	400	825	1,850	29,000

Seated Liberty Quarter
Seated Liberty, stars around top 1/2 of border, date below. Eagle with arrows in talons, value below.

KM# 64.1 • 6.68 g., 0.900 Silver 0.1933 oz. ASW, 24.3 mm. • **Rev. Legend:** UNITED STATES OF AMERICA **Designer:** Christian Gobrecht

Date	Mintage	G4	VG8	F12	VF20	XF40	AU50	MS60	MS65
1838	Inc. above	35.00	42.00	53.00	120	450	860	1,625	36,500
1839	491,146	37.00	46.00	58.00	126	465	885	1,700	38,000
1840O	425,200	40.00	54.00	75.00	145	485	925	1,650	48,500

Drapery added to Liberty's left elbow, stars around top 1/2 of border. Eagle with arrows in talons, value below.

KM# 64.2 • 6.68 g., 0.900 Silver 0.1933 oz. ASW, 24.3 mm. • **Rev. Legend:** UNITED STATES OF AMERICA **Designer:** Christian Gobrecht

Date	Mintage	G4	VG8	F12	VF20	XF40	AU50	MS60	MS65
1840	188,127	31.00	36.50	55.00	100	225	325	900	14,500
1840O	Inc. above	45.00	55.00	90.00	200	350	525	1,100	17,500
1841	120,000	52.00	75.00	95.00	190	275	400	850	11,000
1841O	452,000	34.00	43.50	58.00	125	285	375	750	10,000
1842 small date	88,000	—	—	—	—	—	—	—	—
1842 large date	Inc. above	80.00	140	235	325	390	750	1,550	14,500
1842O small date	769,000	500	1,000	1,750	2,650	4,500	9,000	20,000	—
1842O large date	Inc. above	33.00	44.50	55.00	95.00	275	400	1,350	—
1843	645,600	28.00	31.50	34.00	45.00	85.00	185	400	6,750
1843O	968,000	33.00	44.50	100	325	450	825	2,000	—

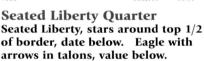

Date	Mintage	G4	VG8	F12	VF20	XF40	AU50	MS60	MS65
1844	421,200	28.00	31.50	34.00	45.00	95.00	215	450	8,250
1844O	740,000	33.00	44.50	58.00	90.00	200	350	1,100	8,250
1845	922,000	28.00	31.50	34.00	45.00	110	200	475	6,650
1846	510,000	30.00	33.50	36.00	48.00	200	275	500	10,000
1847	734,000	28.00	31.50	34.00	45.00	85.00	200	450	6,650
1847O	368,000	36.00	55.00	100	200	950	1,850	4,850	—
1848	146,000	38.00	52.00	90.00	175	275	465	1,075	14,500
1849	340,000	30.00	33.50	38.00	75.00	145	290	700	15,000
1849O	—	550	800	1,300	2,450	4,000	8,500	18,500	—
1850	190,800	31.00	44.50	75.00	135	180	360	850	11,000
1850O	412,000	36.00	44.50	85.00	150	245	575	1,550	15,000
1851	160,000	37.50	65.00	125	200	285	400	875	9,000
1851O	88,000	200	350	550	950	1,650	3,250	5,850	—
1852	177,060	45.00	62.00	85.00	185	285	400	750	6,200
1852O	96,000	210	300	600	1,250	2,850	4,250	11,000	—
1853 recut date	44,200	750	800	1,050	1,250	1,750	2,650	3,850	13,500

Seated Liberty, arrows at date. Rays around eagle.

KM# 78 • 6.22 g., 0.900 Silver 0.180 oz. ASW, 24.3 mm. • **Rev. Legend:** UNITED STATES OF AMERICA **Designer:** Christian Gobrecht

Date	Mintage	G4	VG8	F12	VF20	XF40	AU50	MS60	MS65	Prf65
1853	15,210,020	27.50	31.00	34.00	44.00	170	425	1,025	17,000	175,000
1853/4	Inc. above	40.00	70.00	110	200	400	650	1,750	55,000	—
1853O	1,332,000	35.50	45.00	54.00	85.00	300	1,000	2,850	35,000	—

Seated Liberty, arrows at date. Eagle with arrows in talons, value below.

KM# 81 • 6.22 g., 0.900 Silver 0.180 oz. ASW, 24.3 mm. • **Rev. Legend:** UNITED STATES OF AMERICA **Designer:** Christian Gobrecht

Date	Mintage	G4	VG8	F12	VF20	XF40	AU50	MS60	MS65	Prf65
1854	12,380,000	27.50	31.00	33.00	42.00	77.50	255	610	8,900	37,500
1854O	1,484,000	29.50	40.00	45.00	60.00	125	300	950	10,000	—
1854O huge O	Inc. above	800	1,400	2,650	4,350	7,400	12,500	—	—	—
1855	2,857,000	27.50	31.00	33.00	42.00	77.50	255	610	9,400	37,500
1855O	176,000	40.00	55.00	115	250	475	975	2,900	—	—
1855S	396,400	48.00	60.00	120	225	550	1,150	2,400	45,000	—

Seated Liberty, date below. Eagle with arrows in talons, value below.

KM# A64.2 • 6.22 g., 0.900 Silver 0.180 oz. ASW, 24.3 mm. • **Rev. Legend:** UNITED STATES OF AMERICA **Designer:** Christian Gobrecht

Date	Mintage	G4	VG8	F12	VF20	XF40	AU50	MS60	MS65	Prf65
1856	7,264,000	28.00	31.50	34.00	45.00	75.00	185	330	4,350	18,500
1856O	968,000	30.00	43.50	50.00	60.00	115	260	925	9,350	—
1856S	286,000	60.00	120	200	350	1,600	2,450	5,000	—	—
1856S/S	Inc. above	175	320	550	1,250	2,450	6,000	—	—	—
1857	9,644,000	28.00	31.50	34.00	45.00	75.00	185	330	4,000	11,500
1857O	1,180,000	35.00	33.50	50.00	47.00	175	420	950	—	—
1857S	82,000	100	150	250	400	700	1,350	2,900	—	—
1858	7,368,000	28.00	31.50	34.00	45.00	75.00	185	350	4,000	8,500
1858O	520,000	34.00	41.50	50.00	60.00	110	325	1,300	24,000	—
1858S	121,000	75.00	120	250	800	2,850	4,750	13,500	—	—
1859	1,344,000	30.00	33.50	36.00	47.00	80.00	185	350	7,750	7,000
1859O	260,000	36.00	33.50	50.00	65.00	185	400	1,100	13,500	—
1859S	80,000	150	250	400	900	3,250	15,500	—	—	—
1860	805,400	32.00	35.50	38.00	49.00	85.00	195	375	4,500	5,650
1860O	388,000	36.00	44.00	52.00	70.00	120	360	950	13,000	—
1860S	56,000	350	750	1,350	2,500	6,600	14,500	24,500	—	—
1861	4,854,600	30.00	33.50	36.00	47.00	80.00	195	360	3,350	5,650
1861S	96,000	175	325	750	1,850	4,100	9,750	—	—	—

Date	Mintage	G4	VG8	F12	VF20	XF40	AU50	MS60	MS65	Prf65
1862	932,550	32.00	35.50	44.00	53.00	90.00	190	350	4,450	5,650
1862S	67,000	65.00	130	250	475	880	1,400	3,500	—	—
1863	192,060	48.00	57.00	75.00	140	250	360	650	4,850	5,650
1864	94,070	80.00	100	130	225	400	450	775	5,000	5,650
1864S	20,000	450	650	1,150	2,150	3,450	4,850	12,500	—	—
1865	59,300	85.00	95.00	150	235	340	450	850	6,950	5,650
1865S	41,000	105	180	255	400	825	1,250	2,800	15,000	—
1866 unique	—	—	—	—	—	—	—	—	—	—

Seated Liberty, date below. "In God We Trust" above eagle.

KM# 98 • 6.22 g., 0.900 Silver 0.180 oz. ASW, 24.3 mm. • **Rev. Legend:** UNITED STATES OF AMERICA **Designer:** Christian Gobrecht **Note:** The 1873 closed-3 and open-3 varieties are distinguished by the amount of space between the upper left and lower left serifs in the 3.

Date	Mintage	G4	VG8	F12	VF20	XF40	AU50	MS60	MS65	Prf65
1866	17,525	450	600	750	1,050	1,400	1,700	2,350	6,950	2,750
1866S	28,000	295	390	750	1,400	1,950	2,600	3,500	17,500	—
1867	20,625	260	325	500	850	1,325	1,575	1,950	—	2,550
1867S	48,000	250	450	850	1,350	2,850	7,000	13,500	—	—
1868	30,000	150	200	275	385	500	675	900	7,350	2,650
1868S	96,000	100	185	325	450	775	1,350	2,850	15,000	—
1869	16,600	300	450	560	700	935	1,150	1,600	7,500	2,650
1869S	76,000	100	185	325	475	840	1,325	2,650	15,500	—
1870	87,400	55.00	65.00	130	190	275	360	850	6,500	2,650
1870CC	8,340	10,000	16,000	21,000	29,500	40,000	60,000	—	—	—
1871	119,160	33.00	47.50	60.00	125	300	425	725	8,500	2,500
1871CC	10,890	3,450	7,500	11,500	16,000	26,500	40,000	66,500	350,000	—
1871S	30,900	500	750	1,650	2,400	3,750	5,250	7,400	35,000	—
1872	182,950	30.00	55.00	75.00	110	270	400	1,100	8,500	2,550
1872CC	22,850	1,450	2,000	3,250	6,000	13,000	21,000	44,500	—	—
1872S	83,000	850	1,250	2,250	3,350	5,000	6,750	8,750	100,000	—
1873 closed 3	212,600	250	425	550	800	1,850	2,500	7,500	—	2,650
1873 open 3	Inc. above	32.00	47.50	62.00	130	175	200	450	8,250	—
1873CC 6 known	4,000	—	75,000	—	—	100,000	124,000	150,000	650,000	—

Note: 1873CC, Heritage, April 1999, MS-62, $106,375.

Seated Liberty, arrows at date. "In God We Trust" above eagle.

KM# 106 • 6.25 g., 0.900 Silver 0.1808 oz. ASW, 24.3 mm. • **Rev. Legend:** UNITED STATES OF AMERICA **Designer:** Christian Gobrecht

Date	Mintage	G4	VG8	F12	VF20	XF40	AU50	MS60	MS65	Prf65
1873	1,271,700	28.00	32.00	37.50	62.00	195	425	850	4,400	8,000
1873CC	12,462	5,000	9,500	12,500	18,500	26,500	48,500	100,000	175,000	—
1873S	156,000	35.00	45.00	85.00	175	325	525	1,450	20,000	—
1874	471,900	28.00	32.00	37.50	62.00	195	425	850	4,500	8,000
1874S	392,000	33.00	37.00	52.00	110	275	485	900	3,750	—

Seated Liberty, date below. "In God We Trust" above eagle.

KM# A98 • 6.25 g., 0.900 Silver 0.1808 oz. ASW, 24.3 mm. • **Rev. Legend:** UNITED STATES OF AMERICA **Designer:** Christian Gobrecht **Note:** The 1876-CC fine-reeding variety has a more finely reeded edge.

Date	Mintage	G4	VG8	F12	VF20	XF40	AU50	MS60	MS65	Prf65
1875	4,293,500	27.50	31.50	33.50	40.00	67.50	155	290	1,800	2,350
1875CC	140,000	95.00	160	270	450	900	1,250	3,800	30,000	—
1875S	680,000	40.00	50.00	67.00	110	190	275	575	3,350	—
1876	17,817,150	27.50	31.50	33.50	40.00	67.50	155	290	1,850	2,350
1876CC Ty1 rev. sm wide CC	4,944,000	60.00	80.00	95.00	125	185	310	600	5,500	—
1876CC Ty1 rev. sm close CC	Inc. above	55.00	73.00	87.50	110	175	275	500	4,250	—
1876CC Ty1 rev. tall CC	Inc. above	48.00	65.00	75.00	95.00	160	235	450	4,000	—
1876CC Ty2 rev. sm CC	Inc. above	48.00	65.00	75.00	95.00	160	235	450	4,150	—

Date	Mintage	G4	VG8	F12	VF20	XF40	AU50	MS60	MS65	Prf65
1876CC Ty2 rev tall CC	Inc. above	58.00	75.00	90.00	115	180	300	550	4,400	—
1876S	8,596,000	27.50	31.50	33.50	40.00	67.50	155	290	2,350	—
1877	10,911,710	27.50	31.50	33.50	40.00	67.50	155	290	1,800	2,350
1877CC	4,192,000	50.00	68.00	80.00	100	165	235	450	2,600	—
1877S	8,996,000	27.50	31.50	33.50	40.00	67.50	155	290	1,850	—
1877S over horizontal S	Inc. above	34.00	44.00	85.00	175	285	335	650	4,750	—
1878	2,260,800	27.50	31.50	33.50	40.00	67.50	165	310	3,000	2,350
1878CC	996,000	58.00	75.00	90.00	140	300	265	550	3,650	—
1878S	140,000	150	225	345	500	785	1,150	1,950	—	—
1879	14,700	180	235	255	325	375	485	600	2,000	2,350
1880	14,955	155	215	275	325	375	435	575	2,100	2,350
1881	12,975	200	250	280	350	400	455	550	2,250	2,350
1882	16,300	210	260	290	350	400	435	600	2,150	2,350
1883	15,439	200	240	280	365	400	465	585	2,800	2,350
1884	8,875	235	285	475	550	600	650	725	2,150	2,350
1885	14,530	165	225	340	280	400	475	610	2,900	2,350
1886	5,886	335	450	550	750	850	925	1,050	3,250	2,350
1887	10,710	225	300	385	450	500	550	700	2,500	2,350
1888	10,833	200	275	325	425	475	520	660	2,000	2,350
1888S	1,216,000	27.50	31.50	33.50	40.00	67.50	165	340	4,000	—
1889	12,711	185	275	300	350	425	475	600	1,900	2,350
1890	80,590	60.00	75.00	100	135	200	300	440	1,900	2,350
1891	3,920,600	27.50	31.50	33.50	42.00	67.50	155	290	1,800	2,350
1891O	68,000	240	400	500	1,350	2,350	3,500	4,850	28,500	—
1891S	2,216,000	28.50	32.50	35.50	43.00	73.00	165	295	2,100	—

Barber Quarter
Laureate head right, flanked by stars, date below.   Heraldic eagle.

KM# 114 • 6.25 g., 0.900 Silver 0.1808 oz. ASW, 24.3 mm. • **Obv. Legend:** IN GOD WE TRUST **Rev. Legend:** UNITED STATES OF AMERICA **Designer:** Charles E. Barber

Date	Mintage	G4	VG8	F12	VF20	XF40	AU50	MS60	MS65	Prf65
1892	8,237,245	12.00	15.50	30.00	50.00	76.00	155	285	—	2,450
1892 Type 2 Rev	Inc. above	10.75	12.50	25.00	44.00	70.00	130	250	1,350	2,450
1892O	2,640,000	22.00	30.00	51.00	80.00	125	185	400	—	—
1892O Type 2 Rev	Inc. above	15.00	23.50	44.00	61.00	98.00	155	340	1,600	—
1892S	964,079	50.00	75.00	115	160	225	350	650	—	—
1892S Type 2 Rev	Inc. above	35.00	59.00	92.00	145	210	310	500	4,500	—
1893	5,484,838	10.50	12.50	20.00	37.00	68.00	130	255	1,550	2,450
1893O	3,396,000	13.50	18.00	35.00	70.00	128	190	300	—	—
1893O MM far right	Inc. above	11.50	15.50	30.00	58.00	118	170	255	1,850	—
1893S	1,454,535	26.00	46.00	80.00	165	225	350	615	—	—
1893S MM far right	Inc. above	20.00	38.00	65.00	125	190	320	435	6,350	—
1894	3,432,972	10.75	12.50	30.00	46.00	87.00	145	255	1,300	2,450
1894O	2,852,000	12.25	24.00	50.00	105	159	235	420	—	—
1894O MM far right	Inc. above	11.75	18.50	42.00	81.00	138	210	315	2,000	—
1894S	2,648,821	12.00	17.50	41.00	76.00	147	210	410	—	—
1894S MM far right	Inc. above	11.75	13.00	34.50	71.00	126	190	295	2,650	—
1895	4,440,880	10.50	12.50	28.00	37.00	73.00	135	255	1,650	2,450
1895O	2,816,000	17.50	27.00	46.00	88.00	165	245	525	—	—
1895O MM far right	Inc. above	12.50	19.50	42.00	74.00	140	215	385	2,650	—
1895S	1,764,681	26.50	40.00	85.00	165	210	320	560	—	—
1895S MM far right	Inc. above	19.50	36.00	73.00	125	180	280	430	3,650	—
1896	3,874,762	10.50	12.00	23.00	39.00	82.00	135	255	1,150	2,450
1896O	1,484,000	62.00	98.00	210	355	650	900	1,150	6,950	—
1896S	188,039	725	1,525	2,450	3,950	5,425	7,250	9,750	50,000	—
1897	8,140,731	10.50	12.00	19.50	30.50	67.50	130	255	1,450	2,450
1897O	1,414,800	44.00	75.00	200	390	535	595	900	3,550	—
1897S	542,229	145	160	310	615	950	1,150	1,800	6,850	—
1898	11,100,735	10.50	12.00	20.50	34.00	72.00	130	255	1,150	2,450
1898O	1,868,000	16.00	29.00	74.00	150	290	425	680	8,950	—
1898S	1,020,592	12.50	19.50	50.00	67.00	103	215	395	7,950	—
1899	12,624,846	10.50	12.00	20.50	34.00	72.00	130	255	1,150	2,450
1899O	2,644,000	13.50	22.50	38.00	67.00	140	285	425	2,850	—
1899S	708,000	30.00	45.00	105	120	155	275	425	3,650	—
1900	10,016,912	10.50	12.00	44.00	35.00	72.00	133	265	1,550	2,450
1900O	3,416,000	15.50	29.00	127	120	175	345	565	3,750	—
1900S	1,858,585	11.75	14.50	35.00	50.00	75.00	133	350	4,950	—
1901	8,892,813	30.50	36.00	44.00	72.00	86.00	133	255	1,550	2,450
1901O	1,612,000	70.00	115	210	385	640	825	1,085	5,450	—
1901S	72,664	4,500	9,000	18,500	26,500	31,000	38,500	41,500	77,500	—
1902	12,197,744	8.75	9.75	17.50	30.50	63.00	128	255	1,100	2,450

Date	Mintage	G4	VG8	F12	VF20	XF40	AU50	MS60	MS65	Prf65
1902O	4,748,000	10.75	15.50	49.00	81.00	140	220	460	4,000	—
1902S	1,524,612	14.50	22.50	50.00	86.00	170	240	490	3,600	—
1903	9,670,064	8.75	9.75	18.50	33.00	70.00	128	255	2,150	2,450
1903O	3,500,000	10.75	13.50	37.00	61.00	123	245	425	4,850	—
1903S	1,036,000	15.50	26.00	42.00	86.00	145	265	425	2,450	—
1904	9,588,813	8.75	12.50	18.50	33.00	65.50	128	260	1,200	2,450
1904O	2,456,000	30.50	45.00	87.00	160	215	435	850	2,650	—
1905	4,968,250	30.50	36.00	47.00	62.00	69.00	133	255	1,500	2,450
1905O	1,230,000	44.00	62.50	125	235	255	340	460	6,850	—
1905S	1,884,000	32.50	42.00	70.00	105	110	205	325	3,650	—
1906	3,656,435	8.75	9.75	17.50	30.50	62.50	128	255	1,100	2,450
1906D	3,280,000	9.25	17.50	44.00	39.00	64.50	143	255	1,675	—
1906O	2,056,000	10.50	15.75	38.00	57.00	110	187	275	1,150	—
1907	7,192,575	8.75	9.75	16.00	30.50	60.00	125	255	1,100	2,450
1907D	2,484,000	8.75	9.75	25.00	47.00	74.00	170	255	2,650	—
1907O	4,560,000	10.50	13.00	17.50	37.00	62.50	133	255	1,950	—
1907S	1,360,000	10.50	18.50	44.00	67.00	130	250	465	5,650	—
1908	4,232,545	8.75	9.75	17.50	30.00	62.50	125	255	1,100	2,450
1908D	5,788,000	8.75	9.75	16.00	34.00	62.50	125	255	1,100	—
1908O	6,244,000	10.50	12.50	16.00	35.00	69.00	135	255	1,100	—
1908S	784,000	32.00	67.50	140	160	290	465	710	4,750	—
1909	9,268,650	8.75	9.75	16.00	30.50	60.00	125	255	1,100	2,450
1909D	5,114,000	8.75	9.75	20.00	37.00	82.00	150	255	1,350	—
1909O	712,000	42.00	120	445	875	1,625	2,300	3,050	8,750	—
1909S	1,348,000	10.75	14.50	34.00	51.00	87.00	180	285	2,250	—
1910	2,244,551	8.75	10.25	27.00	41.00	74.00	133	255	1,100	2,450
1910D	1,500,000	9.00	11.00	42.00	67.00	120	240	340	1,875	—
1911	3,720,543	8.75	9.75	18.50	30.50	69.00	125	255	1,100	2,450
1911D	933,600	30.50	45.00	165	310	455	650	485	5,750	—
1911S	988,000	10.50	13.00	52.00	92.00	170	275	385	1,425	—
1912	4,400,700	8.75	9.75	16.00	30.50	53.50	125	255	1,100	2,485
1912S	708,000	26.00	33.00	72.00	100	128	215	400	1,675	—
1913	484,613	29.00	47.00	120	180	375	490	900	4,450	2,485
1913D	1,450,800	12.50	14.00	34.50	52.00	88.00	170	255	1,200	—
1913S	40,000	1,625	2,450	5,200	7,950	10,550	13,750	14,750	31,500	—
1914	6,244,610	8.75	9.75	16.00	30.50	53.50	125	255	1,100	2,550
1914D	3,046,000	8.75	9.75	16.00	28.50	53.50	125	255	1,100	—
1914S	264,000	139	205	425	625	925	1,080	1,375	3,450	—
1915	3,480,450	8.75	9.75	16.00	27.50	60.50	125	255	1,100	2,485
1915D	3,694,000	8.75	9.75	16.00	27.50	60.50	125	255	1,100	—
1915S	704,000	28.00	42.00	61.00	92.00	98.00	200	290	1,200	—
1916	1,788,000	8.75	9.75	16.00	27.50	53.50	125	255	1,100	—
1916D	6,540,800	8.75	9.75	16.00	27.50	53.50	125	235	1,100	—
1916D/D	Inc. above	12.50	15.50	21.00	32.00	59.00	148	300	—	—

Standing Liberty Quarter
Right breast exposed; Type 1.

KM# 141 • 6.25 g., 0.900 Silver 0.1808 oz. ASW, 24.3 mm. • **Designer:** Hermon A. MacNeil

Right breast exposed

Date	Mintage	G4	VG8	F12	VF20	XF40	AU50	MS60	MS65	MS65FH
1916	52,000	2,850	5,650	6,900	9,000	9,500	12,000	14,000	25,000	36,500
1917	8,792,000	—	50.00	63.50	85.00	120	182	230	695	850
1917D	1,509,200	28.00	67.50	90.00	130	200	240	310	1,225	1,650
1917S	1,952,000	30.00	75.00	105	155	220	280	340	1,150	3,200

Right breast covered; Type 2.   Three stars below eagle.

KM# 145 • 6.25 g., 0.900 Silver 0.1808 oz. ASW, 24.3 mm. • **Designer:** Hermon A. MacNeil

Right breast covered   Mint mark

Date	Mintage	G4	VG8	F12	VF20	XF40	AU50	MS60	MS65	MS65FH
1917	13,880,000	25.00	35.00	52.00	72.00	97.50	135	200	600	900
1917D	6,224,400	40.00	45.00	86.00	120	155	210	265	1,550	3,350
1917S	5,522,000	40.00	45.00	88.00	115	148	200	255	1,085	3,650
1918	14,240,000	17.00	21.00	27.50	30.00	43.00	75.00	150	510	1,750
1918D	7,380,000	26.00	36.00	68.50	75.00	135	190	275	1,750	4,850
1918S	11,072,000	17.00	21.00	30.00	35.00	50.00	85.00	170	1,150	10,500
1918/17S	Inc. above	1,550	2,250	3,650	4,850	7.500	11,750	15,000	90,000	320,000
1919	11,324,000	33.00	44.00	58.50	70.00	80.00	118	170	510	1,275
1919D	1,944,000	85.00	110	200	400	595	775	950	2,875	37,500
1919S	1,836,000	80.00	105	170	285	490	675	735	3,850	31,500
1920	27,860,000	15.00	18.00	24.00	37.00	50.00	88.00	150	510	1,850
1920D	3,586,400	48.00	65.00	82.00	120	160	220	335	2,050	6,850
1920S	6,380,000	19.00	25.00	28.00	37.00	57.00	155	225	2,250	24,000
1921	1,916,000	165	210	400	635	810	1,100	1,650	3,850	5,500
1923	9,716,000	15.00	18.00	33.00	37.00	43.00	95.00	155	550	3,850
1923S	1,360,000	300	425	665	1,000	1,550	2,000	2,600	5,250	7,500
1924	10,920,000	15.00	18.00	23.00	35.00	46.00	110	185	525	1,550
1924D	3,112,000	56.00	68.00	105	135	185	235	295	540	4,350
1924S	2,860,000	27.00	32.00	43.00	60.00	120	220	310	1,650	5,650
1925	12,280,000	7.90	8.90	10.50	18.00	44.00	88.00	170	520	950
1926	11,316,000	7.90	8.50	9.60	14.00	36.00	72.50	168	495	1,650
1926D	1,716,000	6.50	10.00	25.00	47.50	92.00	135	170	465	25,000
1926S	2,700,000	8.20	8.80	11.50	24.00	105	215	325	1,850	26,000
1927	11,912,000	7.90	8.50	9.60	11.00	28.00	72.50	125	515	1,150
1927D	976,400	14.00	19.00	30.00	73.50	145	210	250	565	2,450
1927S	396,000	35.00	48.00	110	295	925	2,600	4,500	11,000	185,000
1928	6,336,000	7.90	8.50	9.60	12.00	28.00	72.50	125	515	1,850
1928D	1,627,600	8.40	9.00	10.60	20.00	42.50	84.00	130	465	4,950
1928S Large S	2,644,000	9.90	11.00	15.00	25.00	65.00	115	200	—	—
1928S Small S	Inc. above	8.20	8.80	10.30	16.50	38.00	75.00	130	525	900
1929	11,140,000	7.90	8.50	9.60	12.00	28.00	72.50	125	465	795
1929D	1,358,000	8.40	9.00	10.60	16.00	38.50	77.50	130	465	5,850
1929S	1,764,000	8.20	8.80	10.10	15.00	34.00	77.50	130	465	795
1930	5,632,000	7.90	8.50	9.60	11.00	28.00	72.50	125	465	795
1930S	1,556,000	8.20	8.80	9.60	11.50	34.00	77.50	130	465	845

Washington Quarter

KM# 164 • 6.25 g., 0.900 Silver 0.1808 oz. ASW, 24.3 mm. • **Designer:** John Flanagan

Mint mark 1932-64

Date	Mintage	G4	VG8	F12	VF20	XF40	AU50	MS60	MS65	Prf65
1932	5,404,000	5.00	5.10	5.20	5.30	9.50	14.50	25.00	300	—
1932D	436,800	115	125	140	180	290	440	1,150	12,500	—
1932S	408,000	125	140	150	165	225	260	465	4,000	—
1934 Medium Motto	31,912,052	5.00	5.60	5.90	6.30	7.60	10.50	26.00	100	—
1934 Heavy Motto	Inc. Above	4.80	4.90	9.00	12.50	18.00	30.00	50.00	265	—
1934 Light motto	Inc. Above	5.40	6.20	10.00	12.00	15.00	26.00	45.00	340	—
1934 Doubled Die Obverse	Inc. Above	75.00	100	165	200	320	450	850	4,250	—
1934D Medium Motto	3,527,200	4.80	4.90	11.50	18.50	29.00	85.00	235	825	—
1934D Heavy Motto	Inc. Above	5.00	7.50	12.50	20.00	34.00	100	265	1,350	—
1935	32,484,000	4.80	5.00	5.30	5.80	7.30	10.00	20.00	110	—
1935D	5,780,000	5.50	5.80	6.50	16.50	33.50	125	245	595	—
1935S	5,660,000	5.00	5.20	6.20	7.30	15.50	36.50	95.00	310	—
1936	41,303,837	4.80	5.00	5.30	5.80	7.30	9.50	26.00	100	1,550
1936D	5,374,000	5.50	5.80	10.50	26.00	52.00	255	585	975	—
1936S	3,828,000	5.20	5.50	6.20	6.70	14.50	48.50	108	345	—

QUARTER

Date	Mintage	G4	VG8	F12	VF20	XF40	AU50	MS60	MS65	Prf65
1937	19,701,542	4.80	5.00	5.30	7.20	10.00	16.50	22.00	90.00	475
1937 Double Die Obverse	Inc. Above	75.00	100	235	340	450	850	1,850	11,500	—
1937D	7,189,600	5.00	5.20	6.20	6.60	16.50	38.00	67.50	150	—
1937S	1,652,000	5.50	5.80	6.60	22.00	34.00	95.00	160	430	—
1938	9,480,045	5.00	5.20	6.20	6.60	18.00	49.00	90.00	215	350
1938S	2,832,000	5.50	5.70	5.90	9.75	22.50	55.00	108	215	—
1939	33,548,795	4.80	5.00	5.30	5.80	6.90	7.00	15.50	55.00	250
1939D	7,092,000	5.00	5.20	5.80	7.30	12.00	19.50	42.00	122	—
1939S	2,628,000	5.50	5.80	6.30	12.00	26.00	60.00	105	275	—
1940	35,715,246	4.80	5.00	5.30	5.80	6.80	7.50	17.50	53.50	160
1940D	2,797,600	5.00	5.20	5.30	12.50	26.00	65.00	130	300	—
1940S	8,244,000	5.00	5.20	5.30	5.40	9.00	16.50	28.50	52.00	—
1941	79,047,287	—	—	—	—	5.00	5.20	9.50	36.00	175
1941 Double Die Obv.	Inc. Above	—	—	—	20.00	40.00	50.00	65.00	120	—
1941D	16,714,800	—	—	—	5.50	6.60	15.00	33.00	66.00	—
1941S	16,080,000	—	—	—	5.70	5.80	12.50	30.00	65.00	—
1941 Lg S	Inc. Above	—	5.80	12.00	20.00	30.00	50.00	100	350	—
1942	102,117,123	—	—	—	—	4.90	5.10	6.60	29.00	135
1942D	17,487,200	—	—	—	5.50	6.70	11.00	18.00	38.00	—
1942D Double Die Obv.	Inc. Above	—	115	250	440	650	1,350	2,150	5,000	—
1942D Double Die Rev.	Inc. Above	—	22.00	40.00	60.00	75.00	150	350	1,850	—
1942S	19,384,000	—	—	—	5.60	11.00	22.50	70.00	135	—
1943	99,700,000	—	—	—	—	4.90	5.10	6.60	39.00	—
1943 Double Die Obv.	Inc. Above	—	12.00	20.00	35.00	50.00	90.00	175	450	—
1943D	16,095,600	—	—	—	5.70	6.80	16.50	29.00	50.00	—
1943S	21,700,000	—	—	5.40	5.80	6.20	14.50	27.00	51.50	—
1943S Double Die Obv.	Inc. Above	30.00	60.00	80.00	110	150	265	400	1,200	—
1943 Trumpet tail S	Inc. Above	10.00	15.00	25.00	40.00	60.00	100	175	675	—
1944	104,956,000	—	—	—	—	4.90	5.10	5.70	29.00	—
1944D	14,600,800	—	—	—	5.40	5.50	11.00	19.00	38.50	—
1944S	12,560,000	—	—	—	5.40	5.50	9.50	14.50	31.00	—
1945	74,372,000	—	—	—	—	4.90	5.10	5.70	34.00	—
1945D	12,341,600	—	—	—	5.50	7.50	11.00	18.00	37.00	—
1945S	17,004,001	—	—	—	5.30	5.40	5.60	8.50	32.00	—
1946	53,436,000	—	—	—	—	4.90	5.10	5.70	38.00	—
1946D	9,072,800	—	—	—	5.40	6.00	6.20	9.75	40.00	—
1946S	4,204,000	—	—	—	5.40	6.00	6.20	6.90	34.00	—
1947	22,556,000	—	—	—	—	6.00	6.20	11.50	39.00	—
1947D	15,338,400	—	—	—	5.40	5.90	6.10	11.00	39.00	—
1947S	5,532,000	—	—	—	5.40	5.90	6.10	9.25	28.00	—
1948	35,196,000	—	—	—	5.40	5.90	6.10	5.90	30.00	—
1948D	16,766,800	—	—	—	5.40	6.00	6.40	13.00	45.00	—
1948S	15,960,000	—	—	—	5.40	5.90	6.10	6.70	40.00	—
1949	9,312,000	—	—	—	5.50	6.50	15.00	36.00	62.00	—
1949D	10,068,400	—	—	—	5.30	6.00	9.50	16.50	48.00	—
1950	24,971,512	—	—	—	—	5.50	7.00	10.00	30.00	65.00
1950D	21,075,600	—	—	—	—	5.00	5.20	5.90	32.00	—
1950D/S	Inc. Above	30.00	37.00	45.00	75.00	140	225	350	5,000	—
1950S	10,284,004	—	—	—	—	5.60	7.50	13.50	34.00	—
1950S/D	Inc. Above	32.00	44.00	65.00	125	180	285	400	1,250	—
1950S/S	Inc. Above	6.00	7.00	8.00	10.00	14.00	18.00	35.00	135	—
1951	43,505,602	—	—	—	—	4.90	5.10	8.00	27.00	60.00
1951D	35,354,800	—	—	—	—	5.10	5.70	8.50	26.00	—
1951S	9,048,000	—	—	4.70	5.60	7.50	11.00	21.00	40.00	—
1952	38,862,073	—	—	—	—	4.90	5.80	9.10	28.00	46.00
1952D	49,795,200	—	—	—	—	4.90	5.10	6.70	32.00	—
1952S	13,707,800	—	—	—	5.50	5.60	11.00	15.00	32.00	—
1953	18,664,920	—	—	—	—	5.50	6.40	10.00	25.00	44.00
1953D	56,112,400	—	—	—	—	4.90	5.10	6.20	22.00	—
1953S	14,016,000	—	—	—	—	4.90	5.10	6.50	28.00	—
1954	54,645,503	—	—	—	—	4.90	5.10	5.70	24.00	18.00
1954D	42,305,500	—	—	—	—	4.90	5.10	5.70	24.00	—
1954S	11,834,722	—	—	—	—	4.90	5.10	6.20	22.00	—
1955	18,558,381	—	—	—	—	4.90	5.10	5.70	26.00	22.00
1955D	3,182,400	—	—	—	—	5.60	6.00	6.70	24.00	—
1956	44,813,384	—	—	—	—	4.90	5.10	5.70	22.00	15.00
1956 Double Bar 5	Inc. Above	—	5.60	5.70	5.80	6.50	9.00	20.00	125	—
1956 Type B rev, proof rev die	Inc. Above	—	—	8.00	12.00	18.00	25.00	35.00	275	—
1956D	32,334,500	—	—	—	—	4.90	5.10	5.70	15.00	—
1957	47,779,952	—	—	—	—	4.90	5.10	5.70	14.00	12.00
1957 Type B rev, proof rev die	Inc. Above	—	—	—	5.60	10.00	20.00	40.00	125	—
1957D	77,924,160	—	—	—	—	4.90	5.10	5.70	16.00	—
1958	7,235,652	—	—	—	—	4.90	5.10	5.70	12.00	12.00
1958 Type B rev, proof rev die	Inc. Above	—	—	—	5.60	10.00	16.00	24.00	90.00	—
1958D	78,124,900	—	—	—	—	4.90	5.10	5.70	15.00	—
1959	25,533,291	—	—	—	—	4.90	5.10	5.70	12.00	12.00
1959 Type B rev, proof rev die	Inc. Above	—	—	—	5.80	8.00	12.00	18.00	65.00	—

Date	Mintage	G4	VG8	F12	VF20	XF40	AU50	MS60	MS65	Prf65
1959D	62,054,232	—	—	—	—	4.90	5.10	5.70	18.00	—
1960	30,855,602	—	—	—	—	4.90	5.10	5.70	14.00	12.00
1960 Type B rev, proof rev die	Inc. Above	—	—	—	5.10	10.00	16.00	24.00	90.00	—
1960D	63,000,324	—	—	—	—	4.90	5.10	5.70	14.00	—
1961	40,064,244	—	—	—	—	4.90	5.10	5.70	15.00	12.00
1961 Type B rev, proof rev die	Inc. Above	—	—	—	5.80	10.00	14.00	20.00	200	—
1961D	83,656,928	—	—	—	—	4.90	5.10	5.70	20.00	—
1962	39,374,019	—	—	—	—	4.90	5.10	5.70	15.00	12.00
1962 Type B rev, proof rev die	Inc. Above	—	—	—	8.00	12.00	15.00	30.00	175	—
1962D	127,554,756	—	—	—	—	4.90	5.10	5.70	22.00	—
1963	77,391,645	—	—	—	—	4.90	5.10	5.70	12.00	12.00
1963 Type B rev, proof rev die	Inc. Above	—	—	—	5.80	5.90	8.00	15.00	50.00	—
1963D	135,288,184	—	—	—	—	4.90	5.10	5.70	15.00	—
1964	564,341,347	—	—	—	—	4.90	5.10	5.70	12.00	12.00
1964 Type B rev, proof rev die	Inc. Above	—	—	—	5.80	9.00	10.00	18.00	75.00	—
1964 SMS	Inc. Above	—	—	—	—	—	250	750	1,400	—
1964D	704,135,528	—	—	—	—	4.90	5.10	5.70	12.00	—
1964D Type C rev, clad rev die	Inc. Above	—	—	—	40.00	55.00	75.00	125	450	—

KM# 164a • 5.67 g., Copper-Nickel Clad Copper, 24.3 mm. • **Designer:** John Flanagan

Date	Mintage	MS65	Prf65
1965	1,819,717,540	10.00	—
1965 SMS	2,360,000	9.00	—
1966	821,101,500	7.50	—
1966 SMS	2,261,583	9.00	—
1967	1,524,031,848	10.00	—
1967 SMS	1,863,344	9.00	—
1968	220,731,500	10.00	—
1968D	101,534,000	7.00	—
1968S	3,041,506	—	2.00

Date	Mintage	MS65	Prf65
1969	176,212,000	14.00	—
1969D	114,372,000	8.00	—
1969S	2,934,631	—	2.25
1970	136,420,000	12.00	—
1970D	417,341,364	6.00	—
1970S	2,632,810	—	2.00
1971	109,284,000	12.00	—
1971D	258,634,428	6.00	—
1971S	3,220,733	—	2.00
1972	215,048,000	7.50	—
1972D	311,067,732	6.00	—
1972S	3,260,996	—	2.00
1973	346,924,000	8.00	—
1973D	232,977,400	7.00	—
1973S	2,760,339	—	1.75
1974	801,456,000	6.00	—
1974D	353,160,300	8.00	—
1974S	2,612,568	—	2.10
1975 none minted		—	—
1975D none minted		—	—
1975S none minted		—	—

Colonial drummer, torch at top left within ring of stars.

KM# 204 • 5.67 g., Copper-Nickel Clad Copper, 24.3 mm. • **Rev. Designer:** Jack L. Ahr

Date	Mintage	G4	VG8	F12	VF20	XF40	MS60	MS65	Prf65
1976	809,784,016	—	—	—	—	—	0.50	7.00	—
1976D	860,118,839	—	—	—	—	—	0.50	8.00	—
1976S	4,149,730	—	—	—	—	—	—	—	3.25

Bicentennial design, drummer boy.

KM# 204a • 5.75 g., Silver Clad, 24.3 mm. • **Rev. Designer:** Jack L. Ahr

Date	Mintage	G4	VG8	F12	VF20	XF40	MS60	MS65	Prf65
1976S	4,908,319	—	—	—	—	—	1.85	6.00	—
1976S	3,998,621	—	—	—	—	—	1.85	6.00	4.50

Eagle, regular design resumed.

KM# A164a • 5.67 g., Copper-Nickel Clad Copper, 24.3 mm. • **Edge:** Reeded **Note:** KM#164 design and composition resumed. The 1979-S and 1981 Type II proofs have clearer mint marks than the Type I proofs for those years.

Date	Mintage	MS65	Prf65
1977	468,556,000	7.50	—
1977D	256,524,978	8.00	—
1977S	3,251,152	—	2.75
1978	521,452,000	6.00	—
1978D	287,373,152	7.00	—

Date	Mintage	MS65	Prf65
1978S	3,127,781	—	2.75
1979	515,708,000	8.00	—
1979D	489,789,780	7.00	—
1979S T-I	3,677,175	—	2.50
1979S T-II	Inc. above	—	4.00

QUARTER

Date	Mintage	MS65	Prf65
1980P	635,832,000	8.00	—
1980D	518,327,487	8.50	—
1980S	3,554,806	—	2.75
1981P	601,716,000	7.50	—
1981D	575,722,833	6.50	—
1981S T-I	4,063,083	—	2.75
1981S T-II	Inc. above	—	7.50
1982P	500,931,000	28.00	—
1982D	480,042,788	15.00	—
1982S	3,857,479	—	4.00
1983P	673,535,000	50.00	—
1983D	617,806,446	30.00	—
1983S	3,279,126	—	3.00
1984P	676,545,000	14.50	—
1984D	546,483,064	12.50	—
1984S	3,065,110	—	3.00
1985P	775,818,962	12.50	—
1985D	519,962,888	10.00	—
1985S	3,362,821	—	3.00
1986P	551,199,333	11.00	—
1986D	504,298,660	15.00	—
1986S	3,010,497	—	3.00
1987P	582,499,481	10.50	—
1987D	655,594,696	8.50	—
1987S	4,227,728	—	3.00
1988P	562,052,000	10.00	—
1988D	596,810,688	7.50	—
1988S	3,262,948	—	3.00
1989P	512,868,000	16.00	—
1989D	896,535,597	7.50	—
1989S	3,220,194	—	3.00
1990P	613,792,000	12.00	—
1990D	927,638,181	6.00	—
1990S	3,299,559	—	4.50
1991P	570,968,000	10.00	—
1991D	630,966,693	12.00	—
1991S	2,867,787	—	3.00
1992P	384,764,000	20.00	—
1992D	389,777,107	12.00	—
1992S	2,858,981	—	3.00
1993P	639,276,000	7.50	—
1993D	645,476,128	8.50	—
1993S	2,633,439	—	3.00
1994P	825,600,000	8.00	—
1994D	880,034,110	8.00	—
1994S	2,484,594	—	3.00
1995P	1,004,336,000	7.50	—
1995D	1,103,216,000	6.50	—
1995S	2,117,496	—	6.00
1996P	925,040,000	7.50	—
1996D	906,868,000	11.00	—
1996S	1,750,244	—	4.00
1997P	595,740,000	22.50	—
1997D	599,680,000	17.00	—
1997S	2,055,000	—	9.00
1998P	896,268,000	14.00	—
1998D	821,000,000	18.00	—
1998S	2,086,507	—	9.00

KM# A164b • 6.25 g., 0.900 Silver 0.1808 oz. ASW, 24.3 mm. •

Date	Mintage	Prf65
1992S	1,317,579	6.80
1993S	761,353	—
1994S	785,329	—
1995S	838,953	8.00
1996S	775,021	—
1997S	741,678	8.00
1998S	878,792	6.80

50 State Quarters

Delaware

KM# 293 • 5.67 g., Copper-Nickel Clad Copper, 24.3 mm.

Date	Mintage	MS63	MS65	Prf65
1999P	373,400,000	1.00	5.00	—
1999D	401,424,000	1.00	7.00	—
1999S	3,713,359	—	—	3.50

KM# 293a • 6.25 g., 0.900 Silver 0.1808 oz. ASW, 24.3 mm.

Date	Mintage	MS63	MS65	Prf65
1999S	804,565	—	—	20.00

Pennsylvania

KM# 294 • 5.67 g., Copper-Nickel Clad Copper, 24.3 mm.

Date	Mintage	MS63	MS65	Prf65
1999P	349,000,000	1.00	5.00	—
1999D	358,332,000	1.00	4.00	—
1999S	3,713,359	—	—	3.50

KM# 294a • 6.25 g., 0.900 Silver 0.1808 oz. ASW, 24.3 mm.

Date	Mintage	MS63	MS65	Prf65
1999S	804,565	—	—	20.00

New Jersey

KM# 295 • 5.67 g., Copper-Nickel Clad Copper, 24.3 mm.

Date	Mintage	MS63	MS65	Prf65
1999P	363,200,000	1.00	5.00	—
1999D	299,028,000	1.00	4.00	—
1999S	3,713,359	—	—	3.50

KM# 295a • 6.25 g., 0.900 Silver 0.1808 oz. ASW, 24.3 mm.

Date	Mintage	MS63	MS65	Prf65
1999S	804,565	—	—	20.00

QUARTER

Georgia

KM# 296 • 5.67 g., Copper-Nickel Clad Copper, 24.3 mm.

Date	Mintage	MS63	MS65	Prf65
1999P	451,188,000	1.00	4.50	—
1999D	488,744,000	1.00	4.50	—
1999S	3,713,359	—	—	3.50

KM# 296a • 6.25 g., 0.900 Silver 0.1808 oz. ASW, 24.3 mm.

Date	Mintage	MS63	MS65	Prf65
1999S	804,565	—	—	20.00

Connecticut

KM# 297 • 5.67 g., Copper-Nickel Clad Copper, 24.3 mm.

Date	Mintage	MS63	MS65	Prf65
1999P	688,744,000	0.80	6.00	—
1999D	657,480,000	0.80	5.00	—
1999S	3,713,359	—	—	3.50

KM# 297a • 6.25 g., 0.900 Silver 0.1808 oz. ASW, 24.3 mm.

Date	Mintage	MS63	MS65	Prf65
1999S	804,565	—	—	20.00

Massachusetts

KM# 305 • 5.67 g., Copper-Nickel Clad Copper, 24.3 mm.

Date	Mintage	MS63	MS65	Prf65
2000P	629,800,000	0.80	7.00	—
2000D	535,184,000	0.80	8.00	—
2000S	4,078,747	—	—	3.00

KM# 305a • 6.25 g., 0.900 Silver 0.1808 oz. ASW, 24.3 mm.

Date	Mintage	MS63	MS65	Prf65
2000S	965,921	—	—	9.00

Maryland

KM# 306 • 5.67 g., Copper-Nickel Clad Copper, 24.3 mm.

Date	Mintage	MS63	MS65	Prf65
2000P	678,200,000	0.80	6.00	—
2000D	556,526,000	0.80	6.00	—
2000S	4,078,747	—	—	3.00

KM# 306a • 6.25 g., 0.900 Silver 0.1808 oz. ASW, 24.3 mm.

Date	Mintage	MS63	MS65	Prf65
2000S	965,921	—	—	9.00

South Carolina

KM# 307 • 5.67 g., Copper-Nickel Clad Copper, 24.3 mm.

Date	Mintage	MS63	MS65	Prf65
2000P	742,756,000	0.80	6.00	—
2000D	566,208,000	0.80	9.00	—
2000S	4,078,747	—	—	3.00

KM# 307a • 6.25 g., 0.900 Silver 0.1808 oz. ASW, 24.3 mm.

Date	Mintage	MS63	MS65	Prf65
2000S	965,921	—	—	9.00

New Hampshire

KM# 308 • 5.67 g., Copper-Nickel Clad Copper, 24.3 mm.

Date	Mintage	MS63	MS65	Prf65
2000P	673,040,000	0.80	8.00	—
2000D	495,976,000	0.80	9.00	—
2000S	4,078,747	—	—	3.00

KM# 308a • 6.25 g., 0.900 Silver 0.1808 oz. ASW, 24.3 mm.

Date	Mintage	MS63	MS65	Prf65
2000S	965,921	—	—	9.00

Virginia

KM# 309 • 5.67 g., Copper-Nickel Clad Copper, 24.3 mm.

Date	Mintage	MS63	MS65	Prf65
2000P	943,000,000	0.80	6.50	—
2000D	651,616,000	0.80	6.50	—
2000S	4,078,747	—	—	3.00

KM# 309a • 6.25 g., 0.900 Silver 0.1808 oz. ASW, 24.3 mm.

Date	Mintage	MS63	MS65	Prf65
2000S	965,921	—	—	9.50

QUARTER

New York

KM# 318 • 5.67 g., Copper-Nickel Clad Copper, 24.3 mm.

Date	Mintage	MS63	MS65	Prf65
2001P	655,400,000	0.80	5.50	—
2001D	619,640,000	0.80	5.50	—
2001S	3,094,140	—	—	4.00

KM# 318a • 6.25 g., 0.900 Silver 0.1808 oz. ASW, 24.3 mm.

Date	Mintage	MS63	MS65	Prf65
2001S	889,697	—	—	9.50

North Carolina

KM# 319 • 5.67 g., Copper-Nickel Clad Copper, 24.3 mm.

Date	Mintage	MS63	MS65	Prf65
2001P	627,600,000	1.00	5.50	—
2001D	427,876,000	1.00	6.50	—
2001S	3,094,140	—	—	4.00

KM# 319a • 6.25 g., 0.900 Silver 0.1808 oz. ASW, 24.3 mm.

Date	Mintage	MS63	MS65	Prf65
2001S	889,697	—	—	9.50

Rhode Island

KM# 320 • 5.67 g., Copper-Nickel Clad Copper, 24.3 mm.

Date	Mintage	MS63	MS65	Prf65
2001P	423,000,000	0.80	5.50	—
2001D	447,100,000	0.80	6.00	—
2001S	3,094,140	—	—	4.00

KM# 320a • 6.25 g., 0.900 Silver 0.1808 oz. ASW, 24.3 mm.

Date	Mintage	MS63	MS65	Prf65
2001S	889,697	—	—	9.50

Vermont

KM# 321 • 5.67 g., Copper-Nickel Clad Copper, 24.3 mm.

Date	Mintage	MS63	MS65	Prf65
2001P	423,400,000	0.80	6.50	—
2001D	459,404,000	0.80	6.50	—
2001S	3,094,140	—	—	4.00

KM# 321a • 6.25 g., 0.900 Silver 0.1808 oz. ASW, 24.3 mm.

Date	Mintage	MS63	MS65	Prf65
2001S	889,697	—	—	9.50

Kentucky

KM# 322 • 5.67 g., Copper-Nickel Clad Copper, 24.3 mm.

Date	Mintage	MS63	MS65	Prf65
2001P	353,000,000	1.00	6.50	—
2001D	370,564,000	1.00	7.00	—
2001S	3,094,140	—	—	4.00

KM# 322a • 6.25 g., 0.900 Silver 0.1808 oz. ASW, 24.3 mm.

Date	Mintage	MS63	MS65	Prf65
2001S	889,697	—	—	9.50

Tennessee

KM# 331 • 5.67 g., Copper-Nickel Clad Copper, 24.3 mm.

Date	Mintage	MS63	MS65	Prf65
2002P	361,600,000	1.40	6.50	—
2002D	286,468,000	1.40	7.00	—
2002S	3,084,245	—	—	2.30

KM# 331a • 6.25 g., 0.900 Silver 0.1808 oz. ASW, 24.3 mm.

Date	Mintage	MS63	MS65	Prf65
2002S	892,229	—	—	8.50

QUARTER

Ohio

KM# 332 • 5.67 g., Copper-Nickel Clad Copper, 24.3 mm.

Date	Mintage	MS63	MS65	Prf65
2002P	217,200,000	0.80	5.50	—
2002D	414,832,000	0.80	5.50	—
2002S	3,084,245	—	—	2.30

KM# 332a • 6.25 g., 0.900 Silver 0.1808 oz. ASW, 24.3 mm.

Date	Mintage	MS63	MS65	Prf65
2002S	892,229	—	—	8.50

Louisiana

KM# 333 • 5.67 g., Copper-Nickel Clad Copper, 24.3 mm.

Date	Mintage	MS63	MS65	Prf65
2002P	362,000,000	0.80	5.50	—
2002D	402,204,000	0.80	6.00	—
2002S	3,084,245	—	—	2.30

KM# 333a • 6.25 g., 0.900 Silver 0.1808 oz. ASW, 24.3 mm.

Date	Mintage	MS63	MS65	Prf65
2002S	892,229	—	—	8.50

Indiana

KM# 334 • 5.67 g., Copper-Nickel Clad Copper, 24.3 mm.

Date	Mintage	MS63	MS65	Prf65
2002P	362,600,000	0.80	5.00	—
2002D	327,200,000	0.80	5.00	—
2002S	3,084,245	—	—	2.30

KM# 334a • 6.25 g., 0.900 Silver 0.1808 oz. ASW, 24.3 mm.

Date	Mintage	MS63	MS65	Prf65
2002S	892,229	—	—	8.50

Mississippi

KM# 335 • 5.67 g., Copper-Nickel Clad Copper, 24.3 mm.

Date	Mintage	MS63	MS65	Prf65
2002P	290,000,000	0.80	5.00	—
2002D	289,600,000	0.80	5.00	—
2002S	3,084,245	—	—	2.30

KM# 335a • 6.25 g., 0.900 Silver 0.1808 oz. ASW, 24.3 mm.

Date	Mintage	MS63	MS65	Prf65
2002S	892,229	—	—	8.50

Illinois

KM# 343 • 5.67 g., Copper-Nickel Clad Copper, 24.3 mm.

Date	Mintage	MS63	MS65	Prf65
2003P	225,800,000	1.10	5.00	—
2003D	237,400,000	1.10	5.00	—
2003S	3,408,516	—	—	2.30

KM# 343a • 6.25 g., 0.900 Silver 0.1808 oz. ASW, 24.3 mm.

Date	Mintage	MS63	MS65	Prf65
2003S	1,257,555	—	—	8.50

Alabama

KM# 344 • 5.67 g., Copper-Nickel Clad Copper, 24.3 mm.

Date	Mintage	MS63	MS65	Prf65
2003P	225,000,000	0.65	5.00	—
2003D	232,400,000	0.65	5.00	—
2003S	3,408,516	—	—	2.30

KM# 344a • 6.25 g., 0.900 Silver 0.1808 oz. ASW, 24.3 mm.

Date	Mintage	MS63	MS65	Prf65
2003S	1,257,555	—	—	8.50

Maine

KM# 345 • 5.67 g., Copper-Nickel Clad Copper, 24.3 mm.

Date	Mintage	MS63	MS65	Prf65
2003P	217,400,000	0.65	5.00	—
2003D	213,400,000	0.65	5.00	—
2003S	3,408,516	—	—	2.30

KM# 345a • 6.25 g., 0.900 Silver 0.1808 oz. ASW, 24.3 mm.

Date	Mintage	MS63	MS65	Prf65
2003S	1,257,555	—	—	8.50

Missouri

KM# 346 • 5.67 g., Copper-Nickel Clad Copper, 24.3 mm.

Date	Mintage	MS63	MS65	Prf65
2003P	225,000,000	0.65	5.00	—
2003D	228,200,000	0.65	5.00	—
2003S	3,408,516	—	—	2.30

KM# 346a • 6.25 g., 0.900 Silver 0.1808 oz. ASW, 24.3 mm.

Date	Mintage	MS63	MS65	Prf65
2003S	1,257,555	—	—	8.50

Arkansas

KM# 347 • 5.67 g., Copper-Nickel Clad Copper, 24.3 mm.

Date	Mintage	MS63	MS65	Prf65
2003P	228,000,000	0.65	5.00	—
2003D	229,800,000	0.65	5.00	—
2003S	3,408,516	—	—	2.30

KM# 347a • 6.25 g., 0.900 Silver 0.1808 oz. ASW, 24.3 mm.

Date	Mintage	MS63	MS65	Prf65
2003S	1,257,555	—	—	8.50

Michigan

KM# 355 • 5.67 g., Copper-Nickel Clad Copper, 24.3 mm.

Date	Mintage	MS63	MS65	Prf65
2004P	233,800,000	0.65	5.00	—
2004D	225,800,000	0.65	5.00	—
2004S	2,740,684	—	—	2.30

KM# 355a • 6.25 g., 0.900 Silver 0.1808 oz. ASW, 24.3 mm.

Date	Mintage	MS63	MS65	Prf65
2004S	1,775,370	—	—	8.50

Florida

KM# 356 • 5.67 g., Copper-Nickel Clad Copper, 24.3 mm.

Date	Mintage	MS63	MS65	Prf65
2004P	240,200,000	0.65	5.00	—
2004D	241,600,000	0.65	5.00	—
2004S	2,740,684	—	—	2.30

KM# 356a • 6.25 g., 0.900 Silver 0.1808 oz. ASW, 24.3 mm.

Date	Mintage	MS63	MS65	Prf65
2004S	1,775,370	—	—	8.50

Texas

KM# 357 • 5.67 g., Copper-Nickel Clad Copper, 24.3 mm.

Date	Mintage	MS63	MS65	Prf65
2004P	278,800,000	0.65	5.00	—
2004D	263,000,000	0.65	5.00	—
2004S	2,740,684	—	—	2.30

KM# 357a • 6.25 g., 0.900 Silver 0.1808 oz. ASW, 24.3 mm.

Date	Mintage	MS63	MS65	Prf65
2004S	1,775,370	—	—	8.50

Iowa

KM# 358 • 5.67 g., Copper-Nickel Clad Copper, 24.3 mm.

Date	Mintage	MS63	MS65	Prf65
2004P	213,800,000	0.65	5.00	—
2004D	251,800,000	0.65	5.00	—
2004S	2,740,684	—	—	2.30

KM# 358a • 6.25 g., 0.900 Silver 0.1808 oz. ASW, 24.3 mm.

Date	Mintage	MS63	MS65	Prf65
2004S	—	—	—	8.50

Wisconsin

KM# 359 • 5.67 g., Copper-Nickel Clad Copper, 24.3 mm.

Date	Mintage	MS63	MS65	Prf65
2004P	226,400,000	0.65	5.00	—
2004D	226,800,000	0.65	5.00	—
2004D Extra Leaf Low	Est. 9000	135	190	—
2004D Extra Leaf High	Est. 3000	175	285	—
2004S	—	—	—	2.30

KM# 359a • 6.25 g., 0.900 Silver 0.1808 oz. ASW, 24.3 mm.

Date	Mintage	MS63	MS65	Prf65
2004S	1,775,370	—	—	8.50

Minnesota

KM# 371 • 5.67 g., Copper-Nickel Clad Copper, 24.3 mm.

Date	Mintage	MS63	MS65	Prf65
2005P	226,400,000	0.65	5.00	—
2005P Satin Finish	Inc. above	1.50	4.50	—
2005D	226,800,000	0.65	5.00	—
2005D Satin Finish	Inc. above	1.50	4.50	—
2005S	3,262,960	—	—	2.30

KM# 371a • 6.25 g., 0.900 Silver 0.1808 oz. ASW, 24.3 mm.

Date	Mintage	MS63	MS65	Prf65
2005S	1,679,600	—	—	8.50

Oregon

KM# 372 • 5.67 g., Copper-Nickel Clad Copper, 24.3 mm.

Date	Mintage	MS63	MS65	Prf65
2005P	316,200,000	0.65	5.00	—
2005P Satin Finish	Inc. above	1.50	4.50	—
2005D	404,000,000	0.65	5.00	—
2005D Satin Finish	Inc. above	1.50	4.50	—
2005S	3,262,960	—	—	2.30

KM# 372a • 6.25 g., 0.900 Silver 0.1808 oz. ASW, 24.3 mm.

Date	Mintage	MS63	MS65	Prf65
2005S	1,679,600	—	—	8.50

Kansas

KM# 373 • 5.67 g., Copper-Nickel Clad Copper, 24.3 mm.

Date	Mintage	MS63	MS65	Prf65
2005P	263,400,000	0.65	5.00	—
2005P Satin Finish	Inc. above	1.50	4.50	—
2005D	300,000,000	0.65	5.00	—
2005D Satin Finish	Inc. above	1.50	4.50	—
2005S	3,262,960	—	—	2.30

KM# 373a • 6.25 g., 0.900 Silver 0.1808 oz. ASW, 24.3 mm.

Date	Mintage	MS63	MS65	Prf65
2005S	1,679,600	—	—	8.50

West Virginia

KM# 374 • 5.67 g., Copper-Nickel Clad Copper, 24.3 mm.

Date	Mintage	MS63	MS65	Prf65
2005P	365,400,000	0.65	5.00	—
2005P Satin Finish	Inc. above	1.50	4.50	—
2005D	356,200,000	0.65	5.00	—
2005D Satin Finish	Inc. above	1.50	4.50	—
2005S	3,262,960	—	—	2.30

KM# 374a • 6.25 g., 0.900 Silver 0.1808 oz. ASW, 24.3 mm.

Date	Mintage	MS63	MS65	Prf65
2005S	1,679,600	—	—	8.50

California

KM# 370 • 5.67 g., Copper-Nickel Clad Copper, 24.3 mm.

Date	Mintage	MS63	MS65	Prf65
2005P	257,200,000	0.65	5.00	—
2005P Satin Finish	Inc. above	1.50	4.50	—
2005D	263,200,000	0.65	5.00	—
2005D Satin Finish	Inc. above	1.50	4.50	—
2005S	3,262,960	—	—	2.30

KM# 370a • 6.25 g., 0.900 Silver 0.1808 oz. ASW, 24.3 mm.

Date	Mintage	MS63	MS65	Prf65
2005S	1,679,600	—	—	8.50

QUARTER

QUARTER

Nevada

KM# 382 • 5.67 g., Copper-Nickel Clad Copper, 24.3 mm.

Date	Mintage	MS63	MS65	Prf65
2006P	277,000,000	0.65	5.00	—
2006P Satin Finish	Inc. above	1.50	4.50	—
2006D	312,800,000	0.65	5.00	—
2006D Satin Finish	Inc. above	1.50	4.50	—
2006S	2,862,078	—	—	2.30

KM# 382a • 6.25 g., 0.900 Silver 0.1808 oz. ASW, 24.3 mm.

Date	Mintage	MS63	MS65	Prf65
2006S	1,571,839	—	—	8.50

Nebraska

KM# 383 • 5.67 g., Copper-Nickel Clad Copper, 24.3 mm.

Date	Mintage	MS63	MS65	Prf65
2006P	318,000,000	0.65	5.00	—
2006P Satin Finish	Inc. above	1.50	4.50	—
2006D	273,000,000	0.65	5.00	—
2006D Satin Finish	Inc. above	1.50	4.50	—
2006S	2,862,078	—	—	2.30

KM# 383a • 6.25 g., 0.900 Silver 0.1808 oz. ASW, 24.3 mm.

Date	Mintage	MS63	MS65	Prf65
2006S	1,571,839	—	—	8.50

Colorado

KM# 384 • 5.67 g., Copper-Nickel Clad Copper, 24.3 mm.

Date	Mintage	MS63	MS65	Prf65
2006P	274,800,000	0.65	5.00	—
2006P Satin Finish	Inc. above	1.50	4.50	—
2006D	294,200,000	0.65	5.00	—
2006D Satin Finish	Inc. above	1.50	4.50	—
2006S	2,862,078	—	—	2.30

KM# 384a • 6.25 g., 0.900 Silver 0.1808 oz. ASW, 24.3 mm.

Date	Mintage	MS63	MS65	Prf65
2006S	1,571,839	—	—	8.50

North Dakota

KM# 385 • 5.67 g., Copper-Nickel Clad Copper, 24.3 mm.

Date	Mintage	MS63	MS65	Prf65
2006P	305,800,000	0.65	5.00	—
2006P Satin Finish	Inc. above	1.50	4.50	—
2006D	359,000,000	0.65	5.00	—
2006D Satin Finish	Inc. above	1.50	4.50	—
2006S	2,862,078	—	—	2.30

KM# 385a • 6.25 g., 0.900 Silver 0.1808 oz. ASW, 24.3 mm.

Date	Mintage	MS63	MS65	Prf65
2006S	1,571,839	—	—	8.50

South Dakota

KM# 386 • 5.67 g., Copper-Nickel Clad Copper, 24.3 mm.

Date	Mintage	MS63	MS65	Prf65
2006P	245,000,000	0.65	5.00	—
2006P Satin Finish	Inc. above	1.50	4.50	—
2006D	265,800,000	0.65	5.00	—
2006D Satin Finish	Inc. above	1.50	4.50	—
2006S	2,862,078	—	—	2.30

KM# 386a • 6.25 g., 0.900 Silver 0.1808 oz. ASW, 24.3 mm.

Date	Mintage	MS63	MS65	Prf65
2006S	1,571,839	—	—	8.50

Montana

KM# 396 • 5.67 g., Copper-Nickel Clad Copper, 24.3 mm.

Date	Mintage	MS63	MS65	Prf65
2007P	257,000,000	0.65	5.00	—
2007P Satin Finish	—	1.50	4.50	—
2007D	256,240,000	0.65	5.00	—
2007D Satin Finish	—	1.50	4.50	—
2007S	2,374,778	—	—	2.30

KM# 396a • 6.25 g., 0.900 Silver 0.1808 oz. ASW, 24.3 mm.

Date	Mintage	MS63	MS65	Prf65
2007S	1,299,878	—	—	8.50

QUARTER

Washington

KM# 397 • 5.67 g., Copper-Nickel Clad Copper, 24.3 mm.

Date	Mintage	MS63	MS65	Prf65
2007P	265,200,000	0.65	5.00	—
2007P Satin Finish	—	1.50	4.50	—
2007D	280,000,000	0.65	5.00	—
2007D Satin Finish	—	1.50	4.50	—
2007S	2,374,778	—	—	2.30

KM# 397a • 6.25 g., 0.900 Silver 0.1808 oz. ASW, 24.3 mm.

Date	Mintage	MS63	MS65	Prf65
2007S	1,299,878	—	—	8.50

Idaho

KM# 398 • 5.67 g., Copper-Nickel Clad Copper, 24.3 mm.

Date	Mintage	MS63	MS65	Prf65
2007P	294,600,000	0.65	5.00	—
2007P Satin finish	—	1.50	4.50	—
2007D	286,800,000	0.65	5.00	—
2007D Satin finish	—	1.50	4.50	—
2007S	2,374,778	—	—	2.30

KM# 398a • 6.25 g., 0.900 Silver 0.1808 oz. ASW, 24.3 mm.

Date	Mintage	MS63	MS65	Prf65
2007S	1,299,878	—	—	8.50

Wyoming

KM# 399 • 5.67 g., Copper-Nickel Clad Copper, 24.3 mm.

Date	Mintage	MS63	MS65	Prf65
2007P	243,600,000	0.65	5.00	—
2007P Satin finish	—	1.50	4.50	—
2007D	320,800,000	0.65	5.00	—
2007 Satin finish	—	1.50	4.50	—
2007S	2,374,778	—	—	2.30

KM# 399a • 6.25 g., 0.900 Silver 0.1808 oz. ASW, 24.3 mm.

Date	Mintage	MS63	MS65	Prf65
2007S	1,299,878	—	—	8.50

Utah

KM# 400 • 5.67 g., Copper-Nickel Clad Copper, 24.3 mm.

Date	Mintage	MS63	MS65	Prf65
2007P	255,000,000	0.65	5.00	—
2007P Satin finish	—	1.50	4.50	—
2007D	253,200,000	0.65	5.00	—
2007D Satin finish	—	1.50	4.50	—
2007S	2,374,778	—	—	2.30

KM# 400a • 6.25 g., 0.900 Silver 0.1808 oz. ASW

Date	Mintage	MS63	MS65	Prf65
2007S	1,299,878	—	—	8.50

Oklahoma

KM# 421 • 5.67 g., Copper-Nickel Clad Copper, 24.3 mm.

Date	Mintage	MS63	MS65	Prf65
2008P	222,000,000	0.65	5.00	—
2008P Satin finish	—	1.50	4.50	—
2008D	194,600,000	0.65	5.00	—
2008D Satin finish	—	1.50	4.50	—
2008S	2,100,000	—	—	2.30

KM# 421a • 6.25 g., 0.900 Silver 0.1808 oz. ASW, 24.3 mm.

Date	Mintage	MS63	MS65	Prf65
2008S	1,200,000	—	—	8.50

New Mexico

KM# 422 • 5.67 g., Copper-Nickel Clad Copper, 24.3 mm.

Date	Mintage	MS63	MS65	Prf65
2008P	244,200,000	0.65	5.00	—
2008P Satin finish	—	1.50	4.50	—
2008D	244,400,000	0.65	5.00	—
2008D Satin finish	—	1.50	4.50	—
2008S	2,100,000	—	—	2.30

KM# 422a • 6.25 g., 0.900 Silver 0.1808 oz. ASW, 24.3 mm.

Date	Mintage	MS63	MS65	Prf65
2008S	1,200,000	—	—	8.50

QUARTER

Arizona

KM# 423 • 5.67 g., Copper-Nickel Clad Copper, 24.3 mm.

Date	Mintage	MS63	MS65	Prf65
2008P	244,600,000	0.65	5.00	—
2008P Satin finish	—	1.50	4.50	—
2008D	265,000,000	0.65	5.00	—
2008D Satin finish	—	1.50	4.50	—
2008S	2,100,000	—	—	2.30

KM# 423a • 6.25 g., 0.900 Silver 0.1808 oz. ASW, 24.3 mm.

Date	Mintage	MS63	MS65	Prf65
2008S	1,200,000	—	—	8.50

Alaska

KM# 424 • 5.67 g., Copper-Nickel Clad Copper, 24.3 mm.

Date	Mintage	MS63	MS65	Prf65
2008P	251,800,000	0.65	5.00	—
2008P Satin finish	—	1.50	4.50	—
2008D	254,000,000	0.65	5.00	—
2008D Satin finish	—	1.50	4.50	—
2008S	2,100,000	—	—	2.30

KM# 424a • 6.25 g., 0.900 Silver 0.1808 oz. ASW, 24.3 mm.

Date	Mintage	MS63	MS65	Prf65
2008S	1,200,000	—	—	8.50

Hawaii

KM# 425 • 5.67 g., Copper-Nickel Clad Copper, 24.3 mm.

Date	Mintage	MS63	MS65	Prf65
2008P	254,000,000	0.65	5.00	—
2008P Satin finish	—	1.50	4.50	—
2008D	263,600,000	0.65	5.00	—
2008D Satin finish	—	1.50	4.50	—
2008S	2,100,000	—	—	2.30

KM# 425a • 6.25 g., 0.900 Silver 0.1808 oz. ASW, 24.3 mm.

Date	Mintage	MS63	MS65	Prf65
2008S	1,200,000	—	—	8.50

DC and Territories

District of Columbia

KM# 445 • 5.67 g., Copper-Nickel Clad Copper, 24.3 mm.

Date	Mintage	MS63	MS65	Prf65
2009P	83,600,000	0.75	5.00	—
2009D	88,800,000	0.75	5.00	—
2009S	2,113,478	—	—	3.75

KM# 445a • 6.25 g., 0.900 Silver 0.1808 oz. ASW, 24.3 mm.

Date	Mintage	MS63	MS65	Prf65
2009S	996,548	—	—	7.75

Puerto Rico

KM# 446 • 5.67 g., Copper-Nickel Clad Copper, 24.3 mm.

Date	Mintage	MS63	MS65	Prf65
2009P	53,200,000	0.75	5.00	—
2009D	86,000,000	0.75	5.00	—
2009S	2,113,478	—	—	3.75

KM# 446a • 6.25 g., 0.900 Silver 0.1808 oz. ASW, 24.3 mm.

Date	Mintage	MS63	MS65	Prf65
2009S	996,548	—	—	7.75

Guam

KM# 447 • 5.67 g., Copper-Nickel Clad Copper, 24.3 mm.

Date	Mintage	MS63	MS65	Prf65
2009P	45,000,000	0.75	5.00	—
2009D	42,600,000	0.75	5.00	—
2009S	2,113,478	—	—	3.75

KM# 447a • 6.25 g., 0.900 Silver 0.1808 oz. ASW, 24.3 mm.

Date	Mintage	MS63	MS65	Prf65
2009S	996,548	—	—	7.75

American Samoa

KM# 448 • 5.67 g., Copper-Nickel Clad Copper, 24.3 mm.

Date	Mintage	MS63	MS65	Prf65
2009P	42,600,000	0.75	5.00	—
2009D	39,600,000	0.75	5.00	—
2009S	2,113,478	—	—	3.75

KM# 448a • 6.25 g., 0.900 Silver 0.1808 oz. ASW, 24.3 mm.

Date	Mintage	MS63	MS65	Prf65
2009S	996,548	—	—	7.75

US Virgin Islands

KM# 449 • 5.67 g., Copper-Nickel Clad Copper, 24.3 mm.

Date	Mintage	MS63	MS65	Prf65
2009P	41,000,000	0.75	5.00	—
2009D	41,000,000	0.75	5.00	—
2009S	2,113,478	—	—	3.75

KM# 449a • 6.25 g., 0.900 Silver 0.1808 oz. ASW, 24.3 mm.

Date	Mintage	MS63	MS65	Prf65
2009S	996,548	—	—	7.75

Northern Mariana Islands

KM# 466 • 5.67 g., Copper-Nickel Clad Copper

Date	Mintage	MS63	MS65	Prf65
2009P	35,200,000	0.75	5.00	—
2009D	37,600,000	0.75	5.00	—
2009S	2,113,478	—	—	3.75

KM# 466a • 6.25 g., 0.900 Silver 0.1808 oz. ASW

Date	Mintage	MS63	MS65	Prf65
2009S	996,548	—	—	7.75

America the Beautiful

Hot Springs, Ark.

KM# 469 • 5.67 g., Copper-Nickel Clad Copper, 24.3 mm.

Date	Mintage	MS63	MS65	Prf65
2010P	35,600,000	0.75	5.00	—
2010D	34,000,000	0.75	5.00	—
2010S	1,401,903	—	—	3.75

KM# 469a • 6.25 g., 0.900 Silver 0.1808 oz. ASW

Date	Mintage	MS63	MS65	Prf65
2010S	859,435	—	—	7.75

Yellowstone National Park

KM# 470 • 5.67 g., Copper-Nickel Clad Copper, 24.3 mm.

Date	Mintage	MS63	MS65	Prf65
2010P	33,600,000	0.75	5.00	—
2010D	34,800,000	0.75	5.00	—
2010S	1,402,756	—	—	3.75

KM# 470a • 6.25 g., 0.900 Silver 0.1808 oz. ASW

Date	Mintage	MS63	MS65	Prf65
2010	859,435	—	—	7.75

Yosemite National Park

KM# 471 • 5.67 g., Copper-Nickel Clad Copper, 24.3 mm.

Date	Mintage	MS63	MS65	Prf65
2010P	35,200,000	0.75	5.00	—
2010D	34,800,000	0.75	5.00	—
2010S	1,400,215	—	—	3.75

KM# 471a • 6.25 g., 0.900 Silver 0.1808 oz. ASW

Date	Mintage	MS63	MS65	Prf65
2010	859,435	—	—	7.75

QUARTER

QUARTER

Grand Canyon National Park

KM# 472 • 5.67 g., Copper-Nickel Clad Copper, 24.3 mm.

Date	Mintage	MS63	MS65	Prf65
2010P	34,800,000	0.75	5.00	—
2010D	35,400,000	0.75	5.00	—
2010S	1,399,970	—	—	3.75

KM# 472a • 6.25 g., 0.900 Silver 0.1808 oz. ASW

Date	Mintage	MS63	MS65	Prf65
2010	859,435	—	—	7.75

Mount Hood National Park

KM# 473 • 5.67 g., Copper-Nickel Clad Copper, 24.3 mm.

Date	Mintage	MS63	MS65	Prf65
2010P	34,400,000	0.75	5.00	—
2010D	34,400,000	0.75	5.00	—
2010S	1,397,101	—	—	3.75

KM# 473a • 6.25 g., 0.900 Silver 0.1808 oz. ASW

Date	Mintage	MS63	MS65	Prf65
2010S	859,435	—	—	7.75

Gettysburg National Military Park

KM# 494 • 5.67 g., Copper-Nickel Clad Copper, 24 mm.

Date	Mintage	MS63	MS65	Prf65
2011P	30,800,000	0.75	5.00	—
2011D	30,400,000	0.75	5.00	—
2011S	1,271,553	—	—	3.75

KM# 494a • 6.25 g., 0.900 Silver 0.1808 oz. ASW

Date	Mintage	MS63	MS65	Prf65
2011S	722,076	—	—	7.75

Glacier National Park

KM# 495 • 5.67 g., Copper-Nickel Clad Copper, 24 mm.

Date	Mintage	MS63	MS65	Prf65
2011P	30,400,000	0.75	5.00	—
2011D	31,200,000	0.75	5.00	—
2011S	1,268,452	—	—	3.75

KM# 495a • 6.25 g., 0.900 Silver 0.1808 oz. ASW

Date	Mintage	MS63	MS65	Prf65
2011S	722,076	—	—	7.75

Olympic National Park

KM# 496 • 5.67 g., Copper-Nickel Clad Copper, 24 mm.

Date	Mintage	MS63	MS65	Prf65
2011P	30,400,000	0.75	5.00	—
2011D	30,600,000	0.75	5.00	—
2011S	1,267,361	—	—	3.75

KM# 496a • 6.25 g., 0.900 Silver 0.1808 oz. ASW

Date	Mintage	MS63	MS65	Prf65
2011S	722,076	—	—	7.75

Vicksburg National Military Park

KM# 497 • 5.67 g., Copper-Nickel Clad Copper, 24 mm.

Date	Mintage	MS63	MS65	Prf65
2011P	30,800,000	0.75	5.00	—
2011D	33,400,000	0.75	5.00	—
2011S	1,267,691	—	—	3.75

KM# 497a • 6.25 g., 0.900 Silver 0.1808 oz. ASW

Date	Mintage	MS63	MS65	Prf65
2011S	722,076	—	—	7.75

Chickasaw National Recreation Area

KM# 498 • 5.67 g., Copper-Nickel Clad Copper, 24 mm.

Date	Mintage	MS63	MS65	Prf65
2011P	73,800,000	0.75	5.00	—
2011D	69,400,000	0.75	5.00	—
2011S	1,266,010	—	—	3.75

KM# 498a • 6.25 g., 0.900 Silver 0.1808 oz. ASW

Date	Mintage	MS63	MS65	Prf65
2011S	722,076	—	—	7.75

El Yunque National Forest

KM# 519 • 5.67 g., Copper-Nickel Clad Copper, 24.3 mm.

Date	Mintage	MS63	MS65	Prf65
2012P	25,800,000	0.75	5.00	—
2012D	25,800,000	0.75	5.00	—
2012S	1,010,361	—	7.50	—
2012S	1,679,240	—	—	3.75

KM# 519a • 6.25 g., 0.900 Silver 0.1808 oz. ASW, 24.3 mm.

Date	Mintage	MS63	MS65	Prf65
2012S	557,891	—	—	7.75

Chaco Culture National Historic Park

KM# 520 • 5.71 g., Copper-Nickel Clad Copper, 24.3 mm.

Date	Mintage	MS63	MS65	Prf65
2012P	22,000,000	0.75	8.00	—
2012D	22,000,000	0.75	8.00	—
2012S	960,049	—	10.00	—
2012S	1,389,020	—	—	4.00

KM# 520a • 6.25 g., 0.900 Silver 0.1808 oz. ASW, 24.3 mm.

Date	Mintage	MS63	MS65	Prf65
2012S	557,891	—	—	7.75

Acadia National Park

KM# 521 • 5.67 g., Copper-Nickel Clad Copper, 24.3 mm.

Date	Mintage	MS63	MS65	Prf65
2012P	24,800,000	0.75	5.00	—
2012D	21,606,000	0.75	5.00	—
2012S	960,409	—	7.50	—
2012S	1,409,120	—	—	3.75

KM# 521a • 6.25 g., 0.900 Silver 0.1808 oz. ASW, 24.3 mm.

Date	Mintage	MS63	MS65	Prf65
2012S	557,891	—	—	7.75

Hawai'i Volcanoes National Park

KM# 522 • 5.67 g., Copper-Nickel Clad Copper, 24.3 mm.

Date	Mintage	MS63	MS65	Prf65
2012P	46,200,000	0.75	5.00	—
2012D	78,600,000	0.75	5.00	—
2012S	961,272	—	7.50	—
2012S	1,407,520	—	—	3.75

KM# 522a • 6.25 g., 0.900 Silver 0.1808 oz. ASW, 24.3 mm.

Date	Mintage	MS63	MS65	Prf65
2012S	557,891	—	—	7.75

Denali National Park

KM# 523 • 5.67 g., Copper-Nickel Clad Copper, 24.3 mm.

Date	Mintage	MS63	MS65	Prf65
2012P	135,400,000	0.75	5.00	—
2012D	166,600,000	0.75	5.00	—
2012S	957,856	—	7.50	—
2012S	1,401,920	—	—	3.75

KM# 523a • 6.25 g., 0.900 Silver 0.1808 oz. ASW, 24.3 mm.

Date	Mintage	MS63	MS65	Prf65
2012S	557,891	—	—	7.75

White Mountain National Forest

KM# 542 • 5.67 g., Copper-Nickel Clad Copper, 24.3 mm.

Date	Mintage	MS63	MS65	Prf65
2013P	68,800,000	0.75	5.00	—
2013D	107,600,000	0.75	5.00	—
2013S	950,080	—	7.50	—
2013S	—	—	—	3.75

KM# 542a • 6.25 g., 0.900 Silver 0.1808 oz. ASW, 24.3 mm.

Date	Mintage	MS63	MS65	Prf65
2013S	579,409	—	—	7.75

QUARTER

QUARTER

Perry's Victory and International Peace Memorial

KM# 543 • 5.67 g., Copper-Nickel Clad Copper, 24.3 mm.

Date	Mintage	MS63	MS65	Prf65
2013P	107,800,000	0.75	5.00	—
2013D	131,600,000	0.75	5.00	—
2013S	913,563	—	7.50	—
2013S	—	—	—	3.75

KM# 543a • 6.25 g., 0.900 Silver 0.1808 oz. ASW, 24.3 mm.

Date	Mintage	MS63	MS65	Prf65
2013S	579,409	—	—	7.75

Great Basin National Park

KM# 544 • 5.67 g., Copper-Nickel Clad Copper, 24.3 mm.

Date	Mintage	MS63	MS65	Prf65
2013P	122,400,000	0.75	5.00	—
2013D	141,400,000	0.75	5.00	—
2013S	911,525	—	7.50	—
2013S	—	—	—	3.75

KM# 544a • 6.25 g., 0.900 Silver 0.1808 oz. ASW, 24.3 mm.

Date	Mintage	MS63	MS65	Prf65
2013S	579,409	—	—	7.75

Fort McHenry National Monument and Historic Shrine

KM# 545 • 5.67 g., Copper-Nickel Clad Copper, 24.3 mm.

Date	Mintage	MS63	MS65	Prf65
2013P	120,000,000	0.75	5.00	—
2013D	151,400,000	0.75	5.00	—
2013S	911,451	—	7.50	—
2013S	—	—	—	3.75

KM# 545a • 6.25 g., 0.900 Silver 0.1808 oz. ASW, 24.3 mm.

Date	Mintage	MS63	MS65	Prf65
2013S	579,409	—	—	7.75

Mount Rushmore National Memorial

KM# 546 • 5.67 g., Copper-Nickel Clad Copper, 24.3 mm.

Date	Mintage	MS63	MS65	Prf65
2013P	231,800,000	0.75	5.00	—
2013D	272,400,000	0.75	5.00	—
2013S	920,695	—	7.50	—
2013S	—	—	—	3.75

KM# 546a • 6.25 g., 0.900 Silver 0.1808 oz. ASW, 24.3 mm.

Date	Mintage	MS63	MS65	Prf65
2013S	579,409	—	—	7.75

Great Smokey Mountains National Park

KM# 566 • 5.67 g., Copper-Nickel Clad Copper, 24.3 mm.

Date	Mintage	MS63	MS65	Prf65
2014P	—	0.75	5.00	—
2014D	—	0.75	5.00	—
2014S	—	—	—	3.75

KM# 566a • 6.25 g., 0.900 Silver 0.1808 oz. ASW, 24.3 mm.

Date	Mintage	MS63	MS65	Prf65
2014S	—	—	—	7.75

Shenandoah National Park

KM# 567 • 5.67 g., Copper-Nickel Clad Copper, 24.3 mm.

Date	Mintage	MS63	MS65	Prf65
2014P	—	0.75	5.00	—
2014D	—	0.75	5.00	—
2014S	—	—	—	3.75

KM# 567a • 6.25 g., 0.900 Silver 0.1808 oz. ASW, 24.3 mm.

Date	Mintage	MS63	MS65	Prf65
2014S	—	—	—	7.75

Arches National Park

KM# 568 • 5.67 g., Copper-Nickel Clad Copper, 24.3 mm.

Date	Mintage	MS63	MS65	Prf65
2014P	—	0.75	5.00	—
2014D	—	0.75	5.00	—
2014S	—	—	—	3.75

KM# 568a • 6.25 g., 0.900 Silver 0.1808 oz. ASW, 24.3 mm.

Date	Mintage	MS63	MS65	Prf65
2014S	—	—	—	7.75

Great Sand Dunes National Park

KM# 569 • 5.67 g., Copper-Nickel Clad Copper, 24.3 mm.

Date	Mintage	MS63	MS65	Prf65
2014P	—	0.75	5.00	—
2014D	—	0.75	5.00	—
2014S	—	—	—	3.75

KM# 569a • 6.25 g., 0.900 Silver 0.1808 oz. ASW, 24.3 mm.

Date	Mintage	MS63	MS65	Prf65
2014S	—	—	—	7.75

Everglades National Park

KM# 570 • 5.67 g., Copper-Nickel Clad Copper, 24.3 mm.

Date	Mintage	MS63	MS65	Prf65
2014P	—	0.75	5.00	—
2014D	—	0.75	5.00	—
2014S	—	—	—	3.75

KM# 570a • 6.25 g., 0.900 Silver 0.1808 oz. ASW, 24.3 mm.

Date	Mintage	MS63	MS65	Prf65
2014S	—	—	—	7.75

HALF DOLLAR

Flowing Hair Half Dollar

KM# 16 • 13.48 g., 0.892 Silver 0.3866 oz. ASW, 32.5 mm. • **Designer:** Robert Scot **Note:** The 1795 "recut date" variety had the date cut into the dies twice, so both sets of numbers are visible on the coin. The 1795 "3 leaves" variety has three leaves under each of the eagle's wings on the reverse.

Date	Mintage	G4	VG8	F12	VF20	XF40	MS60
1794	23,464	2,850	5,750	8,850	19,500	37,500	225,000
1795	299,680	1,025	1,450	2,850	4,850	13,850	46,500
1795 recut date	Inc. above	1,040	1,470	2,895	5,200	14,250	46,500
1795 3 leaves	Inc. above	2,600	3,150	5,350	8,350	17,500	59,500

Draped Bust Half Dollar
Draped bust right.   Small eagle.

KM# 26 • 13.48 g., 0.892 Silver 0.3866 oz. ASW, 32.5 mm. • **Designer:** Robert Scot

Date	Mintage	G4	VG8	F12	VF20	XF40	MS60
1796 15 obverse stars	3,918	36,500	46,000	62,000	73,500	118,000	300,000
1796 16 obverse stars	Inc. above	39,500	50,000	67,000	79,500	128,000	320,000
1797	Inc. above	36,700	46,300	62,500	74,300	121,000	310,000

Draped bust right, flanked by stars, date at angle below.   Heraldic eagle.

KM# 35 • 13.48 g., 0.892 Silver 0.3866 oz. ASW, 32.5 mm. • **Obv. Legend:** LIBERTY **Rev. Legend:** UNITED STATES OF AMERICA **Designer:** Robert Scot **Note:** The two varieties of the 1803 strikes are distinguished by the size of the 3 in the date. The several varieties of the 1806 strikes are distinguished by the style of 6 in the date, size of the stars on the obverse, and whether the stem of the olive branch held by the reverse eagle extends through the claw.

Date	Mintage	G4	VG8	F12	VF20	XF40	MS60
1801	30,289	850	1,250	2,550	4,250	10,500	50,000
1802	29,890	900	1,350	2,750	4,500	11,000	52,000
1803 small 3	188,234	255	325	425	825	2,325	17,250
1803 large 3	Inc. above	195	235	295	715	1,925	14,750
1805	211,722	195	235	295	685	1,865	10,750
1805/4	Inc. above	270	385	570	1,515	3,325	30,000
1806 knobbed 6, large stars	839,576	195	235	295	665	1,825	—
1806 knobbed 6, small stars	Inc. above	195	235	295	680	2,025	13,500
1806 knobbed 6, stem not through claw	Inc. above	20,000	35,000	42,000	57,500	95,000	—
1806 pointed-top 6, stem not through claw	Inc. above	195	235	295	665	1,825	15,250
1806 pointed-top 6, stem through claw	Inc. above	195	235	295	665	1,825	9,750
1806/5	Inc. above	215	270	355	775	2,050	10,075
1806 /inverted 6	Inc. above	255	355	845	1,615	4,375	28,500
1807	301,076	195	235	295	665	1,825	9,750

Capped Bust
Draped bust left, flanked by stars, date at angle below.   "50 C." below eagle.

KM# 37 • 13.48 g., 0.892 Silver 0.3866 oz. ASW, 32.5 mm. • **Rev. Legend:** UNITED STATES OF AMERICA **Designer:** John Reich **Note:** There are three varieties of the 1807 strikes. Two are distinguished by the size of the stars on the obverse. The third was struck from a reverse die that had a 5 cut over a 2 in the "50C" denomination. Two varieties of the 1811 are distinguished by the size of the 8 in the date. A third has a period between the 8 and second 1 in the date. One variety of the 1817 has a period between the 1 and 7 in the date. Two varieties of the 1820 are distinguished by the size of the date. On the 1823 varieties, the "broken 3" appears to be almost separated in the middle of the 3 in the date; the "patched 3" has the error reparied; the "ugly 3" has portions of its detail missing. The 1827 "curled-2" and "square-2" varieties are distinguished by the numeral's base -- either curled or square. Among the 1828 varieties, "knobbed 2" and "no knob" refers to whether the upper left serif of the digit is rounded. The 1830 varieties are distinguished by the size of the 0 in the date. The four 1834 varieties are distinguished by the sizes of the stars, date and letters in the inscriptions. The 1836 "50/00" variety was struck from a reverse die that has "50" recut over "00" in the denomination.

Date	Mintage	G4	VG8	F12	VF20	XF40	AU50	MS60	MS65
1807 small stars	750,500	125	175	350	750	1,900	6,500	9,850	54,000
1807 large stars	Inc. above	115	165	300	660	1,750	5,650	8,900	—
1807 50/20 C.	Inc. above	85.00	125	195	450	1,500	3,150	6,500	30,000
1807 bearded goddess	—	450	775	1,500	3,350	6,850	22,500	—	—
1808	1,368,600	67.00	84.00	97.00	145	350	550	1,800	20,000
1808/7	Inc. above	90.00	110	135	240	440	1,850	5,400	32,500
1809 IIIIIII edge	Inc. above	85.00	110	140	210	450	850	4,000	—
1809 Normal edge	1,405,810	65.00	82.00	94.00	140	375	750	1,500	12,650
1809 XXXX edge	Inc. above	80.00	105	135	185	550	950	4,450	—
1810	1,276,276	64.00	81.00	91.00	135	265	650	1,950	19,500
1811 small 8	1,203,644	70.00	80.00	88.00	125	350	800	2,350	28,500
1811 large 8	Inc. above	80.00	107	119	175	425	1,000	2,400	28,500
1811 dated 18.11	Inc. above	78.00	100	110	165	650	1,250	3,500	28,500
1812	1,628,059	64.00	81.00	88.00	114	254	440	1,350	13,450
1812/1 small 8	Inc. above	80.00	97.00	119	200	500	1,350	2,500	—
1812/1 large 8	Inc. above	1,650	2,450	4,500	6,750	12,000	21,000	—	—
1812 Single leaf below wing	Inc. above	750	950	1,250	2,400	4,000	6,800	12,500	—
1813	1,241,903	64.00	81.00	88.00	114	184	480	1,400	12,650
1813 50/UNI reverse	1,241,903	74.00	101	124	179	650	1,350	3,650	27,500
1814	1,039,075	64.00	81.00	88.00	124	285	650	1,650	11,450
1814/3	Inc. above	100	165	245	300	850	1,650	3,250	—
1814 E/A in States	Inc. above	85.00	110	150	225	385	950	3,950	—
1814 Single leaf below wing	Inc. above	75.00	97.00	124	194	575	1,350	2,250	—
1815/2	47,150	1,100	1,550	2,250	3,650	5,500	7,950	14,500	85,000
1817	1,215,567	67.00	84.00	91.00	119	195	450	1,300	11,650
1817/3	Inc. above	115	175	280	525	1,150	2,350	4,850	—
1817/4	—	60,000	80,000	150,000	200,000	240,000	—	—	—
1817 dated 181.7	Inc. above	100	87.00	94.00	104	575	1,350	3,950	27,500
1817 Single leaf below wing	Inc. above	75.00	98.00	124	209	550	2,100	2,750	—
1818	1,960,322	64.00	81.00	88.00	119	225	440	1,350	11,250
1818/7 Large 8	Inc. above	100	115	145	190	325	950	1,850	17,500
1818/7 Small 8	Inc. above	98.00	110	130	150	250	850	1,650	16,500
1819	2,208,000	64.00	81.00	88.00	119	175	430	1,350	13,650
1819/8 small 9	Inc. above	75.00	92.00	109	184	290	650	1,900	11,650
1819/8 large 9	Inc. above	85.00	105	150	275	385	850	2,000	25,650
1820 Curl Base 2, small date	751,122	70.00	85.00	96.00	124	285	950	2,250	11,650
1820 Square Base 2 with knob, large date	Inc. above	72.00	90.00	104	139	400	800	2,400	13,150
1820 Square Base 2 without knob, large date	Inc. above	72.00	90.00	104	154	475	1,100	2,500	26,500
1820 E's without Serifs	Inc. above	260	450	900	2,150	3,500	5,500	—	—
1820/19 Square Base 2	Inc. above	110	130	165	240	775	1,650	3,250	25,000
1820/19 Curled Base 2	Inc. above	95.00	115	140	200	650	1,450	2,900	24,500
1821	1,305,797	58.00	76.00	89.00	101	185	575	1,350	11,250
1822	1,559,573	58.00	76.00	89.00	101	180	450	1,250	10,950
1822/1	Inc. above	83.00	100	129	275	385	800	1,900	—
1823	1,694,200	58.00	76.00	89.00	101	175	425	1,150	11,150
1823 broken 3	Inc. above	68.00	88.00	104	139	500	1,500	3,200	—
1823 patched 3	Inc. above	73.00	94.00	119	159	550	950	2,000	15,150
1823 ugly 3	Inc. above	78.00	99.00	129	184	750	1,750	4,200	—
1824	3,504,954	58.00	76.00	89.00	101	175	360	1,075	10,150
1824/21	Inc. above	63.00	82.00	99.00	126	275	650	2,000	15,650
1824/4	Inc. above	61.00	80.00	91.00	114	225	500	1,350	—
1824 1824/various dates	Inc. above	60.00	79.00	91.00	104	300	875	2,000	15,150
1825	2,943,166	58.00	76.00	89.00	101	175	385	1,050	10,150
1826	4,004,180	58.00	76.00	89.00	101	175	385	1,050	10,150
1827 curled 2	5,493,400	61.00	81.00	99.00	134	185	485	1,400	12,650
1827 square 2	Inc. above	58.00	76.00	89.00	101	175	385	1,050	10,150
1827/6	Inc. above	85.00	95.00	120	155	265	650	1,450	11,650
1828 curled-base 2, no knob	3,075,200	58.00	76.00	89.00	101	175	385	1,150	11,150
1828 curled-base 2, knobbed 2	Inc. above	78.00	99.00	129	184	245	460	1,300	—
1828 small 8s, square-base 2, large letters	Inc. above	60.00	80.00	99.00	124	175	385	1,050	12,650

Date	Mintage	G4	VG8	F12	VF20	XF40	AU50	MS60	MS65
1828 small 8s, square-base 2, small letters	Inc. above	58.00	76.00	89.00	106	250	750	1,900	—
1828 large 8s, square-base 2	Inc. above	58.00	76.00	89.00	101	175	385	1,050	11,150
1829	3,712,156	55.00	72.00	79.00	89.00	159	350	1,000	10,150
1829 Large letters	Inc. above	59.00	79.00	89.00	104	180	420	1,250	12,650
1829/7	Inc. above	78.00	99.00	129	174	200	475	1,250	12,650
1830 Small O rev	4,764,800	55.00	72.00	79.00	89.00	159	350	1,000	10,150
1830 Large O	Inc. above	60.00	78.00	88.00	109	189	550	2,000	13,150
1830 Large letter rev	Inc. above	1,500	2,250	3,000	3,750	4,800	9,800	—	—
1831	5,873,660	55.00	72.00	79.00	89.00	159	350	1,000	10,150
1832 small letters	4,797,000	55.00	72.00	79.00	89.00	159	350	1,000	10,150
1832 large letters	Inc. above	58.00	75.00	85.00	99.00	175	410	1,350	12,650
1833	5,206,000	55.00	72.00	79.00	89.00	159	360	1,000	10,150
1834 small date, large stars, small letters	6,412,004	55.00	74.00	81.00	91.00	163	360	1,025	10,400
1834 small date, small stars, small letters	Inc. above	55.00	74.00	81.00	9.00	163	360	1,025	10,400
1834 large date, small letters	Inc. above	55.00	74.00	81.00	91.00	163	360	1,025	10,400
1834 large date, large letters	Inc. above	55.00	72.00	79.00	89.00	159	350	1,000	10,150
1835	5,352,006	55.00	72.00	79.00	89.00	159	350	1,000	10,150
1836	6,545,000	55.00	72.00	79.00	89.00	159	350	1,000	10,150
1836	Inc. above	80.00	95.00	120	265	450	1,000	2,500	—
1836 50/00	Inc. above	93.00	112	129	165	300	800	1,750	19,500

Bust Half Dollar
Draped bust left, flanked by stars, date at angle below.   "50 Cents" below eagle.
KM# 58 • 13.48 g., 0.892 Silver 0.3866 oz. ASW, 30 mm. • **Rev. Legend:** UNITED STATES OF AMERICA
Edge: Reeded. **Designer:** Christian Gobrecht

Date	Mintage	G4	VG8	F12	VF20	XF40	AU50	MS60	MS65
1836	1,200	850	1,075	1,600	2,000	3,350	4,400	8,850	66,500

KM# 58a • 13.36 g., 0.900 Silver 0.3866 oz. ASW, 30 mm. • **Rev. Legend:** UNITED STATES OF AMERICA
Edge: Reeded. **Designer:** Christian Gobrecht

Date	Mintage	G4	VG8	F12	VF20	XF40	AU50	MS60	MS65
1837	3,629,820	58.00	73.00	80.00	115	200	345	1,100	24,500

Draped bust left, flanked by stars, date below. "HALF DOL." below eagle.

KM# 65 • 13.36 g., 0.900 Silver 0.3866 oz. ASW, 30 mm. • **Rev. Legend:** UNITED STATES OF AMERICA
Designer: Christian Gobrecht

Date	Mintage	G4	VG8	F12	VF20	XF40	AU50	MS60	MS65
1838	3,546,000	58.00	70.00	82.00	120	205	420	1,200	17,500
1838O proof only	Est. 20	—	—	—	—	250,000	300,000	—	—
1839	1,392,976	60.00	76.00	92.00	130	245	410	1,350	39,500
1839O	116,000	240	325	425	650	1,350	2,350	4,500	46,500

Seated Liberty Half Dollar
Seated Liberty, date below. "Half Dol." below eagle.

KM# 68 • 13.36 g., 0.900 Silver 0.3866 oz. ASW, 30.6 mm. • **Rev. Legend:** UNITED STATES OF AMERICA
Designer: Christian Gobrecht

Date	Mintage	G4	VG8	F12	VF20	XF40	AU50	MS60	MS65
1839 no drapery from elbow	Inc. above	55.00	95.00	365	580	1,275	2,875	6,900	200,000
1839 drapery	Inc. above	52.00	60.00	75.50	110	225	345	1,000	25,000
1840 small letters	1,435,008	54.00	60.00	70.00	108	170	325	600	7,500
1840 reverse 1838	Inc. above	150	185	310	385	850	1,350	3,500	30,000
1840O	855,100	52.00	62.00	76.00	115	250	440	1,050	—
1841	310,000	52.00	65.00	110	165	235	375	1,200	6,850
1841O	401,000	50.00	65.00	75.00	110	265	375	1,250	7,000
1842 small date	2,012,764	48.00	60.00	80.00	135	200	325	1,300	13,500
1842 medium date	Inc. above	44.00	60.00	74.50	90.00	152	300	750	8,800
1842O small date	957,000	650	950	1,550	2,450	4,650	7,750	25,000	—
1842O medium date	Inc. above	44.00	60.00	76.00	90.00	175	350	1,250	10,500
1843	3,844,000	49.00	55.00	71.50	89.00	125	245	500	4,500
1843O	2,268,000	60.00	65.00	73.50	89.00	165	320	550	—
1844	1,766,000	52.50	55.00	71.50	89.00	160	210	525	4,500
1844O	2,005,000	46.00	55.00	71.50	90.00	165	320	675	—
1844/1844O	Inc. above	500	850	1,150	1,400	3,000	6,250	10,000	—
1845	589,000	49.00	65.00	79.50	125	220	365	1,250	12,000
1845O	2,094,000	46.00	60.00	71.50	89.00	165	325	700	9,400
1845O no drapery	Inc. above	48.00	70.00	90.00	165	350	650	1,450	—
1846 medium date	2,210,000	46.00	60.00	77.00	86.00	175	340	900	9,000
1846 tall date	Inc. above	47.00	61.00	90.00	135	350	550	750	12,000
1846 /horizontal 6	Inc. above	160	250	325	550	775	1,350	3,800	—
1846O medium date	2,304,000	49.00	60.00	79.50	86.00	220	300	1,100	12,000
1846O tall date	Inc. above	200	325	425	675	1,750	2,450	6,650	—
1847/1846 (1847)	1,156,000	2,000	2,750	4,000	5,500	10,000	13,500	23,500	—
1847	Inc. above	44.00	52.00	67.50	80.00	125	245	450	9,000
1847O	2,584,000	54.00	65.00	71.50	86.00	160	355	640	7,000
1848	580,000	54.00	75.00	110	185	275	485	1,050	9,000
1848O	3,180,000	46.00	55.00	71.50	86.00	210	375	850	9,000
1849	1,252,000	49.00	70.00	79.50	90.00	165	365	1,250	15,000
1849O	2,310,000	54.00	65.00	71.50	90.00	175	325	750	9,000
1850	227,000	275	325	450	585	700	1,000	2,200	—
1850O	2,456,000	50.00	57.00	73.50	95.00	185	275	950	9,000
1851	200,750	375	475	850	850	1,350	1,650	3,000	—
1851O	402,000	49.00	65.00	125	135	225	325	1,500	9,000
1852	77,130	425	500	700	925	1,100	1,350	2,350	—

HALF DOLLAR

HALF DOLLAR

Date	Mintage	G4	VG8	F12	VF20	XF40	AU50	MS60	MS65
1852O	144,000	70.00	160	210	350	750	1,650	3,850	26,000
1853O mintage unrecorded	—	—	250,000	—	—	600,000	—	—	—

Seated Liberty, arrows at date. Rays around eagle.

KM# 79 • 12.44 g., 0.900 Silver 0.360 oz. ASW **Rev. Legend:** UNITED STATES OF AMERICA **Designer:** Christian Gobrecht

Date	Mintage	G4	VG8	F12	VF20	XF40	AU50	MS60	MS65	Prf65
1853	3,532,708	36.50	48.00	72.00	97.50	270	615	1,500	24,500	175,000
1853O	1,328,000	48.50	56.50	81.00	124	325	695	2,250	29,500	—

Seated Liberty, arrows at date. "HALF DOL." below eagle.

KM# 82 • 12.44 g., 0.900 Silver 0.360 oz. ASW **Rev. Legend:** UNITED STATES OF AMERICA **Designer:** Christian Gobrecht

Date	Mintage	G4	VG8	F12	VF20	XF40	AU50	MS60	MS65	Prf65
1854	2,982,000	36.50	48.00	60.00	73.50	145	305	585	8,500	37,500
1854O	5,240,000	36.50	48.00	60.00	73.50	145	305	610	8,000	—
1855	759,500	38.50	50.00	64.00	87.00	375	575	1,250	9,000	39,500
1855/4	Inc. above	65.00	75.00	135	175	400	600	2,350	17,500	37,000
1855O	3,688,000	39.50	55.00	65.00	78.50	145	305	650	8,000	—
1855S	129,950	350	575	800	1,600	3,650	6,850	19,500	—	—

Seated Liberty, date below. "HALF DOL." below eagle.

KM# A68 • 12.44 g., 0.900 Silver 0.360 oz. ASW **Rev. Legend:** UNITED STATES OF AMERICA **Designer:** Christian Gobrecht

Date	Mintage	G4	VG8	F12	VF20	XF40	AU50	MS60	MS65	Prf65
1856	938,000	44.00	57.00	67.50	84.00	135	245	550	6,500	12,500
1856O	2,658,000	49.00	57.00	67.50	95.00	135	245	450	12,500	—
1856S	211,000	85.00	110	175	275	750	1,500	6,500	19,000	—
1857	1,988,000	44.00	52.00	67.50	84.00	125	245	450	5,150	12,500
1857O	818,000	49.00	55.00	71.00	85.00	150	275	1,150	12,500	—
1857S	158,000	90.00	125	185	400	1,050	1,650	4,500	19,000	—
1858	4,226,000	44.00	52.00	67.50	84.00	125	245	450	6,500	12,500
1858O	7,294,000	49.00	57.00	67.50	84.00	125	245	485	12,500	—
1858S	476,000	50.00	65.00	90.00	140	365	475	1,350	12,500	—
1859	748,000	40.00	57.00	72.00	90.00	145	245	600	6,600	5,500
1859O	2,834,000	44.00	62.00	67.50	84.00	125	245	450	6,500	—
1859S	566,000	45.00	68.00	79.50	100	275	375	950	12,500	—
1860	303,700	48.00	56.00	71.50	100	150	325	750	6,500	5,500

Date	Mintage	G4	VG8	F12	VF20	XF40	AU50	MS60	MS65	Prf65
1860O	1,290,000	44.00	56.00	67.50	84.00	135	260	450	5,150	—
1860S	472,000	49.00	70.00	72.50	88.00	215	335	850	12,500	—
1861	2,888,400	54.00	60.00	67.50	84.00	130	255	485	5,150	5,500
1861O	2,532,633	60.00	68.00	77.00	88.00	175	285	650	5,150	—
1861O CSA Obv, cracked die	Inc. above	55.00	65.00	74.50	110	170	325	875	9,500	—
1861S	939,500	250	350	600	750	1,200	2,350	—		—
1862	253,550	56.00	69.00	92.50	120	235	425	650	5,150	5,500
1862S	1,352,000	54.00	62.00	67.50	80.00	125	265	485	9,000	—
1863	503,660	59.00	73.00	92.50	145	240	350	750	5,150	5,500
1863S	916,000	52.00	69.00	82.50	105	220	295	600	9,000	—
1864	379,570	64.00	75.00	97.50	150	275	400	750	5,150	5,500
1864S	658,000	56.00	69.00	81.50	145	250	350	1,250	9,000	—
1865	511,900	52.00	71.00	88.00	100	265	375	1,000	5,150	5,500
1865S	675,000	56.00	68.00	82.50	100	250	450	900	9,000	—
1866 proof, unique	—	—	—	—	—	—	—	—	—	—
1866S	60,000	485	650	925	1,250	2,550	3,500	6,500	68,000	—

Seated Liberty, date below.   IN GOD WE TRUST above eagle.

KM# 99 • 12.44 g., 0.900 Silver 0.360 oz. ASW **Rev. Legend:** UNITED STATES OF AMERICA **Designer:** Christian Gobrecht

Date	Mintage	G4	VG8	F12	VF20	XF40	AU50	MS60	MS65	Prf65
1866	745,625	54.00	72.50	82.00	95.00	175	300	565	4,800	3,750
1866S	994,000	48.50	62.50	80.00	85.00	200	275	650	5,000	—
1867	449,925	53.50	67.50	88.00	165	275	290	450	4,800	3,750
1867S	1,196,000	47.50	61.50	80.00	100	200	285	775	7,000	—
1868	418,200	58.50	70.00	105	185	275	350	750	7,100	3,750
1868S	1,160,000	48.50	55.50	70.00	95.00	175	285	550	7,000	—
1869	795,900	48.50	64.50	78.00	95.00	165	275	550	4,600	3,750
1869S	656,000	50.00	66.50	80.00	95.00	210	325	850	7,000	—
1870	634,900	47.50	59.50	70.00	98.00	165	275	625	7,000	3,750
1870CC	54,617	1,450	2,650	4,500	7,250	16,000	30,000	110,000	—	—
1870S	1,004,000	43.50	59.50	72.00	110	200	425	1,250	7,000	—
1871	1,204,560	41.00	51.50	71.00	85.00	160	285	650	7,000	3,750
1871CC	153,950	375	650	950	1,450	3,350	6,000	22,500	—	—
1871S	2,178,000	48.50	60.00	68.00	88.00	175	275	675	7,000	—
1872	881,550	48.50	59.50	68.00	88.00	185	310	575	2,850	3,750
1872CC	272,000	210	265	500	950	2,350	4,850	16,500	50,000	—
1872S	580,000	48.50	62.00	86.00	135	300	375	1,150	7,000	—
1873 closed 3	801,800	48.50	57.50	83.00	115	165	280	675	4,500	3,750
1873 open 3	Inc. above	3,550	4,450	5,600	7,250	10,000	13,500	30,000	—	—
1873CC	122,500	275	440	650	1,150	2,350	6,500	17,500	80,000	—
1873S no arrows	5,000	—	—	—	—	—	—	—	—	—

Note: 1873S no arrows, no specimens known to survive.

Seated Liberty, arrows at date.   IN GOD WE TRUST above eagle.

KM# 107 • 12.50 g., 0.900 Silver 0.3617 oz. ASW **Rev. Legend:** UNITED STATES OF AMERICA **Designer:** Christian Gobrecht

Date	Mintage	G4	VG8	F12	VF20	XF40	AU50	MS60	MS65	Prf65
1873	1,815,700	48.00	62.00	78.00	105	265	470	925	17,500	9,000
1873CC	214,560	275	400	650	1,100	2,350	3,900	11,500	42,000	—
1873S	233,000	55.00	130	175	245	475	850	3,850	40,000	—

Date	Mintage	G4	VG8	F12	VF20	XF40	AU50	MS60	MS65	Prf65
1874	2,360,300	44.00	56.00	72.00	90.00	250	455	900	15,500	9,000
1874CC	59,000	775	1,550	2,200	3,650	5,400	9,750	12,500	—	—
1874S	394,000	54.00	70.00	85.00	225	365	685	2,500	20,000	—

Seated Liberty, date below.   IN GOD WE TRUST above eagle.

KM# A99 • 12.50 g., 0.900 Silver 0.3617 oz. ASW **Rev. Legend:** UNITED STATES OF AMERICA **Designer:** Christian Gobrecht

Date	Mintage	G4	VG8	F12	VF20	XF40	AU50	MS60	MS65	Prf65
1875	6,027,500	38.50	49.50	66.00	88.00	128	225	450	3,500	3,375
1875CC	1,008,000	55.00	85.00	135	225	325	500	1,450	8,350	—
1875S	3,200,000	38.50	49.50	66.00	95.00	130	210	390	2,700	—
1876	8,419,150	38.50	49.50	66.00	88.00	118	210	390	5,300	3,775
1876CC	1,956,000	52.00	65.00	100	140	265	375	1,250	4,200	—
1876S	4,528,000	36.50	47.50	66.00	88.00	118	210	390	2,700	—
1877	8,304,510	36.50	47.50	66.00	88.00	118	210	390	2,700	3,825
1877CC	1,420,000	52.00	75.00	110	140	265	350	1,150	3,250	—
1877S	5,356,000	36.50	47.50	66.00	88.00	118	210	390	2,700	—
1878	1,378,400	38.50	57.50	100	130	150	210	485	3,650	3,900
1878CC	62,000	900	1,300	2,350	2,750	3,750	6,500	12,500	43,500	—
1878S	12,000	28,500	42,000	49,500	60,000	75,000	95,000	135,000	175,000	—
1879	5,900	275	310	375	450	540	575	775	3,650	3,150
1880	9,755	260	300	350	425	510	600	800	3,750	3,150
1881	10,975	270	325	345	425	500	565	750	4,000	3,150
1882	5,500	340	410	460	600	650	675	850	3,850	3,150
1883	9,039	325	390	480	560	625	650	1,000	3,950	3,150
1884	5,275	385	425	500	610	700	685	1,000	3,850	3,150
1885	6,130	390	450	485	575	660	700	825	3,850	3,150
1886	5,886	400	550	630	725	850	875	1,150	3,900	3,150
1887	5,710	475	600	700	800	875	950	1,100	3,900	3,150
1888	12,833	280	310	365	410	525	550	800	3,900	3,150
1889	12,711	275	315	400	465	510	575	800	3,900	3,150
1890	12,590	275	310	365	415	500	550	800	3,850	3,150
1891	200,600	55.00	75.00	125	140	165	240	480	3,850	3,150

Barber Half Dollar
Laureate head right, flanked by stars, date below.   Heraldic eagle.

KM# 116 • 12.50 g., 0.900 Silver 0.3617 oz. ASW, 30.6 mm. • **Obv. Legend:** IN GOD WE TRUST **Rev. Legend:** UNITED STATES OF AMERICA **Designer:** Charles E. Barber

Date	Mintage	G4	VG8	F12	VF20	XF40	AU50	MS60	MS65	Prf65
1892	935,245	29.50	44.00	73.50	120	200	395	610	3,100	3,750
1892O	390,000	300	420	515	600	675	700	850	3,950	—
1892O micro O	Inc. above	2,250	3,950	5,000	7,000	11,500	17,500	24,000	80,000	—
1892S	1,029,028	240	330	425	550	650	700	985	4,400	—
1893	1,826,792	22.50	36.00	78.00	150	205	395	625	4,250	3,750
1893O	1,389,000	36.00	70.00	130	230	360	445	700	8,250	—
1893S	740,000	165	240	550	750	1,000	1,525	1,275	22,000	—
1894	1,148,972	32.50	54.00	115	220	280	405	610	3,050	3,750
1894O	2,138,000	21.50	36.00	95.00	180	320	430	660	5,600	—
1894S	4,048,690	21.00	30.00	75.00	130	195	410	575	8,350	—
1895	1,835,218	22.00	28.00	72.00	165	195	410	595	4,050	3,750
1895O	1,766,000	40.00	68.00	130	195	285	435	650	5,950	—

Date	Mintage	G4	VG8	F12	VF20	XF40	AU50	MS60	MS65	Prf65
1895S	1,108,086	32.00	56.00	140	255	345	440	635	6,350	—
1896	950,762	22.50	30.00	88.00	160	265	405	625	5,000	3,750
1896O	924,000	48.00	65.00	210	350	650	1,050	2,450	19,500	—
1896S	1,140,948	120	160	235	400	560	850	1,575	9,750	—
1897	2,480,731	21.50	26.00	48.50	125	200	395	610	3,150	3,750
1897O	632,000	170	240	510	835	1,050	1,350	2,700	7,350	—
1897S	933,900	155	230	410	600	925	1,275	2,600	7,250	—
1898	2,956,735	20.50	24.00	55.50	131	200	405	610	3,150	3,750
1898O	874,000	37.50	100	240	400	575	640	1,250	8,950	—
1898S	2,358,550	29.00	52.50	95.00	175	340	440	985	9,400	—
1899	5,538,846	19.50	24.00	55.50	131	200	415	610	3,350	3,750
1899O	1,724,000	26.00	37.50	85.00	180	300	435	700	8,000	—
1899S	1,686,411	25.00	45.00	92.00	165	275	405	660	5,750	—
1900	4,762,912	18.50	24.50	55.50	131	200	405	610	3,650	3,750
1900O	2,744,000	18.50	22.50	62.00	190	315	435	900	13,500	—
1900S	2,560,322	18.50	24.50	48.50	131	215	400	660	8,250	—
1901	4,268,813	18.50	24.50	57.00	125	200	385	610	3,750	3,750
1901O	1,124,000	18.50	29.50	85.00	235	400	500	1,500	14,850	—
1901S	847,044	34.00	55.00	175	375	825	1,300	2,350	16,500	—
1902	4,922,777	18.50	24.50	57.00	125	200	395	610	3,750	3,750
1902O	2,526,000	18.50	24.50	55.00	115	240	420	850	9,850	—
1902S	1,460,670	18.50	28.50	66.00	165	285	420	825	7,500	—
1903	2,278,755	18.50	24.50	48.50	131	215	405	610	7,000	3,750
1903O	2,100,000	18.50	24.50	55.00	135	225	435	665	8,750	—
1903S	1,920,772	18.50	24.50	60.00	145	265	465	675	4,850	—
1904	2,992,670	18.50	24.50	55.50	125	200	405	610	4,100	3,750
1904O	1,117,600	19.00	33.00	90.00	250	435	610	1,375	11,000	—
1904S	553,038	42.00	100	325	775	1,450	2,450	9,850	38,500	—
1905	662,727	23.50	34.00	95.00	195	270	420	650	5,650	3,750
1905O	505,000	30.00	44.50	130	245	340	460	760	4,400	—
1905S	2,494,000	18.50	26.50	50.00	135	240	410	725	8,750	—
1906	2,638,675	18.50	24.50	50.50	131	200	385	600	3,150	3,750
1906D	4,028,000	18.50	24.50	53.50	139	195	385	600	3,650	—
1906O	2,446,000	18.50	24.50	48.50	131	210	400	650	5,850	—
1906S	1,740,154	18.50	26.50	57.50	135	230	430	650	4,650	—
1907	2,598,575	17.50	22.50	48.50	125	195	385	600	3,600	3,750
1907D	3,856,000	17.50	22.50	48.50	125	195	385	600	2,950	—
1907O	3,946,000	17.50	22.50	50.50	125	195	385	600	3,050	—
1907S	1,250,000	22.00	25.00	85.00	190	385	675	1,275	12,000	—
1908	1,354,545	17.50	22.50	48.50	125	195	385	600	3,350	3,750
1908D	3,280,000	17.50	22.50	48.50	125	195	385	600	2,950	—
1908O	5,360,000	17.50	22.50	48.50	125	195	395	600	2,950	—
1908S	1,644,828	17.50	29.50	75.00	175	285	475	875	5,500	—
1909	2,368,650	17.00	24.00	51.50	131	195	385	600	2,950	3,750
1909O	925,400	19.80	23.50	58.00	185	440	725	1,500	4,850	—
1909S	1,764,000	17.50	23.50	48.50	131	215	395	600	3,950	—
1910	418,551	20.00	30.00	95.00	180	365	495	675	3,750	3,750
1910S	1,948,000	19.00	27.50	54.50	131	200	405	640	6,250	—
1911	1,406,543	17.50	22.50	48.50	125	195	385	600	2,950	3,750
1911D	695,080	17.50	24.00	55.50	141	195	395	625	3,750	—
1911S	1,272,000	17.50	24.50	48.50	131	210	395	650	5,350	—
1912	1,550,700	17.50	22.50	48.50	125	195	385	600	3,450	3,750
1912D	2,300,800	17.50	22.50	48.50	125	195	385	600	2,950	—
1912S	1,370,000	17.80	22.00	55.50	141	210	435	650	4,250	—
1913	188,627	77.00	88.00	235	400	615	875	1,600	4,950	3,750
1913D	534,000	19.00	22.50	48.50	131	200	395	625	3,750	—
1913S	604,000	21.00	25.00	53.50	151	260	435	760	4,000	—
1914	124,610	145	170	335	525	775	1,000	1,475	7,850	3,750
1914S	992,000	17.50	22.50	48.50	131	210	405	625	4,250	—
1915	138,450	100	140	285	410	650	920	1,350	5,850	3,750
1915D	1,170,400	19.50	22.50	48.50	125	195	385	600	2,950	—
1915S	1,604,000	19.00	24.50	55.50	144	210	400	625	2,950	—

HALF DOLLAR

Walking Liberty Half Dollar
Liberty walking left wearing U.S. flag gown, sunrise at left. Eagle advancing left.

KM# 142 • 12.50 g., 0.900 Silver 0.3617 oz. ASW, 30.6 mm. • **Designer:** Adolph A. Weinman **Note:** The mint mark appears on the obverse below the word "Trust" on 1916 and some 1917 issues. Starting with some 1917 issues and continuing through the remainder of the series, the mint mark was changed to the reverse, at about the 8 o'clock position near the rim.

Obverse mint mark 1916-1917

Reverse mint mark 1917-1947

Date	Mintage	G4	VG8	F12	VF20	XF40	AU50	MS60	MS65	Prf65
1916	608,000	52.00	55.00	95.00	170	235	320	355	1,875	—
1916D	1,014,400	50.00	55.00	80.00	135	200	255	385	2,350	—
1916S	508,000	100	135	280	440	595	720	1,050	6,600	—
1917	12,292,000	9.10	14.20	18.00	22.00	40.00	72.00	130	1,225	—
1917D obv. mint mark	765,400	23.50	33.00	80.00	155	225	335	595	8,300	—
1917S obv. mint mark	952,000	26.00	44.00	135	365	650	1,100	2,325	22,500	—
1917D rev. mint mark	1,940,000	16.30	18.00	45.00	135	275	550	950	17,500	—
1917S rev. mint mark	5,554,000	16.00	17.00	19.00	32.00	60.00	155	370	14,000	—
1918	6,634,000	16.00	17.00	19.00	64.00	150	245	545	3,760	—
1918D	3,853,040	17.50	22.00	40.00	90.00	220	500	1,325	24,000	—
1918S	10,282,000	16.00	17.00	18.00	34.00	73.00	190	500	17,800	—
1919	962,000	25.50	32.50	78.50	265	510	875	1,400	7,550	—
1919D	1,165,000	25.00	38.50	95.00	320	760	2,200	5,900	155,000	—
1919S	1,552,000	19.50	27.50	72.00	310	820	1,750	3,550	18,400	—
1920	6,372,000	17.00	18.00	20.00	42.00	75.00	155	350	4,725	—
1920D	1,551,000	17.50	19.00	65.00	240	445	900	1,550	17,500	—
1920S	4,624,000	17.00	18.00	19.00	90.00	240	510	875	14,700	—
1921	246,000	150	210	315	750	2,250	3,150	6,750	22,750	—
1921D	208,000	295	370	575	900	2,850	4,450	13,500	33,500	—
1921S	548,000	43.00	65.00	200	775	4,100	4,450	19,250	122,000	—
1923S	2,178,000	16.00	17.00	27.50	110	500	1,150	1,625	17,750	—
1927S	2,392,000	15.50	16.00	17.50	46.00	165	425	1,000	9,550	—
1928S Large S	1,940,000	19.50	22.00	28.00	110	325	650	1,800	—	—
1928S Small S	Inc. above	16.00	18.00	19.00	66.00	195	475	1,070	11,500	—
1929D	1,001,200	12.90	16.00	18.00	42.50	94.00	195	415	2,975	—
1929S	1,902,000	12.90	16.00	17.00	28.50	113	220	435	2,950	—
1933S	1,786,000	15.60	16.50	17.50	22.00	57.50	260	640	3,600	—
1934	6,964,000	12.60	14.00	16.00	18.00	21.00	25.00	85.00	430	—
1934D	2,361,400	12.90	15.00	17.00	19.50	33.00	88.00	145	1,425	—
1934S	3,652,000	12.90	14.00	16.00	17.50	31.00	100	375	3,975	—
1935	9,162,000	10.60	11.20	13.50	16.00	19.50	26.00	44.00	280	—
1935D	3,003,800	12.90	14.00	16.00	20.00	31.50	66.00	140	2,175	—
1935S	3,854,000	12.10	13.00	15.00	17.50	49.00	95.00	280	2,750	—
1936	12,617,901	10.60	11.20	11.50	13.60	19.50	26.00	37.00	280	3,675
1936D	4,252,400	11.60	12.20	12.50	16.00	24.00	52.00	77.00	410	—
1936S	3,884,000	11.60	12.20	12.50	16.00	31.00	58.00	147	825	—
1937	9,527,728	9.90	10.50	10.70	12.60	20.00	26.00	38.00	190	940
1937D	1,676,000	11.60	12.20	12.70	13.60	34.00	105	215	690	—
1937S	2,090,000	11.60	12.20	12.50	13.10	26.50	62.00	165	600	—
1938	4,118,152	10.10	10.70	11.10	12.60	21.95	38.00	63.00	330	785
1938D	491,600	55.00	71.00	100	110	72.00	250	500	1,500	—
1939	6,820,808	9.60	10.20	10.50	11.10	20.00	24.00	42.00	175	730
1939D	4,267,800	9.60	10.70	11.00	12.10	21.25	26.00	46.00	145	—
1939S	2,552,000	10.10	11.20	11.50	13.90	25.50	76.00	155	280	—
1940	9,167,279	9.60	10.20	10.50	10.60	19.50	24.00	35.00	130	575
1940S	4,550,000	9.60	10.50	10.70	12.10	21.00	21.00	50.00	335	—
1941	24,207,412	9.90	10.20	10.50	10.60	17.50	23.00	34.00	115	580
1941D	11,248,400	9.60	10.50	11.00	11.10	19.95	24.00	40.00	155	—
1941S Small S	8,098,000	9.90	10.50	11.00	11.10	24.30	28.00	74.00	710	—
1941S Large S	Inc. above	12.20	13.20	15.50	20.00	35.00	60.00	—	—	—
1942	47,839,120	9.90	10.20	10.50	10.60	17.50	23.00	34.00	114	605
1942D	10,973,800	9.60	10.50	10.70	11.10	19.95	24.00	40.00	280	—
1942S	12,708,000	9.90	10.50	10.70	11.10	19.95	25.00	40.00	440	—
1943	53,190,000	9.90	10.20	10.50	10.60	17.80	23.00	34.00	114	—
1943D	11,346,000	9.60	10.50	10.70	11.10	19.95	25.00	43.00	225	—
1943D Double Die Obverse	Inc. above	12.00	15.00	17.00	19.00	22.00	30.00	58.00	450	—

Date	Mintage	G4	VG8	F12	VF20	XF40	AU50	MS60	MS65	Prf65
1943S	13,450,000	9.90	10.50	10.70	11.10	19.95	24.00	43.00	265	—
1944	28,206,000	9.60	10.20	10.50	10.60	17.80	23.00	34.00	114	—
1944D	9,769,000	9.90	10.50	10.70	11.10	19.95	24.00	40.00	150	—
1944S	8,904,000	9.90	10.20	10.70	11.10	19.95	26.00	45.00	440	—
1945	31,502,000	9.60	10.50	10.50	10.60	17.80	23.00	34.00	114	—
1945D	9,966,800	9.90	10.50	10.70	11.10	19.95	24.00	40.00	124	—
1945S	10,156,000	9.90	10.20	10.70	11.10	19.95	24.00	45.00	150	—
1946	12,118,000	9.60	10.25	10.50	10.60	17.80	23.00	34.00	150	—
1946 Double Die Reverse	Inc. above	16.00	24.00	35.00	50.00	85.00	175	325	3,200	—
1946D	2,151,000	8.60	10.70	11.00	12.60	23.75	42.00	49.00	124	—
1946S	3,724,000	8.10	10.50	10.50	11.10	20.75	35.00	54.00	115	—
1947	4,094,000	8.10	10.20	10.50	11.10	19.95	26.00	47.00	160	—
1947D	3,900,600	8.60	10.70	11.00	12.60	19.95	32.00	47.00	125	—

Franklin Half Dollar
Franklin bust right.   Liberty Bell, small eagle at right.

KM# 199 • 12.50 g., 0.900 Silver 0.3617 oz. ASW, 30.6 mm. • **Designer:** John R. Sinnock **Note:** The type I reverse is distinguished by the eagle having four full feathers on the wing closest the bell, whereas the type II reverse eagle has three full feathers.

Mint mark

Date	Mintage	G4	VG8	F12	VF20	XF40	AU50	MS60	MS65	65FBL	65CAM
1948	3,006,814	—	7.70	7.80	8.40	9.00	9.20	20.00	63.00	190	—
1948D	4,028,600	—	7.70	7.80	8.40	8.50	8.90	19.50	107	260	—
1949	5,614,000	—	—	—	—	9.50	15.00	36.00	115	250	—
1949D	4,120,600	—	—	—	8.20	10.50	25.00	42.00	517	1,750	—
1949S	3,744,000	—	—	—	8.40	16.50	30.00	80.00	132	700	—
1950	7,793,509	—	—	—	—	7.80	13.00	27.75	86.00	285	2,000
1950D	8,031,600	—	—	—	—	8.80	9.00	21.00	230	900	—
1951	16,859,602	—	—	—	—	7.50	10.50	17.50	50.00	340	1,500
1951D	9,475,200	—	—	—	—	12.80	17.50	36.00	143	540	—
1951S	13,696,000	—	—	—	7.80	8.50	15.00	25.50	55.00	750	—
1952	21,274,073	—	—	—	—	7.70	10.50	22.50	50.00	210	775
1952D	25,395,600	—	—	—	—	7.70	10.50	18.50	109	450	—
1952S	5,526,000	—	—	7.80	10.40	16.00	32.00	64.00	89.50	1,500	—
1953	2,796,920	—	—	7.80	7.90	8.30	16.00	26.00	88.50	1,000	475
1953D	20,900,400	—	—	—	—	7.50	7.70	19.00	101	400	—
1953S	4,148,000	—	—	—	7.80	8.50	18.50	30.00	46.00	160	—
1954	13,421,503	—	—	—	—	7.50	7.70	16.30	40.00	225	175
1954D	25,445,580	—	—	—	—	7.50	7.70	16.30	80.00	235	—
1954S	4,993,400	—	—	—	—	7.90	8.50	17.50	33.00	440	—
1955	2,876,381	—	15.50	16.00	17.50	18.00	18.50	19.50	42.50	140	120
1955 Bugs Bunny	Inc. above	—	20.00	22.00	23.00	25.00	26.00	28.00	120	750	—
1956 Type 1 rev.	4,701,384	—	7.50	7.50	7.60	7.90	8.70	19.50	29.00	125	300
1956 Type 2 rev.	Inc. above	—	—	—	—	—	—	—	—	—	40.00
1957 Type 1 rev.	6,361,952	—	—	—	—	7.50	8.70	16.50	31.00	95.00	—
1957 Type 2 rev.	Inc. above	—	—	—	—	—	—	—	—	—	55.00
1957D	19,966,850	—	—	—	—	7.50	8.70	16.00	33.00	100	—
1958 Type 1 rev.	4,917,652	—	—	—	—	7.50	8.70	16.50	30.00	110	—
1958 Type 2 rev.	Inc. above	—	—	—	—	8.20	20.00	26.00	—	—	60.00
1958D	23,962,412	—	—	—	—	7.50	8.70	16.30	30.00	80.00	—
1959 Type 1 rev.	7,349,291	—	—	—	—	7.50	8.70	16.30	50.00	250	—
1959 Type 2 rev.	Inc. above	—	—	—	—	8.00	16.00	30.00	115	—	75.00
1959D	13,053,750	—	—	—	—	7.50	8.70	16.30	72.00	215	—
1960 Type 1 rev.	7,715,602	—	—	—	—	7.50	8.70	16.00	82.75	340	—
1960 Type 2 rev.	Inc. above	—	—	—	—	—	—	—	—	—	45.00
1960D	18,215,812	—	—	—	—	7.50	8.70	16.00	195	1,350	—
1961 Type 1 rev.	11,318,244	—	—	—	—	7.50	8.70	16.00	41.00	1,300	—
1961 Type 2 rev.	Inc. above	—	—	—	—	25.00	—	—	—	—	40.00
1961 Double die rev.	Inc. above	—	—	—	—	—	—	—	—	—	3,500
1961D	20,276,442	—	—	—	—	7.50	8.70	16.00	103	875	—
1962 Type 1 rev.	12,932,019	—	—	—	—	7.50	8.70	16.00	76.00	1,850	—
1962 Type 2 rev.	Inc. above	—	—	—	—	—	—	—	—	—	35.00
1962D	35,473,281	—	—	—	—	7.50	8.70	16.00	92.00	800	—
1963 Type 1 rev.	25,239,645	—	—	—	—	7.50	8.70	15.50	28.50	1,200	—

Date	Mintage	G4	VG8	F12	VF20	XF40	AU50	MS60	MS65	65FBL	65CAM
1963 Type 2 rev.	Inc. above	—	—	—	—	—	—	—	—	—	35.00
1963D	67,069,292	—	—	—	—	7.50	8.70	15.50	30.00	165	—

Kennedy Half Dollar

KM# 202 • 12.50 g., 0.900 Silver 0.3617 oz. ASW, 30.6 mm. • **Obv. Designer:** Gilroy Roberts **Rev. Designer:** Frank Gasparro **Edge:** Reeded

Mint mark 1964

Date	Mintage	G4	VG8	F12	VF20	XF40	MS60	MS65	Prf65
1964	277,254,766	—	—	—	—	12.30	12.50	22.00	15.00
1964 Accented Hair	Inc. above	—	—	—	—	—	—	—	40.00
1964D	156,205,446	—	—	—	—	12.40	12.70	24.00	—

KM# 202a • 11.50 g., 0.400 Silver 0.1479 oz. ASW, 30.6 mm. • **Obv. Designer:** Gilroy Roberts **Rev. Designer:** Frank Gasparro **Edge:** Reeded

Mint mark 1968 - present

Date	Mintage	G4	VG8	F12	VF20	XF40	MS60	MS65	Prf65
1965	65,879,366	—	—	—	—	—	6.10	14.50	—
1965 SMS	2,360,000	—	—	—	—	—	—	15.00	—
1966	108,984,932	—	—	—	—	—	6.10	22.50	—
1966 SMS	2,261,583	—	—	—	—	—	—	17.00	—
1967	295,046,978	—	—	—	—	—	6.10	18.50	—
1967 SMS	1,863,344	—	—	—	—	—	—	18.00	—
1968D	246,951,930	—	—	—	—	—	6.10	16.50	—
1968S	3,041,506	—	—	—	—	—	—	—	8.56
1969D	129,881,800	—	—	—	—	—	6.10	20.00	—
1969S	2,934,631	—	—	—	—	—	—	—	8.56
1970D	2,150,000	—	—	—	—	—	8.50	40.00	—
1970S	2,632,810	—	—	—	—	—	—	—	12.00

KM# 202b • 11.34 g., Copper-Nickel Clad Copper, 30.6 mm. • **Obv. Designer:** Gilroy Roberts **Rev. Designer:** Frank Gasparro

Date	Mintage	G4	VG8	F12	VF20	XF40	MS60	MS65	Prf65
1971	155,640,000	—	—	—	—	—	1.00	17.50	—
1971D	302,097,424	—	—	—	—	—	1.00	12.00	—
1971S	3,244,183	—	—	—	—	—	—	—	5.00
1972	153,180,000	—	—	—	—	—	1.00	15.50	—
1972D	141,890,000	—	—	—	—	—	1.00	14.50	—
1972S	3,267,667	—	—	—	—	—	—	—	5.00
1973	64,964,000	—	—	—	—	—	1.00	20.00	—
1973D	83,171,400	—	—	—	—	—	—	12.00	—
1973S	2,769,624	—	—	—	—	—	—	—	5.00
1974	201,596,000	—	—	—	—	—	1.00	25.00	—
1974D	79,066,300	—	—	—	—	—	1.00	17.00	—
1974D DDO	Inc. above	—	—	—	—	24.00	32.00	165	—
1974S	2,617,350	—	—	—	—	—	—	—	5.00
1975 none minted		—	—	—	—	—	—	—	—
1975D none minted		—	—	—	—	—	—	—	—
1975S none minted		—	—	—	—	—	—	—	—

HALF DOLLAR

Independence Hall.

KM# 205 • 11.20 g., Copper-Nickel, 30.6 mm. • **Obv. Designer:** Gilroy Roberts **Rev. Designer:** Seth Huntington

Date	Mintage	G4	VG8	F12	VF20	XF40	MS60	MS65	Prf65
1976	234,308,000	—	—	—	—	—	1.00	16.50	—
1976D	287,565,248	—	—	—	—	—	1.00	14.00	—
1976S	7,059,099	—	—	—	—	—	—	—	5.00

Bicentennial design, Independence Hall.

KM# 205a • 11.50 g., 0.400 Silver 0.1479 oz. ASW, 30.6 mm. • **Rev. Designer:** Seth Huntington

Date	Mintage	G4	VG8	F12	VF20	XF40	MS60	MS65	Prf65
1976S	4,908,319	—	—	—	—	—	—	12.00	8.70
1976S	3,998,621	—	—	—	—	—	—	—	8.70

Regular design resumed.

KM# A202b • 11.34 g., Copper-Nickel Clad Copper, 30.61 mm. • **Edge:** Reeded **Note:** KM#202b design and composition resumed. The 1979-S and 1981-S Type II proofs have clearer mint marks than the Type I proofs of those years.

Date	Mintage	MS65	Prf65
1977	43,598,000	12.50	—
1977D	31,449,106	16.50	—
1977S	3,251,152	—	4.50
1978	14,350,000	12.00	—
1978D	13,765,799	15.00	—
1978S	3,127,788	—	5.00
1979	68,312,000	13.50	—
1979D	15,815,422	13.50	—
1979S Type I	3,677,175	—	5.00
1979S Type II	Inc. above	—	18.00
1980P	44,134,000	12.50	—
1980D	33,456,449	17.50	—
1980S	3,547,030	—	5.00
1981P	29,544,000	9.00	—
1981D	27,839,533	12.00	—
1981S Type I	4,063,083	—	5.00
1981S Type II	Inc. above	—	18.50
1982P	10,819,000	18.50	—
1982P no initials FG	Inc. above	110	—
1982D	13,140,102	20.00	—
1982S	38,957,479	—	5.00
1983P	34,139,000	22.50	—
1983D	32,472,244	12.50	—
1983S	3,279,126	—	5.00
1984P	26,029,000	12.00	—
1984D	26,262,158	18.00	—
1984S	3,065,110	—	6.00
1985P	18,706,962	16.50	—
1985D	19,814,034	12.50	—
1985S	3,962,138	—	5.00
1986P	13,107,633	17.50	—
1986D	15,336,145	14.00	—
1986S	2,411,180	—	6.00
1987P	2,890,758	16.50	—
1987D	2,890,758	12.50	—
1987S	4,407,728	—	5.00
1988P	13,626,000	16.50	—
1988D	12,000,096	10.00	—
1988S	3,262,948	—	5.00
1989P	24,542,000	13.00	—
1989D	23,000,216	13.00	—
1989S	3,220,194	—	5.00
1990P	22,780,000	17.50	—
1990D	20,096,242	20.00	—
1990S	3,299,559	—	5.00
1991P	14,874,000	12.50	—
1991D	15,054,678	16.00	—
1991S	2,867,787	—	5.00
1992P	17,628,000	10.00	—
1992D	17,000,106	10.00	—
1992S	2,858,981	—	5.00
1993P	15,510,000	12.00	—
1993D	15,000,006	10.00	—
1993S	2,633,439	—	5.00
1994P	23,718,000	12.00	—
1994D	23,828,110	8.50	—
1994S	2,484,594	—	5.00
1995P	26,496,000	10.00	—
1995D	26,288,000	8.00	—
1995S	2,010,384	—	12.00
1996P	24,442,000	10.00	—
1996D	24,744,000	10.00	—
1996S	2,085,191	—	9.00
1997P	20,882,000	14.00	—
1997D	19,876,000	13.50	—
1997S	1,975,000	—	10.00
1998P	15,646,000	12.50	—
1998D	15,064,000	12.50	—
1998S	2,078,494	—	7.00
1999P	8,900,000	11.00	—
1999D	10,682,000	10.00	—
1999S	2,557,897	—	8.00
2000P	22,600,000	12.00	—
2000D	19,466,000	12.00	—
2000S	3,082,944	—	5.00
2001P	21,200,000	10.00	—

HALF DOLLAR

Date	Mintage	MS65	Prf65
2001D	19,504,000	9.00	—
2001S	2,235,000	—	5.00
2002P	3,100,000	10.00	—
2002D	2,500,000	10.50	—
2002S	2,268,913	—	5.00
2003P	2,500,000	6.00	—
2003D	2,500,000	6.00	—
2003S	2,076,165	—	5.00
2004P	2,900,000	4.50	—
2004D	2,900,000	4.50	—
2004S	1,789,488	—	6.00
2005P	3,800,000	6.00	—
2005P Satin finish	1,160,000	8.00	—
2005D	3,500,000	5.00	—
2005D Satin finish	1,160,000	10.00	—
2005S	2,275,000	—	5.00
2006P	2,400,000	4.50	—
2006P Satin finish	847,361	12.00	—
2006D	2,000,000	4.50	—
2006D Satin finish	847,361	14.00	—
2006S	1,934,965	—	6.00
2007P	2,400,000	4.50	—
2007P Satin finish	—	8.00	—
2007D	2,400,000	4.50	—
2007D Satin finish	—	8.00	—
2007S	1,702,116	—	6.00
2008P	1,700,000	4.50	—
2008P Satin finish	—	8.50	—
2008D	1,700,000	4.50	—
2008D Satin finish	—	8.50	—
2008S	1,405,674	—	9.00
2009P	1,900,000	4.50	—
2009P Satin finish	—	8.50	—
2009D	1,900,000	4.50	—
2009D Satin finish	—	8.50	—
2009S	1,482,502	—	6.00
2010P	1,800,000	4.50	—
2010P Satin finish	—	8.50	—
2010D	1,700,000	4.50	—
2010D Satin finish	—	8.50	—
2010S	1,103,815	—	13.00
2011P	1,750,000	4.50	—
2011D	1,700,000	4.50	—
2011S	1,098,835	—	9.00
2012P	1,800,000	4.50	—
2012D	1,700,000	4.50	—
2012S	841,972	—	9.00
2013P	5,000,000	4.50	—
2013D	4,600,000	4.50	—

Date	Mintage	MS65	Prf65
2013S	821,031	—	9.00
2014D	—	4.50	—
2014P	—	4.50	—
2014S	—	—	9.00
2015D	—	4.50	—
2015P	—	4.50	—
2015S	—	—	9.00

KM# A202c • 12.50 g., 0.900 Silver 0.3617 oz. ASW, 30.6 mm. • **Designer:** Gilroy Roberts

Date	Mintage	MS65	PF65
1992S	1,317,579	—	13.20
1993S	761,353	—	15.20
1994S	785,329	—	13.20
1995S	838,953	—	46.00
1996S	830,021	—	15.20
1997S	821,678	—	35.00
1998S Matte Finish	62,350	225	—
1998S	878,792	—	13.20
1999S	804,565	—	15.20
2000S	965,921	—	13.20
2001S	849,600	—	13.20
2002S	888,816	—	13.20
2003S	1,040,425	—	13.20
2004S	1,175,935	—	13.20
2005S	1,069,679	—	14.20
2006S	988,140	—	14.20
2007S	1,384,797	—	15.70
2008S	620,684	—	14.20
2009S	697,365	—	13.20
2010S	585,401	—	14.20
2011S	574,175	—	14.20
2012S	395,443	—	14.20
2013S	451,342	—	14.20
2014S	—	—	12.00
2015S	—	—	9.00

DOLLAR

Flowing Hair Dollar

KM# 17 • 26.96 g., 0.892 Silver 0.7732 oz. ASW, 39-40 mm. • **Designer:** Robert Scot **Note:** The two 1795 varieties have either two or three leaves under each of the eagle's wings on the reverse.

Date	Mintage	G4	VG8	F12	VF20	XF40	MS60	MS63
1794	1,758	57,500	90,000	120,000	170,000	245,000	575,000	950,000
1795 2 leaves	203,033	1,950	2,250	4,450	7,800	16,150	80,500	196,500
1795 3 leaves	Inc. above	1,850	2,100	4,200	7,250	14,500	69,500	182,500
1795 Silver plug	Inc. above	3,500	6,500	9,850	13,950	28,500	115,000	235,000

Draped Bust Dollar
Small eagle.

KM# 18 • 26.96 g., 0.892 Silver 0.7732 oz. ASW, 39-40 mm. • **Designer:** Robert Scot

Date	Mintage	G4	VG8	F12	VF20	XF40	MS60	MS63
1795 Off-center bust	Inc. above	1,350	2,050	3,850	5,850	12,500	52,000	126,000
1795 Centered bust	Inc. above	1,370	2,075	3,900	5,950	12,700	52,500	126,000
1796 small date, small letters	72,920	1,450	2,150	4,100	6,300	13,750	70,000	—
1796 small date, large letters	Inc. above	1,360	2,070	3,875	6,400	13,700	—	—
1796 large date, small letters	Inc. above	1,385	2,085	4,250	6,750	14,350	57,000	136,000
1797 9 stars left, 7 stars right, small letters	7,776	2,000	3,250	5,200	9,000	18,850	—	—
1797 9 stars left, 7 stars right, large letters	Inc. above	1,560	2,325	4,250	6,850	13,950	55,500	—
1797 10 stars left, 6 stars right	Inc. above	1,450	2,250	4,050	6,350	13,600	53,500	125,000
1798 13 stars	327,536	1,450	2,250	4,150	6,300	13,750	85,000	—
1798 15 stars	Inc. above	2,050	2,750	4,700	7,450	16,150	95,000	—

Draped bust right, flanked by stars, date below.   Heraldic eagle.

KM# 32 • 26.96 g., 0.892 Silver 0.7732 oz. ASW, 39-40 mm. • **Obv. Legend:** LIBERTY **Rev. Legend:** UNITED STATES OF AMERICA **Designer:** Robert Scot **Note:** The 1798 "knob 9" variety has a serif on the lower left of the 9 in the date. The 1798 varieties are distinguished by the number of arrows held by the eagle on the reverse and the number of berries on the olive branch. On the 1798 "high-8" variety, the 8 in the date is higher than the other numerals. The 1799 varieties are distinguished by the number and positioning of the stars on the obverse and by the size of the berries in the olive branch on the reverse. On the 1700 "irregular date" variety, the first 9 in the date is smaller than the other numerals. Some varieties of the 1800 strikes had letters in the legend cut twice into the dies; as between the numerals in the date are wider than other varieties and the 8 is lower than the other numerals. The 1800 "small berries" variety refers to the size of the berries in the olive branch on the reverse. The 1800 "12 arrows" and "10 arrows" varieties refer to the number of arrows held by the eagle. The 1800 "Americai" variety appears to have the faint outline of an "I" after "America" in the reverse legend. The "close" and "wide" varieties of the 1802 refer to the amount of space between the numerals in the date. The 1800 large-3 and small-3 varieties are distinguished by the size of the 3 in the date.

Date	Mintage	G4	VG8	F12	VF20	XF40	MS60	MS63
1798 knob 9, 4 stripes	423,515	1,025	1,185	1,785	2,735	5,550	21,750	95,000
1798 knob 9, 10 arrows	Inc. above	1,025	1,185	1,785	2,735	5,550	21,750	87,000
1798 knob 9, 5 stripes	Inc. above	—	—	—	—	—	—	124,500
1798 pointed 9, 4 berries	Inc. above	1,025	1,185	1,785	2,735	5,550	21,750	43,500
1798 5 berries, 12 arrows	Inc. above	1,025	1,185	1,785	2,735	5,550	21,750	43,500
1798 high 8	Inc. above	1,025	1,185	1,785	2,735	5,550	21,750	43,500
1798 13 arrows	Inc. above	1,025	1,185	1,785	2,735	5,550	21,750	45,000
1799/98 13-star reverse	Inc. above	1,065	1,250	2,000	2,950	4,300	23,500	45,000
1799/98 15-star reverse	Inc. above	1,050	1,225	1,875	2,850	4,000	24,500	47,500
1799 irregular date, 13-star reverse	Inc. above	1,010	1,170	1,825	3,000	3,900	23,500	45,000
1799 irregular date, 15-star reverse	Inc. above	1,000	1,160	1,825	3,200	5,550	21,500	42,500
1799 perfect date, 7- and 6-star obverse, no berries	Inc. above	990	1,150	1,750	2,700	3,850	18,500	42,500

DOLLAR

DOLLAR

Date	Mintage	G4	VG8	F12	VF20	XF40	MS60	MS63
1799 perfect date, 7- and 6-star obverse, small berries	Inc. above	990	1,150	1,750	2,700	3,850	18,500	42,500
1799 perfect date, 7- and 6-star obverse, medium large berries	Inc. above	990	1,150	1,750	2,700	3,850	18,500	42,500
1799 perfect date, 7- and 6-star obverse, extra large berries	Inc. above	1,000	1,180	1,750	2,700	3,850	18,500	51,500
1799 8 stars left, 5 stars right on obverse	Inc. above	1,075	1,200	1,825	2,800	3,900	24,000	45,000
1800 R" in "Liberty" double cut	220,920	1,040	1,225	1,825	2,775	5,550	21,500	45,000
1800 first "T" in "States" double cut	Inc. above	1,040	1,200	1,800	2,750	5,550	21,500	45,000
1800 both letters double cut	Inc. above	1,040	1,200	1,800	2,750	5,550	21,500	45,000
1800 T' in "United" double cut	Inc. above	1,040	1,200	1,800	2,750	5,550	21,500	45,000
1800 very wide date, low 8	Inc. above	1,040	1,200	1,800	2,750	5,550	21,500	—
1800 small berries	Inc. above	1,040	1,200	1,850	2,800	3,900	22,000	48,500
1800 dot date	Inc. above	1,040	1,250	2,000	3,000	4,300	21,500	45,000
1800 12 arrows	Inc. above	1,040	1,200	1,825	3,200	5,550	31,000	—
1800 10 arrows	Inc. above	1,040	1,200	1,825	3,200	5,550	—	—
1800 Americai	Inc. above	1,065	1,250	2,000	3,300	4,300	21,500	49,000
1801	54,454	1,065	1,300	2,050	3,200	4,000	25,000	—
1801 proof restrike	—	—	—	—	—	—	—	—
1802/1 close	Inc. above	1,090	1,275	2,000	3,300	4,300	20,500	—
1802/1 wide	Inc. above	1,090	1,275	2,000	3,300	4,300	20,500	—
1802 close, perfect date	Inc. above	1,090	1,275	1,850	2,800	3,900	20,500	—
1802 wide, perfect date	Inc. above	1,090	1,250	1,825	2,775	3,950	21,500	—
1802 proof restrike, mintage unrecorded	—	—	—	—	—	—	—	—
1803 large 3	85,634	1,100	1,300	1,875	3,000	4,000	20,500	47,500
1803 small 3	Inc. above	1,100	1,300	2,000	3,300	4,300	21,500	48,500
1803 proof restrike, mintage unrecorded	—	—	—	—	—	—	—	—
1804 15 known	—	—	—	—	—	—	—	—

Note: 1804, Childs Sale, Aug. 1999, Prf-68, $4,140,000.

Gobrecht Dollar
"C Gobrecht F." in base.   Eagle flying left amid stars.
KM# 59.1 • 26.73 g., 0.900 Silver 0.7734 oz. ASW, 38.1 mm. • **Obv. Designer:** Christian Gobrecht **Rev. Legend:** UNITED STATES OF AMERICA **Edge:** Plain.

Date	Mintage	G4	VG8	F12	VF20	XF40	AU50	MS60	MS63	MS65	Prf65
1836	1,000	—	—	—	11,500	14,850	18,000	—	—	—	75,000

C. Gobrecht F." in base.   Eagle flying in plain field.
KM# 59.2 • 26.73 g., 0.900 Silver 0.7734 oz. ASW, 38.1 mm. • **Obv. Designer:** Christian Gobrecht. **Edge:** Plain.

Date	Mintage	G4	VG8	F12	VF20	XF40	AU50	MS60	MS63	MS65	Prf65
1836 Restrike	—	—	—	—	—	—	17,500	—	—	—	68,000

C. Gobrecht F." in base.

KM# 59a.1 • 26.73 g., 0.900 Silver 0.7734 oz. ASW, 38.1 mm. • **Obv. Legend:** Eagle flying left amid stars.
Edge: Plain.

Date	Mintage	G4	VG8	F12	VF20	XF40	AU50	MS60	MS63	MS65	Prf65
1836	600	—	—	—	—	—	—	—	—	—	—

C. Gobrecht F." in base.   Eagle flying left amid stars.

KM# 59a.2 • 26.73 g., 0.900 Silver 0.7734 oz. ASW, 38.1 mm. • **Edge:** Reeded.

Date	Mintage	G4	VG8	F12	VF20	XF40	AU50	MS60	MS63	MS65	Prf65
1836 Restrike		—	—	—	—	—	—	—	—	—	—

Designer's name omitted in base.   Eagle in plain field.

KM# 59a.3 • 26.73 g., 0.900 Silver 0.7734 oz. ASW, 38.1 mm. • **Edge:** Reeded.

Date	Mintage	G4	VG8	F12	VF20	XF40	AU50	MS60	MS63	MS65	Prf65
1839	300	—	—	—	—	—	27,500	—	—	—	95,000

KM# 59a.4 • 26.73 g., 0.900 Silver 0.7734 oz. ASW, 38.1 mm. •

Date	Mintage	G4	VG8	F12	VF20	XF40	AU50	MS60	MS63	MS65	Prf65
1839 Restrike		—	—	—	—	—	26,500	—	—	—	90,000

Note: All other combinations are restrikes of the late 1850's.

DOLLAR

Seated Liberty Dollar
Seated Liberty, date below. No motto above eagle.
KM# 71 • 26.73 g., 0.900 Silver 0.7734 oz. ASW, 38.1 mm. • **Rev. Legend:** UNITED STATES OF AMERICA
Designer: Christian Gobrecht

Date	Mintage	G4	VG8	F12	VF20	XF40	AU50	MS60	MS63	MS65	Prf65
1840	61,005	290	320	340	420	680	1,075	4,000	21,500	—	—
1841	173,000	265	295	315	395	610	1,000	2,950	5,500	100,000	—
1842	184,618	265	295	315	395	630	925	2,650	4,700		—
1843	165,100	265	295	315	395	465	925	2,750	9,000		—
1844	20,000	280	313	360	455	785	1,250	6,450	15,000	100,000	—
1845	24,500	300	335	385	455	900	1,750	10,500	26,500	—	75,000
1846	110,600	275	313	345	490	650	1,100	2,750	5,200	98,000	125,000
1846O	59,000	285	330	370	480	775	1,325	8,750	20,000		—
1847	140,750	265	295	315	395	465	900	2,950	7,500	100,000	—
1848	15,000	325	385	515	795	1,250	1,700	4,100	12,500	100,000	—
1849	62,600	275	305	350	420	600	1,000	3,200	7,950	100,000	155,000
1850	7,500	465	545	380	845	1,750	2,650	7,850	15,000	—	80,000
1850O	40,000	335	400	515	750	1,550	3,950	12,850	34,500		—
1851	1,300	4,000	4,850	5,750	7,750	18,000	27,000	43,500	68,500	150,000	225,000
1851 Restrike	—										90,000
1852	1,100	3,500	4,150	5,200	7,000	15,000	26,000	38,500	60,000	150,000	200,000
1852 Restrike	—										70,000
1853	46,110	335	400	550	660	1,100	1,425	4,000	7,950	100,000	90,000
1853 Restrike	—										
1854	33,140	1,100	1,450	2,000	2,850	4,500	5,750	8,500	13,500	100,000	80,000
1855	26,000	900	1,150	1,500	2,150	3,750	4,950	8,850	31,500	—	55,000
1856	63,500	400	450	515	775	1,650	2,850	4,350	11,500	—	39,500
1857	94,000	450	525	675	800	1,500	1,850	3,650	9,000	95,000	39,500
1858 proof only	Est. 800	3,200	3,600	4,000	4,800	7,250	8,850	—	—	—	42,500
Note: Later restrike.											
1859	256,500	285	335	400	515	655	1,000	2,850	5,850	95,000	17,500
1859O	360,000	265	295	315	395	465	800	2,250	4,150	56,000	—
1859S	20,000	330	390	515	750	1,550	3,500	15,000	36,500	—	—
1860	218,930	275	310	380	510	660	900	2,550	5,500	90,000	15,700
1860O	515,000	265	295	315	395	465	800	2,250	3,850	56,000	—
1861	78,500	600	750	900	985	1,750	1,975	2,950	5,650	90,000	15,700
1862	12,090	440	600	850	945	1,450	1,650	3,250	5,750	90,000	15,700
1863	27,660	375	525	575	660	985	1,400	3,250	6,000	90,000	18,000
1864	31,170	350	410	500	565	920	1,375	3,350	6,400	90,000	15,700
1865	47,000	300	350	420	585	1,050	1,750	3,250	6,250	90,000	15,700
1866 2 known without motto	—										

DOLLAR

Seated Liberty, date below.   IN GOD WE TRUST above eagle.

KM# 100 • 26.73 g., 0.900 Silver 0.7734 oz. ASW, 38.1 mm. • **Rev. Legend:** UNITED STATES OF AMERICA
Designer: Christian Gobrecht **Note:** In 1866 the motto was added to the reverse above the eagle.

Date	Mintage	G4	VG8	F12	VF20	XF40	AU50	MS60	MS63	MS65	Prf65
1866	49,625	320	350	440	590	795	1,250	2,400	5,000	85,000	16,000
1867	47,525	315	345	405	565	670	895	2,435	5,050	85,000	16,000
1868	162,700	325	355	395	535	650	920	3,500	7,350	85,000	16,000
1869	424,300	290	320	370	490	640	985	2,400	5,000	85,000	16,000
1870	416,000	280	320	350	430	595	970	2,300	4,950	67,500	16,000
1870CC	12,462	475	600	825	1,375	3,650	8,250	27,500	44,500	—	—
1870S 12-15 known	—	150,000	235,000	350,000	600,000	850,000	1,350,000	1,850,000	2,500,000	—	—
Note: 1870S, Eliasberg Sale, April 1997, EF-45 to AU-50, $264,000.											
1871	1,074,760	270	300	330	410	545	970	2,300	4,950	67,500	16,000
1871CC	1,376	2,000	2,850	4,750	7,450	14,500	25,000	68,500	175,000	—	—
1872	1,106,450	270	300	330	410	495	820	2,300	4,850	67,500	16,000
1872CC	3,150	900	1,400	2,850	4,300	4,850	13,500	28,500	120,000	385,000	—
1872S	9,000	310	365	550	700	2,000	4,500	11,000	26,000	—	—
1873	293,600	275	310	340	420	510	840	2,350	4,900	67,500	16,000
1873CC	2,300	6,250	7,250	11,500	19,000	31,500	43,500	125,000	225,000	625,000	—
1873S none known	700	—	—	—	—	—	—	—	—	—	—

Trade Dollar
Seated Liberty, IN GOD WE TRUST in base above date.   TRADE DOLLAR below eagle.

KM# 108 • 27.22 g., 0.900 Silver 0.7876 oz. ASW, 38.1 mm. • **Rev. Legend:** UNITED STATES OF AMERICA.
Designer: William Barber

Date	Mintage	G4	VG8	F12	VF20	XF40	AU50	MS60	MS65	Prf65
1873	397,500	115	155	165	185	280	360	1,200	15,500	10,250
1873CC	124,500	245	295	335	460	875	1,875	10,000	120,000	—
1873S	703,000	115	155	160	210	280	355	1,475	18,500	—
1874	987,800	125	155	160	185	280	365	1,100	18,250	10,250
1874CC	1,373,200	255	295	335	385	625	775	3,450	33,000	—
1874S	2,549,000	115	155	160	170	280	340	1,125	17,500	—
1875	218,900	145	185	350	425	550	800	2,450	18,000	15,000
1875CC	1,573,700	235	275	315	350	525	800	2,650	38,500	—
1875S	4,487,000	105	155	155	160	260	330	1,050	12,500	—
1875S/CC	Inc. above	210	285	365	560	925	1,450	4,650	59,000	—
1876	456,150	115	155	160	170	280	340	1,100	12,500	10,250
1876CC	509,000	245	285	310	365	585	985	8,000	76,500	—
1876CC DDR	Inc. above	—	—	375	650	1,250	2,000	8,500	—	—
1876S	5,227,000	105	145	150	160	255	330	1,050	17,500	—
1877	3,039,710	115	155	160	170	265	340	1,150	23,500	10,250
1877CC	534,000	255	295	335	425	700	825	2,650	59,000	—
1877S	9,519,000	105	145	150	160	255	330	1,050	12,500	—

DOLLAR

Mintage	G4	VG8	F12	VF20	XF40	AU50	MS60	MS65	Prf65
900	—	—	—	1,200	1,300	1,500	—	—	11,000
97,000	425	625	935	1,475	2,750	4,000	13,500	112,500	—
4,162,000	105	145	150	160	225	330	1,050	12,500	—
1,541	—	—	—	1,175	1,275	1,400	—	—	10,250

Date	Mintage	G4	VG8	F12	VF20	XF40	AU50	MS60	MS65	Prf65
1880 proof only	1,987	—	—	—	1,150	1,250	1,350	—	—	10,250
1881 proof only	960	—	—	—	1,200	1,300	1,400	—	—	10,250
1882 proof only	1,097	—	—	—	1,175	1,275	1,375	—	—	10,250
1883 proof only	979	—	—	—	1,200	1,300	1,400	—	—	10,250
1884 proof only	10	—	—	—	—	—	100,000	—	—	650,000

Note: 1884, Eliasberg Sale, April 1997, Prf-66, $396,000.

Date	Mintage	G4	VG8	F12	VF20	XF40	AU50	MS60	MS65	Prf65
1885 proof only	5	—	—	—	—	—	—	—	—	3,000,000

Note: 1885, Eliasberg Sale, April 1997, Prf-65, $907,500.

Morgan Dollar

Laureate head left, date below flanked by stars.   Eagle within 1/2 wreath.

KM# 110 • 26.73 g., 0.900 Silver 0.7734 oz. ASW, 38.1 mm. • **Obv. Legend:** E • PLURIBUS • UNUM **Rev. Legend:** UNITED STATES OF AMERICA **Designer:** George T. Morgan **Note:** "65DMPL" values are for coins grading MS-65 deep-mirror prooflike. The 1878 "8 tail feathers" and "7 tail feathers" varieties are distinguished by the number of feathers in the eagle's tail. On the "reverse of 1878" varieties, the top of the top feather in the arrows held by the eagle is straight across and the eagle's breast is concave. On the "reverse of 1879 varieties," the top feather in the arrows held by the eagle is slanted and the eagle's breast is convex. The 1890-CC "tail-bar" variety has a bar extending from the arrow feathers to the wreath on the reverse, the result of a die gouge. The Pittman Act of 1918 authorized the melting of 270 Million pieces of various dates. They were not individually recorded.

7 Tail feathers   7/8 Tail feathers   8 Tail feathers

Date	Mintage	VG8	F12	VF20	XF40	AU50	MS60	MS63	MS64	MS65	65DMPL	Prf65
1878 8 tail feathers	750,000	66.00	71.00	76.50	93.00	115	188	300	500	1,625	23,500	10,000
1878 7 over 8 tail feathers	9,759,550	44.00	46.25	49.00	50.00	55.00	115	220	535	2,650	24,500	185,000
1878 7 tail feathers, reverse of 1878	Inc. above	44.00	46.25	49.00	52.00	71.50	195	300	500	2,425	17,000	—
1878 7 tail feathers, reverse of 1879	Inc. above	44.00	46.25	49.00	51.00	55.00	91.00	150	2,750	1,150	11,500	11,500
1878CC	2,212,000	115	120	127	137	180	445	510	620	1,950	10,800	—
1878S	9,744,000	42.00	46.25	48.50	38.90	55.00	68.00	105	120	315	10,350	—
1879	14,807,100	29.50	30.00	33.50	34.50	44.00	60.00	100	160	895	17,250	7,200
1879CC	756,000	145	155	315	755	2,400	4,700	8,000	11,500	31,500	49,000	—
1879CC capped CC	Inc. above	145	180	250	640	1,850	4,470	6,800	10,150	43,000	63,500	—
1879O	2,887,000	38.50	43.00	45.00	46.50	48.50	110	270	595	4,450	28,500	—
1879S reverse of 1878	9,110,000	39.50	40.50	45.00	51.00	71.00	193	645	1,560	6,000	24,000	—
1879S reverse of 1879	Inc. above	29.50	30.00	33.50	34.50	44.00	61.00	67.00	89.50	170	1,450	—
1880	12,601,335	30.00	36.50	39.50	37.10	46.00	55.00	83.00	160	800	6,350	7,200
1880CC reverse of 1878	591,000	165	195	220	300	355	585	745	1,160	2,375	21,500	—
1880CC 80/79 reverse of 1878	Inc. above	190	230	270	335	410	640	850	1,750	4,000	—	—
1880CC 8/7 reverse of 1878	Inc. above	170	200	235	290	360	600	750	1,300	2,800	—	—
1880CC reverse of 1879	Inc. above	150	190	235	285	345	580	660	700	1,265	9,850	—
1880CC 8/7 high 7 reverse of 1879	Inc. above	175	205	245	290	355	525	685	775	1,800	—	—
1880CC 8/7 low 7 reverse of 1879	Inc. above	175	205	245	290	355	525	665	775	1,800	10,500	—
1880O	5,305,000	36.00	41.00	41.00	39.90	46.00	98.00	395	2,000	29,500	70,000	—
1880S	8,900,000	29.50	30.00	33.00	34.50	46.00	55.00	63.00	86.00	170	1,025	—

Date	Mintage	VG8	F12	VF20	XF40	AU50	MS60	MS63	MS64	MS65	65DMPL	Prf65
1880S 8/7 crossbar	—	35.40	31.70	40.60	45.00	75.00	90.00	265	335	450	—	—
1881	9,163,975	29.50	30.00	33.00	38.50	46.00	56.00	83.00	170	700	21,750	7,300
1881CC	296,000	365	375	390	425	460	580	635	635	935	3,050	—
1881O	5,708,000	35.50	37.50	36.50	39.50	46.00	53.00	77.50	195	1,375	35,000	—
1881S	12,760,000	29.50	30.00	33.00	34.50	46.00	56.00	57.00	83.00	170	1,100	—
1882	11,101,100	29.50	30.00	33.00	34.50	46.00	56.50	68.00	155	570	6,800	7,200
1882CC	1,133,000	98.00	99.00	100	130	155	240	270	295	575	2,000	—
1882O	6,090,000	35.50	37.50	39.50	39.50	46.00	55.00	83.00	135	1,600	4,950	—
1882O/S	Inc. above	46.50	53.50	61.00	67.50	99.50	245	775	1,925	61,500	65,000	—
1882S	9,250,000	29.50	30.00	33.00	34.50	46.00	58.00	71.00	83.00	170	4,100	—
1883	12,291,039	29.50	30.00	33.00	34.50	46.00	56.00	77.50	110	225	1,675	7,600
1883CC	1,204,000	97.00	99.00	100	128	148	225	248	270	570	1,450	—
1883O	8,725,000	35.00	42.00	44.00	42.90	49.20	52.00	59.00	86.00	202	1,550	—
1883S	6,250,000	29.50	30.50	34.00	39.90	145	1,020	2,750	5,950	51,500	94,500	—
1884	14,070,875	29.50	30.00	33.50	34.50	44.00	53.00	77.50	110	375	4,350	7,200
1884CC	1,136,000	137	150	155	170	174	225	250	275	583	1,485	—
1884O	9,730,000	35.50	37.50	39.50	39.50	44.00	53.00	57.00	81.00	170	1,100	—
1884S	3,200,000	29.50	30.50	34.00	43.00	310	8,950	37,000	110,000	235,000	220,000	—
1885	17,787,767	29.50	30.00	33.00	34.50	44.00	52.00	68.00	81.00	190	1,050	7,200
1885CC	—	585	615	615	625	650	800	900	950	1,155	2,650	—
1885O	9,185,000	35.00	37.00	39.50	39.50	44.00	52.00	59.00	81.00	170	1,075	—
1885S	1,497,000	29.50	31.00	49.00	64.00	110	285	365	745	2,325	42,500	—
1886	19,963,886	29.50	30.75	33.50	34.50	44.00	52.00	57.00	81.00	170	1,400	7,200
1886O	10,710,000	35.30	39.00	44.50	42.90	78.00	1,015	3,575	12,600	190,000	300,000	—
1886S	750,000	54.00	59.00	83.00	120	145	395	540	870	3,375	30,000	—
1887	20,290,710	29.50	30.00	33.00	34.50	44.50	53.00	57.00	81.00	170	1,430	7,200
1887/6	Inc. above	46.00	47.30	48.50	55.00	165	420	565	800	2,300	44,750	—
1887O	11,550,000	29.50	30.00	33.00	35.50	44.50	77.00	175	425	2,550	12,000	—
1887/6O	—	47.00	47.50	49.00	65.00	190	495	2,050	4,800	29,500	—	—
1887S	1,771,000	29.50	30.00	34.00	38.90	45.50	145	335	755	2,875	29,500	—
1888	19,183,833	29.50	30.50	39.00	39.40	46.00	55.00	66.00	80.00	255	3,000	7,200
1888O	12,150,000	35.50	39.00	41.00	41.00	50.00	66.00	77.50	122	560	4,850	—
1888O Hot Lips	Inc. above	50.00	125	250	600	3,000	—	—	—	—	—	—
1888S	657,000	120	176	182	225	235	375	530	65.00	3,550	16,500	—
1889	21,726,811	29.50	30.00	33.00	35.50	45.00	52.00	65.00	90.00	385	4,050	7,200
1889CC	350,000	650	940	1,305	3,150	8,500	27,500	52,000	85,000	320,000	—	—
1889O	11,875,000	29.50	30.00	33.00	35.50	43.00	210	400	1,000	8,350	18,000	—
1889S	700,000	52.00	62.00	65.00	82.00	125	290	395	680	2,350	38,500	—
1890	16,802,590	29.50	30.00	35.50	35.50	44.00	53.00	94.00	170	2,050	19,750	7,200
1890CC	2,309,041	96.00	99.00	102	140	220	605	990	1,500	5,350	15,500	—
1890CC tail bar	Inc. above	155	175	225	400	700	1,450	3,600	5,500	—	—	—
1890O	10,701,000	29.50	30.00	33.00	35.50	46.00	83.00	110	335	2,700	10,000	—
1890S	8,230,373	29.50	30.00	33.00	35.50	46.00	72.00	110	330	1,300	10,500	—
1891	8,694,206	29.50	30.00	33.00	35.50	50.00	80.00	225	950	8,900	27,500	7,200
1891CC	1,618,000	96.00	99.00	100	135	215	625	890	1,415	5,300	34,500	—
1891CC Spitting Eagle	Inc. above	105	115	135	185	260	605	865	1,375	5,500	—	—
1891O	7,954,529	29.50	30.00	33.00	39.50	46.50	215	400	885	8,550	37,500	—
1891S	5,296,000	29.50	30.00	33.00	38.50	47.50	85.00	155	360	1,925	21,500	—
1892	1,037,245	42.00	43.00	45.50	55.00	88.00	365	550	1,265	5,500	20,500	7,200
1892CC	1,352,000	185	200	245	485	725	1,630	2,425	3,450	9,500	39,500	—
1892O	2,744,000	29.50	30.00	36.00	42.50	77.00	315	445	1,225	8,150	52,500	—
1892S	1,200,000	36.00	40.50	135	290	1,650	45,000	72,500	112,500	205,000	225,000	—
1893	378,792	225	230	237	300	400	835	1,125	2,450	8,950	66,000	7,200
1893CC	677,000	255	310	710	1,455	2,575	5,750	9,350	18,150	70,000	90,000	—
1893O	300,000	195	240	355	555	850	3,550	6,950	17,600	210,000	235,000	—
1893S	100,000	3,000	4,150	5,625	9,500	23,200	143,000	245,000	365,000	715,000	735,000	—
1894	110,972	900	1,050	1,150	1,225	1,825	3,650	5,200	10,150	38,500	78,000	8,150
1894O	1,723,000	47.50	49.50	51.00	105	310	1,275	5,100	12,100	68,500	61,500	—
1894S	1,260,000	58.00	65.00	98.00	155	485	965	1,400	2,450	7,200	26,000	—
1895 proof only	12,880	27,000	31,000	37,000	38,000	40,000	—	—	—	—	—	75,000
1895O	450,000	305	335	450	595	1,040	15,500	57,500	79,000	165,000	—	—
1895S	400,000	405	525	890	1,325	1,865	4,450	7,000	10,800	28,000	42,500	—
1896	9,967,762	29.50	30.75	33.00	38.50	44.00	53.00	65.00	85.00	265	1,450	7,200
1896O	4,900,000	37.50	40.50	41.00	42.40	155	1,675	8,500	44,000	180,000	180,000	—
1896S	5,000,000	42.00	43.00	55.00	235	895	2,500	3,975	5,675	19,500	110,000	—
1897	2,822,731	29.50	30.00	33.00	38.50	46.50	54.00	70.00	99.00	365	3,950	7,200
1897O	4,004,000	29.50	30.00	33.00	50.90	93.50	1,000	4,400	15,900	70,000	72,500	—
1897S	5,825,000	29.50	30.00	33.00	34.50	44.50	91.00	137	172	635	3,250	—
1898	5,884,735	29.50	30.00	33.00	34.50	44.50	53.50	65.00	90.00	265	1,350	7,200
1898O	4,440,000	29.50	30.00	33.00	34.50	44.50	55.50	61.50	81.00	170	1,175	—
1898S	4,102,000	42.00	43.25	46.00	55.00	93.50	275	510	750	2,500	18,000	—
1899	330,846	165	180	190	205	220	265	335	415	935	2,650	7,200
1899O	12,290,000	29.50	30.00	33.00	34.50	44.50	55.50	68.00	83.00	190	1,650	—
1899S	2,562,000	42.00	43.00	46.00	61.00	155	440	550	845	2,365	26,000	—
1900	8,880,938	29.50	30.00	33.00	34.50	44.00	53.50	65.00	88.00	170	42,500	7,200
1900O	12,590,000	29.50	30.00	33.00	34.50	44.00	56.50	65.00	79.00	170	6,250	—
1900O/CC	Inc. above	42.00	61.00	67.50	100	190	305	810	965	2,260	19,000	—

Date	Mintage	VG8	F12	VF20	XF40	AU50	MS60	MS63	MS64	MS65	65DMPL	Prf65
1900S	3,540,000	42.00	43.00	46.00	42.40	88.00	330	415	665	1,875	38,500	—
1901	6,962,813	42.00	48.50	56.00	105	280	3,150	17,250	55,000	375,000	—	500
1901 doubled die reverse	Inc. above	275	450	900	2,000	3,850	—	—	—	—	—	—
1901O	13,320,000	35.30	38.50	40.00	40.50	47.00	56.00	71.00	90.00	215	10,000	—
1901S	2,284,000	35.80	39.00	41.00	61.00	200	575	900	1,320	3,800	24,500	—
1902	7,994,777	35.50	37.50	39.50	45.90	53.00	71.00	132	180	480	19,500	200
1902O	8,636,000	35.30	37.50	39.50	39.50	45.00	55.50	64.00	85.00	226	16,000	—
1902S	1,530,000	99.00	105	145	210	275	445	690	910	3,000	15,000	—
1903	4,652,755	47.00	48.00	49.00	50.00	52.00	68.00	82.50	120	345	36,850	200
1903O	4,450,000	325	340	365	390	398	440	470	510	690	6,150	—
1903S	1,241,000	85.00	115	190	365	1,925	4,950	7,150	8,575	11,750	40,000	—
1903S Micro S	Inc. above	135	225	450	1,150	3,000	—	—	—	—	—	—
1904	2,788,650	30.50	36.50	38.00	44.40	53.00	105	265	600	2,850	86,500	200
1904O	3,720,000	36.50	47.30	54.00	55.00	57.00	60.00	61.00	83.00	173	1,385	—
1904S	2,304,000	42.00	48.50	80.00	230	525	2,585	4,950	5,665	10,350	24,500	—
1921	44,690,000	25.00	25.30	31.75	33.00	37.50	46.50	66.00	175	11,500		75,000
1921D	20,345,000	25.00	25.50	33.00	33.00	41.50	52.00	95.00	335	—	—	
1921S	21,695,000	29.30	31.00	34.00	33.00	40.50	51.00	140	1,600	—	—	

Peace Dollar
Liberty Head left.   Eagle facing right perched on rock.

KM# 150 • 26.73 g., 0.900 Silver 0.7734 oz. ASW, 38.1 mm. • **Designer:** Anthony DeFrancisci **Note:** Prices with a letter after them mean, e=estimated, a=auction realization, h=historical record over 5 years old.

Date	Mintage	G4	VG8	F12	VF20	XF40	AU50	MS60	MS63	MS64	MS65
1921	1,006,473	70.00	115	120	133	140	165	300	485	960	2,200
1921 rev ray over first L in DOLLAR Vam 3	—	—	—	—	—	200	250	475	—	—	—
1922	51,737,000	23.00	23.00	23.50	27.00	33.00	37.00	44.00	48.50	61.00	145
1922D	15,063,000	23.30	23.00	23.50	27.00	33.00	37.00	52.00	94.00	149	610
1922S	17,475,000	23.30	23.00	23.50	27.00	33.00	37.00	52.00	102	360	2,400
1923	30,800,000	23.00	23.00	23.50	27.00	33.00	36.00	44.00	48.50	61.00	145
1923D	6,811,000	23.30	23.00	23.50	27.30	33.00	37.00	75.00	160	420	1,225
1923S	19,020,000	23.30	23.00	23.50	33.50	33.00	37.00	50.00	94.00	520	6,000
1924	11,811,000	23.00	23.00	28.00	385	33.00	36.00	44.00	48.50	61.00	145
1924S	1,728,000	23.00	23.30	23.80	46.00	41.50	64.00	245	520	1,560	8,725
1925	10,198,000	23.00	23.00	28.00	46.00	28.00	30.80	46.00	53.00	61.00	145
1925S	1,610,000	23.90	23.30	23.80	27.00	28.90	43.00	105	300	1,165	22,500
1926	1,939,000	24.10	23.30	28.30	27.00	29.30	31.00	55.00	105	138	580
1926D	2,348,700	24.10	23.30	23.80	27.00	28.00	48.50	93.50	245	445	985
1926S	6,980,000	23.60	23.30	23.80	27.00	28.60	33.80	59.00	100	330	1,075
1927	848,000	25.30	30.20	31.30	29.30	34.00	50.00	87.00	205	660	2,900
1927D	1,268,900	25.30	30.20	34.00	36.00	36.00	38.00	87.00	220	1,130	4,650
1927S	866,000	25.30	30.20	31.30	36.00	38.00	80.00	205	635	1,320	9,100
1928	360,649	345	375	380	390	400	425	540	1,025	1,375	4,440
1928S	1,632,000	34.00	35.00	40.00	43.00	48.00	66.00	178	570	1,335	21,700
1934	954,057	35.00	44.00	46.00	48.00	52.00	57.50	127	215	420	735
1934D Large D	1,569,500	36.00	45.00	46.00	48.00	56.00	68.00	180	600	925	2,100
1934S Lg D, DDO Vam 3	—	—	—	—	—	75.00	510	2,335	4,680	5,900	8,850
1934D Small D	—	35.00	44.00	45.00	50.00	55.00	65.00	160	385	630	2,175
1934D SmD, DDO Vam 4	—	—	—	—	—	300	150	275	500	—	—
1934C	1,011,000	38.00	45.00	53.00	46.00	185	440	850	2,000	—	—
1935	1,576,000	35.00	44.00	45.00	80.00	47.50	57.50	85.00	135	288	760
1935S 3 Rays	1,964,000	35.00	44.00	45.00	46.00	47.50	99.00	300	510	710	1,515
1935S 4 Rays	—	36.00	45.00	46.00	50.00	58.00	122	365	600	850	1,850

DOLLAR

Eisenhower Dollar

KM# 203 • 22.80 g., Copper-Nickel Clad Copper, 38 mm. • **Designer:** Frank Gasparro

Date	Mintage	MS63	MS65	Prf65
1971	47,799,000	5.00	185	—
1971D	68,587,424	4.00	40.00	—
1972 Low Relief	75,890,000	18.00	80.00	—
1972 High Relief	Inc. above	100	1,500	—
1972 Modified High Relief	Inc. above	25.00	125	—
1972D	92,548,511	8.00	27.00	—
1973	2,000,056	12.00	65.00	—
1973D	2,000,000	12.00	45.00	—
1973S	2,769,624	—	—	12.00
1974	27,366,000	9.00	45.00	—
1974D	35,466,000	7.50	22.00	—
1974S	2,617,350	—	—	11.00

KM# 203a • 24.59 g., 0.400 Silver 0.3162 oz. ASW, 38.1 mm. • **Designer:** Frank Gasparro

Date	Mintage	MS63	MS65	Prf65
1971S	6,868,530	7.50	22.00	11.00
1971S	4,265,234	—	—	—
1971S Peg Leg "R" Variety	Inc. above	—	—	17.00
1971S Partial Peg Leg "R" Variety	Inc. above	—	—	18.00
1972S	2,193,056	7.50	18.50	—
1972S	1,811,631	—	—	9.00
1973S	1,833,140	7.50	20.00	—
1973S	1,005,617	—	—	45.00
1974S	1,720,000	7.50	18.50	—
1974S	1,306,579	—	—	11.00

Moon behind Liberty Bell.

KM# 206 • 22.68 g., Copper-Nickel Clad Copper, 38.1 mm. • **Rev. Designer:** Dennis R. Williams **Note:** In 1976 the lettering on the reverse was changed to thinner letters, resulting in the Type II variety for that year. The Type I variety was minted 1975 and dated 1976.

	Type I		Type II	
	Squared "T"		Slant-top "T"	

Date	Mintage	MS63	MS65	Prf65
1976 type I	117,337,000	12.00	125	—
1976 type II	Inc. above	7.50	24.00	—
1976D type I	103,228,274	10.00	50.00	—
1976D type II	Inc. above	7.00	22.00	—
1976S type I	2,909,369	—	—	10.00
1976S type II	4,149,730	—	—	9.00

Bicentennial design, moon behind Liberty Bell.

KM# 206a • 24.59 g., 0.400 Silver 0.3162 oz. ASW **Rev. Designer:** Dennis R. Williams

Date	Mintage	MS63	MS65	Prf65
1976S	4,908,319	7.50	18.00	14.00
1976S	3,998,621	—	—	—

Regular design resumed.

KM# A203 • Copper-Nickel Clad Copper, 38.1 mm. • **Designer:** Frank Gasparro

Date	Mintage	MS63	MS65	Prf65
1977	12,596,000	5.50	20.00	—
1977D	32,983,006	8.00	25.00	—
1977S	3,251,152	—	—	9.00
1978	25,702,000	6.50	35.00	—
1978D	33,012,890	6.50	30.00	—
1978S	3,127,788	—	—	9.00

Susan B. Anthony Dollar
Susan B. Anthony bust right. Eagle landing on moon, symbolic of Apollo manned moon landing.

KM# 207 • 8.10 g., Copper-Nickel Clad Copper, 26.5 mm. • **Edge:** Reeded **Designer:** Frank Gasparro **Note:** The 1979-S and 1981-S Type II coins have a clearer mint mark than the Type I varieties for those years.

Date	Mintage	MS63	PF65
1979P Near date	360,222,000	30.00	—
1979P	Inc. above	2.50	—
1979D	288,015,744	2.50	—
1979S Proof, Type I	3,677,175	—	6.00

DOLLAR

Date	Mintage	MS63	PF65
1979S Proof, Type II	Inc. above	—	85.00
1979S	109,576,000	2.50	—
1980P	27,610,000	2.50	—
1980D	41,628,708	2.50	—
1980S	20,422,000	5.00	—
1980S Proof	3,547,030	—	5.00
1981P	3,000,000	5.00	—
1981D	3,250,000	5.00	—
1981S	3,492,000	5.00	—
1981S Proof, Type I	4,063,083	—	7.00
1981S Proof, Type II	Inc. above	—	225
1999P	29,592,000	3.00	—
1999P Proof	Est. 750000	—	22.00
1999D	11,776,000	3.00	—

Sacagawea Dollar
Sacagawea bust right, with baby on back. Eagle in flight left.
KM# 310 • 8.07 g., Copper-Zinc-Manganese-Nickel Clad Copper, 26.5 mm. • **Obv. Designer:** Glenda Goodacre **Rev. Designer:** Thomas D. Rodgers

Date	Mintage	MS63	PF65
2000P	767,140,000	2.00	—
2000P Goodacre Presentation	5,000	—	—
2000D	518,916,000	2.00	—
2000D from Millennium Set	5,500	10.00	—
2000S	4,048,000	—	5.00
2001P	62,468,000	2.25	—
2001D	70,909,500	2.25	—
2001S	3,084,000	—	16.00
2002P	3,865,610	3.00	—
2002D	3,732,000	2.75	—
2002S	3,157,739	—	10.00
2003P	3,090,000	4.50	—
2003D	3,090,000	4.75	—
2003S	3,116,590	—	8.00
2004P	2,660,000	3.50	—
2004D	2,660,000	4.00	—
2004S	2,992,069	—	7.50
2005P	2,520,000	3.00	—
2005P Satin Finish	1,160,000	5.00	—
2005D	2,520,000	3.00	—
2005D Satin Finish	1,160,000	5.00	—
2005S	3,273,000	—	6.00
2006P	4,900,000	3.25	—
2006P Satin Finish	847,361	4.50	—
2006D	2,800,000	3.50	—
2006D Satin Finish	847,361	4.00	—
2006S	3,054,436	—	9.00
2007P	3,640,000	2.25	—
2007P Satin Finish	895,628	4.00	—
2007D	3,920,000	2.25	—
2007D Satin Finish	895,628	4.00	—
2007S	2,577,166	—	6.50
2008P	1,820,000	2.00	—
2008P Satin Finish	745,464	4.00	—
2008D	1,820,000	3.50	—
2008D Satin Finish	745,464	4.00	—
2008S	2,169,561	—	16.00

Native American Dollar - Planting crops reverse
Sacagawea bust right with baby on back. Native American female planting corn, beans and squash.
KM# 467 • 8.07 g., Copper-Zinc-Manganese-Nickel Clad Copper, 26.5 mm. • **Obv. Designer:** Glenda Goodacre **Rev. Designer:** Norm Nemeth **Edge Lettering:** E PLURIBUS UNUM, date, mint mark **Note:** Date and mint mark on edge

Date	Mintage	MS63	PF65
2009P	37,380,000	2.00	—
2009P Satin finish	784,614	4.00	—
2009D	33,880,000	2.00	—
2009D Satin finish	784,614	4.00	—
2009S	2,179,867	—	6.00

Native American Dollar - Hiawatha belt reverse
Sacagawea bust right with baby on back. Hiawatha belt and bundle of five arrows.
KM# 474 • 8.07 g., Copper-Zinc-Manganese-Nickel Clad Copper, 26.5 mm. • **Obv. Designer:** Glenda Goodacre **Rev. Designer:** Thomas Cleveland and Charles L. Vickers **Edge Lettering:** E PLURIBUS UNUM, date, mint mark **Note:** Date and mint mark on edge

Date	Mintage	MS63	PF65
2010P	32,060,000	2.00	—
2010P Satin Finish	583,897	4.00	—
2010D	48,720,000	2.00	—
2010D Satin Finish	583,897	4.00	—
2010S	1,689,364	—	12.50

Native American Dollar - Peace Pipe reverse
Sacagawea bust right with baby on back. Hands passing peace pipe.
KM# 503 • 8.07 g., Copper-Zinc-Manganese-Nickel Clad Copper, 26.5 mm. • **Obv. Designer:** Glenna Goodacre **Rev. Designer:** Richard Masters and Joseph Menna **Edge Lettering:** E PLURIBUS UNUM, date, mint mark **Note:** Date and mint mark on edge

Date	Mintage	MS63	PF65
2011P	29,400,000	2.00	—
2011D	48,160,000	2.00	—
2011S	1,453,276	—	8.00

Native American Dollar - Horse reverse

Sacagawea bust right with baby on back. Horse and Native American profile facing left.

KM# 528 • 8.07 g., Copper-Zinc-Manganese-Nickel Clad Copper, 26.5 mm. • **Obv. Designer:** Glenda Goodacre **Rev. Designer:** Thomas Cleveland and Phebe Hemphill **Edge Lettering:** E PLURIBUS UNUM, date, mint mark **Note:** Date and mint mark on edge

Date	Mintage	MS63	PF65
2012P	2,800,000	2.00	—
2012D	3,080,000	2.00	—
2012S	1,189,445	—	12.50

Native American Dollar - Delaware Treaty of 1778

Turtle, turkey and wolf.

KM# 551 • 8.07 g., Copper-Zinc-Manganese-Nickel Clad Copper, 26.5 mm. • **Edge:** E PLURIBUS UNUM, date, mint mark **Note:** Date and mint mark on edge.

Date	Mintage	MS63	PF65
2013P	1,820,000	2.00	—
2013D	1,820,000	2.00	—
2013S	1,192,690	—	12.50

Native Hospitality

KM# 575 • 8.07 g., Copper-Zinc-Manganese-Nickel Clad Copper, 26.5 mm. •

Date	Mintage	MS63	PF65
2014P	—	2.00	—
2014D	—	2.00	—
2014S	—	—	12.50

Presidents

George Washington

KM# 401 • 8.07 g., Copper-Zinc-Manganese-Nickel Clad Copper, 26.5 mm. **Note:** Date and mint mark incuse on edge.

Date	Mintage	MS63	MS65	Prf65
2007P	176,680,000	2.00	3.00	—
2007P Satin Finish	895,628	2.00	4.00	—
2007 Plain edge error	Inc. above	175	275	—
2007D	163,680,000	2.00	3.00	—
2007D Satin Finish	895,628	2.00	4.00	—
2007S	3,883,103	—	—	3.00

John Adams

KM# 402 • 8.07 g., Copper-Zinc-Manganese-Nickel Clad Copper, 26.5 mm. **Note:** Date and mint mark incuse on edge.

Date	Mintage	MS63	MS65	Prf65
2007P	112,420,000	2.00	4.00	—
2007S Double edge lettering	Inc. above	—	—	3.00
2007D Satin Finish	895,628	—	4.00	—
2007D	112,140,000	60.00	70.00	—
2007P Plain edge error	Inc. above	45.00	65.00	—
2007D Satin Finish	895,628	2.00	3.00	—
2007P	3,877,409	2.00	3.00	—

DOLLAR

DOLLAR

Thomas Jefferson

KM# 403 • 8.07 g., Copper-Zinc-Manganese-Nickel Clad Copper, 26.5 mm. **Note:** Date and mint mark incuse on edge.

Date	Mintage	MS63	MS65	Prf65
2007P	100,800,000	2.00	3.00	—
2007P Satin Finish	895,628	2.00	4.00	—
2007D	102,810,000	2.00	3.00	—
2007D Satin Finish	895,628	2.00	4.00	—
2007S	3,877,573	—	—	3.00

James Madison

KM# 404 • 8.07 g., Copper-Zinc-Manganese-Nickel Clad Copper, 26.5 mm. **Note:** Date and mint mark incuse on edge.

Date	Mintage	MS63	MS65	Prf65
2007P	84,560,000	2.00	3.00	—
2007P Satin Finish	895,628	2.00	4.00	—
2007D	87,780,000	2.00	3.00	—
2007D Satin Finish	895,628	2.00	4.00	—
2007S	3,876,829	—	—	3.00

James Monroe

KM# 426 • 8.07 g., Copper-Zinc-Manganese-Nickel Clad Copper, 26.5 mm.

Date	Mintage	MS63	MS65	Prf65
2008P	64,260,000	2.00	3.00	—
2008P Satin Finish	745,464	2.00	4.00	—
2008D	60,230,000	2.00	3.00	—
2008D Satin Finish	745,464	2.00	4.00	—
2008S	3,000,000	—	—	4.00

John Quincy Adams

KM# 427 • 8.07 g., Copper-Zinc-Manganese-Nickel Clad Copper, 26.5 mm. **Note:** Date and mint mark incuse on edge.

Date	Mintage	MS63	MS65	Prf65
2008P	57,540,000	2.00	3.00	—
2008P Satin Finish	745,464	2.00	4.00	—
2008D	57,720,000	2.00	3.00	—
2008D Satin Finish	745,464	2.00	4.00	—
2008S	3,000,000	—	—	4.00

Andrew Jackson

KM# 428 • 8.07 g., Copper-Zinc-Manganese-Nickel Clad Copper, 26.5 mm. **Note:** Date and mint mark incuse on edge.

Date	Mintage	MS63	MS65	Prf65
2008P	61,180,000	2.00	3.00	—
2008P Satin Finish	745,464	2.00	4.00	—
2008D	61,070,000	2.00	3.00	—
2008D Satin Finish	745,464	2.00	4.00	—
2008S	3,000,000	—	—	4.00

Martin van Buren

KM# 429 • 8.07 g., Copper-Zinc-Manganese-Nickel Clad Copper, 26.5 mm. **Note:** Date and mint mark incuse on edge.

Date	Mintage	MS63	MS65	Prf65
2008P	51,520,000	2.00	3.00	—
2008P Satin Finish	745,464	2.00	4.00	—
2008D	50,960,000	2.00	3.00	—
2008D Satin Finish	745,464	2.00	4.00	—
2008S	3,000,000	—	—	4.00

William Henry Harrison

KM# 450 • 8.07 g., Copper-Zinc-Manganese-Nickel Clad Copper, 26.5 mm. **Note:** Date and mint mark on edge

Date	Mintage	MS63	MS65	Prf65
2009P	43,260,000	2.00	3.00	—
2009P Satin Finish	784,614	2.00	4.00	—
2009D	55,160,000	2.00	3.00	—
2009P Satin Finish	784,614	2.00	4.00	—
2009S	2,224,827	—	—	3.00

John Tyler

KM# 451 • 8.07 g., Copper-Zinc-Manganese-Nickel Clad Copper, 26.5 mm. **Note:** Date and mint mark on edge.

Date	Mintage	MS63	MS65	Prf65
2009P	43,540,000	2.00	3.00	—
2009P Satin Finish	784,614	2.00	4.00	—
2009D	43,540,000	2.00	3.00	—
2009D Satin Finish	784,614	2.00	4.00	—
2009S	2,224,827	—	—	3.00

James K. Polk

KM# 452 • 8.07 g., Copper-Zinc-Manganese-Nickel Clad Copper, 26.5 mm. **Note:** Date and mint mark on edge

Date	Mintage	MS63	MS65	Prf65
2009P	46,620,000	2.00	3.00	—
2009P Satin Finish	784,614	2.00	4.00	—
2009D	41,720,000	2.00	3.00	—
2009D Satin Finish	784,614	2.00	4.00	—
2009S	2,224,827	—	—	3.00

Zachary Taylor

KM# 453 • 8.07 g., Copper-Zinc-Manganese-Nickel Clad Copper, 26.5 mm. **Note:** Date and mint mark on edge.

Date	Mintage	MS63	MS65	Prf65
2009P	41,580,000	2.00	3.00	—
2009P Satin Finish	784,614	2.00	4.00	—
2009D	36,680,000	2.00	3.00	—
2009D Satin Finish	784,614	2.00	4.00	—
2009S	2,224,827	—	—	3.00

Millard Filmore

KM# 475 • 8.07 g., Copper-Zinc-Manganese-Nickel Clad Copper, 26.5 mm. **Note:** Date and mint mark on edge.

Date	Mintage	MS63	MS65	Prf65
2010P	37,520,000	2.00	3.00	—
2010P Satin Finish	583,897	2.00	4.00	—
2010D	36,960,000	2.00	3.00	—
2010D Satin Finish	583,897	2.00	4.00	—
2010S	2,224,827	—	—	4.00

Franklin Pierce

KM# 476 • 8.07 g., Copper-Zinc-Manganese-Nickel Clad Copper, 26.5 mm. **Note:** Date and mint mark on edge.

Date	Mintage	MS63	MS65	Prf65
2010P	38,220,000	2.00	3.00	—
2010P Satin Finish	583,897	2.00	4.00	—
2010D	38,360,000	2.00	3.00	—
2010D Satin Finish	583,897	2.00	4.00	—
2010S	2,224,827	—	—	4.00

DOLLAR

DOLLAR

James Buchanan

KM# 477 • 8.07 g., Copper-Zinc-Manganese-Nickel Clad Copper, 26.5 mm. **Note:** Date and mint mark on edge.

Date	Mintage	MS63	MS65	Prf65
2010P	36,820,000	2.00	3.00	—
2010P Satin Finish	583,897	2.00	4.00	—
2010D	36,540,000	2.00	3.00	—
2010D Satin Finish	583,897	2.00	4.00	—
2010S	2,224,827	—	—	4.00

Abraham Lincoln

KM# 478 • 8.07 g., Copper-Zinc-Manganese-Nickel Clad Copper, 26.5 mm. **Note:** Date and mint mark on edge.

Date	Mintage	MS63	MS65	Prf65
2010P	49,000,000	2.00	3.00	—
2010P Satin Finish	583,897	2.00	4.00	—
2010D	48,020,000	2.00	3.00	—
2010D Satin Finish	583,897	2.00	4.00	—
2010S	2,224,827	—	—	4.00

Andrew Johnson

KM# 499 • 8.07 g., Copper-Zinc-Manganese-Nickel Clad Copper, 26.5 mm. **Note:** Date and mint mark on edge.

Date	Mintage	MS63	MS65	Prf65
2011P	35,560,000	2.00	3.00	—
2011D	37,100,000	2.00	3.00	—
2011S	1,706,916	—	—	4.00

Ulysses S. Grant

KM# 500 • 8.07 g., Copper-Zinc-Manganese-Nickel Clad Copper, 26.5 mm. **Note:** Date and mint mark on edge.

Date	Mintage	MS63	MS65	Prf65
2011P	38,080,000	2.00	3.00	—
2011D	37,940,000	2.00	3.00	—
2011S	1,706,916	—	—	4.00

Rutherford B. Hayes

KM# 501 • 8.07 g., Copper-Zinc-Manganese-Nickel Clad Copper, 26.5 mm. **Note:** Date and mint mark on edge.

Date	Mintage	MS63	MS65	Prf65
2011P	37,660,000	2.00	3.00	—
2011D	36,820,000	2.00	3.00	—
2011S	1,706,916	—	—	4.00

James Garfield

KM# 502 • 8.07 g., Copper-Zinc-Manganese-Nickel Clad Copper, 26.5 mm. **Note:** Date and mint mark on edge.

Date	Mintage	MS63	MS65	Prf65
2011P	37,100,000	2.00	3.00	—
2011D	37,100,000	2.00	3.00	—
2011S	1,706,916	—	—	4.00

Chester A. Arthur

KM# 524 • 8.07 g., Copper-Zinc-Manganese-Nickel Clad Copper, 26.5 mm. **Note:** Date and mintmark on edge

Date	Mintage	MS63	MS65	Prf65
2012P	6,020,000	2.00	3.00	—
2012D	4,060,000	2.00	3.00	—
2012S	—	—	—	5.00

Grover Cleveland, first term

KM# 525 • 8.07 g., Copper-Zinc-Manganese-Nickel Clad Copper, 26.5 mm. **Note:** Date and mint mark on edge.

Date	Mintage	MS63	MS65	Prf65
2012P	5,460,000	2.00	3.00	—
2012D	4,060,000	2.00	3.00	—
2012S	1,438,710	—	—	5.00

Benjamin Harrison

KM# 526 • 8.07 g., Copper-Zinc-Manganese-Nickel Clad Copper, 26.5 mm. **Note:** Date at mint mark on edge

Date	Mintage	MS63	MS65	Prf65
2012P	5,640,001	2.00	3.00	—
2012D	4,200,000	2.00	3.00	—
2012S	1,438,710	—	—	5.00

Grover Cleveland, second term

KM# 527 • 8.07 g., Copper-Zinc-Manganese-Nickel Clad Copper, 26.5 mm. **Note:** Date and mint mark on edge.

Date	Mintage	MS63	MS65	Prf65
2012P	10,680,000	2.00	3.00	—
2012D	3,920,000	2.00	3.00	—
2012S	1,438,710	—	—	5.00

William McKinley

KM# 547 • 8.07 g., Copper-Zinc-Manganese-Nickel Clad Copper, 26.5 mm. **Note:** Date and mint mark on edge.

Date	Mintage	MS63	MS65	Prf65
2013P	4,760,000	2.00	3.00	—
2013D	3,365,100	2.00	3.00	—
2013S	1,449,415	—	—	5.00

Theodore Roosevelt

KM# 548 • 8.07 g., Copper-Zinc-Manganese-Nickel Clad Copper, 26.5 mm. **Note:** Date and mint mark on edge.

Date	Mintage	MS63	MS65	Prf65
2013P	5,310,700	2.00	3.00	—
2013D	3,920,000	2.00	3.00	—
2013S	1,449,415	—	—	5.00

William Howard Taft

KM# 549 • 8.07 g., Copper-Zinc-Manganese-Nickel Clad Copper, 26.5 mm. **Note:** Date and mint mark on edge.

Date	Mintage	MS63	MS65	Prf65
2013P	4,760,000	2.00	3.00	—
2013D	3,360,000	2.00	3.00	—
2013S	1,449,415	—	—	5.00

Woodrow Wilson

KM# 550 • 8.07 g., Copper-Zinc-Manganese-Nickel Clad Copper, 26.5 mm. **Note:** Date and mint mark on edge.

DOLLAR

Date	Mintage	MS63	MS65	Prf65
2013P	4,620,000	2.00	3.00	—
2013D	3,360,000	2.00	3.00	—
2013S	1,449,415	—	—	5.00

Warren G. Harding

KM# 571 • 8.07 g., Copper-Zinc-Manganese-Nickel Clad Copper, 26.5 mm. **Note:** Date and mint mark on edge.

Date	Mintage	MS63	MS65	Prf65
2014P	—	2.00	3.00	—
2014D	—	2.00	3.00	—
2014S	—	—	—	5.00

Calvin Coolidge

KM# 572 • 8.07 g., Copper-Zinc-Manganese-Nickel Clad Copper, 26.5 mm. **Note:** Date and mint mark on edge.

Date	Mintage	MS63	MS65	Prf65
2014P	—	2.00	5.00	—

Date	Mintage	MS63	MS65	Prf65
2014D	—	2.00	5.00	—
2014S	—	—	—	5.00

Herbert Hoover

KM# 573 • 8.07 g., Copper-Zinc-Manganese-Nickel Clad Copper, 26.5 mm. **Note:** Date and mint mark on edge.

Date	Mintage	MS63	MS65	Prf65
2014P	—	2.00	3.00	—
2014D	—	2.00	3.00	—
2014S	—	—	—	5.00

Franklin D. Roosevelt

KM# 574 • 8.07 g., Copper-Zinc-Manganese-Nickel Clad Copper, 26.5 mm. **Note:** Date and mint mark on edge.

Date	Mintage	MS63	MS65	Prf65
2014P	—	2.00	3.00	—
2014D	—	2.00	3.00	—
2014S	—	—	—	5.00

GOLD

Liberty Head - Type 1
Liberty head left within circle of stars. Value, date within 3/4 wreath.

KM# 73 1.67 g., 0.900 Gold 0.0484 oz. AGW, 13 mm. • **Rev. Legend:** UNITED STATES OF AMERICA **Designer:** James B. Longacre **Note:** On the "closed wreath" varieties of 1849, the wreath on the reverse extends closer to the numeral 1.

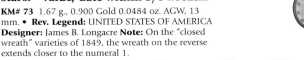

Date	Mintage	F12	VF20	XF40	AU50	MS60
1849 open wreath	688,567	160	225	245	345	650
1849 small head, no L	—	—	—	—	—	—
1849 closed wreath	Inc. above	160	210	225	325	475
1849C closed wreath	11,634	800	950	1,450	2,400	8,850
1849C open wreath	Inc. above	135,000	240,000	320,000	475,000	600,000
1849D open wreath	21,588	1,050	1,300	1,875	2,600	6,000
1849O open wreath	215,000	20.00	235	290	365	800
1850	481,953	160	210	225	260	475
1850C	6,966	900	1,150	1,600	2,650	9,000
1850D	8,382	1,050	1,250	1,725	2,950	12,500
1850O	14,000	200	275	390	750	3,300
1851	3,317,671	160	210	225	245	475
1851C	41,267	840	1,150	1,500	1,700	3,150
1851D	9,882	1,000	1,250	1,675	2,500	5,650
1851O	290,000	160	195	240	275	775
1852	2,045,351	160	210	225	245	475
1852C	9,434	845	1,040	1,400	1,750	5,100
1852D	6,360	1,025	1,250	1,675	2,300	10,000

Date	Mintage	F12	VF20	XF40	AU50	MS60
1852O	140,000	130	175	260	385	1,400
1853	4,076,051	160	210	225	245	475
1853C	11,515	900	1,100	1,400	2,000	5,600
1853D	6,583	1,040	1,250	1,700	2,650	9,700
1853O	290,000	135	160	235	265	665
1854	736,709	160	210	225	245	475
1854D	2,935	1,050	1,400	2,350	5,500	13,000
1854S	14,632	260	360	525	775	2,450

Indian Head - Type 2
Indian head with headdress left.
Value, date within wreath.

KM# 83 1.67 g., 0.900 Gold 0.0484 oz. AGW, 15 mm. • **Obv. Legend:** UNITED STATES OF AMERICA **Designer:** James B. Longacre

Date	Mintage	F12	VF20	XF40	AU50	MS60
1854	902,736	275	350	420	525	1,850
1855	758,269	275	350	420	525	1,850
1855C	9,803	975	1,450	3,750	9,500	33,000
1855D	1,811	3,250	4,750	9,800	22,000	48,000
1855O	55,000	345	440	600	1,500	7,800
1856S	24,600	525	820	1,325	2,500	8,650

Indian Head - Type 3
Indian head with headdress left.
Value, date within wreath.

KM# 86 • 1.67 g., 0.900 Gold 0.0484 oz. AGW, 15 mm. • **Obv. Legend:** UNITED STATES OF AMERICA **Designer:** James B. Longacre **Note:** The 1856 varieties are distinguished by whether the 5 in the date is slanted or upright. The 1873 varieties are distinguished by the amount of space between the upper left and lower left serifs in the 3.

Date	Mintage	F12	VF20	XF40	AU50	MS60	Prf65
1856 upright 5	1,762,936	190	235	265	295	590	—
1856 slanted 5	Inc. above	185	225	240	260	440	55,000
1856D	1,460	2,350	3,650	5,800	8,000	32,000	—
1857	774,789	175	220	240	260	440	32,000
1857C	13,280	900	1,150	1,750	3,750	13,250	—
1857D	3,533	1,000	1,300	2,300	4,400	11,000	—
1857S	10,000	260	520	650	1,300	6,200	—
1858	117,995	175	220	240	260	440	28,500
1858D	3,477	1,025	1,250	1,600	2,850	10,000	—
1858S	10,000	300	400	575	1,450	5,350	—
1859	168,244	175	220	240	260	440	17,000
1859C	5,235	885	1,050	1,700	4,250	9,850	—
1859D	4,952	1,050	1,500	2,100	3,250	10,500	—
1859S	15,000	210	265	525	1,250	5,500	—
1860	36,668	175	220	240	260	440	16,500
1860D	1,566	2,150	2,500	4,200	7,000	19,500	—
1860S	13,000	300	380	500	750	2,900	—
1861	527,499	175	220	240	260	440	14,850
1861D mintage unrecorded	—	4,950	7,000	11,000	21,000	41,500	—
1862	1,361,390	175	220	240	260	440	15,000
1863	6,250	370	500	925	2,100	3,900	18,000
1864	5,950	290	370	475	825	1,050	18,000
1865	3,725	290	370	590	750	1,600	18,000
1866	7,130	300	385	470	685	1,025	18,000
1867	5,250	325	420	525	675	1,160	17,500
1868	10,525	265	290	415	500	1,025	19,000
1869	5,925	315	460	530	725	1,150	17,000
1870	6,335	255	290	410	500	875	16,000
1870S	3,000	300	475	785	1,250	2,650	—
1871	3,930	260	290	390	480	750	18,000
1872	3,530	260	295	400	480	975	18,500
1873 closed 3	125,125	325	425	825	950	1,650	—
1873 open 3	Inc. above	175	220	240	260	440	—
1874	198,820	175	220	240	260	440	30,000
1875	420	1,650	2,350	4,650	5,200	10,000	32,500
1876	3,245	240	300	360	475	725	16,750
1877	3,920	175	210	340	460	725	18,000
1878	3,020	195	250	365	480	675	15,500
1879	3,030	175	225	285	330	525	14,000

DOLLAR GOLD

Date	Mintage	F12	VF20	XF40	AU50	MS60	Prf65
1880	1,636	200	180	255	290	555	14,000
1881	7,707	200	245	255	290	540	11,500
1882	5,125	210	250	255	290	540	24,500
1883	11,007	200	240	255	290	540	25,000
1884	6,236	200	240	255	290	540	24,000
1885	12,261	200	240	255	290	540	24,000
1886	6,016	200	240	255	290	540	24,000
1887	8,543	200	240	255	290	540	24,000
1888	16,580	200	240	255	290	540	24,000
1889	30,729	200	240	255	290	470	24,000

$2.50 (QUARTER EAGLE)

Liberty Cap
Liberty cap on head, right, flanked by stars. Heraldic eagle.

KM# 27 • 4.37 g., 0.916 Gold 0.1287 oz. AGW, 20 mm. • **Obv. Legend:** LIBERTY **Rev. Legend:** UNITED STATES OF AMERICA **Designer:** Robert Scot **Note:** The 1796 "no stars" variety does not have stars on the obverse. The 1804 varieties are distinguished by the number of stars on the obverse.

Date	Mintage	F12	VF20	XF40	MS60
1796 no stars	963	55,000	71,500	100,000	245,000
1796 stars	432	26,500	32,500	65,000	185,000
1797	427	20,000	25,000	45,000	125,000
1798 close date	1,094	6,250	8,650	16,500	60,000
1798 wide date	Inc. above	5,250	7,650	15,500	57,500
1802/1	3,035	4,250	6,650	14,500	34,500
1804 13-star reverse	3,327	45,000	65,000	125,000	—
1804 14-star reverse	Inc. above	4,550	7,150	15,500	46,500
1805	1,781	4,250	6,650	14,500	37,000
1806/4	1,616	4,250	6,650	15,000	38,000
1806/5	Inc. above	6,250	8,650	21,500	95,000
1807	6,812	4,250	6,650	14,500	34,500

Turban Head
Turban on head left flanked by stars. Banner above eagle.

KM# 40 • 4.37 g., 0.916 Gold 0.1287 oz. AGW, 20 mm. • **Rev. Legend:** UNITED STATES OF AMERICA **Designer:** John Reich

Date	Mintage	F12	VF20	XF40	MS60
1808	2,710	26,500	36,500	54,500	175,000

Turban on head left within circle of stars. Banner above eagle.

KM# 46 • 4.37 g., 0.916 Gold 0.1287 oz. AGW, 18.5 mm. • **Rev. Legend:** UNITED STATES OF AMERICA **Designer:** John Reich

Date	Mintage	F12	VF20	XF40	MS60
1821	6,448	6,250	8,250	12,350	32,500
1824/211	2,600	6,250	8,250	12,250	32,000
1825	4,434	6,250	8,250	12,250	30,000
1826/255	760	6,750	9,000	13,000	80,000
1827	2,800	6,350	8,450	12,750	31,500

Turban on head left within circle of stars. Banner above eagle.

KM# 49 • 4.37 g., 0.916 Gold 0.1287 oz. AGW, 18.2 mm. • **Rev. Legend:** UNITED STATES OF AMERICA **Designer:** John Reich

Date	Mintage	F12	VF20	XF40	MS60
1829	3,403	5,400	6,950	9,950	21,500
1830	4,540	5,400	6,950	9,950	21,500
1831	4,520	5,400	6,950	9,950	22,000
1832	4,400	5,400	6,950	9,950	21,500
1833	4,160	5,400	6,950	9,950	22,000
1834	4,000	9,000	12,450	20,000	49,500

DOLLAR GOLD

Classic Head
Classic head left within circle of stars. No motto above eagle.
KM# 56 • 4.18 g., 0.899 Gold 0.1208 oz. AGW, 18.2 mm. • **Rev. Legend:** UNITED STATES OF AMERICA
Designer: William Kneass

Date	Mintage	F12	VF20	XF40	MS60
1834	112,234	260	475	675	3,300
1835	131,402	260	475	675	3,200
1836	547,986	260	475	675	3,100
1837	45,080	280	500	800	4,000
1838	47,030	260	500	625	3,200
1838C	7,880	950	1,700	3,000	27,000
1839	27,021	260	500	900	5,500
1839C	18,140	880	1,500	2,650	26,500
1839/8	Inc. above	—	—	—	—
1839D	13,674	880	1,750	3,450	24,000
1839O	17,781	400	700	1,100	7,250

Coronet Head
Coronet head left within circle of stars. No motto above eagle.
KM# 72 • 4.18 g., 0.900 Gold 0.121 oz. AGW, 18 mm. • **Rev. Legend:** UNITED STATES OF AMERICA
Designer: Christian Gobrecht

1848 "Cal." reverse

Date	Mintage	F12	VF20	XF40	AU50	MS60	Prf65
1840	18,859	275	375	900	2,950	6,000	—
1840C	12,822	1,250	1,400	1,600	6,000	13,000	—
1840D	3,532	2,500	3,200	8,700	15,500	35,000	—
1840O	33,580	325	400	825	2,100	11,000	—
1841	—	—	48,000	100,000	—	—	—
1841C	10,281	1,100	1,500	2,000	3,500	18,500	—
1841D	4,164	1,350	2,100	4,750	11,000	25,000	—
1842	2,823	1,100	900	2,600	6,500	20,000	140,000
1842C	6,729	1,250	1,700	3,500	8,000	27,000	—
1842D	4,643	1,300	2,100	4,000	11,750	—	—
1842O	19,800	325	390	1,200	2,500	14,000	—
1843	100,546	275	345	450	915	3,000	140,000
1843C small date, Crosslet 4	26,064	1,500	2,400	5,500	9,000	29,000	—
1843C large date, Plain 4	Inc. above	1,200	1,600	2,200	3,500	8,800	—
1843D small date, Crosslet 4	36,209	1,350	1,800	2,350	3,250	10,500	—
1843O small date, Crosslet 4	288,002	285	315	375	400	1,700	—
1843O large date, Plain 4	76,000	295	370	465	1,600	8,000	—
1844	6,784	350	400	850	2,000	7,500	140,000
1844C	11,622	1,050	1,600	2,600	7,000	20,000	—
1844D	17,332	1,100	1,650	2,200	3,200	7,800	—
1845	91,051	325	395	360	600	1,275	140,000
1845D	19,460	1,100	1,900	2,600	3,900	15,000	—
1845O	4,000	575	1,050	2,300	9,000	20,000	—
1846	21,598	320	365	500	950	6,000	140,000
1846C	4,808	1,100	1,575	3,500	8,950	18,750	—
1846D	19,303	1,000	1,400	2,000	3,000	12,000	—
1846O	66,000	350	385	400	1,150	6,500	—
1847	29,814	275	350	360	825	3,800	—
1847C	23,226	900	1,800	2,300	3,500	7,250	—
1847D	15,784	950	1,650	2,250	3,250	10,500	—
1847O	124,000	275	365	400	1,000	4,000	—
1848	7,497	340	500	850	2,400	7,000	125,000
1848 CAL.	1,389	35,000	40,000	45,000	50,000	55,000	—
1848C	16,788	950	1,600	2,100	3,800	13,750	—
1848D	13,771	1,100	2,000	2,500	4,500	12,000	—
1849	23,294	295	375	475	1,000	2,600	—
1849C	10,220	975	1,475	2,150	5,150	23,500	—
1849D	10,945	1,050	2,000	2,500	4,500	18,000	—
1850	252,923	265	310	360	385	1,100	—
1850C	9,148	800	1,500	2,000	3,600	13,500	—
1850D	12,148	950	1,700	2,350	3,450	1,600	—
1850O	84,000	300	345	485	1,300	4,500	—
1851	1,372,748	265	300	330	345	495	—

$2.50 GOLD

Date	Mintage	F12	VF20	XF40	AU50	MS60	Prf65
1851C	14,923	900	1,650	2,250	3,450	9,850	—
1851D	11,264	1,000	1,800	2,500	3,850	12,000	—
1851O	148,000	300	335	370	900	4,450	—
1852	1,159,681	265	300	330	345	495	—
1852C	9,772	975	1,500	2,050	4,250	16,500	—
1852D	4,078	1,100	1,650	2,950	7,000	17,500	—
1852O	140,000	300	335	365	1,000	5,000	—
1853	1,404,668	265	300	330	345	495	—
1853D	3,178	1,250	1,975	3,450	4,850	18,000	—
1854	596,258	265	300	330	345	495	—
1854C	7,295	1,100	1,450	2,450	4,750	13,500	—
1854D	1,760	2,100	3,350	6,950	11,500	27,500	—
1854O	153,000	300	335	365	420	1,600	—
1854S	246	95,000	175,000	300,000	—	—	—
1855	235,480	270	305	335	350	495	—
1855C	3,677	1,050	1,675	3,250	6,350	19,500	—
1855D	1,123	2,100	3,350	7,500	16,500	50,000	—
1856	384,240	270	305	335	350	515	75,000
1856C	7,913	985	1,600	2,500	4,000	14,500	—
1856D	874	3,850	6,500	12,850	30,000	72,500	—
1856O	21,100	300	345	750	1,350	7,500	—
1856S	71,120	300	335	425	950	4,350	—
1857	214,130	270	305	335	350	515	75,000
1857D	2,364	1,025	1,650	2,775	3,700	13,200	—
1857O	34,000	300	335	425	1,050	4,450	—
1857S	69,200	300	335	365	875	5,350	—
1858	47,377	275	310	340	395	1,250	59,000
1858C	9,056	965	1,500	2,100	3,350	9,250	—
1859	39,444	275	310	350	425	1,250	61,000
1859D	2,244	1,150	1,850	3,100	3,950	18,500	—
1859S	15,200	310	365	950	2,350	5,000	—
1860	22,675	275	310	340	450	1,150	58,000
1860C	7,469	985	1,475	2,175	3,100	20,000	—
1860S	35,600	310	365	625	1,150	3,850	—
1861	1,283,878	270	305	335	350	850	31,500
1861S	24,000	320	400	900	3,250	7,250	—
1862	98,543	310	340	600	1,950	5,150	32,500
1862/1	Inc. above	650	875	1,850	3,450	7,500	—
1862S	8,000	650	875	2,050	4,200	17,500	—
1863	30	—	—	—	—	—	95,000
1863S	10,800	465	475	1,475	3,150	13,500	—
1864	2,874	3,750	5,450	11,500	22,500	47,500	27,000
1865	1,545	2,950	4,750	7,750	18,000	37,500	30,000
1865S	23,376	320	335	595	1,450	4,400	—
1866	3,110	775	1,250	3,150	5,750	11,500	25,000
1866S	38,960	365	400	625	1,500	5,950	—
1867	3,250	350	395	850	1,150	4,750	27,000
1867S	28,000	300	335	575	1,600	4,100	—
1868	3,625	300	335	395	640	1,625	27,000
1868S	34,000	270	305	365	1,050	3,850	—
1869	4,345	300	335	435	685	2,750	24,500
1869S	29,500	300	365	445	800	4,000	—
1870	4,555	290	375	550	900	4,150	33,500
1870S	16,000	270	345	465	1,000	4,900	—
1871	5,350	295	360	385	850	3,100	36,500
1871S	22,000	270	345	415	550	2,350	—
1872	3,030	305	450	800	1,250	4,650	33,500
1872S	18,000	275	340	485	1,150	4,350	—
1873 closed 3	178,025	270	330	375	395	435	42,500
1873 open 3	Inc. above	270	325	355	375	405	—
1873S	27,000	280	345	395	900	2,800	—
1874	3,940	285	345	425	850	2,250	42,500
1875	420	1,950	3,500	5,500	11,000	24,000	70,000
1875S	11,600	270	330	375	850	3,950	—
1876	4,221	285	345	675	1,250	3,350	27,500
1876S	5,000	285	345	625	1,150	2,850	—
1877	1,652	310	395	875	1,250	3,250	35,000
1877S	35,400	265	325	355	415	750	—
1878	286,260	265	320	345	370	410	35,000
1878S	178,000	265	320	345	375	415	—
1879	88,990	270	325	355	385	435	26,000
1879S	43,500	270	340	365	765	2,500	—
1880	2,996	275	345	385	750	1,400	26,000
1881	691	950	2,150	3,150	5,250	9,850	26,500
1882	4,067	270	330	375	550	1,050	23,500
1883	2,002	280	395	750	1,350	3,350	23,500
1884	2,023	275	375	440	750	1,600	23,500

Date	Mintage	F12	VF20	XF40	AU50	MS60	Prf65
1885	887	400	750	1,850	2,650	4,850	22,500
1886	4,088	275	340	375	650	1,150	23,500
1887	6,282	275	340	365	500	850	17,500
1888	16,098	270	335	365	450	520	18,000
1889	17,648	270	335	365	450	535	20,500
1890	8,813	275	340	365	500	600	18,500
1891	11,040	—	—	—	—	—	17,500
1891 Double die reverse	Inc. above	275	335	365	475	585	—
1892	2,545	275	330	365	500	950	15,500
1893	30,106	270	330	355	375	400	15,500
1894	4,122	275	330	365	440	800	18,000
1895	6,199	265	325	355	400	525	16,750
1896	19,202	265	325	350	370	400	16,750
1897	29,904	270	325	350	370	400	16,750
1898	24,165	265	325	345	365	385	15,000
1899	27,350	265	325	345	365	385	15,000
1900	67,205	265	325	345	365	385	15,000
1901	91,322	265	325	345	365	385	15,000
1902	133,733	265	320	345	365	385	15,000
1903	201,257	265	320	345	365	385	15,000
1904	160,960	265	320	345	365	385	15,000
1905	217,944	265	320	345	365	385	15,000
1906	176,490	265	320	345	365	385	15,000
1907	336,448	265	320	345	365	385	15,000

Indian Head

KM# 128 • 4.18 g., 0.900 Gold 0.121 oz. AGW, 18 mm. • **Designer:** Bela Lyon Pratt

Date	Mintage	VF20	XF40	AU50	MS60	MS63	MS65	Prf65
1908	565,057	260	285	315	425	1,050	2,510	70,000
1909	441,899	260	285	315	425	1,650	6,540	90,000
1910	492,682	260	285	315	350	1,550	7,500	80,000
1911	704,191	260	285	315	350	855	8,500	70,000
1911D D strong D	55,680	2,350	3,550	4,450	7,650	19,000	70,000	—
1911D D weak D	Inc. above	1,150	1,950	2,850	4,950	—	—	—
1912	616,197	260	285	320	375	1,750	11,850	70,000
1913	722,165	260	285	315	350	975	7,500	70,000
1914	240,117	265	310	375	585	4,950	34,500	75,000
1914D	448,000	260	285	325	365	1,700	36,500	—
1915	606,100	260	285	310	350	850	6,500	77,500
1925D	578,000	260	285	310	340	565	1,910	—
1926	446,000	260	285	310	340	565	1,910	—
1927	388,000	260	285	310	340	565	1,910	—
1928	416,000	260	285	310	340	565	1,910	—
1929	532,000	260	295	325	370	655	7,000	—

$3

Indian head with headdress, left. Value, date within wreath.

KM# 84 • 5.02 g., 0.900 Gold 0.1451 oz. AGW, 20.5 mm. • **Obv. Legend:** UNITED STATES OF AMERICA **Designer:** James B. Longacre **Note:** The 1873 "closed-3" and "open-3" varieties are distinguished by the amount of space between the upper left and lower left serifs of the 3 in the date.

Date	Mintage	VF20	XF40	AU50	MS60	MS65	Prf65
1854	138,618	860	1,150	1,290	2,650	19,500	175,000
1854D	1,120	8,300	16,500	35,000	77,500	—	—
1854O	24,000	1,150	2,650	5,000	50,000	—	—
1855	50,555	840	1,175	1,750	3,200	44,000	150,000
1855S	6,600	1,055	2,750	6,950	25,000	—	—
1856	26,010	830	1,125	1,650	3,250	45,000	115,000
1856S	34,500	930	1,600	2,650	12,500	—	—
1857	20,891	830	1,125	1,415	3,500	44,000	105,000
1857S	14,000	980	2,775	5,350	21,000	—	—
1858	2,133	980	1,900	3,650	9,300	50,000	95,000
1859	15,638	930	1,725	1,975	3,250	32,500	60,000
1860	7,155	930	1,625	2,150	3,600	33,000	60,000
1860S	7,000	980	2,450	8,650	26,000	—	—
1861	6,072	955	2,550	3,650	6,900	37,500	60,000
1862	5,785	955	2,350	3,650	6,900	44,500	60,000

$3 GOLD

Date	Mintage	VF20	XF40	AU50	MS60	MS65	Prf65
1863	5,039	930	2,350	3,650	6,900	34,500	60,000
1864	2,680	980	2,350	3,650	6,900	39,500	60,000
1865	1,165	1,275	2,700	6,500	11,700	55,000	60,000
1866	4,030	1,000	1,500	2,250	3,500	38,500	60,000
1867	2,650	1,025	1,550	2,650	3,600	39,500	60,000
1868	4,875	875	1,475	2,125	3,350	33,000	60,000
1869	2,525	1,150	1,550	2,350	4,300	50,000	60,000
1870	3,535	1,030	1,625	2,450	4,400	—	60,000
1870S unique	—	—	4,000,000	—	—	—	—
Note: H. W. Bass Collection. AU50, cleaned. Est. value, $1,250,000.							
1871	1,330	1,030	1,575	2,375	4,000	42,500	60,000
1872	2,030	930	1,525	2,250	3,850	4,500	60,000
1873 closed 3, mintage unknown	—	4,000	9,000	16,000	27,500	—	95,000
1873 open 3, proof only	25	—	—	—	—	—	90,000
1874	41,820	830	1,125	1,265	2,250	16,750	62,500
1875 proof only	20	20,000	28,000	47,500	—	—	225,000
1876	45	6,000	11,500	18,000	—	—	97,500
1877	1,488	1,350	3,150	7,500	23,000	—	65,000
1878	82,324	830	1,125	1,265	2,250	14,500	65,000
1879	3,030	880	1,325	2,000	3,200	22,500	50,000
1880	1,036	950	2,100	3,375	4,700	27,000	42,000
1881	554	1,400	3,350	6,750	12,000	38,500	36,500
1882	1,576	955	1,475	2,350	3,600	30,000	35,500
1883	989	1,000	1,625	2,950	3,800	34,500	35,500
1884	1,106	1,285	2,000	2,800	3,650	34,500	35,500
1885	910	1,300	2,050	3,450	5,200	38,500	34,500
1886	1,142	1,250	2,250	2,875	5,000	47,500	34,500
1887	6,160	930	1,550	2,175	3,250	22,500	34,500
1888	5,291	980	1,525	2,125	3,150	15,000	34,500
1889	2,429	955	1,475	2,000	3,200	22,500	34,500

$5 (HALF EAGLE)

Liberty Cap
Liberty Cap on head, right, flanked by stars. Small eagle.
KM# 19 • 8.75 g., 0.916 Gold 0.2577 oz. AGW

Date	Mintage	F12	VF20	XF40	MS60
1795	8,707	19,500	25,000	31,000	79,500
1796/955	6,196	20,500	25,350	32,750	84,500
1797 15 obverse stars	Inc. above	23,000	27,500	42,250	—
1797 16 obverse stars	Inc. above	21,000	25,850	41,000	210,000
1798	—	112,000	185,000	350,000	—

Liberty cap on head, right, flanked by stars. Large Heraldic eagle.
KM# 28 • 8.75 g., 0.916 Gold 0.2577 oz. AGW, 25 mm. • **Obv. Legend:** LIBERTY **Rev. Legend:** UNITED STATES OF AMERICA **Designer:** Robert Scot

Date	Mintage	F12	VF20	XF40	MS60
1795	Inc. above	10,000	16,500	22,500	85,000
1797/955	3,609	10,850	17,500	24,000	155,000
1797 15 star obv.; Unique	—	—	—	—	—
Note: Smithsonian collection					
1797 16 star obv.; Unique	—	—	—	—	—
Note: Smithsonian collection					
1798 small 8	24,867	4,850	6,650	10,100	—
1798 large 8, 13-star reverse	Inc. above	4,050	5,050	8,350	33,500
1798 large 8, 14-star reverse	Inc. above	5,050	6,650	10,950	—
1799 small reverse stars	7,451	3,850	4,900	11,100	21,500
1799 large reverse stars	Inc. above	3,950	4,750	14,200	31,700
1800	37,628	3,850	4,650	7,100	15,850
1802/1	53,176	3,850	4,650	7,100	15,850
1803/2	33,506	3,850	4,650	7,100	15,850
1804 small 8	30,475	3,850	4,650	7,100	15,850
1804 small 8 over large 8	Inc. above	3,950	4,850	7,600	17,850

Date	Mintage	F12	VF20	XF40	MS60
1805	33,183	3,850	4,650	7,100	15,850
1806 pointed 6	64,093	3,850	4,650	7,100	17,750
1806 round 6	Inc. above	3,850	4,650	7,100	15,850
1807	32,488	3,850	4,650	7,100	15,850

Turban Head
Capped draped bust, left, flanked by stars. Heraldic eagle.

KM# 38 • 8.75 g., 0.916 Gold 0.2577 oz. AGW, 25 mm. • **Rev. Legend:** UNITED STATES OF AMERICA **Designer:** John Reich

Date	Mintage	F12	VF20	XF40	MS60
1807	51,605	3,100	3,850	5,100	13,850
1808	55,578	3,600	4,500	5,950	18,850
1808/7	Inc. above	3,100	3,850	5,100	13,850
1809/8	33,875	3,100	3,850	5,100	13,850
1810 small date, small 5	100,287	17,500	32,500	48,500	125,000
1810 small date, large 5	Inc. above	3,100	3,850	5,100	16,250
1810 large date, small 5	Inc. above	17,500	37,500	60,000	135,000
1810 large date, large 5	Inc. above	3,100	3,850	5,100	13,850
1811 small 5	99,581	3,100	3,850	5,100	13,850
1811 tall 5	Inc. above	3,100	3,850	5,100	13,850
1812	58,087	3,100	3,850	5,100	13,850

Capped head, left, within circle of stars. Heraldic eagle.

KM# 43 • 8.75 g., 0.916 Gold 0.2577 oz. AGW, 25 mm. • **Rev. Legend:** UNITED STATES OF AMERICA **Designer:** John Reich

Date	Mintage	F12	VF20	XF40	MS60
1813	95,428	3,150	3,850	6,250	13,250
1814/133	15,454	5,000	6,250	8,250	19,000
1815	635	32,500	50,000	200,000	245,000
Note: 1815, private sale, Jan. 1994, MS-61, $150,000					
1818	48,588	5,000	6,450	13,500	20,000
1818 5D over 50 Inc. Above	—	5,500	6,450	10,500	23,500
1819	51,723	8,800	16,500	50,000	64,000
1819 5D over 50 Inc. Above	—	5,500	11,000	35,000	64,000
1820 curved-base 2, small letters	263,806	5,250	6,600	12,850	22,500
1820 curved-base 2, large letters	Inc. above	5,100	6,400	12,000	20,000
1820 square-base 2	Inc. above	5,000	6,250	11,500	19,000
1821	34,641	12,000	22,000	43,000	115,000
1822 3 known	—	500,000	90,000	1,250,000	1,000,000
1823	14,485	5,500	6,250	13,500	27,500
1824	17,340	5,500	10,500	32,000	38,000
1825/211	29,060	5,750	9,500	25,000	39,500
1825/244	Inc. above	—	—	550,000	750,000
Note: 1825/24, Bowers & Merena, March 1989, XF, $148,500.					
1826	18,069	5,500	7,800	16,500	30,000
1827	24,913	6,000	10,000	23,500	34,500
1828/7	28,029	15,000	28,500	66,000	125,000
Note: 1828/7, Bowers & Merena, June 1989, XF, $20,900.					
1828	Inc. above	6,000	13,000	30,000	60,000
1829 large planchet	57,442	15,000	28,500	65,000	125,000
Note: 1829 large planchet, Superior, July 1985, MS-65, $104,500.					
1829 small planchet	Inc. above	37,500	54,000	86,500	140,000
Note: 1829 small planchet, private sale, 1992 (XF-45), $89,000.					
1830 small "5D.	126,351	16,500	33,500	50,000	70,000
1830 large "5D.	Inc. above	16,500	33,500	50,000	70,000
1831	140,594	16,500	33,500	50,000	70,000
1832 curved-base 2, 12 stars	157,487	50,000	80,000	175,000	—
1832 square-base 2, 13 stars	Inc. above	16,500	33,500	50,000	70,000
1833 large date	Inc. above	16,500	33,500	50,000	70,000
1833 small date	193,630	17,500	35,500	60,000	90,000
1834 plain 4	50,141	16,500	33,500	50,000	70,000
1834 crosslet 4	Inc. above	17,500	35,500	60,000	80,000

$5 GOLD

Classic Head
Classic head, left, within circle of stars. No motto above eagle.

KM# 57 • 8.36 g., 0.899 Gold 0.2416 oz. AGW, 22.5 mm. • **Rev. Legend:** UNITED STATES OF AMERICA **Designer:** William Kneass

Date	Mintage	VF20	XF40	MS60	MS65	PF65
1834 plain 4	658,028	585	795	4,750	65,000	—
1834 crosslet 4	Inc. above	1,850	3,150	25,000	—	—
1835	371,534	585	795	4,900	50,000	—
1836	553,147	585	795	4,750	80,000	—
1837	207,121	585	845	5,000	110,000	—
1838	286,588	585	975	5,400	70,000	—
1838C	17,179	4,150	8,750	42,500	—	—
1838D	20,583	2,100	4,650	31,000	—	—

Coronet Head
Coronet head, left, within circle of stars. No motto above eagle.

KM# 69 • 8.36 g., 0.900 Gold 0.2419 oz. AGW, 21.6 mm. • **Rev. Legend:** UNITED STATES OF AMERICA **Designer:** Christian Gobrecht **Note:** Varieties for 1843 are distinguished by the size of the numerals in the date. One 1848 variety has "Cal." incsribed on the reverse, indicating it was made from California gold. The 1873 "closed-3" and "open-3" varieties are distinguished by the amount of space between the upper left and lower left serifs in the 3 in the date.

Date	Mintage	VF20	XF40	MS60	MS65	PF65
1839	118,143	540	655	3,850	—	—
1839C	17,205	1,900	3,200	20,000	—	—
1839D	18,939	1,950	4,250	24,500	—	—
1840	137,382	540	645	3,300	—	—
1840C	18,992	1,775	2,900	22,000	—	—
1840D	22,896	1,750	3,000	15,000	—	—
1840O	38,700	540	825	10,000	—	—
1841	15,833	500	875	4,850	—	—
1841C	21,467	1,750	2,150	14,500	—	—
1841D	30,495	1,775	2,350	12,500	90,000	—
1841O 2 known	50	—	—	—	—	—
1842 small letters	27,578	490	1,000	13,500	85,000	—
1842 large letters	Inc. above	660	1,850	11,000	—	—
1842C small date	28,184	9,400	17,500	90,000	—	—
1842C large date	Inc. above	1,650	2,150	15,000	—	—
1842D small date	59,608	1,850	2,475	13,500	—	—
1842D large date	Inc. above	2,350	5,950	48,000	—	—
1842O	16,400	1,000	3,650	22,000	—	—
1843	611,205	490	565	1,825	42,500	—
1843C	44,201	1,600	2,200	10,500	—	—
1843D	98,452	1,750	2,250	10,600	—	—
1843O small letters	82,000	610	1,400	17,500	—	—
1843O large letters	Inc. above	604	1,050	11,000	—	—
1844	340,330	490	565	2,000	26,000	—
1844C	23,631	1,700	2,750	185,800	—	—
1844D	88,982	1,700	2,200	10,000	—	—
1844O	364,600	524	595	4,000	43,000	—
1845	417,099	490	565	2,100	—	—
1845D	90,629	1,800	2,275	10,500	85,000	—
1845O	41,000	520	725	8,750	—	—
1846	395,942	510	565	2,350	—	—
1846C	12,995	1,700	2,600	18,500	—	—
1846D	80,294	1,750	2,250	11,500	—	—
1846O	58,000	540	900	11,000	—	—
1847	915,981	490	565	1,850	21,500	—
1847C	84,151	1,725	2,150	10,000	75,000	—
1847D	64,405	1,800	2,250	9,000	—	—
1847O	12,000	1,800	5,800	24,500	—	—
1848	260,775	490	565	1,900	36,000	—
1848C	64,472	1,750	2,150	17,000	—	—
1848D	47,465	1,800	2,250	12,750	—	—
1849	133,070	490	565	2,450	24,000	—

$5 GOLD

Date	Mintage	VF20	XF40	MS60	MS65	PF65
1849C	64,823	1,750	2,200	10,000	—	—
1849D	39,036	1,850	2,300	12,500	—	—
1850	64,491	510	565	3,350	80,000	—
1850C	63,591	1,750	2,100	10,500	—	—
1850D	43,984	1,800	2,250	24,500	—	—
1851	377,505	490	565	2,400	—	—
1851C	49,176	1,700	2,150	11,750	—	—
1851D	62,710	1,700	2,250	13,000	—	—
1851O	41,000	590	1,400	12,500	—	—
1852	573,901	490	565	1,850	—	—
1852C	72,574	1,750	2,100	6,250	—	—
1852D	91,584	1,850	2,250	10,500	—	—
1853	305,770	490	565	1,850	—	—
1853C	65,571	1,750	2,150	7,750	—	—
1853D	89,678	1,850	2,250	8,250	—	—
1854	160,675	490	565	2,000	—	—
1854C	39,283	1,750	2,150	12,500	—	—
1854D	56,413	1,850	2,250	9,000	—	—
1854O	46,000	520	595	7,500	—	—
1854S	268	—	—	—	—	—
Note: 1854S, Bowers & Merena, Oct. 1982, AU-55, $170,000.						
1855	117,098	490	565	2,000	—	—
1855C	39,788	1,750	2,150	13,500	—	—
1855D	22,432	1,850	2,300	1,500	—	—
1855O	11,100	625	1,950	20,000	—	—
1855S	61,000	620	900	15,500	—	—
1856	197,990	490	565	2,300	—	—
1856C	28,457	1,750	2,100	20,000	—	—
1856D	19,786	1,850	2,250	11,000	—	—
1856O	10,000	650	1,200	14,000	—	—
1856S	105,100	550	615	7,350	—	—
1857	98,188	490	565	2,000	—	123,500
1857C	31,360	1,750	2,150	8,400	—	—
1857D	17,046	1,850	2,300	12,000	—	—
1857O	13,000	640	1,350	15,000	—	—
1857S	87,000	500	615	9,000	—	—
1858	15,136	500	625	3,500	—	190,000
1858C	38,856	1,750	2,150	9,500	—	—
1858D	15,362	1,850	2,275	11,000	—	—
1858S	18,600	750	2,200	31,000	—	—
1859	16,814	520	575	6,500	—	—
1859C	31,847	1,750	2,150	11,000	11,000	—
1859D	10,366	1,900	2,300	10,500	—	—
1859S	13,220	1,125	3,250	26,000	—	—
1860	19,825	500	575	4,000	—	100,000
1860C	14,813	1,900	2,400	12,000	—	—
1860D	14,635	1,950	2,450	13,000	—	—
1860S	21,200	1,050	2,000	23,000	—	—
1861	688,150	510	575	1,850	31,000	100,000
1861C	6,879	2,250	4,850	23,000	—	—
1861D	1,597	7,900	18,500	63,500	—	—
1862	4,465	675	3,650	19,000	—	96,000
1862S	9,500	2,900	5,500	40,000	—	—
1861S	18,000	975	4,100	—	—	—
1863	2,472	2,150	4,000	32,000	—	90,000
1863S	17,000	1,325	7,250	35,500	—	—
1864	4,220	675	1,800	13,500	45,000	72,000
1864S	3,888	4,450	20,000	50,000	225,000	—
1865	1,295	1,450	6,750	21,000	—	82,500
1865S	27,612	1,200	2,400	16,000	—	—
1866S	9,000	1,700	4,000	36,000	—	—

Coronet head, left, within circle of stars. IN GOD WE TRUST above eagle.

KM# **101** • 8.36 g., 0.900 Gold 0.2419 oz. AGW, 21.6 mm. • **Rev. Legend:** UNITED STATES OF AMERICA **Designer:** Christian Gobrecht

Date	Mintage	VF20	XF40	AU50	MS60	MS63	MS65	Prf65
1866	6,730	750	1,650	3,500	16,500	—	—	70,000
1866S	34,920	900	2,600	8,800	25,000	—	—	—
1867	6,920	500	1,500	3,300	11,500	—	—	70,000
1867S	29,000	1,400	2,900	8,000	34,500	—	—	—
1868	5,725	650	1,000	3,500	11,500	—	—	70,000
1868S	52,000	486	1,550	4,000	20,000	—	—	—
1869	1,785	925	2,400	3,500	17,500	34,000	—	65,000
1869S	31,000	500	1,750	4,000	26,000	—	—	—
1870	4,035	800	2,000	2,850	18,000	—	—	75,000
1870CC	7,675	5,250	15,000	30,000	110,000	137,500	200,000	—
1870S	17,000	950	2,600	8,250	29,000	—	—	—
1871	3,230	900	1,700	3,300	12,500	—	—	70,000
1871CC	20,770	1,250	3,000	12,000	60,000	—	—	—
1871S	25,000	500	950	2,950	13,000	—	—	—
1872	1,690	850	1,925	3,000	15,000	18,000	—	60,000
1872CC	16,980	1,250	5,000	20,000	60,000	—	—	—
1872S	36,400	537	800	3,400	13,500	—	—	—
1873 closed 3	49,305	472	486	500	1,200	6,500	24,000	70,000
1873 open 3	63,200	467	477	487	850	3,650	—	—
1873CC	7,416	2,600	12,500	27,500	60,000	—	—	—
1873S	31,000	525	1,400	3,250	21,000	—	—	—
1874	3,508	660	1,675	2,500	13,000	26,000	—	66,000
1874CC	21,198	850	1,700	9,500	36,000	—	—	—
1874S	16,000	640	2,100	4,800	22,500	—	—	—
1875	220	34,000	45,000	60,000	190,000	—	—	185,000
1875CC	11,828	1,400	4,500	11,500	52,000	—	—	—
1875S	9,000	715	2,250	5,000	16,500	32,500	—	—
1876	1,477	1,100	2,500	4,125	11,000	14,500	55,000	60,000
1876CC	6,887	1,450	5,000	14,000	46,500	82,500	165,000	—
1876S	4,000	2,000	3,600	9,500	30,000	—	—	—
1877	1,152	900	2,750	4,000	13,750	29,000	—	75,000
1877CC	8,680	1,000	3,300	11,000	52,500	—	—	—
1877S	26,700	499	650	1,400	9,200	—	—	—
1878	131,740	469	480	524	550	2,000	—	50,000
1878CC	9,054	3,100	7,200	20,000	60,000	—	—	—
1878S	144,700	467	475	3,000	675	4,250	—	—
1879	301,950	467	475	485	520	2,000	12,000	55,000
1879CC	17,281	1,000	1,500	3,150	22,000	—	—	—
1879S	426,200	469	480	524	950	3,300	—	—
1880	3,166,436	462	470	480	500	840	7,500	54,000
1880CC	51,017	625	815	1,375	9,900	—	—	—
1880S	1,348,900	462	470	480	490	800	5,750	—
1881	5,708,802	462	470	480	500	775	4,800	54,000
1881/800	Inc. above	465	600	750	1,500	4,500	—	—
1881CC	13,886	650	1,500	7,000	22,500	60,000	—	—
1881S	969,000	462	470	480	500	775	7,150	—
1882	2,514,568	462	470	480	500	800	6,150	54,000
1882CC	82,817	625	625	900	7,500	40,000	—	—
1882S	969,000	462	470	480	510	800	4,500	—
1883	233,461	479	487	497	530	1,200	—	40,000
1883CC	12,958	625	1,100	3,200	18,000	—	—	—
1883S	83,200	479	478	490	1,000	2,950	—	—
1884	191,078	479	480	497	650	2,250	—	35,000
1884CC	16,402	625	975	3,000	17,000	—	—	—
1884S	177,000	479	487	497	490	2,000	—	—
1885	601,506	462	470	480	505	825	4,800	35,000
1885S	1,211,500	462	470	480	510	790	4,000	—
1886	388,432	462	470	480	510	1,125	5,600	44,000
1886S	3,268,000	462	470	480	510	815	4,500	—
1887	87	—	14,500	20,000	—	—	—	120,000
1887S	1,912,000	462	470	480	510	800	4,800	—
1888	18,296	477	485	497	550	1,500	—	29,000
1888S	293,900	467	475	547	1,200	4,000	—	—
1889	7,565	576	584	557	1,150	2,400	—	30,000
1890	4,328	499	507	550	2,200	6,500	—	27,000
1890CC	53,800	576	584	615	1,600	7,500	55,000	—
1891	61,413	469	480	524	640	2,000	5,400	29,000
1891CC	208,000	561	565	800	1,350	3,500	28,500	—

$5 GOLD

Date	Mintage	VF20	XF40	AU50	MS60	MS63	MS65	Prf65
1892	753,572	462	470	480	530	1,350	7,000	30,000
1892CC	82,968	562	584	750	1,500	6,500	33,500	—
1892O	10,000	524	1,000	1,375	3,300	15,000	—	—
1892S	298,400	462	470	485	525	2,850	—	—
1893	1,528,197	462	470	480	510	1,150	3,900	34,000
1893CC	60,000	596	634	825	1,550	6,650	—	—
1893O	110,000	477	581	585	950	5,950	—	—
1893S	224,000	462	470	485	510	1,040	9,000	—
1894	957,955	462	470	480	500	905	2,600	35,000
1894O	16,600	479	487	570	1,300	5,500	—	—
1894S	55,900	489	487	575	2,900	10,000	—	—
1895	1,345,936	462	470	480	495	905	4,500	29,000
1895S	112,000	467	487	497	3,150	6,500	26,000	—
1896	59,063	462	470	485	510	1,650	4,500	30,000
1896S	155,400	469	480	524	1,150	6,000	24,500	—
1897	867,883	462	470	480	495	905	4,500	35,000
1897S	354,000	462	470	485	865	5,150	—	—
1898	633,495	462	470	480	500	905	6,000	30,000
1898S	1,397,400	462	470	480	495	1,310	—	—
1899	1,710,729	462	470	480	495	890	3,600	30,000
1899S	1,545,000	462	470	480	495	1,260	9,600	—
1900	1,405,730	462	470	480	495	890	3,600	30,000
1900S	329,000	462	470	480	500	1,260	14,000	—
1901	616,040	462	470	480	495	890	3,650	27,000
1901S	3,648,000	462	470	480	495	890	3,600	—
1902	172,562	462	470	480	495	890	4,400	27,000
1902S	939,000	462	470	480	495	890	3,600	—
1903	227,024	462	470	480	500	905	4,000	27,000
1903S	1,855,000	462	470	480	495	890	3,600	—
1904	392,136	462	470	480	495	890	3,600	27,000
1904S	97,000	469	480	524	885	4,000	9,600	—
1905	302,308	462	470	480	500	905	4,000	27,000
1905S	880,700	462	470	480	495	3,350	9,600	—
1906	348,820	462	470	480	495	890	3,600	26,000
1906D	320,000	462	470	480	495	905	3,200	—
1906S	598,000	462	470	480	500	1,190	4,400	—
1907	626,192	462	470	480	495	890	3,400	23,000
1907D	888,000	462	470	480	495	890	3,400	—
1908	421,874	462	470	485	510	905	3,400	—

Indian Head

KM# 129 • 8.36 g., 0.900 Gold 0.2419 oz. AGW,
21.6 mm. • **Designer:** Bela Lyon Pratt

Date	Mintage	VF20	XF40	AU50	MS60	MS63	MS65	Prf65
1908	578,012	420	430	465	545	1,630	12,950	39,500
1908D	148,000	420	430	465	615	1,750	39,500	—
1908S	82,000	495	555	1,150	2,750	8,950	24,500	—
1909	627,138	420	430	465	540	1,570	13,750	50,500
1909D	3,423,560	420	430	465	525	1,050	12,200	—
1909O	34,200	4,950	6,850	12,750	36,500	105,000	500,000	—
1909S	297,200	450	470	525	1,400	15,500	51,000	—
1910	604,250	420	430	465	525	1,650	13,450	46,000
1910D	193,600	420	430	465	545	4,200	38,500	—
1910S	770,200	460	485	535	1,150	10,600	87,000	—
1911	915,139	420	430	465	525	1,475	13,200	39,500
1911D	72,500	625	825	1,840	8,000	43,500	275,000	—
1911S	1,416,000	430	465	520	780	5,900	57,500	—
1912	790,144	420	430	465	525	1,475	13,600	39,500
1912S	392,000	465	495	610	1,675	17,500	190,000	—
1913	916,099	420	430	465	525	1,475	13,200	39,500
1913S	408,000	460	490	650	2,325	20,500	155,000	—
1914	247,125	420	430	465	545	2,250	18,500	39,500
1914D	247,000	420	430	465	545	2,550	27,600	—
1914S	263,000	465	485	560	1,375	15,500	135,000	—
1915	588,075	420	430	465	525	1,825	14,200	54,500
1915S	164,000	475	505	555	1,900	20,000	135,000	—
1916S	240,000	445	465	550	950	7,200	37,000	—
1929	662,000	12,000	15,475	18,800	31,000	49,000	130,000	—

$10 (EAGLE)

Liberty Cap
Small eagle.
KM# 21 • 17.50 g., 0.916 Gold 0.5154 oz. AGW, 33 mm. • **Designer:** Robert Scot

Date	Mintage	F12	VF20	XF40	MS60
1795 13 leaves	5,583	28,500	33,850	48,500	122,500
1795 9 leaves	Inc. above	30,000	45,000	73,500	250,000
1796	4,146	27,500	36,000	50,000	135,000
1797 small eagle	3,615	31,500	40,000	55,000	200,000

Liberty cap on head, right, flanked by stars. Heraldic eagle.
KM# 30 • 17.50 g., 0.916 Gold 0.5154 oz. AGW, 33 mm. • **Obv. Legend:** LIBERTY **Rev. Legend:** UNITED STATES OF AMERICA **Designer:** Robert Scot

Date	Mintage	F12	VF20	XF40	MS60
1797 large eagle	10,940	9,800	12,850	21,400	58,500
1798/977 9 stars left, 4 right	900	13,500	19,000	34,500	127,500
1798/977 7 stars left, 6 right	842	28,500	38,500	87,500	235,000
1799 large star obv	37,449	9,350	10,750	18,200	37,500
1799 small star obv	Inc. above	9,350	10,750	18,200	37,500
1800	5,999	9,500	10,750	18,350	39,500
1801	44,344	9,250	10,900	17,400	37,500
1803 extra star	15,017	9,600	11,850	19,550	67,500
1803 large stars rev	Inc. above	9,250	11,400	17,800	37,500
1804 crosslet 4	3,757	16,500	22,750	31,500	92,500
1804 plain 4	—	—	—	—	400,000

Coronet Head
Old-style head, left, within circle of stars. No motto above eagle.
KM# 66.1 • 16.72 g., 0.900 Gold 0.4837 oz. AGW, 27 mm. • **Rev. Legend:** UNITED STATES OF AMERICA **Designer:** Christian Gobrecht

Date	Mintage	VF20	XF40	MS60	MS65	PF65
1838	7,200	2,650	6,850	43,500	—	1,500,000
1839/8 Type of 1838	25,801	1,450	5,850	28,500	220,000	1,500,000
1839 large letters	Inc. above	1,150	2,150	32,000	—	—

New-style head, left, within circle of stars. No motto above eagle.

KM# 66.2 • 16.72 g., 0.900 Gold 0.4837 oz. AGW, 27 mm. • **Rev. Legend:** UNITED STATES OF AMERICA **Designer:** Christian Gobrecht

Date	Mintage	VF20	XF40	MS60	MS65	PF65
1839 small letters	12,447	1,550	6,850	75,000	—	—
1840	47,338	1,059	1,333	11,500	—	—
1841	63,131	1,049	1,233	9,000	—	—
1841O	2,500	3,450	6,950	—	—	—
1842 small date	81,507	1,049	1,158	15,000	—	—
1842 large date	Inc. above	1,049	1,148	9,500	104,000	—
1842O	27,400	1,059	1,463	22,500	—	—
1843	75,462	1,049	1,263	16,750	—	—
1843O	175,162	1,059	1,218	12,000	—	—
1844	6,361	1,350	3,200	16,750	—	—
1844O	118,700	1,059	1,403	15,000	—	—
1845	26,153	1,219	1,343	17,500	—	—
1845O	47,500	1,059	875	16,500	—	—
1845O repunched	Inc. above	1,419	3,850	—	—	—
1846	20,095	1,289	1,250	—	—	—
1846O	81,780	1,059	1,150	—	—	—
1846/5	Inc. above	1,419	1,135	—	—	—
1847	862,258	1,049	1,093	3,450	—	—
1847O	571,500	1,049	1,093	6,500	—	—
1848	145,484	1,049	1,158	5,000	—	—
1848O	38,850	1,239	1,850	17,750	98,000	—
1849	653,618	1,049	1,093	3,400	—	—
1849O	23,900	1,239	2,450	27,500	—	—
1850 large date	291,451	1,049	1,093	4,500	—	—
1850 small date	Inc. above	1,239	1,150	8,500	—	—
1850O	57,500	1,074	1,275	19,500	225,000	—
1851	176,328	1,049	1,093	5,150	—	—
1851O	263,000	1,059	1,148	6,650	—	—
1852	263,106	1,049	1,093	5,250	105,500	—
1852O	18,000	1,219	1,650	27,500	—	—
1853	201,253	1,059	1,093	3,600	—	—
1853/2	Inc. above	1,074	1,428	14,950	—	—
1853O	51,000	1,074	1,158	14,500	—	—
1854	54,250	1,049	1,118	6,250	—	—
1854O small date	52,500	1,074	1,398	11,000	—	—
1854O large date	Inc. above	1,214	925	9,450	—	—
1854S	123,826	1,049	1,118	10,500	—	—
1855	121,701	1,049	1,093	4,750	—	—
1855O	18,000	1,074	2,100	28,000	—	—
1856	60,490	1,049	1,093	4,250	—	—
1856O	14,500	1,374	2,150	18,500	—	—
1856S	68,000	1,049	1,168	9,000	—	—
1857	16,606	1,074	1,050	13,500	—	—
1857O	5,500	1,800	3,650	—	—	—
1857S	26,000	1,059	1,050	11,500	—	—
1858	2,521	5,200	8,250	35,000	—	—
1858O	20,000	1,049	1,418	10,000	—	—
1858S	11,800	1,600	3,950	—	—	—
1859	16,093	1,074	1,278	10,500	—	—
1859O	2,300	4,250	10,500	—	—	—
1859S	7,000	2,600	5,250	—	—	—
1860	15,105	1,114	1,328	8,450	—	175,000
1860O	11,100	1,214	1,850	13,750	—	—
1860S	5,000	2,950	6,400	—	—	—
1861	113,233	1,049	1,093	6,250	105,000	170,000
1861S	15,500	1,600	3,750	—	—	—
1862	10,995	1,204	1,200	—	—	170,000
1862S	12,500	2,000	3,450	—	—	—
1863	1,248	4,000	10,000	52,500	—	165,000
1863S	10,000	1,600	3,750	29,500	—	—
1864	3,580	1,800	4,950	18,000	—	165,000
1864S	2,500	5,100	17,500	—	—	—
1865	4,005	1,950	4,850	34,500	—	165,000
1865S	16,700	4,850	12,500	—	—	—
1865S over inverted 186	Inc. above	3,450	8,750	50,000	—	—
1866S	8,500	2,650	5,950	—	—	—

$10 GOLD

New-style head, left, within circle of stars. IN GOD WE TRUST above eagle.

KM# 102 • 16.72 g., 0.900 Gold 0.4837 oz. AGW, 27 mm. • **Rev. Legend:** UNITED STATES OF AMERICA **Designer:** Christian Gobrecht

Date	Mintage	VF20	XF40	AU50	MS60	MS63	MS65	Prf65
1866	3,780	1,175	2,600	5,000	45,000	—	—	120,000
1866S	11,500	1,600	3,850	8,000	—	—	—	—
1867	3,140	1,550	2,750	5,000	35,000	—	—	—
1867S	9,000	2,350	6,650	9,850	—	—	—	—
1868	10,655	880	1,200	2,000	19,000	—	—	120,000
1868S	13,500	1,350	2,400	3,900	—	—	—	—
1869	1,855	1,550	3,000	5,150	36,000	—	—	—
1869S	6,430	1,450	2,700	5,750	30,000	60,000	—	—
1870	4,025	1,200	1,650	3,750	20,000	—	—	—
1870CC	5,908	32,500	50,000	85,000	—	—	—	—
1870S	8,000	1,250	2,850	6,500	33,500	—	—	—
1871	1,820	1,500	3,000	4,850	28,000	—	—	120,000
1871CC	8,085	2,600	6,400	22,500	65,000	—	—	—
1871S	16,500	1,300	2,200	5,500	—	—	—	—
1872	1,650	2,400	5,000	8,700	25,000	42,500	—	90,000
1872CC	4,600	5,250	9,850	26,500	—	—	—	—
1872S	17,300	880	1,175	1,900	19,500	—	—	—
1873 closed 3	825	4,500	20,000	24,000	55,000	—	—	—
1873CC	4,543	6,000	23,500	32,000	—	—	—	—
1873S	12,000	1,150	2,650	4,850	27,500	—	—	—
1874	53,160	850	925	913	1,750	6,750	42,500	120,000
1874CC	16,767	2,850	4,650	12,000	52,500	100,000	200,000	—
1874S	10,000	1,275	2,950	6,500	—	—	—	—
1875	120	110,000	225,000	300,000	—	—	—	—

Note: 1875, Akers, Aug. 1990, Proof, $115,000.

Date	Mintage	VF20	XF40	AU50	MS60	MS63	MS65	Prf65
1875CC	7,715	4,250	9,850	25,000	75,000	150,000	—	—
1876	732	3,950	8,500	18,500	60,000	—	—	—
1876CC	4,696	3,850	10,500	21,500	—	—	—	—
1876S	5,000	1,300	3,750	7,500	—	—	—	—
1877	817	3,350	6,350	10,000	37,500	—	—	—
1877CC	3,332	2,400	6,750	15,000	—	—	—	—
1877S	17,000	832	1,050	2,450	20,000	—	—	—
1878	73,800	820	868	925	1,050	7,000	30,000	—
1878CC	3,244	3,850	8,650	19,000	—	—	—	—
1878S	26,100	1,000	1,150	2,050	14,000	29,500	—	—
1879	384,770	823	868	905	1,000	5,000	14,500	83,000
1879/788	Inc. above	830	880	1,100	1,250	2,850	—	—
1879CC	1,762	8,350	12,500	42,500	75,000	—	—	—
1879O	1,500	2,150	8,000	10,850	—	—	—	—
1879S	224,000	823	868	935	1,150	6,500	35,000	—
1880	1,644,876	805	830	875	980	2,000	25,000	—
1880CC	11,190	955	1,250	2,450	17,500	—	—	—
1880O	9,200	925	1,450	2,450	10,000	—	—	—
1880S	506,250	805	830	875	930	2,600	25,000	—
1881	3,877,260	805	830	875	910	1,350	15,000	63,000
1881CC	24,015	951	1,300	1,950	6,850	36,500	—	—
1881O	8,350	807	868	1,375	10,000	35,000	—	—
1881S	970,000	805	830	875	920	3,450	—	—
1882	2,324,480	805	830	875	910	1,200	19,500	63,000
1882CC	6,764	985	1,900	3,250	—	—	—	—
1882O	10,820	833	1,010	1,250	6,500	42,500	—	—
1882S	132,000	833	868	913	992	3,650	20,000	—
1883	208,740	805	830	875	920	1,500	40,000	63,000
1883CC	12,000	1,005	1,250	2,600	22,500	—	—	—
1883O	800	4,400	12,000	37,500	—	—	—	—
1883S	38,000	833	868	913	1,650	10,500	23,500	—
1884	76,905	833	868	913	1,000	4,200	15,000	53,000
1884CC	9,925	1,025	1,600	2,500	12,850	60,000	—	—
1884S	124,250	805	830	875	925	6,500	—	—
1885	253,527	805	830	875	910	3,000	23,000	57,500
1885S	228,000	805	830	875	910	4,400	—	—
1886	236,160	805	830	875	910	3,500	—	63,000
1886S	826,000	805	830	875	920	1,500	—	—
1887	53,680	833	868	925	975	6,500	—	95,000
1887S	817,000	805	830	875	920	2,000	17,500	—
1888	132,996	833	868	925	1,000	7,500	—	—

$10 GOLD

Date	Mintage	VF20	XF40	AU50	MS60	MS63	MS65	Prf65
1888O	21,335	833	868	925	1,200	5,750	—	—
1888S	648,700	805	830	875	910	1,500	—	—
1889	4,485	863	1,025	1,075	3,500	10,000	—	53,000
1889S	425,400	805	830	875	920	1,650	53,000	—
1890	58,043	843	888	933	1,000	4,500	20,000	46,000
1890CC	17,500	1,085	1,145	1,350	4,000	20,000	—	—
1891	91,868	863	908	953	988	2,650	20,000	48,000
1891CC	103,732	1,085	1,145	1,350	2,300	7,500	85,000	—
1892	797,552	805	830	875	910	1,500	9,100	48,000
1892CC	40,000	1,085	1,145	1,200	4,000	30,000	—	—
1892O	28,688	863	888	933	986	8,000	—	—
1892S	115,500	833	892	937	972	2,700	—	—
1893	1,840,895	805	830	875	910	1,200	8,500	46,000
1893CC	14,000	1,085	1,230	2,100	8,500	—	—	—
1893O	17,000	833	868	955	1,190	5,000	—	—
1893S	141,350	833	868	925	985	2,500	20,000	—
1894	2,470,778	805	830	875	910	1,100	16,000	46,000
1894O	107,500	833	868	970	1,100	6,000	28,000	—
1894S	25,000	833	892	1,050	3,850	—	—	—
1895	567,826	805	830	875	910	1,075	11,500	43,500
1895O	98,000	833	868	925	1,200	6,500	—	—
1895S	49,000	833	880	890	2,400	9,500	—	—
1896	76,348	805	830	875	920	1,500	10,000	43,500
1896S	123,750	833	863	935	1,600	10,000	35,000	—
1897	1,000,159	805	830	875	910	1,085	7,000	—
1897O	42,500	833	868	913	1,110	6,500	28,000	—
1897S	234,750	833	863	908	1,020	5,750	22,500	—
1898	812,197	805	830	875	910	1,350	8,000	43,500
1898S	473,600	833	830	875	920	3,300	18,500	—
1899	1,262,305	805	830	875	910	1,035	3,350	43,500
1899O	37,047	833	868	915	1,000	7,500	35,000	—
1899S	841,000	805	830	875	920	1,850	14,000	—
1900	293,960	805	830	875	920	1,250	5,500	43,500
1900S	81,000	833	868	913	980	6,500	25,000	—
1901	1,718,825	805	830	875	910	1,035	3,350	43,500
1901O	72,041	833	868	913	1,050	3,500	12,500	—
1901S	2,812,750	805	830	875	910	1,035	3,350	—
1902	82,513	805	830	875	930	1,600	9,000	43,500
1902S	469,500	805	830	875	910	1,135	6,000	—
1903	125,926	805	830	875	920	2,450	7,000	43,500
1903O	112,771	833	868	913	1,020	1,260	17,500	—
1903S	538,000	805	830	875	920	1,035	3,350	—
1904	162,038	805	830	875	920	1,750	8,000	46,000
1904O	108,950	833	868	913	1,020	3,000	22,500	—
1905	201,078	805	830	875	920	1,085	8,500	43,500
1905S	369,250	833	863	920	1,100	6,000	30,000	—
1906	165,497	805	830	875	920	1,500	10,500	43,500
1906D	981,000	805	830	875	910	1,100	7,000	—
1906O	86,895	833	868	913	1,060	4,800	15,000	—
1906S	457,000	833	863	913	960	4,500	15,000	—
1907	1,203,973	805	830	875	910	1,035	5,000	43,500
1907D	1,030,000	805	830	875	920	1,700	14,000	—
1907S	210,500	833	863	935	975	5,450	17,500	—

Indian Head
No motto to left of eagle.

KM# 125 • 16.72 g., 0.900 Gold 0.4837 oz. AGW, 27 mm. • **Designer:** Augustus Saint-Gaudens **Note:** 1907 varieties are distinguished by whether the edge is rolled or wired, and whether the legend E PLURIBUS UNUM has periods between each word.

Date	Mintage	VF20	XF40	AU50	MS60	MS63	MS65	Prf65
1907 wire edge, periods before and after legend	500	13,850	17,500	21,000	26,500	44,500	72,500	—
1907 same, without stars on edge, unique	—	—	—	—	—	—	—	—
1907 rolled edge, periods	42	26,000	38,500	49,000	66,500	135,000	325,000	—
1907 without periods	239,406	730	750	785	1,215	3,400	10,500	—
1908 without motto	33,500	715	735	770	1,200	5,350	15,500	—
1908D without motto	210,000	715	735	770	1,240	8,250	37,500	—

$10 GOLD

IN GOD WE TRUST left of eagle.
KM# 130 • 16.72 g., 0.900 Gold 0.4837 oz. AGW, 27 mm. • **Designer:** Augustus Saint-Gaudens

Date	Mintage	VF20	XF40	AU50	MS60	MS63	MS65	Prf65
1908	341,486	710	725	755	1,050	2,500	12,250	145,000
1908D	836,500	715	745	775	1,225	8,000	29,000	
1908S	59,850	725	1,085	1,150	2,950	13,100	25,500	
1909	184,863	710	725	755	950	4,550	20,250	150,000
1909D	121,540	715	730	760	1,235	7,750	39,500	—
1909S	292,350	715	730	760	2,050	7,950	22,250	—
1910	318,704	710	725	755	775	1,210	12,750	146,500
1910D	2,356,640	705	720	755	775	1,125	10,250	—
1910S	811,000	715	730	760	1,600	11,050	55,000	—
1911	505,595	705	720	750	790	1,425	10,000	145,000
1911D	30,100	1,350	1,600	2,250	10,750	34,500	255,000	—
1911S	51,000	745	1,150	1,200	2,750	11,750	24,750	—
1912	405,083	710	725	755	775	1,475	12,000	145,000
1912S	300,000	715	730	1,975	8,750	46,000	—	
1913	442,071	710	725	755	775	1,310	11,000	145,000
1913S	66,000	760	1,200	1,300	6,950	31,500	125,000	—
1914	151,050	710	725	755	785	2,320	12,000	148,000
1914D	343,500	710	725	755	775	2,550	18,000	—
1914S	208,000	720	1,165	1,250	2,100	8,850	33,500	—
1915	351,075	710	725	755	775	2,000	12,000	145,000
1915S	59,000	760	790	1,200	5,400	19,750	83,000	—
1916S	138,500	745	760	823	1,900	7,800	26,500	—
1920S	126,500	12,500	16,850	21,000	37,500	88,500	325,000	—
1926	1,014,000	705	720	750	770	1,010	3,150	—
1930S	96,000	8,500	11,250	14,850	23,500	47,500	93,500	—
1932	4,463,000	705	720	750	770	1,010	3,250	—
1933	312,500	—	140,000	160,000	180,000	225,000	600,000	—

$20

Liberty Head
Coronet head, left, within circle of stars.   TWENTY D. below eagle, no motto above eagle.
KM# 74.1 • 33.44 g., 0.900 Gold 0.9675 oz. AGW, 34 mm. • **Rev. Legend:** UNITED STATES OF AMERICA
Designer: James B. Longacre

Date	Mintage	VF20	XF40	AU50	MS60	MS63	MS65	Prf65
1849 unique, in Smithsonian collection	1	—	—	—	—	—	—	—
1850	1,170,261	2,295	2,475	3,800	11,500	46,500	175,000	—
1850O	141,000	2,345	4,350	9,800	45,000	—	—	—
1851	2,087,155	2,175	2,235	2,550	5,000	22,500	—	—
1851O	315,000	2,410	4,200	6,150	23,000	—	—	—
1852	2,053,026	2,175	2,225	2,550	4,950	18,500	—	—
1852O	190,000	2,365	3,850	6,000	22,500	—	—	—
1853	1,261,326	2,335	2,235	2,550	5,000	27,500	—	—
1853/2	Inc. above	2,415	2,465	5,000	34,500	—	—	—
1853O	71,000	2,425	3,650	7,950	32,500	—	—	—
1854 Small date	757,899	2,175	2,225	2,550	9,750	—	—	—
1854 Large Date	Inc. above	2,575	3,350	6,000	30,000	—	—	—
1854O	3,250	125,000	250,000	375,000	—	—	—	—
1854S	141,468	23,315	3,400	7,500	17,500	26,000	90,000	—

$10 GOLD

Date	Mintage	VF20	XF40	AU50	MS60	MS63	MS65	Prf65
1855	364,666	2,175	2,225	2,550	8,850	66,500	—	—
1855O	8,000	10,500	19,500	42,500	110,000	—	—	—
1855S	879,675	2,315	2,475	2,800	6,750	15,500	—	—
1856	329,878	2,175	2,225	2,550	8,400	28,000	—	—
1856O	2,250	175,000	275,000	400,000	550,000	1,100,000	—	—
1856S	1,189,750	2,315	2,475	2,800	5,900	15,000	35,000	—
1857	439,375	2,175	2,225	2,550	4,250	24,500	—	—
1857O	30,000	2,390	4,250	9,400	37,500	115,000	—	—
1857S	970,500	2,315	2,475	2,900	4,750	9,300	12,850	—
1858	211,714	2,175	2,225	2,550	6,750	34,500	—	—
1858O	35,250	2,515	5,000	11,000	42,000	—	—	—
1858S	846,710	2,295	2,495	3,000	8,500	—	—	—
1859	43,597	2,360	2,450	6,950	28,000	—	—	280,000
1859O	9,100	5,000	18,500	40,000	110,000	—	—	—
1859S	636,445	2,175	2,225	2,550	8,000	35,000	—	—
1860	577,670	2,315	2,475	2,800	5,500	18,000	63,500	—
1860O	6,600	4,350	14,500	35,000	120,000	—	—	—
1860S	544,950	2,175	2,225	3,090	7,350	18,500	48,000	—
1861	2,976,453	2,200	2,325	2,650	6,750	19,500	70,000	275,000
1861O	17,741	4,200	21,000	37,500	88,000	—	—	—
1861S	768,000	2,250	2,575	2,925	10,500	37,500	—	—

Coronet head, left, within circle of stars.   Paquet design, TWENTY D. below eagle.

KM# 93 • 33.44 g., 0.900 Gold 0.9675 oz. AGW **Rev. Legend:** UNITED STATES OF AMERICA **Note:** In 1861 the reverse was redesigned by Anthony C. Paquet, but it was withdrawn soon after its release. The letters in the inscriptions on the Paquet-reverse variety are taller than on the regular reverse.

Date	Mintage	VF20	XF40	AU50	MS60	MS63	MS65	Prf65
1861 2 Known	—	—	—	—	—	—	—	—
Note: 1861 Paquet reverse, Bowers & Merena, Nov. 1988, MS-67, $660,000.								
1861S	—	22,000	55,000	92,500	275,000	—	—	—
Note: Included in mintage of 1861S, KM#74.1								

Longacre design resumed.

KM# A74.1 • 33.44 g., 0.900 Gold 0.9675 oz. AGW

Date	Mintage	VF20	XF40	AU50	MS60	MS63	MS65	Prf65
1862	92,133	2,315	4,850	10,000	17,500	36,500	—	250,000
1862S	854,173	2,300	2,425	2,800	12,400	60,000	—	—
1863	142,790	2,415	3,100	7,900	19,500	55,000	—	250,000
1863S	966,570	2,300	2,430	2,755	8,350	28,500	—	—
1864	204,285	2,315	2,465	3,250	21,500	—	—	250,000
1864S	793,660	2,300	2,425	2,735	8,850	32,000	125,000	—
1865	351,200	2,315	2,450	2,840	6,200	23,500	90,000	250,000
1865S	1,042,500	2,300	2,430	2,750	5,350	13,500	28,000	—
1866S	Inc. below	2,750	11,500	37,500	—	—	—	—

Coronet head, left, within circle of stars. TWENTY D. below eagle. IN GOD WE TRUST above eagle.

KM# 74.2 • 33.44 g., 0.900 Gold 0.9675 oz. AGW, 34 mm. • **Rev. Legend:** UNITED STATES OF AMERICA
Designer: James B. Longacre

Date	Mintage	VF20	XF40	AU50	MS60	MS63	MS65	Prf65
1866	698,775	1,810	1,980	2,155	11,000	65,000	—	200,000
1866S	842,250	1,810	1,990	3,350	15,500	—	—	—
1867	251,065	1,810	2,000	2,155	4,650	40,000	—	200,000
1867S	920,750	1,810	1,990	2,175	15,000	—	—	—
1868	98,600	1,850	2,100	3,450	17,500	60,000	—	200,000
1868S	837,500	1,810	1,960	2,150	14,500	—	—	—
1869	175,155	1,820	1,950	2,175	7,250	40,000	350,000	—
1869S	686,750	1,810	1,980	2,075	7,100	45,000	—	—
1870	155,185	1,830	1,980	2,300	10,500	55,000	—	215,000
1870CC	3,789	215,000	275,000	410,000	—	—	—	—
1870S	982,000	1,810	1,935	2,110	5,450	—	—	—
1871	80,150	1,820	1,935	2,100	7,950	55,000	—	—
1871CC	17,387	10,000	25,000	50,000	97,500	300,000	650,000	—
1871S	928,000	1,810	1,950	2,150	4,750	25,000	—	—
1872	251,880	1,810	1,980	2,180	4,000	24,500	—	—
1872CC	26,900	2,750	6,500	11,500	38,500	—	—	—
1872S	780,000	1,810	1,980	2,155	3,700	23,500	—	—
1873 closed 3	Est. 208925	1,810	2,040	2,215	3,500	—	—	200,000
1873 open 3	Est. 1500900	1,810	1,980	1,960	2,425	12,200	235,000	—
1873CC	22,410	3,250	9,000	14,500	37,500	150,000	—	—
1873S closed 3	1,040,600	1,700	1,950	2,150	2,400	30,000	—	—
1873S open 3	Inc. above	1,810	1,980	2,155	2,375	—	—	—
1874	366,800	1,810	1,980	1,950	2,325	20,000	—	—
1874CC	115,085	2,350	2,850	5,250	16,500	—	—	—
1874S	1,214,000	1,700	1,950	1,950	2,175	24,500	—	—
1875	295,740	1,810	1,980	2,155	2,380	11,000	—	—
1875CC	111,151	2,450	4,250	3,450	6,400	33,500	—	—
1875S	1,230,000	1,700	1,950	1,950	2,175	16,850	—	—
1876	583,905	1,700	1,970	1,950	2,175	13,500	—	—
1876CC	138,441	2,350	3,250	4,750	9,850	50,000	—	—
1876S	1,597,000	1,700	1,950	1,950	2,175	12,200	235,000	—

Coronet head, left, within circle of stars. TWENTY DOLLARS below eagle.

KM# 74.3 • 33.44 g., 0.900 Gold 0.9675 oz. AGW **Rev. Legend:** UNITED STATES OF AMERICA

Date	Mintage	VF20	XF40	AU50	MS60	MS63	MS65	Prf65
1877	397,670	1,520	1,700	1,720	1,775	16,000	35,000	—
1877CC	42,565	2,350	3,450	5,650	19,500	—	—	—
1877S	1,735,000	1,510	1,570	1,720	1,775	17,500	35,000	—
1878	543,645	1,530	1,670	1,800	1,965	15,000	—	—
1878CC	13,180	3,000	11,500	18,500	36,000	—	—	—
1878S	1,739,000	1,510	1,545	1,720	1,775	20,500	—	—
1879	207,630	1,590	1,725	175	1,845	20,500	—	—
1879CC	10,708	3,350	10,000	16,500	37,500	—	—	—

Date	Mintage	VF20	XF40	AU50	MS60	MS63	MS65	Prf65
1879O	2,325	16,500	32,000	40,000	105,000	—	—	—
1879S	1,223,800	1,510	1,545	1,720	2,450	40,000	—	—
1880	51,456	1,620	1,750	1,825	7,250	25,000	—	110,000
1880S	836,000	1,510	1,545	1,720	1,795	42,500	125,000	—
1881	2,260	12,500	21,000	34,500	98,500	—	—	110,000
1881S	727,000	1,510	1,545	1,655	1,845	22,500	—	—
1882	630	11,800	39,500	88,000	135,000	225,000	—	130,000
1882CC	39,140	2,350	3,250	4,550	11,000	85,000	—	—
1882S	1,125,000	1,580	1,545	1,635	1,915	18,500	—	—
1883 proof only	92	—	—	27,500	—	—	—	195,000
1883CC	59,962	2,350	3,200	4,850	8,750	45,000	—	—
1883S	1,189,000	1,510	1,545	1,745	1,845	8.500	—	—
1884 proof only	71	—	—	35,000	—	—	—	225,000
1884CC	81,139	2,350	3,000	4,600	7,950	32,500	—	—
1884S	916,000	1,510	1,545	1,645	1,785	6,150	55,000	—
1885	828	8,450	24,500	39,500	75,000	125,000	—	115,000
1885CC	9,450	2,650	6,500	9,850	23,500	—	—	—
1885S	683,500	1,510	1,545	1,655	1,785	5,700	—	—
1886	1,106	21,000	36,000	70,000	135,000	160,000	—	105,000
1887	121	—	—	40,000	—	—	—	142,500
1887S	283,000	1,510	1,545	1,645	1,845	16,500	40,000	—
1888	226,266	1,510	1,545	1,665	1,895	10,000	36,500	93,500
1888S	859,600	1,510	1,545	1,645	1,785	4,850	45,000	—
1889	44,111	1,670	1,800	1,990	2,450	16,500	—	105,000
1889CC	30,945	2,600	4,250	5,000	10,500	24,000	—	—
1889S	774,700	1,510	1,545	1,645	1,795	5,950	—	—
1890	75,995	1,510	1,570	1,770	1,845	10,000	—	100,000
1890CC	91,209	2,350	2,650	3,950	6,000	40,000	—	—
1890S	802,750	1,510	1,545	1,645	1,785	6,650	—	—
1891	1,442	9,250	15,000	22,500	75,000	145,000	—	108,000
1891CC	5,000	6,000	12,500	17,500	28,500	—	—	—
1891S	1,288,125	1,510	1,545	1,645	1,785	3,000	—	—
1892	4,523	2,000	4,100	6,750	16,500	35,000	75,000	90,000
1892CC	27,265	2,350	2,850	4,350	9,000	46,500	—	—
1892S	930,150	1,510	1,545	1,700	1,775	3,500	34,500	—
1893	344,339	1,510	1,565	1,710	1,815	2,750	12,500	95,000
1893CC	18,402	2,350	3,000	7,000	9,850	45,000	—	—
1893S	996,175	1,470	1,500	1,595	1,620	3,950	45,000	—
1894	1,368,990	1,470	1,500	1,595	1,620	2,350	25,000	85,000
1894S	1,048,550	1,470	1,500	1,595	1,620	2,850	25,000	—
1895	1,114,656	1,470	1,500	1,595	1,620	1,875	22,000	82,500
1895S	1,143,500	1,470	1,500	1,595	1,620	1,875	16,500	—
1896	792,663	1,470	1,500	1,595	1,620	1,875	30,000	200,000
1896S	1,403,925	1,470	1,500	1,595	1,620	1,875	23,500	—
1897	1,383,261	1,470	1,500	1,595	1,620	1,975	30,000	200,000
1897S	1,470,250	1,470	1,500	1,595	1,620	1,875	21,500	—
1898	170,470	1,475	1,530	1,695	1,920	5,300	—	200,000
1898S	2,575,175	1,475	1,500	1,595	1,620	1,875	9,500	—
1899	1,669,384	1,470	1,500	1,595	1,620	1,875	10,500	200,000
1899S	2,010,300	1,470	1,500	1,595	1,620	2,075	21,500	—
1900	1,874,584	1,470	1,500	1,595	1,620	1,910	5,750	200,000
1900S	2,459,500	1,470	1,500	1,595	1,620	1,875	25,000	—
1901	111,526	1,470	1,500	1,595	1,620	2,010	6,850	200,000
1901S	1,596,000	1,470	1,500	1,595	1,620	3,850	22,000	—
1902	31,254	1,470	1,695	1,855	2,030	13,000	37,500	200,000
1902S	1,753,625	1,470	1,500	1,595	1,620	2,900	23,500	—
1903	287,428	1,470	1,500	1,595	1,620	1,910	4,250	200,000
1903S	954,000	1,470	1,500	1,595	1,620	2,340	13,500	—
1904	6,256,797	1,470	1,500	1,595	1,620	1,875	3,725	200,000
1904S	5,134,175	1,470	1,500	1,595	1,620	1,875	6,000	—
1905	59,011	1,475	1,520	1,630	1,920	14,500	65,000	200,000
1905S	1,813,000	1,470	1,500	1,595	1,620	4,000	25,000	—
1906	69,690	1,381	1,505	1,650	1,800	7,700	31,500	200,000
1906D	620,250	1,470	1,500	1,595	1,620	3,700	23,500	—
1906S	2,065,750	1,470	1,500	1,595	1,620	2,650	24,500	—
1907	1,451,864	1,470	1,500	1,595	1,620	1,975	8,800	200,000
1907D	842,250	1,470	1,500	1,595	1,620	3,500	7,500	—
1907S	2,165,800	1,470	1,500	1,595	1,620	3,000	27,000	—

$20 GOLD

Saint-Gaudens High Relief
Roman numerals in date.   No motto below eagle.

KM# 126 • 33.44 g., 0.900 Gold 0.9675 oz. AGW, 34 mm. • **Edge:** Plain. **Designer:** Augustus Saint-Gaudens

Date	Mintage	VF20	XF40	AU50	MS60	MS63	MS65	Prf65
MCMVII (1907) high relief, unique	—	—	—	—	—	—	—	—
Note: AU-55, $150,000								
MCMVII (1907) high relief, wire rim	11,250	7,650	9,350	11,000	14,350	24,500	47,500	—
MCMVII (1907) high relief, flat rim	Inc. above	7,900	9,850	12,000	15,600	26,000	49,000	—

Saint-Gaudens
Arabic numerals in date.   No motto below eagle.

KM# 127 • 33.44 g., 0.900 Gold 0.9675 oz. AGW, 34 mm. • **Edge:** Lettered; large letters. **Designer:** Augustus Saint-Gaudens

Date	Mintage	VF20	XF40	AU50	MS60	MS63	MS65	Prf65
1907 large letters on edge, unique	—	—	—	—	—	—	—	—
1907 small letters on edge	361,667	1,500	1,525	1,620	1,665	1,920	4,600	—
1908	4,271,551	1,490	1,515	1,600	1,625	1,710	2,150	—
1908D	663,750	1,500	5,125	1,610	1,650	1,820	11,800	—

IN GOD WE TRUST below eagle.

KM# 131 • 33.44 g., 0.900 Gold 0.9675 oz. AGW, 34 mm. • **Designer:** Augustus Saint-Gaudens

Date	Mintage	VF20	XF40	AU50	MS60	MS63	MS65	Prf65
1908	156,359	1,350	1,355	1,365	1,710	2,580	23,000	76,500
1908 Roman finish; Rare	—	—	—	—	—	—	—	—
1908D	349,500	1,355	1,360	1,375	1,445	1,800	7,500	—
1908S	22,000	2,450	3,150	5,000	11,350	23,225	53,500	
1909/8	161,282	1,355	1,360	1,415	2,325	5,250	53,500	—
1909	Inc. Above	1,365	1,380	1,385	1,470	2,950	48,000	92,500
1909D	52,500	1,395	1,400	1,510	3,225	7,250	57,500	—
1909S	2,774,925	1,355	1,360	1,375	1,405	1,555	7,525	—
1910	482,167	1,350	1,355	1,365	1,470	1,570	9,600	84,500

Date	Mintage	VF20	XF40	AU50	MS60	MS63	MS65	Prf65
1910D	429,000	1,350	1,355	1,365	1,455	1,520	4,000	—
1910S	2,128,250	1,355	1,360	1,380	1,455	2,100	9,900	—
1911	197,350	1,355	1,360	1,385	1,470	2,675	21,500	76,500
1911D	846,500	1,350	1,355	1,365	1,450	1,520	2,650	—
1911S	775,750	1,350	1,355	1,365	1,460	1,570	7,350	—
1912	149,824	1,355	1,360	1,380	1,520	2,550	32,000	76,500
1913	168,838	1,355	1,360	1,380	1,470	3,150	56,500	82,500
1913D	393,500	1,350	1,355	1,365	1,450	2,075	6,900	—
1913S	34,000	1,405	1,410	1,415	2,475	5,000	39,000	—
1914	95,320	1,365	1,370	1,415	1,520	3,550	26,650	81,500
1914D	453,000	1,350	1,355	1,365	1,470	1,570	4,650	—
1914S	1,498,000	1,350	1,355	1,365	1,450	1,570	2,350	—
1915	152,050	1,355	1,360	1,375	1,470	2,550	27,500	125,000
1915S	567,500	1,350	1,355	1,365	1,470	1,570	2,380	—
1916S	796,000	1,355	1,360	1,375	1,460	2,050	3,625	—
1920	228,250	1,345	1,350	1,355	1,470	2,260	105,000	—
1920S	558,000	14,500	18,500	28,500	52,500	95,000	345,000	—
1921	528,500	35,000	43,500	55,000	118,000	285,000	865,000	—
1922	1,375,500	1,345	1,350	1,355	1,385	1,520	8,375	—
1922S	2,658,000	1,465	1,150	1,300	2,760	5,500	51,750	—
1923	566,000	1,345	1,350	1,355	1,385	1,875	9,400	—
1923D	1,702,250	1,355	1,360	1,365	1,385	1,520	2,525	—
1924	4,323,500	1,345	1,350	1,355	1,385	1,520	1,865	—
1924D	3,049,500	1,568	1,573	2,100	4,725	8,300	120,000	—
1924S	2,927,500	1,665	1,750	2,200	4,520	11,200	185,000	—
1925	2,831,750	1,345	1,350	1,355	1,385	1,450	2,150	—
1925D	2,938,500	1,510	2,100	2,375	4,825	11,950	135,000	—
1925S	3,776,500	1,900	2,850	4,850	10,075	15,950	210,000	—
1926	816,750	1,345	1,350	1,355	1,385	1,495	2,190	—
1926D	481,000	12,000	15,900	19,350	17,250	27,500	240,000	—
1926S	2,041,500	1,548	1,550	1,725	3,450	6,225	36,850	—
1927	2,946,750	1,345	1,350	1,355	1,385	1,495	1,865	—
1927D	180,000	155,000	200,000	245,000	635,000	1,500,000	1,975,000	—
1927S	3,107,000	6,850	8,850	13,250	27,150	54,000	157,500	—
1928	8,816,000	1,345	1,350	1,355	1,385	1,520	1,865	—
1929	1,779,750	9,850	13,500	15,500	21,250	37,500	92,500	—
1930S	74,000	35,000	42,500	49,500	66,000	105,000	250,000	—
1931	2,938,250	10,500	13,500	20,500	38,250	63,000	113,000	—
1931D	106,500	8,850	11,500	21,000	44,000	66,000	130,000	—
1932	1,101,750	12,500	14,500	17,850	31,250	75,000	110,000	—
1933	445,500	—	—	—	—	—	9,000,000	—

COMMEMORATIVE COINAGE
1892-1954

All commemorative half dollars of 1892-1954 have the following specifications: diameter — 30.6 millimeters; weight — 12.500 grams; composition — 0.900 silver, 0.3617 ounces actual silver weight. Values for PDS sets contain one example each from the Philadelphia, Denver and San Francisco mints. Type coin prices are the most inexpensive single coin available from the date and mint mark combinations listed.

QUARTER

Columbian Exposition

KM# 115 • 6.25 g., 0.900 Silver 0.1808 oz. ASW, 24.3 mm. • **Obv.** Queen Isabella bust left **Rev:** Female kneeling with distaff and spindle

Date	Mintage	AU50	MS60	MS63	MS64	MS65
1893	24,214	450	525	650	950	2,750

HALF DOLLAR

Columbian Exposition

KM# 117 • 12.50 g., 0.900 Silver 0.3617 oz. ASW, 30.6 mm. • **Obv.** Christopher Columbus bust right **Rev:** Santa Maria sailing left, two globes below **Obv. Designer:** Charles E. Barber **Rev. Designer:** George T. Morgan

Date	Mintage	AU50	MS60	MS63	MS64	MS65
1892	950,000	18.50	28.00	80.00	135	525
1893	1,550,405	17.00	28.00	75.00	145	465

Panama-Pacific Exposition

KM# 135 • 12.50 g., 0.900 Silver 0.3617 oz. ASW, 30.6 mm. • **Obv.** Columbia standing, sunset in background **Rev:** Eagle standing on shield **Designer:** Charles E. Barber

Date	Mintage	AU50	MS60	MS63	MS64	MS65
1915 S	27,134	465	535	825	1,250	2,650

Illinois Centennial-Lincoln

KM# 143 • 12.50 g., 0.900 Silver 0.3617 oz. ASW, 30.6 mm. • **Obv.** Abraham Lincon bust right **Rev:** Eagle standing left **Obv. Designer:** George T. Morgan **Rev. Designer:** John R. Sinnock

Date	Mintage	AU50	MS60	MS63	MS64	MS65
1918	100,058	135	150	165	200	565

Maine Centennial

KM# 146 • 12.50 g., 0.900 Silver 0.3617 oz. ASW, 30.6 mm. • **Obv.** Arms of the State of Maine **Rev:** Legend within wreath **Designer:** Anthony de Francisci

Date	Mintage	AU50	MS60	MS63	MS64	MS65
1920	50,028	130	165	185	250	500

Pilgrim Tercentenary

KM# 147.1 • 12.50 g., 0.900 Silver 0.3617 oz. ASW, 30.6 mm. • **Obv.** William Bradford half-length left **Rev:** Mayflower sailing left **Designer:** Cyrus E. Dallin

Date	Mintage	AU50	MS60	MS63	MS64	MS65
1920	152,112	80.00	100	110	120	375

COMMEMORATIVE COINAGE 1892-1954

Pilgrim Tercentenary

KM# 147.2 • 12.50 g., 0.900 Silver 0.3617 oz. ASW, 30.6 mm. • **Obv.** William Bradford half-length left, 1921 added at left **Rev:** Mayflower sailing left **Designer:** Cyrus E. Dallin

Date	Mintage	AU50	MS60	MS63	MS64	MS65
1921	20,053	170	200	220	235	515

Missouri Centennial

KM# 149.1 • 12.50 g., 0.900 Silver 0.3617 oz. ASW, 30.6 mm. • **Obv.** Frontiersman in coonskin cap left **Rev:** Frontiersman and Native American standing left **Designer:** Robert Aitken

Date	Mintage	AU50	MS60	MS63	MS64	MS65
1921	15,428	400	600	885	1,275	3,650

2x2

Alabama Centennial

KM# 148.1 • 12.50 g., 0.900 Silver 0.3617 oz. ASW, 30.6 mm. • **Obv.** William W. Bibb and T.E. Kilby conjoint busts left. "2x2" at right above stars **Rev:** Ealge left on shield **Designer:** Laura G. Fraser **Note:** Fake 2x2" counterstamps exist.

Date	Mintage	AU50	MS60	MS63	MS64	MS65
1921	6,006	315	330	525	675	1,600

2x4

Missouri Centennial

KM# 149.2 • 12.50 g., 0.900 Silver 0.3617 oz. ASW, 30.6 mm. • **Obv.** Frontiersman in coonskin cap left, 2(star)4 in field at left **Rev:** Frontiersman and Native American standing left **Designer:** Robert Aitken **Note:** Fake "2*4" counterstamps exist.

Date	Mintage	AU50	MS60	MS63	MS64	MS65
1921	5,000	620	720	1,050	1,500	3,450

Alabama Centennial

KM# 148.2 • 12.50 g., 0.900 Silver 0.3617 oz. ASW, 30.6 mm. • **Obv.** William W. Bibb and T.E. Kilby conjoint busts left **Rev:** Eagle standing left on shield **Obv. Designer:** Laura G. Fraser

Date	Mintage	AU50	MS60	MS63	MS64	MS65
1921	59,038	190	215	525	685	1,800

Grant Memorial

KM# 151.1 • 12.50 g., 0.900 Silver 0.3617 oz. ASW, 30.6 mm. • **Obv.** Grant bust right **Rev:** Birthplace in Point Pleasant, Ohio **Designer:** Laura G. Fraser

Date	Mintage	AU50	MS60	MS63	MS64	MS65
1922	67,405	120	125	155	250	700

COMMEMORATIVE COINAGE 1892-1954

Grant Memorial

KM# 151.2 • 12.50 g., 0.900 Silver 0.3617 oz. ASW, 30.6 mm. • **Obv.** Grant bust left, star above the word GRANT **Rev:** Birthplace in Point Pleasant, Ohio **Designer:** Laura G. Fraser **Note:** Fake star" counterstamps exist.

Date	Mintage	AU50	MS60	MS63	MS64	MS65
1922	4,256	925	1,275	1,750	3,450	7,850

Monroe Doctrine Centennial

KM# 153 • 12.50 g., 0.900 Silver 0.3617 oz. ASW, 30.6 mm. • **Obv.** James Monroe and John Quincy Adams conjoint busts left **Rev:** Western Hemisphere portraied by two female figures **Designer:** Chester Beach

Date	Mintage	AU50	MS60	MS63	MS64	MS65
1923 S	274,077	56.00	72.50	125	250	1,950

Huguenot-Walloon Tercentenary

KM# 154 • 12.50 g., 0.900 Silver 0.3617 oz. ASW, 30.6 mm. • **Obv.** Huguenot leader Gaspard de Coligny and William I of Orange conjoint busts right **Rev:** Nieuw Nederland sailing left **Designer:** George T. Morgan

Date	Mintage	AU50	MS60	MS63	MS64	MS65
1924	142,080	135	145	150	215	385

California Diamond Jubilee

KM# 155 • 12.50 g., 0.900 Silver 0.3617 oz. ASW, 30.6 mm. • **Obv.** Fourty-Niner kneeling panning for gold **Rev:** Grizzly bear walking left **Designer:** Jo Mora

Date	Mintage	AU50	MS60	MS63	MS64	MS65
1925 S	86,594	195	225	270	485	900

Lexington-Concord Sesquicentennial

KM# 156 • 12.50 g., 0.900 Silver 0.3617 oz. ASW, 30.6 mm. • **Obv.** Concord's Minute Man statue **Rev:** Old Belfry at Lexington **Designer:** Chester Beach

Date	Mintage	AU50	MS60	MS63	MS64	MS65
1925	162,013	95.00	105	110	145	615

Stone Mountain Memorial

KM# 157 • 12.50 g., 0.900 Silver 0.3617 oz. ASW, 30.6 mm. • **Obv.** Generals Robert E. Lee and Thomas "Stonewall" Jackson mounted left. **Rev:** Eagle on rock at right **Designer:** Gutzon Borglum

Date	Mintage	AU50	MS60	MS63	MS64	MS65
1925	1,314,709	62.00	67.50	80.00	190	315

Fort Vancouver Centennial

KM# 158 • 12.50 g., 0.900 Silver 0.3617 oz. ASW, 30.6 mm. • **Obv.** John McLoughlin bust left **Rev:** Frontiersmen standing with musket, Ft. Vancouver in background **Designer:** Laura G. Fraser

Date	Mintage	AU50	MS60	MS63	MS64	MS65
1925	14,994	320	360	420	475	1,250

Oregon Trail Memorial

KM# 159 • 12.50 g., 0.900 Silver 0.3617 oz. ASW, 30.6 mm. • **Obv.** Native American standing in full headdress and holding bow, US Map in background **Rev:** Conestoga wagon pulled by oxen left towards sunset **Designer:** James E. and Laura G. Fraser

Date	Mintage	AU50	MS60	MS63	MS64	MS65
1926	47,955	135	165	175	195	315
1926 S	83,055	135	165	180	195	320
1928	6,028	220	245	275	285	375
1933 D	5,008	365	380	385	390	465
1934 D	7,006	195	205	215	220	365
1936	10,006	165	190	205	220	340
1936 S	5,006	175	190	210	235	350
1937 D	12,008	175	200	210	225	325
1938	6,006	155	170	205	210	335
1938 D	6,005	155	170	205	220	335
1938 S	6,006	155	170	205	215	335
1939	3,004	510	585	600	620	675
1939 D	3,004	510	585	610	620	675
1939 S	3,005	510	585	590	600	665

U.S. Sesquicentennial

KM# 160 • 12.50 g., 0.900 Silver 0.3617 oz. ASW, 30.6 mm. • **Obv.** George Washington and Calvin Coolidge conjoint busts right **Rev:** Liberty Bell **Designer:** John R. Sinnock

Date	Mintage	AU50	MS60	MS63	MS64	MS65
1926	141,120	85.00	110	118	465	4,800

Vermont Sesquicentennial

KM# 162 • 12.50 g., 0.900 Silver 0.3617 oz. ASW, 30.6 mm. • **Obv.** Ira Allen bust right **Rev:** Catamount advancing left **Obv. Designer:** Charles Keck

Date	Mintage	AU50	MS60	MS63	MS64	MS65
1927	28,142	250	275	290	335	880

Hawaiian Sesquicentennial

KM# 163 • 12.50 g., 0.900 Silver 0.3617 oz. ASW, 30.6 mm. • **Obv.** Captain James Cook bust left **Rev:** Native Hawaiian standing over view of Diamond Head **Designer:** Juliette May Fraser and Chester Beach **Note:** Counterfeits exist.

Date	Mintage	AU50	MS60	MS63	MS64	MS65
1928	10,008	1,785	2,650	3,350	3,775	6,200

Daniel Boone Bicentennial

KM# 165.2 • 12.50 g., 0.900 Silver 0.3617 oz. ASW, 30.6 mm. • **Obv.** Daniel Boone bust left **Rev:** Daniel Boone and Native American standing, "1934" added above the word "PIONEER." **Designer:** Augustus Lukeman

Date	Mintage	AU50	MS60	MS63	MS64	MS65
1935	10,008	125	135	140	145	260
1935 D	2,003	360	390	425	450	835
1935 S	2,004	360	390	425	450	815
1936	12,012	120	125	135	140	250
1936 D	5,005	130	135	145	155	295
1936 S	5,006	130	135	145	155	285
1937	9,810	135	135	138	145	260
1937 D	2,506	320	375	385	400	515
1937 S	2,506	320	375	385	400	540
1938	2,100	340	380	390	400	535
1938 D	2,100	340	380	390	410	525
1938 S	2,100	340	380	390	400	565

Texas Centennial

KM# 167 • 12.50 g., 0.900 Silver 0.3617 oz. ASW, 30.6 mm. • **Obv.** Eagle standing left, large star in background **Rev:** Winged Victory kneeling beside Alamo Mission, small busts of Sam Houston and Stephen Austin at sides **Designer:** Pompeo Coppini

Date	Mintage	AU50	MS60	MS63	MS64	MS65
1934	61,463	135	140	150	165	300
1935	9,994	140	145	155	160	300
1935 D	10,007	140	145	155	160	300
1935 S	10,008	140	145	155	160	300
1936	8,911	140	145	155	160	310
1936 D	9,039	140	145	155	160	310
1936 S	9,055	140	145	155	160	325
1937	6,571	140	145	155	160	310
1937 D	6,605	140	145	155	160	300
1937 S	6,637	140	145	155	160	300
1938	3,780	235	250	260	305	425
1938 D	3,775	240	255	265	305	415
1938 S	3,814	235	250	260	305	415

Arkansas Centennial

KM# 168 • 12.50 g., 0.900 Silver 0.3617 oz. ASW, 30.6 mm. • **Obv.** Liberty and Indian Chief's conjoint heads left **Rev:** Eagle with outstretched wings and flag of Arkansas in background **Designer:** Edward E. Burr

Date	Mintage	AU50	MS60	MS63	MS64	MS65
1935	13,012	90.00	100	110	120	215
1935 D	5,505	105	110	120	130	250
1935 S	5,506	105	110	120	130	250
1936	9,660	90.00	100	110	120	225
1936 D	9,660	105	110	120	130	255
1936 S	9,662	105	110	120	130	255
1937	5,505	105	115	120	135	275
1937 D	5,505	105	115	120	130	265
1937 S	5,506	105	115	120	135	290
1938	3,156	155	180	190	200	590
1938 D	3,155	160	180	190	200	580
1938 S	3,156	160	180	190	200	640
1939	2,104	320	375	380	400	940
1939 D	2,104	320	375	380	400	910
1939 S	2,105	320	375	380	400	925

Daniel Boone Bicentennial

KM# 165.1 • 12.50 g., 0.900 Silver 0.3617 oz. ASW, 30.6 mm. • **Obv.** Daniel Boone bust left **Rev:** Daniel Boone and Native American standing **Designer:** Augustus Lukeman

Date	Mintage	AU50	MS60	MS63	MS64	MS65
1934	10,007	120	125	135	140	250
1935	10,010	120	125	135	140	250
1935 D	5,005	130	135	145	155	295
1935 S	5,005	130	135	145	155	285

Maryland Tercentenary

KM# 166 • 12.50 g., 0.900 Silver 0.3617 oz. ASW, 30.6 mm. • **Obv.** Lord Baltimore, Cecil Calvert bust right **Rev:** Maryland state arms **Designer:** Hans Schuler

Date	Mintage	AU50	MS60	MS63	MS64	MS65
1934	25,015	150	175	185	200	375

San Diego-Pacific International Exposition

KM# 171 • 12.50 g., 0.900 Silver 0.3617 oz. ASW, 30.6 mm. • **Obv.** Seated female with bear at her side **Rev:** State of California exposition building **Designer:** Robert Aitken

Date	Mintage	AU50	MS60	MS63	MS64	MS65
1935 S	70,132	95.00	98.00	105	110	240
1936 D	30,092	100	120	125	135	275

Connecticut Tercentenary

KM# 169 • 12.50 g., 0.900 Silver 0.3617 oz. ASW, 30.6 mm. • **Obv.** Eagle standing left **Rev:** Charter oak tree **Designer:** Henry Kreiss

Date	Mintage	AU50	MS60	MS63	MS64	MS65
1935	25,018	240	265	275	325	500

Hudson, N.Y., Sesquicentennial

KM# 170 • 12.50 g., 0.900 Silver 0.3617 oz. ASW, 30.6 mm. • **Obv.** Hudson's ship, the Half Moon sailing right **Rev:** Seal of the City of Hudson **Designer:** Chester Beach

Date	Mintage	AU50	MS60	MS63	MS64	MS65
1935	10,008	750	875	1,050	1,550	2,100

Old Spanish Trail

KM# 172 • 12.50 g., 0.900 Silver 0.3617 oz. ASW, 30.6 mm. • **Obv.** Long-horn cow's head facing **Rev:** The 1535 route of Cabeza de Vaca's expedition and a yucca tree **Designer:** L.W. Hoffecker **Note:** Counterfeits exist.

Date	Mintage	AU50	MS60	MS63	MS64	MS65
1935	10,008	1,250	1,375	1,650	1,750	2,000

Albany, N.Y., Charter Anniversary

KM# 173 • 12.50 g., 0.900 Silver 0.3617 oz. ASW, 30.6 mm. • **Obv.** Beaver knawing on maple branch **Rev:** Standing figures of Thomas Dongan, Peter Schyuyler and Robert Livingston **Designer:** Gertrude K. Lathrop

Date	Mintage	AU50	MS60	MS63	MS64	MS65
1936	17,671	300	310	330	350	440

San Francisco-Oakland Bay Bridge

KM# 174 • 12.50 g., 0.900 Silver 0.3617 oz. ASW, 30.6 mm. • **Obv.** Grizzly bear facing **Rev:** Oakland Bay Bridge **Designer:** Jacques Schnier

Date	Mintage	AU50	MS60	MS63	MS64	MS65
1936	71,424	155	160	165	185	365

Bridgeport, Conn., Centennial

KM# 175 • 12.50 g., 0.900 Silver 0.3617 oz. ASW, 30.6 mm. • **Obv.** P.T. Barnum bust left **Rev:** Eagle standing right **Designer:** Henry Kreiss

Date	Mintage	AU50	MS60	MS63	MS64	MS65
1936	25,015	130	140	150	175	320

Cincinnati Music Center

KM# 176 • 12.50 g., 0.900 Silver 0.3617 oz. ASW, 30.6 mm. • **Obv.** Stephen Foster bust right **Rev:** Kneeling female with lyre **Designer:** Constance Ortmayer

Date	Mintage	AU50	MS60	MS63	MS64	MS65
1936	5,005	295	310	335	410	725
1936 D	5,005	295	310	335	410	750
1936 S	5,006	295	310	335	410	750

Cleveland-Great Lakes Exposition

KM# 177 • 12.50 g., 0.900 Silver 0.3617 oz. ASW, 30.6 mm. • **Obv.** Moses Cleveland bust left **Rev:** Dividers and map of the Great Lakes **Designer:** Brenda Putnam

Date	Mintage	AU50	MS60	MS63	MS64	MS65
1936	50,030	110	115	120	160	215

Columbia, S.C., Sesquicentennial

KM# 178 • 12.50 g., 0.900 Silver 0.3617 oz. ASW, 30.6 mm. • **Obv.** Figure of Justice between capitols of 1786 and 1936 **Rev:** Palmetto tree **Designer:** A. Wolfe Davidson

Date	Mintage	AU50	MS60	MS63	MS64	MS65
1936	9,007	250	265	270	275	310
1936 D	8,009	260	270	280	285	340
1936 S	8,007	260	270	280	285	340

Delaware Tercentenary

KM# 179 • 12.50 g., 0.900 Silver 0.3617 oz. ASW, 30.6 mm. • **Obv.** Old Swedes Church in Wilmington **Rev:** Kalmar Nyckel sailing left **Designer:** Carl L. Schmitz

Date	Mintage	AU50	MS60	MS63	MS64	MS65
1936	20,993	255	265	275	290	465

Elgin, Ill., Centennial

KM# 180 • 12.50 g., 0.900 Silver 0.3617 oz. ASW, 30.6 mm. • **Obv.** Pioneer head left **Rev:** Statue group **Designer:** Trygve Rovelstad

Date	Mintage	AU50	MS60	MS63	MS64	MS65
1936	20,015	195	205	215	225	355

Battle of Gettysburg 75th Anniversary

KM# 181 • 12.50 g., 0.900 Silver 0.3617 oz. ASW, 30.6 mm. • **Obv.** Union and Confederate veteran conjoint busts right **Rev:** Double blased fasces seperating two shields **Designer:** Frank Vittor

Date	Mintage	AU50	MS60	MS63	MS64	MS65
1936	26,928	435	460	485	565	925

Long Island Tercentenary

KM# 182 • 12.50 g., 0.900 Silver 0.3617 oz. ASW, 30.6 mm. • **Obv.** Dutch settler and Native American conjoint head right **Rev:** Dutch sailing vessel **Designer:** Howard K. Weinman

Date	Mintage	AU50	MS60	MS63	MS64	MS65
1936	81,826	85.00	92.00	98.00	105	325

Lynchburg, Va., Sesquicentennial

KM# 183 • 12.50 g., 0.900 Silver 0.3617 oz. ASW, 30.6 mm. • **Obv.** Sen. Carter Glass bust left **Rev:** Liberty standing, old Lynchburg courthouse at right **Designer:** Charles Keck

Date	Mintage	AU50	MS60	MS63	MS64	MS65
1936	20,013	220	230	265	275	365

Norfolk, Va., Bicentennial

KM# 184 • 12.50 g., 0.900 Silver 0.3617 oz. ASW, 30.6 mm. • **Obv.** Seal of the City of Norfolk **Rev:** Royal Mace of Norfolk **Designer:** William M. and Marjorie E. Simpson

Date	Mintage	AU50	MS60	MS63	MS64	MS65
1936	16,936	425	435	445	460	575

Rhode Island Tercentenary

KM# 185 • 12.50 g., 0.900 Silver 0.3617 oz. ASW, 30.6 mm. • **Obv.** Roger Williams in canoe hailing Native American **Rev:** Shield with anchor **Designer:** Arthur G. Carey and John H. Benson

Date	Mintage	AU50	MS60	MS63	MS64	MS65
1936	20,013	98.00	105	110	120	290
1936 D	15,010	100	110	120	125	305
1936 S	15,011	100	110	120	130	320

Roanoke Island, N.C.

KM# 186 • 12.50 g., 0.900 Silver 0.3617 oz. ASW, 30.6 mm. • **Obv.** Sir Walter Raleigh bust left **Rev:** Ellinor Dare holding baby Virginia, two small ships flanking **Designer:** William M. Simpson

Date	Mintage	AU50	MS60	MS63	MS64	MS65
1937	29,030	220	225	235	245	315

Arkansas Centennial

KM# 187 • 12.50 g., 0.900 Silver 0.3617 oz. ASW, 30.6 mm. • **Obv.** Eagle with wings outstreatched, Arkansas flag in backgorund **Rev:** Sen. Joseph T. Robinson bust right **Obv. Designer:** Henry Kreiss **Rev. Designer:** Edward E. Burr

Date	Mintage	AU50	MS60	MS63	MS64	MS65
1936	25,265	140	175	210	220	385

Wisconsin Territorial Centennial

KM# 188 • 12.50 g., 0.900 Silver 0.3617 oz. ASW, 30.6 mm. • **Obv.** Badger from the Territorial seal **Rev:** Pick axe and mound of lead ore **Designer:** David Parsons

Date	Mintage	AU50	MS60	MS63	MS64	MS65
1936	25,015	215	240	255	265	365

COMMEMORATIVE COINAGE 1892-1954

COMMEMORATIVE COINAGE 1892-1954

York County, Maine, Tercentenary

KM# 189 • 12.50 g., 0.900 Silver 0.3617 oz. ASW, 30.6 mm. • **Obv.** Stockade **Rev:** York County seal **Designer:** Walter H. Rich

Date	Mintage	AU50	MS60	MS63	MS64	MS65
1936	25,015	210	215	225	235	340

Battle of Antietam 75th Anniversary

KM# 190 • 12.50 g., 0.900 Silver 0.3617 oz. ASW, 30.6 mm. • **Obv.** Generals Robert E. Lee and George McClellan conjoint busts left **Rev:** Burnside Bridge **Designer:** William M. Simpson

Date	Mintage	AU50	MS60	MS63	MS64	MS65
1937	18,028	695	735	750	775	950

New Rochelle, N.Y.

KM# 191 • 12.50 g., 0.900 Silver 0.3617 oz. ASW, 30.6 mm. • **Obv.** John Pell and a calf **Rev:** Fleur-de-lis from the seal of the city **Designer:** Gertrude K. Lathrop

Date	Mintage	AU50	MS60	MS63	MS64	MS65
1938	15,266	375	385	425	440	600

Booker T. Washington

KM# 198 • 12.50 g., 0.900 Silver 0.3617 oz. ASW, 30.6 mm. • **Obv.** Booker T. Washington bust right **Rev:** Cabin and NYU's Hall of Fame **Designer:** Isaac S. Hathaway **Note:** Actual mintages are higher, but unsold issues were melted to produce Washington Carver issues.

Date	Mintage	AU50	MS60	MS63	MS64	MS65
1946	1,000,546	14.00	18.00	21.00	23.00	64.00
1946 D	200,113	16.50	20.00	32.00	37.00	72.00
1946 S	500,729	15.00	18.50	23.00	27.00	66.00
1947	100,017	30.00	36.00	56.00	65.00	80.00
1947 D	100,017	32.00	38.00	62.00	70.00	100
1947 S	100,017	32.00	38.00	59.00	65.00	76.00
1948	8,005	46.00	64.00	77.00	80.00	84.00
1948 D	8,005	46.00	62.00	77.00	80.00	84.00
1948 S	8,005	46.00	65.00	78.00	82.00	88.00
1949	6,004	67.00	82.00	85.00	96.00	115
1949 D	6,004	67.00	82.00	85.00	96.00	115
1949 S	6,004	67.00	82.00	85.00	102	105
1950	6,004	46.00	68.00	78.00	82.00	90.00
1950 D	6,004	46.00	68.00	75.00	82.00	88.00
1950 S	512,091	18.00	20.00	24.00	26.00	65.00
1951	51,082	17.00	22.00	24.00	26.00	65.00
1951 D	7,004	47.00	68.00	80.00	85.00	90.00
1951 S	7,004	47.00	68.00	80.00	84.00	88.00

Iowa Statehood Centennial

KM# 197 • 12.50 g., 0.900 Silver 0.3617 oz. ASW, 30.6 mm. • **Obv.** First Capitol building at Iowa City **Rev:** Iowa state seal **Designer:** Adam Pietz

Date	Mintage	AU50	MS60	MS63	MS64	MS65
1946	100,057	100	105	108	112	160

Booker T. Washington and George Washington Carver

KM# 200 • 12.50 g., 0.900 Silver 0.3617 oz. ASW, 30.6 mm. • **Obv.** Booker T. Washington and

George Washington Carver conjoint busts right
Rev: Map of the United States **Designer:** Isaac S. Hathaway

Date	Mintage	AU50	MS60	MS63	MS64	MS65
1951	110,018	18.00	20.00	25.00	44.00	290
1951 D	10,004	42.00	50.00	80.00	82.00	140
1951 S	10,004	42.00	50.00	80.00	86.00	90.00
1952	2,006,292	17.00	18.00	24.00	42.00	83.00
1952 D	8,006	40.00	50.00	80.00	85.00	190
1952 S	8,006	40.00	50.00	80.00	84.00	185
1953	8,003	40.00	50.00	80.00	85.00	260
1953 D	8,003	40.00	50.00	80.00	85.00	175
1953 S	108,020	17.00	18.00	24.00	42.00	120
1954	12,006	39.00	48.00	70.00	75.00	200
1954 D	12,006	39.00	48.00	70.00	80.00	83.00
1954 S	122,024	17.00	18.00	24.00	42.00	83.00

DOLLAR

Lafayette

KM# 118 • 26.73 g., 0.900 Silver 0.7734 oz. ASW, 38.1 mm. • **Obv.** George Washington and Marquis de Lafayette conjoint busts right **Rev:** Lafayette on horseback left **Designer:** Charles E. Barber

Date	Mintage	AU50	MS60	MS63	MS64	MS65
1900	36,026	550	950	1,875	3,250	11,500

Louisiana Purchase Exposition - Jefferson bust

KM# 119 • 1.67 g., 0.900 Gold 0.0484 oz. AGW, 15 mm. • **Obv.** Jefferson bust left **Rev:** Legend and laurel branch **Designer:** Charles E. Barber

Date	Mintage	AU50	MS60	MS63	MS64	MS65
1903	17,500	600	660	925	1,450	2,150

Louisiana Purchase Exposition - McKinley bust

KM# 120 • 1.67 g., 0.900 Gold 0.0484 oz. AGW, 15 mm. • **Obv.** William McKinley bust left **Rev:** Legend and laurel branch **Obv. Designer:** Charles E. Barber

Date	Mintage	AU50	MS60	MS63	MS64	MS65
1903	17,500	590	650	800	1,400	2,100

Lewis and Clark Exposition

KM# 121 • 1.67 g., 0.900 Gold 0.0484 oz. AGW, 15 mm. • **Obv.** Lewis bust left **Rev:** Clark bust left **Obv. Designer:** Charles E. Barber

Date	Mintage	AU50	MS60	MS63	MS64	MS65
1904	10,025	950	1,100	1,850	3,650	7,900
1905	10,041	975	1,450	2,250	3,950	15,000

Panama-Pacific Exposition

KM# 136 • 1.67 g., 0.900 Gold 0.0484 oz. AGW, 15 mm. • **Obv.** Canal laborer bust left **Rev:** Value within two dolphins **Obv. Designer:** Charles Keck

Date	Mintage	AU50	MS60	MS63	MS64	MS65
1915 S	15,000	565	625	775	1,100	1,700

McKinley Memorial

KM# 144 • 1.67 g., 0.900 Gold 0.0484 oz. AGW, 15 mm. • **Obv.** William McKinley head left **Rev:** Memorial building at Niles, Ohio **Obv. Designer:** Charles E. Barber **Rev. Designer:** George T. Morgan

Date	Mintage	AU50	MS60	MS63	MS64	MS65
1916	9,977	520	600	685	1,000	1,750
1917	10,000	575	700	900	1,475	2,250

Grant Memorial

KM# 152.1 • 1.67 g., 0.900 Gold 0.0484 oz. AGW, 15 mm. • **Obv.** U.S. Grant bust right **Rev:** Birthplace **Obv. Designer:** Laura G. Fraser **Note:** Without an incuse "star" above the word GRANT on the obverse.

Date	Mintage	AU50	MS60	MS63	MS64	MS65
1922	5,000	1,875	1,900	2,350	3,650	4,900

COMMEMORATIVE COINAGE 1892-1954

   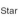 Star

Grant Memorial

KM# 152.2 • 1.67 g., 0.900 Gold 0.0484 oz.
AGW, 15 mm. • **Obv.** U.S. Grant bust right **Rev:**
Birthplace **Obv. Designer:** Laura G. Fraser **Note:**
Variety with an incuse "star" above the word GRANT
on the obverse.

Date	Mintage	AU50	MS60	MS63	MS64	MS65
1922	5,016	1,650	1,775	2,100	2,150	3,100

$2.50 (QUARTER EAGLE)

Panama-Pacific Exposition

KM# 137 • 4.18 g., 0.900 Gold 0.121 oz. AGW, 18
mm. • **Obv.** Columbia holding cadueus while
seated on a hippocamp **Rev:** Eagle standing left
Obv. Designer: Charles E. Barber **Rev. Designer:**
George T. Morgan

Date	Mintage	AU50	MS60	MS63	MS64	MS65
1915 S	6,749	1,550	1,950	4,100	5,650	6,750

U.S. Sesquicentennial

KM# 161 • 4.18 g., 0.900 Gold 0.121 oz. AGW, 18
mm. • **Obv.** Liberty standing holding torch and
scroll **Rev:** Independence Hall **Obv. Designer:**
John R. Sinnock

Date	Mintage	AU50	MS60	MS63	MS64	MS65
1926	46,019	425	500	800	1,375	3,450

$50

Panama-Pacific Exposition Round

KM# 138 • 83.59 g., 0.900 Gold 2.4187 oz. AGW,
44 mm. • **Obv.** Minerva bust helmeted left **Rev:**
Owl pearched on California pin branch **Obv.**
Designer: Robert Aitken **Shape:** Round

Date	Mintage	AU50	MS60	MS63	MS64	MS65
1915 S	483	46,500	57,500	90,000	105,000	160,000

Panama-Pacific Exposition Octagonal

KM# 139 • 83.59 g., 0.900 Gold 2.4187 oz. AGW,
44 mm. • **Obv.** Minerva bust helmeted left **Rev:**
Owl perched on California pine branch **Obv.**
Designer: Robert Aitken **Shape:** Octagon

Date	Mintage	AU50	MS60	MS63	MS64	MS65
1915 S	645	50,000	52,500	84,500	98,000	146,000

COMMEMORATIVE COINAGE 1982-PRESENT

All commemorative silver dollar coins of 1982-present have the following specifications: diameter — 38.1 millimeters; weight — 26.730 grams; composition — 0.900 silver, 0.7736 ounces actual silver weight. All commemorative $5 coins of 1982-present have the following specificiations: diameter — 21.6 millimeters; weight — 8.359 grams; composition: 0.900 gold, 0.242 ounces actual gold weight.

Note: In 1982, after a hiatus of nearly 30 years, coinage of commemorative half dollars resumed. Those designated with a 'W' were struck at the West Point Mint. Some issues were struck in copper-nickel. Those struck in silver have the same size, weight and composition as the prior commemorative half-dollar series.

HALF DOLLAR

George Washington, 250th Birth Anniversary

KM# 208 • 12.50 g., 0.900 Silver 0.3617 oz. ASW, 30.6 mm. • **Obv.** George Washington on horseback facing **Rev:** Mount Vernon **Obv. Designer:** Elizabeth Jones **Rev. Designer:** Matthew Peloso

Date	Mintage	MS65	Prf65
1982D	2,210,458	13.70	—
1982S	4,894,044	—	13.70

Congress Bicentennial

KM# 224 • 11.34 g., Copper-Nickel Clad Copper **Obv.** Statue of Freedom head **Rev:** Capitol building **Obv. Designer:** Patricia L. Verani **Rev. Designer:** William Woodward and Edgar Z. Steever

Date	Mintage	MS65	Prf65
1989D	163,753	7.50	—
1989S	762,198	—	7.50

Statue of Liberty Centennial

KM# 212 • 11.34 g., Copper-Nickel Clad Copper **Obv.** Statue of Liberty and sunrise **Rev:** Emigrant family looking toward mainland **Obv. Designer:** Edgar Z. Steever **Rev. Designer:** Sherl Joseph Winter

Date	Mintage	MS65	Prf65
1986D	928,008	3.25	—
1986S	6,925,627	—	3.50

Mount Rushmore 50th Anniversary

KM# 228 • 11.34 g., Copper-Nickel Clad Copper **Rev:** Mount Rushmore portraits **Obv. Designer:** Marcel Jovine **Rev. Designer:** T. James Ferrell **Edge:** Bison standing left

Date	Mintage	MS65	Prf65
1991D	172,754	17.50	—
1991S	753,257	—	16.00

COMMEMORATIVE COINAGE 1982-PRESENT

1992 Olympics

KM# 233 • 11.34 g., Copper-Nickel Clad Copper
Obv. Torch and laurel **Rev:** Female gymnast and
large flag **Obv. Designer:** William Cousins **Rev.
Designer:** Steven M. Bieda

Date	Mintage	MS65	Prf65
1992P	161,607	8.50	—
1992S	519,645	—	8.50

Columbus Voyage - 500th Anniversary

KM# 237 • 11.34 g., Copper-Nickel Clad Copper
Obv. Columbus standing on shore **Rev:** Nina, Pinta
and Santa Maria sailing right **Obv. Designer:** T.
James Ferrell **Rev. Designer:** Thomas D. Rogers, Sr.

Date	Mintage	MS65	Prf65
1992D	135,702	11.50	—
1992S	390,154	—	8.75

James Madison - Bill of Rights

KM# 240 • 12.50 g., 0.900 Silver 0.3617 oz.
ASW **Obv.** James Madison writing, Montpelier
in background **Rev:** Statue of Liberty torch **Obv.
Designer:** T. James Ferrell **Rev. Designer:** Dean
McMullen

Date	Mintage	MS65	Prf65
1993W	193,346	19.00	—
1993S	586,315	—	19.00

World War II 50th Anniversary

KM# 243 • 11.34 g., Copper-Nickel Clad Copper
Obv. Three portraits, plane above, large V in
background **Rev:** Pacific island battle scene **Obv.
Designer:** George Klauba and T. James Ferrell **Rev.
Designer:** William J. Leftwich and T. James Ferrell

Date	Mintage	MS65	Prf65
ND(1993)P	317,396	—	16.50
ND(1993)P	197,072	17.00	—

1994 World Cup Soccer

KM# 246 • 11.34 g., Copper-Nickel Clad Copper
Obv. Soccer player with ball **Rev:** World Cup 94
logo **Obv. Designer:** Richard T. LaRoche **Rev.
Designer:** Dean McMullen

Date	Mintage	MS65	Prf65
1994D	168,208	8.25	—
1994P	609,354	—	8.00

Civil War Battlefield Preservation

KM# 254 • 11.34 g., Copper-Nickel Clad Copper
Obv. Drummer and fenceline **Rev:** Canon
overlooking battlefield **Obv. Designer:** Don
Troiani **Rev. Designer:** T. James Ferrell

Date	Mintage	MS65	Prf65
1995S	119,510	36.50	—
1995S	330,099	—	33.50

1996 Atlanta Olympics - Basketball

KM# 257 • 11.34 g., Copper-Nickel Clad Copper **Obv.** Three players, one jumping for a shot **Rev:** Hemisphere and Atlanta Olympics logo **Obv. Designer:** Clint Hansen and Al Maletsky **Rev. Designer:** T. James Ferrell

Date	Mintage	MS65	Prf65
1995S	171,001	17.00	—
1995S	169,655	—	18.00

1996 Atlanta Olympics - Baseball

KM# 262 • 11.34 g., Copper-Nickel Clad Copper **Obv.** Baseball batter at plate, catcher and umpire **Rev:** Hemisphere and Atlanta Olympics logo **Obv. Designer:** Edgar Z. Steever **Rev. Designer:** T. James Ferrell

Date	Mintage	MS65	Prf65
1995S	164,605	19.50	—
1995S	118,087	—	17.50

1996 Atlanta Olympics - Soccer

KM# 271 • 11.34 g., Copper-Nickel Clad Copper **Obv.** Two female soccer players **Rev:** Atlanta Olympics logo

Date	Mintage	MS65	Prf65
1996S	52,836	130	—
1996S	122,412	—	88.00

1996 Atlanta Olympics - Swimming

KM# 267 • 11.34 g., Copper-Nickel Clad Copper **Obv.** Swimmer right in butterfly stroke **Rev:** Atlanta Olympics logo **Obv. Designer:** William J. Krawczewicz and Edgar Z. Steever **Rev. Designer:** Malcolm Farley and Thomas D. Rogers, Sr.

Date	Mintage	MS65	Prf65
1996S	49,533	140	—
1996S	114,315	—	31.00

U. S. Capitol Visitor Center

KM# 323 • 11.34 g., Copper-Nickel Clad Copper **Obv.** Capitol sillouete, 1800 structure in detail **Rev:** Legend within circle of stars **Obv. Designer:** Dean McMullen **Rev. Designer:** Alex Shagin and Marcel Jovine

Date	Mintage	MS65	Prf65
2001P	99,157	14.50	—
2001P	77,962	—	15.50

First Flight Centennial

KM# 348 • 11.34 g., Copper-Nickel Clad Copper **Obv.** Wright Monument at Kitty Hawk **Rev:** Wright Flyer in flight **Obv. Designer:** John Mercanti **Rev. Designer:** Donna Weaver

Date	Mintage	MS65	Prf65
2003P	57,726	15.00	—
2003P	111,569	—	17.00

COMMEMORATIVE COINAGE 1982-PRESENT

COMMEMORATIVE COINAGE 1982-PRESENT

American Bald Eagle

KM# 438 • 11.34 g., Copper-Nickel Clad Copper, 30.6 mm. • **Obv.** Two eaglets in nest with egg **Rev:** Eagle Challenger facing right, American Flag in background **Obv. Designer:** Susan Gamble and Joseph Menna **Rev. Designer:** Donna Weaver and Charles Vickers

Date	Mintage	MS65	Prf65
2008S	120,180	12.50	—
2008S	222,577	—	14.00

U.S. Army

KM# 506 • 11.34 g., Copper-Nickel Clad Copper, 30.6 mm. • **Obv.** Army contributions during peacetime, surveying, building a flood wall and space exploration **Rev:** Continental soldier with musket **Obv. Designer:** Donna Weaver and Charles L. Vickers **Rev. Designer:** Thomas Cleveland and Joseph Menna **Edge:** Reeded

Date	Mintage	MS65	Prf65
2011D	39,461	69.00	—
2011S	68,349	—	35.00

Five-Star Generals - Henry "Hap" Arnold and Omar N. Bradley

KM# 554 • Silver, 30.6 mm. • **Obv.** Two portraits facing **Rev:** Shield

Date	Mintage	MS65	Prf65
2013P	38,097	50.00	—
2013S	47,337	—	60.00

KM# 587 JOHN F. KENNEDY HALF DOLLAR, 50TH ANNIVERSARY • 23.33 g., 0.9999 Gold 0.750 oz. AGW, 30.61 mm. • **Obv.** Kennedy head left, dual dates below **Rev:** Presidential seal **Obv. Designer:** Gilroy Roberts **Rev. Designer:** Frank Gasparro

Date	Mintage	MS65	PF65
1964-2014W	—	—	1,500

Baseball Hall of Fame

KM# 576 • 11.34 g., Copper-Nickel Clad Copper, 30.6 mm. • **Obv.** Glove **Rev:** Baseball

Date	Mintage	MS65	Prf65
2014S	—	—	60.00
2014D	—	50.00	—

DOLLAR

1984 Los Angeles Olympics - Discus

KM# 209 • 26.73 g., 0.900 Silver 0.7734 oz. ASW, 38.1 mm. • **Obv.** Trippled discus thrower and five star logo **Rev:** Eagle bust left **Obv. Designer:** Elizabeth Jones

Date	Mintage	MS65	Prf65
1983P	294,543	34.80	—
1983D	174,014	34.70	—
1983S	174,014	34.80	—
1983S	1,577,025	—	36.80

Constitution Bicentennial

KM# 220 • 26.73 g., 0.900 Silver 0.7734 oz. ASW, 38.1 mm. • **Obv.** Feather pen and document **Rev:** Group of people **Obv. Designer:** Patricia L. Verani

Date	Mintage	MS65	Prf65
1987P	451,629	34.80	—
1987S	2,747,116	—	36.80

1984 Los Angeles Olympics - Stadium Statues

KM# 210 • 26.73 g., 0.900 Silver 0.7734 oz. ASW, 38.1 mm. • **Obv.** Statues at exterior of Los Angeles Memorial Coliseum **Rev:** Eagle standing on rock **Obv. Designer:** Robert Graham

Date	Mintage	MS65	Prf65
1984P	217,954	34.80	—
1984D	116,675	35.30	—
1984S	116,675	35.30	—
1984S	1,801,210	—	36.80

1988 Olympics

KM# 222 • 26.73 g., 0.900 Silver 0.7734 oz. ASW, 38.1 mm. • **Obv.** Olympic torch and Statue of Liberty torch within laurel wreath **Rev:** Olympic rights within olive wreath **Obv. Designer:** Patricia L. Verani **Rev. Designer:** Sherl Joseph Winter

Date	Mintage	MS65	Prf65
1988D	191,368	34.80	—
1988S	1,359,366	—	36.80

Statue of Liberty Centennial

KM# 214 • 26.73 g., 0.900 Silver 0.7734 oz. ASW, 38.1 mm. • **Obv.** Statue of Liberty and Ellis Island great hall **Rev:** Statue of Liberty torch **Obv. Designer:** John Mercanti **Rev. Designer:** John Mercanti and Matthew Peloso

Date	Mintage	MS65	Prf65
1986P	723,635	34.80	—
1986S	6,414,638	—	36.80

COMMEMORATIVE COINAGE 1982-PRESENT

Congress Bicentennial

KM# 225 • 26.73 g., 0.900 Silver 0.7734 oz.
ASW, 38.1 mm. • **Obv.** Statue of Freedom in
clouds and sunburst **Rev:** Mace from the House of
Represenatives **Designer:** William Woodward and
Chester Y. Martin

Date	Mintage	MS65	Prf65
1989D	135,203	34.80	—
1989S	762,198	—	36.80

Eisenhower Centennial

KM# 227 • 26.73 g., 0.900 Silver 0.7734 oz. ASW,
38.1 mm. • **Obv.** Two Eisenhower profiles, as
general, left, as President, right **Rev:** Eisenhower
home at Gettysburg **Obv. Designer:** John Mercanti
Rev. Designer: Marcel Jovine and John Mercanti

Date	Mintage	MS65	Prf65
1990W	241,669	34.80	—
1990P	1,144,461	—	36.80

Mount Rushmore
50th Anniversary

KM# 229 • 26.73 g., 0.900 Silver 0.7734 oz. ASW,
38.1 mm. • **Obv.** Mount Rushmore portraits,
wreath below **Rev:** Great seal in rays, United States
map in background **Obv. Designer:** Marika
Somogyi and Chester Martin **Rev. Designer:** Frank
Gasparro

Date	Mintage	MS65	Prf65
1991P	133,139	39.80	—
1991S	738,419	—	42.80

Korean War - 38th Anniversary

KM# 231 • 26.73 g., 0.900 Silver 0.7734 oz. ASW,
38.1 mm. • **Obv.** Soldier advancing right up a
hill; planes above, ships below **Rev:** Map of Korean
peninsula, eagle's head at right **Obv. Designer:**
John Mercanti **Rev. Designer:** T. James Ferrell

Date	Mintage	MS65	Prf65
1991D	213,049	37.80	—
1991P	618,488	—	36.80

USO 50th Anniversary

KM# 232 • 26.73 g., 0.900 Silver 0.7734 oz. ASW, 38.1 mm. • **Obv.** USO banner **Rev:** Eagle pearched right atop globe **Obv. Designer:** Robert Lamb **Rev. Designer:** John Mercanti

Date	Mintage	MS65	Prf65
1991D	124,958	37.80	—
1991S	321,275	—	38.80

White House Bicentennial

KM# 236 • 26.73 g., 0.900 Silver 0.7734 oz. ASW, 38.1 mm. • **Obv.** White House's north portico **Rev:** John Hoban bust left, main entrance doorway **Obv. Designer:** Edgar Z. Steever **Rev. Designer:** Chester Y. Martin

Date	Mintage	MS65	Prf65
1992D	123,803	37.80	—
1992W	375,851	—	38.80

1992 Olympics - Baseball

KM# 234 • 26.73 g., 0.900 Silver 0.7734 oz. ASW, 38.1 mm. • **Obv.** Baseball pitcher, Nolan Ryan as depicted on card **Rev:** Shield flanked by stylized wreath, olympic rings above **Obv. Designer:** John R. Deecken and Chester Y. Martin **Rev. Designer:** Marcel Jovine

Date	Mintage	MS65	Prf65
1992D	187,552	37.80	—
1992S	504,505	—	38.80

Columbus Discovery - 500th Anniversary

KM# 238 • 26.73 g., 0.900 Silver 0.7734 oz. ASW, 38.1 mm. • **Obv.** Columbus standing with banner, three ships in background **Rev:** Half view of Santa Maria on left, Space Shuttle Discovery on right **Obv. Designer:** John Mercanti **Rev. Designer:** Thomas D. Rogers, Sr.

Date	Mintage	MS65	Prf65
1992D	106,949	40.80	—
1992P	385,241	—	37.80

COMMEMORATIVE COINAGE 1982-PRESENT

COMMEMORATIVE COINAGE 1982-PRESENT

James Madison - Bill of Rights

KM# 241 • 26.73 g., 0.900 Silver 0.7734 oz. ASW, 38.1 mm. • **Obv.** James Madison bust right, at left **Rev:** Montpelier home **Obv. Designer:** William Krawczewicz and Thomas D. Rogers, Sr. **Rev. Designer:** Dean McMullen and Thomas D. Rogers, Sr.

Date	Mintage	MS65	Prf65
1993D	98,383	37.80	—
1993S	534,001	—	38.80

1994 World Cup Soccer

KM# 247 • 26.73 g., 0.900 Silver 0.7734 oz. ASW, 38.1 mm. • **Obv.** Two players with ball **Rev:** World Cup 94 logo **Obv. Designer:** Dean McMullen and T. James Ferrell **Rev. Designer:** Dean McMullen

Date	Mintage	MS65	Prf65
1994D	81,698	38.80	—
1994S	576,978	—	36.80

World War II 50th Anniversary

KM# 244 • 26.73 g., 0.900 Silver 0.7734 oz. ASW, 38.1 mm. • **Obv.** Soldier on Normandy beach **Rev:** Insignia of the Supreme Headquarters of the AEF above Eisenhower quote **Designer:** Thomas D. Rogers, Sr.

Date	Mintage	MS65	Prf65
1993D	94,708	36.80	—
1993W	342,041	—	40.80

Thomas Jefferson 250th Birth Anniversary

KM# 249 • 26.73 g., 0.900 Silver 0.7734 oz. ASW, 38.1 mm. • **Obv.** Jefferson's head left **Rev:** Monticello home **Designer:** T. James Ferrell

Date	Mintage	MS65	Prf65
1993P	266,927	36.80	—
1993S	332,891	—	40.80

Vietnam Veterans Memorial

KM# 250 • 26.73 g., 0.900 Silver 0.7734 oz. ASW, 38.1 mm. • **Obv.** Outstretched hand touching names on the Wall, Washington Monument in background **Rev:** Service Medals **Obv. Designer:** John Mercanti **Rev. Designer:** Thomas D. Rogers, Sr.

Date	Mintage	MS65	Prf65
1994W	57,317	79.00	—
1994P	226,262	—	63.00

Women in Military Service Memorial

KM# 252 • 26.73 g., 0.900 Silver 0.7734 oz. ASW, 38.1 mm. • **Obv.** Five uniformed women left **Rev:** Memorial at Arlington National Cemetery **Obv. Designer:** T. James Ferrell **Rev. Designer:** Thomas D. Rogers, Sr.

Date	Mintage	MS65	Prf65
1994W	53,054	38.80	—
1994P	213,201	—	38.80

National Prisoner of War Museum

KM# 251 • 26.73 g., 0.900 Silver 0.7734 oz. ASW, 38.1 mm. • **Obv.** Eagle in flight left within circle of barbed wire **Rev:** National Prisioner of War Museum **Obv. Designer:** Thomas Nielson and Alfred Maletsky **Rev. Designer:** Edgar Z. Steever

Date	Mintage	MS65	Prf65
1994W	54,790	84.00	—
1994P	220,100	—	39.80

U.S. Capitol Bicentennial

KM# 253 • 26.73 g., 0.900 Silver 0.7734 oz. ASW, 38.1 mm. • **Obv.** Capitol dome, Statue fo Freedom surrounded by stars **Rev:** Eagle on shield, flags flanking **Obv. Designer:** William C. Cousins **Rev. Designer:** John Mercanti

Date	Mintage	MS65	Prf65
1994D	68,352	38.80	—
1994S	279,416	—	40.80

Civil War

KM# 255 • 26.73 g., 0.900 Silver 0.7734 oz. ASW, 38.1 mm. • **Obv.** Soldier giving water to wounded soldier **Rev:** Chamberlain quote and battlefield monument **Obv. Designer:** Don Troiani and Edgar Z. Steever **Rev. Designer:** John Mercanti

Date	Mintage	MS65	Prf65
1995P	45,866	65.00	—
1995S	437,114	—	54.00

1996 Atlanta Paralympics - Blind runner

KM# 259 • 26.73 g., 0.900 Silver 0.7734 oz. ASW, 38.1 mm. • **Obv.** Blind runner **Rev:** Two clasped hands, Atlanta Olympic logo above **Obv. Designer:** Jim C. Sharpe and Thomas D. Rogers, Sr. **Rev. Designer:** William J. Krawczewicz and T. James Ferrell

Date	Mintage	MS65	Prf65
1995D	28,649	67.00	—
1995P	138,337	—	45.00

1996 Atlanta Olympics - Gymnastics

KM# 260 • 26.73 g., 0.900 Silver 0.7734 oz. ASW, 38.1 mm. • **Obv.** Two gymnasts, female on floor exercise and male on rings **Rev:** Two clasped hands, Atlanta Olympic logo above **Obv. Designer:** James C. Sharpe and Thomas D. Rogers, Sr. **Rev. Designer:** William J. Krawczewicz and T. James Ferrell

Date	Mintage	MS65	Prf65
1995D	42,497	55.00	—
1995P	182,676	—	36.80

1996 Atlanta Olympics - Cycling

KM# 263 • 26.73 g., 0.900 Silver 0.7734 oz. ASW, 38.1 mm. • **Obv.** Three cyclists approaching **Rev:** Two clasped hands, Atlanta Olympic logo above **Obv. Designer:** John Mercanti **Rev. Designer:** William J. Krawczewicz and T. James Ferrell

Date	Mintage	MS65	Prf65
1995D	19,662	135	—
1995P	118,795	—	45.00

1996 Atlanta Olympics - Track and field

KM# 264 • 26.73 g., 0.900 Silver 0.7734 oz. ASW, 38.1 mm. • **Obv.** Two runners on a track, one crossing finish line **Rev:** Two clasped hands, Atlanta Olympic logo above **Obv. Designer:** John Mercanti **Rev. Designer:** William J. Krawczewicz and T. James Ferrell

Date	Mintage	MS65	Prf65
1995D	24,796	88.00	—
1995P	136,935	—	38.80

1996 Atlanta Paralympics - Wheelchair racer

KM# 268 • 26.73 g., 0.900 Silver 0.7734 oz. ASW, 38.1 mm. • **Obv.** Wheelchair racer approaching with uplifted arms **Rev:** Atlanta Olympics logo **Obv. Designer:** James C. Sharpe and Alfred F. Maletsky **Rev. Designer:** Thomas D. Rogers, Sr.

Date	Mintage	MS65	Prf65
1996D	14,497	305	—
1996P	84,280	—	71.00

Special Olympics World Games

KM# 266 • 26.73 g., 0.900 Silver 0.7734 oz. ASW, 38.1 mm. • **Obv.** Eunice Schriver head left; founder of the Special Olympics **Rev:** Special Olympics Logo on an award medal, rose, quote from Schriver **Obv. Designer:** Jamie Wyeth and T. James Ferrell **Rev. Designer:** Thomas D. Rogers, Sr.

Date	Mintage	MS65	Prf65
1995W	89,301	40.80	—
1995P	351,764	—	41.80

1996 Atlanta Olympics - Tennis

KM# 269 • 26.73 g., 0.900 Silver 0.7734 oz. ASW, 38.1 mm. • **Obv.** Female tennis player **Rev:** Atlanta Olympics logo **Obv. Designer:** James C. Sharpe and T. James Ferrell **Rev. Designer:** Thomas D. Rogers, Sr.

Date	Mintage	MS65	Prf65
1996D	15,983	245	—
1996P	92,016	—	83.00

1996 Atlanta Olympics - High Jump

KM# A272 • 26.73 g., 0.900 Silver 0.7734 oz. ASW
Obv. High jumper **Obv. Designer:** T. James Ferrell
Rev. Designer: Thomas D. Rogers, Sr.

Date	Mintage	MS65	Prf65
1996D	15,697	310	—
1996P	124,502	—	43.00

1996 Atlanta Olympics - Rowing

KM# 272 • 26.73 g., 0.900 Silver 0.7734 oz. ASW,
38.1 mm. • **Obv.** Four man crew rowing left **Rev:**
Atlanta Olympic logo **Obv. Designer:** Bart Forbes
and T. James Ferrell **Rev. Designer:** Thomas D.
Rogers, Sr.

Date	Mintage	MS65	Prf65
1996D	16,258	290	—
1996P	151,890	—	62.00

National Community Service

KM# 275 • 26.73 g., 0.900 Silver 0.7734 oz. ASW,
38.1 mm. • **Obv.** Female standing with lamp and
shield **Rev:** Legend within wreath **Obv. Designer:**
Thomas D. Rogers, Sr. **Rev. Designer:** William C.
Cousins

Date	Mintage	MS65	Prf65
1996S	101,543	—	51.00
1996S	23,500	170	—

Smithsonian Institution 150th Anniversary

KM# 276 • 26.73 g., 0.900 Silver 0.7734 oz. ASW,
38.1 mm. • **Obv.** Original Smithsonian building,
the "Castle" designed by James Renwick **Rev:**
Female seated with torch and scroll on globe **Obv.
Designer:** Thomas D. Rogers, Sr. **Rev. Designer:**
John Mercanti

Date	Mintage	MS65	Prf65
1996D	31,230	122	—
1996P	129,152	—	49.00

U.S. Botanic Gardens
175th Anniversary

KM# 278 • 26.73 g., 0.900 Silver 0.7734 oz. ASW, 38.1 mm. • **Obv.** National Botanic Gardens Conservatory building **Rev:** Rose **Obv. Designer:** Edgar Z. Steever **Rev. Designer:** William C. Cousins

Date	Mintage	MS65	Prf65
1997P	57,272	42.00	—
1997P	264,528	—	42.00

National Law Enforcement
Officers Memorial

KM# 281 • 26.73 g., 0.900 Silver 0.7734 oz. ASW, 38.1 mm. • **Obv.** Male and female officer admiring name on monument **Rev:** Rose on a plain shield **Designer:** Alfred F. Maletsky

Date	Mintage	MS65	Prf65
1997P	28,575	135	—
1997P	110,428	—	78.00

Jackie Robinson

KM# 279 • 26.73 g., 0.900 Silver 0.7734 oz. ASW, 38.1 mm. • **Obv.** Jackie Robinson sliding into base **Rev:** Anniversary logo **Obv. Designer:** Alfred Maletsky **Rev. Designer:** T. James Ferrell

Date	Mintage	MS65	Prf65
1997S	30,007	72.00	—
1997S	110,495	—	90.00

Robert F. Kennedy

KM# 287 • 26.73 g., 0.900 Silver 0.7734 oz. ASW, 38.1 mm. • **Obv.** Kennedy bust facing **Rev:** Eagle on sheild, Senate Seal **Obv. Designer:** Thomas D. Rogers, Sr. **Rev. Designer:** James M. Peed and Thomas D. Rogers, Sr.

Date	Mintage	MS65	Prf65
1998S	106,422	47.50	—
1998S	99,020	—	47.50

COMMEMORATIVE COINAGE 1982-PRESENT

Black Revolutionary War Patriots

KM# 288 • 26.73 g., 0.900 Silver 0.7734 oz. ASW, 38.1 mm. • **Obv.** Crispus Attucks bust right **Rev:** Family standing **Obv. Designer:** John Mercanti **Rev. Designer:** Edward Dwight and Thomas D. Rogers, Sr.

Date	Mintage	MS65	Prf65
1998S	37,210	145	—
1998S	75,070	—	89.00

Yellowstone

KM# 299 • 26.73 g., 0.900 Silver 0.7734 oz. ASW, 38.1 mm. • **Obv.** Old Faithful gyser erupting **Rev:** Bison and vista as on National Parks shield **Obv. Designer:** Edgar Z. Steever **Rev. Designer:** William C. Cousins

Date	Mintage	MS65	Prf65
1999P	82,563	44.00	—
1999P	187,595	—	40.30

Dolley Madison

KM# 298 • 26.73 g., 0.900 Silver 0.7734 oz. ASW, 38.1 mm. • **Obv.** Madison bust right, at left **Rev:** Montpelier home **Obv. Designer:** Tiffany & Co. and T. James Ferrell **Rev. Designer:** Tiffany & Co. and Thomas D. Rogers, Sr.

Date	Mintage	MS65	Prf65
1999P	22,948	38.30	—
1999P	158,247	—	38.30

Library of Congress Bicentennial

KM# 311 • 26.73 g., 0.900 Silver 0.7734 oz. ASW **Obv.** Open and closed book, torch in background **Rev:** Skylight dome above the main reading room **Obv. Designer:** Thomas D. Rogers, Sr. **Rev. Designer:** John Mercanti

Date	Mintage	MS65	Prf65
2000P	52,771	40.80	—
2000P	196,900	—	38.30

Leif Ericson

KM# 313 • 26.73 g., 0.900 Silver 0.7734 oz. ASW
Obv. Ericson bust helmeted right **Rev:** Viking ship
sailing left **Obv. Designer:** John Mercanti **Rev.
Designer:** T. James Ferrell

Date	Mintage	MS65	Prf65
2000P	28,150	69.00	—
2000P	58,612	—	62.50
2000 Iceland	15,947	—	26.80

Native American - Bison

KM# 325 • 26.73 g., 0.900 Silver 0.7734 oz. ASW
Obv. Native American bust right **Rev:** Bison
standing left **Designer:** James E. Fraser

Date	Mintage	MS65	Prf65
2001D	197,131	165	—
2001P	272,869	—	169

Capitol Visitor Center

KM# 324 • 26.73 g., 0.900 Silver 0.7734 oz. ASW
Obv. Original and current Capital facades **Rev:**
Eagle with sheild and ribbon **Obv. Designer:**
Marika Somogyi **Rev. Designer:** John Mercanti

Date	Mintage	MS65	Prf65
2001P	66,636	40.80	—
2001P	143,793	—	40.80

2002 Winter Olympics - Salt Lake City

KM# 336 • 26.73 g., 0.900 Silver 0.7734 oz. ASW,
38.1 mm. • **Obv.** Salt Lake City Olympic logo **Rev:**
Stylized skyline with mountains in background
Obv. Designer: John Mercanti **Rev. Designer:**
Donna Weaver

Date	Mintage	MS65	Prf65
2002P	35,388	40.80	—
2002P	142,873	—	38.30

COMMEMORATIVE COINAGE 1982-PRESENT

U.S. Military Academy at West Point -Bicentennial

KM# 338 • 26.73 g., 0.900 Silver 0.7734 oz. ASW, 38.1 mm. • **Obv.** Cadet Review flagbearers, Academy buildings in background **Rev:** Academy emblems - Corinthian helmet and sword **Obv. Designer:** T. James Ferrell **Rev. Designer:** John Mercanti

Date	Mintage	MS65	Prf65
2002W	103,201	38.30	—
2002W	288,293	—	39.80

Thomas A. Edison - Electric Light 125th Anniversary

KM# 362 • 23.73 g., 0.900 Silver 0.6866 oz. ASW **Obv.** Edison half-length figure facing holding light bulb **Rev:** Light bulb and rays **Obv. Designer:** Donna Weaver **Rev. Designer:** John Mercanti

Date	Mintage	MS65	Prf65
2004P	68,031	40.80	—
2004P	213,409	—	41.80

First Flight Centennial

KM# 349 • 26.75 g., 0.900 Silver 0.774 oz. ASW, 38.1 mm. • **Obv.** Orville and Wilbur Wright busts left **Rev:** Wright Flyer over dunes **Obv. Designer:** T. James Ferrell **Rev. Designer:** Norman E. Nemeth **Edge:** Reeded

Date	Mintage	MS65	Prf65
2003P	53,761	40.80	—
2003P	193,086	—	46.80

Lewis and Clark Corps of Discovery Bicentennial

KM# 363 • 26.73 g., 0.900 Silver 0.7734 oz. ASW **Obv.** Lewis and Clark standing **Rev:** Jefferson era clasped hands peace medal **Designer:** Donna Weaver

Date	Mintage	MS65	Prf65
2004P	90,323	40.80	—
2004P	288,492	—	46.80

John Marshall, 250th Birth Anniversary

KM# 375 • 26.73 g., 0.900 Silver 0.7734 oz. ASW, 38.1 mm. • **Obv.** Marshall bust left **Rev:** Marshall era Supreme Court Chamber **Obv. Designer:** John Mercanti **Rev. Designer:** Donna Weaver

Date	Mintage	MS65	Prf65
2005P	48,953	37.30	—
2005P	141,993	—	35.80

Benjamin Franklin, 300th Birth Anniversary

KM# 387 • 26.73 g., 0.900 Silver 0.7734 oz. ASW, 38.1 mm. • **Obv.** Youthful Franklin flying kite **Rev:** Revolutionary era "JOIN, or DIE" snake cartoon illustration **Obv. Designer:** Norman E. Nemeth **Rev. Designer:** Charles Vickers

Date	Mintage	MS65	Prf65
2006P	58,000	40.80	—
2006P	142,000	—	45.00

U.S. Marine Corps, 230th Anniversary

KM# 376 • 26.73 g., 0.900 Silver 0.7734 oz. ASW, 38.1 mm. • **Obv.** Flag Raising at Mt. Suribachi on Iwo Jima **Rev:** Marine Corps emblem **Obv. Designer:** Norman E. Nemeth **Rev. Designer:** Charles Vickers

Date	Mintage	MS65	Prf65
2005P	130,000	48.00	—
2005P	370,000	—	52.50

Benjamin Franklin, 300th Birth Anniversary

KM# 388 • 26.73 g., 0.900 Silver 0.7734 oz. ASW, 38.1 mm. • **Obv.** Bust 3/4 right, signature in oval below **Rev:** Continental Dollar of 1776 in center **Obv. Designer:** Don Everhart II **Rev. Designer:** Donna Weaver

Date	Mintage	MS65	Prf65
2006P	58,000	40.80	—
2006P	142,000	—	51.00

San Francisco Mint Museum

KM# 394 • 26.73 g., 0.900 Silver 0.7734 oz. ASW, 38.1 mm. • **Obv.** 3/4 view of building **Rev:** Reverse of 1880s Morgan silver dollar **Obv. Designer:** Sherl J. Winter **Rev. Designer:** George T. Morgan

Date	Mintage	MS65	Prf65
2006S	65,609	40.80	—
2006S	255,700	—	40.80

Central High School Desegregation

KM# 418 • 26.73 g., 0.900 Silver 0.7734 oz. ASW, 38.1 mm. • **Obv.** Children's feet walking left with adult feet in military boots **Rev:** Little Rock's Central High School **Obv. Designer:** Richard Masters and Charles Vickers **Rev. Designer:** Don Everhart II

Date	Mintage	MS65	Prf65
2007P	66,093	40.80	—
2007P	124,618	—	43.00

Jamestown - 400th Anniversary

KM# 405 • 26.73 g., 0.900 Silver 0.7734 oz. ASW, 38.1 mm. • **Obv.** Two settlers and Native American **Rev:** Three ships **Obv. Designer:** Donna Weaver and Don Everhart II **Rev. Designer:** Susan Gamble and Charles Vickers

Date	Mintage	MS65	Prf65
2007P	79,801	40.80	—
2007P	258,802	—	38.30

American Bald Eagle

KM# 439 • 26.73 g., 0.900 Silver 0.7734 oz. ASW, 38.1 mm. • **Obv.** Eagle with flight, mountain in background at right **Rev:** Great Seal of the United States **Obv. Designer:** Joel Iskowitz and Don Everhart II **Rev. Designer:** James Licaretz

Date	Mintage	MS65	Prf65
2008P	110,073	44.00	—
2008P	243,558	—	38.30

Lincoln Bicentennial

KM# 454 • 26.73 g., 0.900 Silver 0.7734 oz. ASW, 38.1 mm. • **Obv.** 3/4 portrait facing right **Rev:** Part of Gettysburg Address within wreath **Obv. Designer:** Justin Kunz and Don Everhart II **Rev. Designer:** Phebe Hemphill

Date	Mintage	MS65	Prf65
2009P	125,000	55.00	—
2009P	375,000	—	55.00

Louis Braille Birth Bicentennial

KM# 455 • 26.73 g., 0.900 Silver 0.7734 oz. ASW, 38.1 mm. • **Obv.** Louis Braille bust facing **Rev:** School child reading book in Braille, BRL in Braille code above **Obv. Designer:** Joel Iskowitz and Phebe Hemphill **Rev. Designer:** Susan Gamble and Joseph Menna

Date	Mintage	MS65	Prf65
2009P	82,639	38.50	—
2009P	135,235	—	38.30

American Veterans Disabled for Life

KM# 479 • 0.900 Silver **Obv.** Soldier's feet, crutches **Rev:** Legend within wreath **Obv. Designer:** Don Everhart II **Rev. Designer:** Thomas Cleveland and Joseph Menna

Date	Mintage	MS65	Prf65
2010W	77,859	40.80	—
2010W	189,881	—	42.30

Boy Scouts of America, 100th Anniversary

KM# 480 • 0.900 Silver **Obv.** Cub Scout, Boy Scout and Venturer saluting **Rev:** Boy Scouts of America logo **Obv. Designer:** Donna Weaver **Rev. Designer:** Jim Licaretz

Date	Mintage	MS65	Prf65
2010P	105,020	38.50	—
2010P	244,963	—	42.00

COMMEMORATIVE COINAGE 1982-PRESENT

Medal of Honor

KM# 504 • 26.73 g., 0.900 Silver 0.7734 oz. ASW,
38.1 mm. • **Obv.** Medal of Honor designs for
Army, Navy and Air Force awards **Rev:** Army infantry
doldier carrying another to safety **Obv. Designer:**
James Licaretz **Rev. Designer:** Richard Masters and
Phebe Hemphill **Edge:** Reeded

Date	Mintage	MS65	Prf65
2011S	44,769	46.50	—
2011S	112,850	—	43.50

U.S. Army

KM# 507 • 26.73 g., 0.900 Silver 0.7734 oz. ASW,
38.1 mm. • **Obv.** Male and femlae soldier heads
looking outward **Rev:** Seven core values of the Army,
Eagle from the great seal **Obv. Designer:** Richard
Masters and Michael Gaudioso **Rev. Designer:**
Susan Gamble and Don Everhart, II **Edge:** Reeded

Date	Mintage	MS65	Prf65
2011S	43,512	45.00	—
2011S	119,829	—	43.50

National Infantry Museum and Soldier Center

KM# 529 • 26.73 g., 0.900 Silver 0.7734 oz. ASW,
38.1 mm. • **Obv.** Infantry soldier advancing left
Rev: Crossed rifles insignia **Obv. Designer:** Joel
Iskowitz and Michael Gaudioso **Rev. Designer:**
Ronald D. Sanders and Norman E. Nemeth

Date	Mintage	MS65	Prf65
2012	—	50.00	—
2012	—	—	60.00

Star-Spangled Banner

KM# 530 • 26.73 g., 0.900 Silver 0.7734 oz. ASW,
38.1 mm. • **Obv.** Liberty waving 15 star and stripe
flag, Ft. McHenry in background **Rev:** Modern
American Flag **Obv. Designer:** Joel Iskowitz and
Phebe Hemphill **Rev. Designer:** William C Burgard
III and Don Everhart

Date	Mintage	MS65	Prf65
2012	—	50.00	—
2012	—	—	60.00

Girl Scouts of the USA, 100th Anniversary

KM# 552 • 26.73 g., 0.900 Silver 0.7734 oz. ASW,
38.1 mm. • **Obv.** Three busts right **Rev:** Trefoil
logo

Date	Mintage	MS65	Prf65
2013W	37,461	50.00	—
2013W	86,353	—	60.00

Five-Star Generals - George C. Marshall and Dwight D. Eisenhower

KM# 553 • 26.73 g., 0.900 Silver 0.7734 oz. ASW, 38.1 mm. • **Obv.** Two busts facing, strips from flag in background **Rev:** Lamp from U.S. Army Command and General Staff College

Date	Mintage	MS65	Prf65
2013W	34,639	50.00	—
2013S	69,290	—	60.00

Baseball Hall of Fame

KM# 577 • 26.73 g., 0.900 Silver 0.7734 oz. ASW **Obv.** Baseball glove **Rev:** Baseball

Date	Mintage	MS65	Prf65
2014P	—	50.00	—
2014P	—	—	60.00

Civil Rights Act of 1964

KM# 579 • 26.73 g., 0.900 Silver 0.7734 oz. ASW **Obv.** Three Civil Rights marchers **Rev:** Torch

Date	Mintage	MS65	Prf65
2014P	—	50.00	—
2014P	—	—	60.00

$5 (HALF EAGLE)

Statue of Liberty Centennial

KM# 215 • 8.36 g., 0.900 Gold 0.2419 oz. AGW, 21.6 mm. • **Obv.** Statue of Liberty head right **Rev:** Eagle in flight left **Designer:** Elizabeth Jones

Date	Mintage	MS65	Prf65
1986W	95,248	442	—
1986W	404,013	—	442

Constitution Bicentennial

KM# 221 • 8.36 g., 0.900 Gold 0.2419 oz. AGW, 21.6 mm. • **Obv.** Eagle left with quill pen in talon **Rev:** Upright quill pen **Designer:** Marcel Jovine

Date	Mintage	MS65	Prf65
1987W	214,225	442	—
1987W	651,659	—	442

COMMEMORATIVE COINAGE 1982-PRESENT

1988 Olympics

KM# 223 • 8.36 g., 0.900 Gold 0.2419 oz. AGW, 21.6 mm. • **Obv.** Nike head wearing olive wreath **Rev:** Stylized olympic couldron **Obv. Designer:** Elizabeth Jones **Rev. Designer:** Marcel Jovine

Date	Mintage	MS65	Prf65
1988W	62,913	442	—
1988W	281,456	—	442

Congress Bicentennial

KM# 226 • 8.36 g., 0.900 Gold 0.2419 oz. AGW, 21.6 mm. • **Obv.** Capitol dome **Rev:** Eagle atop of the canopy from the Old Senate Chamber **Designer:** John Mercanti

Date	Mintage	MS65	Prf65
1989W	46,899	442	—
1989W	164,690	—	442

Mount Rushmore 50th Anniversary

KM# 230 • 8.36 g., 0.900 Gold 0.2419 oz. AGW, 21.6 mm. • **Obv.** Eagle in flight towards Mount Rushmore **Rev:** Legend at center **Obv. Designer:** John Mercanti **Rev. Designer:** Robert Lamb and William C. Cousins

Date	Mintage	MS65	Prf65
1991W	31,959	442	—
1991W	111,991	—	442

1992 Olympics

KM# 235 • 8.36 g., 0.900 Gold 0.2419 oz. AGW, 21.6 mm. • **Obv.** Sprinter, U.S. Flag in background **Rev:** Heraldic eagle, olympic rings above **Obv. Designer:** James C. Sharpe and T. James Ferrell **Rev. Designer:** James M. Peed

Date	Mintage	MS65	Prf65
1992W	27,732	442	—
1992W	77,313	—	442

Columbus Quincentenary

KM# 239 • 8.36 g., 0.900 Gold 0.2419 oz. AGW, 21.6 mm. • **Obv.** Columbus' profile left, at right, map of Western Hemisphere at left **Rev:** Arms of Spain, and parchment map **Obv. Designer:** James Ferrell **Rev. Designer:** Thomas D. Rogers, Sr.

Date	Mintage	MS65	Prf65
1992W	24,329	442	—
1992W	79,730	—	442

James Madison - Bill of Rights

KM# 242 • 8.36 g., 0.900 Gold 0.2419 oz. AGW, 21.6 mm. • **Obv.** Madison at left holding document **Rev:** Eagle above legend, torch and laurel at sides **Obv. Designer:** Scott R. Blazek **Rev. Designer:** Joseph D. Peña

Date	Mintage	MS65	Prf65
1993W	22,266	442	—
1993W	78,651	—	442

World War II 50th Anniversary

KM# 245 • 8.36 g., 0.900 Gold 0.2419 oz. AGW, 21.6 mm. • **Obv.** Soldier with expression of victory **Rev:** Morse code dot-dot-dot-dash for V, large in background; V for Victory **Obv. Designer:** Charles J. Madsen and T. James Ferrell **Rev. Designer:** Edward S. Fisher and T. James Ferrell

Date	Mintage	MS65	Prf65
1993W	23,089	442	—
1993W	65,461	—	442

1994 World Cup Soccer

KM# 248 • 8.36 g., 0.900 Gold 0.2419 oz. AGW, 21.6 mm. • **Obv.** World Cup trophy **Rev:** World Cup 94 logo **Obv. Designer:** William J. Krawczewicz **Rev. Designer:** Dean McMullen

Date	Mintage	MS65	Prf65
1994W	22,464	442	—
1994W	89,619	—	442

Civil War

KM# 256 • 8.36 g., 0.900 Gold 0.2419 oz. AGW, 21.6 mm. • **Obv.** Bugler on horseback right **Rev:** Eagle on shield **Designer:** Don Troiani and Alfred F. Maletsky

Date	Mintage	MS65	Prf65
1995W	55,246	—	442
1995W	12,735	950	—

1996 Olympics - Torch runner

KM# 261 • 8.36 g., 0.900 Gold 0.2419 oz. AGW, 21.6 mm. • **Obv.** Torch runner, Atlanta skyline and logo in background **Rev:** Eagle advancing right **Designer:** Frank Gasparro

Date	Mintage	MS65	Prf65
1995W	14,675	885	—
1995W	57,442	—	442

1996 Olympics - Stadium

KM# 265 • 8.36 g., 0.900 Gold 0.2419 oz. AGW, 21.6 mm. • **Obv.** Atlanta Stadium and logo **Rev:** Eagle advancing right **Obv. Designer:** Marvel Jovine and William C. Cousins **Rev. Designer:** Frank Gasparro

Date	Mintage	MS65	Prf65
1995W	10,579	2,500	—
1995W	43,124	—	442

1996 Olympics - Cauldron

KM# 270 • 8.36 g., 0.900 Gold 0.2419 oz. AGW, 21.6 mm. • **Obv.** Torch bearer lighting cauldron **Rev:** Atlanta Olympics logo flanked by laurel **Designer:** Frank Gasparro and T. James Ferrell **Rev. Designer:** William J. Krawczewicz and Thomas D. Rogers, Sr.

Date	Mintage	MS65	Prf65
1996W	9,210	2,600	—
1996W	38,555	—	442

1996 Olympics - Flag bearer

KM# 274 • 8.36 g., 0.900 Gold 0.2419 oz. AGW, 21.6 mm. • **Obv.** Flag bearer advancing **Rev.** Atlanta Olympic logo flanked by laurel **Obv. Designer:** Patricia Verani and John Mercanti **Rev. Designer:** William J. Krawczewicz and Thomas D. Rogers, Sr.

Date	Mintage	MS65	Prf65
1996W	9,174	2,600	—
1996W	32,886	—	442

Smithsonian Institution 150th Anniversary

KM# 277 • 8.36 g., 0.900 Gold 0.2419 oz. AGW, 21.6 mm. • **Obv.** Smithson bust left **Rev:** Sunburst museum logo **Obv. Designer:** Alfred Maletsky **Rev. Designer:** T. James Ferrell

Date	Mintage	MS65	Prf65
1996W	9,068	850	—
1996W	29,474	—	442

Jackie Robinson

KM# 280 • 8.36 g., 0.900 Gold 0.2419 oz. AGW, 21.6 mm. • **Obv.** Robinson head right **Rev:** Legend on baseball **Obv. Designer:** William C. Cousins **Rev. Designer:** James M. Peed

Date	Mintage	MS65	Prf65
1997W	5,202	2,900	—
1997W	24,072	—	590

Franklin Delano Roosevelt

KM# 282 • 8.36 g., 0.900 Gold 0.2419 oz. AGW, 21.6 mm. • **Obv.** Roosevelt bust right **Rev:** Eagle shield **Obv. Designer:** T. James Ferrell **Rev. Designer:** James M. Peed and Thomas D. Rogers, Sr.

Date	Mintage	MS65	Prf65
1997W	11,894	1,275	—
1997W	29,474	—	442

COMMEMORATIVE COINAGE 1982-PRESENT

COMMEMORATIVE COINAGE 1982-PRESENT

George Washington Death Bicentennial

KM# 300 • 8.36 g., 0.900 Gold 0.2419 oz. AGW, 21.6 mm. • **Obv.** Washington's head right **Rev:** Eagle with wings outstretched **Designer:** Laura G. Fraser

Date	Mintage	MS65	Prf65
1999W	22,511	452	—
1999W	41,693	—	447

Capitol Visitor Center

KM# 326 • 8.54 g., 0.900 Gold 0.2471 oz. AGW **Obv.** Column at right **Rev:** First Capital building **Designer:** Elizabeth Jones

Date	Mintage	MS65	Prf65
2001W	6,761	1,750	—
2001W	27,652	—	442

2002 Winter Olympics

KM# 337 • 8.36 g., 0.900 Gold 0.2419 oz. AGW, 21.6 mm. • **Obv.** Salt Lake City Olympics logo **Rev:** Stylized cauldron **Designer:** Donna Weaver

Date	Mintage	MS65	Prf65
2002W	10,585	452	—
2002W	32,877	—	442

San Francisco Mint Museum

KM# 395 • 8.36 g., 0.900 Gold 0.2419 oz. AGW **Obv.** Front entrance façade **Rev:** Eagle as on 1860's $5. Gold **Obv. Designer:** Charles Vickers and Joseph Menna **Rev. Designer:** Christian Gobrecht

Date	Mintage	MS65	Prf65
2006S	16,230	442	—
2006S	41,517	—	442

Jamestown - 400th Anniversary

KM# 406 • 8.36 g., 0.900 Gold 0.2419 oz. AGW **Obv.** Settler and Native American **Rev:** Jamestown Memorial Church ruins **Obv. Designer:** John Mercanti **Rev. Designer:** Susan Gamble and Norman Nemeth

Date	Mintage	MS65	Prf65
2007W	18,843	442	—
2007W	47,050	—	442

American Bald Eagle

KM# 440 • 8.36 g., 0.900 Gold 0.2419 oz. AGW, 21.6 mm. • **Obv.** Two eagles on branch **Rev:** Eagle with shield **Obv. Designer:** Susan Gamble adn Phebe Hemphill **Rev. Designer:** Don Everhart II

Date	Mintage	MS65	Prf65
2008W	13,467	457	—
2008W	59,269	—	442

Medal of Honor

KM# 505 • 8.36 g., 0.900 Gold 0.2419 oz. AGW, 21.1 mm. • **Obv.** 1861 Medal of Honor design for the Navy **Rev:** Minerva standing with shield and Union flag, field artillery canon flanking **Obv. Designer:** Joseph Menna **Rev. Designer:** Joel Iskowitz and Michael Gaudioso **Edge:** Reeded

Date	Mintage	MS65	Prf65
2011S	18,012	—	500
2011S	8,251	585	—

U.S. Army

KM# 508 • 8.36 g., 0.900 Gold 0.2419 oz. AGW, 21.1 mm. • **Obv.** Five Soldiers of different eras **Rev:** Elements from the Army's emblem **Obv. Designer:** Joel Iskowitz and Phebe Hemphill **Rev. Designer:** Joseph Menna **Edge:** Reeded

Date	Mintage	MS65	Prf65
2011P	8,062	585	—
2011W	17,173	—	495

Star-Spangled Banner

KM# 531 • 8.36 g., 0.900 Gold 0.2419 oz. AGW, 21.1 mm. • **Obv.** Naval battle scene from the War of 1812. American ship in foreground, damaged British ship in background **Rev:** 15 stars and 15 stripes, opening words to the Star-Spangled Banner: O say can you see. **Obv. Designer:** Donna Weaver **Rev. Designer:** Joseph Menna

Date	Mintage	MS65	Prf65
2012	—	585	—
2012	—	—	600

Five-Star Generals - Douglas MacArthur

KM# 555 • 8.36 g., 0.900 Gold 0.2419 oz. AGW, 21.1 mm. • **Obv.** Head facing at left **Rev:** Lamp

Date	Mintage	MS65	Prf65
2013P	5,658	—	—
2013S	15,843	—	—

Baseball Hall of Fame

KM# 578 • 8.36 g., 0.900 Gold 0.2419 oz. AGW, 21.1 mm. • **Obv.** Baseball glove **Rev:** Baseball

Date	Mintage	MS65	Prf65
2014W	—	—	—
2014W	—	—	—

$10 (EAGLE)

1984 Olympics

KM# 211 • 16.72 g., 0.900 Gold 0.4837 oz. AGW, 27 mm. • **Obv.** Male and female runner with torch **Rev:** Heraldic eagle **Obv. Designer:** James M. Peed and John Mercanti **Rev. Designer:** John Mercanti

Date	Mintage	MS65	Prf65
1984W	75,886	883	—
1984W	381,085	—	893
1984P	33,309	—	893

Date	Mintage	MS65	Prf65
1984D	34,533	—	893
1984S	48,551	—	893

Library of Congress

KM# 312 • 16.26 g., Bi-Metallic, 48% platinum center in 48% gold ring **Obv.** Torch and partial facade **Rev:** Stylized eagle within laurel wreath **Obv. Designer:** John Mercanti **Rev. Designer:** Thomas D. Rogers, Sr.

Date	Mintage	MS65	Prf65
2000W	6,683	4,500	—
2000W	27,167	—	1,300

First Flight Centennial

KM# 350 • 16.72 g., 0.900 Gold 0.4837 oz. AGW **Obv.** Orvile and Wilbur Wright busts facing **Rev:** Wright flyer and eagle **Obv. Designer:** Donna Weaver **Rev. Designer:** Norman Nemeth

Date	Mintage	MS65	Prf65
2003P	10,129	1,050	—
2003W	21,846	—	893

$20 (DOUBLE EAGLE)

KM# 464 • 31.11 g., 0.999 Gold 0.999 oz. AGW, 27 mm. • **Obv.** Ultra high relief Liberty holding torch, walking forward **Rev:** Eagle in flight left, sunrise in background **Designer:** Augustus Saint-Gaudens

Date	Mintage	MS65	Prf65
2009	115,178	2,150	—

COMMEMORATIVE COINAGE 1982-PRESENT

AMERICA THE BEAUTIFUL
SILVER BULLION

SILVER QUARTER

KM# 489 HOT SPRINGS NATIONAL PARK • 155.55 g., 0.999 Silver 4.996 oz. ASW **Rev:** Park Headquarters and fountain **Rev. Designer:** Don Everhart II and Joseph Menna

Date	Mintage	MS65	MS69
2010	33,000	290	360
2010P Vapor Blast finish	27,000	250	375

KM# 490 YELLOWSTONE NATIONAL PARK • 155.55 g., 0.999 Silver 4.996 oz. ASW **Rev:** Old Faithful geyser and bison **Rev. Designer:** Don Everhart II

Date	Mintage	MS65	MS69
2010	33,000	275	360
2010P Vapor Blast finish	27,000	240	325

KM# 491 YOSEMITE NATIONAL PARK • 155.55 g., 0.999 Silver 4.996 oz. ASW **Rev:** El Capitan, largest monolith of granite in the world **Rev. Designer:** Joseph Menna and Phebe Hemphill

Date	Mintage	MS65	MS69
2010	33,000	275	385
2010P Vapor blast finish	27,000	225	260

BULLION COINAGE

KM# 492 GRAND CANYON NATIONAL PARK

- 155.55 g., 0.999 Silver 4.996 oz. ASW **Rev:** Grabarues above the Nankoweap Delta in Marble Canyon near the Colorado River **Rev. Designer:** Phebe Hemphill

Date	Mintage	MS65	MS69
2010	33,000	250	325
2010P Vapor blast finish	26,019	225	325

KM# 513 GETTYSBURG NATIONAL MILITARY PARK

- 155.55 g., 0.999 Silver 4.996 oz. ASW **Rev:** 72nd Pennsylvania Infantry Monumnet on the battle line of the Union Army at Cemetery Ridge **Rev. Designer:** Joel Iskowitz and Phebe Hemphill

Date	Mintage	MS65	MS69
2011	126,700	200	260
2011P Vapor blast finish	24,625	190	240

KM# 493 MOUNT HOOD NATIONAL PARK

• 155.55 g., 0.999 Silver 4.996 oz. ASW **Rev:** Mt. Hood with Lost Lake in the foreground **Rev. Designer:** Phebe Hemphill

Date	Mintage	MS65	MS69
2010	33,000	275	360
2010P Vapor blast finish	25,318	200	260

KM# 514 GLACIER NATIONAL PARK

• 155.55 g., 0.999 Silver 4.996 oz. ASW **Rev:** Northeast slope of Mount Reynolds **Rev. Designer:** Barbara Fox and Charles L. Vickers

Date	Mintage	MS65	MS69
2011	126,700	200	260
2011P Vapor blast finish	20,503	190	240

BULLION COINAGE

ULLION COINAGE

KM# 515 OLYMPIC NATIONAL PARK • 155.55 g., 0.999 Silver 4.996 oz. ASW **Rev:** Roosevelt elk on a gravel river bar along the Hoh River, Mount Olympus in the background **Rev. Designer:** Susan Gambel and Michael Gaudioso

Date	Mintage	MS65	MS69
2011	85,900	200	260
2011P Vapor blast finish	17,988	190	240

KM# 517 CHICKASAW NATIONAL RECREATION AREA • 155.55 g., 0.999 Silver 4.996 oz. ASW **Rev:** Limestone Lincoln Bridge **Rev. Designer:** Donna Weaver and James Licaretz

Date	Mintage	MS65	MS69
2011	29,700	200	260
2011P Vapor blast finish	16,386	190	240

KM# 516 VICKSBURG NATIONAL MILITARY PARK • 155.55 g., 0.999 Silver 4.996 oz. ASW **Rev:** U.S.S. Cairo on the Yazoo River **Rev. Designer:** Thomas Cleveland and Joseph menna

Date	Mintage	MS65	MS69
2011	39,500	200	260
2011P Vapor blast finish	18,181	190	240

KM# 536 EL YUNGUE NATIONAL FOREST • 155.55 g., 0.999 Silver 4.996 oz. ASW **Rev:** Coquin tree frog and Puerto Rico parrot

Date	Mintage	MS65	MS69
2012	21,900	200	260
2012P Vapor blast finish	15,271	190	240

KM# 537 CHACO CULTURE NATIONAL HISTORIC PARK
• 155.52 g., 0.999 Silver 4.9951 oz. ASW **Rev:** Two elevated kivas at Chetro Ketl complex

Date	Mintage	MS65	MS69
2012	20,000	200	260
2012P Vapor blast finish	12,679	190	240

KM# 539 HAWAII VOLCANOES NATIONAL PARK
• 155.52 g., 0.999 Silver 4.9951 oz. ASW **Rev:** Volcano erupting

Date	Mintage	MS65	MS69
2012	20,000	200	260
2012P Vapor blast finish	13,789	190	240

KM# 538 ACADIA NATIONAL PARK
• 155.52 g., 0.999 Silver 4.9951 oz. ASW **Rev:** Bass Harbor Head Lighthouse

Date	Mintage	MS65	MS69
2012	25,400	200	260
2012P Vapor blast finish	13,196	190	240

KM# 540 DENALI NATIONAL PARK
• 155.55 g., 0.999 Silver 4.9961 oz. ASW **Rev:** Dall sheep and Mount McKinley

Date	Mintage	MS65	MS69
2012	20,000	200	260
2012P Vapor blast finish	10,180	190	240

BULLION COINAGE

BULLION COINAGE

KM# 556 WHITE MOUNTAIN NATIONAL FOREST • 155.55 g., 0.999 Silver 4.996 oz. ASW **Rev:** Mountain vista

Date	Mintage	MS65	MS69
2013	35,000	200	260
2013P Vapor blast finish	20,530	190	240

KM# 558 GREAT BASIN NATIONAL PARK • 155.55 g., 0.999 Silver 4.996 oz. ASW **Rev:** Ancient weatherworn tree

Date	Mintage	MS65	MS69
2013	30,000	190	240
2013P Vapor blast finish	17,792	200	260

KM# 557 PERRY'S VICTORY AND INTERNATIONAL PEACE MEMORIAL • 155.55 g., 0.999 Silver 4.996 oz. ASW **Rev:** Perry standing and Memorial column

Date	Mintage	MS65	MS69
2013	30,000	200	260
2013P Vapor blast finsih	17,707	190	240

KM# 559 FORT MCHENRY NATIONAL MONUMENT AND HISTORIC SITE • 155.55 g., 0.999 Silver 4.996 oz. ASW **Rev:** Fort McHenry and flag

Date	Mintage	MS65	MS69
2013	30,000	200	260
2013 Vapor blast finish	19,802	190	240

KM# 560 MT. RUSHMORE NATIONAL MEMORIAL • 155.55 g., 0.999 Silver 4.996 oz. ASW **Rev:** Presidential head sculpture on Mt. Rushmore

Date	Mintage	MS65	MS69
2013	35,000	190	240
2013P Vapor blast finish	23,547	200	260

KM# 581 SHENANDOAH NATIONAL PARK • 155.55 g., 0.999 Silver 4.996 oz. ASW

Date	Mintage	MS65	MS69
2014	—	—	260
2014P Vapor blast finish	—	—	240

KM# 580 GREAT SMOKEY MOUNTAINS NATIONAL PARK 155.550 Silver, .999 ASW

Date	Mintage	MS65	MS69
2014	29,500	200	260
2014P Vapor blast finish	24,705	190	240

KM# 582 ARCHES NATIONAL PARK • 155.55 g., 0.999 Silver 4.996 oz. ASW

Date	Mintage	MS65	MS69
2014	—	200	260
2014P Vapor blast finish	—	190	240

BULLION COINAGE

KM# 583 GREAT SAND DUNES NATIONAL PARK
- 155.55 g., 0.999 Silver 4.996 oz. ASW

Date	Mintage	MS65	MS69
2014	—	200	260
2014P Vapor blast finish	—	190	240

KM# 584 EVERGLADES NATIONAL PARK •
155.55 g., 0.999 Silver 4.996 oz. ASW

Date	Mintage	MS65	MS69
2014	—	200	260
2014P Vapor blast finish	—	190	240

AMERICAN EAGLE BULLION COINS

GOLD $5

KM# 216 • 3.39 g., 0.9167 Gold 0.100 oz. AGW, 16.5 mm. • **Obv. Designer:** Augustus Saint-Gaudens **Rev. Designer:** Miley Busiek

Date	Mintage	MS65	PF65
MCMLXXXVI -1986	912,609	200	—
MCMLXXXVII -1987	580,266	200	—
MCMLXXXVIII -1988	159,500	200	—
MCMLXXXVIII (1988)P	143,881	—	190
MCMLXXXIX -1989	264,790	200	—
MCMLXXXIX (1989)P	84,647	—	205
MCMXC -1990	210,210	200	—
MCMXC (1990)P	99,349	—	225
MCMXCI -1991	165,200	245	—
MCMXCI (1991)P	70,334	—	210
1992	209,300	160	—
1992P	64,874	—	185
1993	210,709	200	—
1993P	45,960	—	210
1994	206,380	175	159
1994W	62,849	—	169
1995	223,025	205	—
1995W	62,667	—	205
1996	401,964	145	159
1996W	57,047	—	169
1997	528,515	195	159
1997W	34,977	—	169
1998	1,344,520	165	159
1998W	39,395	—	169
1999	2,750,338	169	159
1999W	48,428	160	—

Date	Mintage	MS65	PF65
1999W Unfinished Proof die	Est. 6000	1,050	—
Note: The 1999 W issues are standard matte finished gold that were struck with unfinished proof dies.			
2000	569,153	176	159
2000W	49,971	—	169
2001	269,147	145	159
2001W	37,530	—	169
2002	230,027	205	159
2002W	40,864	—	169
2003	245,029	195	159
2003W	40,027	—	169
2004	250,016	195	—
2004W	35,131	—	225
2005	300,043	195	—
2005W	49,265	—	225
2006	285,006	195	159
2006W Burnished Unc.	20,643	205	—
2006W	47,277	—	169
2007	190,010	195	159
2007W Burnished Unc.	22,501	210	—
2007W	58,553	—	169
2008	305,000	145	—
2008W Burnished Unc.	12,657	360	—
2008W	Est. 29000	—	159
2009	27,000	145	—
2010	435,000	145	159
2010W	54,285	—	169
2011	350,000	185	159
2011W	42,697	—	169
2012W	—	145	—
2012W	20,740	—	225
2013W	—	165	—
2013	21,879	—	225
2014	—	165	—
2014	—	—	225

BULLION COINAGE

GOLD $10

KM# 217 • 8.48 g., 0.9167 Gold 0.250 oz. AGW, 22 mm. • **Obv. Designer:** Augustus Saint-Gaudens **Rev. Designer:** Miley Busiek

Date	Mintage	MS65	PF65
MCMLXXXVI -1986	726,031	550	—
MCMLXXXVII -1987	269,255	550	—
MCMLXXXVIII -1988	49,000	660	395
MCMLXXXVIII (1988)P	98,028	—	419
MCMLXXXIX -1989	81,789	660	—
MCMLXXXIX (1989)P	54,170	—	510
MCMXC -1990	41,000	780	—
MCMXC (1990)P	62,674	—	495
MCMXCI -1991	36,100	780	—
MCMXCI (1991)P	50,839	—	470
1992	59,546	605	385
1992P	46,269	—	409
1993	71,864	605	—
1993P	33,775	—	510
1994	72,650	605	415
1994W	47,172	—	439
1995	83,752	605	385
1995W	47,526	—	409
1996	60,318	605	375
1996W	38,219	—	399
1997	108,805	341	375
1997W	29,805	—	399
1998	309,829	341	375
1998W	29,503	—	399
1999	564,232	641	375
1999W	34,417	—	399
1999W Unfinished Proof die	Est. 6000	1,850	—

Note: The 1999 W issues are standard matte finished gold that were struck with unfinished proof dies.

Date	Mintage	MS65	PF65
2000	128,964	321	375
2000W	36,036	—	399
2001	71,280	605	375
2001W	25,613	—	399
2002	62,027	605	375
2002W	29,242	—	399
2003	74,029	341	375
2003W	30,292	—	399
2004	72,014	341	375
2004W	28,839	—	399
2005	72,015	341	375
2005W	37,207	—	399
2006	60,004	341	375
2006W Burnished Unc.	15,188	715	—
2006W	36,127	—	399
2007	34,004	610	375
2007W Burnished Unc.	12,786	660	—
2007W	46,189	—	399
2008	Est. 58000	341	—
2008W Burnished Unc.	8,883	1,675	—
2008W	28,000	—	475
2009	110,000	341	—
2010	86,000	341	375
2010W	44,507	—	399
2011	80,000	341	375
2011W	28,782	—	399
2012	—	341	—
2012W	13,375	—	—
2013	—	341	—
2013	12,642	—	475
2014	—	364	—
2014	—	—	475

GOLD $25

KM# 218 • 16.97 g., 0.9167 Gold 0.500 oz. AGW, 27 mm. • **Obv. Designer:** Augustus Saint-Gaudens **Rev. Designer:** Miley Busiek

Date	Mintage	MS65	PF65
MCMLXXXVI -1986	599,566	1,065	—
MCMLXXXVII -1987	131,255	1,320	—
MCMLXXXVII (1987)P	143,398	—	760
MCMLXXXVIII -1988	45,000	2,050	7,901
MCMLXXXVIII (1988)P	76,528	—	838
MCMLXXXIX -1989	44,829	2,150	—
MCMLXXXIX (1989)P	44,798	—	1,015
MCMXC -1990	31,000	2,475	—
MCMXC (1990)P	51,636	—	1,000
MCMXCI -1991	24,100	3,650	—
MCMXCI (1991)P	53,125	—	1,015
1992	54,404	1,520	770
1992P	40,976	—	818
1993	73,324	1,050	830
1993P	31,130	—	878
1994	62,400	1,035	760
1994W	44,584	—	808
1995	53,474	1,700	760
1995W	45,388	—	808
1996	39,287	1,725	760
1996W	35,058	—	808
1997	79,605	1,050	760
1997W	26,344	—	808
1998	169,029	641	760
1998W	25,374	—	808
1999	263,013	641	780
1999W	30,427	—	828
2000	79,287	995	760
2000W	32,028	—	808
2001	48,047	1,550	760
2001W	23,240	—	808
2002	70,027	1,050	760
2002W	26,646	—	808
2003	79,029	641	760
2003W	28,270	—	808
2004	98,040	641	760
2004W	27,330	—	808
2005	80,023	641	760
2005W	34,311	—	808
2006	66,004	644	760
2006W Burnished Unc.	15,164	1,185	—
2006W	34,322	—	808
2007	47,002	1,115	760
2007W Burnished Unc.	11,458	1,185	—
2007W	44,025	—	808
2008	61,000	644	—
2008W Burnished Unc.	15,683	1,650	—
2008W	27,800	—	920
2009	55,000	644	—
2010	81,000	641	760
2010W	44,527	—	808
2011	70,000	641	760
2011W	26,781	—	808
2012W	—	641	—
2013W	12,570	689	—
2013	—	641	975
2014	—	689	—
2014	—	—	975

BULLION COINAGE

GOLD $50

KM# 219 • 33.93 g., 0.9167 Gold 1.000 oz. AGW, 32.7 mm. • **Obv. Designer:** Augustus Saint-Gaudens **Rev. Designer:** Miley Busiek

Date	Mintage	MS65	PF65
MCMLXXXVI -1986	1,362,650	1,225	—
MCMLXXXVI (1986)W	446,290	—	1,450
MCMLXXXVII -1987	1,045,500	1,225	1,545
MCMLXXXVII (1987)W	147,498	1,316	—
MCMLXXXVIII -1988	465,000	1,225	—
MCMLXXXVIII (1988)W	87,133	—	1,450
MCMLXXXIX -1989	415,790	1,225	1,450
MCMLXXXIX (1989)W	54,570	—	1,545
MCMXC -1990	373,219	1,225	1,710
MCMXC (1990)W	62,401	—	1,805
MCMXCI -1991	243,100	1,225	1,750
MCMXCI (1991)W	50,411	—	1,845
1992W	275,000	—	1,510
1992	44,826	1,225	1,415
1993W	480,192	—	1,960
1993	34,369	1,225	1,865
1994W	221,663	—	1,610
1994	46,674	1,225	1,515
1995W	200,636	—	1,610
1995	46,368	1,225	1,515
1995W 10th Anniversary	—	—	—
1996W	189,148	—	1,610
1996	36,153	1,225	1,515
1997	664,508	1,225	1,515
1997W	28,034	—	1,610
1998	1,468,530	1,225	1,515
1998W	25,886	—	1,610
1999	1,505,026	1,225	1,715
1999W	31,427	—	1,810
1999W Die error	—	3,300	—

Note: The 1999 W issues are standard matte finished gold that were struck with unfinished proof dies.

Date	Mintage	MS65	PF65
2000	433,319	1,225	1,415
2000W	33,007	—	1,510
2001	143,605	1,225	1,415
2001W	24,555	—	1,510
2002	222,029	1,225	1,415
2002W	27,499	—	1,510
2003	416,032	1,225	1,415
2003W	28,344	—	1,510
2004	417,149	1,225	1,415
2004W	28,215	—	1,510
2005W	356,555	—	1,510
2005	35,246	1,225	1,415
2006	237,510	1,225	1,415
2006W Burnished Unc.	45,912	—	1,885
2006W	47,000	—	1,510
2006W Reverse Proof	10,000	2,800	—
2007W	140,016	—	1,510
2007W Burnished Unc.	18,609	1,980	—

Date	Mintage	MS65	PF65
2007	51,810	1,237	1,415
2008W	710,000	—	2,150
2008W Burnished Unc.	11,908	2,100	—
2008W Reverse of '07	—	—	—
2008W	29,000	1,316	—
2009	122,000	1,225	—
2010W	1,125,000	—	1,510
2010	59,480	1,225	1,415
2011	857,000	1,225	1,415
2011 Burnished Unc.	8,729	2,350	—
2011W	48,306	—	1,510
2012W	—	1,316	—
2012 Burnished Unc.	5,829	2,975	—
2013W	24,753	1,316	—
2013	—	1,225	1,850
2014	—	—	1,850
2014	—	1,316	—

PLATINUM $10

KM# 283 • 3.11 g., 0.9995 Platinum 0.0999 oz. APW, 17 mm. • **Rev:** Eagle flying right over sunrise **Obv. Designer:** John Mercanti **Rev. Designer:** Thomas D. Rogers Sr

Date	Mintage	MS65	PF65
1997	70,250	155	—
1997W	36,996	—	180
1998	39,525	155	—
1999	55,955	155	—
2000	34,027	155	—
2001	52,017	155	—
2002	23,005	155	—
2003	22,007	155	—
2004	15,010	155	—
2005	14,013	155	—
2006	11,001	155	—
2006W Burnished Unc.	—	425	—
2007	13,003	180	—
2007W Burnished Unc.	—	280	—
2008	17,000	155	—
2008 Burnished Unc.	—	390	—

KM# 289 • 3.11 g., 0.9995 Platinum 0.0999 oz. APW, 17 mm. • **Rev:** Eagle in flight over New England costal lighthouse **Obv. Designer:** John Mercanti

Date	Mintage	MS65	PF65
1998W	19,847	—	180

KM# 301 • 3.11 g., 0.9995 Platinum 0.0999 oz. APW, 17 mm. • **Rev:** Eagle in flight over Southeastern Wetlands **Obv. Designer:** John Mercanti

Date	Mintage	MS65	PF65
1999W	19,133	—	180

BULLION COINAGE

KM# 314 • 3.11 g., 0.9995 Platinum 0.0999 oz. APW, 17 mm. • **Rev:** Eagle in flight over Heartland **Obv. Designer:** John Mercanti

Date	Mintage	MS65	PF65
2000W	15,651	—	180

KM# 327 • 3.11 g., 0.9995 Platinum 0.0999 oz. APW, 17 mm. • **Rev:** Eagle in flight over Southwestern cactus desert **Obv. Designer:** John Mercanti

Date	Mintage	MS65	PF65
2001W	12,174	—	180

KM# 339 • 3.11 g., 0.9995 Platinum 0.0999 oz. APW, 17 mm. • **Rev:** Eagle fishing in America's Northwest **Obv. Designer:** John Mercanti

Date	Mintage	MS65	PF65
2002W	12,365	—	180

KM# 351 • 3.11 g., 0.9995 Platinum 0.0999 oz. APW, 17 mm. • **Rev:** Eagle pearched on a Rocky Mountain Pine branch against a flag backdrop **Series:** Patrotic Vigilance **Obv. Designer:** John Mercanti **Rev. Designer:** Al Maletsky

Date	Mintage	MS65	PF65
2003W	9,534	—	250

KM# 364 • 3.11 g., 0.9995 Platinum 0.0999 oz. APW, 17 mm. • **Rev:** Chester French, 1907. The sculpture is outside the N.Y. Customs House, now part of the Smithsonian's Museum of the American Indian **Obv. Designer:** John Mercanti

Date	Mintage	MS65	PF65
2004W	7,161	—	445

KM# 377 • 3.11 g., 0.9995 Platinum 0.0999 oz. APW, 17 mm. • **Rev:** Eagle with cornucopiae **Obv. Designer:** John Mercanti **Rev. Designer:** Donna Weaver

Date	Mintage	MS65	PF65
2005W	8,104	—	265

KM# 389 LEGISLATIVE • 3.11 g., 0.9995 Platinum 0.0999 oz. APW, 17 mm. • **Rev:** Liberty seated writing between two columns **Obv. Designer:** John Mercanti

Date	Mintage	MS65	PF65
2006W	10,205	—	180

KM# 414 EXECUTIVE BRANCH • 3.11 g., 0.9995 Platinum 0.0999 oz. APW, 17 mm. • **Rev:** Eagle with shield **Obv. Designer:** John Mercanti

Date	Mintage	MS65	PF65
2007W	8,176	—	180

KM# 434 • 3.11 g., 0.9995 Platinum 0.0999 oz. APW, 17 mm. • **Rev:** Justice standing before eagle **Obv. Designer:** John Mercanti

Date	Mintage	MS65	PF65
2008W	8,176	—	495

KM# 460 JUDICIAL • 3.11 g., 0.9995 Platinum 0.0999 oz. APW, 17 mm. • **Obv. Designer:** John Mercanti

Date	Mintage	MS65	PF65
2009W	5,600	—	—

PLATINUM $25

KM# 284 • 7.79 g., 0.9995 Platinum 0.2502 oz. APW, 22 mm. • **Rev:** Eagle in flight over sunrise **Obv. Designer:** John Mercanti **Rev. Designer:** Thomas D. Rogers Sr

BULLION COINAGE

BULLION COINAGE

Date	Mintage	MS65	PF65
1997	27,100	363	—
1997W	18,628	—	407
1998	38,887	363	—
1999	39,734	363	—
2000	20,054	363	—
2001	21,815	363	—
2002	27,405	363	—
2003	25,207	363	—
2004	18,010	363	—
2005	12,013	363	—
2006	12,001	363	—
2006W Burnished Unc.	—	590	—
2007	8,402	363	—
2007W Burnished Unc.	—	590	—
2008	—	363	—
2008 Burnished Unc.	22,800	665	—

KM# 290 • 7.79 g., 0.9995 Platinum 0.2502 oz. APW, 22 mm. • **Rev:** Eagle in flight over New England costal lighthouse **Obv. Designer:** John Mercanti

Date	Mintage	MS65	PF65
1998W	14,873	—	374

KM# 302 • 7.79 g., 0.9995 Platinum 0.2502 oz. APW, 22 mm. • **Rev:** Eagle in flight over Southeastern Wetlands **Obv. Designer:** John Mercanti

Date	Mintage	MS65	PF65
1999W	13,507	—	374

KM# 315 • 7.79 g., 0.9995 Platinum 0.2502 oz. APW, 22 mm. • **Rev:** Eagle in flight over Heartland **Obv. Designer:** John Mercanti

Date	Mintage	MS65	PF65
2000W	11,995	—	374

KM# 328 • 7.79 g., 0.9995 Platinum 0.2502 oz. APW, 22 mm. • **Rev:** Eagle in flight over Southwestern cactus desert **Obv. Designer:** John Mercanti

Date	Mintage	MS65	PF65
2001W	8,847	—	374

KM# 340 • 7.79 g., 0.9995 Platinum 0.2502 oz. APW, 22 mm. • **Rev:** Eagle fishing in America's Northwest **Obv. Designer:** John Mercanti

Date	Mintage	MS65	PF65
2002W	9,282	—	374

KM# 352 • 7.79 g., 0.9995 Platinum 0.2502 oz. APW, 22 mm. • **Rev:** Eagle pearched on a Rocky Mountain Pine branch against a flag backdrop. **Series:** Patrotic Vigilance **Obv. Designer:** John Mercanti **Rev. Designer:** Al Maletsky

Date	Mintage	MS65	PF65
2003W	7,044	—	374

KM# 365 • 7.79 g., 0.9995 Platinum 0.2502 oz. APW, 22 mm. • **Rev:** Chester French, 1907. The sculpture is outside the N.Y. Customs House, now part of the Smithsonian's Museum of the American Indian **Obv. Designer:** John Mercanti

Date	Mintage	MS65	PF65
2004W	5,193	—	1,000

KM# 378 • 7.79 g., 0.9995 Platinum 0.2502 oz. APW, 22 mm. • **Rev:** Eagle with cornucopiae **Obv. Designer:** John Mercanti **Rev. Designer:** Donna Weaver

Date	Mintage	MS65	PF65
2005W	6,592	—	610

KM# 390 LEGISLATIVE • 7.79 g., 0.9995 Platinum 0.2502 oz. APW, 22 mm. • **Rev:** Liberty seated writing between two columns **Obv. Designer:** John Mercanti

Date	Mintage	MS65	PF65
2006W	7,813	—	374

KM# 415 EXECUTIVE • 7.79 g., 0.9995 Platinum 0.2502 oz. APW, 22 mm. • **Rev:** Eagle with shield **Obv. Designer:** John Mercanti

Date	Mintage	MS65	PF65
2007W Polished Freedom	6,017	—	407
2007W Frosted Freedom, Rare	—	—	—

KM# 435 JUDICIAL • 7.79 g., 0.9995 Platinum 0.2502 oz. APW, 22 mm. • **Rev:** Justice holding scales, standing before eagle **Obv. Designer:** John Mercanti

Date	Mintage	MS65	PF65
2008W	6,017	—	715

KM# 461 • 7.79 g., 0.9995 Platinum 0.2502 oz. APW, 22 mm. • **Obv. Designer:** John Mercanti

Date	Mintage	MS65	PF65
2009W	3,800	—	374

PLATINUM $50

KM# 285 • 15.55 g., 0.9995 Platinum 0.4998 oz. APW, 27 mm. • **Rev:** Eagle flying right over sunrise **Obv. Designer:** John Mercanti **Rev. Designer:** Thomas D. Rogers Sr

Date	Mintage	MS65	PF65
1997	20,500	730	—
1997W	15,432	—	742
1998	32,419	730	—
1999	32,309	730	—
2000	18,892	730	—
2001	12,815	730	—
2002	24,005	730	—
2003	17,409	730	—
2004	13,236	730	—
2005	9,013	730	—
2006	9,602	730	—
2006W Burnished Unc.	—	889	—
2007	7,001	730	—
2007W Burnished Unc.	—	925	—
2008	14,000	730	—
2008W Burnished Unc.	—	1,200	—

KM# 291 • 15.55 g., 0.9995 Platinum 0.4998 oz. APW, 27 mm. • **Rev:** Eagle in flight over New England costal lighthouse **Obv. Designer:** John Mercanti

Date	Mintage	MS65	PF65
1998W	13,836	—	742

KM# 303 • 15.55 g., 0.9995 Platinum 0.4998 oz. APW, 27 mm. • **Rev:** Eagle in flight over Southeastern Wetlands **Obv. Designer:** John Mercanti

Date	Mintage	MS65	PF65
1999W	11,103	—	742

KM# 316 • 15.55 g., 0.9995 Platinum 0.4998 oz. APW, 27 mm. • **Rev:** Eagle in flight over Heartland **Obv. Designer:** John Mercanti

Date	Mintage	MS65	PF65
2000W	11,049	—	742

KM# 329 • 15.55 g., 0.9995 Platinum 0.4998 oz. APW, 27 mm. • **Rev:** Eagle in flight over Southwestern cactus desert **Obv. Designer:** John Mercanti

Date	Mintage	MS65	PF65
2001W	8,254	—	742

BULLION COINAGE

KM# 341 • 15.55 g., 0.9995 Platinum 0.4998 oz. APW, 27 mm. • **Rev:** Eagle fishing in America's Northwest **Obv. Designer:** John Mercanti

Date	Mintage	MS65	PF65
2002W	8,772	—	742

KM# 353 PATROTIC VIGILANCE • 15.55 g., 0.9995 Platinum 0.4998 oz. APW, 27 mm. • **Rev:** Eagle pearched on a Rocky Mountain Pine branch against a flag backdrop **Obv. Designer:** John Mercanti **Rev. Designer:** Al Maletsky

Date	Mintage	MS65	PF65
2003W	7,131	—	742

KM# 366 • 15.55 g., 0.9995 Platinum 0.4998 oz. APW, 27 mm. • **Rev:** Chester French, 1907. The sculpture is outside the N.Y. Customs House, now part of the Smithsonian's Museum of the American Indian **Obv. Designer:** John Mercanti

Date	Mintage	MS65	PF65
2004W	5,063	—	1,550

KM# 379 • 15.55 g., 0.9995 Platinum 0.4998 oz. APW, 27 mm. • **Rev:** Eagle with cornucopiae **Obv. Designer:** John Mercanti **Rev. Designer:** Donna Weaver

Date	Mintage	MS65	PF65
2005W	5,942	—	1,175

KM# 391 LEGISLATIVE • 15.55 g., 0.9995 Platinum 0.4998 oz. APW, 27 mm. • **Rev:** Liberty seated writing between two columns **Obv. Designer:** John Mercanti

Date	Mintage	MS65	PF65
2006W	7,649	—	742

KM# 416 EXECUTIVE • 15.55 g., 0.9995 Platinum 0.4998 oz. APW, 27 mm. • **Rev:** Eagle with shield **Obv. Designer:** John Mercanti

Date	Mintage	MS65	PF65
2007W Reverse Proof	22,873	—	742
2007W Frosted Freedom, Rare	—	—	—

KM# 436 JUDICIAL • 15.55 g., 0.9995 Platinum 0.4998 oz. APW, 27 mm. • **Rev:** Justice standing before eagle **Obv. Designer:** John Mercanti

Date	Mintage	MS65	PF65
2008W	22,873	—	1,225

KM# 462 • 15.55 g., 0.9995 Platinum 0.4998 oz. APW, 27 mm. • **Obv. Designer:** John Mercanti

Date	Mintage	MS65	PF65
2009	3,600	—	—

PLATINUM $100

KM# 286 • 31.11 g., 0.9995 Platinum 0.9995 oz. APW, 33 mm. • **Rev:** Eagle in flight over sun rise **Obv. Designer:** John Mercanti **Rev. Designer:** Thomas D. Rogers Sr

Date	Mintage	MS65	PF65
1997W	15,885	—	1,388
1997	56,000	1,340	—
1998	133,002	1,340	—
1999	56,707	1,340	—
2000	10,003	1,340	—
2001	14,070	1,340	—

BULLION COINAGE

Date	Mintage	MS65	PF65
2002	11,502	1,340	—
2003	8,007	1,340	—
2004	7,009	1,340	—
2005	6,310	1,340	—
2006	6,000	1,340	—
2006W Burnished Unc.	—	1,340	—
2007W	—	—	1,375
2007 Burnished Unc.	7,202	2,100	—
2008	21,800	1,340	—
2008W Burnished Unc.	—	2,300	—
2011	—	1,426	—

KM# 292 • 31.11 g., 0.9995 Platinum 0.9995 oz. APW, 33 mm. • **Rev:** Eagle in flight over New England costal lighthouse **Obv. Designer:** John Mercanti

Date	Mintage	MS65	PF65
1998W	14,912	—	1,375

KM# 304 • 31.11 g., 0.9995 Platinum 0.9995 oz. APW, 33 mm. • **Rev:** Eagle in flight over Southeastern Wetlands **Obv. Designer:** John Mercanti

Date	Mintage	MS65	PF65
1999W	12,363	—	1,375

KM# 317 • 31.11 g., 0.9995 Platinum 0.9995 oz. APW **Rev:** Eagle in flight over Heartland **Obv. Designer:** John Mercanti

Date	Mintage	MS65	PF65
2000W	12,453	—	1,375

KM# 330 • 31.11 g., 0.9995 Platinum 0.9995 oz. APW, 33 mm. • **Rev:** Eagle in flight over Southwestern cactus desert **Obv. Designer:** John Mercanti

Date	Mintage	MS65	PF65
2001W	8,969	—	1,375

KM# 342 • 31.11 g., 0.9995 Platinum 0.9995 oz. APW, 33 mm. • **Rev:** Eagle fishing in America's Northwest **Obv. Designer:** John Mercanti

Date	Mintage	MS65	PF65
2002W	9,834	—	1,375

KM# 354 • 31.11 g., 0.9995 Platinum 0.9995 oz. APW, 33 mm. • **Rev:** Eagle pearched on a Rocky Mountain Pine branch against a flag backdrop **Series:** Patrotic Vigilance **Obv. Designer:** John Mercanti **Rev. Designer:** Al Maletsky

Date	Mintage	MS65	PF65
2003W	8,246	—	1,388

KM# 367 • 31.11 g., 0.9995 Platinum 0.9995 oz. APW, 33 mm. • **Rev:** Inspired by the sculpture

BULLION COINAGE

"America" by Daniel Chester French, 1907. The sculpture is outside the N.Y. Customs House, now part of the Smithsonian's Museum of the American Indian **Obv. Designer:** John Mercanti **Rev. Designer:** Donna Weaver

Date	Mintage	MS65	PF65
2004W	6,007	—	1,655

KM# 380 • 31.11 g., 0.9995 Platinum 0.9995 oz. APW, 33 mm. • **Rev:** Eagle with cornucopiae **Obv. Designer:** John Mercanti **Rev. Designer:** Donna Weaver

Date	Mintage	MS65	PF65
2005W	6,602	—	1,510

KM# 392 LEGISLAIVE • 31.11 g., 0.9995 Platinum 0.9995 oz. APW, 33 mm. • **Rev:** Liberty seated writing between two columns **Obv. Designer:** John Mercanti

Date	Mintage	MS65	PF65
2006W	9,152	—	1,375

KM# 417 EXECUTIVE BRANCH • 31.11 g., 0.9995 Platinum 0.9995 oz. APW, 33 mm. • **Rev:** Eagle with shield **Obv. Designer:** John Mercanti

Date	Mintage	MS65	PF65
2007W Freedom Frosted	8,363	—	1,375
2007W Freedom Polished	—	—	50,000

KM# 437 JUDICIAL • 31.11 g., 0.9995 Platinum 0.9995 oz. APW, 33 mm. • **Rev:** Justice standing before eagle **Obv. Designer:** John Mercanti

Date	Mintage	MS65	PF65
2008W	8,363	—	3,000

KM# 463 A MORE PERFECT UNION • 31.10 g., 0.9995 Platinum 0.9995 oz. APW, 33 mm. • **Rev:** Four portraits **Obv. Designer:** John Mercanti

Date	Mintage	MS65	PF65
2009W Proof	4,900	—	2,260

KM# 488 TO ESTABLISH JUSTICE • 31.11 g., 0.999 Platinum 0.999 oz. APW, 33 mm. • **Rev:** Statue of Justice holding scales **Obv. Designer:** John Mercanti

Date	Mintage	MS65	PF65
2010W	—	—	2,175

KM# 518 TO INSURE DOMESTIC TRANQUILITY • 31.11 g., 0.9995 Platinum 0.9995 oz. APW, 33 mm. • **Rev:** Female with dove, walking in field

Date	Mintage	MS65	PF65
2011W	10,299	—	2,000

KM# 541 TO PROVIDE FOR THE COMMON
DEFENSE • 31.11 g., 0.9995 Platinum 0.9995 oz.
APW, 33 mm. • **Rev:** Colonial soldier and flag

Date	Mintage	MS65	PF65
2012	—	—	1,692

KM# 585 TO PROVIDE FOR THE COMMON
WELFARE • 31.11 g., 0.9995 Platinum 0.9995 oz.
APW, 33 mm. • **Rev:** Female and gears of industry

Date	Mintage	MS65	PF65
2013	—	—	1,538

KM# 586 TO SECURE THE BLESSINGS
OF LIBERTY TO OURSELVES AND OUR
PROSPERITY • 31.11 g., 0.9995 Platinum 0.9995
oz. APW, 33 mm. •

Date	Mintage	MS65	PF65
2014W	—	—	1,620

SILVER DOLLAR

KM# 273 • 31.11 g., 0.9993 Silver 0.9993 oz. ASW,
40.6 mm. • **Obv.** Liberty walking left **Rev:** Eagle
with shield **Obv. Designer:** Adolph A. Weinman
Rev. Designer: John Mercanti **Edge:** Reeded

Date	Mintage	MS65	PF65
1986	5,393,005	34.30	60.00
1986S	1,446,778	—	63.00

Date	Mintage	MS65	PF65
1987	11,442,335	26.60	60.00
1987S	904,732	—	63.00
1988	5,004,646	26.60	60.00
1988S	557,370	—	63.00
1989	5,203,327	—	60.00
1989S	617,694	—	63.00
1990	5,840,110	26.60	60.00
1990S	695,510	—	63.00
1991	7,191,066	26.60	60.00
1991S	511,924	—	63.00
1992	5,540,068	26.60	60.00
1992S	498,543	—	63.00
1993	6,763,762	29.60	—
1993P	405,913	—	105
1994	4,227,319	44.00	—
1994P	372,168	—	198
1995	4,672,051	—	4,450
1995	407,822	42.00	79.00
1995P 10th Anniversary	30,102	—	90.00
1996P	3,603,386	—	82.00
1996	498,293	70.00	—
1997P	4,295,004	—	95.00
1997	440,315	39.50	—
1998P	4,847,547	—	71.50
1998	450,728	34.00	—
1999P	7,408,640	—	63.00
1999	549,330	28.30	60.00
2000	9,239,132	28.30	53.00
2000P	600,743	—	56.00
2001	9,001,711	26.30	50.00
2001W	746,398	—	53.00
2002W	10,539,026	—	63.00
2002	647,342	26.30	60.00
2003W	8,495,008	—	63.00
2003	747,831	22.80	60.00
2004	801,602	22.80	60.00
2004W	8,882,754	—	63.00
2005	8,891,025	22.80	50.00
2005W	816,663	—	53.00
2006	10,676,522	22.80	50.00
2006P Burnished Unc.	468,000	—	265
2006W	1,093,600	—	53.00
2006W Reverse Proof	Est. 250000	85.00	—
2006 20th Aniv. 3 pc. set	—	—	415
2007W	9,028,036	—	53.00
2007W Burnished Unc.	690,891	22.80	—
2007	821,759	22.80	50.00
2008W	20,583,000	22.80	—
2008 Burnished Unc.	Est. 550000	71.50	—
2008 Reverse of '07, U in United with rounded bottom.	Est. 47000	565	—
2008W	713,353	—	50.00
2009	30,459,000	22.80	—
2010	34,764,500	—	50.00
2010	—	22.80	—
2011W	39,764,500	50.00	—
2011P Reverse Proof	100,000	—	305
2011 Burnished Unc.	100,000	21.80	53.00
2011S Burnished Unc.	—	285	—
2011W	850,000	—	56.00
2012	—	19.80	—
2012S Reverse Proof	—	—	53.00
2012	60,203	—	125
2012W Burnished Unc.	33,742,500	62.00	—
2013W	178,941	22.10	—
2013W Enhanced Finish	—	93.50	—
2013	—	19.80	54.00
2013 Enhanced Finish	—	26.00	—
2013W Enhanced Finish Reverse Proof	—	—	88.00
2014	—	—	60.00
2014	—	24.00	—

BULLION COINAGE

BISON BULLION COINAGE

GOLD $5

KM# 411 • 3.11 g., 0.9999 Gold 0.100 oz. AGW
Obv. Indian Head right **Rev:** Bison

Date	Mintage	MS65	PF65
2008W	17,429	600	—
2008W	18,884	—	660

GOLD $10

KM# 412 • 7.79 g., 0.9999 Gold 0.2503 oz. AGW
Obv. Indian Head right **Rev:** Bison

Date	Mintage	MS65	PF65
2008W	9,949	1,375	—
2008W	13,125	—	1,550

GOLD $25

KM# 413 • 15.55 g., 0.999 Gold 0.4995 oz. AGW
Obv. Indian Head right **Rev:** Bison

Date	Mintage	MS65	PF65
2008W	16,908	1,350	—
2008W	12,169	—	1,850

GOLD $50

KM# 393 • 31.11 g., 0.9999 Gold 0.9999 oz. AGW,
32 mm. • **Obv.** Indian head right **Rev:** Bison
standing left on mound **Designer:** James E. Fraser

Date	Mintage	MS65	PF65
2006	337,012	1,225	—
2006W Proof	246,267	—	1,390
2007	136,503	1,225	—
2007W Proof	58,998	—	1,390
2008	189,500	1,225	—
2008W Burnished	18,863	—	3,200
2008W Moy Family Chop, Proof	—	—	3,950
2009	200,000	1,225	—
2009W Proof	49,306	—	1,360
2010	209,000	1,225	—
2010W Proof	49,263	—	1,390
2011W	174,500	—	1,390
2011 Proof	28,693	1,225	—
2012	132,000	1,225	—
2012W Proof	19,765	—	2,000
2013W	—	1,225	—
2013 Reverse Proof	47,836	1,950	—
2014	—	1,316	—
2014	—	—	1,475

FIRST SPOUSE GOLD COINAGE

GOLD $10

KM# 407 MARTHA WASHINGTON • 15.55 g.,
0.9999 Gold 0.500 oz. AGW, 26.5 mm. • **Obv.**
Bust 3/4 facing **Rev:** Martha Washington seated
sewing **Series:** Presidential Spouse Bullion **Obv.
Designer:** Joseph Menna **Rev. Designer:** Susan
Gamble and Don Everhart

Date	Mintage	MS65	PF65
2007W	17,661	630	—
2007W	19,169	—	630

KM# 408 ABIGAIL ADAMS • 15.55 g., 0.9999
Gold 0.500 oz. AGW, 26.5 mm. • **Obv.** Bust 3/4
facing **Rev:** Abigail Adams seated at desk writing
to John during the Revolutionary War **Series:**
Presidential Spouse Bullion **Obv. Designer:** Joseph
Menna **Rev. Designer:** Thomas Cleveland and
Phebe Hemphill

Date	Mintage	MS65	PF65
2007W	17,142	—	677
2007W	17,149	677	—

BULLION COINAGE

KM# 409 JEFFERSON - BUST COINAGE DESIGN
- 15.55 g., 0.9999 Gold 0.500 oz. AGW, 26.5 mm.
- **Obv.** Bust design from coinage **Rev:** Jefferson's tombstone **Series:** Presidential Spouse Bullion **Obv. Designer:** Robert Scot and Phebe Hemphill **Rev. Designer:** Charles Vickers

Date	Mintage	MS65	PF65
2007W	19,823	—	630
2007W	19,815	630	—

KM# 410 DOLLEY MADISON
- 15.55 g., 0.9999 Gold 0.500 oz. AGW, 26.5 mm. • **Obv.** Bust 3/4 facing **Rev:** Dolley standing before painting of Washington, which she saved from the White House **Series:** Presidential Spouse Bullion **Obv. Designer:** Don Everhart **Rev. Designer:** Joel Iskowitz and Don Everhart

Date	Mintage	MS65	PF65
2007W	11,813	677	—
2007W	17,661	—	677

KM# 430 ELIZABETH MONROE
- 15.55 g., 0.999 Gold 0.4995 oz. AGW, 26.5 mm. • **Obv.** Bust 3/4 facing right **Rev:** Elizabeth standing before mirror **Series:** Presidential Spouse Bullion **Obv. Designer:** Joel Iskowitz and Don Everhart **Rev. Designer:** Donna Weaver and Charles Vickers

Date	Mintage	MS65	PF65
2008W	4,519	975	—
2008W	7,933	—	950

KM# 431 LOUSIA ADAMS
- 15.55 g., 0.999 Gold 0.4995 oz. AGW, 26.5 mm. • **Obv.** Bust 3/4 facing right **Rev:** Lousia and son Charles before entrance

Series: Presidential Spouse Bullion **Obv. Designer:** Susan Gamble and Phebe Hemphill **Rev. Designer:** Joseph Menna

Date	Mintage	MS65	PF65
2008W	4,223	1,175	—
2008W	7,454	—	1,125

KM# 432 JACKSON'S LIBERTY
- 15.55 g., 0.999 Gold 0.4995 oz. AGW, 26.5 mm. • **Obv.** Capped and draped bust left **Rev:** Andrew Jackson on horseback right **Series:** Presidential Spouse Bullion **Obv. Designer:** John Reich **Rev. Designer:** Justin Kunz and Don Everhart

Date	Mintage	MS65	PF65
2008W	4,281	1,575	—
2008W	7,454	—	1,325

KM# 433 VAN BUREN'S LIBERTY
- 15.55 g., 0.999 Gold 0.4995 oz. AGW, 26.5 mm. • **Obv.** Seated Liberty with shiled **Rev:** Youthful van Buren seated under tree, family tavern in distance **Series:** Presidential Spouse Bullion **Obv. Designer:** Christian Gobrecht **Rev. Designer:** Thomas Cleveland and James Licaretz

Date	Mintage	MS65	PF65
2008W	3,443	1,500	—
2008W	6,187	—	1,525

KM# 456 ANNA HARRISON
- 15.55 g., 0.999 Gold 0.4995 oz. AGW, 26.5 mm. • **Obv.** Bust 3/4 left **Rev:** Anna reading to her three children **Series:** Presidential Spouse Bullion **Obv. Designer:** Donna Weaver and Joseph Menna **Rev. Designer:** Thomas Cleveland and Charles Vickers

Date	Mintage	MS65	PF65
2009W	2,993	1,225	—
2009W	5,801	—	1,150

BULLION COINAGE

KM# 457 LETTIA TYLER • 15.55 g., 0.999 Gold 0.4995 oz. AGW, 26.5 mm. • **Obv.** Bust facing **Rev:** Letitia and two children playing outside of Cedar Grove Plantation **Series:** Presidential Spouse Bullion **Obv. Designer:** Phebe Hemphill **Rev. Designer:** Susan Gamble and Norm Nemeth

Date	Mintage	MS65	PF65
2009W	2,381	1,525	—
2009W	4,341	—	1,325

KM# 458 JULIA TYLER • 15.55 g., 0.999 Gold 0.4995 oz. AGW **Obv.** Bust facing **Rev:** Julia and John Tyler dancing **Series:** Presidential Spouse Bullion **Rev. Designer:** 26.5 **Designer:** Joel Iskowitz and Don Everhart

Date	Mintage	MS65	PF65
2009W	2,188	1,650	—
2009W	3,878	—	1,800

KM# 459 SARAH POLK • 15.55 g., 0.999 Gold 0.4995 oz. AGW, 26.5 mm. • **Obv.** Bust 3/4 right **Rev:** Sarah seated at desk as personal secretary to James Polk **Series:** Presidential Spouse Bullion **Designer:** Phebe Hemphill

Date	Mintage	MS65	PF65
2009W	1,893	1,300	—
2009W	3,512	—	1,100

KM# 465 MARGARET TAYLOR • 15.55 g., 0.999 Gold 0.4995 oz. AGW, 26.5 mm. • **Obv.** Bust 3/4 left **Rev:** Margaret Taylor nurses wounded soldier during the Seminole War **Series:** Presidential Spouse Bullion **Obv. Designer:** Phebe Hemphill and Charles Vickers **Rev. Designer:** Mary Beth

Zeitz and James Licaretz

Date	Mintage	MS65	PF65
2009W	3,430	1,050	—
2009W	4,787	—	1,225

KM# 481 ABIGAIL FILMORE • 15.52 g., 0.999 Gold 0.4985 oz. AGW, 26.5 mm. • **Rev:** Abigail Filmore placing books on library shelf **Series:** Presidential Spouse Bullion **Obv. Designer:** Phebe Hemphill **Rev. Designer:** Susan Gamble and Joseph Menna

Date	Mintage	MS65	PF65
2010W	3,482	1,300	—
2010W	6,130	—	1,025

KM# 482 JANE PIERCE • 15.52 g., 0.999 Gold 0.4985 oz. AGW, 26.5 mm. • **Rev:** Jane Pierce seated on porch **Series:** Presidential Spouse Bullion **Obv. Designer:** Donna Weaver and Don Everhart **Rev. Designer:** Donna Weaver and Charles Vickers

Date	Mintage	MS65	PF65
2010W	3,338	1,000	—
2010W	4,775	—	1,225

KM# 483 BUCHANAN'S LIBERTY • 15.52 g., 0.999 Gold 0.4985 oz. AGW, 26.5 mm. • **Rev:** Buchanan as clerk **Series:** Presidential Spouse Bullion **Obv. Designer:** Christian Gobrecht **Rev. Designer:** Joseph Menna

Date	Mintage	MS65	PF65
2010W	5,162	1,000	—
2010W	7,110	—	1,075

KM# 484 MARY TODD LINCOLN • 15.52 g., 0.999 Gold 0.4985 oz. AGW, 26.5 mm. • **Rev:** Mary Lincoln visiting soldiers at hospital **Series:**

Presidential Spouse Bullion **Obv. Designer:** Phebe Hemphill **Rev. Designer:** Joel Iskowitz and Pheve Hemphill

Date	Mintage	MS65	PF65
2010W	3,965	1,000	—
2010W	6,861	—	975

KM# 509 ELIZA JOHNSON • 15.55 g., 0.999 Gold 0.4994 oz. AGW, 26.5 mm. • **Obv.** Bust of Eliza Johnson **Series:** Presidential Spouse Bullion

Date	Mintage	MS65	PF65
2011W	2,915	1,075	—
2011W	3,907	—	1,075

KM# 510 JULIA GRANT • 15.55 g., 0.999 Gold 0.4995 oz. AGW, 26.5 mm. • **Obv.** Bust of Julia Grant **Series:** Presidential Spouse Bullion

Date	Mintage	MS65	PF65
2011W	2,952	1,075	—
2011W	3,969	—	1,075

KM# 511 LUCY HAYES • 15.55 g., 0.999 Gold 0.4995 oz. AGW, 26.5 mm. • **Obv.** Bust of Lucy Hayes **Series:** Presidential Spouse Bullion

Date	Mintage	MS65	PF65
2011W	2,263	1,325	—
2011W	3,885	—	1,075

KM# 512 LUCRETIA GARFIELD • 15.55 g., 0.999 Gold 0.4995 oz. AGW, 26.5 mm. • **Obv.** Bust of Lucretia Garfield **Series:** Presidential Spouse Bullion

Date	Mintage	MS65	PF65
2011W	2,498	1,325	—
2011W	3,652	—	1,075

KM# 532 ALICE PAUL, SUFFRAGIST • 15.55 g., 0.999 Gold 0.4995 oz. AGW, 26.5 mm. • **Series:** Presidential Spouse Bullion

Date	Mintage	MS65	PF65
2012W	2,798	1,050	—
2012W	3,506	—	1,075

KM# 533 FRANCES CLEVELAND (FIRST TERM) • 15.55 g., 0.999 Gold 0.4995 oz. AGW, 26.5 mm. • **Obv.** Frances Cleveland **Series:** Presidential Spouse Bullion

Date	Mintage	MS65	PF65
2012W	2,454	1,050	—
2012W	3,158	—	1,075

KM# 534 CAROLINE HARRISON • 15.55 g., 0.999 Gold 0.4995 oz. AGW, 26.5 mm. • **Obv.** Caroline Harrison **Series:** Presidential Spouse Bullion

Date	Mintage	MS65	PF65
2012W	2,436	1,050	—
2012W	3,046	—	1,075

KM# 535 FRANCES CLEVELAND (SECOND TERM) • 15.55 g., 0.999 Gold 0.4995 oz. AGW, 26.5 mm. • **Obv.** Frances Cleveland **Series:** Presidential Spouse Bullion

Date	Mintage	MS65	PF65
2012W	2,425	1,050	—
2012W	3,104	—	1,075

BULLION COINAGE

BULLION COINAGE

KM# 561 IDA McKINLEY • 15.55 g., 0.999 Gold
0.4995 oz. AGW, 26.5 mm. • **Obv.** Bust of Ida
McKinley **Series:** Presidential Spouse Bullion

Date	Mintage	MS65	PF65
2013W	—	800	—
2013W	—	—	825

KM# 565 EDITH WILSON • 15.55 g., 0.999 Gold
0.4995 oz. AGW, 26.5 mm. • **Obv.** Bust of Edith
Wilson **Series:** Presidential Spouse Bullion

Date	Mintage	MS65	PF65
2013W	—	800	—
2013W	—	—	825

KM# 562 EDITH ROOSEVELT • 15.55 g., 0.999
Gold 0.4995 oz. AGW, 26.5 mm. • **Obv.** Bust of
Edith Roosevelt **Series:** Presidential Spouse Bullion

Date	Mintage	MS65	PF65
2013W	—	800	—
2013W	—	—	825

KM# 563 HELEN TAFT • 15.55 g., 0.999 Gold
0.4995 oz. AGW, 26.5 mm. • **Obv.** Bust of Helen
Taft **Series:** Presidential Spouse Bullion

Date	Mintage	MS65	PF65
2013W	—	800	—
2013W	—	—	825

KM# 564 ELLEN WILSON • 15.55 g., 0.999 Gold
0.4995 oz. AGW, 26.5 mm. • **Obv.** Bust of Ellen
Wilson **Series:** Presidential Spouse Bullion

Date	Mintage	MS65	PF65
2013W	—	800	—
2013W	—	—	825

MINT SETS

Mint, or uncirculated, sets contain one uncirculated coin of each denomination from each mint produced for circulation that year. Values listed here are only for those sets sold by the U.S. Mint. Sets were not offered in years not listed. In years when the Mint did not offer the sets, some private companies compiled and marketed uncirculated sets. Mint sets from 1947 through 1958 contained two examples of each coin mounted in cardboard holders, which caused the coins to tarnish. Beginning in 1959, the sets have been packaged in sealed Pliofilm packets and include only one specimen of each coin struck for that year (both P & D mints). Listings for 1965, 1966 and 1967 are for "special mint sets," which were of higher quality than regular mint sets and were prooflike. They were packaged in plastic cases. The 1970 large-date and small-date varieties are distinguished by the size of the date on the coin. The 1976 three-piece set contains the quarter, half dollar and dollar with the Bicentennial design. The 1971 and 1972 sets do not include a dollar coin; the 1979 set does not include an S-mint-marked dollar. Mint sets issued prior to 1959 were double sets (containing two of each coin) packaged in cardboard with a paper overlay. Origional sets will always be toned and can bring large premiums if nicely preserved with good color.

Date	Sets Sold	Issue Price	Value	Date	Sets Sold	Issue Price	Value
1947 Est. 5,000	—	4.87	2,950	1980 Susan B. Anthony PDS	—	—	6.50
1948 Est. 6,000	—	4.92	1,815	Souvenir Set			
1949 Est. 5,200	—	5.45	2,400	1981 Type I	2,908,145	11.00	8.60
1950 None issued	—	—	—	1981 Susan B. Anthony PDS	—	—	22.00
1951	8,654	6.75	1,975	Souvenir Set			
1952	11,499	6.14	1,700	1982 & 1983 None issued	—	—	—
1953	15,538	6.14	1,325	1982 Souvenir set	—	—	59.00
1954	25,599	6.19	670	1983 Souvenir set	—	—	65.00
1955 flat pack	49,656	3.57	445	1984	1,832,857	7.00	2.80
1956	45,475	3.34	450	1985	1,710,571	7.00	3.60
1957	32,324	24.50	685	1986	1,153,536	7.50	6.35
1958	50,314	4.43	425	1987	2,890,758	7.00	2.85
1959	187,000	2.40	41.00	1988	1,646,204	7.00	4.40
1960 large date	260,485	2.40	35.00	1989	1,987,915	7.00	3.10
1961	223,704	2.40	35.25	1990	1,809,184	7.00	3.30
1962	385,285	2.40	33.75	1991	1,352,101	7.00	3.90
1963	606,612	2.40	32.00	1992	1,500,143	7.00	3.65
1964	1,008,108	2.40	27.50	1993	1,297,094	8.00	3.90
1965 Special Mint Set	2,360,000	4.00	9.65	1994	1,234,813	8.00	2.80
1966 Special Mint Set	2,261,583	4.00	8.80	1995	1,038,787	8.00	3.35
1967 Special Mint Set	1,863,344	4.00	9.65	1996	1,457,949	8.00	17.50
1968	2,105,128	2.50	5.50	1997	950,473	8.00	3.90
1969	1,817,392	2.50	5.50	1998	1,187,325	8.00	3.05
1970 large date	2,038,134	2.50	17.75	1999 9 piece	1,421,625	14.95	6.10
1970 small date	Inc. above	2.50	53.50	2000	1,490,160	14.95	7.15
1971	2,193,396	3.50	3.30	2001	1,066,900	14.95	7.20
1972	2,750,000	3.50	2.75	2002	1,139,388	14.95	7.05
1973	1,767,691	8.00	11.75	2003	1,002,555	14.95	8.25
1974	1,975,981	6.75	6.05	2004	844,484	16.95	8.00
1975	1,921,488	6.00	6.60	2005	—	16.95	7.20
1976 3 coins	4,908,319	9.00	15.25	2006	—	16.95	7.25
1976	1,892,513	6.00	6.90	2007	—	—	17.25
1977	2,006,869	7.00	5.25	2008	—	—	45.00
1978	2,162,609	7.00	6.10	2009 18 piece clad set	—	—	19.00
1979 Type I	2,526,000	8.00	5.00	2010 28 piece clad set	—	—	29.70
1979 Susan B Anthony PDS	—	—	6.50	2010 14 piece clad set	—	—	22.50
Souvenir Set				2011 14 piece clad set	532,059	—	23.50
1980	2,815,066	9.00	6.10	2012 14 piece clad set	365,298	—	74.00

SETS & ROLLS

MODERN COMMEMORATIVE COIN SETS

Olympic, 1983-1984

Date	Price
1983 1983S & 1984S 2 coin set: proof dollars.	74.00
1983 1983 collectors 3 coin set: 1983 PDS uncirculated dollars; KM209.	104
1984 1984 collectors 3 coin set: 1984 PDS uncirculated dollars; KM210.	105
1983 1983 & 1984 3 coin set: 1983 and one 1984 uncirculated dollar and 1984W uncirculated gold $10; KM209, 210, 211.	952
1983 1983S & 1984S 3 coin set: proof 1983 and 1984 dollar and 1984W gold $10; KM209, 210, 211.	956
1983 1983 & 1984 6 coin set in a cherrywood box: 1983S and 1984S uncirculated and proof dollars, 1984W uncirculated and proof gold $10; KM209, 210, 211.	1,909

Statue of Liberty

Date	Price
1986 1986 2 coin set: uncirculated silver dollar and clad half dollar; KM212, 214.	38.00
1986 1986 2 coin set: proof silver dollar and clad half dollar; KM212, 214.	40.00
1986 1986 3 coin set: uncirculated silver dollar, clad half dollar and gold $5; KM212, 214, 215.	480
1986 1986 3 coin set: proof silver dollar, clad half dollar and gold $5; KM212, 214, 215.	483
1986 1986 6 coin set: 1 each of the proof and uncirculated issues; KM212, 214, 215.	963

Constitution

Date	Price
1987 1987 2 coin set: uncirculated silver dollar and gold $5; KM220, 221.	477
1987 1987 2 coin set: proof silver dollar and gold $5; KM220, 221.	479
1987 1987 4 coin set: silver dollar and $5 gold proof and uncirculated issues; KM220, 221.	958

Olympic, 1988

Date	Price
1988 1988 2 coin set: uncirculated silver dollar and gold $5; KM222, 223.	477
1988 1988 2 coin set: proof silver dollar and gold $5; KM222, 223.	479
1988 1988 4 coin set: silver dollar and $5 gold proof and uncirculated issues; KM222, 223.	958

Congress

Date	Price
1989 1989 2 coin set: uncirculated silver dollar and clad half dollar; KM224, 225.	42.00
1989 1989 2 coin set: proof silver dollar and clad half dollar; KM224, 225.	44.00
1989 1989 3 coin set: uncirculated silver dollar, clad half and gold $5; KM224, 225, 226.	485
1989 1989 3 coin set: proof silver dollar, clad half and gold $5; KM224, 225, 226.	487
1989 1989 6 coin set: 1 each of the proof and uncirculated issues; KM224, 225, 226.	973

Mt. Rushmore

Date	Price
1991 1991 2 coin set: uncirculated half dollar and silver dollar; KM228, 229.	57.00
1991 1991 2 coin set: proof half dollar and silver dollar; KM228, 229.	60.00
1991 1991 3 coin set: uncirculated half dollar, silver dollar and gold $5; KM228, 229, 230.	500
1991 1991 3 coin set: proof half dollar, silver dollar and gold $5; KM228, 229, 230.	502
1991 1991 6 coin set: 1 each of proof and uncirculated issues; KM228, 229, 230.	1,004

Olympic, 1992

Date	Price
1992 1992 2 coin set: uncirculated half dollar and silver dollar; KM233, 234.	46.00
1992 1992 2 coin set: proof half dollar and silver dollar; KM233, 234.	47.00
1992 1992 3 coin set: uncirculated half dollar, silver dollar and gold $5; KM233, 234, 235.	489
1992 1992 3 coin set: proof half dollar, silver dollar and gold $5; KM233, 234, 235.	490
1992 1992 6 coin set: 1 each of proof and uncirculated issues; KM233, 234, 235.	978

Columbus Quincentenary

Date	Price
1992 1992 2 coin set: uncirculated half dollar and silver dollar; KM237, 238.	52.00
1992 1992 2 coin set: proof half dollar and silver dollar; KM237, 238.	47.00
1992 1992 3 coin set: uncirculated half dollar, silver dollar and gold $5; KM237, 238, 239.	495
1992 1992 3 coin set: proof half dollar, silver dollar and gold $5; KM237, 238, 239.	489
1992 1992 6 coin set: 1 each of proof and uncirculated issues; KM237, 238, 239.	985

Jefferson

Date	Price
1993 1993 Jefferson: dollar, 1994 matte proof nickel and $2 note; KM249, 192.	109

Madison / Bill of Rights

Date	Price
1993 1993 2 coin set: uncirculated half dollar and silver dollar; KM240, 241.	57.00
1993 1993 2 coin set: proof half dollar and silver dollar; KM240, 241.	58.00
1993 1993 3 coin set: uncirculated half dollar, silver dollar and gold $5; KM240, 241, 242.	499
1993 1993 3 coin set: proof half dollar, silver dollar and gold $5; KM240, 241, 242.	500
1993 1993 6 coin set: 1 each of proof and uncirculated issues; KM240, 241, 242.	999
1993 Coin and stamp set; KM#240 and 20c stamp	21.00

World War II

Date	Price
1993 1993 2 coin set: uncirculated half dollar and silver dollar; KM243, 244.	54.00
1993 1993 2 coin set: proof half dollar and silver dollar; KM243, 244.	57.00
1993 1993 3 coin set: uncirculated half dollar, silver dollar and gold $5; KM243, 244, 245.	496
1993 1993 3 coin set: proof half dollar, silver dollar and gold $5; KM243, 244, 245.	500
1993 1993 6 coin set: 1 each of proof and uncirculated issues; KM243, 244, 245.	1,000

U.S. Veterans

Date	Price
1994 1994 3 coin set: uncirculated POW, Vietnam, Women dollars; KM250, 251, 252.	202
1994 1994 3 coin set: proof POW, Vietnam, Women dollars; KM250, 251, 252.	142

World Cup

Date	Price
1994 1994 2 coin set: uncirculated half dollar and silver dollar; KM246, 247.	48.00
1994 1994 2 coin set: proof half dollar and silver dollar; KM246, 247.	45.00
1994 1994 3 coin set: uncirculated half dollar, silver dollar and gold $5; KM246, 247, 248.	490

SETS & ROLLS

Date	Price
1994 1994 3 coin set: proof half dollar, silver dollar and gold $5; KM246, 247, 248.	487
1994 1994 6 coin set: 1 each of proof and uncirculated issues; KM246, 247, 248.	983

Olympic, 1995-96

Date	Price
1995 1995 4 coin set: uncirculated basketball half, $1 gymnast & blind runner, $5 torch runner; KM257, 259, 260, 261.	1,024
1995 1995 4 coin set: proof basketball half, $1 gymnast & blind runner, $5 torch runner; KM257, 259, 260, 261.	533
1995 1995P 2 coin set: proof $1 gymnast & blind runner; KM259, 260.	82.00
1995 1995P 2 coin set: proof $1 track & field, cycling; KM263, 264.	84.00
1995 1995-96 4 coin set: proof halves, basketball, baseball, swimming, soccer; KM257, 262, 267, 271.	75.00
1995 1995 & 96 8 coins in cherry wood case: proof silver dollars: blind runner, gymnast, cycling, track & field, wheelchair, tennis, rowing, high jump; KM259, 260, 263, 264, 268, 269, 272, 272A.	425
1995 1995 & 96 16 coins in cherry wood case: bu and proof silver dollars: blind runner, gymnast, cycling, track & field, wheelchair, tennis, rowing, high jump; KM259, 260, 263, 264, 268, 269, 272, 272A.	10,400
1995 1995 & 96 16 coins in cherry wood case: proof half dollars: basketball, baseball, swimming, soccer, KM257, 262, 267, 271. Proof silver dollars: blind runner, gymnast, cycling, track & field, wheelchair, tennis, rowing, high jump, KM259, 260, 263, 264, 268, 269, 272, 272A. Proof $5 gold: torch runner, stadium, cauldron, flag bearer KM 261, 265, 270, 274.	2,370
1995 1995 & 96 32 coins in cherry wood case: bu & proof half dollars: basketball, baseball, swimming, soccer, KM257, 262, 267, 271. BU & proof silver dollars: blind runner, gymnast, cycling, track & field, wheelchair, tennis, rowing, high jump, KM259, 260, 263, 264, 268, 269, 272, 272A. BU & proof $5 gold: torch runner, stadium, cauldron, flag bearer, KM261, 265, 270, 274.	12,800
1996 1996P 2 coin set: proof $1 wheelchair & tennis; KM268, 269.	154
1996 1996P 2 coin set: proof $1 rowing & high jump; KM272, 272A.	105
1996 Young collector 4 coin set; Half dollars: KM#257, 262, 267, 271	205

Civil War

Date	Price
1995 1995 2 coin set: uncirculated half and dollar; KM254, 255.	102
1995 Civil War Young Collectors set KM#245	37.50
1995 1995 2 coin set: proof half and dollar; KM254, 255.	88.00
1995 1995 3 coin set: uncirculated half, dollar and gold $5; KM254, 255, 256.	1,055
1995 1995 3 coin set: proof half, dollar and gold $5; KM254, 255, 256.	530
1995 1995 6 coin set: 1 each of proof and uncirculated issues; KM254, 255, 256.	1,585

Smithsonian

Date	Price
1996 1996 2 coin set: proof dollar and $5 gold; KM276, 277.	495
1996 1996 4 coin set: proof and B.U. ; KM276, 277.	1,465

Franklin Delano Roosevelt

Date	Price
1997 1997W 2 coin set: uncirculated and proof; KM282.	3,500

Jackie Robinson

Date	Price
1997 1997 2 coin set: proof dollar & $5 gold; KM279, 280.	680
1997 1997 4 coin set: proof & BU; KM279, 280.	3,660
1997 1997 legacy set.	650

Botanic Garden

Date	Price
1997 1997 2 coin set: dollar, Jefferson nickel and $1 note; KM278, 192.	220

Black Patriots

Date	Price
1998 1998S 2 coin set: uncirculated and proof; KM288.	220

Kennedy

Date	Price
1998 1998 2 coin set: proof; KM287.	88.00
1998 1998 2 coin collectors set: Robert Kennedy dollar and John Kennedy half dollar; KM287, 202b. Matte finished.	225

Dolley Madison

Date	Price
1999 1999 2 coin set: proof and uncirculated silver dollars; KM298.	76.00

Yellowstone National Park

Date	Price
1999 1999 2 coin set: proof and uncirculated silver dollars; KM299.	84.00

George Washington

Date	Price
1999 1999 2 coin set: proof and uncirculated gold $5; KM300.	900

Millennium Coin & Currency

Date	Price
2000 2000 2 coin set: uncirculated Sacagewea $1, silver Eagle & $1 note.	67.50

Leif Ericson

Date	Price
2000 2000 2 coin set: proof and uncirculated silver dollars; KM313.	85.00

American Buffalo

Date	Price
2001 2001 2 coin set: 90% silver unc. & proof $1.; KM325.	330
2001 2001 coin & currency set 90% unc. dollar & replicas of 1899 $5 silver cert.; KM325.	180

Capitol Visitor Center

Date	Price
2001 2001 3 coin set: proof half, silver dollar, gold $5; KM323, 324, 326.	495

Winter Olympics - Salt Lake City

Date	Price
2002 2002 2 coin set: proof 90% silver dollar KM336 & $5.00 Gold KM337.	465
2002 2002 4 coin set: 90% silver unc. & proof $1, KM336 & unc. & proof gold $5, KM337.	925

Thomas Alva Edison

Date	Price
2004 2004 Uncirculated silver dollar and light bulb.	55.00

Lewis and Clark Bicentennial

Date	Price
2004 2004 Coin and pouch set.	65.00
2004 2004 coin and currency set: Uncirculated silver dollar, two 2005 nickels, replica 1901 $10 Bison note, silver plated peace medal, three stamps & two booklets.	58.00
2004 2004 Westward Journey Nickel series coin and medal set: Proof Sacagawea dollar, two 2005 proof nickels and silver plated peace medal.	40.00

Chief Justice John Marshall

Date	Price
2005 2005 Coin and Chronicles set: Uncirculated silver dollar, booklet and BEP intaglio portrait.	57.00

U.S. Marine Corps

Date	Price
2005 2005 Uncirculated silver dollar and stamp set.	63.00

Benjamin Franklin Tercentennary

Date	Price
2006 2006 Coin and Chronicles set: Uncirculated "Scientist" silver dollar, four stamps, Poor Richards Almanac and intaglio print.	49.00

Central High School Desegregation

Date	Price
2007 2007 Little Rock Dollar and medal set, KM#418	47.80

American Bald Eagle

Date	Price
2008 2008 Proof half dollar, dollar and $5 gold, KM438, KM439, KM440	490
2008 2008 Bald Eagle young collector's set; Half Dollar, KM#438	23.00

Louis Braille

Date	Price
2009 Braille Education set, KM#455	43.50

PROOF SETS

Proof coins are produced through a special process involving specially selected, highly polished planchets and dies. They usually receive two strikings from the coin press at increased pressure. The result is a coin with mirrorlike surfaces and, in recent years, a cameo effect on its raised design surfaces. Proof sets have been sold off and on by the U.S. Mint since 1858. Listings here are for sets from what is commonly called the modern era, since 1936. Values for earlier proofs are included in regular date listings. Sets were not offered in years not listed. Since 1968, proof coins have been produced at the San Francisco Mint; before that they were produced at the Philadelphia Mint. In 1942 the five-cent coin was struck in two compositions. Some proof sets for that year contain only one type (five-coin set); others contain both types. Two types of packaging were used in 1955 -- a box and a flat, plastic holder. The 1960 large-date and small-date sets are distinguished by the size of the date on the cent. Some 1968 sets are missing the mint mark on the dime, the result of an error in the preparation of an obverse die. The 1970 large-date and small-date sets are distinguished by the size of the date on the cent. Some 1970 sets are missing the mint mark on the dime, the result of an error in the preparation of an obverse die. Some 1971 sets are missing the mint mark on the five-cent piece, the result of an error in the preparation of an obverse die. The 1976 three-piece set contains the quarter, half dollar and dollar with the Bicentennial designs. The 1979 and 1981 Type II sets have clearer mint marks than the Type I sets for those years. Some 1983 sets are missing the mint mark on the dime, the result of an error in the preparation of an obverse die. Prestige sets contain the five regular-issue coins plus a commemorative silver dollar from that year. Sets issued prior to 1956 came in transparent envelopes stapled together in a small square box. In mid 1955 sets were changed to a flat clear cellophane envelope. In 1968 sets were changed to a clear hard plastic case as they still are currently issued.

SETS & ROLLS

Date	Sets Sold	Issue Price	Value
1936	3,837	1.89	6,975
1937	5,542	1.89	3,900
1938	8,045	1.89	1,765
1939	8,795	—	1,650
1940	11,246	—	1,375
1941	15,287	—	1,350
1942 6 coins	21,120	1.89	1,250
1942 5 coins	Inc. above	1.89	1,325
1950	51,386	2.10	545
1951	57,500	2.10	575
1952	81,980	2.10	230
1953	128,800	2.10	205
1954	233,300	2.10	110
1955 box	378,200	2.10	95.00
1955 flat pack	Inc. above	2.10	124
1956	669,384	2.10	57.00
1957	1,247,952	2.10	26.00
1958	875,652	2.10	34.50
1959	1,149,291	2.10	31.50
1960 large date	1,691,602	2.10	28.50
1960 small date	Inc. above	2.10	32.00
1961	3,028,244	2.10	29.00
1962	3,218,019	2.10	25.50
1964	3,950,762	2.10	30.00
1968S	3,041,509	5.00	6.05
1968S no mint mark dime	Inc. above	5.00	16,500
1969S	2,934,631	5.00	5.50
1970S large date	2,632,810	5.00	9.40
1970S small date	Inc. above	5.00	99.50
1970S no mint mark dime	Inc. above	5.00	825
1971S	3,224,138	5.00	3.05
1971S no mint mark nickel Est. 1,655	1,655	5.00	1,300
1972S	3,267,667	5.00	3.35
1973S	2,769,624	7.00	6.90
1974S	2,617,350	7.00	9.10
1975S	2,909,369	7.00	8.80
1975S no mint mark dime	Inc. above	7.00	275,000
1976S 3 coins	3,998,621	13.00	24.25
1976S	4,149,730	7.00	8.00
1977S	3,251,152	9.00	6.90
1978S	3,127,788	9.00	6.90
1979S Type I	3,677,175	9.00	8.25
1979S Type II	Inc. above	9.00	64.00
1980S	3,547,030	10.00	5.50
1981S Type I	4,063,083	11.00	5.50
1981S Type II	Inc. above	11.00	250
1982S	3,857,479	11.00	3.60
1983S	3,138,765	11.00	3.85
1983S Prestige Set	140,361	59.00	47.50
1983S no mint mark dime	Inc. above	11.00	680
1984S	2,748,430	11.00	4.10
1984S Prestige Set	316,680	59.00	27.50
1985S	3,362,821	11.00	3.30
1986S	2,411,180	11.00	5.50
1986S Prestige Set	599,317	48.50	27.50
1987S	3,972,233	11.00	4.40
1987S Prestige Set	435,495	45.00	26.00
1988S	3,031,287	11.00	5.25
1988S Prestige Set	231,661	45.00	28.00
1989S	3,009,107	11.00	3.85

Date	Sets Sold	Issue Price	Value
1989S Prestige Set	211,087	45.00	29.75
1990S	2,793,433	11.00	6.10
1990S no S 1¢	3,555	11.00	4,800
1990S Prestige Set	506,126	45.00	27.00
1990S Prestige Set, no S 1¢	Inc. above	45.00	5,100
1991S	2,610,833	11.00	3.85
1991S Prestige Set	256,954	59.00	39.50
1992S	2,675,618	12.00	4.40
1992S Prestige Set	183,285	59.00	40.75
1992S Silver	1,009,585	21.00	17.50
1992S Silver premier	308,055	37.00	21.75
1993S	2,337,819	12.50	4.70
1993S Prestige Set	224,045	57.00	45.50
1993S Silver	570,213	21.00	27.50
1993S Silver premier	191,140	37.00	32.00
1994S	2,308,701	13.00	4.15
1994S Prestige Set	175,893	57.00	44.00
1994S Silver	636,009	21.00	22.00
1994S Silver premier	149,320	37.50	31.00
1995S	2,010,384	12.50	11.00
1995S Prestige Set	107,112	57.00	72.00
1995S Silver	549,878	21.00	48.50
1995S Silver premier	130,107	37.50	52.00
1996S	2,085,191	16.00	6.60
1996S Prestige Set	55,000	57.00	310
1996S Silver	623,655	21.00	28.00
1996S Silver premier	151,366	37.50	29.00
1997S	1,975,000	12.50	9.40
1997S Prestige Set	80,000	57.00	55.00
1997S Silver	605,473	21.00	33.00
1997S Silver premier	136,205	37.50	33.50
1998S	2,078,494	12.50	9.65
1998S Silver	638,134	21.00	25.50
1998S Silver premier	240,658	26.50	31.00
1999S 9 piece	2,557,899	19.95	8.00
1999S 5 quarter set	1,169,958	13.95	3.35
1999S Silver	804,565	31.95	107
2000S 10 piece	3,097,442	19.95	5.00
2000S 5 quarter set	995,803	13.95	2.50
2000S Silver	965,421	31.95	32.75
2001S 10 piece	2,249,498	19.95	11.00
2001S 5 quarter set	774,800	13.95	5.00
2001S Silver	849,600	31.95	44.50
2002S 10 piece	2,319,766	19.95	6.10
2002S 5 quarter set	764,419	13.95	3.05
2002S Silver	892,229	31.95	30.50
2003S 10 piece	2,175,684	16.75	5.80
2003S 5 quarter set	1,225,507	13.95	2.25
2003S Silver	1,142,858	31.95	32.50
2004S 11 piece	1,804,396	22.95	9.10
2004S 5 quarter set	987,960	23.95	2.50
2004S Silver 11 piece	1,187,673	37.95	28.50
2004S Silver 5 quarter set	594,137	—	19.00
2005S American Legacy	—	—	77.50
2005S 11 piece	—	22.95	5.00
2005S 5 quarter set	—	15.95	2.25
2005S Silver 11 piece	—	37.95	31.50
2005S Silver 5 quarter set	—	23.95	18.75
2005S American Legacy	—	—	84.50
2006S 10 piece clad	—	22.95	8.25
2006S 5 quarter set	—	15.95	2.80
2006S Silver 10 piece	—	37.95	33.50
2006S Silver 5 quarter set	—	23.95	21.75
2006S American Legacy	—	—	77.50
2007S 5 quarter set	—	13.95	4.40
2007S Silver 5 quarter set	—	22.95	19.00
2007S 14 piece clad	—	—	15.75
2007S Silver 14 piece	—	—	37.00
2007S Presidental $ set	—	—	5.35
2007S American Legacy	—	—	93.50
2008S 5 quarter clad set	—	22.95	41.50
2008S 5 quarter silver set	—	—	20.80
2008 14 piece clad set	—	—	47.50
2008S 14 piece silver set	734,045	—	40.25
2008S Presidental $ set	—	—	11.75
2008S American Legacy	—	—	93.50
2009S 18 piece clad set	1,477,967	—	23.25
2009S 18 piece silver set	694,406	—	52.00
2009S Presidential $ set	627,925	—	10.50
2009S Lincoln Chronicle	—	—	112
2009S Lincoln 4 piece	—	—	10.00
2009S 6 quarter clad set	—	—	5.60
2009S 6 quarter silver set	—	—	22.00
2010S 14 piece clad set	1,103,950	—	45.50
2010S 14 piece silver set	583,912	—	50.00
2010S Presidential $ set	535,463	—	20.50
2010S 6 quarter set	276,335	—	15.25
2010S 6 quarter silver set	274,003	—	21.00
2011S 5 quarter silver set	147,005	—	28.00
2011S 14 piece silver set	572,247	—	72.00
2011S 5 quarter clad set	151,434	—	14.50
2011S Presidential $ set	299,161	—	28.25
2011S 14 piece clad set	1,095,318	—	38.50
2011S 6 quarter set	—	—	15.00
2012S 5 quarter silver set	—	—	35.25
2012S 14 piece silver set	—	—	212
2012S 6 quarter set	—	—	14.50
2012S 14 piece clad set	—	—	105
2012S Presidential $ set	—	—	72.00
2012 8 piece Limited Edition	—	—	225

UNCIRCULATED ROLLS

Listings are for rolls containing uncirculated coins. Large date and small date varieties for 1960 and 1970 apply to the one cent coins.

Date	Cents	Nickels	Dimes	Quarters	Halves
1934	585	3,500	2,350	1,650	2,350
1934D	2,650	4,350	2,950	9,000	—
1934S	—	—	—	—	—
1935	885	1,700	1,450	1,725	1,250
1935D	750	3,150	2,950	8,850	4,000
1935S	2,500	1,725	1,950	4,650	6,500
1936	285	1,450	885	1,300	1,750
1936D	400	1,450	1,700	—	2,750
1936S	885	1,800	1,675	6,250	3,500
1937	250	1,100	710	1,250	1,150
1937D	250	1,200	1,550	3,450	5,000
1937S	335	1,285	1,650	4,850	3,450
1938	665	535	1,100	3,100	1,850
1938D Buffalo	—	1,065	—	—	—
1938D	710	485	1,000	—	—
1938S	440	355	1,350	3,250	—
1939	180	160	630	1,040	1,250

SETS & ROLLS

SETS & ROLLS

1939D	535	3,850	610	1,875	1,975
1939S	265	2,750	1,900	3,200	2,350
1940	225	145	535	1,850	975
1940D	265	120	780	5,350	—
1940S	300	265	675	1,275	1,200
1941	170	215	430	475	750
1941D	335	330	710	2,750	1,200
1941S	360	295	535	2,450	3,000
1942	140	315	465	450	690
1942P	—	600	—	—	—
1942D	140	2,550	740	1,060	1,350
1942S	585	525	1,050	5,350	1,475
1943	60.00	275	470	365	725
1943D	170	210	610	2,000	1,775
1943S	310	325	650	2,100	1,365
1944	30.00	720	460	280	715
1944D	38.00	680	635	725	1,250
1944S	120	565	660	950	1,300
1945	125	375	410	325	730
1945D	110	315	500	1,000	1,000
1945S	80.00	270	525	575	950
1946	39.00	80.00	140	365	1,025
1946D	36.50	75.00	140	380	900
1946S	185	50.00	140	275	900
1947	220	58.00	215	735	1,000
1947D	46.50	72.00	275	385	1,000
1947S	39.00	72.00	210	415	—
1948	72.50	55.00	188	270	450
1948D	175	155	325	645	425
1948S	165	80.00	255	475	—
1949	180	330	1,200	2,350	1,300
1949D	125	215	550	1,285	1,475
1949S	140	138	2,350	—	2,250
1950	115	120	525	395	750
1950D	42.00	385	200	440	875
1950S	78.00	—	1,550	850	—
1951	165	230	140	435	390
1951D	26.50	285	140	325	800
1951S	60.00	265	690	1,350	750
1952	165	145	140	535	385
1952D	26.50	260	140	300	230
1952S	300	42.00	290	1,000	1,585
1953	42.00	24.50	140	635	490
1953D	22.50	17.00	140	280	280
1953S	35.00	39.00	140	280	850
1954	39.00	57.50	140	280	280
1954D	22.50	24.00	140	280	280
1954S	22.50	39.50	140	280	400
1955	24.50	19.00	140	280	300
1955D	19.00	7.00	170	280	—
1955S	27.50	—	140	—	—
1956	10.50	7.50	140	280	280
1956D	12.50	9.25	140	280	—
1957	10.00	12.50	140	280	280
1957D	9.50	4.75	140	280	280
1958	10.50	6.50	140	280	280
1958D	9.75	5.50	140	280	280
1959	2.50	5.00	140	280	280
1959D	2.10	5.25	140	280	280
1960 large date	1.60	4.40	140	280	280
1960 small date	220	—	—	—	—
1960D large date	1.60	5.00	140	280	280
1960D small date	2.85	—	—	—	—
1961	1.60	4.25	140	280	280
1961D	1.90	4.50	140	280	280
1962	1.65	5.25	140	280	280
1962D	1.65	5.50	140	280	280
1963	1.50	4.25	140	280	280
1963D	1.65	4.75	140	280	280
1964	1.50	3.50	140	280	280
1964D	1.60	3.50	140	280	280
1965	2.25	8.75	8.00	25.00	120
1966	3.75	6.00	10.00	53.00	120
1967	4.50	9.75	8.50	25.00	120
1968	1.75	—	8.50	25.00	—
1968D	1.70	6.00	9.50	33.00	120
1968S	1.90	6.25	—	—	—
1969	7.75	—	44.00	100	—

1969D	2.00	6.25	21.50	82.00	120
1969S	3.75	6.75	—	—	—
1970	2.10	—	8.00	26.00	—
1970D	2.10	4.00	7.75	16.00	235
1970S	3.00	4.50	—	—	—
1970S small date	2,650	—	—	—	—
1971	17.00	26.50	16.00	50.00	26.00
1971D	3.00	7.50	9.50	19.50	15.50
1971S	4.00	—	—	—	—
1972	2.00	6.50	11.00	23.00	32.00
1972D	6.00	5.75	10.00	21.50	23.00
1972S	4.75	—	—	—	—
1973	1.75	6.25	10.50	22.00	25.50
1973D	1.75	6.25	9.00	23.00	18.00
1973S	3.00	—	—	—	—
1974	1.75	4.50	7.50	18.50	15.00
1974D	1.75	5.75	7.75	17.50	21.00
1974S	3.50	—	—	—	—
1975	3.75	12.50	8.75	—	—
1975D	1.75	5.25	15.50	—	—
1976	1.75	13.50	21.00	17.50	18.00
1976D	2.50	11.00	18.00	17.50	15.50
1977	1.75	6.25	9.75	16.50	21.50
1977D	2.85	5.75	8.50	17.50	24.00
1978	3.00	4.50	7.25	16.00	32.00
1978D	10.00	5.00	8.00	16.50	46.50
1979	1.75	4.75	8.75	17.00	22.50
1979D	3.00	5.75	8.00	22.50	22.50
1980	1.75	4.25	8.00	16.50	20.50
1980D	2.50	4.50	7.50	16.50	20.50
1981	1.75	4.25	7.50	16.50	16.50
1981D	1.85	4.25	8.00	16.50	19.00
1982 Large date	2.50	—	—	—	—
1982 Small date	25.00	325	270	250	98.00
1982D Large date	4.00	54.00	66.00	165	80.00
1982 Copper plated Zinc	8.00	—	—	—	—
1982 Small date, copper plated zinc	3.00	—	—	—	—
1982D Large date, copper plated zinc	35.00	—	—	—	—
1982D Small date, copper plated zinc	2.50	—	—	—	—
1983	7.50	90.00	235	945	80.00
1983D	17.50	39.00	39.00	410	120
1984	5.50	22.00	8.50	17.00	26.00
1984D	14.50	6.50	21.00	29.00	37.00
1985	4.25	10.00	9.75	31.00	76.00
1985D	9.75	8.00	9.25	22.00	44.00
1986	20.00	8.75	25.00	85.00	75.00
1986D	31.50	24.50	22.50	210	90.00
1987	6.50	6.00	7.75	15.50	52.00
1987D	13.50	4.50	8.75	15.50	52.00
1988	6.25	5.50	9.75	39.00	75.00
1988D	12.50	9.00	9.25	22.50	45.00
1989	3.25	5.50	12.00	19.50	42.00
1989D	3.50	8.75	12.50	17.00	25.00
1990	4.00	11.50	14.50	20.00	39.00
1990D	5.85	13.75	10.00	25.00	52.00
1991	2.60	12.00	10.00	29.00	37.50
1991D	11.50	12.00	11.00	31.00	33.00
1992	3.00	46.00	8.00	42.00	21.00
1992D	5.00	9.00	8.00	27.50	50.00
1993	3.25	13.50	9.50	39.00	64.00
1993D	7.50	17.50	13.00	36.00	17.00
1994	2.00	7.75	12.00	42.00	15.00
1994D	2.00	8.00	12.00	47.50	20.00
1995	1.85	10.50	16.50	45.00	17.00
1995D	2.00	20.00	19.50	53.00	40.00
1996	2.25	8.75	11.00	19.00	17.00
1996D	2.85	8.25	11.50	27.50	19.00
1997	2.75	14.50	29.00	22.50	20.00
1997D	3.35	60.00	11.00	39.00	16.50
1998	2.00	13.75	9.75	17.00	20.00
1998D	1.85	14.00	12.00	18.00	16.50
1999P	2.35	5.50	8.50	—	20.00
1999D	2.25	6.25	8.50	—	19.00
2000P	2.50	6.25	7.75	—	15.00
2000D	1.75	4.75	7.00	—	17.00
2001P	3.75	4.75	7.75	—	16.50
2001D	2.00	6.50	7.25	—	16.00
2002P	2.00	4.00	7.25	—	20.00

SETS & ROLLS

2002D	3.25	4.10	7.25	—	20.00
2003P	3.35	7.50	7.00	—	22.50
2003D	2.00	3.50	7.00	—	19.50
2004P Peace Medal Nickel	1.75	6.75	7.00	—	30.00
2004D Peace Medal Nickel	2.50	7.00	7.00	—	30.00
2004P Keelboat Nickel	—	4.00	—	—	—
2004D Keelboat Nickel	—	3.50	—	—	—
2005P Bison Nickel	1.75	3.25	7.00	—	21.00
2005D Bison Nickel	2.75	3.25	7.00	—	21.00
2005P Ocean in view Nickel	—	3.25	—	—	—
2005D Ocean in view Nickel	—	3.25	—	—	—
2006P	2.75	3.25	8.50	—	29.00
2006D	1.75	3.25	8.50	—	29.00
2007P	1.75	3.50	8.00	—	21.00
2007D	1.75	3.50	7.75	—	21.00
2008P	1.75	3.75	8.00	—	24.50
2008D	1.75	3.75	7.50	—	25.50
2009P Log Cabin	2.00	23.00	13.50	—	18.50
2009D Log Cabin	2.15	13.50	13.50	—	18.50
2009P Log Splitter	1.75	—	—	—	—
2009D Log Splitter	1.75	—	—	—	—
2009P Professional	1.75	—	—	—	—
2009D Professional	1.75	—	—	—	—
2009P President	2.00	—	—	—	—
2009D President	2.00	—	—	—	—

50 STATE QUARTERS

Listings are for rolls containing uncirculated coins.

Date	Philadelphia	Denver
1999 Delaware	15.00	15.50
1999 Pennsylvania	16.00	16.50
1999 New Jersey	16.00	15.50
1999 Georgia	28.00	30.00
1999 Connecticut	26.00	27.00
2000 Massachusetts	14.00	15.00
2000 Maryland	14.00	15.50
2000 South Carolina	15.50	15.50
2000 New Hampshire	13.50	14.50
2000 Virginia	14.50	14.50
2001 New York	14.00	14.00
2001 North Carolina	14.50	15.00
2001 Rhode Island	14.00	15.50
2001 Vermont	14.50	14.50
2001 Kentucky	16.50	18.50
2002 Tennessee	30.00	39.50
2002 Ohio	21.50	21.50
2002 Louisiana	14.00	14.00
2002 Indiana	14.50	15.50
2002 Mississippi	16.50	16.50
2003 Illinois	39.00	45.00
2003 Alabama	17.00	18.50
2003 Maine	14.50	15.50
2003 Missouri	14.50	14.75
2003 Arkansas	14.50	15.50
2004 Michigan	13.75	14.50
2004 Florida	13.75	14.50
2004 Texas	14.00	15.00
2004 Iowa	14.00	14.50
2004 Wisconsin	15.50	16.50
2005 California	21.00	22.50
2005 Minnesota	17.50	17.50
2005 Oregon	13.75	13.75
2005 Kansas	13.75	14.50
2005 West Virginia	13.50	13.75
2006 Nevada	13.75	13.75
2006 Nebraska	13.75	14.00
2006 Colorado	13.75	14.00
2006 North Dakota	13.75	14.50
2006 South Dakota	13.75	13.75
2007 Montana	14.00	17.00
2007 Washington	18.00	18.75
2007 Idaho	15.50	15.50
2007 Wyoming	14.75	15.00
2007 Utah	15.00	14.50
2008 Oklahoma	13.75	13.75
2008 New Mexico	14.00	15.50
2008 Arizona	15.50	13.75
2008 Alaska	13.50	13.75
2008 Hawaii	13.50	13.50

COLONIAL COINAGE

North America was initially explored by the Vikings, but it was not until the age of Discovery, that active and expansive colonization began. The French, Spanish, Dutch, English and Portuguese were all involved in colonizing North, Central and South America.

The Spanish were strongest in Central and South America, taking that whole continent except for Brazil, which went to Portugal. Their expansion also spread into what became modern day Florida, Texas, and California.

The French settled in the Mississippi River Delta, from New Orleans northward to St. Louis, then east to the Ohio River basin, and west to the Rockies; they also progressed to the north, in the St. Lawrence River area in Canada; Quebec and Montreal being their principal cities.

The Dutch had a presence from the 1620's through 1664, mainly in the New York region, but lost that territory to the English, and never again gained a stronghold on the mainland during this period.

The English settled on the East Coast of the United States, from Georgia north to what later became Maine, and east of the Allegheny and Appalachian Mountains. To the north in Canada, they worked their way into Nova Scotia, Newfoundland, and north of the French in Quebec, Ontario, and with the explorers of the Hudson Bay Company, westward on the plains to the Pacific North West.

On the basis of the voyage of John Cabot to the North American mainland in 1497, England initially claimed the entire continent. The first permanent English settlement was established at Jamestown, Va., in 1607. France and Spain had also claimed extensive territory in North America, but at the end of the French and Indian Wars in 1763, England acquired all of the territory east of the Mississippi River, including east and west Florida. From 1776 to 1781, the States were governed by the Continental Congress. From 1781 to 1789, they were organized under the Articles of Confederation, during which period the individual States, formed from the former 13 British- American colonies; New York, New Jersey, New Hampshire, Massachusetts, Rhode Island, Connecticut, Pennsylvania, Delaware, Maryland, Virginia, North Carolina, South Carolina and Georgia, had the right to issue money.

While British and Spanish silver coins circulated freely in the American Colonies, several of the Colonies and later States did issue copper or silver coins. In addition, both merchant and political tokens, mainly in copper, were issued in several locations. The most popularly circulated, and now collected, of these Colonial and State issues are listed here.

The population of the colonies during this political phase of America's history (1781-1789) was about 3 million, most of whom lived on self-sufficient family farms. Fishing, lumbering and the production of grains for export were major economic endeavors. Rapid strides were also being made in industry and manufacturing by 1775, when the North American colonies were accounting for one- seventh of the world's production of raw iron.

Independence from Great Britain was attained with the American Revolution in 1776. The Constitution organized and governs the present United States. It was ratified on Nov. 21, 1788.

MONETARY SYSTEM

12 Pence = 1 Shilling   5 Shillings = 1 Crown   21 Shillings = 1 Guinea

MARYLAND

LORD BALTIMORE

PENNY (DENARIUM)

KM# 1 • Copper **Obv. Legend:** CAECILIVS Dns TERRAE MARIÆ

Date	G4	VG8	F12	VF20	XF40	MS60
(1659) 9 known	—	—	65,000	120,000	200,000	—

Note: Stack's Auction 5-04, Proof realized $241,500

4 PENCE (GROAT)

KM# 2 • Silver **Obv.** Large bust **Rev:** Large shield
Obv. Legend: CAECILIVS Dns TERRAE MARIÆ

Date	AG3	G4	VG8	F12	VF20	XF40	MS60
(1659)	1,250	1,950	3,500	6,250	13,500	22,000	—

KM# 3 • Silver **Obv.** Small bust **Rev:** Small shield
Obv. Legend: CAECILIVS Dns TERRAE MARIÆ

Date	AG3	G4	VG8	F12	VF20	XF40	MS60
(1659) unique	—	—	—	—	—	—	—

Note: Norweb $26,400

6 PENCE

KM# 4 • Silver **Obv.** Small bust **Obv. Legend:**
CAECILIVS Dns TERRAE MARIÆ **Note:** Known
in two other rare small-bust varieties and two rare
large-bust varieties.

Date	AG3	G4	VG8	F12	VF20	XF40	MS60
(1659)	850	1,400	2,400	5,000	9,500	15,000	—

SHILLING

KM# 6 • Silver **Obv. Legend:** CAECILIVS Dns
TERRAE MARIÆ **Note:** Varieties exist; one is very rare.

Date	AG3	G4	VG8	F12	VF20	XF40	MS60
(1659)	1,100	1,850	3,250	6,000	13,500	20,000	—

MASSACHUSETTS

NEW ENGLAND

3 PENCE

KM# 1 • Silver **Obv.** NE **Rev:** III

Date	AG3	G4	VG8	F12	VF20	XF40	MS60
(1652) Unique	—	—	—	—	—	—	—
Note: Massachusetts Historical Society specimen							

6 PENCE

KM# 2 • Silver **Obv.** NE **Rev:** VI

Date	G4	VG8	F12	VF20	XF40
(1652) 8 known	28,000	60,000	115,000	225,000	—
Note: Garrett $75,000					

SHILLING

KM# 3 • Silver **Obv.** NE **Rev:** XII

Date	AG3	G4	VG8	F12	VF20	XF40	MS60
(1652)	—	37,500	75,000	150,000	250,000	—	—

WILLOW TREE

3 PENCE

KM# 4 • Silver **Obv.** Willow tree

Date	AG3	G4	VG8	F12	VF20	XF40	MS60
1652 3 known	—	—	—	—	—	—	—

6 PENCE

KM# 5 • Silver **Obv.** Willow tree

Date	AG3	G4	VG8	F12	VF20	XF40
1652 14 known	9,500	18,500	30,000	60,000	135,000	225,000

SHILLING

KM# 6 • Silver **Obv.** Willow tree

Date	AG3	G4	VG8	F12	VF20	XF40
1652	10,000	20,000	35,000	85,000	165,000	250,000

COLONIAL COINAGE

OAK TREE

2 PENCE

KM# 7 • Silver **Obv.** Oak tree **Note:** Small 2 and large 2 varieites exist

Date	AG3	G4	VG8	F12	VF20	XF40	MS60
1662	—	500	900	2,000	3,850	6,500	15,000

3 PENCE

KM# 8 • Silver **Obv.** Oak tree **Note:** Two types of legends.

Date	AG3	G4	VG8	F12	VF20	XF40	MS60
1652	350	650	1,250	3,000	6,500	12,000	—

6 PENCE

KM# 9 • Silver **Obv.** Oak tree **Note:** Three types of legends.

Date	AG3	G4	VG8	F12	VF20	XF40	MS60
1652	400	900	1,350	3,500	8,000	17,500	35,000

SHILLING

KM# 10 • Silver **Obv.** Oak tree **Note:** Two types of legends.

Date	AG3	G4	VG8	F12	VF20	XF40	MS60
1652	375	750	1,250	3,000	6,000	11,500	27,500

PINE TREE

3 PENCE

KM# 11 • Silver **Obv.** Pine tree without berries

Date	AG3	G4	VG8	F12	VF20	XF40	MS60
1652	250	500	750	1,650	3,250	6,500	18,500

KM# 12 • Silver **Obv.** Pine tree with berries

Date	AG3	G4	VG8	F12	VF20	XF40	MS60
1652	250	500	750	1,650	3,500	6,750	19,500

6 PENCE

KM# 13 • Silver **Obv.** Pine tree without berries; "spiney tree"

Date	AG3	G4	VG8	F12	VF20	XF40	MS60
1652	400	700	1,400	2,000	4,000	7,000	22,000

KM# 14 • Silver **Obv.** Pine tree with berries

Date	AG3	G4	VG8	F12	VF20	XF40	MS60
1652	300	600	1,000	1,850	3,750	6,500	20,000

SHILLING

KM# 15 • Silver **Obv.** Pine tree **Note:** Large planchet. Many varieties exist; some are very rare.

Date	AG3	G4	VG8	F12	VF20	XF40	MS60
1652	375	700	1,100	2,200	4,500	7,750	22,500

KM# 16 • Silver **Obv.** Pine tree **Note:** Small planchet; large dies. All examples are thought to be contemporary fabrications.

Date	AG3	G4	VG8	F12	VF20	XF40	MS60
1652	—	—	—	—	—	—	—

COLONIAL COINAGE

KM# 17 • Silver **Obv.** Pine tree **Note:** Small planchet; small dies. Many varieties exist; some are very rare.

Date	AG3	G4	VG8	F12	VF20	XF40	MS60
1652	285	550	850	1,750	3,750	7,250	25,000

NEW JERSEY

ST. PATRICK OR MARK NEWBY

FARTHING

KM# 1 • Copper **Obv. Legend:** FLOREAT REX **Rev. Legend:** QUIESCAT PLEBS

Date	AG3	G4	VG8	F12	VF20	XF40	MS60
(1682)	70.00	125	285	775	2,750	6,500	—

Note: One very rare variety is known with reverse legend: QUIESAT PLEBS

KM# 1a • Silver **Obv. Legend:** FLOREAT REX **Rev. Legend:** QUIESCAT PLEBS

Date	AG3	G4	VG8	F12	VF20	XF40	MS60
(1682)	800	1,750	2,750	5,500	9,500	17,500	—

HALFPENNY

KM# 2 • Copper **Obv. Legend:** FLOREAT REX **Rev. Legend:** ECCE GREX

Date	AG3	G4	VG8	F12	VF20	XF40	MS60
(1682)	180	365	850	1,650	4,000	12,500	—

EARLY AMERICAN TOKENS

AMERICAN PLANTATIONS

1/24 REAL

KM# Tn5.1 • Tin **Obv. Legend:** ET HIB REX

Date	AG3	G4	VG8	F12	VF20	XF40	MS60
(1688)	125	200	300	450	850	2,000	—

KM# Tn5.2 • Tin **Obv.** Rider's head left of "B" in legend **Note:** Restrikes made in 1828 from two obverse dies.

Date	AG3	G4	VG8	F12	VF20	XF40	MS60
(1828)	75.00	110	175	275	500	1,000	—

KM# Tn5.3 • Tin **Rev:** Horizontal 4

Date	AG3	G4	VG8	F12	VF20	XF40	MS60
(1688)	275	400	900	1,750	4,250	6,750	—

KM# Tn5.4 • Tin **Obv. Legend:** ET HB REX

Date	AG3	G4	VG8	F12	VF20	XF40	MS60
(1688)	—	250	450	850	1,900	3,250	11,500

KM# Tn6 • Tin **Rev:** Arms of Scotland left, Ireland right

Date	AG3	G4	VG8	F12	VF20	XF40	MS60
(1688)	450	750	1,250	2,150	5,000	7,750	—

ELEPHANT

KM# Tn1.1 • 15.55 g., Copper **Note:** Thick planchet.

Date	AG3	G4	VG8	F12	VF20	XF40	MS60
(1664)	125	200	300	550	1,000	1,750	4,500

KM# Tn1.2 • Copper **Note:** Thin planchet.

Date	AG3	G4	VG8	F12	VF20	XF40	MS60
(1664)	175	300	500	900	3,000	5,500	12,500

COLONIAL COINAGE

KM# Tn2 • Copper **Rev:** Diagonals tie shield

Date	AG3	G4	VG8	F12	VF20	XF40	MS60
(1664)	250	450	650	2,250	7,000	11,500	35,000

KM# Tn3 • Copper **Rev:** Sword right side of shield

Date	AG3	G4	VG8	F12	VF20	XF40	MS60
(1664) 3 known	—	—	—	— 25,000	—	—	—

Note: Norweb $1,320

KM# Tn8.2 • Copper **Obv.** Elephant **Rev. Legend:**
GOD / PRESERVE / CAROLINA AND / THE LORDS
/ PROPRIETORS **Note:** O over E in Proprieters

Date	AG3	G4	VG8	F12	VF20	XF40	MS60
1694		1,300	2,500	4,500	7,000	12,500	20,000	—

Note: Norweb $17,600

GLOUCESTER

KM# Tn15 • Copper **Obv. Legend:** GLOVCESTER
• COVRTHOVSE • VIRGINIA / XII **Rev. Legend:**
RIGHAVLT • DAWSON • ANNO • DOM • 1714 •

Date	AG3	G4	VG8	F12	VF20	XF40	MS60
(1714) 2 known	—	—	—	—	—	—	—

Note: Garrett $36,000

KM# Tn4 • Copper **Rev. Legend:** LON DON

Date	AG3	G4	VG8	F12	VF20	XF40	MS60
(1684)	340	650	1,000	2,250	4,250	8,000	20,000

HIBERNIA-VOCE POPULI

FARTHING

KM# Tn21.1 • Copper **Note:** Large letters

Date	AG3	G4	VG8	F12	VF20	XF40	MS60
1760	145	250	375	750	1,850	3,500	11,500

KM# Tn21.2 • Copper **Note:** Small letters

Date	AG3	G4	VG8	F12	VF20	XF40	MS60
1760	—	—	3,250	6,500	25,000	60,000	—

Note: Norweb $5,940.

KM# Tn7 • Copper **Rev. Legend:** GOD / PRESERVE
/ NEW / ENGLAND

Date	G4	VG8	F12	VF20	XF40	MS60
(1694) 2 known	55,000	85,000	110,000	160,000	—	

Note: Norweb $25,300

KM# Tn8.1 • Copper **Obv.** Elephant **Rev. Legend:**
GOD / PRESERVE / CAROLINA AND / THE LORDS
/ PROPRIETORS

Date	AG3	G4	VG8	F12	VF20	XF40	MS60
(1694) 5 known	—	—	4,750	7,500	15,000	25,000	—

Note: Norweb $35,200

HALFPENNY

KM# Tn22 • Copper

Date	AG3	G4	VG8	F12	VF20	XF40	MS60
1700 Extremely rare	—	—	—	—	—	—	—

Note: Date is in error; ex-Roper $575. Norweb $577. Stack's Americana, VF, $2,900

1760	40.00	75.00	145	185	365	675	2,500
1760 P below bust	65.00	120	200	375	750	1,750	8,250
1760 P in front of bust	55.00	110	180	325	650	1,450	6,500
1760		50.00	80.00	135	195	425	775	3,500

Note: legend VOOE POPULI

HIGLEY OR GRANBY

KM# Tn16 • Copper **Obv. Legend:** CONNECTICVT **Rev. Legend:** THE VALVE OF THREE PENCE

Date	AG3	G4	VG8	F12	VF20	XF40	MS60
1737	—	10,000	18,500	40,000	85,000		

Note: Garrett $16,000

KM# Tn17 • Copper **Obv. Legend:** THE VALVE OF THREE PENCE **Rev. Legend:** I AM GOOD COPPER

Date	G4	VG8	F12	VF20	XF40	MS60
1737 2 known	11,000	20,000	42,500	87,500	—	—

Note: ex-Norweb $6,875

KM# Tn18.1 • Copper **Obv. Legend:** VALUE ME AS YOU PLEASE **Rev. Legend:** I AM GOOD COPPER

Date	AG3	G4	VG8	F12	VF20	XF40	MS60
1737	6,500	10,000	18,500	42,000	87,500	—	—

KM# Tn18.2 • Copper **Obv. Legend:** VALVE.ME.AS. YOU.PLEASE. **Rev. Legend:** I AM GOOD COPPER.

Date	G4	VG8	F12	VF20	XF40	MS60
1737 3 known	—	—	—	—	275,000	—

KM# Tn19 • Copper **Rev:** Broad axe

Date	G4	VG8	F12	VF20	XF40	MS60
(1737)	10,000	20,000	45,000	125,000	—	—

Note: Garrett $45,000

| 1739 5 known | | | | | | |

Note: Eliasberg $12,650. Oechsner $9,900. Steinberg (holed) $4,400.

KM# Tn20 • Copper **Rev:** J CUT MY WAY THROUGH **Obv. Legend:** THE WHEELE GOES ROUND

Date	G4	VG8	F12	VF20	XF40	MS60
(1737) unique	—	—	150,000	—	—	—

Note: Roper $60,500

NEW YORKE

KM# Tn9 • Brass **Obv. Legend:** NEW • YORK • IN • AMERICA

Date	AG3	G4	VG8	F12	VF20	XF40	MS60
1700		1,800	3,750	7,250	17,500	28,000	60,000	—

KM# Tn9a • White Metal **Obv. Legend:** NEW • YORK • IN • AMERICA

Date	G4	VG8	F12	VF20	XF40	MS60
1700 4 known	—	7,750	22,500	32,500	75,000	—

PITT
FARTHING

KM# Tn23 • Copper

Date	AG3	G4	VG8	F12	VF20	XF40	MS60
1766	—	3,750	7,000	11,500	28,500	42,500	—

COLONIAL COINAGE

HALFPENNY

KM# Tn24 • Copper

Date	AG3	G4	VG8	F12	VF20	XF40	MS60
1766	145	275	450	750	1,650	3,000	9,500

KM# Tn24a • Silver Plated Copper

Date	AG3	G4	VG8	F12	VF20	XF40	MS60
1766	—	—	—	—	2,250	5,000	12,500

ROYAL PATENT COINAGE

HIBERNIA

FARTHING

KM# 20 • Copper **Note:** Pattern.

Date	AG3	G4	VG8	F12	VF20	XF40	MS60
1722	135	250	400	600	1,250	3,250	11,500

KM# 24 • Copper **Obv.** 1722 obverse **Obv. Legend:** ...D:G:REX.

Date	AG3	G4	VG8	F12	VF20	XF40	MS60
1723	20.00	75.00	120	170	300	550	1,250

KM# 25 • Copper **Obv. Legend:** DEI • GRATIA • REX •

Date	AG3	G4	VG8	F12	VF20	XF40	MS60
1723	25.00	45.00	60.00	180	300	550	950
1724	—	90.00	125	225	700	1,750	4,250

KM# 25a • Silver

Date	AG3	G4	VG8	F12	VF20	XF40	MS60
1723	—	—	1,600	2,250	4,200	6,500	12,000

HALFPENNY

KM# 21 • Copper **Obv.** Bust right **Rev:** Harp left, head left **Obv. Legend:** GEORGIUS • DEI • GRATIA • REX • **Rev. Legend:** • HIBERNIA • 1722 •

Date	AG3	G4	VG8	F12	VF20	XF40	MS60
1722	50.00	90.00	110	160	325	700	1,750

KM# 22 • Copper **Obv.** Bust right **Rev:** Harp left, head right **Obv. Legend:** GEORGIVS D: G: REX **Rev. Legend:** • HIBERNIÆ • **Note:** "Rocks Reverse" pattern.

Date	AG3	G4	VG8	F12	VF20	XF40	MS60
1722	—	—	—	5,000	7,500	12,500	—

KM# 23.1 • Copper **Rev:** Harp right

Date	AG3	G4	VG8	F12	VF20	XF40	MS60
1722	35.00	60.00	80.00	120	285	600	1,750
Note: 850							
1723	20.00	35.00	45.00	75.00	190	285	850
1723/222	35.00	60.00	80.00	150	400	850	2,500
1724	25.00	50.00	90.00	160	400	850	2,500

KM# 23.2 • Copper **Obv.** DEII error in legend

Date	AG3	G4	VG8	F12	VF20	XF40	MS60
1722	75.00	125	160	325	750	1,500	3,000

KM# 26 • Copper **Rev:** Large head **Note:** Rare. Generally mint state only. Probably a pattern.

Date	AG3	G4	VG8	F12	VF20	XF40	MS60
1723	—	—	—	—	—	—	—

KM# 27 • Copper **Rev:** Continuous legend over head

Date	AG3	G4	VG8	F12	VF20	XF40	MS60
1724	45.00	80.00	150	300	900	1,850	4,500

COLONIAL COINAGE

252 • Royal Patent Coinage

ROSA AMERICANA

KM# 1 • Copper **Obv. Legend:** • D : G : REX •

Date	AG3	G4	VG8	F12	VF20	XF40	MS60
1722	20.00	50.00	140	250	525	1,050	4,000

KM# 2 • Copper **Obv.** Uncrowned rose **Obv. Legend:** ... • DEI • GRATIA • REX • **Note:** Several varieties exist.

Date	AG3	G4	VG8	F12	VF20	XF40	MS60
1722	50.00	90.00	135	250	450	975	3,500
1723		385	700	850	1,750	3,600	—	—

KM# 3 • Copper **Rev. Legend:** VTILE DVLCI

Date	AG3	G4	VG8	F12	VF20	XF40	MS60
1722		250	450	850	2,200	3,800	7,500	—

KM# 9 • Copper **Rev:** Crowned rose

Date	AG3	G4	VG8	F12	VF20	XF40	MS60
1723	45.00	85.00	110	165	425	1,100	4,500

PENNY

KM# 4 • Copper **Rev. Legend:** UTILE DULCI **Note:** Several varieties exist.

Date	AG3	G4	VG8	F12	VF20	XF40	MS60
1722	60.00	100	135	240	450	950	3,750

KM# 5 • Copper **Note:** Several varieties exist. Also known in two rare pattern types with long hair ribbons, one with V's for U's on the obverse.

Date	AG3	G4	VG8	F12	VF20	XF40	MS60
1722	18.00	35.00	150	275	750	1,450	6,000

KM# 10 • Copper **Note:** Several varieties exist.

Date	AG3	G4	VG8	F12	VF20	XF40	MS60
1723	40.00	75.00	110	175	425	900	3,600

KM# 12 • Copper **Note:** Pattern.

Date	AG3	G4	VG8	F12	VF20	XF40	MS60
1724 2 known	—	—	—	—	—	—	—

KM# 13 • Copper **Rev. Legend:** ROSA: SINE: SPINA •

Date	AG3	G4	VG8	F12	VF20	XF40	MS60
(1724) 5 known	—	—	—	—	—	—	—

Note: Stack's Bowers 5-05, VF ralized $21,850; Norweb $2,035

KM# 14 • Copper **Obv.** George II **Note:** Pattern.

Date	AG3	G4	VG8	F12	VF20	XF40	MS60
1727 2 known	—	—	—	—	—	—	—

COLONIAL COINAGE

2 PENCE

KM# 6 • Copper **Rev:** Motto in scroll

Date	AG3	G4	VG8	F12	VF20	XF40	MS60
(1722)	80.00	150	200	425	750	1,650	7,000

KM# 7 • Copper **Rev:** Motto without scroll

Date	AG3	G4	VG8	F12	VF20	XF40	MS60
(1722) 3 known	—	—	—	—	—	—	—

KM# 8.1 • Copper **Rev:** Dated **Obv. Legend:** ...REX •

Date	AG3	G4	VG8	F12	VF20	XF40	MS60
1722	70.00	125	175	275	750	1,500	5,500

KM# 8.2 • Copper **Obv. Legend:** ...REX

Date	AG3	G4	VG8	F12	VF20	XF40	MS60
1722	70.00	125	175	275	775	1,600	6,000

KM# 11 • Copper **Obv.** No stop after REX **Rev:** Stop after 1723 **Note:** Several varieties exist.

Date	AG3	G4	VG8	F12	VF20	XF40	MS60
1723	65.00	125	175	300	550	1,200	3,500

KM# 15 • Copper **Note:** Pattern. Two varieties exist; both extremely rare.

Date	AG3	G4	VG8	F12	VF20	XF40	MS60
1724	—	—	—	—	—	—	—

Note: Stack's Bowers 5-05 choice AU realized $25,300. Ex-Garrett $5,775. Stack's Americana, XF, $10,925

KM# 16 • Copper **Obv.** Bust left **Rev:** Crowned rose **Note:** Pattern.

Date	AG3	G4	VG8	F12	VF20	XF40	MS60
1733 4 known	—	—	—	—	—	—	—

Note: Stacks-Bowers 5-05, Gem Proof realized $63,250; Norweb $19,800

VIRGINIA HALFPENNY

KM# Tn25.1 • Copper **Rev:** Small 7s in date. **Note:** Struck on Irish halfpenny planchets.

Date	G4	VG8	F12	VF20	XF40	MS60	PF60
1773	—	—	—	—	—	—	22,000

KM# Tn25.2 • Copper **Rev:** Varieties with 7 or 8 strings in harp **Obv. Legend:** GEORGIVS •...

Date	AG3	G4	VG8	F12	VF20	XF40	MS60
1773	30.00	50.00	70.00	110	235	425	1,000

KM# Tn25.3 • Copper **Rev:** Varieties with 6, 7 or 8 strings in harp **Obv. Legend:** GEORGIVS...

Date	AG3	G4	VG8	F12	VF20	XF40	MS60
1773	35.00	60.00	75.00	135	275	525	1,350

COLONIAL COINAGE

KM# Tn25.4 • Copper **Rev:** 8 harp strings, dot on cross **Obv. Legend:** GEORGIVS

Date	AG3	G4	VG8	F12	VF20	XF40	MS60
1773	—	—	—	—	—	—	—

Note: ex-Steinberg $2,600

KM# Tn26 • Silver **Note:** So-called "shilling" silver proofs.

Date	AG3	G4	VG8	F12	VF20	XF40	MS60
1774 6 known	—	—	—	—	—	—	—

Note: Garrett $23,000

REVOLUTIONARY COINAGE

CONTINENTAL "DOLLAR"

KM# EA1 • Pewter **Obv. Legend:** CURRENCY.

Date	G4	VG8	F12	VF20	XF40	MS60
1776	7,500	9,350	12,000	21,000	32,500	70,000

KM# EA2 • Pewter **Obv. Legend:** CURRENCY, EG FECIT.

Date	G4	VG8	F12	VF20	XF40	MS60
1776	8,000	10,500	13,500	25,000	37,500	80,000

KM# EA2a • Silver **Obv. Legend:** CURRENCY, EG FECIT.

Date	G4	VG8	F12	VF20	XF40	MS60
1776 2 known	—	—	300,000	450,000	—	—

KM# EA3 • Pewter **Obv. Legend:** CURRENCEY

Date	G4	VG8	F12	VF20	XF40	MS60
1776 Rare	—	—	—	—	150,000	—

KM# EA4 • Pewter **Rev:** Floral cross. **Obv. Legend:** CURRENCY.

Date	G4	VG8	F12	VF20	XF40	MS60
1776 3 known	—	—	—	—	400,000	—

Note: Norweb $50,000. Johnson $25,300.

KM# EA5 • Pewter **Obv. Legend:** CURENCY.

Date	AG3	G4	VG8	F12	VF20	XF40	MS60
1776	—	7,500	9,500	12,000	22,500	33,500	75,000

KM# EA5a • Brass **Obv. Legend:** CURENCY. **Note:** Two varieties exist.

Date	G4	VG8	F12	VF20	XF40	MS60
1776	22,500	28,500	40,000	75,000	135,000	—

COLONIAL COINAGE

KM# EA5b • Silver **Obv. Legend:** CURENCY.

Date	G4	VG8	F12	VF20	XF40	MS60
1776 2 known	—	—	285,000	425,000	—	—

Note: Stacks-Bowers 5-2005, VF $345000; Romano $99,000.

STATE COINAGE

CONNECTICUT

KM# 1 • Copper **Obv.** Bust facing right.

Date	AG3	G4	VG8	F12	VF20	XF40	MS60
1785	35.00	55.00	90.00	200	650	1,750	—

KM# 2 • Copper **Obv.** African head.

Date	AG3	G4	VG8	F12	VF20	XF40	MS60
1785	55.00	85.00	150	600	1,500	3,800	—

KM# 3.1 • Copper **Obv.** Mailed bust facing left.

Date	AG3	G4	VG8	F12	VF20	XF40	MS60
1785	125	220	375	750	1,800	3,850	—
1786	30.00	50.00	90.00	175	500	1,400	—
1787	30.00	50.00	85.00	160	450	1,350	—
1788	30.00	50.00	80.00	160	435	1,150	—

KM# 3.3 • Copper **Obv.** Perfect date. **Rev. Legend:** IN DE ET.

Date	AG3	G4	VG8	F12	VF20	XF40	MS60
1787	50.00	80.00	125	350	750	1,850	—

KM# 3.4 • Copper **Obv. Legend:** CONNLC.

Date	AG3	G4	VG8	F12	VF20	XF40	MS60
1788	44.00	65.00	130	265	700	2,150	—

KM# 4 • Copper **Obv.** Small mailed bust facing left. **Rev. Legend:** ETLIB INDE.

Date	AG3	G4	VG8	F12	VF20	XF40	MS60
1786	45.00	90.00	175	400	1,100	2,750	—

KM# 5 • Copper **Obv.** Small mailed bust facing right. **Rev. Legend:** INDE ET LIB.

Date	AG3	G4	VG8	F12	VF20	XF40	MS60
1786	60.00	100	175	450	2,000	4,250	—

KM# 6 • Copper **Obv.** Large mailed bust facing right.

Date	AG3	G4	VG8	F12	VF20	XF40	MS60
1786	55.00	90.00	160	400	1,750	3,750	—

KM# 7 • Copper **Obv.** Hercules head.

Date	AG3	G4	VG8	F12	VF20	XF40	MS60
1786	60.00	110	220	600	2,500	5,800	—

KM# 8.1 • Copper **Obv.** Draped bust.

Date	AG3	G4	VG8	F12	VF20	XF40	MS60
1786	50.00	100	200	500	1,250	2,850	—

COLONIAL COINAGE

KM# 8.2 • Copper **Obv.** Draped bust. **Note:** Many varieties.

Date	AG3	G4	VG8	F12	VF20	XF40	MS60
1787	28.00	42.00	70.00	115	325	775	—

KM# 8.3 • Copper **Obv. Legend:** AUCIORI.

Date	AG3	G4	VG8	F12	VF20	XF40	MS60
1787	30.00	55.00	90.00	175	450	1,100	—

KM# 8.4 • Copper **Obv. Legend:** AUCTOPI.

Date	AG3	G4	VG8	F12	VF20	XF40	MS60
1787	35.00	65.00	110	200	650	1,650	—

KM# 8.5 • Copper **Obv. Legend:** AUCTOBI.

Date	AG3	G4	VG8	F12	VF20	XF40	MS60
1787	35.00	65.00	110	200	625	1,550	—

KM# 8.6 • Copper **Obv. Legend:** CONNFC.

Date	AG3	G4	VG8	F12	VF20	XF40	MS60
1787	32.00	60.00	95.00	185	525	1,100	—

KM# 8.7 • Copper **Obv. Legend:** CONNLC.

Date	AG3	G4	VG8	F12	VF20	XF40	MS60
1787	60.00	90.00	180	375	950	3,000	—

KM# 8.8 • Copper **Rev. Legend:** FNDE.

Date	AG3	G4	VG8	F12	VF20	XF40	MS60
1787	35.00	55.00	85.00	175	525	1,650	—

KM# 8.9 • Copper **Rev. Legend:** ETLIR.

Date	AG3	G4	VG8	F12	VF20	XF40	MS60
1787	32.00	50.00	75.00	160	475	1,275	—

KM# 8.10 • Copper **Rev. Legend:** ETIIB.

Date	AG3	G4	VG8	F12	VF20	XF40	MS60
1787	35.00	50.00	75.00	160	485	1,300	—

KM# 9 • Copper **Obv.** Small head. **Rev. Legend:** ETLIB INDE.

Date	AG3	G4	VG8	F12	VF20	XF40	MS60
1787	65.00	110	180	425	1,750	4,300	—

KM# 10 • Copper **Obv.** Small head. **Rev. Legend:** INDE ET LIB.

Date	AG3	G4	VG8	F12	VF20	XF40	MS60
1787	75.00	135	200	525	2,300	4,600	—

KM# 11 • Copper **Obv.** Medium bust. **Note:** Two reverse legend types exist.

Date	AG3	G4	VG8	F12	VF20	XF40	MS60
1787	60.00	90.00	150	400	1,750	3,450	—

KM# 12 • Copper **Obv.** Muttonhead" variety. **Note:** Extremely rare with legend INDE ET LIB.

Date	AG3	G4	VG8	F12	VF20	XF40	MS60
1787	60.00	90.00	175	575	2,550	5,200	—

KM# 13 • Copper **Obv.** Laughing head

Date	AG3	G4	VG8	F12	VF20	XF40	MS60
1787	35.00	60.00	120	240	650	1,800	—

KM# 14 • Copper **Obv.** Horned head

Date	AG3	G4	VG8	F12	VF20	XF40	MS60
1787	30.00	50.00	80.00	165	450	1,200	—

KM# 15 • Copper **Rev. Legend:** IND ET LIB

Date	AG3	G4	VG8	F12	VF20	XF40	MS60
1787/8	100	150	250	750	2,000	5,000	—
1787/1887	85.00	150	225	600	1,750	4,750	—

KM# 16 • Copper **Obv. Legend:** CONNECT. **Rev. Legend:** INDE ET LIB. **Note:** Two additional scarce reverse legend types exist.

Date	AG3	G4	VG8	F12	VF20	XF40	MS60
1787	35.00	50.00	120	240	675	1,750	—

COLONIAL COINAGE

KM# 20 • Copper Obv. Mailed bust facing right.

Date	AG3	G4	VG8	F12	VF20	XF40	MS60
1788	28.00	45.00	90.00	200	650	1,650	—

KM# 21 • Copper Obv. Small mailed bust facing right.

Date	AG3	G4	VG8	F12	VF20	XF40	MS60
1788	850	1,650	3,750	5,500	12,500	22,500	—

KM# 22.1 • Copper Obv. Draped bust facing left. **Rev. Legend:** INDE ET LIB.

Date	AG3	G4	VG8	F12	VF20	XF40	MS60
1788	49.50	75.00	140	325	750	1,800	—

KM# 22.2 • Copper Rev. Legend: INDLET LIB.

Date	AG3	G4	VG8	F12	VF20	XF40	MS60
1788	60.00	90.00	195	425	875	1,950	—

KM# 22.3 • Copper Obv. Legend: CONNEC. **Rev. Legend:** INDE ET LIB.

Date	AG3	G4	VG8	F12	VF20	XF40	MS60
1788	58.00	85.00	190	400	875	1,850	—

KM# 22.4 • Copper Obv. Legend: CONNEC. **Rev. Legend:** INDL ET LIB.

Date	AG3	G4	VG8	F12	VF20	XF40	MS60
1788	58.00	85.00	190	400	925	2,250	—

MASSACHUSETTS

HALFPENNY

KM# 17 • Copper

Date	AG3	G4	VG8	F12	VF20	XF40	MS60
1776 unique	—	—	—	200,000	—	—	—

Note: Garrett $40,000

PENNY

KM# 18 • Copper

Date	AG3	G4	VG8	F12	VF20	XF40	MS60
1776 unique	—	—	—	—	—	—	—

HALF CENT

KM# 19 • Copper Note: Varieties exist; some are rare.

Date	AG3	G4	VG8	F12	VF20	XF40	MS60
1787	60.00	90.00	140	225	575	1,000	3,250
1788	70.00	115	175	275	600	1,100	3,500

CENT

KM# 20.1 • Copper Rev: Arrows in right talon

Date	G4	VG8	F12	VF20	XF40	MS60
1787 7 known	9,000	22,500	45,000	—	—	350,000

Note: Ex-Bushnell-Brand $8,800. Garrett $5,500

COLONIAL COINAGE

KM# 20.2 • Copper **Rev:** Arrows in left talon

Date	AG3	G4	VG8	F12	VF20	XF40	MS60
1787	60.00	90.00	165	240	650	1,350	6,800

KM# 20.3 • Copper **Rev:** Horned eagle" die break

Date	AG3	G4	VG8	F12	VF20	XF40	MS60
1787	70.00	110	190	275	775	1,550	7,750

KM# 20.4 • Copper **Rev:** Without period after Massachusetts

Date	AG3	G4	VG8	F12	VF20	XF40	MS60
1788	70.00	105	190	260	675	1,600	6,250

KM# 20.5 • Copper **Rev:** Period after Massachusetts, normal S's

Date	AG3	G4	VG8	F12	VF20	XF40	MS60
1788	60.00	90.00	170	235	600	1,350	5,750

KM# 20.6 • Copper **Rev:** Period after Massachusetts, S's like 8's

Date	AG3	G4	VG8	F12	VF20	XF40	MS60
1788	50.00	75.00	135	200	575	1,250	5,400

NEW HAMPSHIRE

KM# 1 • Copper

Date	G4	VG8	F12	VF20	XF40	MS60
1776 extremely rare	—	—	—	—	—	—

Note: Garrett $13,000

NEW JERSEY

KM# 8 • Copper **Obv.** Date below draw bar.

Date	G4	VG8	F12	VF20	XF40	MS60
1786 extremely rare	—	—	75,000	135,000	—	—

Note: Garrett $52,000

KM# 9 • Copper **Obv.** Large horse head, date below plow, no coulter on plow.

Date	AG3	G4	VG8	F12	VF20	XF40	MS60
1786	450	850	1,500	3,000	8,500	22,500	—

KM# 10 • Copper **Rev:** Narrow shield, straight beam.

Date	AG3	G4	VG8	F12	VF20	XF40	MS60
1786	38.00	60.00	140	210	550	1,350	—

COLONIAL COINAGE

KM# 11.1 • Copper Rev: Wide shield, curved beam.
Note: Varieties exist.

Date	AG3	G4	VG8	F12	VF20	XF40	MS60
1786	45.00	75.00	150	225	600	2,000	—

KM# 11.2 • Copper Obv. Bridle variety (die break).
Note: Reverse varieties exist.

Date	AG3	G4	VG8	F12	VF20	XF40	MS60
1786	45.00	70.00	145	235	650	2,400	—

KM# 12.1 • Copper Rev: Plain shield. **Note:** Small planchet. Varieties exist.

Date	AG3	G4	VG8	F12	VF20	XF40	MS60
1787	35.00	55.00	110	200	500	950	—

KM# 12.2 • Copper Rev: Shield heavily outlined.
Note: Small planchet.

Date	AG3	G4	VG8	F12	VF20	XF40	MS60
1787	38.00	60.00	120	215	550	1,150	—

KM# 13 • Copper Obv. Serpent head.

Date	AG3	G4	VG8	F12	VF20	XF40	MS60
1787	55.00	85.00	200	375	1,650	4,200	—

KM# 14 • Copper Rev: Plain shield. **Note:** Large planchet. Varieties exist.

Date	AG3	G4	VG8	F12	VF20	XF40	MS60
1787	45.00	60.00	135	240	750	1,650	—

KM# 15 • Copper Rev. Legend: PLURIBS.

Date	AG3	G4	VG8	F12	VF20	XF40	MS60
1787	85.00	150	275	500	1,500	3,250	—

KM# 16 • Copper Obv. Horse's head facing right.
Note: Varieties exist.

Date	AG3	G4	VG8	F12	VF20	XF40	MS60
1788	42.00	60.00	115	190	700	1,275	—

KM# 17 • Copper Rev: Fox before legend. **Note:** Varieties exist.

Date	AG3	G4	VG8	F12	VF20	XF40	MS60
1788	75.00	145	295	575	2,150	4,750	—

KM# 18 • Copper Obv. Horse's head facing left.
Note: Varieties exist.

Date	AG3	G4	VG8	F12	VF20	XF40	MS60
1788	235	425	900	1,650	4,800	13,000	—

COLONIAL COINAGE

NEW YORK

KM# 1 • Copper Obv. Bust right **Obv. Legend:** NON VI VIRTUTE VICI. **Rev. Legend:** NEO-EBORACENSIS

Date	AG3	G4	VG8	F12	VF20	XF40	MS60
1786	3,250	5,000	7,500	15,000	35,000	—	—

KM# 2 • Copper Obv. Eagle on globe facing right. **Obv. Legend:** EXCELSIOR **Rev. Legend:** E. PLURIBUS UNUM

Date	AG3	G4	VG8	F12	VF20	XF40	MS60
1787	1,400	2,250	3,850	7,000	17,500	33,500	—

KM# 3 • Copper Obv. Eagle on globe facing left. **Obv. Legend:** EXCELSIOR **Rev. Legend:** E. PLURIBUS UNUM

Date	AG3	G4	VG8	F12	VF20	XF40	MS60
1787	1,250	2,000	3,500	6,500	16,500	32,000	—

KM# 4 • Copper Rev: Large eagle, arrows in right talon. **Obv. Legend:** EXCELSIOR **Rev. Legend:** E. PLURIBUS UNUM

Date	AG3	G4	VG8	F12	VF20	XF40	MS60
1787	—	4,500	9,000	16,500	35,000	55,000	—

Note: Norweb $18,700

KM# 5 • Copper Obv. George Clinton. **Rev. Legend:** EXCELSIOR

Date	AG3	G4	VG8	F12	VF20	XF40	MS60
1787	5,000	9,000	15,500	35,000	75,000	185,000	—

KM# 6 • Copper Obv. Indian. **Rev:** New York arms. **Obv. Legend:** LIBERNATUM LIBERTATEM DEFENDO **Rev. Legend:** EXCELSIOR

Date	AG3	G4	VG8	F12	VF20	XF40	MS60
1787	4,500	7,500	12,500	30,000	65,000	160,000	—

KM# 7 • Copper Obv. Indian. **Rev:** Eagle on globe. **Obv. Legend:** LIBERNATUS LIBERTATEM DEFENDO **Rev. Legend:** NEO EBORACUS EXCELSIOR

Date	AG3	G4	VG8	F12	VF20	XF40	MS60
1787	6,500	11,500	17,500	37,500	75,000	145,000	—

KM# 8 • Copper Obv. Indian. **Rev:** George III.

Date	AG3	G4	VG8	F12	VF20	XF40	MS60
1787 3 Known	—	—	75,000	—	—	—	—

MACHIN'S MILL

KM# 9 • Copper Obv. Bust right **Rev:** Figure seated right. **Obv. Legend:** NOVA EBORAC. **Rev. Legend:** VIRT.ET.LIB.

Date	AG3	G4	VG8	F12	VF20	XF40	MS60
1787	75.00	115	220	360	1,150	2,700	—

COLONIAL COINAGE

KM# 10 • Copper **Obv.** Bust right **Rev:** Figure
seated left. **Obv. Legend:** NOVA EBORAC **Rev.**
Legend: VIRT.ET.LIB.

Date	AG3	G4	VG8	F12	VF20	XF40	MS60
1787	60.00	100	200	325	825	1,750	—

NOVA EBORACS

KM# 11 • Copper **Obv.** Small head, star above. **Rev:**
Figure seated left **Obv. Legend:** NOVA EBORAC.
Rev. Legend: VIRT.ET.LIB.

Date	AG3	G4	VG8	F12	VF20	XF40	MS60
1787	2,450	3,750	5,500	9,500	22,500	—	—

KM# 12 • Copper **Obv.** Large head, two quatrefoils
left. **Rev:** Figure seated left **Obv. Legend:** NOVA
EBORAC. **Rev. Legend:** VIRT.ET.LIB.

Date	AG3	G4	VG8	F12	VF20	XF40	MS60
1787	350	600	1,250	2,500	7,750	15,000	—

KM# 13 • Copper **Note:** Crude, lightweight
imitations of the British Halfpenny were struck at
Machin's Mill in large quantities bearing the obverse
legends: GEORGIVS II REX, GEORGIVS III REX, and
GEORGIUS III REX, with the BRITANNIA reverse.

There are many different mulings. Plain crosses in
the shield of Britannia are noticeable on high grade
pieces, unlike common British made imitations,
which usually have outlined crosses in the shield.
Some Machin's Mill varieties are very rare.

Date	AG3	G4	VG8	F12	VF20	XF40	MS60
(1747-1788)	40.00	75.00	145	325	800	2,250	—

Note: Prices are for most common within date ranges.
Examples are dated: 1747, 1771, 1772, 1774, 1775,
1776, 1777, 1778, 1784, 1785, 1786, 1787 and 1788.
Other dates may exist

VERMONT

KM# 1 • Copper **Rev. Legend:** IMMUNE
COLUMBIA

Date	AG3	G4	VG8	F12	VF20	XF40	MS60
(1785)	4,000	6,000	9,500	13,750	35,000	—	—

KM# 2 • Copper **Obv.** Sun rising over field with
plow **Rev:** Eye, with rays and stars **Obv. Legend:**
VERMONTIS. RES. PUBLICA. **Rev. Legend:**
QUARTA. DECIMA. STELLA.

Date	AG3	G4	VG8	F12	VF20	XF40	MS60
1785	140	300	750	1,650	5,250	12,500	—

KM# 3 • Copper **Obv.** Sun rising over field with
plow **Rev:** Eye, with rays and stars **Obv. Legend:**
VERMONTS. RES. PUBLICA. **Rev. Legend:**
QUARTA. DECIMA. STELLA.

Date	AG3	G4	VG8	F12	VF20	XF40	MS60
1785	150	285	600	1,250	3,150	7,500	—

COLONIAL COINAGE

KM# 4 • Copper **Obv.** Sun rising over field with plow **Rev:** Eye, with pointed rays and stars **Obv. Legend:** VERMONTENSIUM.RES.PUBLICA **Rev. Legend:** QUARTA. DECIMA. STELLA.

Date	AG3	G4	VG8	F12	VF20	XF40	MS60
1786	140	235	425	775	2,000	4,400	—

KM# 5 • Copper **Obv.** Baby head. **Rev:** Seated figure left **Obv. Legend:** AUCTORI: VERMON: **Rev. Legend:** ET:LIB: INDE

Date	AG3	G4	VG8	F12	VF20	XF40	MS60
1786	200	350	650	1,750	4,800	12,500	—

KM# 6 • Copper **Obv.** Bust facing left. **Rev:** Seated figure left **Obv. Legend:** VERMON: AUCTORI: **Rev. Legend:** INDE ETLIB

Date	AG3	G4	VG8	F12	VF20	XF40
1786	115	175	350	825	2,850	5,000
1787 extremely rare	—	4,500	10,000	22,500	42,500	—

KM# 7 • Copper **Obv.** Bust facing right. **Rev:** Seated figure left **Obv. Legend:** VERMON. AUCTORI. **Rev. Legend:** INDE ETLIB **Note:** Varieties exist.

Date	AG3	G4	VG8	F12	VF20	XF40	MS60
1787	70.00	150	260	575	1,450	3,000	—

KM# 8 • Copper **Obv.** Bust right **Rev:** Seated figure left **Obv. Legend:** VERMON AUCTORI **Note:** Britannia mule.

Date	AG3	G4	VG8	F12	VF20	XF40	MS60
1787	65.00	120	170	300	700	1,650	—

KM# 9.1 • Copper **Obv.** Bust right **Rev:** Seated figure left **Obv. Legend:** VERMON. AUCTORI. **Rev. Legend:** INDE . ET LIB. **Note:** Varieties exist.

Date	AG3	G4	VG8	F12	VF20	XF40	MS60
1788	65.00	125	200	450	950	2,250	—

KM# 9.2 • Copper **Obv.** Bust right. "C" backward in AUCTORI. **Rev:** Seated figure left

Date	G4	VG8	F12	VF20	XF40
1788 extremely rare	4,200	7,000	17,500	38,000	—

Note: Stack's Americana, Fine, $9,775

KM# 10 • Copper **Obv.** Bust right **Rev:** Seated figure left **Rev. Legend:** .ET LIB. .INDE.

Date	AG3	G4	VG8	F12	VF20	XF40	MS60
1788	200	325	675	1,450	4,750	13,500	—

KM# 11 • Copper **Obv.** Bust right **Rev:** Seated figure left **Note:** George III Rex mule.

Date	AG3	G4	VG8	F12	VF20	XF40	MS60
1788	325	575	950	5,000	12,500	12,000	—

COLONIAL COINAGE

EARLY AMERICAN TOKENS

ALBANY CHURCH "PENNY"

KM# Tn54.1 • Copper **Obv.** Without "D" above church. **Note:** Uniface.

Date	G4	VG8	F12	VF20	XF40	MS60
(1790) 5 known	—	10,000	25,000	45,000	75,000	—

KM# Tn54.2 • Copper **Obv.** With "D" above church. **Note:** Uniface.

Date	AG3	G4	VG8	F12	VF20	XF40	MS60
(1790) rare	—	—	9,000	22,500	42,500	67,500	—

AUCTORI PLEBIS

KM# Tn50 • Copper **Obv.** Bust left **Rev:** Seated figure left **Obv. Legend:** AUCTORI: PLEBIS: **Rev. Legend:** INDEP: ET. LIBER

Date	AG3	G4	VG8	F12	VF20	XF40	MS60
1787	—	100	165	340	700	1,650	15,000

BAR "CENT"

KM# Tn49 • Copper **Obv.** USA monogram **Rev:** Horizontal bars

Date	AG3	G4	VG8	F12	VF20	XF40	MS60
(1785)	—	1,400	1,750	3,100	6,250	9,500	27,500

CASTORLAND "HALF DOLLAR"

KM# Tn87.1 • Silver **Obv. Legend:** FRANCO • AMERICANA / COLONIA **Edge:** Reeded.

Date	AG3	G4	VG8	F12	VF20	XF40	MS60
1796	—	—	—	—	—	4,500	13,500

KM# Tn87.1a • Copper **Obv. Legend:** FRANCO • AMERICANA / COLONIA **Edge:** Reeded.

Date	AG3	G4	VG8	F12	VF20	XF40	MS60
1796 3 known	—	—	—	—	—	3,500	—

KM# Tn87.1b • Brass **Obv. Legend:** FRANCO • AMERICANA / COLONIA **Edge:** Reeded

Date	AG3	G4	VG8	F12	VF20	XF40	MS60
1796	—	—	—	—	—	225	650

KM# Tn87.2 • Copper **Obv. Legend:** FRANCO • AMERICANA / COLONIA **Edge:** Plain. **Note:** Thin planchet.

Date	AG3	G4	VG8	F12	VF20	XF40	MS60
1796 unique	—	—	—	—	—	—	—

KM# Tn87.3 • Silver **Obv. Legend:** FRANCO • AMERICANA / COLONIA **Edge:** Reeded. **Note:** Thin planchet. Restrike.

Date	G4	VG8	F12	VF20	XF40	MS60	PF60
1796	—	—	—	—	—	1,250	—

KM# Tn87.3a • Copper **Obv. Legend:** FRANCO • AMERICANA / COLONIA **Edge:** Reeded. **Note:** Thin planchet. Restrike.

Date	G4	VG8	F12	VF20	XF40	MS60	PF60
1796	—	—	—	—	—	350	—

KM# Tn87.4 • Silver **Obv. Legend:** FRANCO • AMERICANA / COLONIA **Edge:** Lettered. **Edge Lettering:** ARGENT. **Note:** Thin planchet. Restrike.

Date	G4	VG8	F12	VF20	XF40	MS60	PF60
1796	—	—	—	—	—	150	—

KM# Tn87.5 • Copper **Obv. Legend:** FRANCO • AMERICANA / COLONIA **Edge:** Lettered. **Edge Lettering:** CUIVRE. **Note:** Thin planchet. Restrike.

Date	G4	VG8	F12	VF20	XF40	MS60	PF60
1796	—	—	—	—	—	100	—

COLONIAL COINAGE

CHALMERS
3 PENCE

KM# Tn45 • Silver

Date	AG3	G4	VG8	F12	VF20	XF40	MS60
1783	650	1,150	2,200	4,250	9,500	17,500	—

6 PENCE

KM# Tn46.1 • Silver **Rev:** Small date

Date	AG3	G4	VG8	F12	VF20	XF40	MS60
1783	900	1,650	2,750	6,750	16,500	28,500	—

KM# Tn46.2 • Silver **Rev:** Large date

Date	AG3	G4	VG8	F12	VF20	XF40	MS60
1783	775	1,450	2,250	6,000	14,500	27,500	—

SHILLING

KM# Tn47.1 • Silver **Rev:** Birds with long worm

Date	AG3	G4	VG8	F12	VF20	XF40	MS60
1783	450	775	1,350	2,750	6,000	11,500	—

KM# Tn47.2 • Silver **Rev:** Birds with short worm

Date	AG3	G4	VG8	F12	VF20	XF40	MS60
1783	450	750	1,250	2,350	5,500	11,000	—

KM# Tn48 • Silver **Rev:** Rings and stars

Date	G4	VG8	F12	VF20	XF40	MS60
1783 4 known	—	—	—	200,000	—	—
Note: Garrett $75,000						

COPPER COMPANY OF UPPER CANADA
HALFPENNY

KM# Tn86 • Copper **Obv. Legend:** BRITISH SETTLEMENT KENTUCKY

Date	G4	VG8	F12	VF20	XF40	MS60	PF60
1796	—	—	—	—	—	—	10,000

FRANKLIN PRESS

KM# Tn73 • Copper **Obv.** Printing press **Obv. Legend:** SIC ORITUR DOCTRINA SURGETQUE LIBERTAS **Rev. Inscription:** PAYABLE AT THE FRANKLIN PRESS LONDON **Edge:** Plain.

Date	AG3	G4	VG8	F12	VF20	XF40	MS60
1794	30.00	75.00	110	150	285	450	1,350

KENTUCKY TOKEN

KM# Tn70.1 • Copper **Obv. Legend:** UNANIMITY IS THE STRENGTH OF SOCIETY **Rev. Legend:** E. PLURIBUS UNUM **Edge:** Plain. **Note:** 1793 date is circa.

Date	AG3	G4	VG8	F12	VF20	XF40	MS60
(1793)	12.00	25.00	40.00	150	200	375	1,210

KM# Tn70.2 • Copper **Obv. Legend:** UNANIMITY IS THE STRENGTH OF SOCIETY **Rev. Legend:** E. PLURIBUS UNUM **Edge:** Engrailed.

Date	AG3	G4	VG8	F12	VF20	XF40	MS60
(1793)	35.00	75.00	125	200	500	950	3,400

KM# Tn70.3 • Copper **Obv. Legend:** UNANIMITY IS THE STRENGTH OF SOCIETY **Rev. Legend:** E. PLURIBUS UNUM **Edge:** Lettered. **Edge Lettering:** PAYABLE AT BEDWORTH.

Date	AG3	G4	VG8	F12	VF20	XF40	MS60
(1793) unique	—	—	—	—	—	1,980	—

COLONIAL COINAGE

KM# Tn70.4 • Copper **Obv. Legend:** UNANIMITY IS THE STRENGTH OF SOCIETY **Rev. Legend:** E. PLURIBUS UNUM **Edge:** Lettered. **Edge Lettering:** PAYABLE AT LANCASTER.

Date	AG3	G4	VG8	F12	VF20	XF40	MS60
(1793)	14.00	28.00	45.00	65.00	225	400	1,250

KM# Tn70.5 • Copper **Obv. Legend:** UNANIMITY IS THE STRENGTH OF SOCIETY **Rev. Legend:** E. PLURIBUS UNUM **Edge:** Lettered. **Edge Lettering:** PAYABLE AT I.FIELDING.

Date	AG3	G4	VG8	F12	VF20	XF40	MS60
(1793) unique	—	—	—	—	—	—	—

KM# Tn70.6 • Copper **Obv. Legend:** UNANIMITY IS THE STRENGTH OF SOCIETY **Rev. Legend:** E. PLURIBUS UNUM **Edge:** Lettered. **Edge Lettering:** PAYABLE AT W. PARKERS.

Date	AG3	G4	VG8	F12	VF20	XF40	MS60
(1793) unique	—	—	—	—	20,000	—	—

KM# Tn70.7 • Copper **Obv. Legend:** UNANIMITY IS THE STRENGTH OF SOCIETY **Rev. Legend:** E. PLURIBUS UNUM **Edge:** Ornamented branch with two leaves.

Date	AG3	G4	VG8	F12	VF20	XF40	MS60
(1793) unique	—	—	—	—	—	—	—

MOTT TOKEN

KM# Tn52.1 • Copper **Obv.** Clock **Rev:** Eagle with shield **Note:** Thin planchet.

Date	AG3	G4	VG8	F12	VF20	XF40	MS60
1789	50.00	80.00	150	300	550	1,200	1,750

KM# Tn52.2 • Copper **Obv.** Clock **Rev:** Eagle with shield **Note:** Thick planchet. Weight generally about 170 grams.

Date	AG3	G4	VG8	F12	VF20	XF40	MS60
1789	60.00	95.00	175	325	525	100	—

KM# Tn52.3 • Copper **Obv.** Clock **Rev:** Eagle with shield **Edge:** Fully engrailed. **Note:** Specimens struck with perfect dies are scarcer and generally command higher prices.

Date	AG3	G4	VG8	F12	VF20	XF40	MS60
1789	90.00	160	325	450	700	1,750	4,800

MYDDELTON TOKEN

KM# Tn85 • Copper **Obv. Legend:** BRITISH SETTLEMENT KENTUCKY **Rev. Legend:** PAYABLE BY P • P • P • MYDDELTON •

Date	G4	VG8	F12	VF20	XF40	MS60	PF60
1796	—	—	—	—	—	—	37,500

KM# Tn85a • Silver

Date	G4	VG8	F12	VF20	XF40	MS60	PF60
1796	—	—	—	—	—	—	28,000

NEW YORK THEATRE

KM# Tn90 • Copper **Obv.** Theater building **Rev:** Ships at sea, viewed from dock **Obv. Legend:** THE • THEATRE • AT • NEW • YORK • / AMERICA **Rev. Legend:** MAY • COMMERCE • FLOURISH **Note:** 1796 date is circa.

Date	AG3	G4	VG8	F12	VF20	XF40	MS60
1796	—	—	—	—	7,500	10,000	26,500

NORTH AMERICAN
HALFPENNY

KM# Tn30 • Copper **Obv.** Seated figure left, with harp **Rev:** Ship **Obv. Legend:** NORTH AMERICAN TOKEN **Rev. Legend:** COMMERCE

Date	AG3	G4	VG8	F12	VF20	XF40	MS60
1781	32.00	50.00	70.00	140	300	750	3,250

COLONIAL COINAGE

RHODE ISLAND SHIP

KM# Tn27a • Brass **Obv.** Without wreath below ship.

Date	AG3	G4	VG8	F12	VF20	XF40	MS60
1779	—	—	325	550	1,000	2,000	7,500

KM# Tn27b • Pewter **Obv.** Without wreath below ship.

Date	AG3	G4	VG8	F12	VF20	XF40	MS60
1779	—	—	—	—	5,000	8,500	18,500

KM# Tn28a • Brass **Obv.** Wreath below ship.

Date	AG3	G4	VG8	F12	VF20	XF40	MS60
1779	—	—	—	675	1,100	2,100	7,750

KM# Tn28b • Pewter **Obv.** Wreath below ship.

Date	AG3	G4	VG8	F12	VF20	XF40	MS60
1779	—	—	—	—	5,500	9,000	20,000

KM# Tn29 • Brass **Obv.** VLUGTENDE below ship

Date	AG3	G4	VG8	F12	VF20	XF40	MS60
1779 unique	—	—	—	—	35,000		—
Note: Garrett $16,000							

STANDISH BARRY

3 PENCE

KM# Tn55 • Silver **Obv.** Bust left **Rev:**

Denomination **Obv. Legend:** BALTIMORE • TOWN • JULY • 4 • 90 • **Rev. Legend:** STANDISH BARRY •

Date	AG3	G4	VG8	F12	VF20	XF40	MS60
1790	—	—	15,000	23,500	55,000	—	—

TALBOT, ALLUM & LEE
CENT

KM# Tn71.1 • Copper **Rev:** NEW YORK above ship **Edge:** Lettered. **Edge Lettering:** PAYABLE AT THE STORE OF

Date	AG3	G4	VG8	F12	VF20	XF40	MS60
1794	32.00	50.00	85.00	165	275	550	2,000

KM# Tn71.2 • Copper **Rev:** NEW YORK above ship **Edge:** Plain. **Note:** Size of ampersand varies on obverse and reverse dies.

Date	AG3	G4	VG8	F12	VF20	XF40	MS60
1794 4 known	—	—	—	—	10,000	24,000	—

KM# Tn72.1 • Copper **Rev:** Without NEW YORK above ship **Edge:** Lettered. **Edge Lettering:** PAYABLE AT THE STORE OF

Date	AG3	G4	VG8	F12	VF20	XF40	MS60
1794	200	375	600	1,250	3,750	7,500	22,000

KM# Tn72.2 • Copper **Edge:** Lettered. **Edge Lettering:** WE PROMISE TO PAY THE BEARER ONE CENT.

Date	AG3	G4	VG8	F12	VF20	XF40	MS60
1795	30.00	50.00	75.00	135	250	400	1,200

KM# Tn72.3 • Copper **Edge:** Lettered. **Edge Lettering:** CURRENT EVERYWHERE.

Date	AG3	G4	VG8	F12	VF20	XF40	MS60
1795 unique	—	—	—	—	—	—	—

KM# Tn72.4 • Copper **Edge:** Olive leaf.

Date	AG3	G4	VG8	F12	VF20	XF40	MS60
1795 unique	—	—	—	—	15,000		—
Note: Norweb $4,400							

COLONIAL COINAGE

KM# Tn72.5 • Copper **Edge:** Plain.

Date	VG8	F12	VF20	XF40	MS60
1795 Lettered edge; unique	—	—	15,000	—	

Note: Edge: Cambridge Bedford Huntington.X.X.; Norweb, $3,960

1795 plain edge; 2 known	—	—	—	—	—

WASHINGTON PIECES

KM# Tn35 • Copper **Obv. Legend:** GEORGIVS TRIUMPHO.

Date	AG3	G4	VG8	F12	VF20	XF40	MS60
1783	—	95.00	135	285	650	1,150	—

KM# Tn36 • Copper **Obv.** Large military bust.
Note: Varieties exist.

Date	AG3	G4	VG8	F12	VF20	XF40	MS60
1783	—	—	50.00	90.00	185	450	2,600

KM# Tn37.1 • Copper **Obv.** Small military bust.
Edge: Plain.

Date	AG3	G4	VG8	F12	VF20	XF40	MS60
1783	—	—	70.00	95.00	220	525	3,800

Note: One proof example is known. Value: $25,000

KM# Tn37.2 • Copper **Obv.** Small military bust.
Edge: Engrailed.

Date	AG3	G4	VG8	F12	VF20	XF40	MS60
1783	—	75.00	110	150	300	750	4,250

KM# Tn38.1 • Copper **Obv.** Draped bust, no button on drapery.

Date	AG3	G4	VG8	F12	VF20	XF40	MS60
1783	—	40.00	60.00	95.00	185	400	2,250

KM# Tn38.2 • Copper **Obv.** Draped bust, button on drapery.

Date	AG3	G4	VG8	F12	VF20	XF40	MS60
1783	—	85.00	110	150	325	625	4,500

KM# Tn38.4 • Copper **Edge:** Engrailed. **Note:** Restrike.

Date	G4	VG8	F12	VF20	XF40	MS60	PF60
1783	—	—	—	—	—	—	800

KM# Tn38.4a • Copper **Note:** Bronzed. Restrike.

Date	G4	VG8	F12	VF20	XF40	MS60	PF60
1783	—	—	—	—	—	—	—

KM# Tn83.3 • Copper **Obv.** Large modern lettering. **Edge:** Plain. **Note:** Restrike.

Date	G4	VG8	F12	VF20	XF40	MS60	PF60
1783	—	—	—	—	—	—	950

KM# Tn83.4b • Silver **Note:** Restrike.

Date	G4	VG8	F12	VF20	XF40	MS60	PF60
1783	—	—	—	—	—	—	1,750

KM# Tn83.4c • Gold AGW **Note:** Restrike.

Date	AG3	G4	VG8	F12	VF20	XF40	MS60
1783 2 known	—	—	—	—	—	—	—

COLONIAL COINAGE

KM# Tn60.1 • Copper **Obv. Legend:**
WASHINGTON PRESIDENT. **Edge:** Plain.

Date	AG3	G4	VG8	F12	VF20	XF40	MS60
1792		850	1,450	3,000	7,500	18,500	—	—

Note: Steinberg $12,650. Garrett $15,500.

KM# Tn60.2 • Copper **Obv. Legend:**
WASHINGTON PRESIDENT. **Edge:** Lettered. **Edge
Lettering:** UNITED STATES OF AMERICA.

Date	AG3	G4	VG8	F12	VF20	XF40	MS60
1792	—	—	—	—	—	—	—

KM# Tn61.1 • Copper **Obv. Legend:** BORN
VIRGINIA. **Note:** Varieties exist.

Date	AG3	G4	VG8	F12	VF20	XF40	MS60
(1792)		500	1,000	2,000	4,000	7,500	12,000	—

KM# Tn61.1a • Silver **Edge:** Plain.

Date	G4	VG8	F12	VF20	XF40	MS60
(1792) 4 known	—	—	—	200,000	—	—

Note: Roper $16,500

KM# Tn61.2 • Silver **Edge Lettering:** UNITED
STATES OF AMERICA •

Date	G4	VG8	F12	VF20	XF40	MS60
(1792) 2 known	—	—	—	—	—	—

KM# Tn62 • Silver **Rev:** Heraldic eagle. 1792 half
dollar. **Note:** Mule.

Date	AG3	G4	VG8	F12	VF20	XF40	MS60
(1792) 3 known	—	—	—	—	50,000	75,000	—

KM# Tn77.1 • Copper **Obv. Legend:** LIBERTY AND
SECURITY. **Edge:** Lettered. **Note:** "Penny."

Date	AG3	G4	VG8	F12	VF20	XF40	MS60
(1795)	70.00	110	165	300	500	850	3,500

KM# Tn77.2 • Copper **Edge:** Plain. **Note:** "Penny."

Date	G4	VG8	F12	VF20	XF40	MS60
(1795) extremely rare	—	—	—	—	—	—

KM# Tn77.3 • Copper **Note:** "Penny." Engine-
turned borders.

Date	G4	VG8	F12	VF20	XF40	MS60
(1795) 12 known	275	450	650	1,250	2,400	7,500

KM# Tn78 • Copper **Note:** Similar to "Halfpenny"
with date on reverse.

Date	AG3	G4	VG8	F12	VF20	XF40	MS60
1795 very rare	—	—	—	—	—	—	—

Note: Roper $6,600

HALFPENNY

KM# Tn56 • Copper **Obv. Legend:** LIVERPOOL
HALFPENNY

Date	AG3	G4	VG8	F12	VF20	XF40	MS60
1791	40.00	70.00	1,000	125	300	550	3,250

COLONIAL COINAGE

KM# Tn66.1 • Copper **Rev:** Ship **Edge:** Lettered.

Date	AG3	G4	VG8	F12	VF20	XF40	MS60
1793	25.00	45.00	85.00	225	450	825	3,500

KM# Tn66.2 • Copper **Rev:** Ship **Edge:** Plain.

Date	AG3	G4	VG8	F12	VF20	XF40	MS60
1793 5 known	—	—	—	—	15,000	—	—

KM# Tn75.1 • Copper **Obv.** Large coat buttons **Rev:** Grate **Edge:** Reeded.

Date	AG3	G4	VG8	F12	VF20	XF40	MS60
1795	—	—	70.00	110	200	400	900

KM# Tn75.2 • Copper **Rev:** Grate **Edge:** Lettered.

Date	AG3	G4	VG8	F12	VF20	XF40	MS60
1795	90.00	140	210	275	400	800	2,800

KM# Tn75.3 • Copper **Obv.** Small coat buttons **Rev:** Grate **Edge:** Reeded.

Date	AG3	G4	VG8	F12	VF20	XF40	MS60
1795	50.00	75.00	120	190	275	585	2,650

KM# Tn76.1 • Copper **Obv. Legend:** LIBERTY AND SECURITY. **Edge:** Plain.

Date	AG3	G4	VG8	F12	VF20	XF40	MS60
1795	18.00	35.00	60.00	160	350	700	3,250

KM# Tn76.2 • Copper **Edge:** Lettered. **Edge Lettering:** PAYABLE AT LONDON ...

Date	AG3	G4	VG8	F12	VF20	XF40	MS60
1795	40.00	65.00	90.00	140	300	650	3,000

KM# Tn76.3 • Copper **Edge:** Lettered. **Edge Lettering:** BIRMINGHAM ...

Date	AG3	G4	VG8	F12	VF20	XF40	MS60
1795	55.00	85.00	125	175	350	800	3,600

KM# Tn76.4 • Copper **Edge:** Lettered. **Edge Lettering:** AN ASYLUM ...

Date	AG3	G4	VG8	F12	VF20	XF40	MS60
1795	18.00	35.00	60.00	275	600	1,600	6,500

KM# Tn76.5 • Copper **Edge:** Lettered. **Edge Lettering:** PAYABLE AT LIVERPOOL ...

Date	AG3	G4	VG8	F12	VF20	XF40	MS60
1795 unique	—	—	—	—	—	—	—

KM# Tn76.6 • Copper **Edge:** Lettered. **Edge Lettering:** PAYABLE AT LONDON-LIVERPOOL.

Date	AG3	G4	VG8	F12	VF20	XF40	MS60
1795 unique	—	—	—	—	—	—	—

KM# Tn81.1 • Copper **Rev. Legend:** NORTH WALES **Edge:** Plain.

Date	AG3	G4	VG8	F12	VF20	XF40	MS60
(ca.1795)	60.00	110	175	265	625	1,750	—

KM# Tn81.2 • Copper **Rev. Legend:** NORTH WALES **Edge:** Lettered.

Date	AG3	G4	VG8	F12	VF20	XF40	MS60
(1795)	350	550	1,150	1,750	5,500	9,500	—

KM# Tn82 • Copper **Rev:** Four stars at bottom **Rev. Legend:** NORTH WALES

Date	AG3	G4	VG8	F12	VF20	XF40	MS60
(1795)	1,250	2,250	4,750	7,750	21,500	—	—

COLONIAL COINAGE

CENT

KM# Tn39 • Copper **Obv.** Draped Bust left
Rev: Denomination in wreath **Obv. Legend:**
WASHINGTON & INDEPENDENCE **Rev. Legend:**
UNITY STATES OF AMERICA

Date	AG3	G4	VG8	F12	VF20	XF40	MS60
1783	30.00	50.00	70.00	10.00	265	550	2,250

KM# Tn40 • Copper **Note:** Double head.

Date	AG3	G4	VG8	F12	VF20	XF40	MS60
(1783)	25.00	45.00	60.00	95.00	250	500	2,750

KM# Tn41 • Copper **Obv.** Ugly head. **Note:** 3
known in copper, 1 in white metal.

Date	AG3	G4	VG8	F12	VF20	XF40	MS60
1784	—	120,000	—	—	—	—	—
Note: Roper $14,850							

KM# Tn57 • Copper **Obv.** Military bust left
Rev: Small eagle **Obv. Legend:** WASHINGTON
PRESIDENT.

Date	AG3	G4	VG8	F12	VF20	XF40	MS60
1791	—	—	350	500	725	1,000	4,250

KM# Tn58 • Copper **Obv.** Military bust left
Rev: Large eagle **Obv. Legend:** WASHINGTON
PRESIDENT

Date	AG3	G4	VG8	F12	VF20	XF40	MS60
1791	—	200	325	485	650	900	3,200

KM# Tn65 • Copper **Obv.** Roman" head **Obv.**
Legend: WASHINGTON PRESIDENT.

Date	AG3	G4	VG8	F12	VF20	XF40	MS60
1792	—	—	—	—	—	—	—

HALF DOLLAR

KM# Tn59.1 • Copper **Edge Lettering:** UNITED
STATES OF AMERICA

Date	AG3	G4	VG8	F12	VF20	XF40	MS60
1792 2 known	—	—	—	—	—	75,000	—
Note: Roper $2,860. Benson, EF, $48,300							

KM# Tn59.1a • Silver **Edge Lettering:** UNITED
STATES OF AMERICA

Date	AG3	G4	VG8	F12	VF20	XF40	MS60
1792 rare	—	—	—	—	40,000	65,000	—
Note: Roper $35,200							

KM# Tn59.1b • Gold AGW **Edge Lettering:**
UNITED STATES OF AMERICA

Date	AG3	G4	VG8	F12	VF20	XF40	MS60
1792 unique	—	—	—	—	—	—	—

KM# Tn59.2 • Copper **Edge:** Plain.

Date	G4	VG8	F12	VF20	XF40	MS60
1792 3 known	—	—	—	125,000	200,000	—

KM# Tn59.2a • Silver **Edge:** Plain.

Date	AG3	G4	VG8	F12	VF20	XF40	MS60
1792 rare	—	—	—	—	—	—	—

COLONIAL COINAGE

KM# Tn63.1 • Silver **Rev:** Small eagle **Edge:** Plain.

Date	AG3	G4	VG8	F12	VF20	XF40	MS60
1792	—	—	—	—	200,000	300,000	—

KM# Tn63.1a • Copper **Edge:** Plain.

Date	AG3	G4	VG8	F12	VF20	XF40	MS60
1792	—	4,000	6,500	12,500	32,000	65,000	—

Note: Garrett $32,000

KM# Tn63.2 • Silver **Edge:** Ornamented, circles and squares.

Date	G4	VG8	F12	VF20	XF40	MS60
1792 5 known	—	—	—	100,000	175,000	400,000

KM# Tn63.3 • Silver **Edge:** Two olive leaves.

Date	AG3	G4	VG8	F12	VF20	XF40	MS60
1792 unique	—	—	—	—	—	—	—

KM# Tn64 • Silver **Rev:** Large heraldic eagle

Date	G4	VG8	F12	VF20	XF40	MS60
1792 unique	—	—	—	100,000	—	—

Note: Garrett $16,500

EARLY AMERICAN PATTERNS

NOVA CONSTELLATIO

KM# EA6.1 • Copper **Obv.** Pointed rays **Rev:** Small "U•S **Obv. Legend:** NOVA • CONSTELLATIO •

Date	AG3	G4	VG8	F12	VF20	XF40	MS60
1783	50.00	70.00	100	225	440	950	3,750

KM# EA6.2 • Copper **Obv.** Pointed rays **Rev:** Large "US **Obv. Legend:** NOVA • CONSTELLATIO •

Date	AG3	G4	VG8	F12	VF20	XF40	MS60
1783	55.00	75.00	110	250	600	1,400	7,000

KM# EA7 • Copper **Obv.** Blunt rays **Obv. Legend:** NOVA • CONSTELLATIO •

Date	AG3	G4	VG8	F12	VF20	XF40	MS60
1783	50.00	75.00	110	250	575	1,350	5,000

KM# EA8 • Copper **Obv.** Blunt rays **Obv. Legend:** NOVA • CONSTELLATIO •

Date	AG3	G4	VG8	F12	VF20	XF40	MS60
1785	50.00	75.00	110	260	650	1,550	6,500

KM# EA9 • Copper **Obv.** Pointed rays **Obv. Legend:** NOVA • CONSTELLATIO •

Date	AG3	G4	VG8	F12	VF20	XF40	MS60
1785	—	—	100	225	450	1,000	3,600

KM# EA10 • Copper **Note:** Contemporary circulating counterfeit. Similar to previously listed coin.

Date	G4	VG8	F12	VF20	XF40	MS60
1786 extremely rare	—	—	—	—	—	—

COLONIAL COINAGE

5 UNITS

KM# EA12 • Copper **Obv.** Eye, with pointed rays & stars **Obv. Legend:** NOVA CONSTELLATIO **Rev. Legend:** • LIBERTAS • JUSTITIA •

Date	AG3	G4	VG8	F12	VF20	XF40	MS60
1783 unique	—	—	—	—	—	—	—

100 (BIT)

KM# EA13.1 • Silver **Obv.** Eye, with pointed rays & stars **Obv. Legend:** NOVA CONSTELLATIO **Rev. Legend:** • LIBERTAS • JUSTITIA • **Edge:** Leaf.

Date	AG3	G4	VG8	F12	VF20	XF40	MS60
1783 2 known	—	—	—	—	—	—	—

Note: Garrett $97,500. Stack's auction, May 1991, $72,500

KM# EA13.2 • Silver **Obv.** Eye, with pointed rays & stars **Obv. Legend:** NOVA CONSTELLATIO **Rev. Legend:** • LIBERTAS • JUSTITIA • **Edge:** Plain

Date	AG3	G4	VG8	F12	VF20	XF40	MS60
1783 unique	—	—	—	—	—	—	—

500 (QUINT)

KM# EA14 • Silver **Obv.** Eye with pointed rays & stars **Obv. Legend:** NOVA CONSTELLATIO **Rev. Legend:** • LIBERTAS • JUSTITIA •

Date	AG3	G4	VG8	F12	VF20	XF40	MS60
1783 unique	—	—	—	—	250,000	—	—

Note: Garrett $165,000

KM# EA15 • Silver **Obv.** Eye, with rays & stars, no legend **Rev. Legend:** • LIBERTAS • JUSTITIA •

Date	G4	VG8	F12	VF20	XF40	MS60
1783 unique	—	—	—	75,000	—	—

Note: Garrett $55,000

1000 (MARK)

KM# EA16 • Silver **Obv.** Eye, with pointed rays & stars **Obv. Legend:** NOVA CONSTELLATIO **Rev. Legend:** • LIBERTAS • JUSTITIA •

Date	G4	VG8	F12	VF20	XF40	MS60
1783 unique	—	—	—	—	350,000	—

Note: Garrett $190,000

IMMUNE COLUMBIA

KM# EA17 • Copper **Rev:** Eye, with pointed rays & stars **Obv. Legend:** IMMUNE COLUMBIA. **Rev. Legend:** NOVA • CONSTELLATIO

Date	AG3	G4	VG8	F12	VF20	XF40	MS60
1785	—	—	—	—	25,000	45,000	—

KM# EA17a • Silver **Rev:** Eye, with pointed rays & stars **Obv. Legend:** IMMUNE COLUMBIA • **Rev. Legend:** NOVA CONSTELLATIO

Date	AG3	G4	VG8	F12	VF20	XF40	MS60
1785	—	—	—	—	45,000	75,000	—

KM# EA18 • Copper **Rev:** Eye, with pointed rays & stars. Extra star in reverse legend **Obv. Legend:** IMMUNE COLUMBIA • **Rev. Legend:** NOVA • CONSTELLATIO *

Date	AG3	G4	VG8	F12	VF20	XF40	MS60
1785	—	—	—	—	25,000	45,000	—

Note: Caldwell $4,675

KM# EA19 • Copper **Rev:** Blunt rays **Obv. Legend:** IMMUNE COLUMBIA • **Rev. Legend:** NOVA CONSTELATIO

Date	G4	VG8	F12	VF20	XF40	MS60
1785 2 known	—	—	—	—	120,000	—

Note: Norweb $22,000

KM# EA19a • Gold AGW **Rev:** Blunt rays **Obv. Legend:** IMMUNE COLUMBIA • **Rev. Legend:** NOVA CONSTELATIO •

Date	AG3	G4	VG8	F12	VF20	XF40	MS60
1785 Unique	—	—	—	—	—	—	—

Note: In the Smithsonian Collection

KM# EA20 • Copper **Obv.** George III **Obv. Legend:** GEORGIVS III • REX • **Rev. Legend:** IMMUNE COLUMBIA •

Date	AG3	G4	VG8	F12	VF20	XF40	MS60
1785	3,500	5,250	7,750	11,500	22,500	—	—

KM# EA21 • Copper **Obv.** Head right **Obv. Legend:** VERMON AUCTORI **Rev. Legend:** IMMUNE COLUMBIA •

Date	AG3	G4	VG8	F12	VF20	XF40	MS60
1785	—	6,000	9,500	12,500	35,000	—	—

KM# EA24 • Copper **Obv.** Washington **Rev:** Stars in rayed circle **Rev. Legend:** • CONFEDERATIO •

Date	AG3	G4	VG8	F12	VF20	XF40	MS60
1786 3 known	—	—	—	—	60,000	—	—

Note: Garrett $50,000. Steinberg $12,650

KM# EA25 • Copper **Obv.** Eagle, raw shield **Rev:** Shield **Obv. Legend:** * E • PLURIBUS UNUM • **Rev. Legend:** * E * PLURIBUS * UNUM *

Date	AG3	G4	VG8	F12	VF20	XF40	MS60
1786 unique	—	—	—	—	—	—	—

Note: Garrett $37,500

KM# EA26 • Copper **Obv.** Washington **Rev:** Eagle **Obv. Legend:** GEN • WASHINGTON •

Date	AG3	G4	VG8	F12	VF20	XF40	MS60
1786 2 known	—	—	—	—	—	—	—

KM# EA27 • Copper **Rev:** Shield **Obv. Legend:** IMMUNIS COLUMBIA • **Rev. Legend:** * E * PLURIBUS * UNUM *

Date	AG3	G4	VG8	F12	VF20	XF40	MS60
1786	—	—	—	—	40,000	60,000	—

Note: Rescigno, AU, $33,000. Steinberg, VF $11,000

KM# EA28 • Copper **Rev:** Eagle **Obv. Legend:** IMMUNIS COLUMBIA **Rev. Legend:** * E * PLURIBUS * UNUM *

Date	AG3	G4	VG8	F12	VF20	XF40	MS60
1786 3 known	—	—	—	—	50,000	90,000	—

CONFEDERATIO

KM# EA23 • Copper **Obv.** Standing figure with bow & arrow **Rev:** Large circle of stars **Obv. Legend:** INIMICA TYRANNIS • AMERICANA • **Rev. Legend:** • CONFEDERATIO • **Note:** The Confederatio dies were struck in combination with 13 other dies of the period. All surviving examples of these combinations are extremely rare.

Date	AG3	G4	VG8	F12	VF20	XF40	MS60
1785	—	—	—	—	50,000	100,000	—

KM# EA22 • Copper **Obv.** Standing figure with bow & arrow **Rev:** Small circle of stars **Obv. Legend:** INIMICA TYRANNIS • AMERICANA • **Rev. Legend:** • CONFEDERATIO •

Date	AG3	G4	VG8	F12	VF20	XF40	MS60
1785	—	—	—	—	50,000	95,000	—

COLONIAL COINAGE

EARLY FEDERAL COINAGE

FUGIO "CENT"

KM# EA30.1 • Copper **Obv.** Club rays, round ends.

Date	AG3	G4	VG8	F12	VF20	XF40	MS60
1787	225	325	450	950	2,000	3,850	—

KM# EA30.2 • Copper **Obv.** Club rays, concave ends.

Date	AG3	G4	VG8	F12	VF20	XF40	MS60
1787	1,500	2,500	4,500	9,000	27,500	—	—

KM# EA30.3 • Copper **Obv. Legend:** FUCIO.

Date	AG3	G4	VG8	F12	VF20	XF40	MS60
1787	—	2,000	3,000	7,000	25,000	35,000	—

KM# EA31.1 • Copper **Obv.** Pointed rays. **Rev:** UNITED above, STATES below.

Date	AG3	G4	VG8	F12	VF20	XF40	MS60
1787	600	950	1,500	3,250	8,000	11,500	—

KM# EA31.2 • Copper **Rev:** UNITED STATES at sides of ring.

Date	AG3	G4	VG8	F12	VF20	XF40	MS60
1787	110	175	275	550	900	1,800	3,500

KM# EA31.3 • Copper **Rev:** STATES UNITED at sides of ring.

Date	AG3	G4	VG8	F12	VF20	XF40	MS60
1787	110	190	275	550	850	1,650	3,500

KM# EA31.4 • Copper **Rev:** Eight-pointed stars on ring.

Date	AG3	G4	VG8	F12	VF20	XF40	MS60
1787	150	285	475	700	1,250	2,750	9,000

KM# EA31.5 • Copper **Rev:** Raised rims on ring, large lettering in center.

Date	AG3	G4	VG8	F12	VF20	XF40	MS60
1787	185	325	550	950	2,750	6,000	18,500

KM# EA32.1 • Copper **Obv.** No cinquefoils, cross after date. **Obv. Legend:** UNITED STATES.

Date	AG3	G4	VG8	F12	VF20	XF40	MS60
1787	300	—	750	1,450	3,850	6,700	—

KM# EA32.2 • Copper **Obv.** No cinquefoils, cross after date. **Obv. Legend:** STATES UNITED.

Date	AG3	G4	VG8	F12	VF20	XF40	MS60
1787	175	350	750	1,500	4,000	7,200	—

KM# EA32.3 • Copper **Obv.** No cinquefoils, cross after date. **Rev:** Raised rims on ring.

Date	AG3	G4	VG8	F12	VF20	XF40	MS60
1787	—	—	—	—	27,500	—	—

KM# EA33 • Copper **Obv.** No cinquefoils, cross after date. **Rev:** With rays. **Rev. Legend:** AMERICAN CONGRESS.

Date	VG8	F12	VF20	XF40	MS60
1787 extremely rare	—	—	225,000	300,000	—

Note: Norweb $63,800

KM# EA34 • Brass **Note:** New Haven restrike.

Date	AG3	G4	VG8	F12	VF20	XF40	MS60
1787	—	—	—	—	—	450	1,000

KM# EA34a • Copper **Note:** New Haven restrike.

Date	AG3	G4	VG8	F12	VF20	XF40	MS60
1787	—	—	—	—	450	750	1,000

KM# EA34b • Silver **Note:** New Haven restrike.

Date	AG3	G4	VG8	F12	VF20	XF40	MS60
1787 (ca. 1858)	—	—	—	—	—	2,750	4,000

KM# EA34c • Gold AGW **Note:** New Haven restrike.

Date	AG3	G4	VG8	F12	VF20	XF40	MS60
1787 (ca. 1858) 2 known	—	—	—	—	—	—	—

Note: Norweb (holed) $1,430

COLONIAL COINAGE

BRASHER

KM# Tn51.1 • Gold AGW **Obv.** Sunrise over mountains. **Rev:** Displayed eagle with shield on breast, EB counterstamp on wing.

Date	AG3	G4	VG8	F12	VF20	XF40	MS60
1787 6 known						—	—

Note: Heritage FUN Sale, January 2005, AU-55, $2,415,000.

KM# Tn51.2 • Gold AGW **Obv.** Sun rise over mountains **Rev:** Displayed eagle with sheild on breast. EB counterstamp on breast.

Date	AG3	G4	VG8	F12	VF20	XF40	MS60
1787 unique	—	—	—	—	—	—	—

Note: Heritage FUN sale, January 2005, XF-45, $2,9900. Foreign gold coins with EB counterstamp exist. These are valued at over $5,000, with many much higher.

ISSUES OF 1792

CENT

KM# PnE1 • Bi-Metallic, Silver center in Copper ring

Date	VG8	F12	VF20	XF40	MS60
1792 14 known	—	185,000	325,000	475,000	—

Note: Norweb, MS-60, $143,000; Heritage 4-12; MS61 $1.15 million

KM# PnF1 • Copper **Note:** No silver center.

Date	VG8	F12	VF20	XF40	MS60
1792 9 known	—	250,000	500,000	750,000	—

Note: Norweb, EF-40, $35,200; Benson, VG-10, $57,500

KM# PnG1 • Copper **Edge:** Plain **Note:** Commonly called "Birch cent."

Date	G4	VG8	F12	VF20	XF40	MS60
1792 unique	—	—	—	—	650,000	—

KM# PnH1 • Copper **Obv.** One star in edge legend **Note:** Commonly called "Birch cent."

Date	G4	VG8	F12	VF20	XF40	MS60
1792 2 known	—	—	—	—	600,000	—

Note: Norweb, EF-40, $59,400

KM# PnI1 • Copper **Obv.** Two stars in edge legend **Note:** Commonly called "Birch cent."

Date	G4	VG8	F12	VF20	XF40	MS60
1792 8 known	—	—	200,000	400,000	550,000	—

Note: Hawn, strong VF, $57,750

KM# PnJ1 • White Metal **Rev:** G.W.Pt. below wreath tie **Note:** Commonly called "Birch cent."

Date	AG3	G4	VG8	F12	VF20	XF40	MS60
1792 unique	—	—	—	—	—	—	—

Note: Garrett, $90,000

COLONIAL COINAGE

HALF DISME

KM# 5 • Silver

Date	AG3	G4	VG8	F12	VF20	XF40	MS60
1792	25,000	20,000	45,000	65,000	90,000	125,000	450,000

KM# PnA1 • Copper

Date	AG3	G4	VG8	F12	VF20	XF40	MS60
1792 unique	—	—	—	—	—	—	—
Note: Heritage 4-06, Sp-67, $1,322,500							

DISME

KM# PnB1 • Silver

Date	G4	VG8	F12	VF20	XF40	MS60
1792 3 known	—	—	—	700,000	1,000,000	—
Note: Norweb, EF-40, $28,600						

KM# PnC1 • Copper **Edge:** Reeded

Date	G4	VG8	F12	VF20	XF40	MS60
1792 14 known	—	—	—	150,000	250,000	500,000
Note: Hawn, VF, $30,800; Benson, EF-45, $109,250						

KM# PnD1 • Copper **Edge:** Plain

Date	G4	VG8	F12	VF20	XF40	MS60
1792 2 known	—	—	—	450,000	750,000	—
Note: Garrett, $45,000						

QUARTER

KM# PnK1 • Copper **Edge:** Reeded **Note:** Commonly called "Wright quarter."

Date	AG3	G4	VG8	F12	VF20	XF40	MS60
1792 2 known	—	—	—	—	—	—	—

KM# PnL1 • White Metal **Edge:** Plain **Note:** Commonly called "Wright quarter."

Date	AG3	G4	VG8	F12	VF20	XF40	MS60
1792 4 known	—	—	—	—	175,000	—	—
Note: Norweb, VF-30 to EF-40, $28,600							

KM# PnM1 • White Metal **Note:** Commonly called "Wright quarter."

Date	AG3	G4	VG8	F12	VF20	XF40	MS60
1792 die trial	—	—	—	—	—	—	—
Note: Garrett, $12,000							

COLONIAL COINAGE

US TERRITORIAL GOLD

Territorial gold pieces (also referred to as "Private" and "Pioneer" gold) are those struck outside the U.S. Mint and not recognized as official issues by the federal government. The pieces so identified are of various shapes, denominations, and degrees of intrinsic value, and were locally required because of the remoteness of the early gold fields from a federal mint and/or an insufficient quantity of official coinage in frontier areas.

The legality of these privately issued pieces derives from the fact that federal law prior to 1864 prohibited a state from coining money, but did not specifically deny that right to an individual, providing that the privately issued coins did not closely resemble those of the United States.

In addition to coin-like gold pieces, the private minters of the gold rush days also issued gold in ingot and bar form. Ingots were intended for circulation and were cast in regular values and generally in large denominations. Bars represent a miner's deposit after it had been assayed, refined, cast into convenient form (generally rectangular), and stamped with the appropriate weight, fineness, and value. Although occasionally cast in even values for the convenience of banks, bars were more often of odd denomination, and when circulated were rounded off to the nearest figure. Ingots and bars are omitted from this listing.

CALIFORNIA
Fractional and Small Size Gold Coinage

During the California gold rush a wide variety of U.S. and foreign coins were used for small change, but only limited quantities of these coins were available. Gold dust was in common use, although this offered the miner a relatively low value for his gold.

By 1852 California jewelers had begun to manufacture 25¢, 50¢ and $1 gold pieces in round and octagonal shapes. Makers included M. Deriberpe, Antoine Louis Nouizillet, Isadore Routhier, Robert B. Gray, Pierre Frontier, Eugene Dieviercy, Herman J. Brand, and Herman and Jacob Levison. Reuben N. Hershfield and Noah Mitchell made their coins in Leavenworth, Kansas and most of their production was seized in August 1871. Herman Kroll made California gold coins in New York City in the 1890s. Only two or three of these companies were in production at any one time. Many varieties bear the makers initials. Frontier and his partners made most of the large Liberty Head, Eagle reverse, and Washington Head design types. Most of the small Liberty Head types were made first by Nouizillet and later by Gray and then the Levison brothers and lastly by the California Jewelry Co. Coins initialed "G.G." are apparently patterns made by Frontier and Dieviercy for the New York based firm of Gaime, Guillemot & Co.

Most of the earlier coins were struck from gold alloys and had an intrinsic value of about 50-60 percent of face value. They were generally struck from partially hubbed dies and with reeded collars. A few issues were struck with a plain collar or a collar with reeding on only 7 of the 8 sides. Many issues are too poorly struck or too thin to have a clear and complete image of the collar. The later coins and some of the earlier coins were struck from laminated or plated gold planchets, or from gold plated silver planchets. Most of the last dates of issue are extremely thin and contain only token amounts of gold.

Circumstantial evidence exists that the coins issued through 1856 circulated as small change. The San Francisco mint was established in 1854, and by 1856 it had ramped up its production enough to satisfy the local need for small change. However, some evidence exists that these small gold coins may have continued to circulate on occasion through to 1871. After 1871, the gold content of the coins dramatically decreases and it is very unlikely that any of these last issues circulated.

Although the Private Coinages Act of 1864 outlawed all private coinage, this law was not enforced in California and production of small denominated gold continued through 1882. In the spring of 1883, Col. Henry Finnegass of the U.S. Secret Service halted production of the denominated private gold pieces. Non-denominated tokens (lacking DOLLARS, CENTS or the equivalent) were also made during this latter period, sometimes by the same manufacturing jeweler using the same obverse die and the same planchets as the small denomination gold coins. Production of these tokens continues to this day, with most issues made after the 1906 earthquake and fire being backdated to 1847-1865 and struck from brass or gold plated brass planchets.

Approximately 25,000 pieces of California small denomination gold coins are estimated to exist, in a total of over 500 varieties. A few varieties are undated, mostly gold rush era pieces; and a few of the issues are backdated, mostly those from the 1880's. This listing groups varieties together in easily identified categories. The prices quoted are for the most common variety in each group. UNC prices reflect the median auction prices realized of MS60 to MS62 graded coins. BU prices reflect the median auction prices realized of MS63 to MS64 graded coins. Pre-1871 true MS-65 coins are rare and sell for substantial premiums over the prices on this list. Post-1871 coins are rarely found with wear and often have a cameo proof appearance. Auction prices realized are highly volatile and it is not uncommon to find recent records of sales at twice or half of the values shown here. Many of the rarity estimates published in the 1980s and earlier have proven to be too high, so caution is advised when paying a premium for a rare variety. In addition, many varieties that have a refined appearance command higher prices than equivalent grade but scarcer varieties that have a more crude appearance.

Several counterfeits of California Fractional Gold coins exist. Beware of 1854 and 1858 dated round 1/2 dollars, and 1871 dated round dollars that have designs that do not match any of the published varieties. Beware of reeded edge Kroll coins being sold as originals (see the listings below).

For further information consult "California Pioneer Fractional Gold" by W. Breen and R.J. Gillio and "The Brasher Bulletin" the official newsletter of The Society of Private and Pioneer Numismatists.

CALIFORNIA

1/4 DOLLAR (OCTAGONAL)

KM# 1.1 • Gold Obv. Large Liberty head, left **Rev:** Value and date within beaded circle

Date	F12	VF20	XF40	MS60	MS63
1853	—	—	—	250	350
1854	—	—	—	300	400
1855	—	—	—	300	400
1856 FD	—	—	—	310	425

KM# 1.2 • Gold Obv. Liberty head, left **Rev:** Value and date within wreath

Date	F12	VF20	XF40	MS60	MS63
1859	—	—	—	200	450
1864	—	—	—	250	400
1866	—	—	—	250	400
1867	—	—	—	250	400
1868	—	—	—	200	350
1869	—	—	—	200	350
1870	—	—	—	200	350
1871	—	—	—	200	350

KM# 1.3 • Gold Obv. Large Liberty head, left, above date **Rev:** 1/4 DOLLAR and CAL within wreath

Date	F12	VF20	XF40	MS60	MS63
1872	—	—	—	250	400
1873	—	—	—	175	300

KM# 1.4 • Gold Obv. Small Liberty head, left **Rev:** Value and date within beaded circle

Date	F12	VF20	XF40	MS60	MS63
1853	—	—	200	325	475

KM# 1.5 • Gold Obv. Small Liberty head, left, above date **Rev:** Value within wreath

Date	F12	VF20	XF40	MS60	MS63
1854	—	—	—	300	400

KM# 1.6 • Gold Obv. Small Liberty head, left **Rev:** Value and date within wreath

Date	F12	VF20	XF40	MS60	MS63
1855	—	—	—	300	400
1856	—	—	—	275	350
1857 Plain edge	—	—	—	100	150
Note: Kroll type date					
1857 Reeded edge	—	—	—	75.00	110
Note: Kroll type date					
1860 Rare	—	—	—	—	—
1860 G	—	—	—	200	300
1870 G	—	—	—	250	350

KM# 1.7 • Gold Obv. Liberty head, left **Rev:** 1/4 in shield, DOLLAR and date below, all within wreath

Date	F12	VF20	XF40	MS60	MS63
1863 G	—	—	—	500	—
1864 G	—	—	—	240	350
1865 G	—	—	—	250	550
1866 G	—	—	—	250	400
1867 G	—	—	—	200	400
1868 G	—	—	—	200	—
1869 G	—	—	—	190	300
1870 G	—	—	—	200	350

KM# 1.8 • Gold Obv. Small Liberty head, left, above date **Rev:** 1/4 DOLLAR and CAL, all within wreath

Date	F12	VF20	XF40	MS60	MS63
1870 G	—	—	—	225	300
1871 G	—	—	—	200	250
1871 L	—	—	—	200	250
1873	—	—	—	400	—

US TERRITORIAL GOLD

Date	F12	VF20	XF40	MS60	MS63
1874	—	—	—	200	275
1875/3	—	—	—	1,000	—
1876	—	—	—	225	300

KM# 1.9 • Gold **Obv.** Goofy" Liberty head, left
Rev: Value and date within wreath

Date	F12	VF20	XF40	MS60	MS63
1870	—	—	—	200	300

KM# 1.10 • Gold **Obv.** "Oriental" Liberty head, left, above date **Rev:** 1/4 CALDOLL withn wreath

Date	F12	VF20	XF40	MS60	MS63
1881	—	—	—	1,000	3,000

KM# 1.11 • Gold **Obv.** Large Liberty head, left, above 1872 **Rev:** Value and 1871 within wreath

Date	F12	VF20	XF40	MS60	MS63
1872-71	—	—	—	1,000	3,000

KM# 2.1 • Gold **Obv.** Large Indian head, left, above date **Rev:** Value within wreath

Date	F12	VF20	XF40	MS60	MS63
1852	—	—	—	340	500
Note: Back dated issue					
1868	—	—	—	340	500
Note: Back dated issue					
1874	—	—	—	320	450
Note: Back dated issue					
1876	—	—	—	320	450
1878/6	—	—	—	450	650
1880	—	—	—	300	400
1881	—	—	—	320	450

KM# 2.2 • Gold **Obv.** Large Indian head, left, above date **Rev:** Value and CAL within wreath

Date	F12	VF20	XF40	MS60	MS63
1872	—	—	100	260	350
1873/2	—	—	200	600	850
1873	—	—	120	300	400
1874	—	—	100	260	350
1875	—	—	120	300	400
1876	—	—	120	300	400

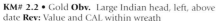

KM# 2.3 • Gold **Obv.** Small Indian head, left, above date **Rev:** 1/4 DOLLAR and CAL, all within wreath

Date	F12	VF20	XF40	MS60	MS63
1875	—	—	—	250	350
1876	—	—	—	250	500
1881	—	—	—	500	1,100

KM# 2.4 • Gold **Obv.** "Aztec" Indian head, left, above date **Rev:** Value and CAL within wreath

Date	F12	VF20	XF40	MS60	MS63
1880	—	—	—	210	300

KM# 2.6 • Gold **Obv.** "Dumb" Indian head, left, date below **Rev:** Value within wreath

Date	F12	VF20	XF40	MS60	MS63
1881	—	—	—	650	—

KM# 2.7 • Gold **Obv.** "Young" Indian head, left, above date **Rev:** Value within wreath

Date	F12	VF20	XF40	MS60	MS63
1881	—	—	—	750	—

KM# 2.8 • Gold **Obv.** Indian head, left, above date **Rev:** 1/4 DOLLAR and CAL, all within wreath

Date	F12	VF20	XF40	MS60	MS63
1882	—	—	—	500	750

KM# 3 • Gold **Obv.** Washington head, left, above date **Rev:** Value and CAL within wreath

Date	F12	VF20	XF40	MS60	MS63
1872	—	—	—	1,250	2,000

1/4 DOLLAR (ROUND)

KM# 4 • Gold **Obv.** Defiant eagle above date **Rev:** 25 CENTS within wreath

Date	F12	VF20	XF40	MS60	MS63
1854	—	—	11,000	33,000	44,000

KM# 5.1 • Gold **Obv.** Large Liberty head, left **Rev:** Value and date within wreath

Date	F12	VF20	XF40	MS60	MS63
1853	—	—	400	1,000	1,500
1853 F.D.	—	—	600	1,500	2,250
1853 G.G.	—	—	600	1,500	2,250
1854	—	—	175	425	625
1858 Rare	—	—	—	—	—
1859	—	—	95.00	250	300
1865	—	—	115	275	375
1866	—	—	—	250	350
1867	—	—	—	250	350
1868	—	—	—	250	350
1870	—	—	—	250	350
1871	—	—	—	250	350

US TERRITORIAL GOLD

KM# 5.2 • Gold **Obv.** Large Liberty head, left, above date **Rev:** Value and CAL within wreath

Date	F12	VF20	XF40	MS60	MS63
1871	—	—	—	250	325
1872	—	—	—	300	375
1873	—	—	—	230	300

KM# 5.3 • Gold **Obv.** Small Liberty head, left **Rev:** 25 CENTS within wreath

Date	F12	VF20	XF40	MS60	MS63
ND	—	—	1,000	2,450	3,500

KM# 5.4 • Gold **Obv.** Small Liberty head, left **Rev:** "1/4 DOLL." or "DOLLAR" and date in wreath

Date	F12	VF20	XF40	MS60	MS63
1853	—	—	500	1,200	2,500
ND	—	—	115	225	375
Note: Rare counterfeit exists					
1855 10 stars	—	—	145	300	400
1855 11 stars	—	—	—	50.00	100
Note: Kroll type					
1856	—	—	125	275	375
1860	—	—	90.00	200	300
1864	—	—	100	225	325
1865	—	—	115	250	375
1866 G	—	—	150	625	375
1867 G	—	—	90.00	200	375
1869 G	—	—	90.00	200	325
1870 G	—	—	150	275	475

KM# 5.5 • Gold **Obv.** Small Liberty head, left **Rev:** Value in shield and date within wreath

Date	F12	VF20	XF40	MS60	MS63
1863/1860 Rare	—	—	—	—	—
Note: Struck over 1/4 Dollar KM#5.4					
1863	—	—	80.00	200	—
1870 G Rare	—	—	—	—	—

KM# 5.6 • Gold **Obv.** Small Liberty head, left, above date **Rev:** 1/4 DOLLAR CAL within wreath

Date	F12	VF20	XF40	MS60	MS63
ND G	—	—	120	500	—
1870 G	—	—	100	200	250
1871 G	—	—	100	200	250
1871 L	—	—	—	210	350
1873	—	—	—	300	500
1874	—	—	—	300	500
1875	—	—	—	250	475
1876	—	—	—	225	400

KM# 5.7 • Gold **Obv.** "Goofy" Liberty head, left **Rev:** Value and date within wreath

Date	F12	VF20	XF40	MS60	MS63
1870	—	—	110	220	275

KM# 5.8 • Gold **Obv.** Liberty head left, H and date below **Rev:** 1/4 DOLLAR CAL within wreath

Date	F12	VF20	XF40	MS60	MS63
1871 H	—	—	180	225	375

KM# 6.1 • Gold **Obv.** Large Indian head left, date below **Rev:** Value within wreath

Date	F12	VF20	XF40	MS60	MS63
1852	—	—	—	350	450
Note: Back dated issue					
1868	—	—	—	400	525
Note: Back dated issue					
1874	—	—	—	350	425
Note: Back dated issue					
1876	—	—	—	350	475
1878/6	—	—	—	350	450
1880	—	—	—	250	375
1881	—	—	—	250	375

KM# 6.2 • Gold **Obv.** Large Indian head left, date below **Rev:** 1/4 DOLLAR CAL within wreath

Date	F12	VF20	XF40	MS60	MS63
1872/1	—	—	—	250	350
1873	—	—	—	325	425
1874	—	—	—	230	325
1875	—	—	—	250	350
1876	—	—	—	250	350

KM# 6.3 • Gold **Obv.** Small Indian head left, date below **Rev:** Value within wreath

Date	F12	VF20	XF40	MS60	MS63
1875	—	—	125	300	450
1876	—	—	115	250	400
1881 Rare	—	—	—	—	—

KM# 6.4 • Gold **Obv.** "Young" Indian head left, date below **Rev:** 1/4 DOLLAR CAL within wreath

Date	F12	VF20	XF40	MS60	MS63
1882	—	—	400	1,225	1,750

KM# 7 • Gold **Obv.** Washington head left, date below **Rev:** 1/4 DOLLAR CAL within wreath

Date	F12	VF20	XF40	MS60	MS63
1872	—	—	—	1,100	1,450

US TERRITORIAL GOLD

1/2 DOLLAR (OCTAGONAL)

KM# 8.1 • Gold Obv. Liberty head left, date below **Rev:** 1/2 DOLLAR in beaded circle, CALIFORNIA GOLD around

Date	F12	VF20	XF40	MS60	MS63
1853 FD	—	—	165	350	450
1854	—	—	110	285	350
Note: Rare counterfeit exists					
1854 FD	—	—	165	350	450
1856	—	—	165	365	450

KM# 8.2 • Gold Obv. Liberty head, left **Rev:** Small eagle with rays ("peacock")

Date	F12	VF20	XF40	MS60	MS63
1853 FD	—	—	800	2,000	3,000

KM# 8.3 • Gold Obv. Large Liberty head, left **Rev:** Large eagle with date

Date	F12	VF20	XF40	MS60	MS63
1853 FD	—	—	5,000	10,000	—

KM# 8.4 • Gold Obv. Liberty head, left **Rev:** Value and date within wreath

Date	F12	VF20	XF40	MS60	MS63
1859	—	—	—	225	300
1866	—	—	—	325	425
1867	—	—	—	250	325
1868	—	—	—	250	325
1869	—	—	—	275	375
1870	—	—	—	275	375
1871	—	—	—	250	325

KM# 8.5 • Gold Obv. Large Liberty head left, date below **Rev:** HALF / DOLLAR / CAL within wreath

Date	F12	VF20	XF40	MS60	MS63
1872	—	—	—	275	375
1873	—	—	—	250	325

KM# 8.6 • Gold Obv. Liberty head, left **Rev:** HALF DOL. CALIFORNIA GOLD around wreath, date within

Date	F12	VF20	XF40	MS60	MS63
1854 N	—	—	100	350	500
1855 N	—	—	90.00	300	400
1856 N	—	—	90.00	265	325
1856 G N	—	—	165	1,100	—
Note: Back date issue struck in 1864					
1868	—	—	70.00	185	275
Note: Kroll type					

KM# 8.7 • Gold Obv. Small Liberty head left **Rev:** HALF / DOLLAR /date all within wreath

Date	F12	VF20	XF40	MS60	MS63
1864 G	—	—	—	275	350
Note: A rare silver strike of 1864G is known					
1870 G	—	—	—	275	—

KM# 8.8 • Gold Obv. Liberty head left **Rev:** CAL. GOLD / HALF DOL and date within wreath

Date	F12	VF20	XF40	MS60	MS63
1869 G	—	—	—	200	350
1870 G	—	—	—	200	350

KM# 8.9 • Gold Obv. Small Liberty head left, date below **Rev:** HALF DOLLAR CAL within wreath

Date	F12	VF20	XF40	MS60	MS63
1870 G	—	—	75.00	200	300
1871 G	—	—	75.00	200	250
1871 L	—	—	75.00	165	250
1873	—	—	95.00	300	600
1874	—	—	95.00	300	600
1875	—	—	250	1,000	—
1876	—	—	75.00	200	250

KM# 8.10 • Gold Obv. "Goofy" Liberty head, left **Rev:** Value and date within wreath

Date	F12	VF20	XF40	MS60	MS63
1870	—	—	75.00	200	300

KM# 8.11 • Gold Obv. "Oriental" Liberty head left, date below **Rev:** 1/2 CALDOLL within wreath

Date	F12	VF20	XF40	MS60	MS63
1881	—	—	250	750	1,150

KM# 9.1 • Gold Obv. Large Indian head left, date below **Rev:** Value within wreath

Date	F12	VF20	XF40	MS60	MS63
1852	—	—	—	700	1,100
Note: Back dated issue					
1868	—	—	—	850	1,200
Note: Back dated issue					
1874	—	—	—	700	1,100
Note: Back dated issue					
1876	—	—	—	350	450
1880	—	—	—	350	450
1881	—	—	—	350	450

US TERRITORIAL GOLD

KM# 9.2 • Gold **Obv.** Large Indian head left, date below **Rev:** 1/2 DOLLAR CAL within wreath

Date	F12	VF20	XF40	MS60	MS63
1852	—	—	—	500	750
Note: Back dated issue					
1868	—	—	—	300	600
Note: Back dated issue					
1872	—	—	—	250	350
1873/2	—	—	—	250	450
1873	—	—	—	250	350
1874/3	—	—	—	300	400
1874	—	—	—	250	475
1875	—	—	—	300	350
1876	—	—	—	300	450
1878/6	—	—	—	300	450
1880	—	—	—	550	1,050
1881	—	—	—	300	450

KM# 9.3 • Gold **Obv.** Small Indian head left, date below **Rev:** Value and CAL within wreath

Date	F12	VF20	XF40	MS60	MS63
1875	—	—	—	350	525
1876	—	—	—	350	525

KM# 9.4 • Gold **Obv.** "Young" Indian head left, date below **Rev:** 1/2 DOLLAR CAL within wreath

Date	F12	VF20	XF40	MS60	MS63
1881	—	—	—	550	850
1882 Rare	—	—	—	—	—

1/2 DOLLAR (ROUND)

KM# 10 • Gold **Obv.** Arms of California and date **Rev:** Eagle and legends

Date	F12	VF20	XF40	MS60	MS63
1853	—	—	—	—	—

KM# 11.1 • Gold **Obv.** Liberty head, left **Rev:** Large eagle and legends

Date	F12	VF20	XF40	MS60	MS63
1854	—	—	1,000	6,000	—
Note: Similar obverse paired with reverse of KM#12.2, or an eagle with no denomination are modern counterfeits					

KM# 11.2 • Gold **Obv.** Liberty head left, date below **Rev:** HALF DOL. CALIFORNIA GOLD around wreath

Date	F12	VF20	XF40	MS60	MS63
1854	—	—	200	450	600

KM# 11.3 • Gold **Obv.** Liberty head left **Rev:** Date in wreath, value and CALIFORNIA GOLD around wreath

Date	F12	VF20	XF40	MS60	MS63
1852	—	—	195	375	500
1852 DN	—	—	195	375	500
1853 DN	—	—	195	375	500
1853 D	—	—	215	400	525
1853	—	—	215	400	525
1854 D	—	—	300	750	1,000
1854 Large head, small stars	—	—	750	1,500	3,000
1854 Small head, small stars	—	—	—	200	300
Note: Kroll type.					
1854 Large stars	—	—	—	—	—
Note: Common counterfeit					
1855	—	—	225	425	650
1856 N	—	—	150	325	425
1860/566	—	—	175	350	500

KM# 11.4 • Gold **Obv.** Liberty head, left **Rev:** Small eagle and legends

Date	F12	VF20	XF40	MS60	MS63
1853 Rare	—	—	—	—	—
1853 GG	—	—	5,000	10,000	15,000

KM# 11.5 • Gold **Obv.** Liberty head left **Rev:** Value in wreath; CALIFORNIA GOLD and date around wreath

Date	F12	VF20	XF40	MS60	MS63
1853 GG	—	—	150	750	1,500

KM# 11.6 • Gold **Obv.** Liberty head left **Rev:** Value and date within wreath

Date	F12	VF20	XF40	MS60	MS63
1854 12 stars	—	—	—	—	—
Note: Rare counterfeit without "FD" beneath truncation					
1854 FD 13 stars	—	—	850	3,000	—
ND Rare	—	—	—	—	—
1855 FD	—	—	180	450	600
1859 FD	—	—	275	750	1,000
1859	—	—	—	275	425
1865	—	—	—	250	375
1866	—	—	—	275	425
1867	—	—	—	250	375
1868	—	—	—	275	425
1869	—	—	—	275	425
1870	—	—	—	250	375
1871	—	—	—	225	325
1873	—	—	—	275	475
Note: A rare counterfeit exists for this date					

US TERRITORIAL GOLD

KM# 11.7 • Gold **Obv.** Liberty head left, date below **Rev:** Value and CAL within wreath

Date	F12	VF20	XF40	MS60	MS63
1870 G	—	—	—	300	450
1871 G	—	—	—	300	450

Note: Common, yet deceptive, counterfeits exist

1871 L	—	—	—	450	
1872	—	—	—	300	450
1873	—	—	—	450	1,000
1874	—	—	—	300	750
1875	—	—	—	350	800
1876	—	—	—	300	—

KM# 11.8 • Gold **Obv.** Liberty head left **Rev:** Value and date within wreath, CALIFORNIA GOLD around

Date	F12	VF20	XF40	MS60	MS63
1863	—	—	275	675	950

Note: This issue is a rare Kroll type. All 1858 dates of this type are counterfeits

KM# 11.9 • Gold **Obv.** Liberty head left **Rev:** HALF DOLLAR and date within wreath

Date	F12	VF20	XF40	MS60	MS63
1864	—	—	150	300	400

Note: A rare silver strike is known

1866 G	—	—	330	800	1,000
1867 G	—	—	150	300	375
1868 G	—	—	150	300	375
1869 G	—	—	175	350	—
1870 G	—	—	—	400	—

KM# 11.11 • Gold **Obv.** "Goofy" Liberty head, left **Rev:** Value and date within wreath

Date	F12	VF20	XF40	MS60	MS63
1870	—	—	150	400	700

KM# 11.12 • Gold **Obv.** Liberty head left, H and date below **Rev:** Value and CAL within wreath

Date	F12	VF20	XF40	MS60	MS63
1871 H	—	—	210	500	575

KM# 12.1 • Gold **Obv.** Large Indian head left, date below **Rev:** Value within wreath **Note:** 1852, 1868 and 1874 are backdated issues

Date	F12	VF20	XF40	MS60	MS63
1852	—	—	—	375	675
1868	—	—	—	325	600
1874	—	—	—	325	600

Note: Similar obverse paired with reverse of KM#11.2 or an eagle with no denomination are modern counterfeits

1876	—	—	—	225	275
1878/6	—	—	—	325	475
1880	—	—	—	275	425
1881	—	—	—	275	425

KM# 12.2 • Gold **Obv.** Large Indian head left, date below **Rev:** Value and CAL within wreath

Date	F12	VF20	XF40	MS60	MS63
1872	—	—	—	250	350
1873/2	—	—	—	400	700
1873	—	—	—	250	350
1874/3	—	—	—	350	500
1874	—	—	—	250	350
1875/3	—	—	—	250	350
1875	—	—	—	350	550
1876/5	—	—	—	250	350
1876	—	—	—	400	650

KM# 12.3 • Gold **Obv.** Small Indian head left, date below **Rev:** Value and CAL within wreath

Date	F12	VF20	XF40	MS60	MS63
1875	—	—	100	300	500
1876	—	—	75.00	250	350

KM# 12.4 • Gold **Obv.** "Young" Indian head left, date above **Rev:** Value and CAL within wreath

Date	F12	VF20	XF40	MS60	MS63
1882	—	—	—	850	—

DOLLAR (OCTAGONAL)

KM# 13.1 • Gold **Obv.** Liberty head left **Rev:** Large eagle and legends

Date	F12	VF20	XF40	MS60	MS63
ND	—	—	1,000	2,200	4,000
1853	—	—	5,000	7,500	—
1854	—	—	1,500	3,200	5,000

KM# 13.2 • Gold **Obv.** Liberty head left **Rev:** Value and date in beaded circle; CALIFORNIA GOLD and initials around

Date	F12	VF20	XF40	MS60	MS63
1853 DERI	—	—	275	750	1,100
1853 DERIB	—	—	450	1,100	—
1853 FD	—	—	300	900	—
1853 N	—	—	325	900	1,450
1854 DERI	—	—	550	1,300	—
1854 FD	—	—	350	1,100	1,900
1855 FD	—	—	425	1,100	—
1856	—	—	2,100	5,000	—
1863 Reeded edge, restrike	—	—	—	175	275
1863 Plain edge	—	—	—	150	250

Note: Plain edge 1863 dates are original Kroll types, while reeded edge examples are Kroll restrikes

US TERRITORIAL GOLD

KM# 13.3 • Gold **Obv.** Liberty head left **Rev:** Value and date inside wreath; legends outside

Date	F12	VF20	XF40	MS60	MS63
1854 GL Rare	—	—	—	—	—
Note: Bowers and Marena sale 5-99, XF $9,775					
1854	—	—	325	900	1,300
1855 NR	—	—	325	900	1,300
1858 K	—	—	180	425	725
Note: 1858 dates are Kroll types					
1859 FD	—	—	1,900	—	—
1860	—	—	—	900	1,200
1868 G	—	—	—	900	1,300
1869 G	—	—	—	800	1,100
1870 G	—	—	—	725	1,100
1871	—	—	—	475	1,000

KM# 13.4 • Gold **Obv.** "Goofy" Liberty head, left **Rev:** Value and date within wreath

Date	F12	VF20	XF40	MS60	MS63
1870	—	—	—	1,200	1,800
Note: Deceptive counterfeits exist					

KM# 13.5 • Gold **Obv.** Liberty head left, date below **Rev:** Value and date within wreath; CALIFORNIA GOLD around

Date	F12	VF20	XF40	MS60	MS63
1871 G	—	—	—	725	1,100
1874	—	—	—	—	—
1875	—	—	—	—	—
1876	—	—	—	—	—

KM# 14.1 • Gold **Obv.** Large Indian head left, date below **Rev:** 1 DOLLAR within wreath; CALIFORNIA GOLD around

Date	F12	VF20	XF40	MS60	MS63
1872	—	—	—	900	1,350
1873/2	—	—	—	1,050	1,650
1873	—	—	—	1,150	—
1874	—	—	—	1,300	1,950
1875	—	—	—	900	1,500
1876/5	—	—	—	1,500	1,950

KM# 14.2 • Gold **Obv.** Small Indian head left, date below **Rev:** 1 DOLLAR CAL within wreath

Date	F12	VF20	XF40	MS60	MS63
1875	—	—	1,050	1,800	—
1876	—	—	—	2,100	—

KM# 14.3 • Gold **Obv.** Indian head left, date below **Rev:** 1 DOLLAR within wreath; CALIFORNIA GOLD around

Date	F12	VF20	XF40	MS60	MS63
1876	—	—	—	1,150	—

DOLLAR (ROUND)

KM# 15.1 • Gold **Obv.** Liberty head left **Rev:** Large eagle and legends

Date	F12	VF20	XF40	MS60	MS63
1853 GG Rare	—	—	—	—	—
Note: Superior sale Sept. 1987 MS-63 $35,200					

KM# 15.2 • Gold **Obv.** Liberty head left **Rev:** Value and date within wreath; CALIFORNIA GOLD around

Date	F12	VF20	XF40	MS60	MS63
1854 GL	—	—	3,000	—	—
1854 FD	—	—	5,000	—	—
1854 Rare	—	—	—	—	—
Note: Superior sale Sept. 1988 Fine $13,200					
1857 4 known	—	—	—	—	—
1870 G	—	—	750	3,000	—
1871	—	—	1,300	3,750	—
Note: Counterfeit exists					

KM# 15.3 • Gold **Obv.** Liberty head left, date below **Rev:** Value within wreath; CALIFORNIA GOLD around

Date	F12	VF20	XF40	MS60	MS63
1870 G	—	—	750	2,100	3,000
1871 G	—	—	750	2,100	3,000

KM# 15.4 • Gold **Obv.** "Goofy" Liberty head left **Rev:** Value and date within wreath; CALIFORNIA GOLD around

Date	F12	VF20	XF40	MS60	MS63
1870	—	—	600	2,250	—

KM# 16 • Gold **Obv.** Large Indian head left, date below **Rev:** Value within wreath; CALIFORNIA GOLD outside

Date	F12	VF20	XF40	MS60	MS63
1872	—	—	975	2,700	3,600

US TERRITORIAL GOLD

U.S. Territorial Gold Coinage
Private Assay Office Issues

CALIFORNIA

Norris, Grieg & Norris produced the first territorial gold coin struck in California, a $5 piece struck in 1849 at Benicia City, though it bears the imprint of San Francisco. The coining facility was owned by Thomas H. Norris, Charles Greig, and Hiram A. Norris, members of a New York engineering firm. A unique 1850 variety of this coin has the name STOCKTON beneath the date, instead of SAN FRANCISCO.

Early in 1849, John Little Moffat, a New York assayer, established an assay office at San Francisco in association with Joseph R. Curtis, Philo H. Perry, and Samuel Ward. The first issues of the **Moffat & Co.** assay office consisted of rectangular $16 ingots and assay bars of various and irregular denominations. In early August, the firm began striking $5 and $10 gold coins which resemble those of the U.S. Mint in design, but carry the legend S.M.V. (Standard Mint Value) CALIFORNIA GOLD on the reverse. Five-dollar pieces of the same design were also issued in 1850.

On Sept. 30, 1850, Congress directed the Secretary of the Treasury to establish an official Assay Office in California. Moffat & Co. obtained a contract to perform the duties of the U.S. Assay Office. **Augustus Humbert**, a New York watchcase maker, was appointed U.S. Assayer of Gold in California. Humbert stamped the first octagonal coin-ingots of the Provisional Government Mint on Jan. 31, 1851. The $50 pieces were accepted at par with standard U.S. gold coins, but were not officially recognized as coins. Officially, they were designated as "ingots." Colloquially, they were known as slugs, quintuple eagles, or 5-eagle pieces.

The $50 ingots failed to alleviate the need of California for gold coins. The banks regarded them as disadvantageous to their interests and utilized them only when compelled to do so by public need or convenience. Being of sound value, the ingots drove the overvalued $5, $10, and $20 territorial gold coins from circulation, bringing about a return to the use of gold dust for everyday transactions. Eventually, the slugs became so great a nuisance that they were discounted 3 percent when accepted. This unexpected turn of events forced Moffat & Co. to resume the issuing of $10 and $20 gold coins in 1852. The $10 piece was first issued with the Moffat & Co. imprint on Liberty's coronet, and later with the official imprint of Augustus Humbert on reverse. The $20 piece was issued with the Humbert imprint.

On Feb. 14, 1852, John L. Moffat withdrew from Moffat & Co. to enter the diving bell business, and Moffat & Co. was reorganized as the **United States Assay Office of Gold**, composed of Joseph R. Curtis, Philo H. Perry, and Samuel Ward. The U.S. Assay Office of Gold issued gold coins in denominations of $50 and $10 in 1852, and $20 and $10 in 1853. With the exception of the $50 slugs, they carry the imprint of the Assay Office on reverse. The .900 fine issues of this facility reflect an attempt to bring the issues of the U.S. Assay Office into conformity with the U.S. Mint standard.

The last territorial gold coins to bear the imprint of Moffat & Co. are $20 pieces issued in 1853, after the retirement of John L. Moffat. These coins do not carry a mark of fineness, and generally assay below the U.S. Mint standard.

Templeton Reid, previously mentioned in connection with the private gold issues of Georgia, moved his coining equipment to California when gold was discovered there, and in 1849 issued $10 and $25 gold pieces. No specimens are available to present-day collectors. The only known $10 piece is in the Smithsonian Collection. The only known specimen of the $25 piece was stolen from the U.S. Mint Cabinet Collection in 1858 and was never recovered.

Little is known of the origin and location of the **Cincinnati Mining & Trading Co.** It is believed that the firm was organized in the East and was forced to abandon most of its equipment while enroute to California. A few $5 and $10 gold coins were struck in 1849. Base metal counterfeits exist.

The **Massachusetts & California Co.** was organized in Northampton, Mass., in May 1849 by Josiah Hayden, S. S. Wells, Miles G. Moies, and others. Coining equipment was taken to San Francisco where $5 gold pieces were struck in 1849. The few pieces extant are heavily alloyed with copper.

Wright & Co., a brokerage firm located in Portsmouth Square, San Francisco, issued an undated $10 gold piece in the autumn of 1849 under the name of **Miners' Bank**. Unlike most territorial gold pieces, the Miners' Bank eagle was alloyed with copper. The coinage proved to be unpopular because of its copper-induced color and low intrinsic value. The firm was dissolved on Jan. 14, 1850.

US TERRITORIAL GOLD

In 1849, Dr. **J. S. Ormsby** and Major William M. Ormsby struck gold coins of $5 and $10 denominations at Sacramento under the name of Ormsby & Co. The coinage, which is identified by the initials J. S. O., is undated. Ormsby & Co. coinage was greatly over-valued, the eagle assaying at as little as $9.37.

The **Pacific Co.** of San Francisco issued $5 and $10 gold coins in 1849. The clouded story of this coinage is based on conjecture. It is believed that the well-struck pattern coins of this type were struck in the East by the Pacific Co. that organized in Boston and set sail for California on Feb. 20, 1849, and that the crudely hand-struck pieces were made by the jewelry firm of Broderick and Kohler after the dies passed into their possession. In any event, the intrinsic value of the initial coinage exceeded face value, but by the end of 1849, when they passed out of favor, the coins had been debased so flagrantly that the eagles assayed for as little as $7.86.

Dubosq & Co., a Philadelphia jewelry firm owned by Theodore Dubosq Sr. and Jr. and Henry Dubosq, took melting and coining equipment to San Francisco in 1849, and in 1850 issued $5 and $10 gold coins struck with dies allegedly made by U.S. Mint Engraver James B. Longacre. Dubosq & Co. coinage was immensely popular with the forty-niners because its intrinsic worth was in excess of face value.

The minting equipment of David C. Broderick and Frederick D. Kohler (see Pacific Co.) was acquired in May 1850 by San Francisco jewelers George C. Baldwin and Thomas S. Holman, who organized a private minting venture under the name of **Baldwin & Co**. The firm produced a $5 piece of Liberty Head design and a $10 piece with Horseman device in 1850. Liberty Head $10 and $20 pieces were coined in 1851. Baldwin & Co. produced the first $20 piece issued in California.

Schultz & Co. of San Francisco, a brass foundry located in the rear of the Baldwin & Co. establishment, and operated by Judge G. W. Schultz and William T. Garratt, issued $5 gold coins from early 1851 until April of that year. The inscription "SHULTS & CO." is a misspelling of SCHULTZ & CO.

Dunbar & Co. of San Francisco issued a $5 gold piece in 1851, after Edward E. Dunbar, owner of the California Bank in San Francisco, purchased the coining equipment of the defunct Baldwin & Co.

The San Francisco-based firm of **Wass, Molitor & Co.** was owned by 2 Hungarian exiles, Count S. C. Wass and A. P. Molitor, who initially founded the firm as a gold smelting and assaying plant. In response to a plea from the commercial community for small gold coins, Wass, Molitor & Co. issued $5 and $10 gold coins in 1852. The $5 piece is coined with small head and large head varieties, and the $10 piece with small head, large head, and small close-date varieties. The firm produced a second issue of gold coins in 1855, in denominations of $10, $20, and $50.

The U.S. Assay Office in California closed its doors on Dec. 14, 1853, to make way for the newly established San Francisco Branch Mint. The Mint, however, was unable to start immediate quantity production due to the lack of refining acids. During the interim, John G. Kellogg, a former employee of Moffat & Co., and John Glover Richter, a former assayer in the U.S. Assay Office, formed **Kellogg & Co.** for the purpose of supplying businessmen with urgently needed coinage. The firm produced $20 coins dated 1854 and 1855, after which Augustus Humbert replaced Richter and the enterprise reorganized as Kellogg & Humbert Melters, Assayers & Coiners. Kellogg & Humbert endured until 1860, but issued coins, $20 pieces, only in 1855.

BALDWIN & COMPANY

5 DOLLARS

KM# 17 • Gold **Obv.** Liberty head left, date below **Rev:** Eagle

Date	F12	VF20	XF40	MS60	MS63
1850	7,500	12,000	22,500	47,500	—

10 DOLLARS

KM# 18 • Gold **Obv.** Figure on horseback right, swinging rope, date and value below **Rev:** Eagle **Obv. Legend:** CALIFORNIA GOLD. / 1850 / CALIFORNIA. **Rev. Legend:** BALDWIN & Co. / SAN FRANCISCO.

Date	F12	VF20	XF40	MS60	MS63
1850 Horsemab	32,500	65,000	97,500	200,000	—

Note: Bass Sale May 2000, MS-64 $149,500

US TERRITORIAL GOLD

KM# 19 • Gold Obv. Coronet head left within circle of stars, date below **Rev:** Eagle **Rev. Legend:** S.M.V. CALIFORNIA GOLD

Date	F12	VF20	XF40	MS60	MS63
1851	10,000	22,000	37,500	125,000	—

20 DOLLARS

KM# 20 • Gold Obv. Coronet head, left, within circle of stars, date below **Rev:** Eagle **Rev. Legend:** S.M.V. CALIFORNIA GOLD

Date	F12	VF20	XF40	MS60	MS63
1851 Rare	—	—	—	—	—

Note: Stack's Superior Sale Dec. 1988, XF-40 $52,800; Beware of copies cast in base metals

BLAKE & COMPANY
20 DOLLARS

KM# 21 • Gold Obv. Value within small center circle, legend around **Rev:** Coining screw press at centre, date and value below **Obv. Legend:** BLAKE & CO. ASSAYERS **Rev. Legend:** ...CALIFORNIA GOLD

Date	F12	VF20	XF40	MS60	MS63
1855	—	—	—	—	—

Note: No original specimens are known. Most experts believe this to be a counterfeit circa 1950. Many modern copies exist

J. H. BOWIE
5 DOLLARS

KM# 22 • Gold Obv. Value at center, Company name above **Rev:** Pine tree **Rev. Legend:** CAL. GOLD 1849

Date	F12	VF20	XF40	MS60	MS63
1849 Rare	—	—	—	—	—

Note: Americana Sale Jan. 2001, AU-58 $253,000

CINCINNATI MINING AND TRADING COMPANY
5 DOLLARS

KM# 23 • Gold Obv. Draped bust with headress left **Rev:** Eagle with shield left, date below **Obv. Legend:** CINCINNATI MINING & TRADING COMPANY.

Date	F12	VF20	XF40	MS60	MS63
1849 Unique	—	—	—	—	—

10 DOLLARS

KM# 24 • Gold Obv. Draped bust with headdress left **Rev:** Eagle with shield left, date below **Obv. Legend:** CINCINNATI MINING & TRADING COMPANY.

Date	F12	VF20	XF40	MS60	MS63
1849 Rare	—	—	—	—	—

Note: Stack's-Bowers sale 2004, XF realized $431,250; Brand Sale 1984, XF $104,500

US TERRITORIAL GOLD

DUBOSQ & COMPANY
5 DOLLARS

KM# 26 • Gold **Obv.** Coronet head left, within circle of stars, date below **Rev:** Eagle **Rev. Legend:** S.M.V. CALIFORNIA GOLD

Date	F12	VF20	XF40	MS60	MS63
1850	120,000	225,000	—	—	—

10 DOLLARS

KM# 27 • Gold **Obv.** Coronet head left, within circle of stars, date below **Rev:** Eagle **Rev. Legend:** S.M.V. CALIFORNIA GOLD

Date	F12	VF20	XF40	MS60	MS63
1850	120,000	200,000	300,000	—	—

DUNBAR & COMPANY
5 DOLLARS

KM# 28 • Gold **Obv.** Coronet head left, within circle of stars, date below **Rev:** Eagle **Rev. Legend:** S.M.V. CALIFORNIA GOLD.

Date	F12	VF20	XF40	MS60	MS63
1851	125,000	200,000	350,000	—	—
Note: Spink & Son Sale 1988, AU $62,000					

AUGUSTUS HUMBERT /
UNITED STATES ASSAYER
10 DOLLARS

KM# 29.1 • Gold **Obv.** Eagle with ribbon, value below **Rev:** Inscription and date **Obv. Legend:** UNITED STATES OF AMERICA. **Note:** "AUGUSTUS

HUMBERT" imprint.

Date	F12	VF20	XF40	MS60	MS63
1852/1	3,000	5,300	8,500	30,000	—
1852	2,750	4,000	7,250	23,500	—

KM# 29.2 • Gold **Obv.** Eagle with ribbon, value below **Rev:** Inscription and date **Note:** Error: IINITED in obverse legend

Date	F12	VF20	XF40	MS60	MS63
1852/1 Rare	—	—	—	—	—
1852 Rare	—	—	—	—	—

20 DOLLARS

KM# 30 • Gold **Obv.** Eagle with ribbon and shield **Rev:** Inscription and date **Obv. Legend:** UNITED STATES OF AMERICA, 884 THOUS on ribbon

Date	F12	VF20	XF40	MS60	MS63
1852/1	6,500	10,000	22,500	—	—
Note: Mory Sale June 2000, AU-53 $13,800; Garrett Sale March 1980, Humbert's Proof $325,000; Private Sale May 1989, Humbert's Proof (PCGS Pr-65) $1,350,000; California Sale Oct. 2000, Humbert's Proof (PCGS Pr-65) $552,000					

50 DOLLARS

KM# 31.1 • Gold **Obv.** Eagle with ribbon and shield **Rev:** Target, 50 stamped incuse in center **Obv. Legend:** UNITED STATES OF AMERICA, 880 THOUS on ribbon **Edge:** Lettered

Date	F12	VF20	XF40	MS60	MS63
1851	22,500	40,000	65,000	—	—

US TERRITORIAL GOLD

KM# 31.1a • Gold **Obv.** 887 THOUS **Rev:** 50 in center **Obv. Legend:** UNITED STATES OF AMERICA

Date	F12	VF20	XF40	MS60	MS63
1851	20,000	32,500	55,000	150,000	—

KM# 31.2 • Gold **Obv.** Eagle with ribbon and shield **Rev:** Target design, without value **Obv. Legend:** UNITED STATES OF AMERICA, 880 THOUS on ribbon

Date	F12	VF20	XF40	MS60	MS63
1851	17,500	28,500	50,000	130,000	—

KM# 31.2a • Gold **Obv.** Eagle with ribbon and shield **Rev:** Target design without value **Obv. Legend:** UNITED STATES OF AMERICA, 887 THOUS on ribbon

Date	F12	VF20	XF40	MS60	MS63
1851	—	45,000	70,000	—	—

KM# 31.3 • Gold **Obv.** Eagle with ribbon and shield **Rev:** Target design, without value **Obv. Legend:** UNITED STATES OF AMERICA **Note:** ASSAYER inverted on edge.

Date	F12	VF20	XF40	MS60	MS63
1851 Unique	—	—	—	—	—

KM# 31.4 • Gold **Obv.** Eagle with ribbon and shield **Rev:** Target design, rays from center, without value **Obv. Legend:** UNITED STATES OF AMERICA, 880 THOUS on ribbon

Date	F12	VF20	XF40	MS60	MS63
1851 Unique	—	—	—	—	—

KM# 32.1 • Gold **Obv.** Eagle with ribbon and shield **Rev:** Target with circular center **Obv. Legend:** UNITED STATES OF AMERICA, 880 THOUS on ribbon

Date	F12	VF20	XF40	MS60	MS63
1851	12,000	20,000	30,000	75,000	—

Note: Garrett Sale March 1980, Humberts Proof $500,000

KM# 32.2 • Gold **Obv.** Eagle with ribbon and shield **Rev:** Target, small design **Obv. Legend:** UNITED STASTES OF AMERICA

Date	F12	VF20	XF40	MS60	MS63
1851	10,000	17,500	35,000	—	—
1852	9,500	16,500	32,000	80,000	—

Note: Bloomfield Sale December 1996, BU $159,500

US TERRITORIAL GOLD

KELLOGG & COMPANY
20 DOLLARS

KM# 33.1 • Gold **Obv.** Coronet head left, thick date **Rev:** Eagle with shield, short arrows **Rev. Legend:** SAN FRANCISCO CALIFORNIA

Date	F12	VF20	XF40	MS60	MS63
1854	2,500	3,500	5,500	19,500	—

KM# 33.2 • Gold **Obv.** Coronet head left, medium date **Rev:** Eagle with shield

Date	F12	VF20	XF40	MS60	MS63
1854	2,500	3,500	5,500	19,500	—

KM# 33.3 • Gold **Obv.** Coronet head left, thin date **Rev:** Eagle with shield, short arrows **Rev. Legend:** SAN FRANCISCO CALIFORNIA

Date	F12	VF20	XF40	MS60	MS63
1854	2,500	3,500	5,500	19,500	—

KM# 33.4 • Gold **Obv.** Coronet head left, thick date **Rev:** Eagle with shield, large and long arrows **Rev. Legend:** SAN FRANCISCO CALIFORNIA

Date	F12	VF20	XF40	MS60	MS63
1854	2,500	3,500	5,750	20,000	—
1855	2,650	3,750	6,500	22,000	—

Note: Garrett Sale March 1980 Proof $230,000

KM# 33.5 • Gold **Obv.** Coronet head left, thick date **Rev:** Eagle with shield, medium arrows **Rev. Legend:** SAN FRANCISCO CALIFORNIA

Date	F12	VF20	XF40	MS60	MS63
1855	2,650	3,750	6,500	22,000	—

KM# 33.6 • Gold **Obv.** Coronet head left **Rev:** Eagle with shield, short arrows

Date	F12	VF20	XF40	MS60	MS63
1855	2,650	3,750	6,000	20,000	—

50 DOLLARS

KM# 34 • Gold **Obv.** Coronet head left, within circle of stars **Rev:** Banner above eagle, FIFTY DOLLS. in legend **Rev. Legend:** SAN FRANCISCO CALIFORNIA.

Date	F12	VF20	XF40	MS60	MS63
1855	—	—	—	—	—

Note: Heritage FUN Sale January 2007, Pr64 $747,500. Heritage ANA Sale August 1977, Proof $156,500

MASSACHUSETTS AND CALIFORNIA COMPANY
5 DOLLARS

KM# 35 • Gold **Obv.** Rearing equestrian figure within shield with bear and dear supporters **Rev:** Value within wreath, date below **Rev. Legend:** MASSACHUSETTS & CALIFORNIA CO.

Date	F12	VF20	XF40	MS60	MS63
1849	120,000	170,000	260,000	—	—

MINERS BANK
10 DOLLARS

KM# 36 • Red Gold **Obv.** Value at center **Rev:** Eagle with shield **Rev. Legend:** CALIFORNIA.

Date	F12	VF20	XF40	MS60	MS63
ND(1849)	—	18,500	35,000	90,000	—

Note: Garrett Sale March 1980, MS-65 $135,000

KM# 36a • Yellow Gold **Obv.** Value within legend **Rev:** Eagle with shield

Date	F12	VF20	XF40	MS60	MS63
ND(1849)	—	—	—	—	—

Note: Rare, as most specimens have heavy copper alloy

MOFFAT & COMPANY
5 DOLLARS

KM# 37.1 • Gold **Obv.** Coronet head left, within circle of stars, date below **Rev:** Eagle with shiled **Rev. Legend:** S.M.V. CALIFORNIA GOLD.

Date	F12	VF20	XF40	MS60	MS63
1849	1,350	2,400	3,750	12,500	—

KM# 37.2 • Gold **Obv.** Coronet head left, within circle of stars, date below **Rev:** Eagle with shield, die break at DOL

Date	F12	VF20	XF40	MS60	MS63
1849	1,350	2,400	3,750	12,500	—

KM# 37.3 • Gold **Obv.** Coronet head left, within circle of stars, date below **Rev:** Eagle with shield, die break on shield

Date	F12	VF20	XF40	MS60	MS63
1849	1,350	2,400	3,750	12,500	—

KM# 37.4 • Gold **Obv.** Coronet head left, within circle of stars, date below **Rev:** Eagle with shield, small letters **Rev. Legend:** S.M.V. CALIFORNIA GOLD

Date	F12	VF20	XF40	MS60	MS63
1850	1,450	2,750	4,500	14,000	—

KM# 37.5 • Gold **Obv.** Coronet head left, within circle of stars, date below **Rev:** Eagle with shield, large letters

Date	F12	VF20	XF40	MS60	MS63
1850	1,450	2,750	4,500	14,000	—

Note: Garrett Sale March 1980, MS-60 $21,000

10 DOLLARS

KM# 38.1 • Gold **Obv.** Coronet head left, within circle of stars, date below **Rev:** Eagle with shield, TEN DOL., middle arrow points below period at end of GOLD **Rev. Legend:** S.M.V. CALIFORNIA GOLD.

Date	F12	VF20	XF40	MS60	MS63
1849	3,250	6,000	12,000	35,000	—

KM# 38.2 • Gold **Obv.** Coronet head left, within circle of stars, date below **Rev:** Eagle with shield, middle arrow points above period at end of GOLD.

Date	F12	VF20	XF40	MS60	MS63
1849	3,250	6,000	12,000	35,000	—

KM# 38.3 • Gold **Obv.** Coronet head, left, within circle of stars, date below **Rev:** Value: "TEN D.", large letters

Date	F12	VF20	XF40	MS60	MS63
1849	3,500	6,500	13,500	40,000	—

KM# 38.4 • Gold **Obv.** Coronet head left, within circle of stars, date below **Rev:** Eagle with shield, small letters

Date	F12	VF20	XF40	MS60	MS63
1849	3,500	6,500	13,500	40,000	—

US TERRITORIAL GOLD

KM# 39.1 • Gold **Obv.** Coronet head left, within circle of stars, wide date below **Rev:** Eagle with ribbon and shield **Rev. Legend:** 264 GRS. CALIFORNIA GOLD **Note:** "MOFFAT & CO." imprint

Date	F12	VF20	XF40	MS60	MS63
1852	3,750	37,500	12,500	70,000	—

KM# 39.2 • Gold **Obv.** Coronet head left, within circle of stars, date below, close date **Rev:** Eagle with ribbon and shield, 880 THOUS. above **Rev. Legend:** 264 GRS. CALIFORNIA GOLD **Note:** Struck by Augustus Humbert.

Date	F12	VF20	XF40	MS60	MS63
1852	3,500	6,000	11,500	70,000	—

20 DOLLARS

KM# 40 • Gold **Obv.** Coronet head left, within circle of stars, date below **Rev:** Eagle and shield, circle of stars and rays above **Rev. Legend:** SAN FRANCISCO CALIFORNIA **Note:** Struck by Curtis, Perry, & Ward.

Date	F12	VF20	XF40	MS60	MS63
1853	4,250	6,750	10,000	32,500	—

NORRIS, GREIG, & NORRIS
HALF EAGLE

KM# 41.1 • Gold **Obv.** Date in center of circle of stars and legend **Rev:** Eagle with laurel and arrows, period after ALLOY **Rev. Legend:** CALIFORNIA GOLD • WITHOUT ALLOY. • **Edge:** Plain

Date	F12	VF20	XF40	MS60	MS63
1849	4,250	6,750	13,500	32,500	—

KM# 41.2 • Gold **Obv.** Date in center of circle of stars and legend **Rev:** Eagle with laurel and arrows, period after ALLOY **Rev. Legend:** CALIFORNIA GOLD • WITHOUT ALLOY. •

Date	F12	VF20	XF40	MS60	MS63
1849	4,250	6,750	13,500	32,500	—

KM# 41.3 • Gold **Obv.** Date in center of circle of stars and legend **Rev:** Eagle with laurel and arrows, period after ALLOY **Edge:** Reeded

Date	F12	VF20	XF40	MS60	MS63
1849	3,750	6,000	12,500	32,000	—

KM# 41.4 • Gold **Obv.** Date in center of circle of stars and legend **Rev:** Eagle with laurel and arrows, without period after ALLOY

Date	F12	VF20	XF40	MS60	MS63
1849	3,750	6,000	12,500	32,000	—

KM# 42 • Gold **Obv.** STOCKTON beneath date **Rev:** Eagle with laurel and arrows

Date	F12	VF20	XF40	MS60	MS63
1850 Unique	—	—	—	—	—

J. S. ORMSBY
5 DOLLARS

KM# 43.1 • Gold **Obv.** J.S.O. in center **Rev:** Value within circle of stars **Obv. Legend:** UNITED STATES OF AMERICA **Edge:** Plain

Date	F12	VF20	XF40	MS60	MS63
ND(1849) Unique	—	—	—	—	—

KM# 43.2 • Gold **Obv.** J.S.O. in center **Rev:** Value within circle of stars **Edge:** Reeded

Date	F12	VF20	XF40	MS60	MS63
ND(1849) Unique	—	—	—	—	—

Note: Superior Auction 1989, VF $137,500

US TERRITORIAL GOLD

10 DOLLARS

KM# 44 • Gold **Obv.** J.S.O. in center **Rev:** Value in center circle of stars **Obv. Legend:** UNITED STATES OF AMERICA

Date	F12	VF20	XF40	MS60	MS63
ND(1849) Rare	—	—	—	—	—

Note: Garrett Sale March 1980, F-12 $100,000; Ariagno Sale June 1999, AU-50 $145,000

PACIFIC COMPANY
1 DOLLAR

KM# A45 • Gold **Obv.** Liberty cap on pole, stars and rays around, value below **Rev:** Eagle

Date	F12	VF20	XF40	MS60	MS63
ND(1849) Rare	—	—	—	—	—

Note: Stack's Old West Sale August 2006, AU $126,500. Mory Sale June 2000, EF-40 $57,500

5 DOLLARS

KM# 45 • Gold **Obv.** Liberty cap on pole, stars and rays around, value below **Rev:** Eagle **Rev. Legend:** PACIFIC COMPANY CALIFORNIA

Date	F12	VF20	XF40	MS60	MS63
1849 Rare	—	—	—	—	—

Note: Garrett Sale March 1980, VF-30 $180,000

10 DOLLARS

KM# 46.1 • Gold **Obv.** Liberty cap on pole, stars and rays around, value below **Rev:** Eagle, date below **Rev. Legend:** PACIFIC COMPANY CALIFORNIA **Edge:** Plain

Date	F12	VF20	XF40	MS60	MS63
1849 Rare	—	—	—	—	—

Note: Waldorf Sale 1964, $24,000

KM# 46.2 • Gold **Obv.** Liberty cap on pole, stars and rays around **Rev:** Eagle **Edge:** Reeded

Date	F12	VF20	XF40	MS60	MS63
1849 Rare	—	—	—	—	—

TEMPLETON REID
10 DOLLARS

KM# 47 • Gold **Obv.** Date in center **Rev:** Value in center **Obv. Legend:** TEMPLETON... **Rev. Legend:** CALIFORNIA * GOLD *

Date	F12	VF20	XF40	MS60	MS63
1849 Unique	—	—	—	—	—

20 DOLLARS

KM# 48 • Gold

Date	F12	VF20	XF40	MS60	MS63
1849 Unknown	—	—	—	—	—

Note: The only known specimen was stolen from the U.S. Mint in 1858 and has never been recovered. For additional listings of Templeton Reid, see listings under Georgia

SCHULTZ & COMPANY
5 DOLLARS

KM# 49 • Gold **Obv.** Coronet head left, within circle of stars, date below **Rev:** Eagle, shield on breast, value below **Rev. Legend:** PURE CALIFORNIA GOLD.

Date	F12	VF20	XF40	MS60	MS63
1851	25,000	55,000	85,000	—	—

UNITED STATES ASSAY OFFICE OF GOLD
10 DOLLARS

KM# 51.1 • Gold **Obv.** Eagle with ribbon and shield **Rev:** O of OFFICE below I of UNITED **Obv. Legend:** UNITED STATES OF AMERICA TEN DOLS 884 THOUS

Date	F12	VF20	XF40	MS60	MS63
1852	—	—	—	—	—

Note: Garrett Sale March 1980, MS-60 $18,000

US TERRITORIAL GOLD

KM# 51.2 • Gold **Obv.** Eagle with ribbon and shield **Rev:** O below N, strong beads **Obv. Legend:** UNITED STATES OF AMERICA TEN DOLS 884 THOUS

Date	F12	VF20	XF40	MS60	MS63
1852	1,750	3,000	5,000	17,500	—

KM# 51.3 • Gold **Obv.** Eagle with ribbon and shield **Rev:** Weak beads **Obv. Legend:** UNITED STATES OF AMERICA TEN DOLS 884 THOUS

Date	F12	VF20	XF40	MS60	MS63
1852	1,750	3,000	5,000	17,500	—

KM# 52 • Gold **Obv.** Eagle with ribbon and shield **Rev:** Inscription, date **Obv. Legend:** UNITED STATES OF AMERICA TEN D, 884 THOUS

Date	F12	VF20	XF40	MS60	MS63
1853	7,500	13,500	25,000	—	—

KM# 52a • Gold **Obv.** Eagle with ribbon and shield **Rev:** Inscription, date **Obv. Legend:** UNITED STATES OF AMERICA TEN D. 900 THOUS

Date	F12	VF20	XF40	MS60	MS63
1853	42,000	6,500	10,000	27,500	—

Note: Garrett Sale March 1980, MS-60 $35,000

20 DOLLARS

KM# 53 • Gold **Obv.** Eagle with ribbon and shield **Rev:** Inscription, date **Obv. Legend:** UNITED STATES OF AMERICA TWENTY D. 884/880 THOUS

Date	F12	VF20	XF40	MS60	MS63
1853	8,500	12,500	18,500	47,500	—

KM# 53a • Gold **Obv.** Eagle with ribbon and

shield **Rev:** Inscription, date **Obv. Legend:** UNITED STATES OF AMERICA TWENTY D. 900/880 THOUS

Date	F12	VF20	XF40	MS60	MS63
1853	2,250	3,250	5,000	12,500	—

Note: 1853 Liberty Head listed under Moffat & Company

50 DOLLARS

KM# 54 • Gold **Obv.** Eagle with ribbon and shield **Rev:** Target **Obv. Legend:** UNITED STATES OF AMERICA FIFTY FOLLS. 887 THOUS **Shape:** 8-sided

Date	F12	VF20	XF40	MS60	MS63
1852	12,500	20,000	32,000	77,500	—

KM# 54a • Gold **Obv.** Eagle and ribbon with shield **Rev:** Target **Obv. Legend:** UNITED STATES OF AMERICA FIFTY DOLLS. 900 THOUS **Shape:** 8-sided

Date	F12	VF20	XF40	MS60	MS63
1852	12,500	20,000	33,500	82,500	—

US TERRITORIAL GOLD

WASS, MOLITOR & COMPANY

5 DOLLARS

KM# 55.1 • Gold **Obv.** Small Liberty head, rounded bust **Rev:** Eagle, shield on breast **Rev. Legend:** • IN CALIFORNIA GOLD • FIVE DOLLARS

Date	F12	VF20	XF40	MS60	MS63
1852	4,500	10,000	20,000	67,500	—

KM# 55.2 • Gold **Obv.** Coronet head, left, within circle of stars **Rev:** Eagle, shield on breast **Rev. Legend:** • IN CALIFORNIA GOLD • FIVE DOLLARS **Note:** Thick planchet.

Date	F12	VF20	XF40	MS60	MS63
1852 Unique	—	—	—	—	—

KM# 56 • Gold **Obv.** Large Liberty head, pointed bust **Rev:** Eagle, shield on breast **Rev. Legend:** • IN CALIFORNIA GOLD • FIVE DOLLARS

Date	F12	VF20	XF40	MS60	MS63
1852	4,000	9,000	17,500	60,000	—

10 DOLLARS

KM# 57 • Gold **Obv.** Liberty head with long neck, large date **Rev:** Eagle, shield on breast **Rev. Legend:** • S.M.V. CALIFORNIA GOLD • TEN D.

Date	F12	VF20	XF40	MS60	MS63
1852	5,500	9,500	18,500	—	—

KM# 58 • Gold **Obv.** Liberty head, short neck, wide date **Rev:** Eagle, shield on breast **Rev. Legend:** • S.M.V. CALIFORNIA GOLD • TEN D.

Date	F12	VF20	XF40	MS60	MS63
1852	2,800	4,650	7,500	27,500	—

KM# 59.1 • Gold **Obv.** Liberty head, short neck, small date **Rev:** Eagle, shield on breast **Rev. Legend:** • S.M.V. CALIFORNIA GOLD • TEN D.

Date	F12	VF20	XF40	MS60	MS63
1852	13,500	28,000	50,000	—	—

Note: Eliasberg Sale May 1996, EF-45 $36,300; S.S. Central America Sale December 2000, VF-30 realized $12,650

KM# 59.2 • Gold **Obv.** Plugged date **Rev:** Eagle, shield on breast **Rev. Legend:** S.M.V.CALIFORNIA GOLD.

Date	F12	VF20	XF40	MS60	MS63
1855	9,000	14,500	22,000	55,000	—

20 DOLLARS

KM# 60 • Gold **Obv.** Large Liberty head **Rev:** Eagle, shield on breast, value in banner above **Rev. Legend:** SAN FRANCISCO CALIFORNIA TWENTY DOL. 900 THOUS

Date	F12	VF20	XF40	MS60	MS63
1855 Rare	—	—	—	—	—

KM# 61 • Gold **Obv.** Small head **Rev:** Eagle, shield on breast, value in banner above **Rev. Legend:** SAN FRANCISCO CALIFORNIA TWENTY DOL.

Date	F12	VF20	XF40	MS60	MS63
1855	12,500	25,000	45,000	—	—

Note: Heritage CSNS Sale May 2007, AU55 $43,125

50 DOLLARS

KM# 62 • Gold **Obv.** Coronet head, left, within circle of stars, date below **Rev:** Value within wreath **Rev. Legend:** SAN FRANCISCO CALIFORNIA WASS MOLITOR & Co 50 DOLLARS

Date	F12	VF20	XF40	MS60	MS63
1855	22,500	32,500	55,000	165,000	—

Note: Heritage Baltimore Sale July-August 2008, MS-61 $207,000, AU-50 $63,250. Heritage FUN Sale January 2008, MS-60 $161,000. Bloomfield Sale December 1996, BU $170,500

COLORADO

The discovery of gold in Colorado Territory was accompanied by the inevitable need for coined money. Austin M. Clark, Milton E. Clark, and Emanuel H. Gruber, bankers of Leavenworth, Kansas, moved to Denver where they established a bank and issued $2.50, $5, $10, and $20 gold coins in 1860 and 1861. To protect the holder from loss by abrasion, Clark, Gruber & Co. made their coins slightly heavier than full value required. The 1860 issues carry the inscription PIKE'S PEAK GOLD on reverse. CLARK, GRUBER & CO. appears on the reverse of the 1861 issues, and PIKE'S PEAK on the coronet of Liberty. The government purchased the plant of Clark, Gruber & Co. in 1863 and operated it as a federal Assay Office until 1906.

In the summer of 1861, John Parsons, an assayer whose place of business was located in South Park at the Tarryall Mines, Colorado, issued undated gold coins in the denominations of $2.50 and $5. They, too, carry the inscription PIKE'S PEAK GOLD on reverse.

J. J. Conway & Co., bankers of Georgia Gulch, Colorado operated the Conway Mint for a short period in 1861. Undated gold coins in the denominations of $2.50, $5, and $10 were issued. A variety of the $5 coin does not carry the numeral 5 on reverse. The issues of the Conway Mint were highly regarded for their scrupulously maintained value.

CLARK, GRUBER & COMPANY
2-1/2 DOLLARS

KM# 63 • Gold **Obv.** Coronet head, left, within circle of stars, date below **Rev:** Eagle, shield on breast **Rev. Legend:** • PIKES PEAK GOLD DENVER • 2 1/2 D.

Date	F12	VF20	XF40	MS60	MS63
1860	1,500	2,500	3,750	12,500	40,000

Note: Garrett Sale March 1980, MS-65 $12,000

KM# 64.1 • Gold **Obv.** Coronet head, left, within circle of stars, date below **Rev:** Eagle, shield on breast **Rev. Legend:** • CLARK GRUBER & CO DENVER • 2 1/2 D

Date	F12	VF20	XF40	MS60	MS63
1861	1,650	2,750	4,000	13,500	—

KM# 64.2 • Gold **Obv.** Coronet head, left, within circle of stars, date below **Rev:** Eagle, shield on breast **Rev. Legend:** • CLARK, GRUBER & CO. DENVER • 2 1/2 D **Note:** Extra high edge.

Date	F12	VF20	XF40	MS60	MS63
1861	1,750	3,000	4,500	14,500	—

5 DOLLARS

KM# 65 • Gold **Obv.** Coronet head, left, within circle of stars, date below **Rev:** Eagle, shield on breast **Rev. Legend:** • PIKES PEAK GOLD DENVER • 2 1/2 D

Date	F12	VF20	XF40	MS60	MS63
1860	2,000	3,200	4,500	12,500	—

Note: Garrett Sale March 1980, MS-63 $9,000

US TERRITORIAL GOLD

KM# 66 • Gold **Obv.** Coronet head, left, within circle of stars, date below **Rev:** Eagle, shield on breast **Rev. Legend:** • CLARK GRUBER & CO DENVER • 2 1/2 D

Date	F12	VF20	XF40	MS60	MS63
1861	2,500	3,650	6,000	35,000	—

10 DOLLARS

KM# 67 • Gold **Obv.** Mountain above value **Rev:** Eagle, shield on breast **Obv. Legend:** PIKES PEAK GOLD / DENVER / TEN D. **Rev. Legend:** CLARK GRUBER & CO.

Date	F12	VF20	XF40	MS60	MS63
1860	7,250	11,000	17,500	47,500	—

KM# 68 • Gold **Obv.** Coronet head, left, within circle of stars, date below **Rev:** Eagle, shield on breast **Rev. Legend:** * CLARK GRUBER & CO DENVER * TEN D.

Date	F12	VF20	XF40	MS60	MS63
1861	2,500	3,850	6,750	27,500	—

20 DOLLARS

KM# 69 • Gold **Obv.** Mountain above value **Rev:**

Eagle, shield on breast **Obv. Legend:** PIKES PEAK GOLD / DENVER / TWENTY D. **Rev. Legend:** CLARK GRUBER & CO.

Date	F12	VF20	XF40	MS60	MS63
1860	50,000	100,000	175,000	525,000	—

Note: Heritage FUN Sale January 2006, MS-64 $690,000. Eliasberg Sale May 1996, AU $90,200. Schoonmaker Sale June 1997, VCF $62,700

KM# 70 • Gold **Obv.** Coronet head, left, within circle of stars, date below **Rev:** Circle of stars and rays above eagle **Rev. Legend:** CLARK GRUBER & CO DENVER .TWENTY D.

Date	F12	VF20	XF40	MS60	MS63
1861	14,500	32,500	57,500	—	—

J. J. CONWAY
2-1/2 DOLLARS

KM# 71 • Gold **Obv.** legend **Rev:** Value in center **Obv. Legend:** * J.J. CONWAY * / & CO. / BANKERS **Rev. Legend:** * PIKES PEAK * 2 1/2 DOLS

Date	F12	VF20	XF40	MS60	MS63
ND(1861)	—	140,000	180,000	—	—

5 DOLLARS

KM# 72.1 • Gold **Obv.** Legend, ring of stars within **Rev:** Large 5 in center **Obv. Legend:** * J.J. CONWAY * / & CO. / BANKERS **Rev. Legend:** PIKES PEAK / FIVE DOLLARS

Date	F12	VF20	XF40	MS60	MS63
ND(1861) Rare	—	—	—	—	—

Note: Brand Sale June 1984, XF-40 $44,000

KM# 72.2 • Gold **Obv.** Legend **Rev:** Legend without large 5 in center **Obv. Legend:** * J.J. CONWAY * / & CO. / BANKERS

Date	F12	VF20	XF40	MS60	MS63
ND(1861) Unique	—	—	—	—	—

US TERRITORIAL GOLD

10 DOLLARS

KM# 73 • Gold **Obv.** & CO. within circle **Rev:**
Numeral value within circle of stars **Obv. Legend:**
* J.J. CONWAY * / & CO. / BANKERS **Obv.**
Inscription: * J.J. CONWAY * BANKERS **Rev.**
Legend: * PIKES PEAK * TEN DOLLARS

Date	F12	VF20	XF40	MS60	MS63
ND(1861) Rare	—	—	—	—	—

JOHN PARSONS
2-1/2 DOLLARS

KM# 74 • Gold **Obv.** Assay office window and
minting machine **Rev:** Eagle, shield on breast, value
below **Obv. Legend:** J PARSON & Co / ORO **Rev.**
Legend: PIKES PEAK GOLD / 2 1/2 D

Date	F12	VF20	XF40	MS60	MS63
ND(1861) Rare	—	—	—	—	—

Note: Garrett Sale March 1980, VF-20 $85,000

5 DOLLARS

KM# 75 • Gold **Obv.** Assay office window and
minting machine **Rev:** Eagle, shield on breast, value
below **Obv. Legend:** J N. PARSON & Co. / ORO
Rev. Legend: PIKES PEAK GOLD / TEN D.

Date	F12	VF20	XF40	MS60	MS63
ND(1861) Rare	—	—	—	—	—

Note: Garrett Sale March 1980, VF-20 $100,000

GEORGIA

The first territorial gold pieces were struck
in 1830 by Templeton Reid, a goldsmith and
assayer who established a private mint at
Gainesville, Georgia, at the time gold was being mined on a relatively large scale in Georgia
and North Carolina. Reid's pieces were issued
in denominations of $2.50, $5, and $10. Ex-
cept for an undated variety of the $10 piece, all
are dated 1830.

CHRISTOPHER BECHTLER
2-1/2 DOLLARS

KM# 76.1 • Gold **Obv.** 2.50 in center **Rev:** 64. G. /
22. in center **Obv. Legend:** BECHTLER . RUTHERF :
Rev. Legend: :GEORGIA GOLD: CARATS

Date	F12	VF20	XF40	MS60	MS63
ND(1831)	4,200	6,750	12,500	28,500	—

KM# 76.2 • Gold **Obv.** 2.50 in center **Rev:** 64. G.
/ 22. in center, even 22 **Obv. Legend:** BECHLER
. RUTHERF : **Rev. Legend:** GEORGIA GOLD :
CATATS :

Date	F12	VF20	XF40	MS60	MS63
ND(1831)	4,500	7,500	13,750	37,500	—

5 DOLLARS

KM# 77 • Gold **Obv.** Value in center **Rev:** 128 G / *
in center **Obv. Legend:** C. BECHTLER. AT RUTHERF
* 5 DOLLARS **Rev. Legend:** GEORGIA GOLD. 22
CARATS.

Date	F12	VF20	XF40	MS60	MS63
ND(1831)	4,000	7,000	11,000	28,500	—

KM# 78.1 • Gold **Obv.** Value in center **Rev:** 128.
G. / * in center **Obv. Legend:** C. BECHTLER.
AT RUTHERFORD * 5 DOLLARS **Rev. Legend:**
GEORGIA GOLD. / 22 CARATS.

Date	F12	VF20	XF40	MS60	MS63
ND(1831)	4,000	7,500	12,000	32,000	—

KM# 78.2 • Gold **Obv.** Value in center **Rev:**
128 G: in center **Obv. Legend:** C. BECHTLER.
AT RUTHERFORD / 5 DOLLARS. **Rev. Legend:**
GEORGIA GOLD. 22 CARATS.

Date	F12	VF20	XF40	MS60	MS63
ND(1831) Rare	—	—	—	—	—

Note: Stack's Americana Sale January 2008 AU-58 $115,000.
Akers Pittman Sale October 1997, VF-XF $26,400.

TEMPLETON REID
2-1/2 DOLLARS

KM# 79 • Gold Obv. Date in center **Rev:** Value in center **Obv. Legend:** GEORGIA /GOLD. / 1830 **Rev. Legend:** T. REID / ASSAYER.

Date	F12	VF20	XF40	MS60	MS63
1830	55,000	85,000	165,000	—	—

Note: Stack's Berngard/S.S. New York Sale July 2008 VF35 $103,500. Stack's Norweb Sale November 2006 AU55 $299,000

5 DOLLARS

KM# 80 • Gold Obv. Value in center **Rev:** Value in center **Obv. Legend:** GEORGIA GOLD. / 1830 / $5 **Rev. Legend:** TEMPLETON REID / ASSAYER. / $5

Date	F12	VF20	XF40	MS60	MS63
1830 Rare, 7 known	—	—	—	—	—

Note: Garrett Sale November 1979, XF-40 $200,000

10 DOLLARS

KM# 81 • Gold Obv. Date at center **Rev:** Written value at center **Obv. Legend:** GEORGIA / GOLD / 1830 **Rev. Legend:** TEMPLETON REID / ASSAYER / TEN / DOLLARS

Date	F12	VF20	XF40	MS60	MS63
1830 Rare, 6 known	—	—	—	—	—

KM# 82 • Gold Obv. Without date at center **Rev:** Written value at center **Obv. Legend:** GEORGIA / GOLD **Rev. Legend:** TEMPLETON REID / ASSAYER / TEN / DOLLARS

Date	F12	VF20	XF40	MS60	MS63
ND(1830) Rare, 3 known	—	—	—	—	—

Note: Also see listings under California

NORTH CAROLINA

The southern Appalachians were also the scene of a private gold minting operation conducted by Christopher Bechtler Sr., his son August, and nephew Christopher Jr. The Bechtlers, a family of German metallurgists, established a mint at Rutherfordton, North Carolina, which produced territorial gold coins for a longer period than any other private mint in American history. Christopher Bechtler Sr. ran the Bechtler mint from July 1831 until his death in 1842, after which the mint was taken over by his son August who ran it until 1852.

The Bechtler coinage includes but 3 denominations -- $1, $2.50, and $5 - but they were issued in a wide variety of weights and sizes. The coinage is undated, except for 3 varieties of the $5 piece which carry the inscription "Aug. 1, 1834" to indicate that they conform to the new weight standard adopted by the U.S. Treasury for official gold coins. Christopher Bechtler Sr. produced $2.50 and $5 gold coins for Georgia, and $1, $2.50, and $5 coins for North Carolina. The dollar coins have the distinction of being the first gold coins of that denomination to be produced in the United States. While under the supervision of August Bechtler, the Bechtler mint issued $1 and $5 coins for North Carolina.

AUGUST BECHTLER
DOLLAR

KM# 83.1 • Gold Obv. Large 1 in center **Rev:** 27. G. in center **Obv. Legend:** A. BECHTLER. / 1 / DOL: * **Rev. Legend:** CAROLINA GOLD. / 21C. **Edge:** Plain

Date	F12	VF20	XF40	MS60	MS63
ND(1842-52)	900	1,450	2,250	4,750	—

KM# 83.2 • Gold Obv. Value in center **Rev:** 27 G. in center **Obv. Legend:** A. BECHTLER . / 1 /DOL: **Rev. Legend:** CAROLINA GOLD . / 21 C. **Edge:** Reeded

Date	F12	VF20	XF40	MS60	MS63
ND(1842-52)	900	1,450	2,250	4,750	—

5 DOLLARS

KM# 84 • Gold Obv. Value in two lines in center

US TERRITORIAL GOLD

Rev: 134 G. at center **Obv. Legend:** A. BECHTLER.
RUTHERFORD * / 5 / DOLLARS **Rev. Legend:**
CAROLINA GOLD. / 21/ CARATS.

Date	F12	VF20	XF40	MS60	MS63
ND(1842-52)	2,650	5,300	9,000	32,500	—

KM# 85 • Gold **Obv.** Value in two lines in center
Rev: 128 G. in center **Obv. Legend:** A. BECHTLER.
RUTHERFORD / 5 / DOLLARS **Rev. Legend:**
CAROLINA GOLD. / 22 / CARATS

Date	F12	VF20	XF40	MS60	MS63
ND(1842-52)	7,000	12,500	18,000	42,500	—

KM# 86 • Gold **Obv.** Value in two lines in center
Rev: 141. G: in center **Obv. Legend:** A. BECHTLER.
RUTHERFORD / 5 / DOLLARS. **Rev. Legend:**
CAROLINA GOLD. / 20 / CARATS

Date	F12	VF20	XF40	MS60	MS63
ND(1842-52)	6,500	11,500	17,000	38,500	—
ND(1842-52) Proof restrike	—	—	—	—	—

> Note: Struck from original dies by Henry Chapman in 1908.
> Stack's Nerngard/S.S. New York Sale July 2008 Pr63
> sold for $34,500. Akers Pittman Sale October 1997 chPr
> $14,300

CHRISTOPHER BECHTLER
DOLLAR

KM# 87 • Gold **Obv.** 28 G. in center **Rev:** ONE
in center, N reversed **Obv. Legend:** * BECHTLER
RUTHERF: / 28. G. **Rev. Legend:** * CAROLINA
DOLLAR / ONE

Date	F12	VF20	XF40	MS60	MS63
ND(1831-42)	1,250	2,200	3,000	7,500	—

KM# 88.1 • Gold **Obv.** 28. G. centered in center
Rev: ONE at center **Obv. Legend:** C: BECHTLER.
RUTHERF: **Rev. Legend:** N: CAROLINA GOLD.
DOLLAR. / ONE

Date	F12	VF20	XF40	MS60	MS63
ND(1831-42)	2,400	4,000	6,000	24,000	—

KM# 88.2 • Gold **Obv.** 28 G high in center
Rev: ONE in center **Obv. Legend:** C: BECHTLER
RUTHERF: / 28 G. **Rev. Legend:** N. CAROLINA
GOLD DOLLAR / ONE

Date	F12	VF20	XF40	MS60	MS63
ND(1831-42)	5,000	8,500	12,500	32,500	—

KM# 89 • Gold **Obv.** 30 G. /* in center **Rev:** ONE
at center **Obv. Legend:** C. BECHTLER. RUTHERF:
/ 30 G. / * **Rev. Legend:** N: CAROLINA GOLD.
DOLLAR. / ONE

Date	F12	VF20	XF40	MS60	MS63
ND(1831-42)	1,650	2,750	4,250	15,000	—

2-1/2 DOLLARS

KM# 90 • Gold **Obv.** 250 in center **Rev:** 67 G.
21 CARATS at center **Obv. Legend:** BECHTLER
RUTHERF: **Rev. Legend:** CAROLINA GOLD.

Date	F12	VF20	XF40	MS60	MS63
ND(1831-42)	2,500	5,500	11,500	27,000	—

> Note: Stack's Old Coloney Sale December 2005 MS62 $23,000

KM# 91 • Gold **Obv.** 250 in center **Rev:** 70 G.
20 CARATS at center **Obv. Legend:** BECHTLER
RUTHERF. **Rev. Legend:** CAROLINA GOLD

Date	F12	VF20	XF40	MS60	MS63
ND(1831-42)	2,750	5,750	12,000	29,500	—

> Note: Stack's Norweb Sale November 2006 MS60 $26,450.
> Stack's Allison Park Sale August 2004 MS62 $28,750.
> Bowers and Merena Long Sale May 1995, MS-63
> $31,900

KM# 92.1 • Gold **Obv.** RUTHERFORD in a circle,
border of large beads **Rev:** 250 / 20 C. / 75 G. in
center **Obv. Legend:** C. BECHTLER, ASSAYER. **Rev.
Legend:** NORTH CAROLINA GOLD

Date	F12	VF20	XF40	MS60	MS63
ND(1831-42)	12,500	22,500	34,500	75,000	—

KM# 92.2 • Gold **Obv.** RUTHERFORD in circle
Rev: 250. / wide 20 C. in center **Obv. Legend:**
C. BECHTLER, ASSAYER. **Rev. Legend:** NORTH
CAROLINA GOLD

US TERRITORIAL GOLD

Date	F12	VF20	XF40	MS60	MS63
ND(1831-42)	15,000	25,000	35,000	85,000	—

Note: Stack's Norweb Sale November 2006 MS62 $83,375

KM# 92.3 • Gold **Obv.** 250 / narrow 20 C in center **Series:** RUTHERFORD in circle in center **Obv. Legend:** C. BECHTLER, ASSAYER **Rev. Legend:** NORTH CAROLINA GOLD

Date	F12	VF20	XF40	MS60	MS63
ND(1831-42)	15,000	25,000	35,000	85,000	—

KM# 93.1 • Gold **Obv.** RUTHERFORD in a circle **Rev:** 250 / 20 G in center **Obv. Legend:** C. BECHTLER, ASSAYER. **Rev. Legend:** NORTH CAROLINA GOLD.

Date	F12	VF20	XF40	MS60	MS63
ND(1831-42) Unique	—	—	—	—	—

KM# 93.2 • Gold **Obv.** * / 75 G in center, border finely serrated **Rev:** 250. / 20 G. in center **Obv. Legend:** C. BECHLER ASSAYER / 75 G **Rev. Legend:** NORTH CAROLINA GOLD

Date	F12	VF20	XF40	MS60	MS63
ND(1831-42) Rare	—	—	—	—	—

5 DOLLARS

KM# 94 • Gold **Obv.** two-line value in center **Rev:** 134 G. / * in center **Obv. Legend:** C. BECHTLER. AT RUTHER. * / 5 / DOLLARS * **Rev. Legend:** CAROLINA GOLD: / 21 CARATS

Date	F12	VF20	XF40	MS60	MS63
ND(1831-42)	2,750	5,500	8,500	22,500	—

KM# 95 • Gold **Obv.** Two-line value in center **Rev:** 134. G at center, 21 above CARATS, no star **Obv. Legend:** C. BECHTLER. AT RUTHERF / 5 / DOLLARS **Rev. Legend:** CAROLINA GOLD / 21 / CARATS

Date	F12	VF20	XF40	MS60	MS63
ND(1831-42) Unique	—	—	—	—	—

KM# 96.1 • Gold **Obv.** Value in center **Rev:** 140 G. in center **Obv. Legend:** C. BECHTLER. AT

RUTHERFORD. **Rev. Legend:** CAROLINA GOLD. / 20 / CARATS **Edge:** Plain

Date	F12	VF20	XF40	MS60	MS63
1834	2,500	5,000	8,000	25,000	—

KM# 96.2 • Gold **Obv.** Value in center **Rev:** 140. G. in center **Obv. Legend:** C. BECHTLER. AT RUTHERFORD / 5 / DOLLARS **Rev. Legend:** CAROLINA GOLD / 20 / CARATS **Edge:** Reeded

Date	F12	VF20	XF40	MS60	MS63
1834	7,500	14,500	27,500	65,000	—

KM# 97.1 • Gold **Obv.** Value at center **Rev:** 140 / G / in center, 20 close to CARATS **Obv. Legend:** C. BECHTLER. AT RUTHER: **Rev. Legend:** CAROLINA GOLD. / 20 / CARATS **Edge:** Plain

Date	F12	VF20	XF40	MS60	MS63
1834	4,000	8,500	16,500	47,500	—

KM# 97.2 • Gold **Obv.** Value in center **Rev:** 140 / G in center, 20 far away from CARATS **Obv. Legend:** C. BECHTLER. AT RUTHERF: / 5 / DOLLARS **Rev. Legend:** CALIFORNIA GOLD. / 20 / CARATS **Edge:** Plain

Date	F12	VF20	XF40	MS60	MS63
1834	2,500	6,500	11,500	32,500	—

Note: Stack's Berngard/S.S. New York Sale July 2008 AU58 $29,900

KM# 98 • Gold **Obv.** Value in center **Rev:** 141. G: in center **Obv. Legend:** C. BECHTLER. AT RUTHERF: / 5 / DOLLARS. **Rev. Legend:** CAROLINA GOLD. / 20 CARATS

Date	F12	VF20	XF40	MS60	MS63
ND(1831-42) Proof restrike	—	—	—	—	—

Note: Struck from original dies by Henry Chapman in 1908. Heritage ANA Sale Auguust 2007 Pr65 $37,375

US TERRITORIAL GOLD

KM# 99.1 • Gold Obv. Legend in double circle **Rev:** 5 / DOLLARS / 20 CARATS / 150 G in center **Obv. Legend:** C. BECHTLER, ASSAYER. / RUTHERFORD COUNTY. **Rev. Legend:** NORTH CAROLINA GOLD.

Date	F12	VF20	XF40	MS60	MS63
ND(1831-42)	12,000	20,000	35,000	85,000	—

Note: Stack's Berngard/S.S. New York Sale July 2008 AU50 $69,000. Stack's Americana Sale January 2008 AU55 $74,750. Heritage ANA Sale August 2007 MS62 $97,750

KM# 99.2 • Gold Obv. Legend in two circles **Rev:** 5 / DOLLARS / 20 CARATS. in center **Obv. Legend:** C. BRECHTLER, ASSAYER. / RUTHERFORD COUNTY. **Rev. Legend:** NORTH CAROLINA GOLD.

Date	F12	VF20	XF40	MS60	MS63
ND(1831-42) Rare	—	—	—	—	—

OREGON

The Oregon Exchange Co., a private mint located at Oregon City, Oregon Territory, issued $5 and $10 pieces of local gold in 1849. The initials K., M., T., A., W. R. C. (G on the $5 piece), and S. on the obverse represent the eight founders of the Oregon Exchange Co.: William Kilborne, Theophilus Magruder, James Taylor, George Abernathy, William Willson, William Rector, John Campbell, and Noyes Smith. Campbell is erroneously represented by a G on the $5 coin. For unknown reasons, the initials A and W are omitted from the $10 piece. O.T. (Oregon Territory) is erroneously presented as T.O. on the $5 coin.

OREGON EXCHANGE COMPANY
5 DOLLARS

KM# 100 • Gold Obv. Beaver above date and sprigs **Rev:** Weight and value in center **Obv. Legend:** R. M. T. A. W. R. C. S. / T. O. / 1849 **Rev. Legend:** OREGON EXCHANGE COMPANY / 130 G. / NATIVE / GOLD. / 5 D.

Date	F12	VF20	XF40	MS60	MS63
1849	22,500	37,500	70,000	—	—

Note: Heritage Internet Sale February 2009 AU53 $69,000. Heritage FUN Sale January 2009 VF25 $37,375

10 DOLLARS

KM# 101 • Gold Obv. Beaver above date and sprigs **Rev:** Weight and value within wreath **Obv. Legend:** R. M. T. R. C. S. / O. T. / 1849 **Rev. Legend:** OREGON EXCHANGE COMPANY. / 10 D. 20 G. / NATIVE / GOLD / TEN D.

Date	F12	VF20	XF40	MS60	MS63
1849	65,000	125,000	225,000	—	—

Note: Heritage Long Beach Sale September 2002 XF40 $126,500

UTAH

In 1894, the Mormons settled in the Great Salt Lake Valley of Utah and established the Deseret Mint in a small adobe building in Salt Lake City. Operating under the direct supervision of Brigham Young, the Deseret Mint issued $2.50, $5, $10, and $20 gold coins in 1849. Additional $5 pieces were struck in 1850 and 1860, the latter in a temporary mint set up in Barlow's jewelery shop. The Mormon $20 piece was the first of that denomination to be struck in the United States. The initials G.S.L.C.P.G. on Mormon coins denotes "Great Salt Lake City Pure Gold." It was later determined that the coinage was grossly deficient in value, mainly because no attempt was made to assay or refine the gold.

MORMON ISSUES
2-1/2 DOLLARS

KM# 102 • Gold Obv. Hat design above eye **Rev:** Clasped hands above date **Obv. Legend:** HOLINESS • TO • THE • LORD • **Rev. Legend:** G. S. L. C. P. C. / TWO . AND . HALF . DO.

Date	F12	VF20	XF40	MS60	MS63
1849	11,500	17,500	28,500	75,000	—

US TERRITORIAL GOLD

5 DOLLARS

KM# 103 • Gold **Obv.** Hat design above eye **Rev:**
Clasped hands above date **Obv. Legend:** HOLINESS
• TO • THE • LORD • **Rev. Legend:** G. S. L. C. P. C.
/ FIVE.DOLLARS

Date	F12	VF20	XF40	MS60	MS63
1849	7,750	18,500	24,500	70,000	—

KM# 104 • Gold **Obv.** Hat design above eye and
stars **Rev:** Clasped hands above date **Obv. Legend:**
HOLINESS •TO • THE • LORD • **Rev. Legend:** G. S.
L. C. P. C. / FIVE DOLLARS

Date	F12	VF20	XF40	MS60	MS63
1850	9,500	18,500	32,000	80,000	—

Note: Heritage Long Beach Sale February 2009 MS61 $54,625

KM# 105 • Gold **Obv.** Seated lion facing left above
date **Rev:** Beehive design on eagle breast

Date	F12	VF20	XF40	MS60	MS63
1860	13,500	27,500	45,000	85,000	—

Note: Heritage Los Angeles Sale August 2009 AU55 $63,250.
Stack's Bergstrom/Husky Sale June 2008 MS61 $74,750

10 DOLLARS

KM# 106 • Gold **Obv.** Hat design above eye **Rev:**
Clasped hands above date **Obv. Legend:** HOLINESS
• TO • THE • LORD **Rev. Legend:** PURE GOLD. /
TEN DOLLARS

Date	F12	VF20	XF40	MS60	MS63
1849	175,000	275,000	385,000	—	—

Note: Heritage ANA Sale July 1988, AU $93,000

20 DOLLARS

KM# 107 • Gold **Obv.** Hat design above eye **Rev:**
Clasped hands above date **Obv. Legend:** HOLINESS
• TO • THE • LORD **Rev. Legend:** G. S. L. C. P. C. /
TWENTY. DOLLARS

Date	F12	VF20	XF40	MS60	MS63
1849	75,000	145,000	225,000	—	—

Note: Stack's Old West Sale August 2006 XF45 $207,000

US TERRITORIAL GOLD

HAWAII, PHILLIPINES, PUERTO RICO

HAWAII

Hawaii, the 50th state, consists of eight main islands and numerous smaller islets of coral and volcanic origin. Situated in the central Pacific Ocean, 2,400 miles from San Francisco, the Hawaiian archipelago has an area of 6,450 square miles. Capital: Honolulu. The principal sources of income are in order: tourism, defense, and agriculture.

The Hawaiian Islands, originally populated by Polynesians from the Society Islands, were rediscovered by British navigator Capt. James Cook in 1778. He named them the Sandwich Islands. King Kamehameha I (the Great) united the islands under one kingdom, which endured until 1893, when Queen Lilioukalani was deposed and a provisional government established. This was followed in 1894 by a republic, which governed Hawaii until 1898, when the islands were ceded to the United States. Hawaii was organized as a territory in 1900 and attained statehood on Aug. 21, 1959.

Official coinage issued under the Kingdom of Hawaii was limited. The 1847 cent or Hapa Haneri coins were ordered by the Minister of Finance through an agent by the name of James Jackson Jarves. Jarves contracted the striking of 100,000 large copper coins from an unknown firm located somewhere in New England. The lack of acceptance by merchants limited the success of the 1847 coppers, which lead to a long gap before the next Hawaiian coinage issue in 1883.

The 1883 Kingdom coinage was contracted through Claus Spreckels, with circulation coins being struck at the San Francisco Mint. Very limited numbers of proof strikes were completed at the Philadelphia Mint, where Charles E. Barber designed these coins. Weights and measures on the 1883 Hawaiian coinage are the same as standard U.S. coins of the time period.

RULERS
Kamehameha I, 1795-1819
Kamehameha II, 1819-1824
Kamehameha III, 1825-1854
Kamehameha IV, 1854-1863
Kamehameha V, 1863-1872
Lunalilo, 1873-1874
Kalakaua, 1874-1891
Liliuokalani, 1891-1893
Provisional Government, 1893-1894
Republic, 1894-1898
Annexed to U.S., 1898-1900
Territory, 1900-1959

MONETARY SYSTEM
100 Hapa Haneri - Akahi Dala
100 Cents - 1 Dollar (Dala)

CENT

KM# 1a • Copper **Obv.** Uniformed bust, facing **Rev:** Value within wreath **Obv. Legend:** KAMEHAMEHA III.KA.MOI. **Rev. Legend:** AUPUNI HAWAII

Date	Mintage	F12	VF20	XF40	MS60	MS63
1847 Plain 4, 13 berries (6 left, 7 right)	100,000	375	475	775	1,150	2,200

KM# 1b • Copper **Obv.** Uniformed bust, facing **Rev:** Value within wreath **Obv. Legend:** KAMEHAMEHA III.KA.MOI. **Rev. Legend:** AUPUNI HAWAII

Date	Mintage	F12	VF20	XF40	MS60	MS63
1847	Inc. above	375	475	775	1,100	2,200

Note: Plain 4, 15 berries (8 left, 7 right)

KM# 1c • Copper **Obv.** Uniformed bust, facing **Rev:** Value within wreath **Obv. Legend:** KAMEHAMEHA III.KA.MOI. **Rev. Legend:** AUPUNI HAWAII

Date	Mintage	F12	VF20	XF40	MS60	MS63
1847	Inc. above	400	500	800	1,300	2,500

Note: Plain 4, 17 berries (8 left, 9 right)

HAWAII, PHILLIPINES, PUERTO RICO

KM# 1d • Copper **Obv.** Uniformed bust, facing **Rev:** Value within wreath **Obv. Legend:** KAMEHAMEHA III.KA.MOI. **Rev. Legend:** AUPUNI HAWAII

Date	Mintage	F12	VF20	XF40	MS60	MS63
1847	Inc. above	375	475	750	1,100	2,200

Note: Crosslet 4, 15 berries (7 left, 8 right)

KM# 1e • Copper **Obv.** Uniformed bust, facing **Rev:** Value within wreath **Obv. Legend:** KAMEHAMEHA III.KA.MOI. **Rev. Legend:** AUPUNI HAWAII

Date	Mintage	F12	VF20	XF40	MS60	MS63
1847	Inc. above	450	600	900	3,500	4,200

Note: Crosslet 4, 18 berries (9 left, 9 right)

KM# 1f • Copper **Obv.** Uniformed bust, facing **Rev:** Value within wreath **Obv. Legend:** KAMEHAMEHA III.KA.MOI. **Rev. Legend:** AUPUNI HAWAII

Date	Mintage	F12	VF20	XF40	MS60	MS63
1847	800	1,500	2,000	2,800	3,250	

Note: Plain 4, 15 berries (7 left, 8 right)

5 CENTS (PATTERN)

KM# 2 • Nickel **Obv.** Head left, date below **Rev:** Value within crowned belt **Obv. Legend:** KALAKAUA KING OF SANDWICH ISLANDS

Date	Mintage	F12	VF20	XF40	MS60	MS63
1881	200	6,500	9,500	14,000	20,000	23,000

Note: Original examples of this pattern were struck on thin nickel planchets, presumably in Paris and some have "MAILLECHORT" stamped on the edge. In the early 1900's, deceptive replicas of the issue were produced in Canada, on thick and thin nickel and aluminum planchets, and thin copper planchets (thick about 2.7 to 3.1mm; thin about 1.4 to 1.7mm). The original patterns have a small cross atop the crown, the replicas do not have the cross.

10 CENTS (UMI KENETA)

KM# 3 • 2.50 g., 0.900 Silver 0.0723 oz. **Obv.** Head right, date below **Rev:** Crown and value within wreath **Obv. Legend:** KALAKAUA I KING OF HAWAII

Date	Mintage		F12	VF20	XF40	MS60	MS63
1883	26	PF60 7,500		PF63 12,000		PF65 15,000	
1883	250,000		65.00	95.00	250	950	2,700

1/8 DOLLAR (HAPAWALU)

KM# 4 • 0.900 Silver **Obv.** Head right **Obv. Legend:** KALAKAUA I KING OF HAWAII **Note:** Pattern issue.

Date	Mintage	F12	VF20	XF40	MS60	MS63
1883	—	PF63 45,000		PF65 50,000		

KM# 4a • Copper **Obv.** Head right **Obv. Legend:** KALAKAUA I KING OF HAWAII **Note:** Pattern issue.

Date	Mintage	F12	VF20	XF40	MS60	MS63
1883	18	PF63 17,000		PF65 25,000		

1/4 DOLLAR (HAPAHA)

KM# 5 • 6.22 g., 0.900 Silver 0.180 oz. **Obv.** Head right, date below **Rev:** Crowned arms divides value **Obv. Legend:** KALAKAUA I KING OF HAWAII **Rev. Legend:** UA MAU KE...

Date	Mintage	F12	VF20	XF40	MS60	MS63
1883	500,000	55.00	75.00	125	250	400
1883/1383	Inc. above	65.00	95.00	150	300	500
1883	—	PF60 10,000	PF63 13,000		PF65 15,000	

KM# 5a • Copper **Obv.** Head right, date below **Rev:** Crowned arms divides value **Obv. Legend:** KALAKAUA I KING OF HAWAII **Rev. Legend:** UA MAU KE... **Note:** Pattern issue.

Date	Mintage	F12	VF20	XF40	MS60	MS63
1883	18	PF60 8,000	PF63 10,000		PF65 12,000	

HAWAII, PHILLIPINES, PUERTO RICO

1/2 DOLLAR (HAPALUA)

KM# 6 • 12.50 g., 0.900 Silver 0.3617 oz. **Obv.**
Head right, date below **Rev:** Crowned arms divides
value **Obv. Legend:** KALAKAUA I KING OF HAWAII
Rev. Legend: UA MAU KE...

Date	Mintage	F12	VF20	XF40	MS60	MS63
1883	700,000	125	175	300	1,000	3,000
1883	—	PF60 14,000	PF63 17,000	PF65 20,000		

KM# 6a • Copper **Obv.** Head right, date below
Rev: Crowned arms divides value **Obv. Legend:**
KALAKAUA I KING OF HAWAII **Rev. Legend:** UA
MAU KE... **Note:** Pattern issue.

Date	Mintage	F12	VF20	XF40	MS60	MS63
1883	18	PF60 10,000	PF63 13,000	PF65 16,000		

DOLLAR (AKAHI DALA)

KM# 7 • 26.73 g., 0.900 Silver 0.7734 oz. **Obv.**
Head right, date below **Rev:** Crowned arms with
supporters within crowned mantle **Obv. Legend:**
KALAKAUA I KING OF HAWAII **Rev. Legend:** UA
MAU KE...

Date	Mintage	F12	VF20	XF40	MS60	MS63
1883	500,000	375	500	800	4,000	10,000
1883	—	PF60 20,000	PF63 25,000	PF65 30,000		

KM# 7a • Copper **Obv.** Head right, date below
Rev: Crowned arms with supporters within crowned
mantle **Obv. Legend:** KALAKAUA I KING OF
HAWAII **Rev. Legend:** UA MAU KE... **Note:** Pattern
issue.

Date	Mintage	F12	VF20	XF40	MS60	MS63
1883	18	PF63 20,000	PF65 25,000			

Note: Official records indicate the following quantities of
the above issues were redeemed and melted: KM#1 -
88,405; KM#3 - 79; KM#5 - 257,400; KM#6 - 612,245;
KM#7 - 453,652. That leaves approximate net mintages
of: KM#1 - 11,600; KM#3 - 250,000; KM#5 (regular
date) - 242,600, (unknown) 40,000; KM#6 - 87,700;
KM#7 - 46,300.

PHILIPPINES
United States Administration
1899-1946

The Philippines, an archipelago in the western Pacific 500 miles (805 km.) from the southeast coast of Asia, has an area of 115,830 square miles (300,000 sq. km.) and a current population of 64.9 million. Its capital city is Manila. From its acquisition in 1898 until 1992, the U.S. has had a military presence in the Philippines.

Migration to the Philippines began about 30,000 years ago when land bridges connected the islands with Borneo and Sumatra. Ferdinand Magellan claimed the islands for Spain in 1521. Miguel de Legazpi established the first permanent settlement at Cebu in April 1565. Manila was established in 1572. A British expedition captured Manila and occupied the Spanish colony in October 1762, but returned it to Spain by the treaty of Paris, 1763. Spain held the Philippines despite growing Filipino nationalism until 1898 when they were ceded to the United States at the end of the Spanish-American War.

A military government was established on the Islands until a civil administration was put in place in 1901. The Philippines became a self-governing commonwealth under the United States in 1935. In 1942, during the Second World War, the Philippines were occupied by the Japanese. U.S forces and Filipinos both fought during 1944-45 to regain control of the Islands. On July 4, 1946, the Philippines became an independent Republic.

The coins listed here were issued under United States Administration of the Philippines. Coins dated 1903 to 1919 were struck at both the Philadelphia and San Francisco Mints, while coins dated 1920 and after were produced at the Manila Mint in the Philippines. With Japanese forces advancing in 1942, much of the Philippine Treasury's silver coinage was returned to the United States for safekeeping. Coinage that remained at the Mint in Manila was crated and dumped in the bay before the Japanese arrived. During the struggle to regain control of the Philippines near the end of WWII, coins dated 1944 to 1945 were struck by the U.S. Mint at Denver, San Francisco and Philadelphia.

Symbolically the first series of U.S. Philippines coins with its American eagle perched on a stars and stripes shield places emphasis on U.S. dominance of the islands. The second series, struck under Commonwealth authority began the move towards independence by placing a new Commonwealth of the Philippines shield on the reverses of all denominations.

MINT MARKS
D - Denver, 1944-1945
S - San Francisco, 1903-1947
M – Manila, 1920-1941

MONETARY SYSTEM
4 Quartos = 1 Real
8 Reales = 1 Peso
1 Peso = 100 Centavos

1/2 CENTAVO

KM# 162 • Bronze **Obv.** Man seated beside hammer and anvil **Rev:** Eagle above stars and striped shield

Date	Mintage	F12	VF20	XF40	MS60	MS63
1903	12,084,000	0.50	1.25	2.50	15.00	40.00
1903	2,558	PF60 100	PF63 125	PF65 150		
1904	5,654,000	1.00	2.25	3.50	20.00	50.00
1904	1,355	PF60 100	PF63 150	PF65 200		
1905	471	PF60 300	PF63 375	PF65 500		
1906	500	PF60 250	PF63 300	PF65 450		
1908	500	PF60 250	PF63 300	PF65 450		

CENTAVO

KM# 163 • 4.70 g., Bronze **Obv.** Man seated beside hammer and anvil **Rev:** Eagle above stars and striped shield

Date	Mintage	F12	VF20	XF40	MS60	MS63
1903	10,790,000	0.50	1.25	2.50	15.00	40.00
1903	2,558	PF60 100	PF63 150	PF65 225		
1904	17,040,000	0.50	1.25	2.75	30.00	60.00
1904	1,355	PF60 100	PF63 175	PF65 250		
1905	10,000,000	0.75	1.25	3.50	30.00	50.00
1905	471	PF60 250	PF63 350	PF65 650		
1906	500	PF60 250	PF63 300	PF65 450		
1908	500	PF60 225	PF63 300	PF65 450		
1908S	2,187,000	2.50	4.00	10.00	50.00	100
1908S/S	—	20.00	30.00	50.00	150	250
1909S	1,738,000	7.00	16.00	25.00	100	225

HAWAII, PHILLIPINES, PUERTO RICO

HAWAII, PHILLIPINES, PUERTO RICO

Date	Mintage	F12	VF20	XF40	MS60	MS63
1910S	2,700,000	2.00	4.00	8.00	50.00	65.00
1911S	4,803,000	1.00	2.50	5.00	25.00	60.00
1912S	3,000,000	3.50	7.50	15.00	75.00	150
1913S	5,000,000	2.00	4.00	7.00	40.00	75.00
1914S	5,000,000	1.75	3.00	7.00	45.00	85.00
1915S	2,500,000	30.00	40.00	90.00	700	1,500
1916S	4,330,000	6.00	12.50	20.00	100	175
1917/6S	7,070,000	40.00	80.00	150	300	500
1917S	Inc. above	2.00	5.00	10.00	75.00	150
1918S	11,660,000	2.00	5.00	8.00	75.00	175
1918S Large S	Inc. above	125	165	250	1,000	1,800
1919S	4,540,000	2.50	5.00	10.00	75.00	150
1920S	2,500,000	4.50	8.00	20.00	125	250
1920	3,552,000	2.00	4.00	7.50	50.00	175
1921	7,283,000	1.00	2.50	5.00	35.00	70.00
1922	3,519,000	0.50	3.00	6.00	40.00	75.00
1925M	9,332,000	0.50	2.50	5.00	35.00	70.00
1926M	9,000,000	0.50	2.50	5.00	30.00	70.00
1927M	9,270,000	0.50	2.50	5.00	30.00	40.00
1928M	9,150,000	0.50	2.00	5.00	30.00	65.00
1929M	5,657,000	1.00	3.00	6.00	35.00	80.00
1930M	5,577,000	0.50	2.00	4.50	30.00	60.00
1931M	5,659,000	0.50	2.00	4.00	25.00	60.00
1932M	4,000,000	1.00	3.00	6.00	50.00	75.00
1933M	8,393,000	0.25	2.00	3.00	20.00	45.00
1934M	3,179,000	0.75	2.50	4.50	50.00	70.00
1936M	17,455,000	0.50	2.50	4.00	30.00	65.00

5 CENTAVOS

KM# 164 • 5.25 g., Copper-Nickel, 21.3 mm. • **Obv.** Man seated beside hammer and anvil **Rev:** Eagle above stars and striped shield

Date	Mintage	F12	VF20	XF40	MS60	MS63
1903	8,910,000	0.50	1.25	2.50	15.00	30.00
1903	2,558	PF60 100		PF63 125		PF65 250
1904	1,075,000	0.75	2.50	4.00	25.00	45.00
1904	1,355	PF60 125		PF63 150		PF65 275
1905	471	PF60 300		PF63 350		PF65 425
1906	500	PF60 225		PF63 275		PF65 375
1908	500	PF60 225		PF63 275		PF65 375
1916S	300,000	40.00	75.00	150	800	1,500
1917S	2,300,000	2.25	5.00	10.00	150	300
1918S/S	—		25.00	50.00	250	—
1918S	2,780,000	3.00	8.00	10.00	150	325
1919S	1,220,000	5.00	8.50	20.00	200	400
1920	1,421,000	3.00	8.50	20.00	175	300
1921	2,132,000	3.00	8.00	20.00	125	200
1925M	1,000,000	8.00	12.00	30.00	175	300
1926M	1,200,000	4.00	6.00	17.50	120	200
1927M	1,000,000	2.50	6.00	12.50	75.00	150
1928M	1,000,000	3.00	7.50	12.50	65.00	125

KM# 173 • Copper-Nickel **Obv.** Man seated beside hammer and anvil **Rev:** Eagle above stars and striped shield **Note:** Mule.

Date	Mintage	F12	VF20	XF40	MS60	MS63
1918S	—	200	500	1,200	4,500	9,500

KM# 175 • 4.75 g., Copper-Nickel, 19 mm. • **Obv.** Man seated beside hammer and anvil **Rev:** Eagle above stars and striped shield

Date	Mintage	F12	VF20	XF40	MS60	MS63
1930M	2,905,000	1.00	3.00	7.50	40.00	85.00
1931M	3,477,000	1.00	3.50	7.50	65.00	150
1932M	3,956,000	1.00	2.00	4.00	50.00	140
1934M	2,154,000	1.00	3.50	9.00	75.00	200
1934M recut 1	—	5.00	15.00	30.00	125	250
1935M	2,754,000	1.00	2.50	10.00	100	220

10 CENTAVOS

KM# 165 • 2.69 g., 0.900 Silver 0.0779 oz. **Obv.** Female standing beside hammer and anvil **Rev:** Eagle above stars and striped shield

Date	Mintage	F12	VF20	XF40	MS60	MS63
1903	5,103,000	2.50	4.00	5.00	35.00	80.00
1903	2,558	PF60 100		PF63 125		PF65 225
1903S	1,200,000	15.00	25.00	40.00	350	1,000
1904	11,000	20.00	30.00	45.00	80.00	150
1904	1,355	PF60 110		PF63 150		PF65 275
1904S	5,040,000	2.50	4.00	7.00	50.00	130
1905	471	PF60 200		PF63 325		PF65 525
1906	500	PF60 150		PF63 275		PF65 500

KM# 169 • 2.00 g., 0.750 Silver 0.0482 oz. **Obv.** Female standing beside hammer and anvil **Rev:** Eagle above stars and striped shield **Edge:** Reeded

Date	Mintage	F12	VF20	XF40	MS60	MS63
1907	1,501,000	1.75	4.00	8.00	50.00	150
1907S	4,930,000	1.75	2.00	7.50	40.00	90.00
1908	500	PF60 190		PF63 250		PF65 475
1908S	3,364,000	BV	2.00	8.00	40.00	70.00
1909S	312,000	25.00	30.00	65.00	450	1,200
1910S	—	—	—			

Note: Unknown in any collection. Counterfeits of the 1910S are commonly encountered

1911S	1,101,000	2.50	4.50	11.50	150	500
1912S	1,010,000	2.50	4.50	12.00	125	250
1913S	1,361,000	2.00	6.00	12.00	85.00	200
1914S Short bar on "4"	1,180,000	2.00	8.00	20.00	175	350
1914S Long bar on "4"	—	2.00	6.50	15.00	125	300
1915S	450,000	12.50	25.00	40.00	275	750
1917S	5,991,000	BV	2.50	5.00	50.00	125
1918S	8,420,000	—	BV	3.00	20.00	65.00
1919S	1,630,000	BV	2.50	4.00	40.00	110
1920	520,000	3.00	7.50	17.50	95.00	200
1921	3,863,000	BV	2.00	3.00	25.00	50.00
1929M	1,000,000	BV	2.00	3.25	20.00	40.00
1935M	1,280,000	BV	2.00	4.00	20.00	50.00

HAWAII, PHILIPPINES, PUERTO RICO

20 CENTAVOS

KM# 166 • 5.38 g., 0.900 Silver 0.1558 oz. **Obv.** Female standing beside hammer and anvil **Rev:** Eagle above stars and striped shield **Edge:** Reeded

Date	Mintage	F12	VF20	XF40	MS60	MS63
1903	5,353,000	BV	5.00	8.00	45.00	100
1903	2,558	PF60 100	PF63 150		PF65 300	
1903S	150,000	12.50	35.00	75.00	600	1,700
1904	11,000	25.00	30.00	45.00	100	200
1904	1,355	PF60 150	PF63 200		PF65 350	
1904S	2,060,000	5.00	7.00	11.00	100	200
1905	471	PF60 250	PF63 450		PF65 800	
1905S	420,000	7.50	20.00	35.00	500	1,500
1906	500	PF60 175	PF63 375		PF65 700	

KM# 170 • 4.00 g., 0.750 Silver 0.0965 oz. **Obv.** Female standing beside hammer and anvil **Rev:** Eagle above stars and striped shield **Edge:** Reeded

Date	Mintage	F12	VF20	XF40	MS60	MS63
1907	1,251,000	3.50	6.00	15.00	200	450
1907S	3,165,000	BV	4.00	6.50	75.00	175
1908	500	PF60 250	PF63 400		PF65 750	
1908S	1,535,000	3.00	4.00	10.00	75.00	200
1909S	450,000	12.50	25.00	50.00	400	1,500
1910S	500,000	12.50	30.00	100	400	1,000
1911S	505,000	10.00	25.00	45.00	350	1,000
1912S	750,000	5.00	12.00	30.00	200	450
1913S/S	949,000	7.00	12.50	35.00	150	350
1913S	Inc. above	4.00	10.00	15.00	175	250
1914S	795,000	3.50	8.50	40.00	250	450
1915S	655,000	15.00	20.00	75.00	600	1,550
1916S	1,435,000	5.00	10.00	25.00	200	575
1917S	3,151,000	BV	3.50	7.50	75.00	200
1918S	5,560,000	BV	3.25	5.00	50.00	125
1919S	850,000	3.50	5.00	15.00	125	225
1920	1,046,000	4.00	10.00	25.00	135	225
1921	1,843,000	—	BV	6.00	70.00	100
1929M	1,970,000	—	BV	5.00	25.00	75.00

KM# 174 • 4.00 g., 0.750 Silver 0.0965 oz. **Obv.** Female standing beside hammer and anvil **Rev:** Eagle above stars and striped shield **Note:** Mule.

Date	Mintage	F12	VF20	XF40	MS60	MS63
1928M	100,000	10.00	25.00	60.00	900	1,800

50 CENTAVOS

KM# 167 • 13.48 g., 0.900 Silver 0.390 oz. **Obv.** Female standing beside hammer and anvil **Rev:** Eagle above stars and striped shield

Date	Mintage	F12	VF20	XF40	MS60	MS63
1903	3,102,000	—	15.00	20.00	70.00	125
1903	2,558	PF60 175	PF63 225		PF65 425	
1903S 2 Known	—	—	—	22,000	—	—
1904	11,000	25.00	40.00	75.00	150	300
1904	1,355	PF60 200	PF63 250		PF65 450	
1904S	2,160,000	—	BV	25.00	125	225
1905	471	PF60 250	PF63 450		PF65 950	
1905S	852,000	BV	20.00	60.00	750	2,250
1906	500	PF60 250	PF63 350		PF65 750	

KM# 171 • 10.00 g., 0.750 Silver 0.2411 oz. **Obv.** Female standing beside hammer and anvil **Rev:** Eagle above stars and striped shield **Edge:** Reeded

Date	Mintage	F12	VF20	XF40	MS60	MS63
1907	1,201,000	BV	15.00	40.00	150	350
1907S	2,112,000	BV	10.00	30.00	150	350
1908	500	PF60 250	PF63 375		PF65 775	
1908S	1,601,000	BV	12.00	45.00	325	2,000
1909S	528,000	10.00	20.00	50.00	350	850
1917S	674,000	BV	15.00	35.00	200	550
1918S	2,202,000	—	BV	15.00	90.00	175
1919S	1,200,000	—	BV	20.00	100	200
1920	420,000	—	BV	10.00	60.00	100
1921	2,317,000	—	BV	7.50	50.00	75.00

PESO

KM# 168 • 26.96 g., 0.900 Silver 0.780 oz. **Obv.**
Female standing beside hammer and anvil **Rev:**
Eagle above stars and striped shield

Date	Mintage	F12	VF20	XF40	MS60	MS63
1903	2,791,000	25.00	35.00	40.00	200	525
1903	2,558	PF60 250	PF63 375	PF65 750		
1903S	11,361,000	25.00	27.50	40.00	125	225
1904	1,361,000	65.00	80.00	125	250	475
1904	1,355	PF60 350	PF63 500	PF65 1,000		
1904S	6,600,000	25.00	30.00	40.00	175	350
1905S curved serif on 1	6,056,000	25.00	35.00	50.00	325	750
1905S straight serif on 1	—	35.00	50.00	75.00	875	2,500
1905	471	PF60 1,200	PF63 1,500	PF65 2,250		
1906	500	PF60 850	PF63 1,150	PF65 2,000		
1906S	201,000	1,000	1,400	2,750	17,500	35,000

Note: Counterfeits of the 1906S exist

KM# 172 • 20.00 g., 0.800 Silver 0.5144 oz. **Obv.**
Female standing beside hammer and anvil **Rev:**
Eagle above stars and striped shield **Edge:** Reeded

Date	Mintage	F12	VF20	XF40	MS60	MS63
1907 Proof, 2 known	—	—	—	—	—	—

Note: Gem $165,000, 6/10/12 Pineda Sale.

1907S	10,276,000	17.00	19.00	22.00	95.00	200
1908	500	PF60 700	PF63 1,200	PF65 2,000		
1908S	20,955,000	17.00	19.00	22.00	90.00	200
1909S	7,578,000	17.00	19.00	25.00	125	300
1910S	3,154,000	19.00	25.00	35.00	225	450
1911S	463,000	30.00	40.00	75.00	750	4,500
1912S	680,000	40.00	50.00	100	2,000	5,500

UNITED STATES ADMINISTRATION
Commonwealth
CENTAVO

KM# 179 • 5.30 g., Bronze, 25 mm. • **Obv.** Male
seated beside hammer and anvil **Rev:** Eagle above

shield

Date	Mintage	F12	VF20	XF40	MS60	MS63
1937M	15,790,000	0.25	2.00	3.00	15.00	40.00
1938M	10,000,000	0.25	1.50	2.50	12.50	35.00
1939M	6,500,000	0.25	2.50	3.50	17.50	45.00
1940M	4,000,000	0.25	1.25	2.50	12.50	30.00
1941M	5,000,000	0.25	1.00	3.50	17.50	35.00
1944S	58,000,000	—	0.25	0.50	2.00	5.25

5 CENTAVOS

KM# 180 • 4.80 g., Copper-Nickel **Obv.** Male
seated beside hammer and anvil **Rev:** Eagle with
wings open above shield

Date	Mintage	F12	VF20	XF40	MS60	MS63
1937M	2,494,000	2.00	3.50	7.50	50.00	110
1938M	4,000,000	0.50	1.00	2.50	25.00	65.00
1941M	2,750,000	2.00	4.00	12.50	55.00	150

KM# 180a • 4.92 g., Copper-Nickel-Zinc, 19 mm.
• **Obv.** Male seated beside hammer and anvil **Rev:**
Eagle with wings open above shield

Date	Mintage	F12	VF20	XF40	MS60	MS63
1944	21,198,000	—	0.50	1.00	1.50	3.00
1944S	14,040,000	—	0.25	0.50	1.00	2.00
1945S	72,796,000	—	0.25	0.50	1.00	2.00

10 CENTAVOS

KM# 181 • 2.00 g., 0.750 Silver 0.0482 oz., 16.7
mm. • **Obv.** Female standing beside hammer
and anvil **Rev:** Eagle with wings open above shield
Edge: Reeded

Date	Mintage	F12	VF20	XF40	MS60	MS63
1937M	3,500,000	1.75	2.25	3.50	25.00	50.00
1938M	3,750,000	1.65	1.85	2.50	10.00	20.00
1941M	2,500,000	1.65	1.85	2.50	10.00	15.00
1944D	31,592,000	—	—	1.85	2.50	5.00
1945D	137,208,000	—	—	1.85	2.50	5.00

Note: 1937, 1938, and 1941 dated strikes have inverted W's for M's

1945D/D	—	—	8.50	16.00	30.00	50.00

HAWAII, PHILLIPINES, PUERTO RICO

HAWAII, PHILLIPINES, PUERTO RICO

20 CENTAVOS

KM# 182 • 4.00 g., 0.750 Silver 0.0965 oz., 21 mm.
• **Obv.** Female standing beside hammer and anvil
Rev: Eagle with wings open above shield **Edge:**
Reeded

Date	Mintage	F12	VF20	XF40	MS60	MS63
1937M	2,665,000	3.50	4.00	6.00	35.00	50.00
1938M	3,000,000	—	BV	3.75	15.00	30.00
1941M	1,500,000	—	BV	3.75	12.50	20.00
1944D	28,596,000	—	—	BV	3.00	5.00
1944D/S	—	—	7.50	10.00	25.00	50.00
1945D	82,804,000	—	—	BV	3.00	5.00

50 CENTAVOS

Establishment of the Commonwealth

KM# 176 • 10.00 g., 0.750 Silver 0.2411 oz., 27.5 mm. • **Obv.** Murphy-Quezon busts facing each other **Rev:** Eagle above shield **Designer:** Ambrosia Morales

Date	Mintage	F12	VF20	XF40	MS60	MS63
1936	20,000	—	25.00	50.00	110	160

KM# 183 • 10.00 g., 0.750 Silver 0.2411 oz., 27.5 mm. • **Obv.** Female standing beside hammer and anvil **Rev:** Eagle with wings open above shield **Edge:** Reeded

Date	Mintage	F12	VF20	XF40	MS60	MS63
1944S	19,187,000	—	BV	8.00	10.00	15.00
1945S	18,120,000	—	BV	8.00	10.00	15.00
1945S/S	—	—	—	50.00	100	200

PESO

Establishment of the Commonwealth

KM# 177 • 20.00 g., 0.900 Silver 0.5787 oz., 35 mm. • **Obv.** Roosevelt-Quezon conjoined busts left **Rev:** Eagle with wings open above shield **Designer:** Ambrosia Morales

Date	Mintage	F12	VF20	XF40	MS60	MS63
1936	10,000	—	60.00	85.00	200	275

Establishment of the Commonwealth

KM# 178 • 20.00 g., 0.900 Silver 0.5787 oz., 35 mm. • **Obv.** Murphy-Quezon conjoined busts left **Rev:** Eagle with wings open above shield **Designer:** Ambrosia Morales

Date	Mintage	F12	VF20	XF40	MS60	MS63
1936	10,000	—	60.00	85.00	200	275

HAWAII, PHILLIPINES, PUERTO RICO

PUERTO RICO

The Commonwealth of Puerto Rico, the eastern-most island of the Greater Antilles in the West Indies, has an area of approximately 3,435 square miles (9,104 sq. km.), with sandy beaches on the costal areas and much mountainous territory inland. Puerto Rico's capital, San Juan, affords the island one of the best natural harbors in the Caribbean and has become an important stop on the Mona Passage shipping route to the Panama Canal.

Columbus discovered Puerto Rico (Rich Port) and took possession for Spain on Nov. 19, 1493 - the only time Columbus set foot on the soil of what is now a possession of the United States. The first settlement, Caparra, was established by Ponce de Leon in 1508. The early years of the colony were not promising. Considerable gold was found, but the supply was soon exhausted. Efforts to enslave the Indians caused violent reprisals. Hurricanes destroyed crops and homes. French, Dutch, and English freebooters burned the towns. Puerto Rico remained a Spanish possession until 1898, when it was ceded to the United States following the Spanish-American War.

When the Spanish first colonized Puerto Rico, native populations were operating on a barter system of exchange. Spanish coinage was introduced and eventually accepted for exchange. As mints developed in the Americas, their coins, first cobs and later milled coins, were also circulated in Puerto Rico. This mix of Spanish and Spanish Colonial coins served Puerto Rico for several centuries, though copper and bronze coins were easier to keep in circulation, while silver and gold tended to be taken away by traders. Paper money was also used in Puerto Rico from the mid 18th century on, though counterfeiting lead to the devaluation of many of these banknotes. Economic conditions were in great disarray by the early part of the 19th century. All sorts of currency and coinage were in circulation with counterfeits diluting the money supply. Cob coins, Spanish coins, cut and countermarked coins of the various West Indies, along with several issues of bank notes were all in circulation, leading to confusion and lack of fluid acceptance.

In 1895 the first coinage specifically struck for the Island of Puerto Rico was produced by Spain. Additional denominations were struck in 1896 completing Puerto Rico's only official coinage series. These coins brought some semblance of order to the daily economic transactions on the island and remained in use until Puerto Rico was taken over by the United States in 1898. Redemption of all peso denominated coins took place from July 1900 until March 1901 at the rate of 60 U.S. cents to the peso.

RULER	ASSAYERS' INITIALS	MONETARY SYSTEM
Spanish, until 1898	G - Antonio Garcia Gonzalez P - Felix Miguel Peiro Rodrigo	100 Centavos = 1 Peso

DECIMAL COINAGE

5 CENTAVOS

KM# 20 • 1.25 g., 0.900 Silver 0.0362 oz. **Obv.** Value, date **Rev:** Crowned arms, pillars

Date	Mintage	F12	VF20	XF40	MS60	MS63
1896 PGV	600,000	30.00	50.00	90.00	225	300

10 CENTAVOS

KM# 21 • 2.50 g., 0.900 Silver 0.0723 oz. **Obv.** Young head left **Rev:** Crowned arms, pillars

Date	Mintage	F12	VF20	XF40	MS60	MS63
1896 PGV	700,000	35.00	65.00	175	375	—

20 CENTAVOS

KM# 22 • 5.00 g., 0.900 Silver 0.1447 oz. **Obv.**
Young head left **Rev:** Crowned arms, pillars

Date	Mintage	F12	VF20	XF40	MS60	MS63
1895 PGV	3,350,000	45.00	100	200	425	—

40 CENTAVOS

KM# 23 • 10.00 g., 0.900 Silver 0.2894 oz. **Obv.**
Young head left **Rev:** Crowned arms, pillars

Date	Mintage	F12	VF20	XF40	MS60	MS63
1896 PGV	725,000	250	375	875	2,850	—

PESO

KM# 24 • 25.00 g., 0.900 Silver 0.7234 oz. **Obv.**
Young head left **Rev:** Crowned arms, pillars

Date	Mintage	F12	VF20	XF40	MS60	MS63
1895 PGV	8,500,000	350	550	950	2,500	4,500

HAWAII, PHILLIPINES, PUERTO RICO

Glossary

Adjustment marks: Marks made by use of a file to correct the weight of overweight coinage planchets prior to striking. Adjusting the weight of planchets was a common practice at the first U.S. Mint in Philadelphia and was often carried out by women hired to weigh planchets and do any necessary filing of the metal.

Altered coin: A coin that has been changed after it left the mint. Such changes are often to the date or mintmark of a common coin in an attempt to increase its value by passing to an unsuspecting buyer as a rare date or mint.

Alloy: A metal or mixture of metals added to the primary metal in the coinage composition, often as a means of facilitating hardness during striking. For example, most U.S. silver coins contain an alloy of 10 percent copper.

Anneal: To heat in order to soften. In the minting process planchets are annealed prior to striking.

Authentication: The act of determining whether a coin, medal, token or other related item is a genuine product of the issuing authority.

Bag marks: Scrapes and impairments to a coin's surface obtained after minting by contact with other coins. The term originates from the storage of coins in bags, but such marks can occur as coins leave the presses and enter hoppers. A larger coin is more susceptible to marks, which affect its grade and, therefore, its value.

Base metal: A metal with low intrinsic value.

Beading: A form of design around the edge of a coin. Beading once served a functional purpose of deterring clipping or shaving parts of the metal by those looking to make a profit and then return the debased coin to circulation.

Blank: Often used in reference to the coinage planchet or disc of metal from which the actual coin is struck. Planchets or blanks are punched out of a sheet of metal by what is known as a blanking press.

Business strike: A coin produced for circulation.

Cast copy: A copy of a coin or medal made by a casting process in which molds are used to produce the finished product. Casting imparts a different surface texture to the finished product than striking and often leaves traces of a seam where the molds came together.

Center dot: A raised dot at the center of a coin caused by use of a compass to aid the engraver in the circular positioning of die devices, such as stars, letters, and dates. Center dots are prevalent on early U.S. coinage.

Chop mark: A mark used by Oriental merchants as a means of guaranteeing the silver content of coins paid out. The merchants' chop marks, or stamped insignia, often obliterated the original design of the host coin. U.S. Trade dollars, struck from 1873 through 1878 and intended for use in trade with China, are sometimes found bearing multiple marks.

Clash marks: Marks impressed in the coinage dies when they come together without a planchet between them. Such marks will affect coins struck subsequently by causing portions of the obverse design to appear in raised form on the reverse, and vice versa.

Clipping: The practice of shaving or cutting small pieces of metal from a coin in circulation. Clipping was prevalent in Colonial times as a means of surreptitiously extracting precious metal from a coin before placing it back into circulation. The introduction of beading and a raised border helped to alleviate the problem.

Coin alignment: U.S. coins are normally struck with an alignment by which, when a coin is held by the top and bottom edge and rotated from side-to-side, the reverse will appear upside down.

Collar: A ring-shaped die between which the obverse and reverse coinage dies are held during striking. The collar contains the outward flow during striking and can be used to produce edge reeding.

Commemorative: A coin issued to honor a special event or person. United States commemorative coins have historically been produced for sale to collectors and not placed in circulation, though the 50-states quarters are circulating commemoratives.

Copy: A replica of an original issue. Copies often vary in quality and metallic composition from the original. Since passage of the Hobby Protection Act (Public Law 93-167) of Nov. 29, 1973, it has been illegal to produce or import copies of coins or other numismatic items that are not clearly and permanently marked with the word "Copy."

Counterfeit: A coin or medal or other numismatic item made fraudulently, either for entry into circulation or sale to collectors.

Denticles: The toothlike pattern found around a coin's obverse or reverse border.

Die: A cylindrical piece of metal containing an incuse image that imparts a raised image when stamped into a planchet.

Die crack: A crack that develops in a coinage die after extensive usage, or if the die is defective or is used to strike harder metals. Die cracks, which often run through border lettering, appear as raised lines on the finished coin.

Device: The principal design element.

Double eagle: Name adopted by the Act of March 3, 1849, for the gold coin valued at 20 units or $20.

Eagle: Name adopted by the Coinage Act of 1792 for a gold coin valued at 10 units or $10. Also a name used to refer to gold, silver, and platinum coins of the American Eagle bullion coinage program begun in 1986.

Edge: The cylindrical surface of a coin between the two sides. The edge can be plain, reeded, ornamented, or lettered.

Electrotype: A copy of a coin, medal, or token made by electroplating.

Exergue: The lower segment of a coin, below the main design, generally separated by a line and often containing the date, designer initials, and mintmark.

Face value: The nominal legal-tender value assigned to a given coin by the governing authority.

Fasces: A Roman symbol of authority consisting of a bound bundle of rods and an axe.

Field: The flat area of a coin's obverse or reverse, devoid of devices or inscriptions.

Galvano: A reproduction of a proposed design from an artist's original model produced in plaster or other substance and then electroplated with metal. The galvano is then used in a reducing lathe to make a die or hub.

Glory: A heraldic term for stars, rays or other devices placed as if in the sky or luminous.

Grading: The largely subjective practice of providing a numerical or adjectival ranking of the condition of a coin, token, or medal. The grade is often a major determinant of value.

Gresham's law: The name for the observation made by Sir Thomas Gresham, 16th century English financier, that when two coins with the same face value but different intrinsic values are in circulation at the same time, the one with the lesser intrinsic value will remain in circulation while the other is hoarded.

Half eagle: Name adopted by the Coinage Act of 1792 for a gold coin valued at five units or $5.

Hub: A piece of die steel showing the coinage devices in relief. The hub is used to produce a die that, in contrast, has the relief details incuse. The die is then used to produce the final coin, which looks much the same as the hub. Hubs may be reused to make new dies.

Legend: A coin' principal lettering, generally shown along its outer perimeter.

Lettered edge: Incuse or raised lettering on a coin's edge.

Matte proof: A proof coin on which the surface is granular or dull. On U.S. coins this type of surface was used on proofs of the early 20th century. The process has since been abandoned.

Magician's coin: A term sometimes used to describe a coin with two heads or two tails. Such a coin is considered impossible in normal production due to physical differences in obverse and reverse die mountings, though as of 2001 two have been certified as genuine by professional coin authenticators. The vast majority are products made outside the Mint as novelty pieces.

Medal: Made to commemorate an event or person. Medals differ from coins in that a medal is not legal tender and, in general, is not produced with the intent of circulating as money.

Medal alignment: Medals are generally struck with the coinage dies facing the same direction during striking. When held by the top and bottom edge and rotated from side-to-side, a piece struck in this manner will show both the obverse and reverse right side up.

Mintage: The total number of coins struck during a given time frame, generally one year.

Mintmark: A letter or other marking on a coin's surface to identify the mint at which the coin was struck.

Mule: The combination of two coinage dies not intended for use together.

Numismatics: The science, study or collecting of coins, tokens, medals, paper money, and related items.

Obverse: The front or "heads" side of a coin, medal, or token.

Overdate: Variety produced when one or more digits of the date are re-engraved over an old date on a die at the Mint, generally to save on dies or correct an error. Portions of the old date can still be seen under the new one.

Overmintmark: Variety created at the Mint when a different mintmark is punched over an already existing mintmark, generally done to make a coinage die already punched for one mint usable at another. Portions of the old mintmark can still be seen under the new one.

Overstrike: A coin, token or medal struck over another coin, token, or medal.

Pattern: A trial strike of a proposed coin design, issued by the Mint or authorized agent of a governing authority. Patterns can be in a variety of metals, thicknesses, and sizes.

Phrygian cap: A close-fitting, egg-shell-shaped hat placed on the head of a freed slave when Rome was in its ascendancy. Hung from a pole, it was a popular symbol of freedom during the French Revolution and in 18th century United States.

Planchet: A disc of metal or other material on which the image of the dies are impressed, resulting in a finished coin. Also sometimes called a blank.

Proof: A coin struck twice or more from specially polished dies and polished planchets. Modern proofs are prepared with a mirror finish. Early 20th century proofs were prepared with a matte surface.

Prooflike: A prooflike coin exhibits some of the characteristics of a proof despite having been struck by regular production processes. Many Morgan dollars are found with prooflike surfaces. The field will have a mirror background similar to that of a proof, and design details are frosted like some proofs.

Quarter eagle: Name adopted by the Coinage Act of 1792 for a gold coin valued at 2.5 units or $2.50.

Reeding: Serrated (toothlike) ornamentation applied to the coin's edge during striking.

Relief: The portion of a design raised above the surface of a coin, medal, or token.

Restrike: A coin, medal or token produced from original dies at a later date, often with the purpose of sale to collectors.

Reverse: The backside or "tails" side of a coin, medal or token, opposite from the principal figure of the design or obverse.

Rim: The raised area bordering the edge and surrounding the field.

Series: The complete group of coins of the same denomination and design and representing all issuing mints.

Token: A privately issued piece, generally in metal, with a represented value in trade or offer of service. Tokens are also produced for advertising purposes.

Type coin: A coin from a given series representing the basic design. A type coin is collected as an example of a particular design rather than for its date and mintmark.

Variety: Any coin noticeably different in dies from another of the same design, date and mint. Overdate and overmintmarks are examples of varieties.

Wire edge: Created when coinage metal flows between the coinage die and collar, producing a thin flange of coin metal at the outside edge or edges of a coin.

Index

Q

R

S

T

U

W

INDEX

· THE BEST BOOKS ·
· THE BEST INFORMATION ·
· THE BEST TIPS ·

for coin and paper money collectors

start exploring now at:
SHOPNUMISMASTER.com